Computational Social Networks

T0135254

Ajith Abraham • Aboul-Ella Hassanien
Editors

Computational Social Networks

Tools, Perspectives and Applications

 Springer

Editors
Dr. Ajith Abraham
Machine Intelligence Research Labs
(MIR Labs)
Scientific Network for Innovation
and Research Excellence
Auburn, Washington
USA

Dr. Aboul-Ella Hassanien
Faculty in Computers and Information
Department of Information Technology
Cairo University
Ahmed Zewal Street 5
Giza, Orman
Egypt

ISBN 978-1-4471-6009-0   ISBN 978-1-4471-4048-1 (eBook)
DOI 10.1007/978-1-4471-4048-1
Springer London Heidelberg New York Dordrecht

Printed on acid-free paper

Springer is part of Springer Science+Business Media (www.springer.com)

Preface

Computational Social Network (CSN) is a new emerging field that has overlapping regions from Mathematics, Psychology, Computer Sciences, Sociology, and Management. E-mails, blogs, instant messages, social network services, wikis, social bookmarking, and other instances of what is often called social software illustrate ideas from social computing. Social network analysis is the study of relationships among social entities.

Very often, all the necessary information are distributed over a number of websites and servers, which brings several research challenges from a data mining perspective. This book is a collection of chapters authored by world-class experts illustrating the concept of social networks from a computational point of view, with a focus on practical tools, applications, and open avenues for further research. The main topics cover the design and use of various computational tools and software, simulations of social networks, representation and analysis of social networks, use of semantic networks in design, and community-based research issues such as knowledge discovery and visualization. The authors present some of the latest advances of computational social networks and illustrate how organizations can gain competitive advantages by applying the different emergent techniques in the real-world scenarios. Experience reports, survey articles, and intelligence techniques and theories with specific networks technology problems are depicted. We hope that this book will be useful for researchers, scholars, postgraduate students, and developers who are interested in social networks research and related issues. In particular, the book will be a valuable companion and comprehensive reference for both postgraduate and senior undergraduate students who are taking a course in Computational Social Networks. The book contains 18 chapters, which are divided into two Parts and all chapters are self-contained to provide greatest reading flexibility.

Part I comprises of eight chapters (including an introductory chapter) and deals with modeling aspects and various computational tools used for social network analysis.

In Chap. 1, Panda et al. provides an overview of a number of social network related concepts from a computational perspective, such as social network analysis, different performance measures, social network services, tools, and applications. In addition, the authors also illustrate some of the current main problems facing social networks, how to address such challenges, opportunities, and future directions of research.

Xu in Chap. 2 proposes a hierarchical graphical knowledge representation (HGKR) to integrate layered abstractions into a coherent structure such that behavior forecasting may propagate downward or aggregate upward in a network. The system consists of a hierarchical graphical model, an evolutionary computation module, inference/forecasting, and decision support to forecast behaviors of groups at different hierarchies.

In Chap. 3, Herbiet and Bouvry illustrate novel social structure mining techniques devoted to the operation of dynamic mobile social networks. The authors focus on the impact of the notion of dynamics and time-evolving characteristics of the social structures and provide the complete state of the art. Further, a novel approach based on epidemic propagation for dynamic clustering and discovery of communities are introduced and the framework is illustrated using case studies.

Labatut and Balasque in Chap. 4 present an interesting problem of community detection in social networks. After presenting the state of the art, the authors focus on the methodological tools to analyze the obtained community structure, both in terms of topological features and nodal attributes. Real-world social network examples are used to illustrate the application of the presented tools and interpret the results from a business science perspective.

In Chap. 5, Bersano-Mendez et al. introduce how social networks can be modeled and analyzed using graph theory. This chapter provides an extensive overview to the mathematical modeling of social networks with an overview of the metrics used to characterize them and the models used to artificially mimic the formation of such networks. The authors illustrate various metrics based on distances, degrees, and neighborhoods as well as the use of such metrics to detect change in the network structure.

Yang et al. in Chap. 6 introduce a number of different ways of studying the macroscopic structure of social networks. The authors focus on the bow-tie decomposition method, and a precise formal definition for the decomposition as well as an algorithm is illustrated. The closely related daisy model and a fractal approach are also discussed.

In Chap. 7, Apolonia et al. describe the design, the development, and resulting evaluation of a web-enabled platform Cycle-Sharing in Social Networks (CSSN). The platform leverages a social network to perform discovery of computational resources, thus giving the possibility for any user to submit their own jobs for remote processing. Walls, messages, and comments in Facebook are used as the underlying transport for CSSN protocol messages, achieving full portability with existing social networks. CSSN gives the chance for common users to unleash the untapped computing power hidden in social networks.

Davidsen and Ortiz-Arroyo in Chap. 8 provide an analysis on the robustness of centrality measures using some examples. Further, the authors present a method to predict edges in dynamic social networks. Experimental results indicate that the robustness of the centrality measures follows a predictable pattern and that the use of temporal statistics could improve the accuracy achieved on edge prediction.

Part II deals with usage of social network tools and conceptual ideas for various applications and consists of ten chapters.

Hall et al. in Chap. 9 introduce the theoretical framework for community action and then discuss some of the revolutionary cognitive technologies that provide tools for implementing the theory, and conclude by presenting some preliminary observations from ongoing case studies where the technology has been recently implemented.

In Chap. 10, Kundu deals with the problem of dynamic Web prediction which is typically done using Markov model. Prediction requires complicated methodologies for selection of a particular hyperlink from the pool of hyperlinks of a current Web page. The author proposes a Web prediction method, which is based on real-time characteristics of users. Minimization of the total number of hyperlinks to be selected is the main aim of the proposed approach for accomplishing superior precision in dynamic prediction mode.

Khodaparast and Kavianfar in Chap. 11 illustrate how to make a reliable public cooperative network of wireless users to exchange intra-city data traffic information without using service providers. The proposed architecture includes a routing algorithm, a forwarding incentive mechanism, a security system, and a resiliency scheme.

In Chap. 12, Huang et al. focus on applications of social networks in peer-to-peer networks using *network coding* and *Named Data Networking,* which is a brand-new framework for future communications.

Pal et al. in Chap. 13 illustrate how digital devices can contribute to a social network used by people. The authors describe the need for such devices to detect user activity and allow other users to interact using that information, thereby creating an immersion of the real and virtual worlds.

In Chap. 14, Luo presents the background of ubiquitous environment, social networks, and media sharing. The author illustrates why and how social network-based media sharing is destined to be indispensable in the ubiquitous environment. Several applications are used as case studies and some future directions are also provided.

Geierhos and Ebrahim in Chap. 15 describe a novel technical service dealing with the integration of social networking channels into existing business processes. By doing so, business process management systems, which are already used to e-mail communication, can benefit of social media and also allow companies to follow general trends in customer opinions on the Internet.

In Chap. 16, Cipresso et al. analyze how to consider real emotions in complex networks by understanding subjects' behaviors in specific situations, such as social network sites navigation and to use these information in modeling complex phenomena. The authors propose a framework comprising of networked agents representing subjects and relationships.

Jones et al. in Chap. 17 develop a social learning environment prototype in a university environment by exploiting the communication and collaborative qualities of social networks. Learners become active participants in the learning process and they could access public Internet content to practice independent information-search and information-discernment skills, which they can share with others, and the virtual learning environment is benefited.

In Chap. 18, Falahi et al. connects social networks with recommender systems clearly illustrating the immediate synergies arising from bringing the two communities together. According to the authors, multiple potentially beneficial mutual synergies still remain to be explored and they provide the state of the art and future opportunities.

We are very much grateful to the authors of this book and to the reviewers for their tremendous service by critically reviewing the chapters. Most of the authors of chapters included in this book also served as referees for chapters written by other authors. Thanks go to all those who provided constructive and comprehensive reviews. The Editors would like to thank Wayne Wheeler and Simon Rees of Springer-Verlag, London, for the editorial assistance and excellent cooperative collaboration to produce this important scientific work. We hope that the reader will share our excitement to present this book on social networks and will find it useful.

Prof. (Dr.) Ajith Abraham
Machine Intelligence Research Labs (MIR Labs)
Scientific Network for Innovation and Research Excellence (SNIRE)
P.O. Box 2259
Auburn, Washington 98071, USA
http://www.mirlabs.org
Email: ajith.abraham@ieee.org
Personal WWW: http://www.softcomputing.net

Prof (Dr.) Aboul Ella Hassanien
Cairo University
Faculty of Computers & Information
Information Technology Department
5 Ahmed Zewal St., Orman, Giza
Email: Aboitcairo@gmail.com
Personal WWW: http://www.fci.cu.edu.eg/~abo/

Contents

Part II Applications

Contributors

Ajith Abraham Machine Intelligence Research Labs (MIR Labs), Scientific Network for Innovation and Research Excellence, WA, USA

Kanna Al Falahi UAE University, Al Ain, United Arab Emirates

Nuno Apolónia INESC ID Lisboa/Technical University of Lisbon, Lisbon, Portugal

Yacine Atif UAE University, Al Ain, United Arab Emirates

Jean-Michel Balasque Business Science & Marketing Department, Galatasaray University, Ortaköy/İstanbul, Turkey

Anna Balgera IULM University, Milan, Italy

Nicolás Ignacio Bersano-Méndez Universidad Diego Portales, Santiago, Chile

Russell Best ISEAL, Victoria University, Melbourne, VIC, Australia

Riddells Creek Landcare, Riddells Creek, VIC, Australia

Chirabrata Bhaumik Tata Consultancy Services, Kolkata, West Bengal, India

Pascal Bouvry Université du Luxembourg, Luxembourg City, Luxembourg

Javier Bustos-Jiménez ORAND, Santiago, Chile

Dah Ming Chiu Department of Information Engineering, Chinese University of Hong Kong (CUHK), Shatin, NT, Hong Kong

Pietro Cipresso Applied Technology for Neuro-Psychology Lab, IRCCS Istituto Auxologico Italiano, Milan, Italy

Søren Atmakuri Davidsen Department of Electronic Systems, Aalborg University, Esbjerg, Denmark

Jean Marie Dembele Université Cheikh Anta Diop, Dakar, Republic of Senegal

Mohamed Ebrahim IPSC, European Commission, Joint Research Centre – Ispra site, Institute for the Protection and Security of the Citizen, Ispra, VA, Italy

Nadia El Assawy Division of Neurology and Neurorehabilitation, San Giuseppe Hospital, IRCCS Istituto Auxologico Italiano, Piancavallo (VB), Italy

Nashwa El-Bendary Arab Academy for Science, Technology, and Maritime Transport, Cairo, Egypt

Paulo Ferreira INESC ID Lisboa/Technical University of Lisbon, Lisbon, Portugal

Federica Galli Division of Neurology and Neurorehabilitation, San Giuseppe Hospital, IRCCS Istituto Auxologico Italiano, Piancavallo (VB), Italy

Michaela Geierhos CIS, Centre for Information and Language Processing, Ludwig-Maximilians-Universität München, München, Germany

Avik Ghose Tata Consultancy Services, Kolkata, West Bengal, India

William P. Hall Engineering Learning Unit, Melbourne School of Engineering, University of Melbourne 2010, VIC, Australia

Kororoit Institute, St Albans, VIC, Australia

Aboul Ella Hassanien Cairo University, Cairo, Egypt

Guillaume-Jean Herbiet Université du Luxembourg, Luxembourg City, Luxembourg

Stephen Hole Swansea Metropolitan University, Wales, UK

Jiaqing Huang Department of Electronics and Information Engineering, Huazhong University of Science and Technology (HUST), Wuhan, Hubei, P.R. China

Karen Jones Swansea Metropolitan University, Wales, UK

Azade Kavianfar Guilan University, Rasht, Iran

Ali Asghar Khodaparast Amirkabir University of Technology, Tehran, Iran

Anirban Kundu Netaji Subhash Engineering College, West Bengal University of Technology, Kolkata, West Bengal, India

Innovation Research Lab (IRL), Capex Technologies, Howrah, West Bengal, India

Vincent Labatut Computer Science Department, Galatasaray University, Ortaköy/İstanbul, Turkey

Zhibin Lei Hong Kong Applied Science and Technology Research Institute Company Limited (ASTRI), Shatin, NT, Hong Kong

Qingyuan Liu Department of Electronics and Information Engineering, Huazhong University of Science and Technology (HUST), Wuhan, Hubei, P.R. China

Xun Luo Qualcomm Inc., San Diego, USA

Nikolaos Mavridis UAE University, Al Ain, United Arab Emirates

Siddharth Nair Spatial Information Architecture Lab, RMIT University, Melbourne, VIC, Australia

Olfa Nasraoui Department of Computer Engineering and Computer Science, University of Louisville, Louisville, KY, USA

Susu Nousala Aalto University, NODUS-Sustainable Design Research Group, Helsinki, Finland

GAMUT, University of Melbourne and Kororoit Institute, St Albans, VIC, Australia

Daniel Ortiz-Arroyo Department of Electronic Systems, Aalborg University, Esbjerg, Denmark

Arpan Pal Tata Consultancy Services, Kolkata, West Bengal, India

Mrutyunjaya Panda Department of ECE, Gandhi Institute for Technological Advancement (GITA), Bhubaneswar, Odisha, India

Rhian Pole Swansea Metropolitan University, Wales, UK

Giuseppe Riva Psychology Department, Catholic University of Milan, Italy, Milan, Italy

Mostafa A. Salama Department of Computer Science, British University in Egypt, Cairo, Egypt

Satu Elisa Schaeffer Universidad Autónoma de Nuevo León, San Nicolás de los Garza, NL, Mexico

Luigi Sellitti Division of Neurology and Neurorehabilitation, San Giuseppe Hospital, IRCCS Istituto Auxologico Italiano, Piancavallo (VB), Italy

Priyanka Sinha Tata Consultancy Services, Kolkata, West Bengal, India

Luís Veiga INESC ID Lisboa/Technical University of Lisbon, Lisbon, Portugal

Marco Villamira IULM University, Milan, Italy

James Williams Swansea Metropolitan University, Wales, UK

Jian-Wu Xu Department of Radiology, The University of Chicago, Chicago, IL, USA

Rong Yang Department of Mathematics and Computer Science, Western Kentucky University, Bowling Green, KY, USA

Leyla Zhuhadar Department of Computer Engineering and Computer Science, University of Louisville, Louisville, KY, USA

Part I
Modeling and Tools

Chapter 1
Computational Social Networks: Tools, Perspectives, and Challenges

Mrutyunjaya Panda, Nashwa El-Bendary, Mostafa A. Salama, Aboul Ella Hassanien, and Ajith Abraham

Abstract Computational social science is a new emerging field that has overlapping regions from mathematics, psychology, computer sciences, sociology, and management. Social computing is concerned with the intersection of social behavior and computational systems. It supports any sort of social behavior in or through computational systems. It is based on creating or recreating social conventions and social contexts through the use of software and technology. Thus, blogs, email, instant messaging, social network services, wikis, social bookmarking, and other instances of what is often called *social software* illustrate ideas from social computing. Social network analysis is the study of relationships among social entities. It is becoming an important tool for investigators. However all the necessary information is often distributed over a number of websites. Interest in this field is blossoming as traditional practitioners in the social and behavioral sciences are being joined by researchers from statistics, graph theory, machine learning,

M. Panda (✉)
Department of ECE, Gandhi Institute for Technological Advancement (GITA),
Bhubaneswar, Odisha, India
e-mail: mrutyunjaya74@gmail.com

N. El-Bendary
Arab Academy for Science, Technology, and Maritime Transport, Cairo, Egypt
e-mail: nashwa_m@aast.edu

M.A. Salama
Department of Computer Science, British University in Egypt, Cairo, Egypt
e-mail: mostafa.salama@gmail.com

A.E. Hassanien
Faculty of Computers and Information, Cairo University, Cairo, Egypt
e-mail: aboitcairo@gmail.com

A. Abraham
Machine Intelligence Research Labs (MIR Labs), Scientific Network for Innovation
and Research Excellence, WA, USA
e-mail: ajith.abraham@ieee.org

A. Abraham and A.-E. Hassanien (eds.), *Computational Social Networks: Tools,
Perspectives and Applications*, DOI 10.1007/978-1-4471-4048-1_1,
© Springer-Verlag London 2012

and data mining. In this chapter, we illustrate the concept of social networks from a computational point of view, with a focus on practical services, tools, and applications and open avenues for further research. Challenges to be addressed and future directions of research are presented and an extensive bibliography is also included.

Introduction

Internet represents an increasingly important role and gradually comes into play in all walks of our lives because of its rich and varied resources. Currently, social networks provide a powerful abstraction for the structure and dynamics of diverse kinds of people or people-to-technology interaction. Web 2.0 has enabled a new generation of web-based communities, and social networks to facilitate collaboration among different communities. During the last few years, social networking sites have become a de facto part of the Internet and a primary destination for many Internet users. Even though the market seems to be saturated with social networking sites for every type of target group, the concepts driving these sites are incredibly similar in form and execution. More and more people would like to spend their time on the Internet especially in order to build some kind of large social entertainment community and then try to communicate with each other as frequently as practicable so as to see that the relationship between them is getting closer [1].

Social computing supports computations that are carried out by groups of people. Examples of social computing include collaborative filtering, online auctions, prediction markets, reputation systems, computational social choice, tagging, and verification games. Social computing has become more widely known because of its relationship to a number of recent trends. These include the growing popularity of social software and web 2.0, increased academic interest in social network analysis, the rise of open source as a viable method of production, and a growing conviction that all of this can have a profound impact on daily life. Accordingly, social network analysis (SNA) has become a widely applied method in research and business for inquiring the web of relationships on the individual, organizational, and societal level. With ready access to computing power, the popularity of social networking websites such as Facebook, Twitter, and Netlog and automated data collection techniques; the demand for solid expertise in SNA has recently exploded.

Social networking covers a wide range of online environments, with many formal definitions broad enough to encompass almost any web 2.0 collaborative environment [2]. While various public social collaborative environments existed on the Internet as early as the 1980s, the emergence of social networking as it is best understood today arose with the large commercially supported sites such as Friendster (2002), LinkedIn and MySpace (2003), and Facebook (2004), along with content-sharing focused sites with limited social network features such as Flickr (2004) and YouTube (2005). Other social networking sites were developing, which have higher usage outside the USA including Orkut (2005), popular in South America and Asia/Pacific regions, Bebo (2005) in Europe and Australia, and QQ (2006) in China. With the development of Twitter in 2006, social networking took a new twist that increased immediacy and incorporated mobile phones into the social mix [3]. In social media, communities take the form of social networks and the communal groups within them. People establish associations, friendships, and allegiances around content, objects, products, services, and ideas. How they communicate is simply subject to the tools and networks that people adopt based on the influence of their social graph – and the culture within [4]. Many of the social networks are enhanced with multiple collaborative tools that go beyond the personal profile and "friending" links, including the ability to post and share files (text, images, audio, and video), participate in discussions or blogs, co-create and edit content with wiki-like tools, and link in and tag external resources from other websites paralleling social bookmarking. Sites such as Flickr or YouTube are in fact more commonly seen as environments primarily for sharing content, digital pictures, and video [3].

This chapter provides an overview of a number of social network-related concepts from a computational perspective, such as social network analysis, social network services, tools, and applications in addition to exploring main problems facing social networks and addressing challenges, opportunities, and future directions of research. The chapter is organized as follows. Section "Social Network Analysis: Concepts" provides an explanation of the some basic related concepts including social networks versus computer networks and the social network sites. Section "Social Networks: Analysis Metrics and Performance" briefly describing the different performance measures, that have been encountered during any network analysis. Section "Social Network Services and Tools" presents different social networking services and tools. Section "Problems in Social Networks" discusses different problems in social networks including uncertainty, missing data in social network, and finding the shortest path. Finally, opportunities and challenges are discussed in section "Conclusion, Challenges, and Opportunities".

Social Network Analysis: Concepts

Social Network Versus Computer Network

Networks can be categorized according to topology, which is the geometric arrangement of a computer system. Common topologies include a bus, star, and ring, protocol which defines a common set of rules and signals that computers on the network use to follow. Or architecture where networks can be broadly classified as either a peer-to-peer or client/server architecture. Computers on a network are sometimes called nodes. Computers and devices that allocate resources for a network are called servers. It is argued that social networks differ from most other types of networks, including technological and biological networks, in two important ways. First, they have nontrivial clustering or network transitivity and second, they show positive correlations, between the degrees of adjacent vertices. Social networks are often divided into groups or communities, and it has recently been suggested that this division could account for the observed clustering. Further, group structure in networks can also account for degree correlations. Hence, assortative mixing in such networks with a variation in the sizes of the groups provides the predicted level compares well with that observed in real-world networks.

Social Network Sites

Social network sites (SNSs) are websites that allow users to register, create their own profile page containing information about themselves (real or virtual), to establish public "Friend" connections with other members and to communicate with other members [5]. Communication typically takes the form of private emails, public comments written on each others' profile pages, blog or pictures, or instant messaging. SNSs like Facebook and MySpace are amongst the ten most popular websites in the world. SNSs are very popular in many countries that include Orkut (Brazil), Cyworld (Korea), and Mixi (Japan).

SNS growth seems to have been driven by youth, with Facebook originating as a college site [5] and MySpace having an average age of 21 for members in early 2008 [6]. However, an increasing proportion of older members are also using these sites. The key motivating factor for using SNS is sociability, however, suggesting that some types of people may never use social network sites extensively [7]. Moreover, it seems that extraversion is beneficial in SNSs [8] and that female MySpace users seem to be more extraverted and more willing to self-disclose than male users [9], which hints that they may be more effective communicators in this environment.

SNS are very much interesting because they support relatively public conversations between friends and acquaintances. Walther et al. [10] view that SNS profiles are known as venues for identity expression of members and since public comments appear in these profiles, they may also be composed or interpreted from the perspective of identity expression rather than performing a pure communicative function. At the same time, the public conversations are interesting because the web now contains millions of informal public messages that researchers can access and analyze. The availability of demographic information about the sender and recipient in their profile pages makes it more interesting and useful with an ethical issue arises from its owners that the dataset are explicitly to be used in research (unlike standard interview or questionnaire protocols). However, if the data has been placed in the most public place online as found though Google then its use does not constitute any kind of invasion of privacy [11]. An ethical issue only arises if feedback is given to the text authors or if a contact is established.

The data mining research has been analyzed using MySpace data for commercially oriented purposes rather than social science goals, but then an IBM study demonstrated how to generate rankings of musicians based upon opinions mined from MySpace comments [12] and a Microsoft team developed a league table system for movies by extracting lists from MySpace profiles, without explicit sentiment analysis [13].

Social Networks: Analysis Metrics and Performance

We describe the different performance measures that are encountered during any network analysis in order to understand the fundamental concepts behind the comprehension. The four most important concepts used in network analysis are closeness, network density, centrality, betweenness, and centralization. In addition to these, there are four other measures of network performance that include robustness, efficiency, effectiveness, and diversity. The first set of measures concerns structure, whereas the second set concerns the dynamics and thus depends on a theory explaining why certain agents do certain things in order to access to information [50].

Social Networks Analysis Metrics

Closeness

This refers to the degree with which an individual is nearer to all others in a network either directly or indirectly. Further, it reflects the ability to access information through the "grapevine" of network members. In this way, the closeness is considered to be the inverse of the sum of the shortest distance (sometimes called as geodesic distance) between each individual and all other available in the network. For a network with n number of nodes, the closeness is represented mathematically as

$$c_c(n_j) = \frac{n-1}{\sum_{k=i, j=k}^{n} d(n_i, n_j)} \qquad (1.1)$$

Where $C_c n_k$ defines the standardized closeness centrality of node j and $d(n_i, n_j)$ denotes the geodesic distance between j and k.

Network Density

Network density is a measure of the connectedness in a network. Density is defined as the actual number of ties in a network, expressed as a proportion of the maximum possible number of ties. It is a number that varies between 0 and 1.0. When density is close to 1.0, the network is said to be dense; otherwise it is sparse. When dealing with directed ties, the maximum possible number of pairs is used instead.

The problem with the measure of density is that it is sensible to the number of network nodes; therefore, it cannot be used for comparisons across networks that vary significantly in size.

Centrality: Local and Global

The concept of centrality comprises of two levels: local and global. A node is said to have local centrality, when it has the higher number of ties with other nodes or else it is referred to as global centrality. Whereas local centrality considers only direct ties (the ties directly connected to that node), global centrality considers indirect ties also (which are not directly connected to that node). For example, in a network with a "star" structure, in which, all nodes have ties with one central node, local centrality of the central node is equal to 1.0. Whereas local centrality measures are expressed in terms of the number of nodes to which a node is connected, global centrality is expressed in terms of the distances among the various nodes. Two nodes are connected by a path if there is a sequence of distinct ties connecting them, and the length of the path is simply the number of ties that make it up . The shortest distance between two points on the surface of the earth lies along the geodesic that connects them, and, by analogy, the shortest path between any particular pair of nodes in a network is termed a geodesic. A node is globally central if it lies at a short distance from many other nodes. Such node is said to be "close" to many of the other nodes in the network, sometimes global centrality is also called closeness centrality. Local and global centrality depends mostly on the size of the network, and therefore they cannot be compared when networks differ significantly in size.

Betweenness

Betweenness is defined as the extent to which a node lies between other nodes in the network. Here, the connectivity of the node's neighbors is taken into account in order to provide a higher value for nodes which bridge clusters. This metrics reflects the number of people who are connecting indirectly through direct links. The betweenness of a node measures the extent to which an agent (represented by a node) can play the part of a broker or gatekeeper with a potential for control over others. Methodologically, betweenness is the most complex of the measures of centrality to calculate and also suffers from the same disadvantages as local and global centrality. The betweenness of the nodes in a network can be defined as:

$$c_b(n_j) = \frac{xx}{\dfrac{(n-2)(n-1)}{2}} \tag{1.2}$$

$$xx = \sum_{k<i, j=k, j=t} \frac{g_{kt}(n_j)}{g_{kt}} \tag{1.3}$$

Where $c_b(n_j)$ denotes the standardized betweenness centrality of node j, $g_{kt}(n_j)$ represents the number of geodesic linking k and I that contains j in between and as the total number of geodesic linking k and i.

Centralization

Centralization is calculated as the ratio between the numbers of links for each node divided by maximum possible sum of differences. Centralization provides a measure on the extent to which a whole network has a centralized structure. Whereas centralization describes the extent to which this connectedness is organized around particular focal nodes, density describes the general level of connectedness in a network. Centralization and density, therefore, are important complementary pair measures. While a centralized network will have many of its links dispersed around one or a few nodes, the decentralized network is one in which there is little variation between the number of links each node possesses. The general procedure involved in any measure of network centralization is to look at the differences between centrality scores of the most central node and those of all other nodes. Basically, centralization can be graphed in three ways: one for each of the three centrality measures: local, global, and betweenness. All three centralization measures vary from 0 to 1.0 where 0 corresponds to a network in which all the nodes are connected to all other nodes whereas a value of 1.0 is achieved on all three measures for "star" networks. However, majority of the real networks lies between these two extremes. Methodologically, the choices of one of these three centralization measures depend on which specific structural features the researcher wants to focus. For example, while a betweenness-based measure is sensitive to the chaining of nodes; a local centrality based measure of network centralization seems to be particularly less sensitive to the local dominance of nodes. It is measured as:

$$R = \frac{\sum_{j=1}^{g}\{\max(D_i) - D_i\}}{(g - 1)^2} \tag{1.4}$$

where D_i represents the number of actors in the network that are directly linked to the actor j and g denoted as the total number of actors present in the network.

Social Networks Performance

Once the network analysis is completed, the network dynamics predicts the performance of the network that can be evaluated as a combination of (1) the network's robustness to the removal of ties and/or nodes, (2) network efficiency in terms of the distance to traverse from one node to another and its non-redundant size, (3) effectiveness of the network in terms of information benefits allocated to central nodes, and finally (4) network diversity in terms of the history of each of the nodes [50].

Robustness

Social network analysts have highlighted the importance of network structure in relation to the network's robustness. The robustness can be evaluated based on how it becomes fragmented when an increasing fraction of nodes is removed. Robustness is measured as an estimate of the tendency of individuals in networks to form local groups or clusters of individuals with whom they share similar characteristics, i.e., clustering. For example, if individuals X, Y, and Z are all computer experts and if X knows Y and Y knows Z, then it is highly likely that X knows Z using the so called chain rule. If the measure of the clustering of individuals is high for a given network, then the robustness of that network increases – within a cluster/group.

Efficiency

Network efficiency can be measures by considering the number of nodes that can access instantly a large number of different nodes – sources of knowledge, status, etc., through a relatively small number of ties. These nodes are treated as non-redundant contacts. For example, with two networks of equal size, the one with more non-redundant contacts provides more benefits than the others. Also, it is quite evident that the gain from a new contact redundant with existing contacts will be minimal. However, it is wise to consume time and energy in cultivating a new contact to un-reached people. Hence, social network analysts measure efficiency by the number of non-redundant contacts and the average number of ties an ego has to traverse to reach any alter, this number is referred to as the average path length. The shorter the average path length relative to the size of the network and the lower the number of redundant contacts and the more efficient is the network.

Effectiveness

Effectiveness targets the cluster of nodes that can be reached through non-redundant contacts. In contrast, efficiency aims at the reduction of the time and energy spent on redundant contacts. Each cluster of contacts is an independent source of information. One cluster around this non-redundant node, no matter how numerous its members are, is only one source of information, because people connected to one another tend to know about the same things at about the same time. For example, a network is more effective when the information benefit provided by multiple clusters of contacts is broader, providing better assurance that the central node will be informed. Moreover, because non-redundant contacts are only connected through the central node, the central node is assured of being the first to see new opportunities created by needs in one group that could be served by skills in another group.

Diversity

While efficiency is about getting a large number of (non-redundant) nodes, node's diversity, on the other hand it suggests a critical performance point of view where those nodes are diverse in nature, i.e., the history of each individual node within the network is important. It is particularly this aspect that can be explored through case studies, which is a matter of intense discussion among social network analysts. It seems to suggest that social scientists should prefer and use network analysis according to the first strand of thought developed by social network analysts instead of actor-attribute-oriented accounts based on the diversity of each the nodes.

Social Network Services and Tools

Social Network Services

Currently available social network services have two main formats: (1) sites that are primarily organized around users' profiles *(profile-based social network services)* and (2) those that are organized around collections of content *(content-based social network services)* [14].

Profile-based social network services are primarily organized around members' profile pages – pages which primarily consist of information about an individual member – including their picture, interests, likes and dislikes. Bebo, Facebook and MySpace are all good examples of this. Users develop their space in various ways, and can often contribute to each other's spaces – typically leaving text, embedded content or links to external content through message walls, comment or evaluation tools. Users often include third-party content (in the form of "widgets") in order to enhance their profiles, or as a way of including information from other web services and social networking services.

On the other hand, in *content-based social network services*, the user's profile remains an important way of organizing connections but plays a secondary role to the posting of content. Photo-sharing site Flickr is an example of this type of service. *Shelfari* is one of the current crop of book-focused sites, with the member's "bookshelf" being a focal point of their profile and membership. Other examples of content-based communities include YouTube for video-sharing and last.fm, where the content is arranged by software that monitors and represents the music that users listen to. In this instance, content is generated by the user's activity. The act of listening to audio files creates and updates profile information ("recently listened to"). This in turn generates data about an individual user's neighbors who are people who have recently listened to the same kind of music.

Figures 1.1 and 1.2 from [15] depict visualizations for two examples of music websites, namely; *last.fm*, founded in the United Kingdom in 2002, and *Musicovery*, which is a website letting users discover new music, using the *last.forward* software

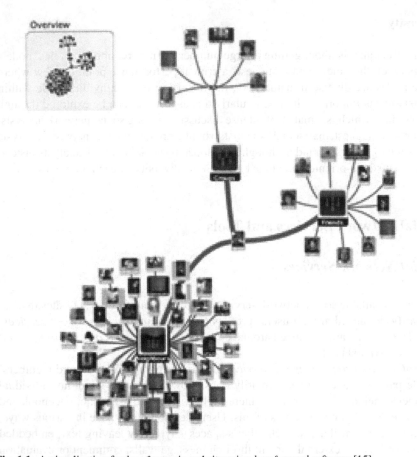

Fig. 1.1 A visualization for *last.fm* music website using *last.forward* software [15]

[15], which is an open source software for analysis and visualization of the social music network of *Last.fm* and *Musicovery*.

Moreover, sites such as Second Life and World of Warcraft represent multi-user online virtual environments in which users to interact with each other's avatars (a virtual representation of the site member). Although the users have profile cards, their functional profiles are the characters they customise or build and control. Friends' lists are usually private and not publicly shared or displayed.

Social Network Tools

Social Bookmarking

Bookmarking is the practice of saving the address of a website users wish to visit in the future on their computer. Social bookmarking, on the other hand, is the practice

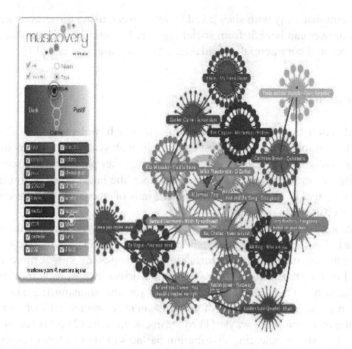

Fig. 1.2 A visualization for *Musicovery* music website using *last.forward* software [15]

of saving bookmarks to a public website and "tagging" them with keywords. Social bookmarking began in unrefined form in the late 1990s. It then fell out of favor online due to changes in the web. It came back in 2005 and has been getting increasingly popular ever since [16].

Social bookmarking is a method for Internet users to organize, store, manages, and search for bookmarks of resources online. In other words, social bookmarking is a user-based online system in which individuals tag their favorite web content and store it in one place, sharing it with others. The favorite content of a person may also be a favorite of another; this will boost the website traffic.

Social Tagging (Social Indexing)

Unlike file sharing, the resources themselves are not shared, but merely bookmarks that reference them. Social tagging – which is also known as collaborative tagging, social classification, and social indexing – allows ordinary users to assign keywords, or tags, to items. It involves linking sites within the various forums, blogs and message boards on social networking websites, blog sites, and content-centric sites and is very useful to share information instantly with other users/friends [16].

Social tagging can be a useful tool for users. Instead of individually saving the site in a variety of folders, just type a few keywords called tags and their sites are organized automatically with sites saved by other users, using those same keywords. All levels of user can benefit from social tagging. Potentially, it is another efficient tool both free and commercially available, which any user can use [17].

Web Syndication

Web syndication is a form of syndication in which website material is made available to multiple other sites. Most commonly, web syndication refers to making web feeds available from a site in order to provide other people with a summary of the website's recently added content (for example, the latest news or forum posts). The term can also be used to describe other kinds of licensing website content so that other websites can use it [18].

Syndication benefits both the websites providing information and the websites displaying it. For the receiving site, content syndication is an effective way of adding greater depth and immediacy of information to its pages, making it more attractive to users. For the transmitting site, syndication drives exposure across numerous online platforms. This generates new traffic for the transmitting site, making syndication a free and easy form of advertisement. Commercial web syndication can be categorized in three ways: (1) by business models, (2) by types of content, or (3) by methods for selecting distribution partners [16]. The term Really Simple Syndication (RSS) is often used to refer to web feeds or web syndication in general, although not all feed formats are RSS-based. A web feed is a data format used for providing users with frequently updated content. Content distributors syndicate a web feed, thereby allowing users to subscribe to it. Making a collection of web feeds accessible in one spot is known as aggregation, which is performed by an aggregator. A web feed is also sometimes referred to as a syndicated feed. RSS is a family of web feed formats used to publish frequently updated works such as blog entries, news headlines, audio, and video in a standardized format. An RSS document includes full or summarized text, plus metadata such as publishing dates and authorship. Web feeds benefit publishers by letting them syndicate content automatically. They benefit readers who want to subscribe to timely updates from favored websites or to aggregate feeds from many sites into one place. RSS feeds can be read using software called an "RSS reader," "feed reader," or "aggregator," which can be web-based, desktop-based, or mobile-device-based.

Knowledge Tagging

Another social networking tool is knowledge tagging. A knowledge tag is a type of meta-information that describes or defines some aspect of an information resource. Knowledge tags are more than traditional nonhierarchical keywords or terms. They are a type of metadata that captures knowledge in the form of descriptions, categorizations, classifications, semantics, comments, notes, annotations, hyperdata, hyperlinks, or references that are collected in tag profiles. These tag profiles reference to an information resource that resides in a distributed, and often heterogeneous, storage repository [19].

Social Search Engines

Social search engines are an important tool that utilize the popularity of social networking services. There are various kinds of social search engines, but sites like Wink and Spokeo generate results by searching across the public profiles of multiple social network sites, allowing the creation of web-based "dossiers" on individuals. This type of people search cuts across the traditional boundaries of social network site membership, although any data retrieved should already be in the public domain.

Mobile Social Networks and Micro-blogging

Many social network sites, for example MySpace and Twitter, offer mobile phone versions of their services, allowing members to interact with their friends via their phones. Increasingly, too, there are mobile-led and mobile-only communities, which include profiles and media-sharing just as with web-based social networking services. MYUBO, for example, allows users to share and view video over mobile networks.

Micro-blogging services such as Twitter and Jaiku allow you to publish short (140 characters, including spaces) messages publicly or within contact groups. They are designed to work as mobile services, but are popularly used and read on the web as well. Many services offer "status updates" – short messages that can be updated to let people know what mood you are in or what you are doing. These can be checked within the site, read as text messages on phones, or exported to be read or displayed elsewhere. They engage users in constantly updated conversation and contact with their online networks.

Social Gaming Applications

A social network game is a type of online game that is played through social networks, and typically features multiplayer and asynchronous gameplay mechanics [20–23]. While they share many aspects of traditional video games, social network games often employ additional ones that make them distinct. Social network games are most often implemented as browser games, but can also be implemented on other platforms such as mobile devices [24]. They are amongst the most popular games played in the world, with several products with tens of millions of players [25]. Green Patch, Happy Farm [26], Farm Town, YoVille, and Mob Wars were some of the first successful games of this genre. Moreover, FrontierVille, CityVille,

Gardens of Time, and The Sims Social are more recent examples of very popular social network games. Companies that make social network games include market leader Zynga, 5 min, Playfish, Playdom, Kabam, Crowdstar, RockYou, Booyah, etc.

Social Networking Tools for Distance Learning

Social networking technologies have many positive uses in educational institutions and libraries. They are an ideal environment for youngsters to share what they are learning or to build something together online. The nature of the medium allows students to receive feedback from teachers, peers, parents, and others. Social networking technologies create a sense of community (as do the physical library and school) and in this way are already aligned with the services and programs at the library/school. Schools and libraries are working to integrate positive uses of social networking into their classrooms, programs, and services. By integrating social networking technologies into educational environments, youngsters have the opportunity to learn from adults how to be safe and smart when participating in online social networks [27].

Based on Internet voting, 63% supported the proposition that social networking will bring large, positive changes to educational methods. Similar debates have occurred elsewhere online, in periodicals, and in schools raising issues of affordances versus challenges common to any new technology. Many advocates promote the use of social networking for community building and increasing student engagement in higher education classrooms. Some critics have suggested that the links between computer-mediated discussion (CMD) and learning or engagement are not well documented, proposing that such advocacy is more hype than reality [28]. But recent studies such as [29] indicate that teacher self-disclosure via social networking can increase motivation and improve classroom climate thus impacting student outcomes. In many of these debates, the focus is often limited to the massive and most well known of the social networks, MySpace and Facebook, particularly because media coverage has ensured that even those who have limited familiarity with social networking have heard about these Internet environments. However, social networking tools are more diverse and in fact, some may better fit specific class needs.

Social networking is a tool, with both its advantages and problems for usage in teaching and learning. When used in a learning context where affordances of the technology are carefully evaluated in terms of pedagogical requirements and student learning outcomes, including those elements that result in a supportive and collaborative learning environment, these tools offer significant advantages for distance learning. Among the positive attributes are impacts on student engagement, motivation, personal interaction, and affective aspects of the learning environment. In the case study reported here, specific positive effects included the balancing of individual creativity and personal interactions with the need for structured learning and collaborative course activities. The direct contribution to student achievement remains to be proven, but when technology supports an affirmative, constructivist-learning environment, and contributes to successful pedagogical strategies without distracting from essential objectives for development of knowledge and skills, the result of formative evaluation of social networking potentials for distance learning is positive [3].

Problems in Social Networks

Uncertainty in Social Network

The uncertainty in digital evidence is not being evaluated at present, thus making it difficult to assess the reliability of evidence stored on and transmitted using computer networks [30]. Uncertainty occurs when the actors are confronted with too many interpretations, causing a shock of confusion. In an ambiguous situation there is no lack of information, no gap that could be filled with a better scanning of available information, rather there are at least two (and often more) different interpretations of the situation [31]. Many research works tackled the problem that the data collected through automated sensors, anonymized communication data, and self-reporting logging on Internet-scale networks as a proxy for real relationships and interactions causes some uncertainty.

Alejandro et al. [32] introduced a methodology that incorporates into the social interaction activity records the uncertainty and time sensitiveness of the events through fuzzy social networks analysis (FSNA). Also, they investigated an approach based on the analysis of current flows in electrical networks for the extraction of primary routes of interaction among key actors in a social network. They proposed that the ability to capture the influence of all nodes involved in a network over a particular path represents a promising avenue for the extraction of characteristics of the social network assuming that uncertainty and time sensitiveness are parameters of the information stored on activity logs that cannot be ignored and must be accounted for. Zhong et al. [33] used an adaptive group fuzzy analytic network process group decision support system under uncertainty that makes up for some deficiencies in the conventional analytic network process. Where the first step fuzzy judgments are used when it is difficult to characterize the uncertainty by point-valued judgments due to partially known information, and a bipartite graph is formulated to model the problem of group decision making under uncertainty. Then, a fuzzy prioritization method is proposed to derive the local priorities from missing or inconsistent fuzzy pairwise comparison judgments. As a result of the unlikeliest for all the decision makers to evaluate all elements under uncertainty, an original aggregation method is developed to cope with the situation where some of the local priorities are missing. Hassan et al. [34] observed that the characteristics of social systems are poorly modeled with crisp attributes. A concrete agent-based system illustrates the analysis of the evolution of values in a society enhanced with fuzzy logic to improve agent models that get closer to reality. This has been explored in five aspects: relationships among agents, some variable attributes that determine agent states, functions of similarity, evolution of agent states, and inheritance. Gabriella et al. [35] proposed new approach to combine survey data with multi agent simulation models of consumer behavior to study the diffusion process of organic food consumption. This methodology is based on rough set theory, which is able to translate survey data into behavioral rules. However, the peculiarity of the rough set approach is that the inconsistencies in a data set about consumer behavior are not aggregated or corrected since lower and upper approximations are computed. Also rough set data analysis provides a suitable link between survey data and multi agent models since it is designed to extract decision rules from large quantitative and qualitative data sets.

Missing Data in Social Network

The inherent problem with much of the data is that it is noisy and incomplete, and at the wrong level of fidelity and abstraction for meaningful data analysis. Thus there is a need for methods which extract and infer "clean" annotated networks from noisy observational network data. This involves inferring missing attribute values (attribute prediction), adding missing links and removing spurious links between the nodes (link prediction), and eliminating duplicate nodes (entity resolution).

Moustafa et al. [36] identified a set of primitives to support the extraction and inference of a network from observational data, and describe a framework that enables network analyst to easily implement and combine new extraction and analysis techniques, and efficiently apply them to large observation networks. Perez et al. [36] proposed linguistic decision analysis to solve decision-making problems based on linguistic information by using the ordinal fuzzy linguistic modeling. In such situations, experts are forced to provide incomplete fuzzy linguistic preference relations. So an additive consistency-based estimation process of missing values to deal with incomplete fuzzy linguistic preference relations is developed.

Finding the Shortest Path

The problem of finding the shortest path is finding the path with minimum distance or cost from a starting node to an ending node. It is one of the most fundamental network optimization problems. The shortest path problem also has a deep connection to the minimum cost low problem, which is an abstraction for various shipping and distribution problems, the minimum weight perfect matching, and the minimum mean-cycle problem. Computing shortest paths in graphs is one of the most well-studied problems in combinatorial optimization [37, 38]. Ant colony optimization algorithm is a very initiative machine learning technique in finding the shortest path. The ants, in their necessity to find food and bring it back to the nest, manage not only to explore a vast area, but also to indicate to their peers the location of the food while bringing it back to the nest. Most of the time, they will find the shortest path and adapt to ground changes, hence proving their great efficiency toward this difficult task. Michlmayr [39] proposed SEMANT algorithm based on ant colony optimization. The proposed algorithm finds the shortest path from every querying peer to one or more appropriate answering peers that possess resources for the given query. An unstructured peer-to-peer networks is designed, which consists of carefully selected constituents of the ant algorithms ant colony system, AntNet, and AntHocNet, which were combined and adapted to fit for the application purpose. Lada et al. [40] applied the ant colony optimization system as a messenger distributing its pheromone, the long-link details, in surrounding area. The subsequence forwarding decision has more option to move to, select among local neighbors or send to node has long link closer to its target. They introduced a novel approach for routing in social network. The authors showed that with additional information, the existence of shortcut in surrounding area is able to find a shorter path than using greedy algorithm. Saiteja et al. [41] proposed AntNet algorithm by using ant colony optimization. Kumar and Kumar [42] proposed open shortest path first protocol by using a genetic algorithm. They had implemented a genetic algorithm to find the set of optimal routes to send the traffic from source to destination. Genetic algorithm is well suited for routing problem as it explores solution space in multiple directions at once and less chances to attain local optimum. The proposed algorithm works on initial population created by some other module, access fitness, generate new population using genetic operators and converges after meeting the specified termination condition.

Hybridization between ants algorithm and genetic algorithm was presented by Cauvery et al. [43] for routing in packet switched data networks. Ant algorithm is found to reduce the size of the routing table. A genetic algorithm cannot use global information of the network. Hence the combination of these two algorithms, which makes the packets to explore the network independently, helps in finding path between pair of nodes effectively. White et al. [44] applied ant system with genetic algorithm (ASGA) system to the problem of path finding in networks, demonstrating by experimentation that the hybrid algorithm exhibits improved performance when compared to the basic ant system. They demonstrated that the ant system can be used to solve hard combinatorial optimization problems as represented by Steiner vertex identification and shortest cycle determination. Araujo et al. [45] proposed a new neural network to solve the shortest path problem for Internet work routing. The proposed solution extends the traditional single-layer recurrent Hopfleld architecture introducing a two-layer architecture that automatically guarantees an entire set of constraints held by any valid solution to the shortest path problem. This solution aims to achieve an increased number of succeeded and valid convergences, which is one of the main limitations of previous solutions based on neural networks. Additionally, in general, it requires less neurons. Sangi et al. [46] applied pulse coupled neural network (PCNN) to compute shortest paths. They proposed dual source PCNN (DSPCNN), which can improve the computational efficiency of pulse-coupled neural networks for shortest path problems. Deng et al. [47] proposed a new algorithm by using a particle swarm optimization algorithm with priority-based encoding scheme based on fluid neural network to search for the shortest path in stochastic traffic networks.

Conclusion, Challenges, and Opportunities

This chapter illustrated the field of social networks from a computational point of view, with a focus on practical services, tools, applications, problems, and performance metrics with addition to open avenues for further research. The popularity and ease of use of social networking services have excited institutions with their potential in a variety of areas. However, effective use of social networking services poses a number of challenges for institutions including long-term sustainability of the services; user concerns over use of social tools in a work or study context; a variety of technical issues and legal issues such as copyright, privacy, accessibility, etc. Institutions would be advised to consider carefully the implications before promoting significant use of such services. Clear understanding of these structural properties of a criminal network may help analysts target critical network members for removal or surveillance, and locate network vulnerabilities where disruptive actions can be effective. Appropriate network analysis techniques, therefore, are needed to mine criminal networks and gain insight into these problems.

Another research area is the usage of social networks and their tools for researchers themselves [48, 49]. Social networking tools enable researchers to communicate, network, and share documents with many people regardless of location, and at little or no expense. Researchers can build relationships and keep up to date with people involved in their areas of interest. This encourages discussion, debate, and engagement within their community. Researchers can also discover, filter, and share information using networks of experts in a field to help deal with information overload and find relevant information. While most researchers still favor traditional channels for disseminating research findings (books, journals, conferences, etc.), in some disciplines scholars may want to disseminate protocols or primary data without undergoing unnecessary and lengthy peer review. Social media tools provide a useful platform to do this. Social networking may also provide a publication outlet for researchers who have difficulty getting published in high-ranking journals, or who feel frustrated by the tight controls of senior scholars and publishers over traditional selection and dissemination of research. This may be a risky strategy on one hand, but may assist in raising a scholar's research profile. For example, promoting your research by posting links to your articles on blogs, Twitter, and LinkedIn can drive readers to your article, potentially increasing the number of citations.

References

1. Snásel, V., Horak, Z., Abraham, A.: Understanding social networks using formal concept analysis. In: Web Intelligence/IAT Workshops'2008, Sydney, pp. 390–393 (2008)
2. Alexander, B.: Web 2.0: a new wave of innovation for teaching and learning? EDUCAUSE Rev. **41**(2), 32–44 (2006)
3. Hoffman, E.: Evaluating social networking tools for distance learning. In: Proceedings of Technology, Colleges and Community Worldwide Online Conference (TCC 2009) Volume 2009, Hawaii, vol. 1, pp. 92–100 (2009)
4. Brian Solis: The Essential Guide to Social Media, e-book (2008)
5. Boyd, D., Ellison, N.: Social network sites: definition, history and scholarship. J. Comput. Mediat. Commun. **13**(1), 210–230 (2007)
6. Thellwal, M.: Social networks, gender and friending, analysis of Myspace profiles. J. Am. Soc. Inf. Sci. Technol. **591**(8), 1321–1330 (2008)
7. Tufekci, Z.: Grooming, gossip Facebook and Myspace: what can we learn about these sites from those who wont assimilate? J. Inf. Commun. Soc. **11**(4), 544–564 (2008)
8. Sheldon, P.: The relationship between unwillingness to communicate and students' Facebook use. J. Media Psychol. **20**(2), 67–75 (2008)
9. Schrock, A.: Eamining social media usage: technology clusters and social network relationships. First Monday Journal, **14**(1) (2009)
10. Walther, J., Heide, B., Kim, S., Westerman, D., Tang, S.T.: The role of friends appearence and behaviour on evaluations of individuals on facebook: are we known by the comapny we keep? Hum. Commun. Res. **34**, 28–49 (2008)
11. Moor, J.H.: Towards a theory of privacy in the information age. SIGCAS Comput. Soc. **27**(3), 27–32 (1997)
12. Grace, I., Gruhl, D., Haas, K., Nagarajan, M., Robson, C., Sahoo, N.: Artist ranking through analysis of online community comments. In: IBM Tech Report, Almaden (2008). http://domino.research.ibm.com/library/cyberdig.nsf/papers/E50790E56F371154852573870 068A184/$File/rj10421.pdf
13. Shani, G., Chickering, M., Meek, C.: Mining recommendations from the web. In: Proceeding of 2008 ACM Conference on Recommender System, Lausanne, Switzerland, pp. 23–25 (2008)
14. Stutzman, F.: Thoughts about information, social networks, identity and technology. Social Network Transitions, Unit Structures (2007)
15. http://www.readwriteweb.com/archives/the_best_tools_for_visualization.php. Accessed Dec 2011
16. Shivalingaiah, D., Naik, U.: Social networking tools: social bookmarking and social tagging. In: Proceedings of the 8th International CALIBER-2011, Goa University, Goa, 02–04 March 2011
17. Brett: 10 Open source social bookmarking platforms. Available at http://webtecker.com/2008/02/23/11-open-source-social-bookmarking-platforms. Accessed Nov 2011
18. Golbeck, J., Halaschek-Wiener, C.: Trust-based revision for expressive web syndication. J. Logic Comput. **19**(5), 771–790 (2008)
19. Sigurbjörnsson, B., Zwol, R.: Flickr tag recommendation based on collective knowledge. In: Proceeding of the 17th International Conference on World Wide Web, ACM, New York, pp. 327–336 (2008)
20. Chen, S.: The social network game boom, Gamasutra (2009). http://www.gamasutra.com/view/feature/132400/the_social_network_game_boom.php?print=1
21. Radoff, J.: History of social games. Available at http://radoff.com/blog/2010/05/24/history-social-games/ Accessed Sept 2010
22. Grossman, L.: The odd popularity of Mafia Wars. TIME (2009). http://invictusrespite.blogspot.com/2009/11/odd-popularity-of-mafia-wars.html
23. Järvinen, A.: Game design for social networks. In: Proceedings of the 13th International MindTrek Conference: Everyday Life in the Ubiquitous Era, Tampere, pp. 224–225 (2009)

24. Kim, R.: The future of social games is mobile. GigaOM. Available at http://gigaom.com/2010/10/12/the-future-of-social-games-is-mobile Accessed Nov 2011
25. Kleinman, Z.: Social network games catch the eye of computer giants. J. Comput.-Mediat. Commun. 12(4), 1143–1168 (2009)
26. Kohler, C.: 14. Happy Farm (2008). The 15 most influential games of the decade, Wired (2011). http://www.sportshawaii.com/sh/viewtopic.php?f=17&t=34425&view=previous
27. YALSA: Teens & Social Networking in the School & Public Library, American Library Association: Young Adult Library Services Association (YALSA) (2007)
28. Godwin, S., Thorpe, M., Richardson, J.: The impact of computer-mediated interaction on distance learning. Br. J. Educ. Technol. 39(1), 52–70 (2008)
29. Mazer, J.P., Murphy, R.E., Simonds, C.J.: I'll see you on "Facebook": the effects of computer-mediated teacher self-disclosure on student motivation, affective learning, and classroom climate. Commun. Edu. 56(1), 1–17 (2007)
30. Saint-Charles, J., Mongeau, P.: Different relationships for coping with ambiguity and uncertainty in organizations. Soc. Netw. 31, 33–39 (2009)
31. Antheunis, M.L., Valkenburg, P.M., Peter, J.: Getting acquainted through social network sites: testing a model of online uncertainty reduction and social attraction. Comput. Hum. Behav. 26, 100–109 (2010)
32. Gutiérrez-Muñoz, A., Kandel, A.: Current flows in electrical networks for Fuzzy social network analysis (FSNA). Master's thesis, Department of Computer Science and Engineering, University of South Florida (2009)
33. Yang, W.Z., Ge, Y.H., He, J.J., Liu, B.: Designing a group decision support system under uncertainty using group Fuzzy analytic network process (ANP). Afr. J. Bus. Manage. 4(12), 2571–2585 (2010)
34. Hassan, S., Garmendia, L., Pavon, J.: Introducing uncertainty into social simulation: using Fuzzy logic for agent-based modelling. Int. J. Reason.-based Intell. Syst. 2(2), 118–124 (2010)
35. Vindigni, G., Janssen, M.A., Jager, W.: Organic food consumption: a multi-theoretical framework of consumer decision making. Br. Food J. 104(8), 624–642 (2002)
36. Moustafa, W., Deshpande, A., Namata, G., Getoor, L.: Declarative analysis of noisy information networks. In: Proceedings of IEEE 27th International Conference on Department of Computer Science, Data Engineering Workshops (ICDEW'11), IEEE Computer Society, pp. 106–111 (2011)
37. Casey, E.: Error, uncertainty, and loss in digital evidence. Int. J. Digit. Evid. 1(2) (2002). https://utica.edu/academic/institutes/ecii/publications/articles/A0472DF7-ADC9-7FDEC80B5E5B306A85C4.pdf
38. Sommer, C.: Approximate shortest path and distance queries in network. PhD Thesis, Department of Computer Science Graduate School of Information Science and Technology, The University of Tokyo (2010)
39. Michlmayr, E.: Ant algorithms for self-organization in social networks. PhD thesis, Vienna University of Technology, Faculty of Informatics (2007)
40. Lertsuwanakul, L., Unger, H.: An improved greedy routing algorithm for grid using pheromone-based landmark. World Academy of Science, Engineering and Technology (2009)
41. Perumbuduru, S., Dhar, J.: Performance evaluation of different network topologies based on Ant colony optimization. Int. J. Wirel. Mob. Netw. 2(4), 141–157 (2010)
42. Kumar, R., Kumar, M.: Exploring Genetic algorithm for shortest path optimization in data networks. Glob. J. Comput. Sci. Technol. 10(11), 8–12 (2010)
43. Cauvery, N., Viswanatha, K.V.: Routing in dynamic network using ants genetic algorithm. IJCSNS 9(3), pp. 194–200 (2009). http://paper.ijcsns.org/07_book/200903/20090326.pdf
44. White, T., Pagurek, B., Oppacher, F.: ASGA: improving the ant system by integration with genetic algorithms. In: Proceedings of the Third Annual Conference, University of Wisconsin, pp. 610–617 (1999)
45. Araujo, F., Ribeiro, B., Rodrigues, L.: A neural network for Shortest path computation. IEEE Trans. Neural Netw. 12(5), 1067–1073 (2001)

46. Sang, Y., YI, Z.: A modified pulse coupled neural network for shortest path computation. J. Comput. Inf. Syst. **6**(9), 3095–3102 (2010)
47. Deng, Y., Tong, H.: Dynamic shortest path algorithm in stochastic traffic networks using PSO based on fluid neural network. J. Intell. Learn. Syst. Appl. **3**, 11–16 (2011)
48. White, C., Plotnick, L., Kushma, J., Hiltz, S.R., Turoff, M.: An online social network for emergency management. Int. J. Emerg. Manage. **6**(3/4), pp. 369–382 (2009)
49. Hobson, J., Cook, S.: Social media for researchers: opportunities and challenges. MAI Review, Issue 3, (2011). http://www.review.mai.ac.nz/index.php/MR/article/view/455
50. http://en.wikipedia.org/wiki/Betweenness. Accessed 05 Jan 2012

Chapter 2
Hierarchical Graphical Models for Social and Behavioral Analysis and Forecasting

Jian-Wu Xu

Abstract Current approaches to forecast human behavior in different applications depend on human experts. The method is slow, static, biased, and imprecise. Existing computational models do not consider the intrinsic hierarchical characteristics of countries, provinces, tribes, groups, organizations, etc. They predominantly focus on a specific level of organization, therefore confining their applications to a particular network. As different entities in an organization need different levels of abstraction, only a hierarchical knowledge representation would be capable of serving various ranks and levels. We propose a hierarchical-graphical-knowledge-representation (HGKR) to integrate layered abstractions into a coherent structure such that behavior forecasting may propagate downward or aggregate upward. The system consists of a hierarchical graphical model, an evolutionary computation module, inference/forecasting, and decision support to forecast behaviors of groups at different hierarchies. The HGKR is based on initial anthropological information and refined through computational genetic algorithm. We develop a hierarchical-evolutionary-engine and a hierarchical-inference-engine, specifically, a two-stage clustering inference algorithm and hierarchical behavior-forecasting algorithm. The HGKR, together with its inference models, will have numerous applications in many culturally aware domains.

Introduction

As military operations transition into urban environments, the civilian and noncombatant population becomes a significant factor in determining the conduct as well as outcome of any operation. Under asymmetric or irregular warfare conditions, it

J.-W. Xu (✉)
Department of Radiology, The University of Chicago, 5841 South Maryland Avenue,
Chicago, IL 60637, USA
e-mail: jwxu@uchicago.edu

A. Abraham and A.-E. Hassanien (eds.), *Computational Social Networks: Tools,*
Perspectives and Applications, DOI 10.1007/978-1-4471-4048-1_2,
© Springer-Verlag London 2012

becomes increasingly difficult to distinguish friends from foes. Such relationships, in fact, take on a dynamic quality whereby your enemies become your friends and vice versa, as the military operations play out. Finally, the military's own command structure has been changing over time, with more autonomy and decision-making power flowing down to squad leaders and noncommissioned officers. Clearly, modern military operations not only require the ability to navigate and understand the enemies, noncombatants, and coalition partners that make up the human terrain, but also the human dimension of the inner works of the military itself. As Sun Tzu succinctly put this golden principle in *The Art of War*, "Know your enemies and yourself, you will fight without danger in battles. If you only know yourself, but not your opponent, you may win or may lose. If you know neither yourself nor your enemy, you will always endanger yourself." The principle holds true in modern times. As Lt. Gen. P. Chiarelli said in December 2006, "I asked my Brigade Commanders what was the number one thing they would have liked to have had more of, and they all said cultural knowledge." Based on the knowledge of enemies, noncombatants, and coalition partners, forces can make accurate forecast of human behavior and wise decisions so that they might win a significant edge over enemies.

As with other forms of battlefield knowledge, the quality and utility of cultural and human terrain knowledge depend on the methods for collection, processing, and dissemination. Current approaches depend on human experts, surveys, and reporting. The method is slow, static, biased, and imprecise. There are no human terrain sensors, and any attempt to form a human terrain map from current data can at best approximate the terrestrial maps of the fifteenth century – a sketch based on human perception rather than unbiased readings of carefully calibrated instruments.

Fortunately, technology is available to allow a more unbiased, automated, and dynamic approach to human terrain modeling and analysis. Human communication forms raw data from which cultural knowledge is assembled. Traditionally, this communication is captured in the form of anthropological surveys, but it can also be acquired through the observation of formal news outlets, informal outlets (blogs), and other social networking forums. Multiple data mining technologies exist for processing unstructured text, and for extracting it from nontextual sources such as audio streams or video. Collectively, these form the human terrain sensors, which not only make knowledge acquisition fast, but also dynamic. Anthropological surveys represent a single snapshot in time; a collection of human terrain sensors can provide a continuous stream of information, allowing changes to be detected as they happen.

Technological solutions are also available for processing the human terrain data, to reduce processing time and bias. Machine learning techniques, particularly those based on Bayesian statistics, enable the development of systems that can learn patterns from streams of unorganized data. Properly stated, these systems do not model factual knowledge, but rather beliefs based on statistical probabilities of truth. Biologically inspired computing, particularly the modeling of evolutionary forces through genetic algorithms, allows beliefs to compete with each other, such that more fit (i.e., accurate) beliefs outlive less accurate ones. Moreover, the driving evolutionary forces themselves can change over time.

Numerous technological solutions are available for disseminating information, but a more pressing concern is how the information is to be *applied*. All military operations are driven by command decisions, which can only be properly made when there is an understanding of the available course of action, the effects of each, and the tactical or strategic effect desired. Many business decisions can now be made with the assistance of software-driven decision support systems (DSS). Similarly, a DSS can provide a military decision maker with a dashboard view of key demographic indicators, such as approval ratings of various cultural leaders, the growth and decline rates of insurgency membership, or the number and location of recent insurgent activity. The DSS can then provide a set of available decisions, such as to increase or decrease patrol frequency, road-side checks, or incarcerations. Finally, through simulation and behavioral prediction, the DSS can play out the consequences of a potential decision, and through the dashboard, provide feedback to the users.

There has been a great amount of interest in applying computational models in analysis of social networks and human behavior forecasting in recent years. Carley proposed an inference network based on dynamic network analysis to handle large dynamic multi-mode and multi-link networks with varying levels of uncertainty [1]. Subrahmanian developed the Cultural Reasoning Architecture (CARA) system to model terror groups, political parties and others, and forecast organizations' social behaviors [2]. CARA uses socio-cultural-political-economic-religious information provided by social scientists and other data sources (surveys, news, etc.) to model organizations' behaviors. Richards at MIT led a team of researchers from multi-university to develop a computational model for belief revision, group decisions, and culture shifts [3]. Other computational models include multi-agent method [4] and genetic algorithm [5]. Agent-based modeling represents a collection of autonomous decision-making entities as agents and simulates the dynamic interaction among them. Sophisticated agent-based technique incorporates neural networks and evolutionary algorithms to allow realistic learning and adaptation. Lawrenz et al. applied genetic algorithm to predict human beings' (traders) behavior in foreign currency exchange market [5].

However, most existing computational models do not consider the intrinsic hierarchical characteristics of groups or organizations. They focus only on a particular level of organization, thus confining their applications to a particular network, or groups. As different military command levels need different levels of abstraction, only a model with hierarchical representation will be satisfactory.

Method

In this study, we propose a computational model, called hierarchical graphical knowledge representation (HGKR), to describe the intrinsic hierarchy of cultural knowledge. HGKR integrates abstractions in different levels into a coherent structure such that behavioral forecasting at certain level will propagate or aggregate into other levels. Therefore, different levels of behavioral prediction will be available to different ranks of military commands for the same situation and external forces. This will facilitate the information flow among military commands.

Fig. 2.1 System overall architecture

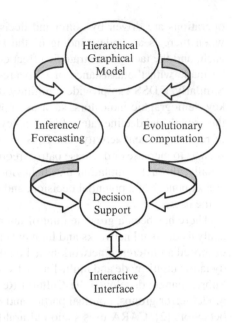

Figure 2.1 illustrates the overall architecture of our proposed methodology. Hierarchical graphical model is the foundation of the system. It represents the targeted groups based on graphical models organized in a hierarchical fashion according to the social, geographical, political, culture, and other information. The initial model takes into account the current anthropological data, information, and knowledge as perceived by the domain expert anthropologists and historians, and continues to incrementally modify the structure of the hierarchy by incorporating the newly acquired and discovered knowledge by the Evolutionary Computation module. The process is introspective to the hierarchy such that it is based entirely on the internal states of the hierarchy at a certain time. The second application of the Evolutionary Computation module is to simulate the graphical model with different combinations of external forces and inputs, such as military actions, economic sanctions, humanitarian aids, etc., to show whether the current model satisfies a fitness function. The core objective of the fitness function should be based on criteria that impute stability to the region under investigation turning the targeted communities and nations from foes to friends. One other application of the Evolutionary Computation module, in its interaction with the Hierarchical Graphical Model, is to notify the human analysts through the Decision Support the discovered beneficial or detrimental patterns of social behaviors. In the former (beneficial patterns) cases, the analysts and the personnel on the field are encouraged to adopt them and in the latter (detrimental patterns) cases the analysts and personnel are encouraged to disband them. In its interaction with the Hierarchical Graphical Model, the Inference/Forecasting module uses machine learning and data mining techniques to *predict* the behavior of the targeted groups at any desired level of the hierarchy. Moreover, the hierarchy would be capable of (1) propagating the prediction downward to the deeper levels of the hierarchy to elucidate the nuances

and fine-grained details of the predicted behavior in the subgraphs at the deeper levels and (2) conversely have them aggregated by abstraction upward to the higher levels to offer a broader perspective of the impact of the targeted predicted behavior. The Decision Support and the Evolutionary Computation module are linked to an interactive user-friendly interface where predictions and discoveries are presented to the outside world (human analysts or simulated environment) as well as receiving questions from the outside and responding to them.

Hierarchical Graphical Model

HGKR Structure

Most of the existing methods represent the studied cultural groups in a nonhierarchi-cal structure which ignores the intrinsic hierarchical organization vital to knowledge management, knowledge scalability, computational tractability and efficiency, and modularity. Our proposed HGKR is naturally amenable to providing the right level of details for variety of personnel with different missions engaging with the systems. For instance, high-level decision makers and strategists may not be interested in detailed nuances which can be derived from deeper levels of the hierarchy, whereas intelligence analysts or game designers might very well be interested in progressively greater details extracted from the system. As demonstrated in Fig. 2.2, each level of the hierarchy is a graph with nodes and edges denoted as $G_i(V_i, E_i)$. Each node V at a certain level of the hierarchy represents a group or community at that level with certain attributes that include, but are not limited to, geographical, culture, social and ideological characteristics, natural resources,

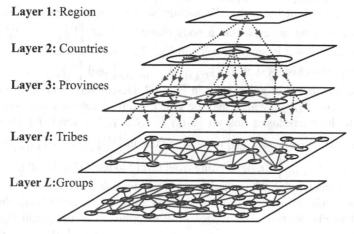

Layer 1: Region

Layer 2: Countries

Layer 3: Provinces

Layer *l*: Tribes

Layer *L*: Groups

Fig. 2.2 Hierarchical graphical knowledge representation

and others. Each edge E between nodes denotes the relationship that can be either inhibitory (adversarial) or excitatory (friendly). Furthermore, quantitative weights are assigned to the edge E to show the degree of the relationship. The weights can be learned and tuned via the Evolutionary Computation module.

The hierarchy will be organized in terms of population, geographical, and other important and relevant characteristics. The highest level represents the broadest geographical region under investigation represented by a single node defined by a small set of attributes shared by all of the subregional nodes in the children levels. The nodes in the second level may denote different countries in that region that not only have the common characteristics defined by the root node but also each containing its own unique attributes. The nodes at the deeper levels in the hierarchy are iteratively further broken down to smaller nodes symbolizing smaller communities inside the larger communities – this decomposition to deeper levels continues to the extent where a community is constrained by either an irreducible territorial heritage/right or ethnic/religious/cultural uniformity.

Similarly links multiply by descending to deeper levels. To see what happens to a graph at a parent level l descending to the child level $(l + 1)$, let $V_{l,1}$ and $V_{l,2}$ be two nodes at level l and let these two nodes be connected by a link $C_{l,(1, 2)}$ characterized by a binary weight vector $(W_{l,(1, 2)}, W_{l,(2, 1)})$, where $W_{l,(1, 2)} > 0$ ($W_{l,(1, 2)} < 0$) implies friendly (adversarial) attitudinal disposition from node $V_{l,1}$ toward node $V_{l,2}$. The binary weight vector clearly indicates that the relationship between nodes $V_{l,1}$ and $V_{l,2}$ is nonsymmetric. We do indeed have many historical cases that attest to this nonsymmetric behavior. For instance, in Second World War, based on historical reasons, Third Reich had bitterness, enmity, and invidious attitude toward Northern and Eastern fronts in Europe with voracious plan to annex a good chunk of Europe to the fascist empire. On the other hand, quite the contrary, Europe at the debut of the war tried very hard, prominently led by Premier Chamberlain of Great Britain, to be appeasing and propitiating. Nodes $V_{l,1}$ and $V_{l,2}$ are decomposed into the node sets $\left\{V^1_{(l+1),1} \cdots V^1_{(l+1),k}\right\}$ and $\left\{V^2_{(l+1),1} \cdots V^2_{(l+1),j}\right\}$ respectively descending from level l to level $(l + 1)$ of the hierarchy. We distinguish between two types of links: intra-cluster links joining nodes within a node cluster such as $\left\{V^1_{(l+1),1} \cdots V^1_{(l+1),k}\right\}$ – these links are shown in maroon color in Fig. 2.2; and inter-cluster links joining nodes across two clusters such as $\left\{V^1_{(l+1),1} \cdots V^1_{(l+1),k}\right\}$ and $\left\{V^2_{(l+1),1} \cdots V^2_{(l+1),j}\right\}$ – these links are shown in green color in Fig. 2.2. Descending from level l to level $(l + 1)$, the link $C_{l,(1, 2)}$, which may be either intra- or inter-cluster, would then multiply to the inter-cluster link set $\{C_{(l+1),1} \cdots C_{(l+1),p}\}$ at level $(l + 1)$, where a link $C_{(l+1),r} \in \{C_{(l+1),1} \cdots C_{(l+1),p}\}$ connects a node in $\left\{V^1_{(l+1),1} \cdots V^1_{(l+1),k}\right\}$ to a node in $\left\{V^2_{(l+1),1} \cdots V^2_{(l+1),j}\right\}$. In descending from level l to level $(l + 1)$, all the intra- or inter-cluster links (at level l) multiply to inter-cluster links (at level $(l + 1)$).

Let the graphs at levels l and $(l + 1)$ be denoted by G_l and $G_{(l+1)}$, the graph G_l is technically defined to be a *projection* mapping P_l of the graph $G_{(l+1)}$ (P_l: $G_{(l+1)} \rightarrow G_l$). The projection P_l projects any node set such as $\left\{V^1_{(l+1),1} \cdots V^1_{(l+1),k}\right\}$ into its parent node $V_{l,1}$ and any link set such as $\{C_{(l+1),1} \cdots C_{(l+1),p}\}$ into its parent link $C_{l,(1,2)}$. Conversely, there exists a *relation* R_l, which we call *extension*, taking the graph G_l onto the graph $G_{(l+1)}$ (R_l: $G_l \rightarrow G_{(l+1)}$), where by extension R_l any l level node such as $V_{l,1}$ extends onto its node set $\left\{ V^1_{(l+1),1} \cdots V^1_{(l+1),k} \right\}$ at level $(l+1)$ (and similarly $V_{l,2}$ extending onto its node set $\left\{ V^2_{(l+1),1} \cdots V^2_{(l+1),j} \right\}$) and any l level link such as $C_{l,(1,2)}$ extends to its link set $\{ C_{(l+1),1} \cdots C_{(l+1),p} \}$. The layered architecture in Fig. 2.2, therefore, generates a sequence of graph *projections* $\{P_1, P_2 \ldots P_{(L-1)}\}$ that allows for an upward chaining and abstraction of information to increasingly more condensed (strategic) information from lower to higher levels. At the same time, it also generates a sequence of *relations* $\{R_1, R_2 \ldots R_{(L-1)}\}$ that allows for a downward chaining and specification of information to increasingly greater (tactical) specificity from higher to lower levels. This forward (backward) chaining over the layered architecture allows for a progressive and tractable addition (deletion) of inherited information desirable for serving various interactive missions, be it high-level strategic decision makers down to deep level intelligence analysts. The inference engine in Fig. 2.1 is the responsible module to trigger such forward (backward) reasoning for inferring relevant data. When asked for explanation on derived information, the inference engine would follow the forward chaining mappings to provide explanation based on deeper levels of the hierarchy. When asked for recommendation steps, the backward chaining can be triggered upward for generating a series of condensed actions.

HGKR Variables

The HGKR variables include the lth level of HGKR where progressively finer details of geo-socio-politico-cultural knowledge (compared to $(l-1)$th level) are inherited from the root node down to the lth level. We denote the deepest level as l_{max} (alternatively L) where HGKR contains the finest and greatest quantity of knowledge represented graphically. l_{max} itself can in principle be considered as a global variable, thus allowing for increase or decrease in the number of HGKR levels.

We denote the graph at the lth level of HGKR as $G(l)$. As a system, $G(l)$ itself is represented by the triplet $< C(l), \mathcal{E}(l), \mathcal{W}(l)>$. $C(l) = \{c(l)_k | k = 1 \ldots K(l)\}$ represents the set of $K(l)$ concepts each representing a node of $G(l)$. We conveniently let K depend on the variable l; where, using the extension relations $R_l \in \{R_1, R_2 \ldots R_{(L-1)}\}$, it is clear that $K(1) < K(2) < \ldots K(l) < \ldots < K(l_{max})$ and we assume $K(l)$ to be fixed. In our model, a node represents a territorial region defined in terms of a set of attributes (size, population, religion, social, political, etc.). The link set is defined as

$$\mathcal{E}(l) = \left\{ e_{k,j} = \left(c(l)_k, c(l)_j\right) = \left(c(l)_j, c(l)_k\right) = e_{j,k} \mid k, j = 1 \ldots K(l); k \neq j \right\}.$$
$$(2.1)$$

$W(k,j) =$

	1	**2**	**...**	**k**	**...**	**K**
	w_{11}	w_{12}	...	w_{1k}	...	w_{1K}
2	w_{21}	w_{22}	...	w_{2k}	...	
	•	•	•	•	•	•
	•	•	•	••••	•	•••• •
	•	•	•	•	•	•
k	w_{k1}	w_{k2}	...	w_{kk}	...	w_{kK}
	•	•	•	•	•	•
	•	•	•	•••	•	••• •
	•	•	•	•	•	•
K	w_{K1}	w_{K2}	...	w_{Kk}	...	w_{KK}

Fig. 2.3 Cross-regional friendly adversarial relationship weight matrix

It represents the set of $\frac{1}{2}K(K-1)$ links, e.g. $e_{k,j}$, connecting $c(l)_k$ to $c(l)_j$. We note that a node is not connected to itself and that $e_{k,j} = e_{j,k}$. The weight set $\mathcal{W}(l) = \{\mathcal{W}_{k,j}|\ k, j = 1\dots K(l)\}$ consists of K^2 scalars; where each pair $(\mathcal{W}_{k,j}, \mathcal{W}_{j,k})$, $k \neq j$, is assigned to a single link $e_{k,j}$ in $\mathcal{E}(l)$. Semantically, we would like these weights to connote friendly or adversarial relationships between regions. By convention we let positive (negative) weights connote friendly (adversarial) relations. We assume zero value weight to be of *measure* zero, thereby assuming all regions having *measurable* cross-regional friendly or adversarial relationships among each other. As analyzed before, we assume in general $\mathcal{W}_{k,j} \neq \mathcal{W}_{j,k}$, thereby making the relationships between any pair of nodes nonsymmetric. We assume the weight $\mathcal{W}_{k,j}$ is bounded from above and below; specifically we let $\mathcal{W}_{k,j} \in [-1, 0] \cup (0, 1)$ – the greater the value of $\mathcal{W}_{k,j}$ $\in (0,1)$ the more friendly the attitude of the node $c(l)_k$ toward the node $c(l)_j$; and the smaller the value of $\mathcal{W}_{k,j} \in [-1, 0]$ the more adversarial the attitude of the node $c(l)_k$ toward the node $c(l)_j$. As for the weight $\mathcal{W}_{k,k}, k = 1\dots K(l)$, we assume each node or region is to a greater or lesser extent in pursuit of its own interest; that is, $\mathcal{W}_{k,k} > 0$. Figure 2.3 represents the weight set $\mathcal{W}(l)$ by a $K \times K$ non-symmetric matrix $W(k,j)$, $k, j = 1\dots K(l)$.

Based on the description above, we assume there exists a sufficiently detailed attribute set $\mathcal{A}(l) = \{a_1, a_2 \dots a_{r(l)}\}$ such that $\mathcal{A}(l)$ is equivalent to the concept set $C(l)$, $l = 1\dots l_{\max}$. $r(l)$ is the size of the attributes. A specific concept, $c_k \in C(l)$, is therefore an instantiation of $A(l)$ denoted by the attribute value vector $vk = \{vk_1, vk_2 \dots vk_{r(l)}\}$, where vk_i is a scalar. Technically, each attribute a_i, $i = 1, 2 \dots r(l)$ is associated with an attribute value domain D_i such that for any concept $c_k \in C(l)$, there exists a mapping f_k: $a_i \rightarrow vk_i \in D_i$ such that it instantiates the concept c_k with the attribute value vector $vk = \{vk_1, vk_2 \ldots vk_{r(l)}\}$. This formalization leads us to a functional $F(l) = \{f_1, f_2 \ldots f_k \ldots f_{K(l)}\}$ such that $F(l)$: $C(l) \rightarrow V(l)$ (or equivalently, $F(l)$: $A(l) \rightarrow V(l)$), where $V(l) = \{vk| k = 1 \ldots K(l)\}$.

We can now define the weight w_{kj} (expressing the attitude of the node c_k towards c_j) in the matrix in Fig. 2.3 as a function of instantiations of c_k and c_j. Specifically, define the mapping $W(l)_{k,j}$: $A(l) \times A(l) \rightarrow V(l) \times V(l)$ such that:

$$W(l)(c_k)\,W(l)(v_k) = w_{k,k}, \tag{2.2}$$

$$W(l)(c_k, c_j) = W(l)(v_k, v_j) = wk. \tag{2.3}$$

In designing the form of $W(l)$, we shall adopt some general rules that hold true across levels. For instance, scarcity of natural resources might be one cause of adversarial behavior, whereas rational and analytic cultures may provide conditions for tolerance and peaceful means for resolving differences and planning for wise resource consumption.

In designing $W(l)$, consider two nodes c_k and c_j at level l of HGKR and let the attribute set at level l be $A(l) = \{a_1, a_2 \ldots a_r\}$. The first step in the design of $W(l)$ is to rank $A(l)$ for each node of $G(l)$. This ranking signifies the preferences of the node; e.g., a node's preferences might be religion over nationalism and individuals' rights, while for another node the preferences might be different. Let $A_k = \{a_{k,1}, a_{k,2} \ldots a_{k,r}\}$ and $A_j = \{a_{j,1}, a_{j,2} \ldots a_{j,r}\}$ be the ranked attribute sequences for the nodes c_k and c_j. Vectors $\Lambda_k = \{d_{k,1}, d_{k,2} \ldots d_{k,r}\}$ and $\Lambda_j = \{d_{j,1}, d_{j,2} \ldots d_{j,r}\}$ denote the attribute value domain sequences for the nodes c_k and c_j, where $d_{k,i} \in D_k$ and $d_{j,i} \in D_j$. The next step is to introduce the weight sequences $U_k = \{u_{k,1}, u_{k,2} \ldots u_{k,r}\}$ and $U_j = \{u_{j,1}, u_{j,2} \ldots u_{j,r}\}$ such that $u_{k,i}, u_{j,i} \in (0, 1)$, $u_{k,1} > u_{k,2} \ldots > u_{k,r}, u_{j,1} > u_{j,2} \ldots > u_{j,r}$ and $\Sigma u_{k,i} = \Sigma u_{j,i} = 1$. Clearly, the inequalities $u_{k,1} > u_{k,2} \ldots > u_{k,r}$ and $u_{j,1} > u_{k,2} \ldots > u_{j,r}$ reflect the partial ordering reigning over the ranked sequences $\{a_{k,1}, a_{k,2} \ldots a_{k,r}\}$ and $\{a_{j,1}, a_{j,2} \ldots a_{j,r}\}$.

Next we must scale the values in the sequences Λ_k and Λ_j by their respective weight sequences $U_k = \{u_{k,1}, u_{k,2} \ldots u_{k,r}\}$ and $U_j = \{u_{j,1}, u_{j,2} \ldots u_{j,r}\}$. One obvious algebraic operation is to form the outer products $U_k \otimes \Lambda_k = (u_{k,1}d_{k,1}, u_{k,2}d_{k,2} \ldots u_{k,r}d_{k,r})$ and $U_j \otimes \Lambda_j = (u_{j,1}d_{j,1}, u_{j,2}d_{j,2} \ldots u_{j,r}d_{j,r})$. We now propose

$$W(l)(c_k, c_j) = W(l)(U_k \otimes L_k, U_j \otimes L_j). \tag{2.4}$$

It is to be noted that $U_k \otimes \Lambda_k$ and $U_j \otimes \Lambda_j$ are vectors but the form $W(l)$ outputs a scalar. Therefore, the operations performed by $W(l)$ will have to be constrained by its scalar output. We also note that, in general,

$$W(l)(c_k, c_j) = W(l)(U_k \otimes \Lambda_k, U_j \otimes \Lambda_j) \neq W(l)(c_j, c_k)$$

$$= W(l)(U_j \otimes \Lambda_j, U_k \otimes \Lambda_k), \tag{2.5}$$

thus satisfying the nonsymmetric requirement for $W(l)(c_k, c_j)$.

In summary, each level l of HGKR is represented by a graph $G(l)$ which is itself represented by the triplet $< C(l), E(l), W(l)>$. $C(l)$ is the concept set, $E(l)$ is the link set, and $W(l)$ is the weight matrix. The concept set $C(l)$ is equivalent to a sufficiently detailed attribute set $A(l) = \{a_1, a_2 \ldots a_{r(l)}\}$ tuned to uniquely define the concepts in $C(l)$ at the level l of HGKR. $c_k \in C(l)$ is an instantiation of $A(l)$.

HGKR Design and Construction

Consider the case of the Middle East as the highest level of HGKR. Clearly, due to the heterogeneity of the Middle East (and its constituent countries), it becomes tenuous defining the concept sets of the top levels of HGKR by detailed attribute sets. It is, therefore, reasonable to suggest that concepts at higher levels in HGKR are defined by a small set of coarse grain attributes. As one penetrates into deeper levels of HGKR, one would incrementally add finer grain attributes to the attribute set.

Unless otherwise explicitly stated for a specific level, by default we admit to inclusion inheritance partial ordering of attribute sets from level l to level $(l + 1)$; that is, by default $A(l) \subset A(l + 1)$. It is important to bear in mind that this inheritance relationship does not hold for the attribute value set $V(l)$. The attribute value v of the attribute a of the concept c at level l of HGKR will in general be different from the attribute values $v_1 \ldots v_n$ of the same attribute a for the children concepts $c_1 \ldots c_n$ of c at level $(l + 1)$ of HGKR. Also of importance, is to note that due to the heterogeneity of top levels, the attribute values at top levels are fuzzy with greater uncertainty while deeper levels would in general be more homogeneous with greater certainty assigned to attribute values.

Step 1 – Generate an over arching attribute ontology that covers the attributes pertaining to HGKR as shown in Fig. 2.4a, b. The structures are fragments of an ontology based on initial anthropological data.

Step 2 – (This and the next step run interactively and in parallel) Select the geographical region of interest and have it hierarchically decomposed into progressively smaller regions that constitute the elements for defining each level of HGKR based on relevant cultural information. The guideline for decomposition of the region of interest into progressively smaller subregions would be greater overall homogeneity of subregions at each level based on the aggregate effect of attribute set specific to each level. The scale of homogeneity is application dependent, and one great advantage of a hierarchical representation is that one can predefine that scale by prefixing the deepest level of hierarchy the application demands.

One natural way for automated territory decomposition is to exploit one of the regular decomposition methods such as QuadTree or Quadratic Binary Triangular (so called Peano-Cesaro) decomposition. From a high-level point of view, the *regionalization* algorithm is made up of two main functions.

Decomposition Function: Decompose the current node provided by the decomposition function into its children nodes and for each compute its

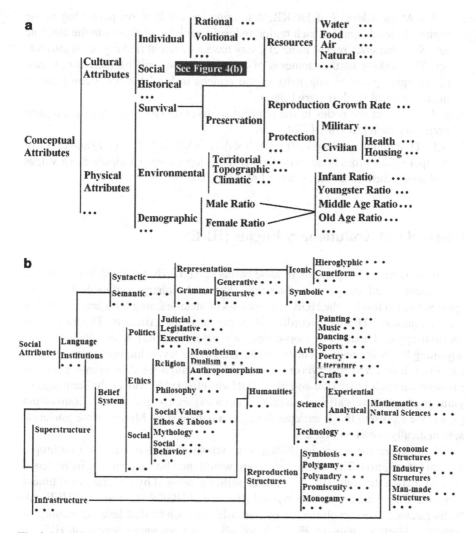

Fig. 2.4 (a): A fragment of conceptual ontology. (b): Social attributes of conceptual ontology

homogeneity. If the difference in homogeneity between the children nodes is above a predefined threshold, we maintain the children and stop the decomposition function. Otherwise we retract to the parent node and declare it as homogeneous – one may want to penetrate one more level to ensure even grandchildren nodes are homogenous.

Regionalization Function: Apply a clustering algorithm to the generated homogeneous nodes in order to merge homogenous neighboring nodes, thereby partitioning the territory into a set of regions.

Step 3 – At each level *l* of HGKR, determine the attribute set pertaining to the regions in level *l* and for each region in level *l*, rank the attributes in the attribute set. Note that each region in level *l* may have a different ranking of its attribute set. The ranking of the elements of the attribute set will be used for at least (1) computing the homogeneity of the regions in level *l* and (2) computation in Hierarchical Evolutionary Engine.

Step 4 – Connect the nodes in the concept set to build $G(l)$, which is a complete graph, for each level of HGKR.

Step 5 – Design the mapping $W(l)_{k,j}$: $A(l) \times A(l) \rightarrow V(l) \times V(l)$ in (2.2) and (2.3) for computing the cross node attitudinal relationship values. Compute these values and assign them to the links in the link set E(*l*).

Hierarchical Evolutionary Engine (HEE)

The Evolutionary Computation module builds upon the HGKR module to simulate the system based on genetic algorithm. The evolutionary computation will be applied to each level of the HGKR. It consists of meta-learning for a *fitness function* which optimizes HGKR according to a pre-designed criterion. The projection (bottom-up) and extension (top-down) movement in HGKR are indicative of adjoining levels interdependencies in HGKR. Higher levels impose structural form on lower levels and vice versa – in Darwinian language they create selection pressure on each other (the so-called Baldwin effect) [6] and in the language of game theory the levels affect each other for convergence to global Nash Equilibrium [7, 8]. We represent this interdependency as a (single step) Markov state transition schematically shown in Fig. 2.5.

We initialize the levels in HGKR with graphical models based on anthropological information. This layered structure would then be subjected to incremental transformation through HEE for optimal utility expressed by a hierarchical fitness function. Concomitant with the layered structure of HGKR the design of HEE will be hierarchical – one evolutionary engine (EE) per each HGKR level. Concomitant with the Markov chain in Fig. 2.5 we allow the adjoining levels of HEE to communicate with each other in transforming the graphical models of HGKR – Fig. 2.6 describes the state of affair. In Fig. 2.6, brown cycles represent the interdependencies of the adjoining levels of HGKR as in Fig. 2.5. The deep blue cycles represent the communication channels between each components of HEE so that collaboratively they optimize the graphical models in HGKR. The green cycles represent the training action of the HEE components on the levels of HGKR.

Fig. 2.5 A Markov state transition exhibiting the interdependencies of the adjoining graphical models in HGKR

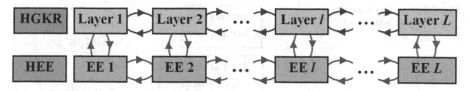

Fig. 2.6 Hierarchical Evolutionary Engine (*HEE*) adapted to transform HGKR

Genetic Algorithm

We use genetic algorithms (GA) to learn the fitness function. GA falls within the stochastic paradigm of learning that is loosely related to Darwinian theory of evolution [6]. Hypothesis (the equivalent of a gene in natural evolution), and in our case $W(l)$ in (2), is represented in bit strings, symbolic expressions, or computational functions. The search for an appropriate hypothesis begins with a population of initial hypotheses randomly generated. GA goes through cycles or generations of evolution changing the patterns of hypotheses representations by shifting and recombining the components of the representations inspired by mutation and crossover operations in biological genetic processes. At each step, the hypotheses in the current population are evaluated relative to a given measure expressed as a fitness function, with the fittest hypothesis having greater probability of multiplying itself and thereby having greater likelihood of entering the next generation. The current population of genes/hypotheses is updated by replacing some fraction of the population by offspring genes of the fittest current genes, thus forming the new generation. Specifically, in each iteration a new population is generated by probabilistically selecting the fittest genes from the current population. Some of the genes are randomly allowed to go to the next generation while other selected fittest genes form the basis for creating new offspring by crossover and mutation operations. Technically, the above process forms a generate-and-test beam search of the hypotheses in which variants of the best current hypotheses are most likely to join the next generation. This process continues until a predominant ratio of the population is occupied by highly fit genes of which a few of the highest fit are recommended as output.

As to the purpose of the fitness function, assume in an application the responsibility of GA is to learn an approximate form of an unknown function (similar to $W(l)$ in (2)) given the training examples of its input and output. For such an application, the fitness could be defined as the accuracy of hypothesis over the training data. If, on the other hand, the task at hand is testing the success or failure of a strategy in operation, then the fitness could be defined as the ratio of the number of successes of the strategy over the total number of trials.

For our application, since we are operating at multiple levels, each level of HEE transforming the respective level of HGKR requires its own fitness function. Let $F(l)$ be the fitness function for EE(l), the lth level evolutionary engine. In the spirit of the problem of approximating the form of a function alluded to above, we would

Fig. 2.7 Learning the form of the weights $W(l)_{k,j}$, $\forall k$, $j = 1, 2 \ldots K(l)$

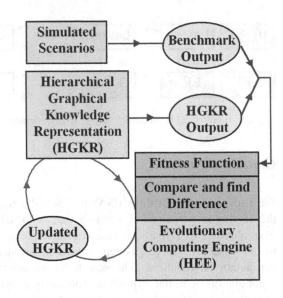

like to learn the form of $W(l)_{k,j}$, $\forall k, j = 1, 2 \ldots K(l)$, where $K(l)$ is the cardinality of $C(l)$, the concept set at level l of HGKR. For learning the form of $W(l)_{k,j}$ we propose to simulate scenarios as a validation platform and running the same scenarios using the proposed system and apply the fitness function $F(l)$ to learn and improve $W(l)_{k,j}$. Figure 2.7 shows the information flow in applying HEE to HGKR and the use of simulation runs in learning $W(l)_{k,j}$. There are many variants of GA [6, 9, 10]. Table 2.1 presents one version of genetic algorithm [6].

Genetic Programming (GP) is a form of evolutionary computation in which the individuals in the evolving population are functions rather than symbols such as bits, numbers, characters, etc. [11–13]. The functions manipulated by GP are typically represented by tree structures corresponding to the parse tree of the program computing the function. Each function call is represented by a node in the tree, and the arguments to the function are given by its descendent nodes. To use the example in [6], in computing the function $f(x, y) = \sin(x) + \sqrt{(x^2 + y)}$, the program represent $f(x, y)$ by a tree structure shown in Fig. 2.8. The fitness of a given individual function in the population is determined by executing the function on some set of training data and see how closely its output compares to the true output.

The task of learning the form of $W(l)_{k,j}$ in (2.4) is considerably more intricate than a simple function such as $f(x, y)$ above. The two sequences with variables involved in (2.4) are $U_k \otimes \Lambda_k = (u_{k,1}d_{k,1}, u_{k,2}d_{k,2} \ldots u_{k,r}d_{k,r})$ and $U_j \otimes \Lambda_j = (u_{j,1}d_{j,1}, u_{j,2}d_{j,2} \ldots u_{j,r}d_{j,r})$ giving rise to $2r(l)$ scalar variables per pair of node sequences per level l of HGKR. For $K(l)$ nodes at level l of HGKR, there are $K(l)^2$ pairs of sequences giving rise to $r(l)K(l)^2$ number of scalar variables per level l of HGKR and for the entire hierarchy the total number of scalar variables counts to

$$\sum_{l=1}^{l=l_{max}} r(l)K(l)^2.$$

To make the epistemological complexity of the functional form of $W(l)_{k,j}$ tractable, we assume that the search in the space of solutions for the mathematical

Table 2.1 Genetic algorithm

Input:

   (a) $FF(.)$ the fitness function; (b) FT, a threshold specifying the termination criterion; (c) p, the number of hypotheses/genes to be included in the population P; (d) r, the fraction of the population to be replaced by Crossover at each step; (e) m, the mutation rate. Also, P_s denotes for the next generation of genes; h denotes a hypotheses; and $Pr(h)$ is the probability of selecting hypotheses h to be added to P_s

Initialization:

   Populate P with p number of hypotheses generated randomly and for each $h{\in}P$, compute $FF(h)$

While $\max_h FF(h) < FT$

   Select: probabilistically select $(1 - r)p$ members of P to add to P_s
      $Pr(h) = FF(h)/\Sigma_{g{\in}P}FF(g)$
   Crossover: probabilistically select $r.p/2$ pairs of hypotheses from P_s according to $Pr(h)$
      in (2.6)
   For each pair h_i, $h_j{\in}P$ in the set of $r.p/2$ pairs produce two offspring by applying the
      Crossover operator
   Mutation: Choose m percent of the members of P_s with uniform probability denoted as
      set P'_s
   For each $h_k{\in} P'_s$, Randomly invert some subset of the gene bit string in their
      representations
   Update: Set $P = P_s$
   Evaluate: For each $h{\in} P_s$, compute $FF(h)$
End

Output:

   The hypotheses h^* from P with highest $FF(h^*)$

---

operators combining $U_k \otimes \Lambda_k$ and $U_j \otimes \Lambda_j$ are between corresponding pairs of their scalar variable. Therefore, mathematical combinations are done pair-wise on attributes of the same type such as (Religion$_k$, Religion$_j$), (Nationalism$_k$, Nationalism$_j$), etc. As the attribute set $A(l) = \{a_1, a_2 \dots a_r\}$ is ranked for each node of $G(l)$ at lth level of HGKR, this homologous type-type attribute correspondence would require two *conjugate* link pairs (c_k, c_j) and (c_j, c_k) depending on which node is the first in the pair. Without loss of generality, we let the two correspondences be: $u_{k,1}d_{k,1}{\leftrightarrow}u_{j,k1}d_{j,k1}$; $u_{k,2}d_{k,2}{\leftrightarrow}u_{j,k2}d_{j,k2} \dots$ $u_{k,r}d_{k,r}{\leftrightarrow}$ $u_{j,kr}d_{j,kr}$ and $u_{j,1}d_{j,1}{\leftrightarrow}u_{k,j1}d_{k,j1}$; $u_{j,2}d_{j,2}{\leftrightarrow}u_{k,j2}d_{k,j2} \dots$ $u_{j,r}d_{j,r}{\leftrightarrow}$ $u_{k,jr}d_{k,jr}$. Once again, the basic rationale for this type-type correspondence is the dictum: "apple for apple" and "orange for orange." In other words, it is plausible that the variables quantifying the same pair of attributes should be combined pair-wise. Let R be the set of binary mathematical operators acting upon corresponding pairs of variables in $U_k \otimes \Lambda_k$ and $U_j \otimes \Lambda_j$. (2.4) would then change to:

$$W(l)\left(c_k, c_j\right) = W(l)\left(R_{k1}\left(u_{k,1}d_{k,1}, u_{j,k1}d_{j,k1}\right), R_{k2}\left(u_{k,2}d_{k,2}, u_{j,k2}d_{j,k2}\right), \dots,\right.$$
$$\left. R_{kr}\left(u_{k,r}d_{k,r}, u_{j,kr}d_{j,kr}\right)\right) \tag{2.6}$$

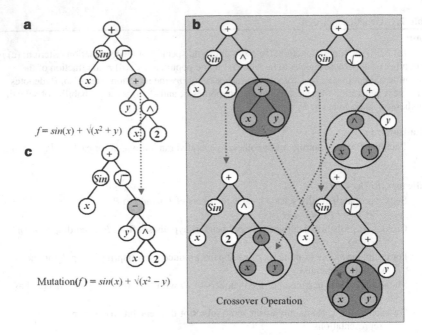

Fig. 2.8 Examples of genetic operations in genetic algorithm

$$W(l)\left(c_j, c_k\right) = W(l)\left(R_{j1}\left(u_{j,1}d_{j,1}, u_{k,j1}d_{k,j1}\right), R_{j2}\left(u_{j,2}d_{j,2}, u_{k,j2}d_{k,j2}\right), \ldots,\right.$$

$$\left.R_{jr}\left(u_{j,r}d_{kjr}, u_{k,jr}d_{k,jr}\right)\right), \tag{2.7}$$

where, $R_z \in R$, $z = 1, 2 \ldots r$. We notice how (2.6) and (2.7) give rise to the non-symmetric $W(l)$ for the pairs (c_k, c_j) and (c_j, c_k).

Next, we need to combine the terms in the sequences $S_k = (R_{k1}(u_{k,1}d_{k,1}, u_{j,k1}d_{j,k1})$, $R_{k2}(u_{k,2}d_{k,2}, u_{j,k2}d_{j,k2}), \ldots, R_{kr}(u_{k,r}d_{k,r}, u_{j,kr}d_{j,kr}))$ and $S_j = (R_{j1}(u_{j,1}d_{j,1}, u_{k,j1}d_{k,j1})$, $R_{j2}(u_{j,2}d_{j,2}, u_{k,j2}d_{k,j2}), \ldots, R_{jr}(u_{j,r}d_{kjr}, u_{k,jr}d_{k,jr}))$.

Once again, we recall that the attribute set $A(l) = \{a_1, a_2 \ldots a_r\}$ for each node at level l is ranked with the ith element having higher rank than $(i + 1)$th element. We therefore reason that the term $R_i(.)$ has higher precedence over the term $R_{i+1}(.)$. An obvious integration would be linear weighted function of the components in sequence S; that is,

$$W(l)\left(c_k, c_j\right) = \omega_{k1} R_{k1}\left(u_{k,1}d_{k,1}, u_{j,k1}d_{j,k1}\right) + \omega_{k2} R_{k2}\left(u_{k,2}d_{k,2}, u_{j,k2}d_{j,k2}\right)$$

$$+ \ldots + \omega_{kr} R_{kr}\left(u_{k,r}d_{k,r}, u_{j,kr}d_{j,kr}\right), \tag{2.8}$$

$$W(l)\left(c_j, c_k\right) = \omega_{j1} R_{j1}\left(u_{j,1}d_{j,1}, u_{k,j1}d_{k,j1}\right) + \omega_{j2} R_{j2}\left(u_{j,2}d_{j,2}, u_{k,j2}d_{k,j2}\right)$$

$$+ \ldots + \omega_{jr} R_{jr}\left(u_{j,r}d_{kjr}, u_{k,jr}d_{k,jr}\right), \tag{2.9}$$

where, ω_{ki}, $\omega_{ji} \in (0, 1)$ $\forall i = 1, 2 \ldots r$, $\forall k$, $j = 1, 2 \ldots K(l)$ and $\Sigma_i \omega_{ki} = \Sigma_i \omega_{ji} = 1$. Another integration alternative might be the receding horizon where the proceeding $(i + 1)$th term affects the overall value for $W(l)$ less than the preceding ith term by an exponent power law form, where the exponent $\varepsilon \in (0, 1)$; that is, the terms in S_k would transform to $[(R_{k1}(u_{k,1}d_{k,1}, u_{j,k1}d_{j,k1}), R_{k2}(u_{k,2}d_{k,2}, u_{j,k2}d_{j,k2})^\varepsilon \ldots R_{kr}(u_{k,r}d_{k,r}, u_{j,kr}d_{j,kr})^{\varepsilon\,(r-1)})]$ and similarly for S_j.

Learning HGKR Weights

There are two sets of variables to be learnt for our proposed social network analysis system. (1) For each level l of HGKR and each node $c_k \in C(l)$, $k = 1, 2 \ldots K(l)$, with ranked attribute sequence $A_k = \{a_{k,1}, a_{k,2} \ldots a_{k,r}\}$ and associated weight sequence $U_k = \{u_{k,1}, u_{k,2} \ldots u_{k,r}\}$, such that $u_{k,i} \in (0, 1)$ and $\Sigma u_{k,i} = 1$, learn the weights in $U_k = \{u_{k,1}, u_{k,2} \ldots u_{k,r}\}$. These weights are needed for learning the weight function $W(l)$ in (2.4). (2) Learn the form of the function $W(l)_{k,j}$ in (2.4) $\forall l = 1, 2 \ldots l_{max}$; and $\forall k$, $j = 1, 2 \ldots K(l)$. We accomplish the tasks in five steps as follows:

First-Order Solution – Learn the weights in $U_k = \{u_{k,1}, u_{k,2} \ldots u_{k,r}\}$ by assuming a single level HGKR with K nodes. We assume given a functional form for $W(l)$. The GA algorithm presented above is ready to be exploited for learning $U_k = \{u_{k,1}, u_{k,2} \ldots u_{k,r}\}$. The only additional concerns are three: The algorithm has to be extended with two (outer and inner) loops to learn all the scalars $u_{k,i}$, $i = 1, 2 \ldots r$; $k = 1, 2 \ldots K$, $u_{k,i} \in (0, 1)$, and $\Sigma u_{k,i} = 1$, $\forall i = 1, 2 \ldots r$.

With respect to the first concern, the outer and inner loops are respectively over $k = 1, 2 \ldots K$, and $i = 1, 2 \ldots r$. The inner loop will have to go through all the current population pools $P^t{}_{k,i}$, current time slice $t = 1, 2 \ldots$ and $i = 1, 2 \ldots r$, before GA algorithm starts the new population pools $P^{t+1}{}_{k,i}$.

With respect to the second concern, we must quantize the open unit interval $U = (0, 1)$ into a digitized (binary) linear grid satisfying the level of accuracy the application requires. Let the grid consist of D partitions. A binary decomposition of U would then output a binary bit string with a length of order $\lceil log_2 D \rceil$. This binarization can be made smart in the sense that (1) the intervals of the partition need not be uniform; and (2) D, the number of partitions, can itself be considered as a global variable so that any level of accuracy can be achieved by selecting an accuracy threshold.

With respect to the third concern, before GA algorithm starts the new population pools $P^{t+1}{}_{k,i}$, the weights $u_{k,i}$ $\forall i = 1, 2 \ldots r$ will have to be renormalize using the substitution $u_{k,i} \Leftarrow u_{k,i}/[\Sigma u_{k,i}{}^2]^{1/2}$.

Second-Order Solution – Learn the weights in $U_k = \{u_{k,1}, u_{k,2} \ldots u_{k,r}\}$ for an l_{max} layered HGKR with $K(l)$ nodes at level l. We assume given a functional form for $W(l)$ for all levels. Again, GA is the main pillar of computation for this solution. Over and above the three concerns addressed for the first solution, the algorithm has to have another overarching outer loop cycling repeatedly through the levels of HGKR until the desired level of fidelity sought for $u_{k,i}$ $\forall i = 1, 2 \ldots r(l)$ and $\forall l = 1, 2 \ldots l_{max}$ is achieved. A cycle starts from the root of HGKR down to the leaf level at $l = l_{max}$ and back to the root node for a new cycle.

Third-Order Solution – Learn the functional form of $W(l)_{k,j}$ by assuming a single level HGKR with K nodes. We assume the weights $U_k = \{u_{k,1}, u_{k,2} \ldots u_{k,r}\}$ are given for that single level. Learning the functional form of $W_{k,j}$ for a single level HGKR requires extending the capabilities of GA presented above to a genetic program (GP) suitable for our application. In the previous section, we have already presented some discussion on GP and conducted some epistemological complexity analysis on the form of $W(l)$ (c_k, c_j). If we apply our analysis to transforming the GA to a GP, we need to generate a bit string, say s_1, representing the mathematical operators in the set R and another bit string, say s_2, representing the set of weights ($\omega_{k1} \ldots \omega_{kr}$). Crossovers and mutations would then be applied to s_1 and s_2 for learning the form of $W(l)$ (c_k, c_j). As in the first-order solution, the core constructed GP will have to be embedded within two loops: the outer loop ranging over k = 1, 2 \ldots K, and the inner loop ranging over $i = 1, 2 \ldots r$.

Fourth-Order Solution – Learn the functional form of $W(l)_{k,j}$ for an l_{max} layered HGKR with $K(l)$ nodes at level l. We assume the weights $U_k = \{u_{k,1}, u_{k,2} \ldots u_{k,r}\}$ are given for all levels. Learning the functional form of $W_{k,j}(l)$ for an l_{max} layered HGKR would take the third-order solution and embed it inside an overarching outer loop cycling repeatedly through the levels of HGKR until the desired level of fidelity sought for $W_{k,j}(l)$, $\forall l = 1, 2 \ldots l_{max}$ is achieved. A cycle starts from the root of HGKR down to the leaf level at $l = l_{max}$ and back to the root node for a new cycle.

Fifth-Order Solution – Learn in an interleaving mode both the weights in $U_k = \{u_{k,1}, u_{k,2} \ldots u_{k,r}\}$ and the functional form of $W(l)_{k,j}$ for an l_{max} layered HGKR with $K(l)$ nodes at level l. Finally, this solution requires interleaving the second- and the third-order solutions. There can be many interleaving variants. The two extremes for interleaving the computations for learning $U_k = \{u_{k,1}, u_{k,2} \ldots u_{k,r}\}$ and $W(l)$ (c_k, c_j) are (1) interleaving the optimizations for U_k and $W(l)$ (c_k, c_j) at each call of the outer loop through the variable $l = 1, 2 \ldots l_{max}$ and (2) letting one complete cycle through $l = 1, 2 \ldots l_{max}$ dedicated to updating U_k and the next cycle dedicated to updating $W(l)$ (c_k, c_j). Clearly, there exist many interleaving linear combination variations in between these two extremes.

Hierarchical Inference Engine (HIE)

The Inference/Reasoning module focuses on inferring underlying and unknown structure of the HGKR. Specifically, we intend to infer which nodes (tribes, villages, groups, etc.) will form allies or conflicting groups and relationship among these formed groups. Inference derived at certain levels in HGKR will propagate or aggregate into other levels. Therefore, the impact on other levels can be inferred when an action is taken toward a certain group at a particular level. The inference module also contains a graph-mining algorithm, which discovers and explores critical links and nodes in the graphs. Critical links and nodes are defined as the ones positioned in the bottleneck of information passage in the graph. Depending on the nature of the links (friendly or adversarial), certain military actions might be considered to encourage and strengthen friendly links, or discourage and eliminate adversarial ones, in order to stabilize and improve the regional situations. It is also beneficial to separate desirable situations and actions from undesirable ones. The important component of this module is to predict how members of the groups at each level may act upon a certain set of determining conditions.

The Hierarchical Inference Engine consists of hierarchical clustering inference (HCI) and hierarchical behavior forecasting algorithm (HBFA). HCI aims to infer clustering structures for the nodes in HGKR and discovers critical links. The most important component of HIE is the HBFA which predicts behavior and (re)action of individual members in HGKR.

Hierarchical Clustering Inference (HCI)

The objective of hierarchical clustering algorithm is to infer which nodes (tribes, villages, groups, etc.) in HGKR will form clusters. A cluster in a graph is defined as a group of nodes sharing similar attributes and having homogeneous links among them. A cluster of nodes with friendly edges forms an ally, whereas a cluster of nodes with adversarial links represents a conflicting group. HCI can be used to facilitate military command to quickly identify clusters of entities (tribes, villages, groups, etc.) and take collective actions. Entities with similar attributes (history, geographical, culture, social and ideological characteristics, natural resources, etc.) might have the tendency to form allies as they share common grounds. However, this is also determined by their links to a great degree such that even two nodes with similar attributes might be in conflict stage to compete for resources as their link is adversarial. On the other hand, nodes with homogenous weight connection (friendly or adversarial) might not form strong allies because they do not share similar backgrounds. Therefore, the attributes of nodes and edges among them are two complementary characteristics to determine the cluster structure of graph.

The attributes of nodes form the first set of features for clustering analysis. We model this set of features as continuous random variables $X_n \in R^K$ where the dimensionality K depends on the number of attributes for the nodes in HGKR. Edges of nodes constitute the second set of feature vectors. Edges can take on positive and negative values. The signs are critical since only nodes with homogenous links can form clusters. So the signs are represented as discrete random variables $S_n \in \{-1, +1\}$. The weights assigned to each edge $W(l)$ are defined in section "HGKR Variables" and are modeled as continuous random variables $w \in [-1, 1]$. Here, we relax the condition that weight can attain zero value which indicates there is no link between two nodes.

We propose a two-stage clustering algorithm for HCI. The first stage separates nodes in graph at any level into different subsets such that all the links inside each subset would be either positive (friendly) or negative (adversarial). In the second stage, we combine the first set of normalized features X_n with the second set of feature w into an augmented feature vector $Y_n = [X_n w]$, and use a graphical clustering method to perform clustering for each subsets obtained from the first-stage analysis.

Stage 1: Graph Partition Based on Weight Matrix

Given the weight matrix $W(k,j)$ defined in section "HGKR Variables," we aim to partition the graph into subgraphs with nodes of homogenous links so that each sub-graph is either a friendly ally or a conflicting group. Due to the high dimensionality of weight matrix, exhaustive search might be computationally expensive. Therefore, we propose a feasible optimization programming methodology to partition graph based on the weight matrix. The intermediate results from stage 1 will serve as candidate sets for stage 2 processing. On the other hand, these intermediate results can also be used to infer grouping patterns of nodes in a broad perspective. While the clustering after stage 2 is able to provide more detailed structures. Therefore, two-stage hierarchical clustering algorithm offers coarse-to-refined resolution and insight into the underlying structure of graph.

Stage 2: Information-Theoretic Spectral Clustering

As the structure of graph represented in the feature vector space would be highly nonlinear and irregular, conventional linear clustering approaches, such as k-means algorithm, would fail to capture the underlying structure. We propose to apply an information-theoretic spectral clustering method to our problem [14]. The information-theoretic spectral clustering method is based on graph cut concept and information theory which utilizes higher order statistical information of data samples. The clustering algorithm aims to minimize the *information cut* which is derived from Cauchy-Schwarz information equality.

The Cauchy-Schwarz information equality is defined as

$$D_{\text{CS}} = -\log \frac{\int p(x)q(x)dx}{\sqrt{\int p^2(x)dx \int q^2(x)dx}}, \qquad (2.10)$$

where $p(x)$ and $q(x)$ are two probability density functions (pdf) for clusters 1 and 2. Using Parzen method to estimate the pdfs with Gaussian kernel, we can direct estimate the argument of D_{CS} which is called the *information cut*:

$$IC = \frac{\sum_{i=1}^{N_1} \sum_{j=1}^{N_2} k_{ij}}{\sqrt{\sum_{i=1}^{N_1} \sum_{i'=1}^{N_1} k_{ii'} \sum_{j=1}^{N_2} \sum_{j'=1}^{N_2} k_{jj'}}}, \qquad (2.11)$$

where k_{ij}, $k_{ii'}$, and $k_{jj'}$ are kernel value for data points, respectively. The information cut can be easily extended into multiple subgroup case. Minimization of information cut leads to a global stationary point of partition of graph.

Critical links/nodes finding: an immediate result obtained after clustering analysis is the discovery of critical links and nodes in the graph. *Critical links* are defined as the edges connecting two clusters. *Critical nodes* are defined as clusters with single node and connecting at least two other clusters. The critical links and nodes position in the bottleneck of information and influence flow in HGKR. Therefore, actions to strengthen or weaken these links or eliminate critical nodes will have greatest impact on the whole graph. To identify these links and nodes is of highly desirable to military# commands.

Rule 1: searching *critical nodes:* it is quite straightforward to search critical nodes after we obtain cluster structure of the graph. First, we count the cardinality of each cluster. If the number of nodes in that cluster is 1, we label that cluster as a candidate. After that, we search the edges linking that node with other clusters, if it has more than two links belonging to two different other clusters, then we identify that node as a critical node.

Rule 2: searching *critical links*: after the clustering algorithm produces subgraphs, external edges among clusters can be identified through searching weight matrix. These external edges are candidates for critical links. Furthermore, if the number of external links connecting two clusters is less than the number of nodes in either of clusters, then those links will be considered as critical links. In extreme case, if there is only one link connecting two clusters, then that link is the most important critical link in graph.

The Hierarchical Clustering Inference can be applied to any levels of the HGKR. Since HGKR is constructed in a hierarchical approach and organized in clusters, the results from HCI can be used to compare against the initial construction. Therefore, HCI offers an alternative perspective toward the whole region under study and provides fresh views on the grouping (friendly or adversarial) patterns.

Hierarchical Behavior Forecasting Algorithm (HBFA)

One of most important components of HGKR is the hierarchical behavior forecasting algorithm, which predicts how members of the modeled group may act under certain conditions. Given the HGKR, HBFA can be readily expressed as a conditional probability under certain constraints. Consider farmers in Pakistan-Afghanistan scenario, we can translate any *what-if* inquiry into a conditional probability. For example, military commands might be interested in seeking answers to *how likely will farmers cultivate poppies if they have a level of debt over t*. This can be quantified as $p(A|G,I)$, where A is the list of actions, G is our HGKR model, and I is a set of conditions. Here $A = farmers\ cultivate\ poppies$ and $I = debt\ level\ over\ t$. HBFA is able to handle complex inquiries. That is, the action list and condition set can have more than one elements, $A = A_1 \cap A_2, ..., \cap A_n$ and $I = I_1 \cap I_2, ..., \cap I_n$. For example, we can investigate the inquiry *how likely will farmers cultivate poppies and be hostile to foreign visitors if they have a level of debt over t and Taliban is active in the local region*.

In a more general term, HBFA is able to compute the conditional probability,

$$p(A|G, I) = \frac{p(I, A|G)}{p(I|G)}, \tag{2.12}$$

where $p(I, A|G)$ and $p(I|G)$ are conditional likelihood probabilities. This general framework can handle any complex inquiry.

More interestingly, given a list of predefined actions, we search which particular action will be the most likely or most unlikely one under certain conditions. This is equivalent to maximization or minimization of $p(A|G,I)$ over action space. The maximum of $p(A|G,I)$ is exactly the predicted behavior of that node in the graph. On the other hand, military commands might also be interested in creating or seeking certain conditions under which a particular behavior outcome will be likely to happen. For example, consider the farmers case again. One of these inquiries could be *under what conditions will farmer stop cultivating poppies and be friendly to foreign visitors*. This can be formulate as maximization of $p(I|G,A)$ by searching the condition space. By Bayes theorem, we can calculate

$$p(I|G, A) = \frac{p(I, G, A)}{p(G, A)} = \frac{p(A|I, G)\, P(I|G)}{p(A|G)}, \tag{2.13}$$

where each term in the expression can be computed. Therefore, HGKR coupled with network inference and Bayes rules can handle any meaningful inquiry, predict most likely behavior outcome for members, and shed light into the complex culture scenarios. HBFA can be applied to each level in HGKR.

As the action space and condition space might be extremely vast, the computation of conditional probabilities might be very computational complex, especially when HBFA is used in the lower level of the graph with large entities. Instead of using the whole graph G, we can limit our search space in certain subgraphs because most inquiries would be confined to a certain local region. This can be readily accomplished by the results we obtain from the Hierarchical Clustering Inference in section "Hierarchical Clustering Inference (HCI)." Given any inquiry, we identify the subgraph, or cluster G_p, from the clustering output and compute the conditional probabilities $p(A|G_p,I)$ and $p(I|G_p,A)$. This simplification not only can reduce our computation, but also might be more meaningful.

Decision Support System

All military operations are driven by command decisions, which can only be properly made when there is an understanding of the available courses of action, the consequences of each, and the tactical or strategic effect desired. Many business decisions can now be made with the assistance of software-driven DSS. A typical DSS is composed of a database or knowledge base, a model, a user interface, and one or more users. From this point of view, the entire architecture depicted in Fig. 2.1 can be considered a DSS. Another key aspect of a DSS is information display and visualization. Hierarchical node and link structure of the HGKR lends itself well to a geospatial style of visualization, where deeper elements of the HGKR are revealed as the user "zooms in." Color, shape, line thickness, and other forms of cartographic symbology can be applied to depict similarities and difference among nodes, and to emphasize the degree of positive or negative relationships between nodes. Similar cartographic techniques can be used to highlight changes between "snapshots" of the HGKR, to help users understand how their proposed courses of action influence nodes and relationships. Finally, a succinct dashboard view can provide the use with quick access to key social, demographic, and tactical indicators – a set of gauges to measure approval ratings, casualty rates, frequency of insurgent activity, or other metrics of interest.

According to Daniel Power [15], Decision Support Systems can be classified as communication driven, data driven, with an emphasis on raw data stores, document driven, with an emphasis on the management of unstructured text, knowledge driven, with an emphasis on automated problem solving, and model driven, with an emphasis on statistical, optimization, and simulation models. Our use of models, simulation, and statistical reasoning make a model-driven DSS a natural fit for our system. As such, users will be able to provide inputs to the system in the form of one or more courses of action, such as the deployment of additional troops to a province, or an increase in patrols and incarcerations in a given community. Through simulation, and our system's evolutionary and inference models, the DSS will run a "what if" analysis and provide one or more possible outcomes of the user's proposed course of action. With this information in-hand, the user will be able to execute the course of action with the optimal predicted result. The simulation output can be stored and referenced at a later time, allowing the underlying models to compare the prediction with what actually happens later on. This store/retrieve/compare capability will allow our system to improve its predictive model over time.

A more sophisticated form of our overall system would use a knowledge-driven DSS. With an embedded problem-solver, a knowledge-driven DSS (KD-DSS) would allow users specify desired outcomes, instead of proposed courses of action. The KD-DSS would then, through simulation, experiment with a set of courses of action and recommend the officers which effects best-fit the desired outcome.

Another key aspect of a DSS is information display and visualization. The geospatial information system (GIS) technology can be applied to display the nodes and edges of the multiple levels of the HKGR as a dynamic zoomable map level that automatically reveals more detail at higher resolution map scales. The GIS will provide a highly flexible environment for experimenting with iconography, color and other forms of symbology, to identify which visualization techniques can best display the similarities and differences across HGKR nodes, and the quality (friendly vs. adversarial) of the relationships between them. The GIS will also be used to compare and detect changes across multiple instances of the HGKR. Specifically, we will compare the "Current World State" HGKR with one or more "Simulated Future World State" HGKRs, allowing the user to rapidly ascertain what effect (e.g., what changes to the HGKR graph) a proposed course of action is likely to cause.

Conclusions

In this study, we present a HGKR to integrate layered abstractions into a coherent structure such that behavior forecasting may propagate or aggregate downward/upward, and thus cater to applications requiring various levels of detail. The system consists of a hierarchical graphical model, an evolutionary computation module, an inference/forecasting module, and decision support to forecast behaviors of groups at different hierarchies. The HGKR is based on initial anthropological information and refined through computational genetic algorithm. We develop a hierarchical-evolutionary-engine and a hierarchical-inference-engine, specifically, a two-stage clustering inference algorithm and hierarchical behavior-forecasting algorithm. The hierarchical graphical knowledge representation, together with its inference models, will have numerous applications in many culturally aware domains.

References

1. Carley, K.: Dynamic network analysis. In: National Research Council Workshop on Social Network Modeling and Analysis, pp. 133–145. The National Academies Press, Washington, DC (2003)
2. Subrahmanian, V.S.: Cultural modeling in real time. Science **317**, 1509–1510 (2007)
3. Richards, W.: Computational Models for Belief Revision, Group Decision-Making and Cultural Shifts. MURI report (2005)
4. Bonabeau, E.: Agent-based modeling: methods and techniques for simulating human systems. Proc. Natl. Acad. Sci. USA **99**, 7280–7287 (2002)
5. Lawrenz, C., Westerhoff, F.: Modeling exchange rate behavior with a genetic algorithm. Comput. Econ. **21**, 209–229 (2003)
6. Mitchell, T.: Machine Learning. McGraw Hill, New York (1997)
7. Osborne, M.J.: An Introduction to Game Theory. Oxford University press, New York (2004)
8. Peytonyoung, H.: Strategic Learning and Its limits. Oxford University press, New York (2004)
9. Goldberg, D.: Genetic Algorithms in Search, Optimization & Machine Learning. Addison-Wesley, Reading (1989)

10. Holland, J.H.: Adaptation in Natural and Artificial Systems. University of Michigan Press, Cambridge (1975)
11. Koza, J.: Genetic Programming: On the Programming of Computers by Means of Natural Selection. MIT Press, Cambridge (1992)
12. Koza, J.: Genetic Programming II: Automatic Discovery of Reusable Programs. MIT Press, Cambridge (1994)
13. Nolfi, S., Floreano, D.: Evolutionary Robotics. MIT Press, Cambridge (1998)
14. Jenssen, R., Erdogmus, D., Hild, K.E., Principe, J.C., Eltoft, T.: Information cut for clustering using a gradient descent approach. Pattern Recognit. **40**, 796–806 (2007)
15. Power, D.J.: Decision Support Systems: Concepts and Resources for Managers. Quorum Books, West Port (2002)

Chapter 3
Social Network Analysis Techniques for Social-Oriented Mobile Communication Networks

Guillaume-Jean Herbiet and Pascal Bouvry

Abstract The recent spread of handheld-size communicating devices has created a dramatic change in the communication opportunities. We are now in the situation where electronic communications can instantly happen not only across the world but *anytime and everywhere* and form a *mobile social network*. However, the study of those new personal, yet public, interactions and their original ubiquitous nature under the light of social network analysis remains an open problem. From all the solutions addressing social structure mining, many are designed for a posteriori analysis of social graphs, and none of them is really suitable for instant and dynamic generation of such structures that, based on social network analysis, would offer an improvement on the organization and robustness of ubiquitous communication between people.

After reviewing the relevance of social analysis on those networks, this chapter presents, analyzes, and evaluates novel social structure mining techniques devoted to operation on those dynamic mobile social networks.

Introduction

The development of powerful, handheld-size communicating devices greatly enhanced the possibility of ubiquitous social exchanges between users. Able to connect with each other anytime and anywhere, users can more easily than ever share their interests, generate and propagate trends, and make what would have been a local phenomenon globally acknowledged. Those smart communicating systems not only offer extended access to Internet-based online social networks but also make possible the creation of ubiquitous networks based on the sporadic device-to-device connections resulting from the users mobility.

G.-J. Herbiet (✉) • P. Bouvry
Université du Luxembourg, 6 Rue Richard Coudenhove-Kalergi, L-1359 Luxembourg
e-mail: guillaume.herbiet@uni.lu; pascal.bouvry@uni.lu

A. Abraham and A.-E. Hassanien (eds.), *Computational Social Networks: Tools, Perspectives and Applications*, DOI 10.1007/978-1-4471-4048-1_3,
© Springer-Verlag London 2012

Relying on wireless communications, the topology of such network instances is tightly related to the evolution of the relative position of users. They shall be close enough for the shared information to be correctly propagated by radio waves, considering the current environment conditions. Contributions studying human mobility models showed that the general behavior tends to create communication networks far from random and where link discrepancies exists: high density in points of interests and lower density in the intermediate locations. Such particularities create communication networks having small-world properties and where community structures (groups of vertices with high internal link density) may emerge. As a consequence, mining of those structures related to the social behavior of the users is important to design efficient protocols and applications on top of them.

However, most of the community mining, and more generally social network analysis tools, have been designed for application to static networks only (like characters, interactions in novels) or for a posteriori analysis of snapshots of dynamic networks (like hyperlinks between Internet pages or friendship relations in social networks). Due to their highly dynamic nature, mobile ad hoc networks require social network technique to be redefined. Not only the considered relations between network elements shall integrate a time-relative component, evaluating the duration and the stability of the relation, but also the applied algorithms shall now consider that those relations are constantly evolving and that the network structure changes over time.

Besides, the ubiquitous nature of the communications and the ability for their components to independently join and leave the mobile social network impose additional requirements to the design of social mining techniques. The algorithms shall be computationally light enough and memory efficient to run on resource-constrained devices. Particularly, it becomes irrelevant to assume a complete knowledge of the network to mine the social structures. Moreover, as each device acts individually and without prior coordination, the mining should be distributed on each device, i.e., the composition of the local decisions, made using local information only, will compose the global mining of social structures over the network.

The dynamic nature of those mobile communication networks and their requirement for distributed operation call for the development of new social network analysis techniques to better understand and take advantage of the inner structure and organization of those interactions. After describing in more details the characteristics of mobile ad hoc networks and their social-oriented application, we will justify the application of social network analysis techniques to this case. Then, we will evaluate the impact of the notion of dynamics and time-evolving characteristics on the sole definition of the social structures. A complete state of the art on current social structure mining solutions is provided, along with a review of their incompatibilities with this particular environment. Then, and based on the requirements expressed above, new techniques for social network analysis, based on epidemic propagation for dynamic clustering and discovery of communities, are introduced. Finally, an extended validation of the various techniques is operated through the use of concrete use cases and realistic simulation tools.

Dynamic and Mobile Social Networks

According to network infrastructure providers, mobile data traffic will increase around 40 times in the next 5 years [8], saturating cellular infrastructure. To relieve part of the traffic volume, this calls for the development of peer-to-peer communications between handheld communicating devices in ad hoc mode.

Ad hoc networks are infrastructure-less communication networks composed, most of the time, by heterogenous wireless-capable devices and using radio waves as a communication medium. Those devices are generally referred to as the network *nodes*. Each node of an ad hoc network can generate data for any other node in the network. All nodes can function, if needed, as relay stations for data packets to be routed to their final destination. A mobile ad hoc network may be connected through dedicated gateways, or nodes functioning as gateways, to other fixed networks or the Internet. In this case, the mobile ad hoc network expands the access to fixed network services. An example of a wireless ad hoc network setup is given in Fig. 3.1.

Examples of potential applications of mobile ad hoc networks range from simple ubiquitous data transfer scenarios to very specific use cases, like disaster relief or battlefield deployments.

Wireless ad hoc networks are heavily constrained by the capacity of the terminals and the lack of reliability of the communication channel, especially on long paths [15, 27]. It is therefore relevant to focus on applications that suit those constraints: social-oriented applications that take benefit of the proximity of users, like enhanced interactivity, gaming, or local streaming, and relay of media exhibiting a shared interest between colocated individuals.

Those dynamic mobile communication networks, when used to facilitate and enhance users, social interactions, are referred to as *Mobile Social Networks* (or MoSoNets). Their main application case considers urban users that will take benefit

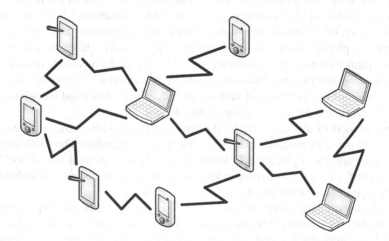

Fig. 3.1 An example of ad hoc network setup

from their terminal for unprompted communications and data sharing either while on the move (by walking or using private or public transportation means) or when standing in some points of interest, like offices, plants, malls, or restaurants.

In this context, ad hoc networks become "tools that support interaction among networked mobile users," which is the characterization of *mobile social services* given by Lugano in [26]. Deployment of social applications over those dynamic networks can be envisioned as the next step further of integration of online social networking in our everyday lives.

As it relies on wireless communications, ad hoc networks of social services or mobile social networks are strongly linked to the mobility of its users. The patterns of this mobility are dictated by sociological aspects, as one important motivation to move is to meet people [20, 28, 29]. Therefore, an efficient mining of the social structures existing and evolving over those dynamic networks would allow to not only reveal the most densely and reliably connected structures but also to determine where it is socially interesting to establish and develop communication opportunities.

Dynamic Social Networks Specificities

As presented in section "Introduction," the notion of social structures has historically been introduced while focusing on static graphs only. In this section, we will consider characteristics of dynamic environments and justify the relevance of and extension to the concept of community. We will also stress the design requirements for algorithms to operate on distributed communication networks such as mobile social networks.

Most graphs that initiated the detection of social structure are issued from social analysis and only abstract from the presence or absence of a symmetric relationship between individuals [39]. However, graphs, as fixed mathematical structures found in graph theory, fail to capture the interactions of evolving systems in many scientific fields such as physics, sociology, or chemistry. They would require a time reference (or a precedence relation) and the ability to evolve over time to become *networks* [5], also called *dynamic graphs*. Those structures are characterized by simple dynamics (the evolution of the valuation of vertices and edges over time) and metadynamics (the appearance and deletion of components of the graph).

In the context of dynamic graphs, the concept of social structure or *community* shall be extended to integrate this new time-based dimension. The high internal connectivity and the high ratio of closed triads [17] (or common neighbors [19]) that characterizes the tight interdependence between the vertices are now in balance with the significance of the graph connections over time.

In [31], a particular attention is drawn to consistently define the importance of links based on their history. The author proposes a set of metrics, measuring the age, the number of appearances, and volatility of dynamic graph elements. Those metrics are extended to graph structures and are applicable to communities. For each edge stability metric, the corresponding structure stability metric is simply the average of the metrics over all the relevant components of the structure.

It remains, however, an open problem to determine whether more importance shall be given to long-lasting social relations, i.e., stable links of a dynamic graph, or to relations that occur often, leading to links with an important volatility. Far from a definitive answer to this question, we propose to focus on an application-oriented definition for the importance of links. Considering the timescale of the envisioned interactions (e.g., the time of a shared game or a streamed video), we will give higher importance to links being robust and stable.

Hence, it is legitimate to complement the search for *tight* communities (the one composed of deeply interconnected nodes) with the search for *robust* communities (the ones presenting higher structure stability metrics, such as average structure link stability). In the rest of this chapter, we will extend the definition of Girvan and Newman [16] and consider communities as "groups of vertices having high *and stable* internal connectivity and much sparser *and less reliable* links to the outside of the group."

Finally, ad hoc communication networks are composed of self-organizing nodes that constantly enter, leave, and move inside the network. This particular aspect calls for the use of decentralized algorithms only: each independent decision from the component of the network will conduct to the generation of social structures. This has to be contrasted with traditional social mining techniques where an omniscient algorithm processes information about the complete network and place nodes in the relevant clusters. Besides, social network analysis should operate here with only local knowledge, in both history and current topology of the network, so as to respect the tight constraints on communication channel, computational power, and memory usage imposed by the handheld devices.

Limitations of Traditional Techniques

As for many complex problems, centralized solutions have been presented first. Then more memory-efficient algorithms, based on local information, have been introduced before the recent emergence of fully decentralized solutions, the only ones suitable for distributed communication networks. However, all those solutions either rely on assumptions unrealistic in a distributed environment or do not cope with issues related to the dynamic nature of the graphs.

Centralized Algorithms for Static Networks

The first algorithms aimed at performing community detection relied on a greedy, centralized approach trying to agglomerate [9] nodes in communities or divide [30] the network in such structures. Basically, they iteratively operate until a measure reflecting the assignment is optimized. Most of the time, the *modularity* measure, Q, (presented in [30]) is used.

The *modularity* measure, Q, is one of the first metrics used to evaluate the quality of a community assignment. It measures how the performed assignment matches the community structure exhibited by the network topology. For a partitioning counting $n_c = |\mathscr{C}|$ communities, we define a squared $n_c \times n_c$ matrix e whose elements e_{ij} represent the fraction of edges from a vertex in community i to a vertex in community j. As a consequence, the sum of rows, or columns, of **e**, $a_i = \sum_j e_{ij}$ corresponds to the fraction of links connected to i. If the community assignment were random, the expected number of intracommunity links would be a_i^2. Hence the definition of Q given in Eq. 3.1:

$$Q = \sum_i \left(e_{ii} - a_i^2 \right).$$ (3.1)

As it is closely related to the underlying community structure of a network, the maximum achievable value for Q is not absolute but topology dependent. The advantage of this metric is that it does not require a reference assignment to compare to but, unfortunately, it does not quantify the distance to an optimal assignment and does not measure the robustness of the assignment to small network changes.

Whenever a *natural* or *predefined* assignment exists for a network, many other metrics have been developed to estimate a normalized distance between the given and the computed classification. In [11], Danon et al. introduced the *normalized mutual information* (NMI) measure based on information theory. This normalized metric evolves between 0 when computed (C) and predetermined (C') assignments are independent, and 1 when they are identical. The NMI is defined as such:

$$I_n(C, C') = \frac{2I(C, C')}{H(C) + H(C')} = \frac{2(H(C) - H(C|C'))}{H(C) + H(C')}.$$ (3.2)

Nodes to group or split are chosen using similarity, betweenness [30], or extremal optimization [13]. Alternative approaches are based on spectral properties of the graph, Laplacian matrix [12] for instance, or on information theory principles, like in the INFOMAP algorithm presented in [33].

A good comparison of those centralized algorithms can be found in [11] or in [24]. They generally perform very well, achieving high *modularity* values on both unit and weighted graphs. However, their iterative nature and their requirement for a centralized computation using a global knowledge of the graph make them hardly applicable to dynamic networks. For the provided solution to be correct, each algorithm shall be run until convergence at each modification of the graph, due to simple or metadynamics, making the required complexity soar.

Algorithms relying only on local information have also been proposed in order to improve the memory efficiency of community detection. In [37], the authors use a cached table representing the network structure and allowing information processing at each vertex to be in $O(1)$ time complexity. In their proposal [36],

Wan et al. use a variation of the L-shell algorithm introduced by Bagrow and Bollt in [3] to iteratively add nodes to a community. They start from the shell origin until the number of added adjacent vertices goes below a given threshold. In [35], the authors introduce the notions of vertex *intensity* (sum of weights of all its attached edges) and vertex *contribution* to a community C (as the ratio of the sum of weights of all its edges to adjacent vertices in community C over its total *intensity*). They then proceed to a greedy agglomerative algorithm, starting with the edge of highest *contribution*. All those algorithms, however, require at some point node coordination or global network knowledge, which is not suitable for use in ad hoc networks.

Distributed Algorithms for Static Networks

Decentralized algorithms appear among most recent contributions to the community detection problem. We distinguish here between *epidemic label propagation algorithms*, where each vertex is responsible for its assignment, and *individual or agent-based algorithms*, where distributed agents (possibly distinct from the network vertices) are in charge of mining the social structures.

Epidemic Label Propagation Algorithms

In [32], Raghavan et al. introduced the *epidemic label propagation* principle for community detection. In this model, the current community of a vertex u is identified by a *label* (integer, string, etc.) $C(u)$ chosen in the space of labels $\mathscr{C}$. Vertices either synchronously or asynchronously beacon their *label* to their adjacent nodes. Then, each vertex adopts the same label as the majority of its neighbors. The behavior generated by this algorithm is depicted in Fig. 3.2.

While directly inheriting from the vertex community definition given in [16], this algorithm is proven to generate label oscillation (subsets of vertices alternating between several different community labels) when run synchronously [32] and to form *monster* communities that plague an extended amount of nodes [25].

In order to address the latter effect, Leung et al. refined this algorithm in [25]. Their version includes a hop attenuation factor δ that fades the infection power of a community and a node preference function (the authors suggest the node degree) weighted by a parameter m. Presented experiments show that the parameter combination ($\delta = 0.1, m = 0.05$) yields the best results, according to the authors' test cases.

The existence of those fixed parameters may not guarantee that this algorithm will perform efficiently whatever the underlying network topology, especially when it is changing, like in dynamic networks with heterogenous mobility. Besides, whether the hop attenuation may limit the creation of *monster* communities,

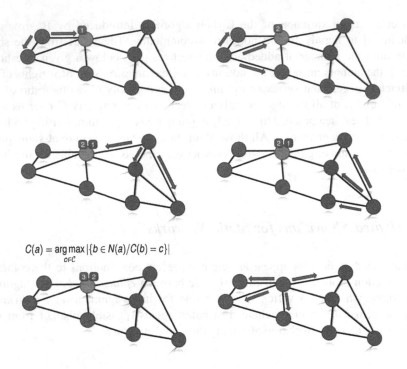

$$C(a) = \underset{c \in C}{\arg\max} |\{b \in N(a)/C(b) = c\}|$$

Fig. 3.2 Principle of the epidemic label propagation algorithm

it also limits the natural span of a label around an arbitrary center. Achieved community assignment might therefore be far from optimal.

Agent-Based Algorithms

In a more recent article, Bo et al. present a distributed autonomy-oriented algorithm for the community assignment problem [38]. In their approach, a set of autonomous agents is spread over the graph to mine. In their paper, one agent is placed inside each vertex of the graph. Each agent iteratively builds a *view*, initialized to its set of adjacent vertices which will converge to the set of vertices of its community. Each agent repeatedly *evaluates* its view (computing a *similarity* measure resembling the one presented in [19]), *shrinks* its view (by deleting from the view vertices whose similarity is below a certain threshold), *enlarges* its view (by adding two-hop adjacent vertices to its view), and *balances* (i.e., normalize the similarities) its view. The algorithm converges to the generation of an overlay network composed of all the agent views, where each community is represented by a nonoverlapping clique.

Although its operation is fully distributed and might perform correctly over a dynamic graph, no detail nor experiments are provided in the corresponding publication. Furthermore, the presented configuration of the algorithm (one agent residing on each of the graph vertex) is very similar to the approach used by epidemic label propagation algorithms. Besides, as communication with nonadjacent vertices is required when the view is *enlarged*, the algorithm is more subject to the limited path reliability of dynamic networks.

Centralized Algorithms for Dynamic Networks

In [4] and [34], Berger-Wolf et al. presented a framework for community identification in dynamic social networks. This work, adopting an optimization-based approach for the problem, is the first major contribution focusing on the impact of dynamic network evolution on social mining.

Assuming that time is discrete, they build an undirected graph G representing the evolution of the assignment of individuals in *groups* (nonempty and pairwise distinct sets of individuals) over time. A *group* $g_{j,t}$ is defined so that every individual of $g_{j,t}$ is not interacting with any individual of group $g_{j',t}$ at time t, for all $j' \neq j$.

Then, they build a graph where there is a vertex $v_{i,t}$ for every individual i at time t, and a vertex $g_{j,t}$ for each group existing at time t. Edges are drawn between all $(v_{i,t}, v_{i,t+1})$ pairs, linking two successive representations of the individual, and between each individual and its group at time t, connecting $v_{i,t}$ to $g_{j,t}$ if and only if $v_{i,t} \in g_{j,t}$.

Finally, the optimization problem is to find a valid graph coloring (i.e., where no two groups g and g' share the same color at any time t) minimizing total cost. Costs are introduced to penalize individual or group actions deviating from a virtuous behavior, like an individual changing its color (i.e., community affiliation), or individuals sharing the color of an incorrect group.

The authors reckon this problem as NP-complete and APX-hard [34] and propose a set of heuristics, such as individual coloring, group coloring, or greedy heuristics, to solve it. However, the building of the interpretation graph G requires a global knowledge of not only the topology but also the complete history of the graph until time T where the computation happens.

While this approach appears as particularly efficient for a posteriori social analysis of dynamic graphs, it is not suitable for distributed communication graphs, where decisions shall be taken *on line* and with a locally limited knowledge in the space and time dimensions.

Distributed Algorithms for Dynamic Networks

In [6], Bertelle, Dutot et al. used an individual-based approach to determine communities (referred as *organizations* in the publication). The algorithm simulates several colonies of ants, each having a distinct color, whose members iteratively travel along the edges of the graph. At each pass, each ant marks the traversed edge with a given amount of pheromone of its color. Ants avoid *hostile* edges that are marked with large amount of pheromones from a different colony and can flee to different zones of the graph, if their surrounding environment is judged too hostile. The different groups of ants tend to colonize different areas of the graph that are bounded by drops in the link density. Each ant colony hence dominates a different community, or organization, in the graph.

This approach is really interesting as it inherently manages the dynamics of the underlying graph: changes in the topology will change the hostility level of the environment and allow or prevent ants to explore and maybe colonize new areas of the graph. However, in this algorithm, the number of detected communities is equal to the number of ant colonies introduced in the computation. An estimation or an a priori knowledge of the number of communities in the graph is therefore required for results to be significant. This estimation may be hard to obtain or even irrelevant as the graph dynamics may make the expected number of communities vary over time.

Distributed Techniques for Dynamic Networks

In the previous section, we have seen that none of the existing techniques and algorithms used so far in social network analysis suited the specificities and design requirements of dynamic networks.

Particularly, we have seen that no decentralized solution presented in the literature, although being the only applicable approaches suitable for such networks, was correctly integrating local information about the network history and topology.

However, this is required to dynamically construct meaningful structures and continuously adapt them to account for the evolution of the network and the impact of its past states. This requires an improved constructive mechanism (to prevent the *monster* community effect and improve robustness of the structure, in the sense given by Siegel et al. in [1] and studied for community detection in [23]), an efficient organization mechanism, but also a dedicated mechanism to cope with the changes in topology and characteristics of the network.

We will present examples of distributed solutions for those challenges, based on the SHARC (Sharper Heuristic for Assignment of Robust Communities) distributed community assignment algorithm. The original SHARC algorithm was first introduced in [19] and proposed an improved distributed constructive mechanism. We complement it here with novel solutions dedicated to operation on dynamic networks.

Improving Distributed Community Detection

The limited performance of traditional epidemic label propagation algorithms can be explained by their limited use of simple information about the adjacent vertices only. However, it has been reckoned in several fields [7, 10] that the tendency to join a community depends not only on the number of connected peers already in this community, but also crucially on how these peers are connected to one another [2].

To express this dependency, we will use the concept of common adjacent vertices set, or *neighborhood similarity*, as heuristic in the community assignment process. This requires each vertex to know not only its set of adjacent vertices, but also the relations (or connections) of those vertices. This principle is referred as *two-hop neighborhood knowledge*. Such heuristic will allow to make the mining sharper and more robust to network changes.

Neighborhood Similarity Measure

While studying relationship networks, sociologist Granovetter isolated the relation between community structures in those networks and the predominance of closed triads in relationships [17]. If A is a friend of both B and C, then B and C are also very likely to be friends. Triads not respecting this closure rule explain the existence of links between communities.

Let $\mathcal{N}$ be a network of n vertices and m edges. We denote $N(u)$, the neighborhood of vertex u, i.e., all the vertices $v \in \mathcal{N}$ that are adjacent to u, and $|N(u)|$ its cardinality, i.e., the *degree* of vertex u.

As a consequence of the triadic closure rule, two neighbor vertices, u and v of the network $\mathcal{N}$, belonging to the same social structure $C(u) = C(v) = c \in \mathcal{C}$ both have a high link density with other vertices of c and should hence have a more similar set of adjacent vertices than with a given vertex w, not belonging to c. The size of this common adjacent vertices set can be used to assess the likelihood of both u and v belonging to the same community. However, it needs to consider the ratio of common neighbors over the total node degree in order not to favor high degree nodes.

Therefore, we propose the following definition of the *neighborhood similarity measure* n_{sim} that is defined for any vertices $u \in \mathcal{N}$ of degree at least 1 $v \in N(u)$ as

$$n_{\text{sim}}(u, v) = 1 - \frac{|(N(u) \setminus N(v)) \cup (N(v) \setminus N(u))|}{|N(u)| + |N(v)|}. \tag{3.3}$$

We have designed this metric so that it respects the similarity set measure properties introduced in [4]. This allows to inherit interesting properties on the evolution of this metric after the removal of an edge based on his relative position and, as a consequence, on the evolution of the choice of the community to join.

Algorithm 1: Neighborhood similarity measure (NS)

Input: Vertex v, $N(v)$, $\mathscr{C} = \{c \mid C(w) = c, \forall w \in N(v)\}$
$C(v) = v$;
CommunityScore = [];
MaxScore = 0;
for *each w in N(v)* **do**
    CommunityScore[$C(w)$] += $n_{sim}(v, w)$;
    if *CommunityScore[C(w)] > MaxScore* **or**
    (CommunityScore[C(w)] = MaxScore **and**
    RandomTieBreakIsWon()) **then**
        $C(v) = C(w)$;
        MaxScore = CommunityScore[$C(w)$];
    end
end
Output: $C(v)$, MaxScore

The neighborhood similarity linearly varies between 0 when the assessed nodes have no neighbor vertex in common and 1 when the neighborhoods are identical. It is a normalized value which does not favor high- or low-degree vertices. This measure is also symmetric for any pair of adjacent vertices of the network $\mathcal{N}$.

The computation of the neighborhood similarity measure is based on simple set operations and can be implemented in linear time (using sorted lists for instance). Therefore, this method is running in $O(\Delta)$, where Δ is the network average degree. An implementation of the neighborhood similarity measure is presented in Algorithm 1.

Community Assignment Using Neighborhood Similarity

Neighborhood similarity can be used as a simple extension of the epidemic label propagation-based algorithm: each neighboring vertex v contributes to the count of its community label $C(v)$ at node u to the extent of its neighborhood similarity with the vertex u. Then, node u will adopt the label of the community $c \in \mathscr{C}$ with the highest *label count*, as shown in Eq. 3.4:

$$C(u) = \arg\max_{c \in \mathscr{C}} \sum_{\substack{v \in N(u) \\ C(v) = c}} n_{sim}(u, v) . \tag{3.4}$$

This heuristic therefore strengthens the gap between community counts as it considers both the number of neighboring vertices with this label and their value in terms of neighborhood similarity, which is high for tightly interconnected nodes. This is the principle of the original SHARC algorithm introduced in [19], and its implementation is presented in Algorithm 2.

Algorithm 2: Sharper Heuristic for Assignment of Robust Communities (SHARC)

Input: $\mathcal{N}$
while not *TerminationCondition()* **do**
    $\mathcal{S}$ = Shuffle({$v \in \mathcal{N}$});
    for *each v in $\mathcal{S}$* **do**
        ($C(v)$, MaxScore) = NS(n);
        Strength(v, $C(v)$) = MaxScore / Degree(v);
    end
end

Community Organization Mechanism

Determining a coherently placed *center* of the social structure is important as this node can then serve as an efficient bridge from the ad hoc community to an infrastructure network, collecting, merging, and reporting information.

A good candidate for playing this role is the community *center* in the sense of *proximity centrality*. This *center* is characterized by having the lowest average shortest path to all the other nodes of the community. However, computing this metric is hard to achieve in a dynamic and distributed environment.

In *epidemic label propagation* algorithms, nodes join a community by adopting the label shared by one of their adjacent vertices. We can hence introduce the notion of *originator* as the node that propagated its original label to all the nodes of its current community. However, the position of the *originator* is fixed and mainly depends on the order in which nodes update their community assignment. Therefore, *originator* and *center* position will likely not match, especially when the structure evolves over time.

A possible solution is to dynamically update the position of the *originator* so that it is always placed far from the community boundaries in areas where the density and reliability of the connections between vertices are high.

Based on the community assignment rule presented in Eq. 3.4, we can also define by extension the *community score*, which reflects, for any vertex $u \in \mathcal{N}$ assigned to community $C(u)$, the total count achieved by this community:

$$\text{score}(u) = \sum_{\substack{v \in N(u) \\ C(v)=C(u)}} n_{\text{sim}}(u, v) . \tag{3.5}$$

The value of the *community score* reflects the strength with which the considered vertex u is tied to the community $C(u)$. Simple graph considerations can show that nodes placed *inside* their community (i.e., having no edge to the outside of their current community) will tend to have a higher score than nodes placed at the border of their community. Passing the *originator* role to nodes with higher scores is hence a first step to place it closer to the community *center*.

Algorithm 3: Local-optimum-favored weighted random walk

Input: Vertex u, $N(u)$, currentOriginator, $score(u)$, $\mathscr{S}(u) = \{s|s = score(v), \forall v \in N(u)\}$
nextOriginator = currentOriginator
if *IsOriginator(u)* **then**
    nextOriginator = u
    if max $\mathscr{S}(u) <= score(u)$ **or**
    randomUniform(0, 1) $<$ max $\mathscr{S}(u)/score(u)$ **then**
        random = *randomUniform(0,* $\sum_{v \in N(u)} score(v))$
        for *each v in N(u)* **do**
            if *random* $<= score(v)$ **then**
                | nextOriginator = v
            else
                | random = random - $score(v)$
            end
        end
    end
end
Output: nextOriginator

The *community score* is computed using local information (the information scope is limited to the two-hop neighborhood); hence nodes have no knowledge whether the chosen *originator* is a local or a global strength optimum over the community. It is therefore very likely that the procedure described above will converge to a node with a *community score* locally optimal.

In order to address this effect, it is required to add diversity to the path followed by the *originator* role but without passing it to weakly assigned nodes. We therefore implemented a *local-optimum-favored weighted random walk* mechanism.

This algorithm described in Algorithm 3 performs as follows. If the node is a local *community score* optimum, then it only passes the *originator* role with a probability equal to the ratio of the highest score found in the adjacent nodes over the score of the current node: this is the local optimum favor phase. If the current is not a local *community score* optimum, or if the local optimum has chosen to pass the role, then a weighted random walk is applied: adjacent nodes with a higher score are more likely to be selected to become *originator* (as detailed in Algorithm 3). Note that if a node leaves its current community, it automatically loses its originator status.

Link Importance Estimation

The relative importance of links shall be introduced to modulate the contribution of each node, based on the stability and lifetime of relations with the other entities of the social structure, reflecting the past history of the network.

As we operate in a heavily constrained dynamic system, it is required that the value of links is estimated independently by each entity, with minimum node coordination, using local information and minimizing computational and memory requirements.

In Eq. 3.4, in order to consider the importance of links in the community assignment process, we propose to substitute the *neighborhood similarity measure* (defined in Eq. 3.3) by the *weighted similarity measure*, defined for each node $u \in \mathcal{N}$ of degree at least 1 and an adjacent vertex $v \in N(u)$:

$$n_{w,\text{sim}}(u, v) = n_{\text{sim}}(u, v) * \hat{s}_u(v) \,, \tag{3.6}$$

where $n_{\text{sim}}(u, v)$ is the *neighborhood similarity measure* as defined in Eq. 3.3 and $\hat{s}_u(v)$ is the *stability estimator* of the edge between u and v at vertex u.

The use of this estimator (instead of referring directly to the stability measure value of the edge) allows to keep the different *weighted similarity measures* consistent to what is the current stability state of a vertex neighborhood: a given absolute stability value s might, at different instants, be considered as corresponding to a really stable or really unstable edge, depending on the value of the other incoming edges.

We therefore propose the following computation formula for the *stability estimator*:

$$\hat{s}_u(v) = \frac{w_{vu}}{\sum_{n \in N(u)} w_{nu}} \,, \tag{3.7}$$

where w_{vu} is the weight (reflecting the stability value) of the incoming edge from v to u (which is equal to w_{uv} if the graph is not directed). Note that this value is not symmetric as $\hat{s}_u(v) \neq \hat{s}_v(u)$ in the general case. We therefore have a *node-centric stability estimation* at each vertex of the graph.

As our algorithm uses beacon messages for the nodes to announce their identity, current community label, and adjacent vertices set, the weight value of each edge can easily be set using one of the stability metrics presented in section "Dynamic Social Networks Specificities." For instance, the age of a link can be estimated by counting the number of consecutive beacons received from the corresponding neighbor node. An illustration of the required beacon information is given in Fig. 3.3.

To account for some requirements in stability (e.g., the link shall live long enough to establish a communication), a *stability estimation threshold* can be set, under which value all estimators $\hat{s}_u(v)$ are set to 0.

Finally, the community assignment rule presented in Eq. 3.4 and the community score computation formula given in Eq. 3.5 can be rewritten as follows:

$$C(u) = \arg \max_{c \in \mathscr{C}} \sum_{\substack{v \in N(u) \\ C(v)=c}} n_{w,\text{sim}}(u, v) \,, \tag{3.8}$$

$$\text{score}(u) = \sum_{\substack{v \in N(u) \\ C(v)=C(u)}} n_{w,\text{sim}}(u, v) \,. \tag{3.9}$$

Sender ID
Freshness counter or timestamp
Distance to originator
Community label
Community score
Break community label (or unset if not break mode)
Neighbor ID 1

. . .

Neighbor ID n

Fig. 3.3 Example of beacon message to be used with SHARC

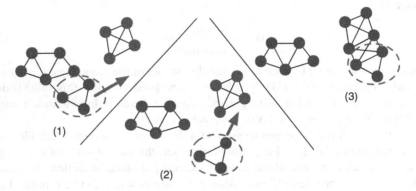

Fig. 3.4 Illustration of the wandering community effect

Social Structure Evolution and Split Mechanism

Many social mining techniques, especially distributed solutions, offer procedures to generate and extend structures reflecting the social organization of the network. On the contrary, few give incentives on when, where, and how reduce or split the generated communities. However, due to the dynamics of the network, link density may decrease in some areas of the community, requiring the structure to split into different entities to maintain a meaningful assignment.

In [19], we have put into light the *wandering community* effect. Being a direct consequence of the dynamic evolution of the network, it may cause a given set of social structures irrelevant, as all entities keep on evolving over time. An illustration of the *wandering community effect* is given in Fig. 3.4.

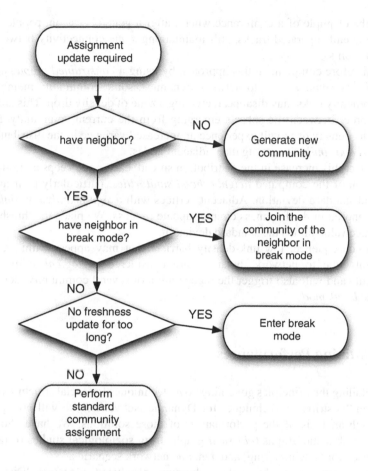

Fig. 3.5 Assignment process with break mode

To cope with this effect, the implementation of a destructive mechanism is required. We present here an example of such a *break mode*. Each originator includes an increasing *freshness counter* value or a timestamp. Nonoriginator nodes simply propagate the highest received value for this counter in their next beacon. Whenever there is a split in a community, all the nodes not anymore connected to the originator of their community will experience a stalling in their freshness and reassign themselves to a different community label. The global behavior of the break is summarized in Fig. 3.5.

This *freshness propagation* mechanism allows to detect the split of a community in disconnected components. However, the connectivity of a dynamic network could evolve so that all the nodes with same label still are in the same connected component but that the link density distribution would require a subdivision in different communities for the assignment to be meaningful. One can envision this case in the example of a conference where, after a general session, people would move to attend separated tracks, still maintaining *some* connectivity between the different rooms.

We therefore complement this approach by using a *constrained propagation of the freshness counter*. Due to network dynamics, some community members or intracommunity links may disappear, creating a zone of density drop. This area will act as border between the subsets emerging from the current community. Nodes around the density drop will experience an increased variance in the distribution of *neighborhood similarity* among their adjacent nodes.

To detect this increase in the distribution spread, each node keeps an up-to-date distribution of the computed *neighborhood similarities*, particularly their average value and standard deviation. Adjacent vertices with a *significantly low similarity* will be ignored in the freshness counter update process. We place the threshold to the average value minus the standard deviation.

As a consequence, low-link-density barriers that may appear within a given community due to network dynamics are considered as *logical splits* of the community and will also trigger the regeneration of several community identifiers, using the *break mode*.

Social Mining Performances

After detailing the principles governing novel techniques for social structure mining in section "Distributed Techniques for Dynamic Networks," we will now present a thorough analysis of the performances of those solutions. We have chosen to consider both static graphs (*classical* graphs from sociological studies or random graphs used for benchmarking) and dynamic network scenarios.

We will focus our study on the techniques introduced in section "Distributed Algorithms for Static Networks," only approaches suitable in a dynamic environment that do not require a prior knowledge of the expected number of communities. We will compare them with the new techniques introduced in section "Distributed Techniques for Dynamic Networks." As stated in section "Dynamic Social Networks Specificities," we will analyze not only on topology-based metrics but also measures evaluating the stability of the generated communities.

Experimentation Setup

All compared algorithms were implemented in Java, based on their description found in the literature. We used GraphStream [14], a dynamic graphs simulation library, to manage the various graphs topology, dynamics, and properties.

In order to ensure the statistical confidence of our results, each unique simulation configuration (unique graph instance, unique algorithm, unique set of configuration

Table 3.1 Comparison of maximum achieved modularity Q by various algorithms on the "karate" network

Algorithm	Year	Max. Q	Type
Newman [30]	2004	0.381	Centralized
Donetti et al. [12]	2004	0.412	Centralized
Wang et al. [37]	2007	0.4188	Local
Wan et al. [36]	2008	0.488	Local
Tian et al. [35]	2009	0.564	Local
Raghavan et al. [32]	2007	0.4151	Distributed
Leung et al. [25]	2008	0.3718	Distributed
SHARC [18]	2009	0.4151	Distributed

parameters), we run 20 simulations using different seeds for the initialization of the random number generator governing stochastic aspects of the algorithms or event management. We provide statistical estimators (average, standard deviation, minimum, maximum) for our results based on those different runs.

Static Networks

In this section, we will first put our results in perspective with local and centralized algorithms in order to assess the gap with our decentralized approach. Then we will compare our contribution with other similar algorithms also relying on epidemic label propagation.

Comparison with Local and Centralized Algorithms

Although they are not directly applicable to ad hoc networks, we want to compare the performance of our contribution with centralized and local algorithms used for community detection. This allows to put our work in perspective with more generic solutions recognized as valuable in the literature for this problem. For this purpose, we will use the maximum modularity Q achieved on the *Zachary karate club* [39] network. This metric and this network are the most used for comparison between algorithms. The corresponding results are shown in Table 3.1.

It appears that SHARC achieves results comparable to, or better than, other distributed algorithms. Besides, this algorithm outperforms early centralized community detection lgorithms, like those introduced by Newman [30] and Donetti et al. [12].

Compared to local algorithms, i.e., greedy algorithms that mostly use local information to perform their community assignment, the performance gap lies between 1% and 33%, when compared to the most efficient algorithm. However, as explained in section "Centralized Algorithms for Static Networks," those local algorithms assume, at some point of their execution, a global knowledge of the network. This assumption makes them not suitable for networks where no global knowledge nor node coordination exists, like ad hoc networks. This results corroborates the general observation that decentralized algorithms, based on a given heuristic like SHARC, offer a suboptimal solution while comparing with results from centralized algorithms.

Girvan-Newman(GN) Experiment

In this experiment, first presented in [30], we generated random networks composed of $N = 128$ nodes, preassigned in four different communities composed of $n_c = 32$ nodes. The average network degree is set to $\langle k \rangle = 16$. The node degrees follow a power law distribution of exponent $\tau_1 = -2$. Edges are created so that each node n of degree k_n has $(1 - \mu_t)k_n$ links with other nodes of its community and $\mu_t k_n$ links outside its community. Sharpness of the assignment is assessed by increasing the value of the mixing factor μ_t until the community structures are no longer properly defined. This experiment will allow us to test the performances of the *neighborhood similarity* of the SHARC algorithm, introduced in section "Community Assignment Using Neighborhood Similarity."

The topmost graph of Fig. 3.6 presents the average (with standard deviation as error bars) achieved normalized mutual information (see Eq. 3.2) by the different distributed algorithms presented in section "Distributed Algorithms for Static Networks" for increasing values of μ_t. Dotted lines present the maximum and minimum values. Those results show SHARC is able to maintain higher value for average NMI, even when the community structures become less clear cut ($\mu_t > 0.4$). The asynchronous epidemic label propagation algorithm [32] performs the poorest and presents the widest variation in its results, making it unreliable for correctly detecting communities in any case. The synchronous epidemic label propagation algorithm [32] and the algorithm presented by Leung et al. [25] perform equivalently in average, with a wider variance in results for the latter.

When communities are not well defined anymore ($\mu_t > 0.7$), SHARC results are comparable with those of other algorithms.

A look at the evolution of the maximum community size, presented in the bottom graph of Fig. 3.6, shows that SHARC good performances are explained by its ability to longer bound the size of the communities to meaningful values. Thanks to the *neighborhood similarity* metric, the assignment performed by SHARC is sharper.

It is also interesting to look at the spread of metrics on the different runs. It appears that SHARC presents less standard deviation in its results. In particular, it does not produce very low results in some configurations. SHARC is hence robust against particular network configurations and initialization parameters.

Weighted LFR Experiment

In order to test algorithms that integrates link-reliability aspects in the community assignment process, we will rely on the weighted version of the Lancicinetti-

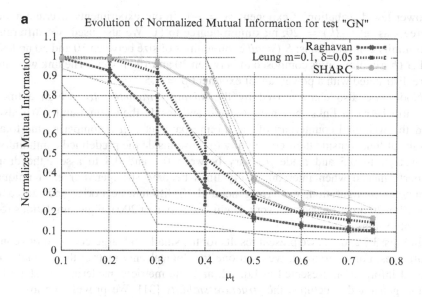

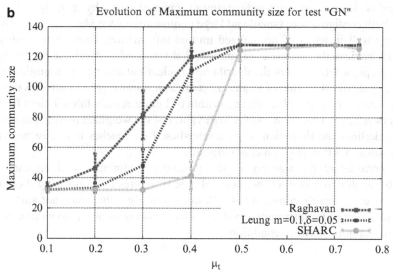

Fig. 3.6 Evolution of NMI (**a**) and maximum community size (**b**) values for the GN benchmark

Fortunato-Radicchi (LFR) benchmark [24]. We will assume that the weight assigned to each link reflects its stability level, as explained in section "Dynamic Social Networks Specificities."

In this test, networks of 5,000 nodes are generated with the tool provided by the LFR benchmark authors [24]. The node degree distribution follows a power law of exponent $\tau_1 = -2$, and sizes of the communities also vary according to a power law distribution of exponent $\tau_2 = -1$. In our experiments, average node degree was set to $\langle k \rangle = 20$, maximum degree to 50. We also used two different community configurations: S (*small* communities of size between 10 and 50 nodes) and B (*big* communities composed of between 20 and 100 nodes). The link weights were distributed with a power law of exponent $\beta = 1.5$.

Nodes are also characterized by the *mixing parameter*, μ_t, which defines the ratio between links they have outside and inside their community. We also used the weighted counterpart of the mixing parameter, μ_w, comparing the total weight of links outside their community to those inside the predefined community. We set μ_t to 0.5 and made μ_w vary between 0.1 and 0.8 to assess the drop of performance when intercommunity links become stronger. For each unique parameter configuration, we have generated 10 different networks, and ran each algorithm 20 times on each network, leading to a total of 200 unique simulations for each algorithm.

In Figs. 3.7 and 3.8, we present results for the small- and large-communities configurations. For assessment, we used one topological-only metric: the normalized mutual information presented in Eq. 3.2, and one metric considering the stability of the generated structures, the *structure stability* [31]. We provide the average, standard deviation, minimum and maximum achieved values by each algorithm.

On both configurations (small and large communities), we observe that SHARC performs well in terms of normalized mutual information, showing its ability to correctly retrieve the *reference* assignment that was used to distribute link weights on the graph, whether or not the distribution is clear-cut among communities. Note that the epidemic algorithm of Raghavan et al., as it is unweighted, performs equally poorly whatever the μ_t value. The algorithm of Leung et al., while efficient for low values of μ_t, performs the worst for high values of the weighted mixing parameter. This underlines the limitation of parameter-based approaches that may not yield good results in different graph configurations.

By considering the stability of the generated communities, it appears that SHARC is able to construct the most reliable structures (i.e., grouping the most-weighted edges *inside* communities). Besides, our algorithm does not suffer any performance drop for intermediate values of μ_t, showing its ability to automatically adapt to changing network conditions.

Dynamic Networks

Although designed with a consideration of the stability of the generated communities, SHARC main objective is to operate on dynamic networks, such as the one created by owners of handheld devices that will form and communicate in a MoSoNet. Therefore, we also assessed the performances of SHARC on three human- and nature-inspired dynamic scenarios.

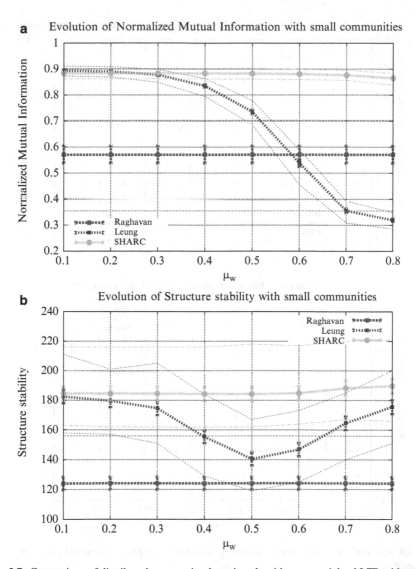

Fig. 3.7 Comparison of distributed community detection algorithms on weighted LFR with small communities

Scenarios Descriptions

We propose to evaluate SHARC, along with the asynchronous and Leung epidemic label propagation algorithms on two different scenarios, reflecting mobility of human users in two urban contexts: a *shopping mall* and a *highway section*. Both derive from the Human Mobility Model, introduced by Hogie in [21]. Their particular characteristics are summed up in Table 3.2.

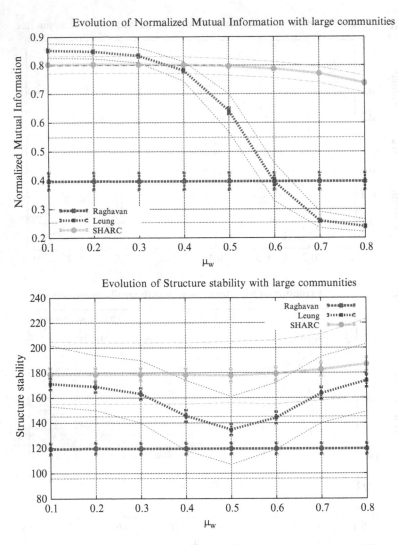

Fig. 3.8 Comparison of distributed community detection algorithms on weighted LFR with large communities

In this model, a mobile node n first chooses a destination spot $d(n)$ as the closest element not contained in a list of recently visited spots $VS(n)$. The node then move toward its destination spot, with a certain degree of random variation in its direction. If all spots have been visited, then $VS(n)$ is emptied. The mobility traces were generated using MadHoc [22], a MANET simulator providing an advanced propagation model, with lognormal shadowing and terrain modeling: spots occupy a given surface on the simulation area and also attenuate signal propagation.

Table 3.2 Parameters of the "mall" and "highway" scenarios

Parameter	Mall	Highway
Nodes	99	80
Playground (m)	300×300	750×900
Duration (s)	120	120
Iterations	480	480
Iterations per second	4	4
Mobility speed (km/h)	[1;10]	[70;140]
Avg. transmission range (m)	43	46
Avg. node degree	8	10
Avg. link lifetime (s)	48	3.4
Avg. link density (m^{-2})	5×10^{-3}	6×10^{-4}

In the *shopping mall* scenario, spots stand for shops, uniformly distributed over the mall area. This scenario generates highly dense wide areas and allows to study the behavior of protocols in dense network conditions.

The *highway section* environment is characterized by nodes moving at a very high speed between a few number of spots (two in our tests). We have chosen this particular scenario as it produces topologies where most links are organized into chains of nodes moving in opposite directions, which favors domination of a single community. As nodes move very fast, link duration is also very short. This is therefore a very aggressive scenario to test the robustness of the algorithms.

Experimentation Results

Results for those two scenarios are given in Figs. 3.9 and 3.10, respectively. While considering the topological quality of the performed assignment (using *modularity* results presented on the topmost graphs), it appears that SHARC achieves the best results. The more demanding the scenario, the bigger the performance gap in favor of our algorithm (this is especially true in the *highway scenario* which involves vehicular mobility and very sporadic connections between cars going in opposite directions).

The good performances of SHARC are explained by looking at the number of communities generated by the algorithms during the different scenarios (plotted in the middle graphs of Figs. 3.9 and 3.10). The constrained freshness propagation regeneration mechanism of SHARC is able to detect local drops of link density, initiate the construction of new structures within a community, and hence maintain the number of communities to a meaningful level. Other algorithms still suffer from the *wandering community* effect [19] that causes quick drops of community labels diversity.

Besides, the community generated by SHARC is also the most reliable. In those experiments, we used the age of the communication links as stability criterion. As shown on the bottom graphs of Figs. 3.9 and 3.10, the communities constructed by SHARC are so that the average stability of interstructure edges, ages is the highest:

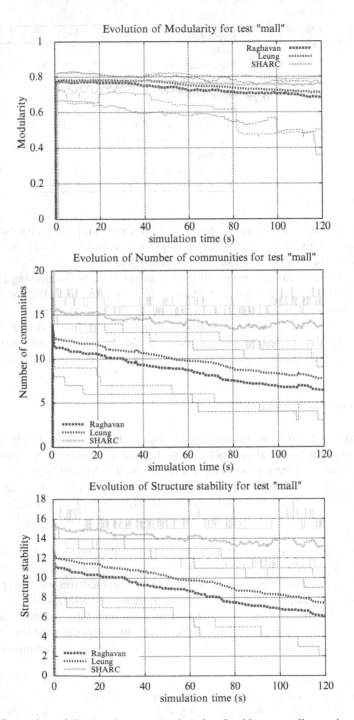

Fig. 3.9 Comparison of distributed community detection algorithms on mall scenario

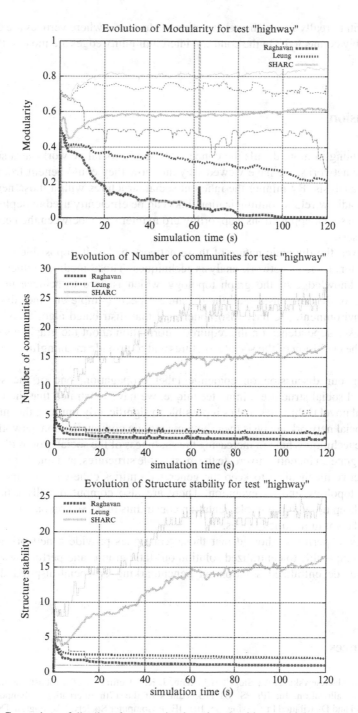

Fig. 3.10 Comparison of distributed community detection algorithms on highway scenario

our algorithm really favors the construction of structures where vertices are densely and reliably connected. On the contrary, intercommunity edges are most of the time short-lived.

Conclusion

After defining in more details the concept of mobile social networks as a subclass of ad hoc networks, we have viewed why and how they could benefit from social network analysis. By mining the inherent social structures within those networks, their sporadic wireless communication links can be efficiently used to deploy next-generation social applications, supporting group interaction between the networked mobile users.

However, the dynamic nature of those network makes it impossible to rely on the traditional social network analysis techniques. Those methods either rely on a global knowledge of the graph topology, which is hard to achieve in ad hoc networks, or do not consider all the dynamic aspects (simple and metadynamics) of the environment. We have also underlined that distributed algorithms, despite their weaker dependency on the required information about the graph, also fail to capture the evolution of the social structures and to provide meaningful results over time.

Basing our discussion on epidemic label propagation, one of the simplest distributed social structure mining technique, we have illustrated that the addition of several novel techniques makes it possible to significantly improve the quality of online social network analysis over dynamic mobile communication networks.

Those techniques help in increasing the sharpness of the social groups identification, integrate an incentive to create the most stable structures, and finally implement a destructive mechanism to keep the generated entities coherent with the current network topology and its evolution. There are also computationally efficient in order to keep up with the implementation constraints that exist on battery-powered handheld communicating devices.

Finally, experiment showed that those techniques provide a network analysis quality comparable to centralized solution on static graphs and perform way better than other decentralized solution on benchmarking or social-inspired dynamic scenarios.

References

1. Ali, S., Maciejewski, A.A., Siegel, H.J., Kim, J.-K.: Definition of a robustness metric for resource allocation. In: IPDPS '03 Proceedings of the 17th International Symposium on Parallel and Distributed Processing, pp. 10+. IEEE Computer Society, Washington, DC (2003)

2. Backstrom, L., Huttenlocher, D., Kleinberg, J., Lan, X.: Group formation in large social networks: membership, growth, and evolution. In: Proceedings of the 12th ACM SIGKDD International Conference on Knowledge Discovery and Data Mining, KDD '06, New York, pp. 44–54. ACM (2006)
3. Bagrow, J., Bollt, E.: A local method for detecting communities. Phys. Rev. E **72**, 046108 (2005)
4. Berger-Wolf, T.Y., Saia, J.: A framework for analysis of dynamic social networks. In: Proceedings of the 12th ACM SIGKDD International Conference on Knowledge Discovery and Data Mining, KDD '06, New York, pp. 523–528. ACM (2006)
5. Bersini, H.: Des réseaux et des sciences – Biologie, informatique, sociologie: l'omniprésence des réseaux. Vuibert Informatique (2005)
6. Bertelle, C., Dutot, A., Guinand, F., Olivier, D.: Organization detection using emergent computing. Int. Trans. Syst. Sci. Appl. **2**(1), 61–69, 09 (2006)
7. Centola, D.M., Macy, M.W., Eguíluz, V.M.: Cascade dynamics of multiplex propagation. In: Garrido, P., Maroo, J., Muñoz, M.A. (eds.) Modeling Cooperative Behavior in the Social Sciences. Volume 779 of American Institute of Physics Conference Series, Granada, pp. 200–200. American Institute of Physics, Melville, July 2005
8. Cisco. Cisco visual networking index: global mobile data traffic forecast update, 2009–2014, Feb 2010
9. Clauset, A., Newman, M.E.J., Moore, C.: Finding community structure in very large networks. Phys. Rev. E **70**, 066111 (2004)
10. Coleman, J.S.: Social capital in the creation of human capital. Am. J. Sociol. **94**, S95–S120 (1988)
11. Danon, L., Duch, J., Diaz-Guilera, A., Arenas, A.: Comparing community structure identification. J. Stat. Mech. **2005**, P09008 (2005)
12. Donetti, L., Munoz, M.A.: Detecting network communities: a new systematic and efficient algorithm. J. Stat. Mech. **2005**, P10012 (2004)
13. Duch, J., Arenas, A.: Community detection in complex networks using extremal optimization. Phys. Rev. E **72**, 027104 (2005)
14. Dutot, A., Guinand, F., Olivier, D., Pigné, Y.: GraphStream: a Tool for bridging the gap between Complex Systems and Dynamic Graphs. In: Emergent Properties in Natural and Artificial Complex Systems. Satellite Conference within the 4th European Conference on Complex Systems (ECCS'2007), Dresden Allemagne, Oct 2007 ANR SARAH
15. Gerharz, M., de Waal, C., Frank, M., Martini, P.: Link stability in mobile wireless ad hoc networks. In: Local Computer Networks, Annual IEEE Conference on, Tampa, p. 30 (2002)
16. Girvan, M., Newman, M.E.J.: Community structure in social and biological networks. Proc. Natl. Acad. Sci. USA **99**, 7821–7826 (2002)
17. Granovetter, M.S.: The strength of weak ties. Am. J. Sociol. **78**(6), 1360–1380 (1973)
18. Herbiet, G.-J., Bouvry, P.: Urbisim: a framework for simulation of ad hoc networks in realistic urban environment. In: GIIS'09: Proceedings of the Second International Conference on Global Information Infrastructure Symposium, Piscataway, pp. 373–378. IEEE (2009)
19. Herbiet, G.-J., Bouvry, P.: SHARC: community-based partitioning for mobile ad hoc networks using neighborhood similarity. In: IEEE WoWMoM 2010 (IEEE WoWMoM 2010), Montreal, June 2010
20. Herrmann, K.: Modeling the sociological aspects of mobility in ad hoc networks. In: Proceedings of the 6th ACM International Workshop on Modeling Analysis and Simulation of Wireless and Mobile Systems, San Diego, pp. 128–129 (2003)
21. Hogie, L., Guinand, F., Bouvry, P.: A heuristic for efficient broadcasting in the metropolitan ad hoc network. In: Knowledge-Based Intelligent Information and Engineering Systems, Wellington, pp. 727–733 (2004)
22. Hogie, L., Bouvry, P., Guinand, F.: An overview of manets simulation. Electron. Notes Theor. Comput. Sci. **150**(1), 81–101 (2006). In: Proceedings of the First International Workshop on Methods and Tools for Coordinating Concurrent, Distributed and Mobile Systems (MTCoord 2005), Namur (2005)

23. Karrer, B., Levina, E., Newman, M.E.J.: Robustness of community structure in networks. Phys. Rev. E **77**, 046119 (2008)
24. Lancichinetti, A., Fortunato, S.: Community detection algorithms: a comparative analysis. In: VALUETOOLS '09 Proceedings of the Fourth International ICST Conference on Performance Evaluation Methodologies and Tools. ICST, Brussel, Aug 2009
25. Leung, I.X., Hui, P., Lio', P., Crowcroft, J.: Towards real-time community detection in large networks. Phys. Rev. E **79**, 066107 (2009)
26. Lugano, G., Kyppö, J., Saariluoma, P.: Designing people's interconnections in mobile social networks. In: Proceedings of the First International Conference on Multidisciplinary Information Sciences and Technologies (InScit), Badajoz, pp. 500–504, 25–27 Oct 2006
27. Mcdonald, A.B., Znati, T.: A path availability model for wireless ad-hoc networks. In: Wireless Communications and Networking Conference, (WCNC), pp. 35–40. IEEE, Sept 1999
28. Musolesi, M., Mascolo, C.: A community based mobility model for ad hoc network research. In: Proceedings of the 2nd International Workshop on Multi-hop ad hoc Networks: From Theory to Reality, pp. 31–38. ACM, New York (2006)
29. Musolesi, M., Hailes, S., Mascolo, C.: An ad hoc mobility model founded on social network theory. In: Proceedings of the 7th ACM International Symposium on Modeling, Analysis and Simulation of Wireless and Mobile Systems, MSWiM '04, New York, pp. 20–24. ACM (2004)
30. Newman, M.E.J., Girvan, M.: Finding and evaluating community structure in networks. Phys. Rev. E **69**, 026113 (2004)
31. Pigné, Y.: Modélisation et traitement décentralisé des graphes dynamiques: Application aux réseaux mobiles ad hoc. PhD thesis, Université du Havre (2008)
32. Raghavan, U.N., Albert, R., Kumara, S.: Near linear time algorithm to detect community structures in large-scale networks. Phys. Rev. E **76**, 036106 (2007)
33. Rosvall, M., Bergstrom, C.T.: Maps of random walks on complex networks reveal community structure. Proc. Natl. Acad. Sci. USA **105**(4), 1118–1123, 01 (2008)
34. Tantipathananandh, C., Berger-Wolf, T., Kempe, D.: A framework for community identification in dynamic social networks. In: Proceedings of the 13th ACM SIGKDD International Conference on Knowledge Discovery and Data Mining, KDD '07, New York, pp. 717–726. ACM (2007)
35. Tian, J., Chen, D., Fu, Y.: A new local algorithm for detecting communities in networks. Education Technology and Computer Science, International Workshop on, vol. 2, Wuhan, pp. 721–724 (2009)
36. Wan, Y., Chen, D., Fu, Y.: A new efficient algorithm for detecting communities in complex networks. In: Network and Parallel Computing Workshops, IFIP International Conference on, Shanghai, pp. 281–286 (2008)
37. Wang, X., Chen, G., Lu, H.: A very fast algorithm for detecting community structures in complex networks. Phys. A **384**(2), 667–674 (2007)
38. Yang, B., Liu, J., Liu, D.: An autonomy-oriented computing approach to community mining in distributed and dynamic networks. Auton. Agents Multi-Agent Syst. **20**(2), 123–157 (2010)
39. Zachary, W.W.: An information flow model for conflict and fission in small groups. J. Anthropol. Res. **33**(4), 452–473 (1977)

Chapter 4
Detection and Interpretation of Communities in Complex Networks: Practical Methods and Application

Vincent Labatut and Jean-Michel Balasque

Abstract Community detection, an important part of network analysis, has become a very popular field of research. This activity resulted in a profusion of community detection algorithms, all different in some not always clearly defined sense. This makes it very difficult to select an appropriate tool when facing the concrete task of having to identify and interpret groups of nodes, relatively to a system of interest. In this chapter, we tackle this problem in a very practical way, from the user's point of view. We first review community detection algorithms and characterize them in terms of the nature of the communities they detect. We then focus on the methodological tools one can use to analyze the obtained community structure, both in terms of topological features and nodal attributes. To be as concrete as possible, we use a real-world social network to illustrate the application of the presented tools and give examples of interpretation of their results from a Business Science perspective.

Introduction

Network modeling has been used for years in many application fields: biological, social, technological, communication, and information (see [1] for a very comprehensive review of applied studies). The necessity to focus on some parts has appeared quite soon, for instance, in sociology [2] and was initially performed

V. Labatut (✉)
Computer Science Department, Galatasaray University, Çırağan Cad. No:36, 34357 Ortaköy/İstanbul, Turkey
e-mail: vlabatut@gsu.edu.tr

J.-M. Balasque
Business Science & Marketing Department, Galatasaray University, Çırağan Cad. No:36, 34357 Ortaköy/İstanbul, Turkey
e-mail: jmbalasque@gsu.edu.tr

A. Abraham and A.-E. Hassanien (eds.), *Computational Social Networks: Tools, Perspectives and Applications*, DOI 10.1007/978-1-4471-4048-1_4,
© Springer-Verlag London 2012

manually, with a qualitative approach. However, this type of analysis changed radically during the last decades, with the coming of the information age, when technology provided scientists with means to store, access, and take advantage of a very large amount of data (databases, internet, computing power). The analysis of very large networks became possible, provided appropriate techniques were used. Network analysis took a quantitative turn, which initiated a very creative phase, leading to the development of powerful tools.

Large real-world networks are characterized by a heterogeneous structure, which leads to particular properties. Various subfields of network analysis focus on different properties: efficiency of information propagation, robustness, stability, synchronization, etc. [1]. In particular, an heterogeneous distribution of links often leads to a so-called community structure [3]. A community roughly corresponds to a group of nodes more densely interconnected, relatively to the rest of the network [4]. Note this concept has been translated into different more formal definitions, which we will review later in this chapter. The way such a structure can be interpreted is obviously dependent on the modeled system. However, independently from the nature of this system, the study of communities constitutes a mesoscopic analysis, complementary to the microscopic (node-wise) and macroscopic (network-wise) approaches one can also adopt. Because of this intermediary position, the community structure conveys some very important information, necessary to the good understanding of the system [5]. Consequently, detecting communities is an essential part of modern network analysis.

In this chapter, we focus on this task with a very practical and operational approach and adopt the user's point of view. To our opinion, someone willing to perform community detection on his data needs to answer three important questions: Which algorithms should I apply? How will I compare their results? How will I interpret the obtained communities? As stated before, networks are used in many application fields. However, modern community detection tools have not significantly penetrated certain research areas yet. We believe one of the reasons for this is the profusion of tools and the lack of information regarding their similarities and differences, which underlines the importance of our first question. Most articles present new community detection algorithms and compare them to existing ones, using real-world and artificially generated data. However, the algorithms are generally compared only in a quantitative way, relying on some performance measures [6]. Yet, algorithms rely on different formal definitions of what a community is. It therefore seems incomplete, or even unfair, to compare algorithms which do not actually try to detect the same objects. Moreover, once communities have been identified, one wants to give them a meaning relative to the studied system, and this task is largely dependent on the selected algorithm.

We aim at offering the user the information he needs to determine which algorithms are adapted to his data, apply and compare them, and interpret their result in meaningful terms, relatively to the applicative context. As an illustration, we will apply the described methods to some data describing a population of 552 university students. These data were gathered during a survey performed in the Galatasaray University at Istanbul, Turkey [7]. Its goal was to retrieve the information needed to extract a network representing the students' social interactions and perform an analysis of their purchasing behavior. Thus, besides the social network itself, the data include a whole set of nodal attributes describing *factual* (age, gender, clubs membership, etc.), *behavioral* (perceived actions in terms of human interaction and purchasing behavior), and *sentimental* (personal thoughts and feelings relative to university, friends, desires, favorite brands, etc.) information. In this chapter, however, we do not mean to conduct an exhaustive analysis of these data, but simply to use them as a practical example (cf. [7] for the details regarding the survey and this analysis).

The rest of this chapter is organized as follows. Section "Community Detection Process" is dedicated to community detection algorithms: we describe their properties, how to compare their results, and how to select the most relevant community structure. In section "Interpretation of the Communities," we show different types of analysis oriented toward the interpretation of the community structure. We focus on different methods allowing to characterize communities, based on both topological information and nodal attributes. Finally, we conclude by mentioning alternative methods which we could not describe in details.

Community Detection Process

Our goal in this section is first to review the existing community detection methods from a user's perspective. Usually, these algorithms are presented from an author's perspective, with emphasis on process, performance, and computational cost [6]. However, the community detection problem is known to be ill-defined [3, 5, 8, 9], which is why so many different algorithms exist: they do not define the concept of community in the same formal way. They consequently do not necessarily detect the same communities. Under these conditions, comparing raw performances obtained from different algorithms seems very little relevant.

We think the final user is basically interested in three properties. First, the type of information the algorithm is able to process. Indeed, there are various ways of describing a network and one can embed different sorts of data: link attributes (weights, directions), node attributes, different classes of links (multiplex networks) or nodes (n-mode or multipartite networks), temporal information, etc. The user may want to select a method able to take advantage of all the available data. In this chapter, we decided to focus on attributes.

Second, the kind of community structure the algorithm produces. One generally distinguishes *partitions* and *covers*, i.e., mutually exclusive and overlapping communities. We decided to focus on the former, because only a few algorithms are able to identify covers already. Most algorithms output a single partition, but some of them are able to produce a collection of community structures estimated for different granularities. In the case of hierarchical algorithms, communities belonging to neighboring granularities are hierarchically related. In a given level, communities may correspond to the merging of several lower level communities, while being a part themselves of larger communities in the upper level. *Multiresolution* methods also estimate the community structure at different granularities, but without looking specifically for hierarchical relationships between them. They either scan automatically various scales or allow to specify them parametrically [10].

Third, the nature of the communities the algorithm is able to identify. As stated before, there are many ways to define formally what a community is. Yet, this concept is at the center of the analysis and is therefore of utmost importance. The user should select his tool mainly based on this feature.

In order to give the user all the information he needs, we reviewed community detection methods according to the three properties we mentioned. Note excellent reviews exist, which describe in great details the points we chose to ignore here [3, 8, 9, 11]. The rest of the section is more practical. We present a list of publicly available tools and summarize their features in the previously mentioned terms. We then consider the very common case where one could estimate several community structures for a network of interest. We present various ways to tackle the problem of selecting the most appropriate community structure depending on the user's criteria and objectives.

Concept of Community

A very widespread informal definition of the community concept considers it as a group of nodes densely interconnected compared to the rest of the network [3, 8, 9, 11]. In other terms, a community is a cohesive subset clearly separated from the rest of the network. Formal interpretations try to formalize and combine both these aspects of cohesion and separation. Note this definition is not always explicit: procedural approaches exist, in which the notion of community is implicitly defined as the result of the processing. Although it is not always straightforward to categorize the definitions, we regroup them in four classes: density-, pattern-, node similarity- and link centrality-based approaches. The last subsection is dedicated to methods which did not fit in the previous definitions.

Density

A whole family of formalizations is based on a direct translation of the informal community definition given above. The general approach consists first of specifying two distinct measures to assess separately cohesion and separation, and then in defining a global measure by considering their difference or ratio. For instance, Mancoridis et al. [12] defined their intra-connectivity and inter-connectivity to measure the cohesion and separation of a community, respectively. The former is simply the regular density processed when considering only the links located inside a community, i.e., connecting two nodes belonging to the community. The latter is the density processed when considering only the links between a pair of communities. Let us note n_C the number of nodes in community C, and m_{CD} the number of links between communities C and D. Then, for an undirected network, community C intra-connectivity is

$$A_C = \frac{m_{CC}}{n_C \left(n_C - 1\right)/2} \tag{4.1}$$

and communities C and D inter-connectivity (C $\neq$ D) is

$$B_{CD} = m_{CD}/n_C n_D. \tag{4.2}$$

Mancoridis et al. proposed to quantify the quality of a whole community structure by considering the difference between these measures averaged over the network ($i \neq j$):

$$MQ = \langle A_i \rangle - \langle B_{ij} \rangle. \tag{4.3}$$

Fortunato gives a different definition of the inter-connectivity in his review [3], by considering the links between the community of interest and the rest of the network:

$$B'_C = \frac{\sum\limits_{i \neq C} m_{Ci}}{n_C \left(n - n_C\right)}, \tag{4.4}$$

where n is the total number of nodes in the network.

Instead of using the density measure, some authors represent cohesion and separation in terms of internal and external degrees, respectively. The former corresponds to the number of links a node has with other nodes from its community, whereas the latter concerns the nodes located out of the community. If we note k_i the number of links a node has with some community i and if we consider a node belonging to community C, then its internal degree is k_C and its external degree is $\sum\limits_{i \neq C} k_i$. This led to the notions of *weak* and *strong* community [13]. The former is characterized by the fact all of its nodes have a greater internal than external degree, whereas the latter applies the same constraint to internal and external degrees of the community as a whole. Certain algorithms are based, sometimes implicitly, on the notion of strong community (or on a related definition), such as the Label Propagation method [14].

Alternatively, in place of deciding what is and what is not a community, it is possible to use these degrees to quantify how good a community is. The *conductance* Φ_C of a community C is the ratio of its external degree to the minimum between its total degree and that of the rest of the network [15]. In the case of a community much smaller than the network, it is therefore its proportion of external links:

$$\Phi_C = \frac{\sum\limits_{i \neq C} m_{Ci}}{\sum\limits_{i} m_{Ci}}. \tag{4.5}$$

Although not explicitly, many algorithms optimize this quantity or one of its variants [3], via spectral analysis of matrices derived from the adjacency matrix [16], use of certain random walk-based distances, simulation of synchronization processes, etc. Lancichinetti et al. defined a similar measure at the level of the node: their *embeddedness* e corresponds to the ratio of the node internal degree k_C to its total degree k [5]:

$$e = k_C / k. \tag{4.6}$$

It can be averaged over the node community or the whole network, to assess the quality of the community or the community structure, respectively. In the latter case, the obtained measure is close to the *coverage* measure, which is the ratio of the intra-community links to the total number of links in the whole network [3]:

$$CV = \sum_i \frac{m_{ii}}{m}, \tag{4.7}$$

where m is the number of links in the network.

Newman's original *modularity* [4] can be viewed as a chance-corrected version of the coverage considered at the level of the communities. Let us note $q_{ij} = m_{ij}$ and m, then the modularity is

$$Q = \sum_i \left(q_{ii} - \left(\sum_j q_{ij} \right)^2 \right). \tag{4.8}$$

First, the proportion of internal links in the whole network is processed over all communities ($\sum_i q_{ii} = CV$), and then the corresponding proportion estimated for a comparable random network is subtracted ($\sum_i (\sum_j q_{ij})^2$). The null model used by Newman is a randomly rewired version of the network of interest, with preserved size (numbers of nodes and links) and degree distribution. Such a network is not supposed to have any community structure because of the uniformly random rewiring. Therefore, in order to have a significant community structure, the network of interest is required to have a much greater proportion of internal links. The modularity is certainly the most popular measure to assess the quality of a partition community structure. Many algorithms were designed to optimize it, explicitly or not: spectral approaches [17], random walk-based distances [18], genetic algorithms, greedy approaches [4, 19–22], simulated annealing [23], mathematical programming [24], extremal optimization, spin glass model [10], etc.

However, the modularity is known to have at least two important limitations. First, its maximal value is not constant, and depends on the considered network structure, which makes it impossible to compare modularity values between different networks. It could be normalized using the maximal modularity of the associated null model, but this value is itself difficult to process [3]. Second, it has a resolution limit, meaning it can detect perfectly valuable communities if they are smaller than a critical size depending on the network itself [25]. Several extensions such as [10] were developed to solve this problem.

Most density-based definitions have been extended for weighted and directed networks (conductance [26], modularity [27, 28]). The extension is generally straightforward, by considering strength instead of degree for weighted links, and by distinguishing in- and out-degree for directed ones. The adaptation of the algorithms is not always as simple though; for instance, spectral approaches are more difficult to apply when the adjacency matrix is asymmetric, which is generally the case when dealing with directed networks [26].

Pattern

Another way to define cohesion and separation consists of identifying maximal subsets composed of small specific interconnection patterns, e.g., cliques. One can consider a community to be either the largest identified pattern, or a set of patterns with common nodes [3, 29]. This approach can be seen as more qualitative than the density-based one, because it does not rely only on numeric values to formalize these concepts. Separation is represented by the fact one is looking for maximal subsets, which implies these are separated from the rest of the network. The nature of this separation and the notion of cohesion both depend on the selected interconnection pattern.

The most basic pattern one can use is the clique, a set of completely interconnected nodes. Luce and Perry present a clique as a group of mutual friends [30]. The connectivity is complete and direct, i.e. for a set of n nodes, each node is connected to the $n - 1$ other nodes from the clique, and is consequently at a distance 1 of anyone of them. However, a clique structure represents a strong constraint, especially for real-world networks [3, 29]. For this reason, many partially relaxed variants exist, which focus either on the complete or the direct aspects of clique connectivity. The patterns called k-plex and k-core belong to the first kind. For the latter, k represents the minimal number of neighbors a certain node must have in the pattern [31]. On the contrary, for the former, it is the maximal number of non-neighbors [32].

The concept of n-clique relaxes the direct aspect of clique connectivity: it does not require all nodes to be connected by a direct link, but at least by a path whose length is at most n [30]. However, this pattern is too relaxed and allows paths to go through nodes located out of the n-clique, possibly leading to an n-clique made of disjoint subsets of nodes. This, of course, is not compatible with the intuitive notion of community, which implies connectedness. For this reason, another pattern called n-clan was defined by adding a constraint on the diameter of an n-clique, stating it should not be greater than n [33].

The approach can be extended to consider directed or weighted links. For instance, an f-group is a maximal subset of weakly and strongly transitive triads.

A triad is a set of three nodes, and it is considered as transitive if it is completely connected (i.e., a three-node clique, or triangle). According to Hanneman, it is strongly transitive if all three links have the same weight, and weakly transitive if the link with the smallest weight is at least above a certain threshold [29]. Palla et al. presented a clique-based method to process both directed and weighted networks [34]. However, to our knowledge, no extension was designed to deal with individual information (i.e., nodal attributes).

Most pattern-based algorithms are computationally demanding [3]. Although this is a drawback in the context of complex networks analysis, due to their size, the pattern-based approach still has an interesting advantage: it allows specifying more precisely the internal structure of the communities. If any *a priori* knowledge of the studied system is available, it is possible to use it to constraint the community identification process. Of course, the pattern has to be chosen thoroughly: some networks do not exhibit certain patterns. For instance, technological networks and certain social networks do not contain many cliques [3].

Node Similarity

By using an appropriate similarity function, the topological notions of cohesion and separation can be translated in terms of intra-community similarity and inter-community dissimilarity. In other terms, a community is viewed as a group of nodes which are similar to each other, but dissimilar from the rest of the network. Once all node-to-node distances are known, detecting a community structure can be performed by applying a distance-based classic cluster analysis algorithm [35]. Such a tool is designed to minimize the internal and maximize the cluster-to-cluster distances. Depending on the desired output (overlapping vs. mutually exclusive community, hierarchy of community), different clustering algorithms can be applied [36, 37].

The strongpoint of this approach is the possibility to include any information in the definition of the similarity function. Purely topological functions exist, such as those based on structural and regular equivalence, which state two nodes are similar if they share the same connection pattern to the same neighbors, or possibly different neighbors, respectively. Structural equivalence can be quantified using, for instance, Jaccard's coefficient [38] (ratio of the intersection cardinality to the union cardinality of two sets of interest) applied to both nodes sets of neighbors (other methods exist, see [3]). If they are structurally similar, two nodes are supposed to be close (and hence to belong to the same community) even if they are not directly linked, because they are likely to be indirectly connected through their neighbors. Note strict equivalence is sometimes too restrictive, and relaxed versions exist (cf. the appendix of [39]).

Other topological functions rely on paths instead of direct connections. One can consider the number of paths, or distinct paths (i.e. the same node or link does not appear twice), or shortest paths between two nodes to assess their similarity: the highest this number, the more similar the nodes. Some authors rather adopt a probabilistic approach, considering random walks. The expected path lengths can be processed; for instance, the *first passage time* is the expected number of steps a random walker would need to go from the source node to the target one [40], while the *commute time* additionally considers the return time [41]. An alternative is to consider instead the probability value itself: probability to visit the target node in a given number of steps [42], probability to reach it before coming back to the source [43], etc.

Finally, similarity can also be defined using both topological and individual information. In [44], Handcock et al. make the assumption the nodes of a network can be characterized by their location in an unobserved so-called *social space*. This location depends on topological information and nodal attributes. Communities are identified by clustering nodes depending on their distance in this social space.

Link Centrality

The concept of community can also be defined in terms of link centrality. There are several definitions for this notion, but link centrality is basically related to two properties: the number of pairs of nodes the link is connecting (directly or not) and how likely these connections are to be used. Under these terms, links located between communities are supposed to be very central, since they allow to connect the nodes from one community to those from the other one, and there are only few of them (by definition inter-community links are sparse) so they are very likely to be used. On the contrary, the links located inside communities connect comparatively few nodes (mainly those from the same community), and the community is supposed to be densely connected, so many different path exist to connect two nodes, making it less likely for a link to be used. In other words, the high centrality of inter-community links and the low centrality of intra-community links relate to separation and cohesion, respectively.

Tyler et al. explicitly defined a community as a set of nodes whose links centrality must not be greater than a certain threshold [45]. They consider the most isolated node a community can contain is a leaf (degree 1 node), whose only link has the maximal centrality in this community. They consequently define their threshold as the centrality exhibited by this link. The fact some node set contains a link more central than this threshold means this link connects two subsets both larger than one node. These subsets could be separated, leading to two communities.

Various edge centrality measures were defined using principles not unlike those employed for path-based node centrality measures. Some of them are not adapted to this case though: number of paths (generally infinite), distinct paths (inefficient on degree 1 nodes). Girvan and Newman defined their *edgebetweenness* measure by considering the total number of shortest paths going through a link [46]. They also used the nondeterministic approach and defined a random walk centrality based on the probability a link has to be passed by the walker, averaged over all pairs of source and target nodes. The extension to directed links is straightforward (one consider only directed paths). Newman proposed extensions of both measures for weighted links [27], by normalizing edgebetweenness with the considered link weight, and by using weights to process the random walker transition probabilities. Although not explicitly stated, the approach described in [47] is related to link centrality, this time defined in terms of currents flow. The network is view as a resistor network and inter-community links are characterized by significant voltage differences.

Radicchi et al. proposed an alternative link centrality called *edge clustering* [13]. It corresponds to the ratio of the number of existing cycles containing the link of interest, to the number of possible cycles given the existing links. Therefore, unlike betweenness centrality, a high value means here the link is likely to be inside a community, since cycles are much more likely to happen there. The measure was extended to weighted links similarly to what was done for the edgebetweenness, i.e., using a normalization based on the weight of the considered link [48].

Others

Certain definitions of the concept of community do not fit the classes we described in the previous subsections. We present here only two of them, because they are used in some of the publicly available algorithms we present in the following section. The reader should notice other specific approaches exist, though (see [3]).

To define the concept of community, Rosvall and Bergstrom [49] do not use an approach based on cohesion and separation like all the previous community definitions. They adopt a data compression perspective and consider the community structure as a set of regularities in the network topology, which can be used to represent the whole network in a more compact way. The best community structure is therefore the one maximizing compactness while minimizing information loss. They implement this definition through the use of the mutual information measure applied to different representations of the network based on the adjacency matrix [49] and on a node nomenclature [50]. Ziv et al. adopted a comparable approach, but used instead a diffusion process to represent the network [51].

Van Dongen proposed to simulate another kind of diffusion process in the network to detect communities [52]. This approach relies on the transfer matrix of the network, which describes the transition probabilities for a random walker evolving in this network. Two specific transformations are iteratively applied on this matrix. First, it is raised to some specified power, in order to get a transfer matrix containing probabilities for longer paths. Second, each element in the matrix is raised to some specified power, in order to favor the higher probability values, which corresponds to nodes presumably belonging to the same community. The resulting matrix is then normalized to get a new transfer matrix. Both steps are repeated until convergence. The resulting matrix can be interpreted as the adjacency matrix of a network with disconnected components. These correspond to communities in the original network.

Table 4.1 List of publicly available community detection tools and their main features

Name	Input	Output	Community	Complexity	Impl.
Edge Betweenness [46]	S, D	H	Link centrality	$O(n^3)$	I, J
Zhou [40]	S, W	H	Node similarity	$O(n^3)$	A
Radetal [13, 48]	S, W	H	Link centrality	$O(n^2)$	A
Fast Greedy [4, 19]	S, W	H	Density	$O(n\log^2 n)$	A
CommFind [16]	S	H	Density	$O(n^3)$	A
NetCarto [23]	S	P	Density	Param. dep.	A
Wu-Huberman [47]	S, W, D	P	Link centrality	$O(n\log n)$	J
WalkTrap [42]	S, W	H, M	Node similarity	$O(n^2\log n)$	A, I
ITmod [51]	S, W	H	Compression	–	A
Leading Eigenvector [17]	S	H	Density	$O(n^2\log n)$	I
SpinGlass [10]	S, W	M	Density	Param. dep.	I
Label Propagation [14]	S, W	P	Density	$O(n)$	I
InfoMod [49]	S	P	Compression	–	A
Wakita-Tsurumi [22]	S	H	Density	$O(n\log^2 n)$	A
Agarwal-Kempe [24]	S	P	Density	$\Theta(n^2)$	A
Louvain [21]	S, W	H	Density	$O(n)$	A, I
MarkovCluster [52]	S, W, D	M	Diffusion	$O(n^3)$	A, G
VBmod [53]	S	P	Density	$O(n^2)$	A
InfoMap [50, 54]	S, W, D	H	Compression	–	A
Multistep Greedy [20]	S, W, D	H	Density	$O(n\log^2 n)$	A
TimeScale [18]	S, W	H, M	Density	–	A
Ierarca [55]	S	H	Node similarity	$O(n\log n)$	A

The inputs are simple (*S*), weighted (*W*), or directed (*D*) networks. The outputs can be a simple partition (*P*), or a collection of partitions hierarchically ordered (*H*) or not (multiresolution, *M*). Only the class of community definition is indicated, see the text for more details. The complexities are expressed for sparse networks, i.e., the number of links is of the order of the number of nodes (*Param. dep.* stands for parameter dependent). Implementations can be author-made (*A*, see the text for details and URL) or belong to the igraph library (*I*) [56] (*R* and Python languages), the Jung package (*J*) [57] (Java) or the Gephi software (*G*) [58] (Java)

Publicly Available Tools

In this section, we present publicly available implementations of community detection algorithms. Table 4.1 shows them in order of publication, with their main features. A large part of these algorithms are dedicated to modularity optimization. The first is *Fast Greedy*, a C implementation of a greedy approach by Newman and Clauset [4, 19] (http://cs.unm.edu/~aaron/research/fastmodularity. htm). It is able to process large networks; however, it suffers from a bias toward large communities. Several variants were defined to correct this: *Wakita-Tsurumi* [22] (Java implementation at http://ken-wakita.net/research/en/software), *Multi-step Greedy* [20] (C++ implementation at http://www.biochem-caflisch.uzh.ch/public/5). The *Louvain* algorithm [21] (C++ code at http://sites.google.com/site/findcommunities) implements a different greedy approach designed for very large networks. Newman also proposed his *Leading Eigenvector* algorithm [17] to optimize modularity by applying a spectral approach on a specific matrix. The *NetCarto* algorithm [23] (C code available on demand to its authors) implements a simulated annealing approach, which allows it to get very close to the actual optimum, but makes it in turn very slow. Reichardt and Bornholdt reformulated the modularity optimization problem using a *Spin Glass* model [10]. Their approach actually generalizes modularity in order to overcome its resolution limit, and let the user specify a resolution parameter. With *TimeScale* [18] (C++ source code available at http://www.lambiotte.be/codes.html) Lambiotte et al. proposed to apply a related extension of the modularity on their Louvain algorithm. Finally, the version of Agarwal and Kempe [24] (C++ and Java codes at http://www-scf.usc.edu/~gaurava) adopts a mathematical programming approach to the same modularity optimization problem.

Besides the modularity, other density-based definitions of the community concept are used. *CommFind* adopts a spectral approach to optimize a partition quality measure related to the conductance [16, 59] (C code at http://wdb.ugr.es/~donetti). *VBmod* [53] (Matlab code at http://www.columbia.edu/~chw2) relies on a Bayesian approach whose probabilistic model is related to the embeddedness measure. *Label Propagation* [14] simulates the spread of values in the network until convergence and identifies communities as sets of nodes associated to the same value. At the end of the process, the value associated to a node is the majority one among its neighbors, so this can be seen as a relaxed version of the strong community concept [13].

Node similarity-based approaches are also fairly represented. *WalkTrap* [42] is based on a random walk distance which considers the probability to go from one node to another in a given number of steps. This parameter affects the resolution of the resulting communities, so the tool can be considered as multiresolution. Zhou also used a random-walk-based distance, but this time considering the excepted number of steps to from one node to another [40] (Fortran implementation at http://www.mpikg-golm.mpg.de/th/people/zhou). *Jerarca* [55] uses an original distance definition based on the detection of patterns (C++ implementation at http://jerarca.sourceforge.net). Three distinct distance functions with different computational complexities are defined based on different patterns.

The *EdgeBetweenness* algorithm [46] was the first link centrality-based tool. Radicchi et al. proposed a variant relying on their edge clustering measure [13, 48] (C code at http://filrad.homelinux.org). Hu and Huberman used a different approach based on currents flow [47].

Several approaches are based on a compression view of the community structure (cf. section "Others"): *InfoMod* [49] and *InfoMap* [50] C++ implementations are available at http://www.tp.umu.se/~rosvall/code.html (the latter was recently extended to output dendrograms), whereas the Matlab code for *ITmod* [51] can be downloaded at http://www.columbia.edu/~chw2. Finally, the diffusion-based approach implemented in *MarkovCluster* [52] can be found at http://www.micans.org/mcl (C code). An inflation parameter allows setting the granularity of the search, making the approach multiresolution.

Pattern-based implementations are mainly used to detect cover and not partitions (e.g., *Cfinder* [60]), which is why they are not represented here. Note some of these algorithms are also very conveniently implemented in libraries dedicated to network analysis, such as *igraph* [56] and *Jung* [57] (see Table 4.1), which gives the user a uniform access to their functionalities.

Most of these algorithms were individually tested on both real-world and randomly generated networks, and several review articles directly compared some of them [6]. However, these performance assessments have to be considered with caution. Concerning real-world networks, the reference communities have to be manually defined and are therefore subjective. On the contrary, in the case of generated networks, they are objective because they are a part of the generative process. However, this process itself is biased in direction of one definition of the community concept (e.g., embeddedness for [6]), and the resulting benchmark therefore favors algorithms based on the same definition. The only relevant comparison concerns algorithms all based on the same community definition, like for instance the various ways of optimizing the modularity.

Comparing Partitions

Thanks to the information provided in the previous sections, the user should be able to choose an appropriate tool based on the data to process, the desired kind of community structure, and most of all a relevant definition of the community concept. However, various situations can lead to results taking the form of several partitions, when one is generally interested in a single one. First, given the profusion of algorithms, several of them might be adapted to a given study, probably resulting in several different partitions. Second, even if a single algorithm is used, one can obtain a collection of community structures if this algorithm has a hierarchical or multiresolution output. In both cases, the user has to make a choice in order to select the community structure he is going to interpret. In this section, we present methods to make this choice.

Different Algorithms

In the case where one has several partitions coming from different algorithms, the simplest way seems to be comparing the quality of the partitions through the use of a quality measure, and ultimately selecting the partition with the highest quality. However, different problems can arise. First, if the algorithms rely on different community definitions, the quality measure, which has itself to implement such a definition, will be biased toward certain algorithms. Second, even when comparing algorithms using the same definition, e.g., modularity optimization methods, the quality measure may present limitations. For instance, the modularity is known to have a resolution limit, which means it will disadvantage partitions displaying communities below this limit, even if these are the actual communities.

A complementary approach consists of comparing the partitions themselves instead of their qualities. The goal is then to assess how much algorithms agree rather than to identify the best partition. This is particularly relevant in the context of an exploratory analysis where one could not choose a community definition adapted to his data and decided to use several algorithms based on various definitions. The fact these algorithms identify similar partitions is a sign of the stability of the community structure, whereas if they are very different, one should question his results.

We propose to use the *adjusted Rand index* (ARI), which is rather popular in cluster analysis. The original Rand index (RI) [61] is defined as

$$RI = \frac{a + d}{a + b + c + d},\qquad(4.9)$$

where a (resp. d) corresponds to the number of pairs of nodes belonging to the same (resp. different) community in both partitions, and b (resp. c) to the number of pairs whose nodes belong to the same community in the first (resp. second) partition, whereas they belong to different communities in the second (resp. first) one. The adjusted version [62] is defined as

$$ARI = \frac{RI - E}{1 - E},\qquad(4.10)$$

where E is the amount of similarity expected to be due to chance, estimated by considering the products of marginals ($E = (a + b)(a + c)/n^2 + (b + d)(c + d)/n^2$). The upper limit of this measure is 1 (the two partitions are exactly the same). The value 0 indicates a partial overlap, equivalent to what would be observed if both partitions were random (i.e. $RI = E$). Negative values indicate a strong divergence between the partitions. Note there are other measures one can use to assess the similarity of two partitions [3, 36]. We can also mention the normalized mutual information, which has been used in recent community detection works [6].

As an example, we applied several community detection algorithms to our social network of university students. Table 4.2 gives the ARI values for some of these results. One can notice the maximal agreement is reached for the two modularity-based algorithms (Fast Greedy and SpinGlass). Moreover, their ARI values when compared to the other algorithms are very close, so we can conclude both partitions are certainly highly similar. The other algorithms differ in the definition of community they rely on, and this shows through the ARI values: InfoMod, with its information theory-based approach, is isolated and largely disagrees with the others. Although they do not use the same approach at all, Label Propagation and MarkovCluster partially agree. Their partitions are nevertheless significantly different from those estimated by the modularity-based approach.

Table 4.2 Agreement measured by the ARI for a selection of community detection algorithms

Algorithm	Fast Greedy	SpinGlass	Label Prop.	InfoMod	MarkovCluster
Fast Greedy	–	0.80	0.52	0.30	0.36
SpinGlass	–	–	0.57	0.26	0.40
Label Prop.	0.57	0.57	–	0.14	0.68
InfoMod	0.26	0.26	0.14	–	0.09
MarkovCluster	0.40	0.40	0.68	0.09	–

Different Granularities

Consider now the case where one wants to compare several partitions corresponding to different granularities output by the same algorithm. If the algorithm is hierarchical, the agreement approach is not relevant, because agreement measures take the hierarchical aspect into account, i.e., two partitions corresponding to different levels in the same hierarchy will necessarily be very similar. The approach can be applied to multiresolution outputs though, in order to check if the partitions obtained at different granularities are really different. If they are similar, on the contrary, one can conclude they are related by a partial hierarchical order.

In both the hierarchical and multiresolution cases, partitions can be compared through their quality, like in the previous subsection. Moreover, here only one algorithm is involved, so it makes sense to rely on the quality measure it optimizes. However, not all algorithms use such a measure, in which case one has to select a measure which would be compatible in terms of community definition. For instance, using the modularity to select the best cut in a dendrogram produced by the EdgeBetweenness algorithm seems rather inappropriate, because the algorithm was not designed to maximize it. But there are not so many quality measures, and in practice the modularity is used most of the time.

The partition quality is important, but is not necessarily the only criterion to take into account. Indeed, one generally wants to identify a community structure in order to subsequently interpret it. He will therefore be interested in the number of communities and in their size: too large or too small values are likely to prevent any meaningful interpretation. Alternatively, some knowledge concerning the studied system might allow for the definition of preferences regarding these quantities. Under these conditions, the selection of the most appropriate partition should result from a compromise between the measured quality and the nature of the community structure.

The partition quality measured over the dendrogram output by a hierarchical algorithm often follows the evolution displayed in Fig. 4.1 for three hierarchical algorithms we applied on our data. In particular, one may notice the partitions surrounding the partition of maximal quality (dotted line) have very similar quality themselves. This situation is favorable to the compromise we mentioned, because it supports the selection of a neighboring partition without losing too much quality. Suppose we want to select a partition containing fewer communities

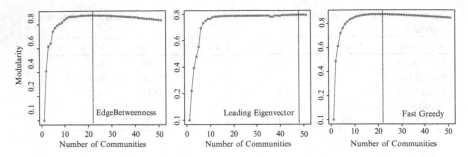

Fig. 4.1 Modularity values obtained for three hierarchical algorithms when applied to our data. Only the higher levels of the hierarchy are represented. The *dotted lines* indicate the partitions of maximal modularity

than the optimal one, i.e., a partition located a few merges away. We have to consider candidates relatively to two criteria: the loss of quality compared to the maximal quality partition and the number of nodes concerned by the merges. This optimization problem is extremely context-dependent, and it is therefore difficult to propose a general method. A reasonable approach consists of defining two limits based on the modeled system and the user's objectives: first the maximal acceptable loss in quality and second the maximal size allowed for a merged community. The user can then select the partition with fewest communities respecting both constraints. Let us consider the hierarchy estimated by Fast Greedy on our data. The best partition has 22 communities, with a modularity of 0.8780. Suppose we allow a quality loss of 0.01 and the merge of communities representing up to 5% of the network nodes. Then we could select the 13-community partition, with a modularity of 0.8696 (loss 0.0084), the largest community merged containing 4.2% of the nodes.

Interpretation of the Communities

Community detection is not an end in itself: once communities have been identified, one wants to understand what they mean. Two kinds of analysis can be performed for this matter. First, it is necessary to study the topology of the community structure. This allows assessing the structural significance and quality of the community structure, but also starting the interpretation process, by discussing the similarities and differences observed between the communities, and by identifying nodes with specific roles. The second phase of the analysis relies on the exploitation of nodal attributes. It is guided by the structures identified during the first phase thanks to the topology of the network (communities, nodes of interest). It consists of characterizing and discussing these structures in terms of the numeric or nominal data specific to the considered system and application domain. In this section, we present consensual tools allowing to perform these analysis. We illustrate their use

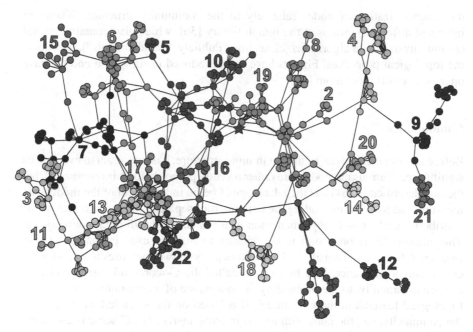

Fig. 4.2 Community structure obtained with Fast Greedy (maximum modularity cut). Each one of the 22 communities is represented by a *different color*. The *two stars* stand for the nodes with minimal embeddedness (0.33)

on our data, commenting from a Business Science perspective the communities identified by Fast Greedy, which are represented on Fig. 4.2. In this field, detecting communities is a very valuable task with huge implications, especially if these communities can be characterized in terms of specific purchase behaviors.

Topological Properties

Classical network analysis can be performed both at macroscopic and microscopic levels, i.e., by considering respectively topological properties of the network as a whole, or of some specific nodes taken individually. Networks can be characterized by a whole set of measures such as density, transitivity (a.k.a. clustering coefficient), and degree distribution (see [63] for a very comprehensive review). However, in this chapter, we rather focus on the community structure, which adds an intermediary level. It allows not only a mesoscopic analysis, but also brings a new point of view regarding individual nodes: one can consider their position in their respective communities or in the community structure (by opposition to their position in the whole network). In this section, we first introduce tools allowing to assess the quality of the communities collectively and separately, and then we consider the characterization of nodes relatively to the community structure. When not indicated differently, we used the igraph library [56], which also contains several community detection algorithms (cf. section "Publicly Available Tools"), to process the topological properties. Figures have been produced using igraph and the Java open source software Gephi [58].

Communities

Before starting the analysis of the community structure, it is important to evaluate its significance. Various methods were rather recently proposed for this purpose [3], but the one described in [64] has the advantage of being independent of the modularity measure, and to allow evaluating the communities separately (instead of the whole distribution). The C++ implementation is available at http://filrad.homelinux.org. This method relies on a null model similar to the one used in the modularity measure (cf. section "Density"). The authors propose two measures to quantify the community significance. The first one is called the C-score and corresponds, for a given community, to the probability of appearance of a community with similar topological features in the null model. It is based on the so-called worst node of the community, i.e., the node with lowest internal degree. The C-score is estimated by considering the probability for its counterpart in the random network to have an equal or larger internal degree. The second measure, called B-score, extends the C-score by considering several nodes instead of a single one. The resulting measure is supposedly more relevant, but also computationally more demanding [64]. We applied it to our data, and Table 4.3 shows 21 communities out of the 22 identified by Fast Greedy are significant ($B < 0.05$), the only exception being the 16th ($B = 0.089$). Note the significance of the community structure can be considered as an additional criterion in the community structure selection problem introduced in section "Different Granularities."

The first step in the analysis of the community structure is generally to characterize the *distribution of community sizes* (expressed in nodes), which is supposed to follow a power-law in many real-world networks [3, 19]. In our case, the number of communities is too small for this distribution to be statistically tested. It can be noticed (cf. Table 4.3) it is right-skewed though, with a single large community and many small ones. However, the difference between the smallest and largest communities is not comparable to what can be observed in other networks [5]. Consequently, we can conclude our community structure is relatively homogenous regarding the community sizes.

One of the most important aspects of the identified communities is their quality in terms of cohesion and separation. Several properties can be used for this assessment. In terms of cohesion, one can consider the *density* of each community, when considered separately from the rest of the network. By definition, communities are denser subgraphs, so their density is supposed to be much larger than for the whole network. Table 4.3 shows this is very much the case for our data, with a network density of 0.01 when most communities are 10 times denser. We remind

Table 4.3 Topological properties of the network and its communities

Community	n	d	$\langle e \rangle$	ℓ	k_{max}	h	B
1	32	0.07	0.96	3.57	10	0.32	0.012
2	39	0.06	0.93	3.99	10	0.26	0.018
3	28	0.08	0.99	3.20	10	0.37	0.001
4	30	0.11	0.98	2.99	10	0.34	0.001
5	23	0.09	0.94	3.45	8	0.36	0.014
6	46	0.07	0.97	3.28	11	0.24	0.001
7	34	0.08	0.93	3.05	11	0.33	0.002
8	23	0.09	0.97	3.14	10	0.45	0.002
9	20	0.11	0.95	3.36	9	0.47	0.001
10	39	0.07	0.96	3.43	10	0.26	0.013
11	20	0.12	0.93	2.64	9	0.47	0.034
12	15	0.13	0.99	2.59	9	0.64	0.002
13	28	0.11	0.96	2.53	12	0.44	0.001
14	13	0.15	0.99	2.21	8	0.67	0.003
15	14	0.16	0.95	2.44	9	0.69	0.038
16	13	0.19	0.86	2.15	7	0.58	0.089
17	28	0.11	0.96	2.63	10	0.37	0.002
18	22	0.15	0.97	2.53	10	0.48	0.005
19	20	0.16	0.97	2.60	8	0.42	0.006
20	12	0.35	0.97	1.74	9	0.82	0.012
21	15	0.24	0.99	1.90	10	0.71	0.001
22	38	0.09	0.97	2.91	12	0.32	0.000
Network	552	0.01	0.96	8.48	12	–	–

n is the number of nodes; d the density; $\langle e \rangle$ the average embeddedness; ℓ the average distance; k_{max} the maximal degree; h the hub dominance and B the B-score

the reader real-world networks are generally sparse, which explains the low density observed on our data. Moreover, sparsity is actually a prerequisite for the existence of a community structure [3]. The density varies much between our communities. It is strongly correlated to their size ($r = -0.72$), which indicates the smaller the communities, the denser they are.

A small *average distance* between nodes of the same community is also a sign of good cohesion. In our data, the average distance of a community is much smaller than its size. Of course, it is also much smaller than the distance averaged over the whole graph, due to its community structure and sparsity. Communities are supposedly small-world, which means the average distance increases logarithmically with the community size [5]. In our case, the distances are highly correlated with the logarithm of the community sizes ($r = -0.77$); however, we could not perform a significant test due to the small number of communities.

A small average distance can be explained by a high density and/or the presence of hubs, i.e., nodes connected to most of the other nodes belonging to the same community [5]. Hub dominance can be assessed using the following ratio:

$$h = \max_C(k) / (n_C - 1), \tag{4.11}$$

where $\max_C(k)$ and n_C represent the maximal degree and number of nodes in community C, respectively. When at least one node is connected to its whole community, it reaches unity. Table 4.3 shows only a few communities have a dominant hub (ratio greater than 0.5), and these are the smallest. Indeed, the correlation between community size and hub dominance is very strong ($r = -0.9$). This is due to the fact the maximal degree a node can reach is biased by construction of the network. Indeed, a student can cite a maximum of 10 friends, which makes it rather easy to get a degree of 10. But to get past this value, the student must be cited by persons he did not cite himself, which proved to be rather rare. Consequently, the maximum degree in a community is always very close to 10, independently from its size. The fact small communities are dominated by hubs while the large ones are not is a common feature of social networks [5].

Community separation can be measured by considering the proportion of links laying in-between them. In our case, only 52 out of the 791 links (6%) connect nodes of different communities. In other terms, the average number of links between two communities is only 0.23. This affects the embeddedness, as seen on Table 4.3. The values are averages over each community (and over the network, for the last one). The fact they are all very close to 1, including the network value, indicates nodes are very dominantly connected to other nodes from the same communities. This remark holds for all communities, independently from their size ($r = -0.02$). It is worth noticing the only nonsignificant community in terms of B-score (16th) exhibits the lowest maximal degree and embeddedness. The embeddedness distribution is also interesting, because unlike what is generally observed in social networks [5], it is not uniform at all. Instead, most nodes are very strongly embedded in their community: only 4% of them have an embeddedness of 0.5 or less. We suppose this is due to the size of our network, which is much smaller than those studied in [5].

Nodes

Weakly embedded nodes are remarkable because they are generally located in-between communities: their small embeddedness reflects the fact there is no clear dominance among the communities of their direct neighbors. For example, Fig. 4.2 shows the two nodes with smallest embeddedness (0.33), under the form of stars. Both are clearly lying at the interface of several communities. How these nodes can be used depends largely on the modeled system, but they generally constitute very valuable information. For instance, in the context of Business Science there are two main uses for them. First, these in-between nodes can be used as a base for certain communication strategies [65], consisting of making these persons as active as possible, in order to have them propagating messages to their contacts [66]. In this diffusion process, they can be considered as bridges between communities and can play the role of accelerators. Second, these people can often be characterized by specific purchase behaviors, constrained by the fact they try to improve part of their social image in order to increase their membership to a group [67].

Other methods exist to characterize the position of a node relatively to the community structure. Guimerà and Amaral defined two measures for this purpose [39]: the first concerns the node community whereas the second focuses on the rest of the network. The *within-community degree* z has more or less the same interpretation than the embeddedness: it quantifies how well a node is connected to the rest of its community. Its expression is different though, since it is defined as the z-score of the node internal degree relatively to its community C:

$$z = (k_C - \langle k_C \rangle)/\sigma, \qquad (4.12)$$

where $\langle k_C \rangle$ is the internal degree averaged over all nodes in community C, and σ is the corresponding standard deviation. A large within-community degree means the node has many more links inside its community than most other nodes belonging to this community. The second measure is the *participation coefficient*, which is defined as

$$P = 1 - \sum_i \left(\frac{k_i}{k} \right)^2, \qquad (4.13)$$

where k is the node total degree, k_i is its number of links with some community i (possibly its own community), and the sum is processed over all communities. It quantifies how much the node of interest is connected to multiple communities, and gets close to unity when it is evenly connected to all of them. On the contrary, when all the neighbors are in the same community ($k_C = k$), the participation coefficient is zero.

Guimerà and Amaral use both measures to characterize a node, and distinguish seven different roles depending on the observed combination of values, and to a set of thresholds. The choice of these thresholds is arbitrary [3] and we present here those determined empirically in [39]. First, nodes with a within-community degree smaller than 2.5 are considered as *hubs*, whereas the remaining ones are *non-hubs*. Finer roles are then defined by applying different thresholds on the participation coefficient. Hubs can be *provincial* (almost all neighbors in the same community, $P \leq 0.3$), *connector* (a majority of neighbors in the same community, $P \leq 0.75$), or *kinless* (less than half the neighbors in the same community, $P > 0.75$). The first can be considered as having an important local role for the cohesion of the community, the second allows connecting communities, and the third does not clearly belong to the community it was assigned to. Nonhubs can be *ultra-peripheral* (all neighbors in the same community, $P \leq 0.05$), *peripheral* (a large majority of neighbors in the same community, $P \leq 0.62$), *connectors* (approximately half the neighbors in the same community, $P \leq 0.80$), and *kinless* (a large majority of neighbors in other communities, $P > 0.80$).

If we consider our data, we get the distribution represented in Fig. 4.3, which is rather similar to the results obtained by Guimerà and Amaral on metabolic networks (appendix of [39]). A large majority of nodes have a zero participation coefficient,

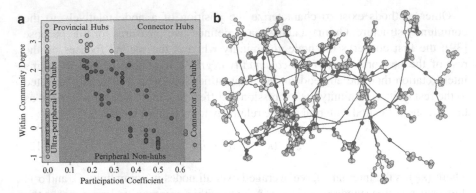

Fig. 4.3 Distribution of roles (**a**) in terms of within-community degree z and participation coefficient P; and (**b**) in the network. The colors are the same than in [39]: *grey*, *red* and *green* for ultra-peripheral, peripheral, and connector nonhubs; *yellow* and *pink* for provincial and connector hubs, respectively

which means all their neighbors belong to their community. This is of course related to the fact only 4% of the nodes have an embeddedness smaller than 0.5. These nodes only differ in their within community degree, and only a few of them are hubs. Consequently, most of the nodes in our network are ultra-peripheral (84%) or peripheral (12%). Three nodes are nonhub connectors, only one is a connector hub, and we have no kinless hub. The rest (3%) are provincial hubs. This is consistent with the community structure of our network, since nonmodular networks exhibits many kinless and very few (ultra-) peripheral nodes [39]. However, it is interesting to note that the hub distribution is not completely compatible with the hub dominance measure. For instance, on the one hand, community 22 has the maximal hub dominance; however, it does not contain any according to the role approach. On the other hand, community 1 has very low hub dominance, when it contains two hubs, including the only connector of the network. In both cases, the hub dominance might be fooled by the community sizes (very small for the first, much larger for the second). Besides these cases, roles and hub dependence agree on most communities. However, this highlights the fact that, when several alternative tools are available, one should confront their results. Another interesting point is the fact community 16 not only contains one of the two minimal embeddedness nodes, but also one of the three connector nonhubs. This seems to confirm our assumption for this community to be an artifact of the algorithm.

Attribute-Based Interpretation

After having described and analyzed the community structure, one is generally interested in giving a context-dependent interpretation, allowing for instance to explain why or how this structure appeared, or to perform some prediction regarding some data not available at the moment of the study. For this matter, in many situations, one has to focus solely on the topological properties described in the previous section. However, it is sometimes possible to associate tabular data to the studied network, defining various attributes for each node. This is particularly true for domains in which the objects composing the networks are complex enough to need being described according to several informative dimensions (e.g., social sciences). When such information is available, one can discuss the topological properties in terms of nodal attributes, which can help a lot in understanding the system. In this section, we present both descriptive and inferential tools adapted to this purpose. Note most of them are implemented in statistical software such as SPSS or R, and even Microsoft Excel for the descriptive methods.

Description

The formation of communities, especially in social networks, can sometimes be explained by homophilic relationships, i.e., a tendency for nodes to connect with other nodes more or less similar to them, relatively to some criteria of interest. Let us consider the sequence of all links present in the network: the values of some attribute for the corresponding source and target nodes can be viewed as two distinct series. The homophily can be measured as the level of association between these two series. For instance, Newman proposed to use the Cohen's Kappa statistic and Pearson's correlation coefficient for nominal and numeric attributes, respectively [68]. It is generally processed over the whole network, but in our case it can also be used to characterize the communities: there is no reason for them to exhibit the same homophily. Table 4.4 shows some results for the gender (G) and class (C) attributes. Most communities have close to zero homophily for gender, except for a few ones for which it reaches a value close to 0.5 (10, 13, 17). This means students do not bond depending on their gender, except for these communities. Homophily values are more contrasted for the class, with values either very close to 0 (6, 14, 22) or to 1 (8, 20).

Another approach consists of considering the community structure instead of the links as the relevant topological information. Under this assumption, communities are simply groups of nodes one wants to characterize relatively to their attributes. This problem is much more general than network analysis, since it also occurs in classic cluster analysis [69]. As an example, we present in Table 4.4 some of the most characteristic attributes of our data. Of course, all communities are not characterized by the same attributes, which is why we selected different types of data: factual (class and department), behavioral (hobbies, mobile phones, digital players), and sentimental (best friend consideration and loan inclination).

For space matters, we focus our comments only on a few communities. Let us consider first community 7. It contains only students of third and fourth year of License, but this holds for other communities too (3, 17), so this property alone is not sufficient to characterize it. However, unlike community 17, its dominating department is Business Science. Communities 3 and 7 can be distinguished by considering the former has no dominant hobby, and their dominant mobile phone

Table 4.4 Description of the network and its communities in terms of attributes

Com.	n	G	C	Class 1		Class 2		Dept.1		H	MP	DP	BF	LI
1	32	0.24	0.30	25	P2	6	L1	7	BS	M	No	Ap	3.80	2.60
2	39	0.36	0.54	15	L2	12	L3	10	IE	C	No	–	3.00	1.78
3	28	0.12	0.00	25	L4	3	L3	12	BS	–	No	–	3.25	2.50
4	30	0.11	−0.04	26	P1	3	P2	6	So	M	No	Cr	2.78	1.78
5	23	0.19	−0.05	17	L2	–	–	15	RI	S	Sa	Ap	2.75	2.25
6	46	0.01	0.65	19	L2	18	L3	14	So	R	Sa	Ap	3.43	1.54
7	34	0.25	0.19	25	L3	9	L4	24	BS	C	Sa	Ap	3.78	2.67
8	23	0.17	0.74	12	P1	10	L1	9	IE	S	Sa	Ap	3.00	3.00
9	20	0.19	0.00	18	P1	2	P2	5	BS	–	No	Ap	2.17	1.67
10	39	0.51	0.55	31	L2	6	L1	17	BS	C	No	Ap	2.92	1.92
11	20	−0.15	0.16	17	L4	2	L3	11	IE	M	No	–	3.80	2.00
12	15	0.11	0.61	7	L1	7	L2	7	La	–	SE	Ap	4.00	1.50
13	28	0.46	0.60	14	L1	13	L2	12	Ma	M	No	So	3.64	1.64
14	13	0.00	0.56	6	L3	5	L4	7	CS	–	No	–	3.50	2.00
15	14	−0.12	0.00	13	L3	–	–	8	RI	P	–	–	2.67	3.50
16	13	−0.10	−0.03	11	L1	–	–	10	Ph	P	–	–	3.67	1.33
17	28	0.48	0.00	25	L4	3	L3	14	IE	C	No	Ap	3.11	2.22
18	22	−0.09	0.54	12	L3	–	–	–	–	–	No	–	3.71	1.17
19	20	−0.06	0.00	19	L1	–	–	9	Ma	–	No	–	3.71	1.71
20	12	−0.14	1.00	12	P1	–	–	2	–	R	No	Ap	2.14	1.71
21	15	−0.16	0.00	13	P2	2	L1	11	La	T	No	–	4.00	1.67
22	38	−0.05	−0.02	34	L1	2	P2	22	BS	C	Sa	Ap	4.00	2.00
Net	552	0.25	0.78	124	L1	107	L2	96	BS	S	No	Ap	3.29	1.94

The G and C columns represent the homophily for the gender and class attributes, respectively. The Class (resp. Dept.) columns describe the two most represented classes (resp. department) in each community: the *left column* is the number of concerned students and the *right one* is the class (resp. department) name. The represented classes are Preparatory (*P1–2*) and License (*L1–4*), the departments are Business Science (*BS*), Computer Science (*CS*), Economics (*Ec*), Industrial Engineering (*IE*), International Relations (*IR*), Law (*La*), Literature (*Li*), Mathematics (*Ma*), Philosophy (*Ph*), Sociology (*So*). *H* is the most popular hobby: music (*M*), cinema (*C*), sport (*S*), photography (*P*), reading (*R*), theater (*T*). The next two columns are the most widespread brands of mobile phones (*MP*) and digital players (*DP*): Nokia (*No*), Samsung (*Sa*), Sony-Ericsson (*SE*), Apple (*Ap*), Creative (*Cr*), Sony (*So*). The two last columns indicate if a student thinks he has his best friends in the university (*BF*) and his inclination to take a loan (*LI*), respectively. Both answers are expressed on a scale ranging from 1 (clear no) to 5 (clear yes)

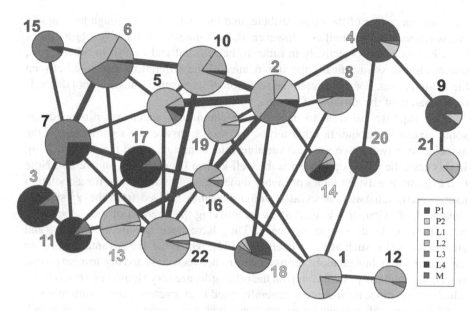

Fig. 4.4 Class distribution in the community network. Each node represents a community from Fig. 4.1, with matching number values and colors. Node diameters and link widths are proportional to community sizes (expressed in number of students) and to number of inter-community links, respectively. Each pie chart represents the class attribute distribution in a community. Possible classes are Preparatory (*P1–2*), License (*L1–4*) and Master (*M*)

brands are different. Students from community 15 are more inclined to take a loan; they have the highest average score for that question (LI). They will certainly be the most receptive to commercial pressure. Detecting such a community can have quite huge implications in the Business field. Community 16 contains almost exclusively first year Licenses from the philosophy department, which is already discriminant when considering the other communities. Moreover, from an application point of view, it is interesting to note that the dominant hobby is photography and there is no dominant brand for electronic devices. Community 20 is very interesting because its students tend to think their best friends are not in the university (BF column): they have the lowest average score for the corresponding question. Nevertheless, this community is quite similar to others regarding hobbies and brands. This may be due to the fact those students are in first year, often in a new city, far away from their family and highschool friends. A similar observation can be on the communities containing a majority of first-year students (e.g., 9), and the effect tends to disappear for the communities of older students (12, 21, 23).

As is shown, the visual inspection of the community composition allows to detect attributes of interest. This inspection can be enhanced by a graphical representation of the network. Figure 4.4 gives an example based on the distribution of the class attribute in the network of communities. This figure includes, among other, the columns Class 1 & 2 from Table 4.4. It confirms our remarks regarding the relatively discriminant power of the class attribute, and the fact it is not enough to uniquely characterize all communities. However, these somewhat subjective observations must be confirmed objectively in order to be relevant and useful. In other terms, one has to assess statistically the significance of the differences observed between the communities. For this matter, the selection of an adapted statistical tool depends on the nature of the attribute of interest.

First, suppose we want to determine if community membership depends on some nominal attribute. In other terms, we want to assess the significance of the association between two nominal variables: the community and the attribute [70]. In this case, the most popular test is the well-known Pearson's chi-square test. Note that extensions exist for tables of higher dimension, allowing to test for association using several attributes. Also, association measures derived from the χ^2 statistic (Pearson's Φ, Cramér's V, etc.) allow quantifying the strength of the association, by opposition to its simple existence. They have been questioned though, and alternatives exist, such as the λ coefficient [71], which has the advantage of being asymmetrical. In our example, the associations between class and department on one side, and community membership on the other side, are very significant ($P < 0.001$), which means those attributes are generally good to characterize our communities.

In the case of a quantitative attribute, one can perform a classic ANOVA to test whether its means are significantly different across communities [69], under the assumptions of independence, normality, and homoscedasticity (variance homogeneous across communities) [70]. Note if several attributes have to be considered at once, an extension called factorial Anova must be used instead. As an example, we performed an Anova on the sentimental attributes (best friend consideration and loan inclination). We first tested for homoscedasticity using Levene's test and got low P-values (respectively 0.068 and 0.085), but not enough to reject the homoscedasticity assumption for $\alpha = 0.05$. For the Anova itself, on the contrary, the P-values were small enough to reject the hypothesis of uniform mean (0.032 and 0.049, respectively). In other words, significant differences exist between communities for both attributes. To identify precisely which communities differ, one has to perform a post-hoc test such as Tuckey's or least significant difference (LSD) tests [70]. We applied the latter to our data, which expose several significant differences, but we limit our comments to the communities on which we focused in this section. It turns out the sentiment of having his best friend at the university is significantly lower in community 20 compared to most others, especially the 16th and 7th, so it can be considered as a characteristic of this community. Students from community 15 are significantly more inclined to take a loan or to delay a payment than most of the other communities, especially the 16th and 20th, whose students are significantly inclined not to take a loan.

Besides the communities, the nodes of interest detected in the previous section can also be interpreted in terms of nodal attributes. In our data, we highlighted five students with very low embeddedness or specific roles (three nonhub connectors and one hub connector). We will here only give some points and remarks to illustrate our purpose. First, it is worth noticing two out of three nonhub connectors are girls, and moreover two of them belong to the same community (16) and department

(Philosophy). One of them is in fourth year of License. She is an outlier on a question concerning the intention to stay in touch with university friends. Students strongly agreed to this assertion in average, whereas this person clearly thinks the opposite. Moreover, she also states she has a high probability to use old-fashioned products, when she owns cutting edge mobile phone and digital player. This information is of major interest in the context of a marketing strategy; for instance, it will allow orienting communication toward social image and acceptance matters. The hub connector is also interesting: he is a boy, in second year of preparatory class in the Law department. Most of his answers to the questions are very close to the average for all the respondents. Nevertheless, contrary to the others, he gives a very high importance to his friends' advice regarding computer and mobile phone purchases. Moreover, contrary to the majority of students, he states he would reduce his other expenditures to be able to afford some products of interest. The marketing strategy has to differ from the case of the previous girl, because he is certainly very well installed socially and possibly aims at keeping a very good social image.

Prediction

The descriptive tools presented in the previous section allow characterizing a community in terms of nodal attributes. This type of analysis is already interesting in terms of interpretation, but predictive methods can bring more precise models regarding the way communities are constituted. First, a model is estimated using the communities as reference groups and taking advantage of the available attributes. Its quality can be assessed in various ways, the simplest being to measure its prediction success rate on instances whose community is known. If the model is considered to fit the data well enough, it can be interpreted by considering which attributes it uses and how it combines them to estimate communities.

We present here two families of statistical tools which can be used to build a predictive model: linear discriminant analysis (LDA) and sigmoid regression. The former was initially designed to predict the value of a nominal variable using numeric attributes and was later extended to the nominal case under the name of discriminant correspondence analysis. The idea sustaining the method is close to PCA (principal component analysis) and other dimension reduction methods. It consists of projecting the data in a new space maximizing the separation between the communities. The result of the projection is defined by a set of discriminant factors, corresponding to linear combinations of the initial attributes. These factors are then used instead of the attributes to estimate the community of an object. The model is valid under the assumptions of multinormality of the attributes conditionally to the communities and homoscedasticity between communities [70]. Note extensions exist for both nonlinear combinations and heteroscedasticity situations.

Two methods exist to derive the discriminant functions: processing all attributes at once (direct approach) or selecting them iteratively (stepwise approach). The second method allows using different criteria [70] to select the attributes and limit their number, it thus results in more parsimonious models. The number of factors is limited by the number of communities and of selected attributes. Each factor can be characterized in terms of its discriminant power and by interpreting the coefficients associated to the attributes in the corresponding function.

As an example, we tested all the numeric attributes related to our behavioral and sentimental data, which represents a total of 57 attributes. The model obtained with the direct approach has 21 discriminant functions and can correctly classify 99.1% of the students. This very high rate has to be nuanced by the fact the model includes many functions, based on all 57 attributes. Obviously, the interpretative value of this model is very weak. We processed separately the behavioral and sentimental attributes and obtained models based on 21 functions using 31 attributes with a prediction rate of 70.5% for the former, whereas the latter led to 21 functions using 26 attributes with a 69.8% prediction rate. The Anova results of the previous sections were rather promising when considering the discriminant power of the two behavioral and sentimental attributes we tested. However, when considering the discriminant analysis results obtained in this section, it does not seem to be the case for the rest of our data. This suggests both kinds of data do not convey sufficient information to efficiently predict community membership. However, note that it is possible to go further, for instance, by preprocessing the data to reduce its dimension before performing the discriminant analysis. This could allow improving the readability of the model without losing much predictive power.

The second family of predictive methods is the sigmoid regression, for which one can use two different models: logit or probit. This type of regression is able to predict the value of a dichotomous variable based on numeric and dichotomous variables (its application to nominal variables therefore requires to recode them). It was extended to the prediction of nominal variables, e.g., communities. The two approaches differ mainly in terms of the assumptions and estimation methods they rely on [70]. Probit allows colinearity in the attributes but requires normality, which is not the case of logit. Unlike for discriminant analysis, homoscedasticity is not required.

We applied a multinomial logit regression to the department and class attributes, which are both nominal. The model could be estimated with significantly good fit for both attributes (compared to a null model implementing the hypothesis of no influence of the attributes on the communities). The overall prediction rate is 46.8%, but varies very much depending on the community. For 4 communities (3, 4, 17, 22), it is greater than 80% (with 89.3% as a maximum), and for 9 others (8, 9, 11, 12, 14, 15, 19–21) it is 0%. For the communities we previously focused on (7, 16 and 20) it is of 64.7%, 61.5% and 0%, respectively. This confirms our previous observation: some communities can be efficiently characterized using these factual attributes, but they are not relevant for others. In marketing, this kind of information is at the origin of classic segmentation approaches. In our case, a marketing strategy based only on factual data would have very different effects depending on the targeted communities. It would certainly perform well on communities 3, 4, 17 and 22, but be inefficient on communities such as the 15th. Yet, we previously showed this community was very attractive from a commercial point of view. The fact the network analysis managed to detect this community illustrates how it can be used to complement classic data analysis.

Conclusion

In this chapter, we tackled the problem of community detection from the user's point of view. The research is very active in this domain, and so many different tools exist that it is difficult to make an accurate and informed choice. Our aim was to present them, with the will of being as operational as possible. We reviewed the various definitions of the concept of community and discussed publicly available community detection tools from this perspective. We emphasized other features allowing the user to make an appropriate choice regarding his data and goals, such as the inputs and outputs these tools are able to process. Our goal was to complete the very detailed existing reviews, which already deal with matters concerning the community detection process itself and related computational properties [3, 8, 9, 11]. We also presented practical means of solving secondary problems such as comparing community structures output by different algorithms or corresponding to different levels estimated by a hierarchical algorithm.

We then considered a practical application of community detection to real-world data describing a population of university students. We first concentrated on the topological properties of the network. We chose to ignore general complex network measures, because there again, reviews already describe them in details [63]. Instead, we focused on measures related to the community structures. We illustrated how one can determine the significance of the communities and assess their quality. We also discussed various ways of characterizing individual nodes relatively to the community structure. We then looked at the various methods allowing to take advantage of nodal attributes, which are rather common in some fields such as social sciences. We reviewed descriptive tools and showed how to characterize and interpret the communities. We also illustrated how the application of predictive methods enhances the understanding of the community composition.

However, due to lack of space, we could not perform an exhaustive review and had to discard some methods at each section of our chapter. First, we ignored community detection algorithms able to identify overlapping communities [3, 34]. Although there are not many of them yet, compared to those outputting partitions, these approaches are very promising, because many real-world networks include nodes located in-between communities (this was illustrated in the analysis of our data). Second, we only presented general families of definitions of the community concept, when specific variants exist among the hundred community detection algorithms one can find in the literature. The same remark holds for the measures designed to study the significance [72, 73] and topological properties [15] of the community structure. Finally, we only mentioned statistical tools in our analysis of the nodal attributes, but some machine learning based approaches are also adapted.

For instance, it would be possible to build a very informative predictive model for each community by applying an association rule mining tool [74].

References

1. da Fontura Costa, L., Oliveira Jr., O.N., Travieso, G., Rodrigues, F.A., Villas Boas, P.R., Antiqueira, L., Viana, M.P., da Rocha, L.E.C.: Analyzing and modeling real-world phenomena with complex networks: a survey of applications. Adv. Phys. **60**(3), 329–412 (2011). doi:10.1080/00018732.2011.572452
2. Freeman, L.C.: The Development of Social Network Analysis: A Study in the Sociology of Science. Empirical Press, New York (2004)
3. Fortunato, S.: Community detection in graphs. Phys. Rep. **486**(3–5), 75–174 (2010). doi:DOI 10.1016/j.physrep. 2009.11.002
4. Newman, M.E.J., Girvan, M.: Finding and evaluating community structure in networks. Phys. Rev. E **69**(2), 026113 (2004). doi:Artn 026113 Doi 10.1103/Physreve.69.026113
5. Lancichinetti, A., Kivelä, M., Saramäki, J., Fortunato, S.: Characterizing the community structure of complex networks. PLoS One **5**(8), e11976 (2010)
6. Lancichinetti, A., Fortunato, S.: Community detection algorithms: a comparative analysis. Phys. Rev. E **80**(5), 056117 (2009)
7. Labatut, V., Balasque, J.-M.: Business-oriented analysis of a social network of University Students. In: Proceeding of the International Conference on Advances in Social Networks Analysis and Mining, Odense, pp. 25–32 (2010)
8. Porter, M.A., Onnela, J.-P., Mucha, P.J.: Communities in networks. Not. Am. Math. Soc. **56**, 1082 (2009)
9. Danon, L., Duch, J., Arenas, A., Díaz-Guilera, A.: Community structure identification. In: Large Scale Structure and Dynamics of Complex Networks: From Information Technology to Finance and Natural Science, pp. 93–113. World Scientific, Singapore (2007)
10. Reichardt, J., Bornholdt, S.: Statistical mechanics of community detection. Phys. Rev. E **74**(1), 016110 (2006)
11. Newman, M.E.J.: Detecting community structure in networks. Eur. Phys. J. B **38**(2), 321–330 (2004). http://www.springerlink.com/content/5gtdacx17bqv6cdc/
12. Mancoridis, S., Mitchell, B.S., Rorres, C., Chen, Y., Gansner, E.R.: Using automatic clustering to produce high-level system organizations of source code. Paper presented at the 6th international workshop on program comprehension, Washington, DC (1998)
13. Radicchi, F., Castellano, C., Cecconi, F., Loreto, V., Parisi, D.: Defining and identifying communities in networks. Proc. Natl. Acad. Sci. USA **101**(9), 2658–2663 (2004). doi:DOI 10.1073/pnas.0400054101
14. Raghavan, U.N., Albert, R., Kumara, S.: Near linear time algorithm to detect community structures in large-scale networks. Phys. Rev. E **76**(3), 036106 (2007)
15. Leskovec, J., Lang, K.J., Dasgupta, A., Mahoney, M.W.: Statistical properties of community structure in large social and information networks. In: Proceeding of the 17th International Conference on World Wide Web, Beijing, pp. 695–704 (2008)
16. Donetti, L., Munoz, M.A.: Detecting network communities: a new systematic and efficient algorithm. J. Stat. Mech. (10), P10012 (2004). doi:10.1088/1742-5468/2004/10/P10012
17. Newman, M.E.J.: Finding community structure in networks using the eigenvectors of matrices. Phys. Rev. E **74**(3), 036104 (2006)
18. Lambiotte, R., Delvenne, J.-C., Barahona, M.: Laplacian dynamics and multiscale modular structure in networks. arXiv:0812.1770v3 [physics.soc-ph] (2009)
19. Clauset, A., Newman, M.E.J., Moore, C.: Finding community structure in very large networks. Phys. Rev. E **70**(6), 066111 (2004)

20. Schuetz, P., Caflisch, A.: Efficient modularity optimization by multistep greedy algorithm and vertex mover refinement. Phys. Rev. E **77**(4), 046112 (2008)
21. Blondel, V.D., Guillaume, J.-L., Lambiotte, R., Lefebvre, E.: Fast unfolding of communities in large networks. J. Stat. Mech. **10**, P10008 (2008)
22. Wakita, K., Tsurumi, T.: Finding community structure in mega-scale social networks. arXiv:cs/0702048v1 [cs.CY] (2007)
23. Guimerà, R., Sales-Pardo, M., Amaral, L.A.N.: Modularity from fluctuations in random graphs and complex networks. Phys. Rev. E **70**(2), 025101 (2004)
24. Agarwal, G., Kempe, D.: Modularity-maximizing graph communities via mathematical programming. Eur. Phys. J. B **66**(3), 409–418 (2008)
25. Fortunato, S., Barthelemy, M.: Resolution limit in community detection. Proc. Natl. Acad. Sci. USA **104**(1), 36–41 (2007)
26. Gleich, D.: Hierarchical Directed Spectral Graph Partitioning. Information Networks, Stanford University (2006)
27. Newman, M.E.J.: Analysis of weighted networks. Phys. Rev. E **70**(5), 056131 (2004). doi:Artn 056131 Doi 10.1103/Physreve.70.056131
28. Leicht, E.A., Newman, M.E.J.: Community structure in directed networks. Phys. Rev. Lett. **100**(11), 118703 (2008)
29. Hanneman, R.A., Riddle, M.: Introduction to Social Network Methods. University of California, Riverside (2005). Available at http://faculty.ucr.edu/~hanneman
30. Luce, R.D.: Connectivity and generalized cliques in sociometric group structure. Psychometrika **15**(2), 169–190 (1950)
31. Seidman, S.B.: Network structure and minimum degree. Soc. Netw. **5**(3), 269–287 (1983)
32. Seidman, S.B., Foster, B.L.: A graph theoretic generalization of the clique concept. J. Math. Sociol. **6**, 139–154 (1978)
33. Mokken, R.J.: Cliques, clubs and clans. Qual. Quant. **13**, 161–173 (1979)
34. Palla, G., Farkas, I.J., Pollner, P., Derenyi, I., Vicsek, T.: Directed network modules. New J. Phys. **9**, 186 (2007). doi:Artn 186 Doi 10.1088/1367–2630/9/6/186 Doi 10.1088/1367–2630/9/6/186 Pii S1367–2630(07)44249–5
35. Fouss, F., Pirotte, A., Renders, J.-M., Saerens, M.: Random-walk computation of similarities between nodes of a graph with application to collaborative recommendation. IEEE Trans. Knowl. Data Eng. **19**(3), 355–369 (2007)
36. Gan, G., Ma, C., Wu, J.: Data Clustering: Theory, Algorithms, and Applications. ASA-SIAM Series on Statistics and Applied Probability. Society for Industrial and Applied Mathematics, Philadelphia (2007)
37. Kaufman, L., Rousseeuw, P.J.: Finding Groups in Data: An Introduction to Cluster Analysis. Wiley, New York (1990)
38. Jaccard, P.: Étude comparative de la distribution florale dans une portion des Alpes et des Jura. Bulletin de la Société Vaudoise des Sciences Naturelles **37**, 547–579 (1901)
39. Guimerà, R., Amaral, L.A.N.: Functional cartography of complex metabolic networks. Nature **433**, 895–900 (2005)
40. Zhou, H.: Network landscape from a Brownian particle's perspective. Phys. Rev. E **67**(4), 041908 (2003)
41. Saerens, M., Fouss, F., Yen, L., Dupont, P.: The principal component analysis of a graph and its relationships to spectral clustering. In: European Conference on Machine Learning, Pisa, 2004
42. Pons, P., Latapy, M.: Computing communities in large networks using random walks. Lect. Notes Comput. Sci. **3733**, 284–293 (2005)
43. Tong, H., Faloutsos, C., Pan, J.-Y.: Random walk with restart: fast solutions and applications. Knowl. Inf. Syst. **14**(3), 327–346 (2008)
44. Handcock, M.S., Raftery, A.E., Tantrum, J.M.: Model-based clustering for social networks. J. Roy. Stat. Soc. A **170**, 301–322 (2007)
45. Tyler, R., Wilkinson, D.M., Huberman, B.A.: Email as spectroscopy: automated discovery of community structure within organizations. In: Deventer, B.V. (ed.) Communities and Technologies, pp. 81–96. Kluwer, Dordrecht (2003)

46. Girvan, M., Newman, M.E.J.: Community structure in social and biological networks. Proc. Natl. Acad. Sci. USA **99**(12), 7821–7826 (2002). doi:DOI 10.1073/pnas.1226539799
47. Wu, F., Huberman, B.A.: Finding communities in linear time: a physics approach. Eur. Phys. J. B **38**(2), 331–338 (2004). doi:DOI 10.1140/epjb/e2004-00125-x
48. Castellano, C., Cecconi, F., Loreto, V., Parisi, D., Radicchi, F.: Self-contained algorithms to detect communities in networks. Eur. Phys. J. B **38**(2), 311–319 (2004)
49. Rosvall, M., Bergstrom, C.T.: An information-theoretic framework for resolving community structure in complex networks. Proc. Natl. Acad. Sci. USA **104**(18), 7327–7331 (2007). doi:DOI 10.1073/pnas.0611034104
50. Rosvall, M., Bergstrom, C.T.: Maps of random walks on complex networks reveal community structure. Proc. Natl. Acad. Sci. USA **105**(4), 1118 (2008)
51. Ziv, E., Middendorf, M., Wiggins, C.H.: Information-theoretic approach to network modularity. Phys. Rev. E **71**(4), 046117 (2005). doi:Artn 046117 Doi 10.1103/Physreve.71.046117
52. van Dongen, S.: Graph clustering via a discrete uncoupling process. SIAM J. Matrix Anal. Appl. **30**(1), 121–141 (2008). doi:Doi 10.1137/040608635
53. Hofman, J.M., Wiggins, C.H.: Bayesian approach to network modularity. Phys. Rev. Lett. **100**(25), 258701 (2008)
54. Rosvall, M., Bergstrom, C.T.: Multilevel compression of random walks on networks reveals hierarchical organization in large integrated systems. PLoS One **6**(4), e18209 (2011). doi:10.1371/journal.pone.0018209
55. Aldecoa, R., Marin, I.: Jerarca: efficient analysis of complex networks using hierarchical clustering. PLoS One **5**(7), e11585 (2010)
56. Csardi, G., Nepusz, T.: The igraph software package for complex network research. InterJ. Complex Syst. **1695** (2006). http://www.interjournal.org/manuscript_abstract.php?361100992
57. O'Madadhain, J., Fisher, D., Smyth, P., White, S., Boey, Y.-B.: Analysis and visualization of network data using. J. Stat. Softw. **10**, 1–35 (2005)
58. Bastian, M., Heymann, S., Jacomy, M.: Gephi: an open source software for exploring and manipulating networks. Paper presented at the international AAAI conference on weblogs and social media, 2009
59. Donetti, L., Munoz, M.A.: Improved spectral algorithm for the detection of network communities. arXiv:physics/0504059v1 [physics.soc-ph] (2005)
60. Palla, G., Derenyi, I., Farkas, I., Vicsek, T.: Uncovering the overlapping community structure of complex networks in nature and society. Nature **435**(7043), 814–818 (2005). doi:Doi 10.1038/Nature03607
61. Rand, W.M.: Objective criteria for the evaluation of clustering methods. J. Am. Stat. Assoc. **66**(336), 846–850 (1971)
62. Hubert, L., Arabie, P.: Comparing partitions. J. Classif. **2**(1), 193–218 (1985)
63. da Fontura Costa, L., Rodrigues, F.A., Travieso, G., Villas Boas, P.R.: Characterization of complex networks: a survey of measurements. Adv. Phys. **56**(1), 167–242 (2007)
64. Lancichinetti, A., Radicchi, F., Ramasco, J.J.: Statistical significance of communities in networks. Phys. Rev. E **81**(4), 046110 (2010)
65. Decaudin, J.M.: La communication Marketing, Concepts, Techniques, Stratégies. Economica, Paris (2003)
66. Watts, D.C., Dodds, P.S.: Influentials, networks and public opinion formation. J. Consum. Res. **34**, 441–458 (2007)
67. Kotler, P., Keller, K.L.: Marketing Management: Analysis, planning, implementation and control, 12th edn. Prentice Hall International Editions, Upper Saddle River (2006)
68. Newman, M.E.J.: Mixing patterns in networks. Phys. Rev. E **67**, 026126 (2003)
69. Evrard, Y., Pras, B., Roux, E.: MARKET: Etudes et recherches en Marketing. Dunod, Paris (2000)
70. Norusis, M.: SPSS 17.0 Guide to Data Analysis. Prentice Hall, Inc., Upper Saddle River (2008)
71. Goodman, L.A., Kruskal, W.H.: Measures of association for cross classification. J. Am. Stat. Assoc. **49**, 732–764 (1954)

72. Rosvall, M., Bergstrom, C.T.: Mapping change in large networks. PLoS One **5**(1), e8694 (2010). doi:Artn E8694 Doi 10.1371/Journal.Pone.0008694
73. Bianconi, G., Pin, P., Marsili, M.: Assessing the relevance of node features for network structure. Proc. Natl. Acad. Sci. USA **106**(28), 11433–11438 (2009)
74. Witten, I.H., Frank, E.: Data Mining: Practical Machine Learning Tools and Techniques. Data Management Systems, 2nd edn. Morgan Kaufmann, Amsterdam (2005)

Chapter 5
Metrics and Models for Social Networks

Nicolás Ignacio Bersano-Méndez, Satu Elisa Schaeffer,
and Javier Bustos-Jiménez

Abstract Social networks can be modeled and analyzed in terms of graph theory. This chapter provides an overview of the mathematical modeling of social networks with an overview of the metrics used to characterize them and the models used to artificially mimic the formation of such networks. We discuss metrics based on distances, degrees, and neighborhoods as well as the use of such metrics to detect change in the network structure. We also discuss the kind of structural differences that distinguish social networks from other types of natural networks together with the implications of these differences about the way in which these networks function.

Introduction

Social networks, as well as nearly any complex system composed of multiple, interconnected actors, can be modeled and analyzed through mathematical models. The purpose of this chapter is to provide an overview on how social networks can be mathematically modeled in terms of *graph theory* together with an overview of the metrics used to characterize them and the models used to artificially mimic the formation of such networks. We discuss metrics based on distances, degrees, and

N.I. Bersano-Méndez (✉)
Universidad Diego Portales, Santiago, Chile
e-mail: nicolas.bersano@mail.udp.cl

S.E. Schaeffer
Universidad Autónoma de Nuevo León, San Nicolás de los Garza, NL, Mexico
e-mail: elisa.schaeffer@uanl.edu.mx

J. Bustos-Jiménez
ORAND, Santiago, Chile
e-mail: javier.bustos@orand.cl

A. Abraham and A.-E. Hassanien (eds.), *Computational Social Networks: Tools,*   115
Perspectives and Applications, DOI 10.1007/978-1-4471-4048-1_5,
© Springer-Verlag London 2012

neighborhoods as well as the use of such metrics to detect change in the network structure. We also discuss the kind of structural differences that distinguish social networks from other types of natural networks together with the implications of these differences about the way in which these networks function.

The structure of the chapter is as follows: In the section "Graph Theory" we introduce the fundamentals of modeling social networks as graphs. In the section "Metrics of Graph Structure" we discuss some of the numerous structural metrics that have been proposed to characterize graphs. Then in the section "Models for Social Networks" we discuss some of the artificial generation models proposed for creating graphs that in some sense mimic social network formation, followed by experimental results in the section "Properties of Social Networks" on detecting changes in network structure, where we also discuss the differences that distinguish social networks from other types of natural networks and the implications of these differences to the way the system functions, after which "Conclusions" section ends this chapter.

Graph Theory

Graph theory has proven to be a strong and widely applicable tool for analyzing systems composed of numerous elements that interact with each other, such as social networks. For decades now, it has been applied not only within computer science, physics, and mathematics, but also in fields such as sociology and psychology. Basic text books on graph theory are numerous; we recommend that of Diestel [9]. The fundamental notion of graph theory is, naturally, a *graph*, which is a set of elements, called *vertices* or *nodes*, together with a set of interactions among these elements, called *edges* or simply *connections*. We will formalize this notion shortly.

Social networks are human-formed systems in which individuals interact in some specific way or within a specific context. Examples include the social interactions we have at work or school, in our hobbies, at online communities, etc. Being essentially sets of individuals combined with interactions among them, social networks are frequently represented as graphs for the purpose of studying the formation of the network, the way it functions, and how different phenomena of interest propagate through the network. The individuals that form the network are modeled as vertices and associated with integer labels for mathematical treatment. We denote the vertex set by

$$V = \{v_1, v_2, \ldots, v_n\}, \tag{5.1}$$

where $n = |V|$ is the number of vertices, called the *order* of the graph. It is common to attach to each vertex a property vector that contains information on the particular individual, including time-related data (in case of social networks, information such as age, latest registered activity, etc.) and categorical data (which for social networks could include gender, education, and profession, for example). The vertices are typically drawn as circles or squares, as shown in Fig. 5.1.

Fig. 5.1 An example of a
graph: the elements, called
vertices, are drawn as *black
circles*, and the interactions,
called edges, are drawn as
black continuous lines. Each
edge connects two interacting
vertices. There are five
vertices and eight edges in the
example graph

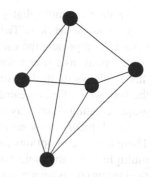

The interactions between individuals are represented as edges; the set of edges is
denoted by E and its members are vertex subsets $S \subset V$. The graph itself is usually
denoted as the pair formed by the vertex set and the edge set: $G = (V, E)$.

Typically, the interactions considered are one-on-one, in which case the edges
are *pairs*, $|S| = 2$, of distinct vertices, (u, v) where $u \in V$ and $v \in V$. If the
interaction is mutual, that is, bidirectional, the order in which the two vertices are
placed, (u, v) or (v, u), makes no difference, but when the interaction is clearly from
v to u, the edge is said to be *directed* and denoted by $\langle v, u \rangle$ and is drawn traditionally
as an arrow (the arrow head indicating the target vertex of the edge),[1] whereas an
undirected edge is drawn as a line; this latter case is illustrated in Fig. 5.1.

For example, in a graph representing the social network created by telephone
calls, each telephone number would be represented as a vertex and the information
on the persons that use this telephone would be stored in the property vector of the
vertex. Then, each phone call would constitute a directed edge, and the timestamps
indicating the time the call began and the time the call was finished would be
properties of this edge.

Graphs where more than one edge may connect a given pair or vertices are called
multigraphs. In the context of the phone call example given above, an alternative to
using would be to merge all calls from v to u into one single edge, which properties
such as total duration of calls, call count, maximum and minimum call duration, to
name a few possibilities.

Another example are social networking web sites such as Facebook or LinkedIn.
Graph models of such communities are formed by representing each user with a
vertex and then using an edge to represent that two users are "friends" or "contacts"
to one another. This would be the base graph of the structure of the social network.
Then, the public and private communications between the users can give rise to
several other graphs. For example, each wall post on Facebook could be a directed
edge from the user who posts to the user on whose wall the post is placed; also the
comments and likings expressed can be represented as edges between the users.

---

[1] Another possible visualization (cf. [19]) is using a line that is thicker at the source and gradually
becomes thinner before reaching the target vertex.

Another example that gives rise to numerous graphs that capture properties of a social network is Twitter, where the base graph is constructed on placing vertices to represent the users and directed edges to indicate who "follows" whom. Additionally, as a user v forwards a message, called a *tweet*, posted by a person w that v follows to all the users that follow v, an implicit interaction between w and the followers of v is created. These so-called retweets propagate through the base graph, creating an overlay of a richer graph.

Graph theory is by no means limited to studying simply pairwise interactions. There are several options for representing repeated interactions, such as permitting multiple edges to connect a vertex pair (one edge per each interaction modeled in the system) or using a property vector on the edge to store such information. When several people take part in a collective interaction, many-to-many instead of one-on-one, the graph-theoretical tool to capture this is a *hypergraph*. An edge, as defined in the previous section, needs not be limited to a vertex pair, but can just as well be vertex subset $S \subseteq V$ or arbitrary cardinality $0 \leq |S| \leq n$.

Application-wise, this would be the case on the comments on a wall post on Facebook: among those who comment, there is communication, although the commentators are not necessarily friends with each other—they only need to be friends with the person on whose wall the commented post appears, not with each other. Yet, an interaction is present as they read and react to each others' comments.

Note that a hyperedge $S \in E$ may as well be directed: some subset of $T \subseteq S$ is considered the source whereas another subset $U \subseteq S$ is considered the target, where $T \cup U = S$ but not necessarily $T \cap U = \emptyset$—the richness and complexity of social interactions can in some cases be better captured in this type of a construction. In practice, however, graphs that are neither multigraphs nor hypergraphs (called *simple graphs*) are the most common model for social networks, as they are generally much easier to construct and manipulate.

Throughout this chapter, we provide a brief overview of some aspects of graph theory that are relevant to social network modeling. We focus on establishing the terminology and notation required in the metrics and models discussed in the rest of the chapter. For a formal and throughout treatment of this versatile and widely applicable topic, we refer the reader to the work of Diestel [9].

Metrics of Graph Structure

Upon studying a social network through a graph model, there are several questions one commonly seeks to answer about the structure and the patterns that the edges form on the vertex set. In this section, we review briefly some of the basic measures used to structurally characterize graphs. The metrics are grouped by the type of information their computation requires. We must, however, first clarify that mathematically a *metric* is a function that measures the *distance* of two members of a set that satisfies the following three properties:

1. The distance of an element to itself must be zero and if the distance from a to b is zero, then it must be that $a = b$.
2. The distance from a to b must be the same as the distance from b to a (this is called symmetry).
3. The distance from a, through c, to b, must not be shorter than that from a directly to b (this is called the *triangle inequality*).

Nonetheless, the use that has been given, somewhat widely, in the field of complex networks to the term "metric" is much looser. In the context of complex network studied, it usually refers simply to a function of any kind that takes a graph $G = (V, E)$ and produces a scalar (usually a real number) that reflects in some sense the structure of the graph. We adopt in this chapter to such nonrigorous use of the term metric. Some authors prefer the term "measure," which also has a formal meaning in mathematics that is not entirely compatible with the use it is given in the literature on complex networks.

Degree-Based Metrics

It is evident that the number of interactions, connections, friends, or followers a vertex has is an important factor in the model. This number is called the *degree* of the vertex and is, formally, the number of edges *incident* to the vertex:

$$\deg(v) = |\{S \in E \mid S \subseteq V, v \in S\}|, \tag{5.2}$$

where V is the vertex set and E is the edge set of the graph, as before. This definition encompasses both hypergraphs and those where edges are pairs.[2] In the latter case, the restriction in mathematical terms is $|S| = 2$. Evidently, for a simple graph, $0 \leq \deg(v) \leq n - 1$.

When the edges are directed, we distinguish between the *in-degree*, which is the number of edges that have v is a target, and the *out-degree*, which is the number of edges that have v as a source. As an example, we define for the non-hyper case that

$$\deg_{in}(v) = |\{\langle u, v \rangle \in E\}|, \tag{5.3}$$

$$\deg_{out}(v) = |\{\langle v, w \rangle \in E\}|, \text{ and} \tag{5.4}$$

$$\deg(v) = \deg_{in}(v) + \deg_{out}(v). \tag{5.5}$$

Within this definition, an undirected edge (u, v) would count as two: as both $\langle u, v \rangle$ and $\langle v, u \rangle$. An example of degrees, mixing directed and undirected edges, is shown in Fig. 5.2.

---

[2]In general graph theory, also edges from a vertex to itself (called loops or reflexive edges) are of interest, but these are not usually present in graphs that represent social networks.

Fig. 5.2 The vertex v (in the *center*) has $\deg_{in}(v) = 3$ and $\deg_{out}(v) = 4$. The undirected edge counts in both partial degrees

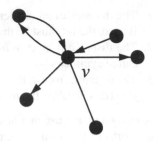

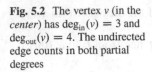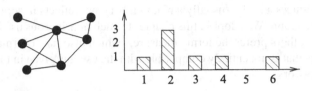

Fig. 5.3 On the *left*, a small undirected simple graph, and on the *right*, its degree distribution as a histogram; each bar of the histogram represents the number of vertices that have that particular degree: one vertex with degree 1, three with degree 2, one with degree 3, one with degree 4, none with degree 5, and one with degree 6

Denoting the number of edges in a graph[3] by $m = |E|$, we observe that if $|S| = k$ for all $S \in E$, it applies that

$$m = \frac{1}{k} \sum_{v \in V} \deg(v), \tag{5.6}$$

as each edge in E is counted k times in the sum of all degrees.

If $\deg(v) = \mathscr{K}$ for all $v \in V$, the graph is said to be *regular* (that is, all vertices have the same degree). In a regular simple graph, $m = \frac{1}{2} \cdot k \cdot n$ as there are n vertices with k edges incident to each, but each edge being incident to two distinct vertices.

A simplistic but often informative metric of network structure is the *average degree*:

$$\mathscr{K} = \frac{1}{n} \sum_{v \in V} \deg(v) = \frac{k \cdot m}{n}, \tag{5.7}$$

the latter expression being in terms of Eq. 5.6.

Often the most descriptive information on degrees is obtained by compiling the entire *degree distribution*, that is, to count the number of vertices that have a certain degree over all degrees present in the graph. An example is given in Fig. 5.3. This can be normalized into a probability distribution, which is particularly useful when one wishes to artificially create graphs with similar degree sequences [10].

---

[3]Whereas the number of vertices is called the *order* of the graph, the number of edges is often called its *size*.

Entropy is a measure used in thermodynamics and in information theory to measure the amount of disorder or randomness in a system [36]. It is defined, in information-theoretical terms, for a random variable X in terms of its distribution function $\Pr[X = i]$ over all possible values Ω that X can take as

$$\mathcal{H}(X) = -\sum_{i \in \Omega} \Pr[X = i] \cdot \log_2 (\Pr[X = i]). \tag{5.8}$$

Wang et al. [41] apply this to the degree distribution of the graph, where

$$\Pr[X = i] = \frac{|\{v \in V \mid \deg(v) = i\}|}{n}, \tag{5.9}$$

which gives a well-defined probability function as

$$\sum_{i=0}^{\infty} \Pr[X = i] = 1 \tag{5.10}$$

and $\Pr[X = i] \geq 0$ for all integers $i \geq 0$. The entropy of a degree distribution attains its maximum value when the degrees are uniformly distributed over the range of all possible degrees (for a simple, undirected graph, this range is $[0, n-1]$) and reaches its minimum, zero, for a regular graph.

Also other interesting properties of a vertex $v \in V$ can be derived from the set of other vertices to which it is *adjacent* in the graph, that is, which which it shares an edge (or one or more edges in the case of a multigraph). This set is called the *neighborhood* of v,

$$\Gamma(v) = \{w \mid w \in S \subseteq V \text{ such that } v \in S \land S \in E\}. \tag{5.11}$$

In a simple, undirected graph, $\deg(v) = |\Gamma(v)|$, as each edge connects it necessarily to a distinct *neighbor*.

Distance-Based Metrics

A *path* is an ordered sequence of adjacent edges in E,

$$\mathcal{P}(u_1, u_k) = [(u_1, u_2), (u_2, u_3), \dots, (u_{k-2}, u_{k-1}), (u_{k-1}, u_k)], \tag{5.12}$$

and its *length* $|\mathcal{P}|$ is the number of edges in it (in this case $k - 1$). Two vertices v and w in V are said to be *connected* in $G = (V, E)$ if there exists there exists at least one path $\mathcal{P}(v, w)$ in E. A vertex is usually considered to be implicitly connected to itself.

If all pairs of (distinct) vertices in V are connected by a path in E, $G = (V, E)$ is said to be *connected* and otherwise *disconnected*. A disconnected graph has two or more vertex subsets $S_1, S_2, \ldots \subset V$ such that there exists at least one path between any two vertices within each S_i, but no path from $v \in S_i$ to $w \in S_j$ when $i \neq j$. Such subsets S_i are referred to as the *(connected) components* of the graph.

For directed graphs, it may well be that v is connected to w by a path but not vice versa, as the adjacent edges on the paths must respect the edge direction, traversing always from the source vertex to the target vertex. If all vertex pairs in V have paths defined in E for both directions in a directed graph, then $G = (V, E)$ is *strongly connected*. Components in which this applies are then strongly connected. , consequently.

The distribution of the orders (that is, a listing of all values of $|S_i|$ of the connected components) of a graph is informative in itself, especially when studying its evolution over time when the network under study changes (through the introduction of new vertices and edges and possibly the removal of some of the existing ones).

The *distance* from v to w in G is the length of the *shortest* of all existing paths:

$$\text{dist}(v, w) = \min_{\mathscr{P}(v,w)} \{|\mathscr{P}(v, w)| \mid \mathscr{P}(v, w) \text{ is a path in } G\}. \tag{5.13}$$

Note that in an undirected graph, $\text{dist}(v, w) = \text{dist}(w, v)$, but this is not necessarily the case in a directed graph as the paths may differ. The theoretical maximum distance is $n - 1$, obtained when the shortest path from v to w requires passing through every single one of the other vertices in the graph. Evidently, the distance from a vertex to itself is defined to be zero as the shortest path is an empty edge sequence. When no path exists, the distance is undefined.

When all distances are defined, implying that the graph is connected, the *average distance* is naturally defined for the undirected case as

$$\mathscr{D} = \frac{1}{\binom{n}{2}} \sum_{\substack{\{u,v\} \subset V \\ u \neq v}} \text{dist}(u, v), \tag{5.14}$$

where $\binom{n}{2}$ is the binomial coefficient,[4] as there are $\binom{n}{2}$ pairs $\{u, w\}$. For the directed case, the number of distances considered doubles as each vertex pair contributes two possibly different distances:

$$\mathscr{D} = \frac{1}{n(n-1)} \sum_{\substack{\{u,v\} \subset V \\ u \neq v}} \text{dist}(u, v) + \text{dist}(v, u). \tag{5.15}$$

---

[4] The *binomial coefficient* is $\binom{n}{k} = \frac{n!}{k!(n-k)!}$, where $k! = 1 \cdot 2 \cdot \ldots \cdot (n-1) \cdot n$ is the *factorial*.

Fig. 5.4 Examples of typical extreme-case topologies, each with $n = 5$. From *left* to *right*: a complete graph, a star graph, a circle graph, a path graph, and an independent set. The edge counts are the following: for the complete graph $m = \binom{n}{2} = 10$, whereas the star graph and the path graph have $m = n - 1 = 4$. The circle graph has $n = m = 5$ and the independent set has $m = 0$

When the graph is not (strongly) connected, average distance of the graph is neither informative not well-defined, and instead the average distances of the (strongly) connected components are studied.

Note that for a complete graph[5] (see Fig. 5.4), all distances are one and so is the average distance, both in the undirected and the directed case, the latter requiring twice as many edges to establish a symmetrical neighborhood relation. A theoretical maximum is obtained when all vertices form on a single path (referred to here as a path graph, see Fig. 5.4), in which case

$$\mathscr{D} = \frac{2}{n(n-1)} \cdot \sum_{i=1}^{n-1} \frac{i(i+1)}{2} \tag{5.16}$$

$$= \frac{1}{n(n-1)} \cdot \left(\sum_{i=1}^{n-1} i^2 + \sum_{i=1}^{n-1} i \right) \tag{5.17}$$

$$= \frac{1}{n(n-1)} \cdot \left(\frac{n(n-1)(2n-1)}{6} + \frac{n(n-1)}{2} \right) \tag{5.18}$$

$$= \frac{1}{n(n-1)} \cdot \frac{n(n^2-1)}{3} \tag{5.19}$$

$$= \frac{n+1}{3}, \tag{5.20}$$

due to symmetry of the extremes, for the undirected case. For the undirected case, the maximum average distance requires a circle graph (see Fig. 5.4) formed by linking the last vertex of a path graph to the first one (and orienting all the edges along the circle to achieve strong connectivity):

$$\mathscr{D} = \sum_{i=1}^{n-1} i = \frac{n(n-1)}{2}. \tag{5.21}$$

as all vertices contribute exactly the same total distances due to symmetry of the circular structure.

---

[5]A *complete* graph is one where all vertices are neighbors among themselves, that is, all possible edges are present.

Fig. 5.5 An example of
distance-based metrics: a
graph with average distance
2 and diameter 3

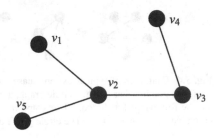

When the graph is (strongly) connected, the distances dist(v, w) form a n-by-n matrix **D** where the elements $d_{i,j}$ are the distances of vertices v_i and v_j under some arbitrary ordering of the vertex set. For an undirected graph, this matrix is necessarily symmetric, whereas for a directed graph it generally is not.

Hence, the average distance $\mathscr{D}$ is the arithmetic average over all elements $d_{i,j}$ in the matrix. The maximum distance over all pairs of vertices is called the *diameter* of the graph:

$$\text{diam}(G) = \max_{i,j}\{d_{i,j}\}. \tag{5.22}$$

The concepts of distance and diameter are exemplified in Fig. 5.5; the distance matrix for the graph in the figure is

$$\mathbf{D} = \begin{pmatrix} 0 & 1 & 2 & 3 & 2 \\ 1 & 0 & 1 & 2 & 1 \\ 2 & 1 & 0 & 1 & 2 \\ 3 & 2 & 1 & 4 & 3 \\ 2 & 1 & 2 & 3 & 0 \end{pmatrix}, \tag{5.23}$$

with the rows and columns ordered by the vertex labels v_i, $i = 1, 2, \ldots, 5$. The element $d_{i,j}$ is the distance between vertex v_i and v_j.

For a complete graph, the diameter is 1 and for a path graph, it is $n - 1$, as well as for a directed circle graph. For an undirected circle graph the diameter is $\lfloor \frac{n-1}{2} \rfloor$.

A measure derived from distances known as *global efficiency* [21] which assumes that the shorter the distance, the more efficient the communication between two vertices is defined as

$$\mathscr{E} = \left((n(n-1)) \sum_{u \neq v \in V} \text{dist}(u, v) \right)^{-1}. \tag{5.24}$$

It attains its minimum when the average distance is maximized, and vice versa.

A widely used metric based on distances is the (betweenness) *centrality* [15, 31], which measures the importance of a vertex in terms of the number of shortest paths it participates in

Fig. 5.6 Examples of betweenness centrality. The value of $\mathscr{B}(v)$ is shown next to each vertex, the highest being $\frac{3}{7} \approx 0.42$ and the lowest being $\frac{1}{4} = 0.25$

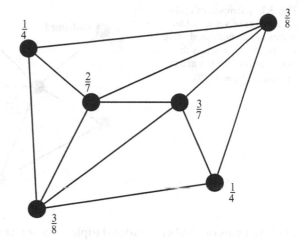

$$\mathscr{B}(v) = \frac{\sum_{u,w} S(u,v,w)}{\sum_{u,w} S'(u,w)}, \qquad (5.25)$$

where $S(u,v,w)$ is the number of paths of length $\mathrm{dist}(u,w)$ in G from vertex u to vertex w that pass through v (not including u and w themselves—although this is a matter of definition and the measure is useful either way), and $S'(u,w)$ is the total number of paths of length $\mathrm{dist}(u,w)$ in G. As a graph measure, the average of $\mathscr{B}(v)$ over $v \in V$ is commonly used. Examples are given in Fig. 5.6. Removing vertices with high centrality is more likely to increase the distance-based measures such as the diameter than the removal of a vertex that is chosen uniformly at random.

A maximum centrality is attained by a vertex that lies on every possible shortest path in the graph, that is a vertex v that is a center of a star graph (see Fig. 5.4) where all the other vertices are connected to v but there are no other edges present. In this case, all paths have length two and there is only one possible path for each vertex pair, yielding $\mathscr{B}(v) = 1$ as v is part of each of the $\binom{n-1}{2}$ distinct paths crossing through v, one for each pair of vertices in $V \setminus \{v\}$. The minimum for this metric is clearly zero, for the case that no shortest path includes a given vertex.

A *cycle* is a nonempty path that repeats no edge that begins and ends at the same vertex. A graph is *acyclic* if no cycles are present. A connected acyclic graph is called a *tree*; a disconnected acyclic graph is a *forest*.

The *cyclic coefficient* [20] is defined for a vertex v as

$$\mathscr{Y}(v) = \frac{2}{(\deg(v)(\deg(v)-1))} \sum_{u,w \in \Gamma(v)} \frac{1}{\ell(u,v,w)}, \qquad (5.26)$$

where $\ell(u,v,w)$ if the length of the shortest cycle containing v and its two neighbors u and w. Note that by definition, vertices with just one neighbor do not have a value for this metric as they produce a division by zero, as the normalization is

Fig. 5.7 Examples of cyclic coefficients of vertices. One vertex has an undefined value for the metric, whereas the maximum is $\frac{2}{3} = 0.\bar{6}$ and the minimum $\frac{17}{100} = 0.17$

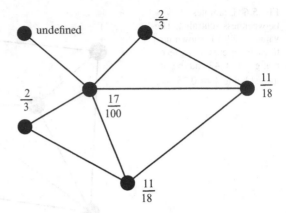

made in terms of number of ordered triples of a vertex with two neighbors). As the summation terms are smaller for larger cycles, vertices that have short cycles for most of their neighbors get higher values of the coefficient than those that also have pairs of neighbors that are further apart in the graph.

In a complete undirected graph, it being $(n-1)$-regular,

$$\mathscr{Y}(v) = \frac{2}{(n-2)(n-1)} \cdot \binom{n-1}{2} \cdot 2 \cdot \left(\frac{1}{3}\right) \tag{5.27}$$

$$= \frac{2}{(n-2)(n-1)} \cdot \frac{(n-1)(n-2)}{2} \cdot \frac{2}{3} \tag{5.28}$$

$$= \frac{2}{3} \tag{5.29}$$

for all $v \in V$, as all possible triplets $\{u, v, w\}$ are connected by a cycle of length three and there are $\binom{n-1}{2}$ pairs of distinct neighbors for each v, each pair considered twice (once in each order), yields the maximum value possible. The minimum (defined) value is attained when all the n vertices form a single cycle, yielding

$$\mathscr{Y}(v) = \frac{2}{2} \cdot 2 \cdot \frac{1}{n} = \frac{2}{n} \tag{5.30}$$

for all $v \in V$, as the graph is 2-regular, each vertex has just one pair or neighbors (considered in the two possible orders) and all cycles have length n. This approaches zero as n goes to infinity. Note that for $n = 3$, the maximum and minimum is given by the same graph: three vertices forming a single cycle. An example on a graph that is neither of these extreme cases is given in Fig. 5.7.

The cyclic coefficient of a graph is obtained, again, by averaging (in this case, typically over those values that are defined, omitting the single-neighbor vertices):

$$\mathscr{Y} = \frac{1}{n} \sum_{v \in V} \mathscr{Y}(v). \tag{5.31}$$

Fig. 5.8 On the *left*, a
triangle; on the *right*, a triplet

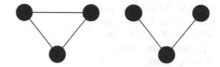

Neighborhood-Based Metrics

A *subgraph* of $G = (V, E)$ is a graph $H = (S, F)$ with the vertex set being $S \subseteq V$
and the edge set being

$$F \subseteq \{(u, v) \mid u \in S, v \in S, (u, v) \in E\}. \tag{5.32}$$

The definition is written in terms of simple graphs, but the concepts extends easily
to multigraphs and hypergraphs; a subgraph is obtained by removing some vertices
and/or edges, making sure that the endpoints of all remaining edges are also kept.
An *induced* subgraph is obtained by keeping a given set of vertices S and all those
edges that have both/all of their endpoints in S.

The *density* of a (sub)graph is the proportion of edges present of the maximum
possible:

$$\delta = \frac{m}{m_{\max}}. \tag{5.33}$$

Defined as a fraction, density takes values from 0 to 1: 0 when no edges are present
and 1 for a complete graph. In an undirected simple graph with n vertices, the
maximum possible value for m is

$$m_{\max} = \binom{n}{2} = \frac{n(n-1)}{2}, \tag{5.34}$$

and in a directed, simple graph, twice as much. Defining density makes little sense
in multigraphs, unless an upper bound is known for the edge multiplicities. A graph
with high density is said to be *dense* and a graph with low density is said to be
sparse.

A *cluster* or a *community* is an induced subgraph $H = (S, F)$ that has high
density but only a few edges to $V \setminus S$ (see the survey of Schaeffer [34] for more
information on graph clustering). Clustering as a graph property [27] refers to
the presence of *clusters* in the structure and is very commonly present in social
networks. There are two approaches that are used to measure the tendency toward
cluster formation.

The first one requires computing for each vertex $v \in V$ the number of *triangles*
it participates in, denoted here by N_t; a triangle being a subgraph of three vertices
where each vertex has an edge to the other two (see Fig. 5.8 for an illustration). Also
the number of *triplets* in which v participates, denoted by N_p is computed; a triplet

Fig. 5.9 An example graph
where for each vertex, the
values of $\mathscr{T}(v)$ (*left*) and
$\mathscr{C}(v)$ (*right*) are shown;
$\mathscr{T} \approx 0.73$ and $\mathscr{C} \approx 0.83$

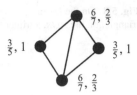

is a path of length two, as illustrated in Fig. 5.8. Then, the tendency for cluster formation in the neighborhood of vertex v is measured as the ratio of triangles to triplets:

$$\mathscr{T}(v) = \frac{3 \cdot N_t}{N_p}; \qquad (5.35)$$

this is known as *transitivity* [32].

Another option is using the density of the subgraph induced by the neighborhood of v, $\Gamma(v)$. We denote this quantity by $\mathscr{C}(v)$ and call it the *clustering coefficient* (cf. [43]).

Both $\mathscr{T}(v)$ and $\mathscr{C}(v)$ are turned into global metrics by averaging over the vertex set:

$$\mathscr{T} = \frac{1}{n} \sum_{v \in V} \mathscr{T}(v), \qquad (5.36)$$

$$\mathscr{C} = \frac{1}{n} \sum_{v \in V} \mathscr{C}(v). \qquad (5.37)$$

We emphasize that the two measures are *not* the same (despite the widespread confusion in literature shortly after their introduction, see [4, 35] for counterexamples). However, for both, the maximum value is 1 (for the complete graph). Both attain their minimum, zero, for any graph with no triangles, especially all trees and forests. There being no triangles, all subgraphs induced by neighborhoods are necessarily independent sets[6] (see Fig. 5.4). An example graph with both metrics computed is shown in Fig. 5.9.

In natural systems, it is often observed that high-degree vertices tend to connect with other high-degree vertices. In the context of social networks, this means that the individuals that maintain many interactions tend to interact with other high-interaction individuals. In the literature, this phenomenon is referred to as *assortativity* and also the *rich-club* phenomenon; the latter by an analogy to the reasoning one would make in selecting a business partner: those that already have many connections (existing partners, clients, distributors, etc.) are more attractive business partners than those who do not.

---

[6]A vertex set $S \subseteq V$ is an *independent set* in $G = (V, E)$ if none of its member vertices are adjacent in E.

Fig. 5.10 The four black vertices form a rich club for $\xi = 5$, with $\mathscr{R}_\xi = \frac{5}{6} = 0.8\overline{3}$, as one of the six possible edges among them is not present. All other vertices have degree less than 5

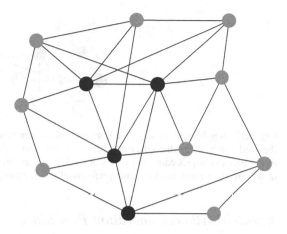

In terms of graphs, we define a *rich club* in terms of a threshold parameter ξ: all vertices $v \in V$ such that $\deg(v) \geq \xi$ "belong to the club." The *rich-club coefficient* $\mathscr{R}(\xi)$ of a graph is then simply the local density of the subgraph induced by the club in it. An example is given in Fig. 5.10.

Models for Social Networks

Natural networks are representations of complex systems present in the nature in terms of graph theory, often considered to include man-made systems. Social networks are in a sense both natural and man-made; the vertices usually represent the actors of a social system and the edges represent the interactions among these actors. Numerous models have been proposed to artificially generate graphs that share some characteristics with natural networks. Typically the goal of such modeling is to better understand some phenomena of interest (such as epidemic spreading, for example [26, 40]).

The proposed generation models for natural network like graphs are numerous. For surveys on the topic, we redirect the reader to works that concentrate on generation models and their properties in general [10, 18, 29, 39].

In this work, we concentrate on three generation models that mimic some properties present in social network formation. These three models operate in an incremental fashion: the vertices join the graph one by one and form some edges to the existing vertices, as well as possible edge formation among the already present vertices. All generation models permit modification to accommodate additional factors such vertices abandoning the network, edge deletion, weighted edges, aging of vertices, and edges; the literature on modifications to make the models fit a new setting or to incorporate an additional property is abundant and often relies on executing random processes on the graph structure (cf. [13]). Again we refer the reader to existing surveys on the specific topic of generation models, mentioned earlier in this section.

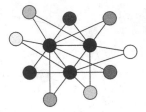

Fig. 5.11 Neighbor selection in the Barabási-Albert generation procedure: the black vertices were the seed graph, after which the other vertices were introduced; the vertex color is lighter the later in the generation procedure the vertex arrived. Each arriving vertex chose two neighbors among those already present, randomly but preferentially to their degree

Barabási-Albert Generation Procedure

The first type of graph generation discussed here is the widely used Barabási-Albert (BA) procedure [3] that takes two parameters in its basic form: the final vertex count n and another integer k. The edge formation is based on *preferential attachment*: when a vertex joins the graph, it randomly—but not uniformly—selects k (usually distinct) existing vertices to form its neighborhood.

When a directed graph is desired, the edges are formed from the new vertex to the existing vertices. In both the undirected and the directed case, the probability of selecting an existing vertex w is directly proportional to its current degree $\deg(w)$ (where in the directed case one uses generally the in-degree). In order for these probabilities to be well-defined, the generation must commence with a connected seed graph. In case that distinct edges are to be formed (hence avoiding generating a multigraph), at least k vertices must initially be present (for the directed case, at having at least one incoming edge each).

The inclusion of new vertices is ceased when the graph order reaches the parameter value n. The preferential attachment is generally implemented simply as roulette-wheel selection: the higher the degree, the more likely the reception of a new edge. Hence the vertices that arrive early have high expected degrees and those that arrive late in the generation process have expected degrees very near the value of the parameter k. The neighbor selection is illustrated in Fig. 5.11.

In the context of social networks, preferential attachment can be interpreted as individuals preferring social contact to persons who already are highly connected, instead of interacting with other individuals of low connectivity.

Bu-Towsley Generation Procedure

A modification, one among several in existing literature, to the Barabási-Albert procedure was proposed by Bu and Towsley [5], where an additional parameter β applies a reduction to the degree at the moment of performing the preferential

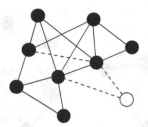

Fig. 5.12 Neighbor selection in the Bu-Towsley model is carried out in one of two possible manners for each arriving vertex: the edges that vertex forms to the existing graph and, with probability controlled by the parameter β, new edges are formed between vertices that are already present. For this example, we assume $k = 3$ and that at least one must be from the arriving vertex at each step. We emphasize those three edges that were added as the white vertex, being the last one added, joined the graph: two to connect it to the existing graph and one among already-present vertices. The new edges are drawn in a *dashed line*

attachment and also includes edge-formation among the existing vertices. One option of implementing this is using β as a probability and for each of the k edges that are to be introduced in each iteration, add an edge between vertices already present with probability β and proceed to the normal preferential attachment of the arriving vertex with probability $1 - \beta$.

Variations of this model are created using alternative selection distributions for selecting the existing vertices that are to connect: whether that selection is also somehow preferential or simply uniform, and whether more than one edge is allowed for a given pair of vertices (that is, whether multigraphs are permitted). Also, if all the k new edges at a particular are allowed to be among the existing vertices, the resulting graph may become disconnected. To assure connectivity, one edge can be forced to be from the new arrival to the rest of the graph whereas the other $k - 1$ are randomly assigned either to this purpose or for adding connections among the existing vertices.

Figure 5.12 illustrates the steps of this generation procedure in one iteration, to which we refer as the Bu-Towsley (BT) procedure. The formation of edges among existing vertices and not only upon arrival is more realistic to the social network scenario, as being part of a social system tends to facilitate the formation of additional connections.

Forest-Fire Generation Procedure

The third and last generation procedure discussed in this chapter, proposed by Leskovec et al. [22], seeks to emulate the propagation of a fire in a forest, interpretable in this context as the propagation of a rumor or a trend in a social system. We refer to this generation method as the *forest-fire* (FF) procedure.

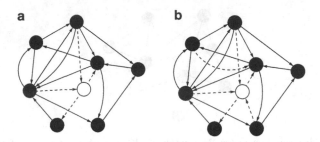

Fig. 5.13 Neighbor selection in the forest-fire model in two phases. (**a**) The *white vertex* arrives; edges that were already present in the graph before the arrival are drawn with *solid lines* and the new $h + k$ edges with *dashed lines*. (**b**) Afterwards, new (*dashed*) edges are created among the existing vertices recursively

The initial graph consists of a single vertex and additional vertices are introduced one at a time. Upon the arrival of a new vertex v, two geometrically distributed pseudo-random numbers are generated, k and h, and a flag is set for each existing vertex as "not visited." The geometric distribution is parametrized to yield mean $(1 - p)^{-1}$ and variance $(1 - rp)^{-1}$, where p and r are model parameters.

Then, a set $A \subseteq V$ such that $|A| = k$ is selected among the presently unvisited vertices, and a directed edge is added from the arriving vertex v to each vertex in A. All vertices in A are flagged as "visited." Then, another set $B \subseteq V$ such that $|B| = h$ is selected uniformly at random among the still unvisited existing vertices and a directed edge is added from each of these vertices to v. Afterwards, these set-selection and edge-formation steps are recursively performed on each vertex in $A \cup B$. The arrival process of a single vertex is illustrated in Fig. 5.13.

While the recursion proceeds, every vertex in the graph becomes either the source or the target of a new edge, possibly except one that has no unvisited vertex left to connect with. Upon concluding the recursion (when there are no more unvisited vertices to choose from), all the visit flags over the vertex set are reset to "unvisited." Then, a new vertex arrives and everything is repeated. The growth continues when the target order n has been reached. The growth and the recursive edge introduction of the FF model can be interpreted as the arrival of a new individual in a social system provoking new interactions between the previously present individuals (rivalry or acquaintance, for example).

Properties of Social Networks

Natural networks in general, as well as social networks specifically, possess properties that affect the way in which the systems under study function and evolve. We summarize here some of the most common properties:

Rich-club phenomenon Highly connected vertices tend to connect to other highly connected vertices. Also referred to as *assortative mixing* [7, 28, 47].

Small-world phenomenon The average distance (and the diameter) in the graph grows sub-linearly to graph order ($\log n$ or even $\log \log n$) or even shrinks over time [22, 42, 43].

Community formation The vertices form dense induced subgraphs with few connections to other parts of the graph [11, 16, 23, 30, 43].

Scale-free degree distribution Most vertices have a low degree, but some vertices (called *hubs*) have a very high degree; the degree distribution plotted on a log-log scale resembles a straight line [1, 3, 14, 24, 37]. It is disputable whether the latter characterization applies in general (cf. [17]), but the presence of hubs is generally accepted.

It is of interest to know how the properties evolve when the graph undergoes growth or some other kind of structural change or perturbation. Throughout the remainder of this section, we study the behavior of four of the metrics defined in the section "Metrics of Graph Structure" for the three network models presented in the section "Models for Social Networks". The metrics used are entropy, average distance, diameter, and clustering coefficient. We are particularly interested in detecting whether the properties of the system undergo change as vertices are added, and if so, when, how, and to what does the structure stabilize.

As experimental work for this study, we grew graphs with the three generation models until the values of entropy and clustering coefficient stabilized (see Fig. 5.14), performing 30 repetitions of each. Over these 30 repetitions, we computed the mean and the standard deviation. The plots in the figures show the average and, technically, the standard deviation, although the latter is mostly so small that the bars are not visible underneath the data point.

Then, we perturb each resulting graph structure by removing edges uniformly at random, attempting to destabilize the two metrics that had previously stabilized, and then resume the growth by continuing with the generation model. The perturbation was performed the iteration number 800, determined by initial experiments to be a moment at which the structure already stabilizes (with the parameters used). Due to the functional differences between the models, the graphs did not all have the same order upon performing the perturbation, much less the same size. The perturbation carried out consists in eliminating k edges, where $k \in [0, m]$ was chosen uniformly at random.

The change resulting from the perturbation is visible for the BT model in both plots in Fig. 5.15, revealing the moment in which it was performed. Also on the FF model, the moment of perturbation is visible on the clustering coefficient. In these cases where a change is in deed clearly visible, we note that the values of entropy and clustering coefficient return to their original stable values relatively soon after the graph growth is resumed, indicating that the value of each is an inherent property of the model (with the used parameters). This implies that these two metrics could be employed to detect when the structure of a network undergoes significant change.

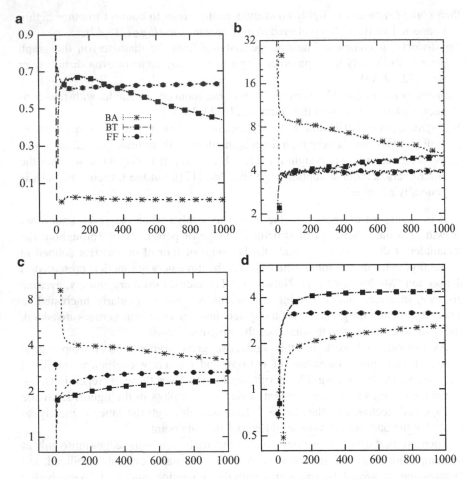

Fig. 5.14 The behavior of the four metrics under the three generation procedures, shown after each vertex arrival until $n = 1,000$ for each method. Note that these plots, with the exception of the clustering coefficient, use a logarithmic scale on the y-axis help reveal the differences between the procedure. The same legend, shown only in the first plot, applies to all four plots; the y-axis indicates the value of the metric in question (notice that the range of possible values depends on the metric, as discussed in the previous section), whereas the x-axis indicates the value of n. The *line* indicates the average after each vertex arrival and the *dots*, accompanied by the mostly invisible error bars to indicate the standard deviation, are only placed in increments of 40 for clarity of the plot. (**a**) Clustering coefficient. (**b**) Diameter. (**c**) Average distance. (**d**) Entropy

Also, as visible in Fig. 5.15, the metrics tends to stabilize, although not to a constant. We define stability for our experiments in terms of the proportional change in each metric from one step of the simulation to the next:

$$\rho_{\mathscr{C}} = \frac{\mathscr{C}_t}{\mathscr{C}_{t+1}}, \tag{5.38}$$

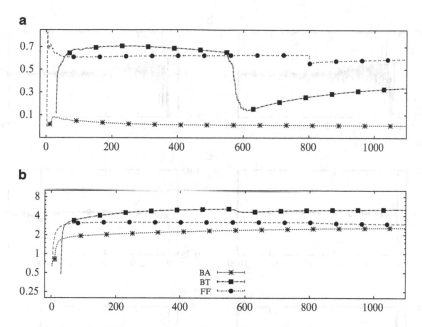

Fig. 5.15 The behavior of the clustering coefficient and entropy for the three generation procedures under perturbation. The value of the metric is shown on the y-axis and n on the x-axis. Again there are very small error bars in increments of 80 by the x-axis, indicating the standard deviation over the set of 30 repetitions. The *lines* show the average after each vertex arrival. (**a**) Clustering coefficient under perturbation. (**b**) Entropy under perturbation

$$\rho_{\mathcal{H}} = \frac{\mathcal{H}_t}{\mathcal{H}_{t+1}}, \tag{5.39}$$

where C_t is the clustering coefficient, and H_t is the entropy at step t of the generation procedure.

Figure 5.16 shows the clustering coefficient ratio $\rho_{\mathscr{C}}$ for the three generation procedures without and with a structural perturbation; Fig. 5.18 shows the entropy ratio $\rho_{\mathscr{H}}$.

All the plots in Fig. 5.16 start with perturbations and then stabilize, in relative terms, by the iteration 500; the plots all show the standard deviation every 100 iterations, which is mostly so small that the bars are not visible. The spike upon perturbation (on the plots on the right) is pronounced in all models; for questions of clarity, the y-range of the plots was limited and the spike is cut off—in fact it rises as high as six in the BT model, although in the other two it remains near 1.1 on average over the 30 repetitions made. This is shown in the close-up plots in Fig. 5.17.

The benefit of observing the ratio instead of the plain metric is that, as shown in Figs. 5.16 and 5.17, the perturbation is observable to the naked eye on all three models, whereas in Fig. 5.15 it was not so for the BA model.

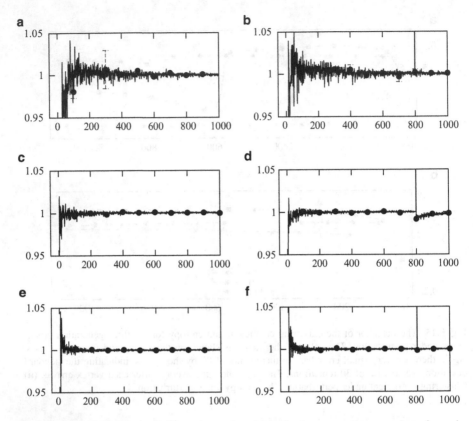

Fig. 5.16 The clustering-coefficient ratio $\rho_{\mathscr{C}}$ (*y*-axis) in the three generation procedures for each iteration. The *left column*, consisting of subfigures (**a**) BA graphs without perturbation, (**c**) BT graphs without perturbation, and (**e**) FF graphs without perturbation, shows the models under normal operation, and the *right column*, consisting of subfigures (**b**) BA graphs under perturbation, (**d**) BT graphs under perturbation, and (**f**) FF graphs under perturbation, shows the behavior when a structural perturbation is performed; the spike reveals the moment in which the perturbation was carried out on the iteration number 800

For the entropy ratio, shown in Fig. 5.18, the FF model shows very little change when perturbed, making the clustering coefficient ratio a much easier-to-use indicator of structural change than the entropy ratio; the close-ups for the entropy ratio are shown in Fig. 5.19 and only there the spike for the FF model becomes visible, although at a very small scale.

We also observe from the above experiments that after the metrics stabilize, both at the beginning of the construction and after recovering from the perturbation, the difference in each step is very small, causing the ratio to remain very close to 1.

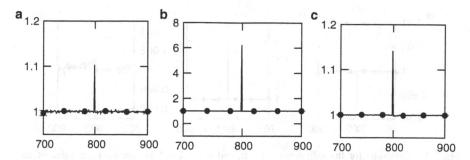

Fig. 5.17 Close-ups for the subfigures (b), (d), and (f) of Fig. 5.16, showing the value of the clustering coefficient ratio to which the spike reaches upon perturbation, carried out at iteration 800. (**a**) BA model. (**b**) BT model. (**c**) FF model

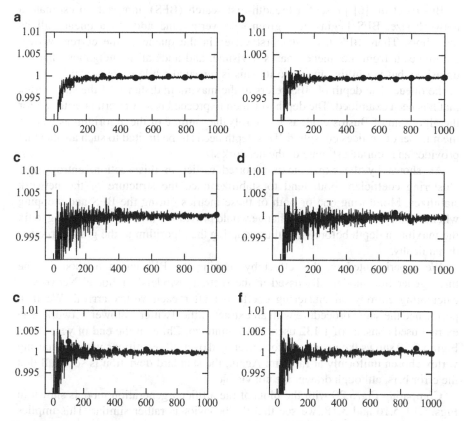

Fig. 5.18 The entropy ratio $\rho_{\mathscr{H}}$ in the three generation procedures without (**a**) BA graphs without perturbation, (**c**) BT graphs without perturbation, (**e**) and with (**b**) BA graphs under perturbation, (**d**) BT graphs under perturbation, (**f**) FF graphs under perturbation, a structural perturbation; the spike reveals again the time of the perturbation

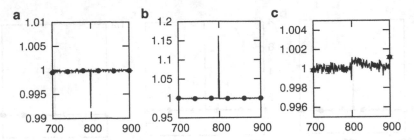

Fig. 5.19 Close-ups for the subfigures (b), (d), and (f) of Fig. 5.18, showing the value of the entropy ratio to which the spike reaches upon perturbation, carried out at iteration 800. (**a**) BA model. (**b**) BT model. (**c**) FF model

Bustos et al. [6] present a breadth-first search (BFS) approach to estimate a network size. BFS begins at a given start vertex and adds to a queue[7] all its neighbors. Then, BFS takes the first vertex in the queue as the current vertex, eliminates it from the queue, marks it visited, and adds all its neighbors that are unvisited, but yet in the queue, to it. This is repeated while there are still vertices in the queue. The depth of BFS refers to the maximum distance of the start vertex that has been examined. The depth to which to proceed is an important criterion for the algorithm of Bustos et al. as it controls the runtime of the algorithm as well as the number of vertices consulted. This depth needs to be limited to such a value that provides an accurate estimate of the network size.

As shown by the experiments reported earlier in this section, entropy and clustering coefficient both tend to stabilize once the structure of the network stabilizes. Monitoring one or both of these metrics during the BFS and stopping whenever there is no significant change would provide an alternative to having to fix the maximum depth beforehand, thus adapting the algorithm to the graph structure dynamically.

We experimented on this effect by running the BFS-based method for the three generation models discussed in the section "Models for Social Networks", calculating entropy an clustering coefficient after each vertex arrival. We then performed the same procedure with an extract of the Twitter follower network. The extract used consists of 1,132 users from Santiago, Chile, at the end of year 2009. Figure 5.20 shows the resulting plots, averaged over 30 repetitions with the starting vertex chosen uniformly at random. Again, the standard deviation is so small that the error bars, although drawn, are not visible.

Comparing Fig. 5.20 with the plots of the artificial generation models shown in Figs. 5.14–5.16 and 5.18, we see that the behavior is rather similar. This implies that once the metrics stabilize, the BFS routine can be terminated, as the network structure has effectively been determined.

---

[7] A *queue* is a data structure where incoming data is appended at the end and removals are only done in the beginning of the structure.

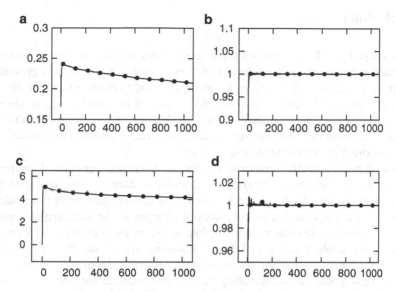

Fig. 5.20 Entropy and clustering coefficient (on the *left*, the plain metric, and on the *right*, the ratios defined in Eq. 5.39) of the extract of the Twitter network for each BFS iteration. The data shown is averaged over 30 repetitions from randomly chosen initial vertices. The error bars every 100 data points show the standard deviation. (**a**) Clustering coefficient for Twitter. (**b**) Clustering-coefficient ratio for Twitter. (**c**) Entropy for Twitter. (**d**) Entropy ratio for Twitter

The effects of entropy on network structure are discussed in detail by Wang et al. [41]. What comes to clustering, social networks are prone to higher values of the clustering coefficient than other natural networks [38]. Among the results regarding the effects of high clustering in networks, we mention a few examples. Firstly, it is well-known in spectral graph theory that the presence of clusters affects the eigenvalues of matrices that represent the graph and that this is related to the mixing time of a random walk on the graphs (cf. [34]; see also [8, 25]). This has implications on the way in which information traverses the network [45] as well as epidemic spreading [46]. The effects of clustering on cooperation have also been studied [12, 33], whereas Arenas et al. [2] discuss in depth structural effects on synchronization. White and Houseman [44] discuss the searchability in the presence of clusters. Virtanen [39] finds that clustered graphs are harder instances of the maximum-clique problem.

The field of mapping structural properties to functional effects has been very active for the past 10 years and still is. Our own ongoing work involves issues regarding the difficulty of graph coloring in terms of structural metrics as well as structural network optimization for rapid synchronization of multi-agent systems.

Conclusions

In this chapter, we have surveyed some metrics and models for natural networks and study experimentally the behavior of some metrics on the models presented. The models included all functions in an incremental fashion, which permits the characterization of the evolution of the metrics over time, step by step, to observe whether and to which value they stabilize and how are the metrics affected by structural perturbations. We also experimented with real-world data for comparison, using an extract of the Twitter follower network.

It was demonstrated that structural metrics, particularly the entropy of the degree distribution and the clustering coefficient, stabilize during network growth and display perturbations to the network structure as abrupt changes in their values. This would permit their use as indicators of changes in the structure of a social network, as well as in determining whether or not an evolving network structure is structurally stable. Using a BFS-based procedure to compute these two metrics on the Twitter network extract, we noted that as soon as the metrics stabilize, the BFS can be stopped, thus saving computational resources, as the value is no longer expected to change on a natural network.

An important concern in network metrics is the computational complexity. For example, entropy is easier to compute than the clustering coefficient, but both require global information and thus fail to be scalable. As future work, locally computable estimations of these metrics are of great interest. We assume that both could be reasonably estimated by performing relatively short random walks on the graph (considering that the diameter of social networks is small), however taking into account that the presence of high clustering increases the mixing time.

Acknowledgements J.B.-J. was supported by grant number IT264-09 by the PAICyT program of the UANL.

References

1. Anghel, M., Toroczkai, Z., Bassler, K.E., Korniss, G.: Competition-driven network dynamics: emergence of a scale-free leadership structure and collective efficiency. Phys. Rev. Lett. **92**, 058701 (2004)
2. Arenas, A., Díaz-Guilera, A., Kurths, J., Moreno, Y., Zhou, C.: Synchronization in complex networks. Phys. Rep. **469**, 93–153 (2008)
3. Barabási, A.L., Albert, R.: Emergence of scaling in random networks. Science **286**, 509–512 (1999)
4. Bollobás, B., Riordan, O.: Mathematical results on scale-free random graphs. In: Handbook of Graphs and Networks, pp. 1–34. Wiley, Weinheim (2005)
5. Bu, T., Towsley, D.: On distinguishing between internet power law topology generators. In: IEEE Infocom: The 21st Annual Joint Conference of the IEEE Computer and Communications Societies in New York, NY, USA. IEEE Computer Society, Los Alamitos (2002)
6. Bustos, J., Bersano, N., Schaeffer, S., Piquer, J., Iosup, A., Ciuffoletti, A.: Estimating the size of peer-to-peer networks using lamberts's w function. In: Golatch, S., Fragopoulou, P., Priol, T. (eds.) Grid Computing – Achievements and Prospects, pp. 61–72. Springer, New York (2008)

7. Catanzaro, M., Caldarelli, G., Pietronero, L.: Assortative model for social networks. Phys. Rev. E **70**(3), 037101 (2004)
8. Dell'Amico, M., Roudier, Y.: A measurement of mixing time in social networks. In: Proceedings of the Fifth International Workshop on Security and Trust Management, Saint Malo, France (2009)
9. Diestel, R.: Graph Theory. Graduate Texts in Mathematics, vol. 173, 4th edn. Springer, Heidelberg (2010)
10. Dorogovtsev, S.N., Mendes, J.F.F.: Evolution of networks. Adv. Phys. **51**(4), 1079–1187 (2002)
11. Du, H., Feldman, M.W., Li, S., Jin, X.: An algorithm for detecting community structure of social networks based on prior knowledge and modularity. Complexity **12**(3), 53–60 (2007)
12. Eguíluz, V.M., Zimmermann, M., Cela-Conde, C., San Miguel, M.: Cooperation and the emergence of role differentiation in the dynamics of social networks. Am. J. Sociol. **110**, 977–1008 (2005)
13. Eubank, S., Vullikanti, A., Khan, M., Marathe, M., Barrett, C.: Beyond degree distributions: local to global structure of social contact graphs. In: Chai, S.-K., Salerno, J., Mabry, P.L. (eds.) Advances in Social Computing. Lecture Notes in Computer Science, vol. 6007 (2010). http://www.springer.com/computer/general+issues/book/978-3-642-12078-7
14. Franks, D.W., Noble, J., Kaufmann, P., Stagl, S.: Extremism propagation in social networks with hubs. Adapt. Behav. **16**(4), 264–274 (2008)
15. Freeman, L.C.: A set of measures of centrality based upon betweenness. Sociometry **40**(1), 35–41 (1977)
16. Girvan, M., Newman, M.E.J.: Community structure in social and biological networks. Proc. Natl. Acad. Sci. USA **99**(12), 7821–7826 (2002)
17. Gjoka, M., Kurant, M., Butts, C.T., Markopoulou, A.: Walking in facebook: a case study of unbiased sampling of osns. In: Proceedins of the IEEE INFOCOM, p. 9. IEEE (2010)
18. Goldenberg, A., Zheng, A.X., Fienberg, S.E., Airoldi, E.M.: A survey of statistical network models. Found. Trends Mach. Learn. **2**(2), 117 (2009)
19. Holten, D., van Wijk, J.J.: A user study on visualizing directed edges in graphs. In: Proceedings of the 27th International Conference on Human Factors in Computing Systems, pp. 2299–2308. ACM, New York (2009)
20. Kim, H.J., Kim, J.M.: Cyclic topology in complex network. Phys. Rev. E **72**(3), 036109 (2005)
21. Latora, V., Marchiori, M.: Efficient behavior of small-world networks. Phys. Rev. Lett. **87**(19), 198701 (2001)
22. Leskovec, J., Kleinberg, J., Faloutsos, C.: Graphs over time: densification laws, shrinking diameters and possible explanations. In: Proceedings of the Eleventh ACM SIGKDD International Conference on Knowledge Discovery and Data Mining, pp. 251–262. ACM, New York (2005)
23. Leskovec, J., Lang, K.J., Dasgupta, A., Mahoney, M.W.: Statistical properties of community structure in large social and information networks. In: Proceedings of the 17th International Conference on World Wide Web. ACM, New York (2008)
24. Liljeros, F., Edling, C.R., Amaral, L.A.N., Stanley, H.E., Aberg, Y.: The web of human sexual contacts. Nature **411**, 907–908 (2001)
25. Mohaisen, A., Yun, A., Kim, Y.: Measuring the mixing time of social graphs. In: Proceedings of the 10th Annual Conference on Internet Measurement, pp. 383–389. ACM, New York (2010)
26. Moore, C., Newman, M.E.J.: Epidemics and percolation in small-world networks. Phys. Rev. E **61**(5), 5678–5682 (2000)
27. Newman, M.E.J.: Scientific collaboration networks: I. Network construction and fundamental results. Phys. Rev. E **64**(1), 016131 (2001)
28. Newman, M.E.: Assortative mixing in networks. Phys. Rev. Lett. **89**, 208701 (2002)
29. Newman, M.: The structure and function of complex networks. SIAM Rev. **45**(2), 167–256 (2003)
30. Newman, M.E.J.: Detecting community structure in networks. Eur. Phys. J. B **38**(2), 321–330 (2004)

31. Newman, M.E.J., Girvan, M.: Mixing patterns and community structure in networks. In: Pastor-Satorras, R., Rubi, M., Diaz-Guilera, A. (eds.) Statistical Mechanics of Complex Networks, Lecture Notes in Physics, vol. 625, pp. 66–87. Springer, Berlin (2003)
32. Newman, M., Strogatz, S., Watts, D.: Random graph models of social networks. Proc. Natl. Acad. Sci. USA **99**, 2566–2572 (2002)
33. Rong, Z., Yang, H.X., Wang, W.X.: Effect of clustering coefficient on cooperation in scale-free public goods game. In: Proceedings of 2010 IEEE International Symposium on Circuits and Systems, pp. 405–408. IEEE (2010)
34. Schaeffer, S.E.: Graph clustering. Comput. Sci. Rev. **1**(1), 27–64 (2007)
35. Schank, T.: Algorithmic aspects of triangle-based network analysis. Ph.D. thesis, Universität Fridericiana zu Karlsruhe (2007)
36. Shannon, C.: A mathematical theory of communication. Bell Syst. Tech. J. **27**, 379–423/ 623–656 (1948)
37. Stephen, A.T., Toubia, O.: Explaining the power-law degree distribution in a social commerce network. Soc. Netw. **31**(4), 262–270 (2009)
38. Toivonen, R., Onnela, J.P., Saramäki, J., Hyvönen, J., Kaski, K.: A model for social networks. Physica A **371**, 851–860 (2006)
39. Virtanen, S.E.: Properties of nonuniform random graph models. In: Research Report A77, Helsinki University of Technology, Laboratory for Theoretical Computer Science, Espoo (2003)
40. Vullikanti, A., Eubank, S., Kumar, V.A., Marathe, M., Srinivasan, A., Wang, N.: Structure of social contact networks, and their impact on epidemics. In: AMS-DIMACS Special Issue on Epidemiology, pp. 181–213. AMS (2006)
41. Wang, B., Tang, H., Guo, C., Xiu, Z.: Entropy optimization of scale-free networks robustness to random failures. Physica A **363**(2), 591–596 (2006)
42. Watts, D.J.: Small Worlds. Princeton University Press, Princeton (1999)
43. Watts, D., Strogatz, S.: Collective dynamics of 'small world' networks. Nature **393**, 440–442 (1998)
44. White, D.R., Houseman, M.: The navigability of strong ties: small worlds, tie strength, and network topology. Complexity **8**(1), 72–81 (2002)
45. Wu, Y., Yang, Y., Wu, H., Wang, G.: Modeling and simulation on information propagation on instant messaging network based on two-layer scale-free networks with tunable clustering. In: IEEE International Conference on Systems, Man and Cybernetics, San Antonio, TX, USA, pp. 5184–5188 (2009)
46. Wua, X., Liu, Z.: How community structure influences epidemic spread in social networks. Phys. A **387**(2–3), 623–630 (2008)
47. Zhou, S., Cox, I., Hansen, L.K.: Second-order assortative mixing in social networks. Techical Report 0903.0687, arXiv.org (2009)

Chapter 6
Structural Decompositions of Complex Networks

Rong Yang, Leyla Zhuhadar, and Olfa Nasraoui

Abstract In complex network research, a number of different ways of studying the macroscopic structure of a network have been developed. This chapter provides an overview of the most important ones. The primary example is the bow-tie decomposition. We provide a precise formal definition for the decomposition as well as an algorithm for computing it. The closely related Daisy model and a fractal approach are also discussed in some detail. Some other approaches are discussed briefly.

Introduction

The web graph is the directed graph which has HTML pages as its nodes and hyperlinks between them as its edges. It is but one particularly important example of the many large complex networks that have become the object of scrutiny and analysis in recent years. Both man-made and natural networks have increasingly become the focus for a great deal of research. The domain of natural networks includes ecological networks such as food webs [23, 24], population biology [36], and epidemiology [30, 37, 38, 41]. On the man-made side, in addition to the web graph, the Internet [17, 52, 53, 57], traffic and airline networks [10, 28, 56, 59], the power grid [4, 18, 32], social and email networks [1, 15, 19, 44], collaboration networks [2, 9, 39, 40], and terrorist networks [6, 21, 33, 47, 48].

R. Yang (✉)
Department of Mathematics and Computer Science, Western Kentucky University,
Bowling Green, KY 42101, USA
e-mail: rong.yang@wku.edu

L. Zhuhadar • O. Nasraoui
Knowledge Discovery and Web Mining Lab, Department of Computer Engineering
and Computer Science, University of Louisville, Louisville, KY 40292, USA
e-mail: leyla.zhuhadar@wku.edu; olfa.nasraoui@louisville.edu

A. Abraham and A.-E. Hassanien (eds.), *Computational Social Networks: Tools,*
Perspectives and Applications, DOI 10.1007/978-1-4471-4048-1_6,
© Springer-Verlag London 2012

While the origin of graph theory as a subject dates back to Euler and the bridges of Königsberg in the eighteenth century, the modern study of large irregular graphs begins with the work of Erdös and Rényi [26,27]. Their work invented random graph theory and introduced probabilistic methods to study these graphs (now commonly known as ER-graphs). The theory of ER-graphs is elegant and they are amenable to mathematical analysis, but the study of new large complex networks quickly revealed that they are not appropriate models for most of the graphs encountered in practice. One of the first discoveries along these lines was made by Barabási and Albert [8]. Since, in an ER-graph, each edge is present or absent with a fixed probability, the degree distribution for these graphs is binomial, which becomes Poisson in the limit as the number of vertices of the graph increases. However, Barabási and Albert discovered that the degree distribution for real-world complex networks is not binomial or Poisson, but rather follows a power-law (scale-free) distribution. That is, the probability that a vertex has degree k is proportional to $k^{-\alpha}$ for some α. These distributions have tails that are much fatter than a binomial or Poisson distribution, which means that vertices of very high degree, while not common, will occur. Barabási and Albert also devised a method called preferential attachment (newly created vertices prefer to attach themselves to vertices of high degree) to create random graphs whose degree distribution follows a power law. These are frequently called BA-graphs.

It was also discovered that most real-world complex networks are "small worlds," meaning that it generally takes only a few steps to get from any vertex to any other vertex connected to it. This is the familiar "six degrees of separation" phenomenon. Indeed, Albert et al. [3] discovered that in the World Wide Web of 1999, which at that time had at least 8×10^8 pages, two documents were typically only 19 clicks apart. This phenomenon is widespread among large sparse graphs, and Watts and Strogatz [54] discovered an effective random model for it. Their method is quite simple. It involves beginning with a regular lattice as the starting graph and then, with some probability p, rewiring the edges of the graph. The probability p serves as a parameter that allows the resulting graph to range from being totally regular ($p = 0$) to totally random ($p = 1$). They discovered that even very small values of p suffice to give rise to a small world. The small-world effect has a bearing on such things as communication, search, and the spread of epidemics.

Another characteristic of real networks which must be mentioned is their tendency to support communities – groups which have more of their ties within the group than outside it. The importance of this property was brought to the attention of the network research community by Girvan and Newman [29]. They devised a new and effective method for identifying communities based on deleting edges from the graph that are in a sense the least central edges. As the graph becomes disconnected through this process, the communities remain intact as connected components. Shortly thereafter in [43], they invented a method called modularity for testing the quality of a proposed decomposition of a network into communities and put the study on a more solid footing. Since then, community detection has become an active and widespread part of the study of networks. Ref. [46] gives a good overview.

The above sketch just begins to give an indication of the breadth and depth of the study of large complex networks as it is practiced today. There are vast areas such as network dynamics, centrality studies, and many others. For an excellent overview, see [42]. Throughout it should be emphasized that understanding the structure of these graphs and their subgraphs is not only of theoretical interest to computer scientists. To mention a few, study of the web graph can be used to improve vital operations on the web such as searching and crawling, understanding metabolic networks can aid in the diagnosis and treatment of disease, and knowing the likely structure of a terrorist network can help prevent attacks.

The purpose of this chapter is to survey some of the approaches which have been taken toward understanding the structural aspects of large complex graphs. These studies attempt to discover ways in which these graphs or their subgraphs can be decomposed into meaningful pieces and how those pieces fit together.

The outline of the rest of the paper is as follows. Section "Notation and Terminology" introduces some of the notations and terminology used in discussing graphs and networks. Section "The Bow-Tie Decomposition" is an in-depth discussion of the bow-tie decomposition including a precise definition of the decomposition and an algorithm for computing it. Section "The Daisy Approach" looks at the Daisy model which provides a more detailed view than the bare bow-tie. Section "A Fractal Attack" considers the possible self-similar, fractal nature of large networks. Section "Others Worth Mentioning" takes a quick look at other approaches that have been taken. Finally section "Conclusions" provides a few parting comments.

Notation and Terminology

The unadorned word graph means an undirected graph. A directed graph is also known as a digraph. When dealing with undirected graphs, the links are called edges, while when dealing with directed graphs they are called arcs. In either case, the graph is denoted by an ordered pair $G = (V, E)$ where V is the set of vertices (or nodes) and E is the set of edges (or arcs). The number of nodes, $|V|$, is called the order of the graph and the number of links, $|E|$, is called the size of the graph. A graph with order p and size q is often called a (p, q)-graph.

We will be particularly concerned with questions of connectivity. Let $G = (V, E)$ be a graph or digraph and let v, $w \varepsilon V$. A path from v to w is a sequence of nodes (distinct except possibly for v and w) $v = v_0, v_1, \ldots, v_n = w$ where for each $i = 0, \ldots, n - 1$, (v_i, v_{i+1}), is an edge or arc. This path is of length n (the number of links). This is also referred to as a (v, w)-path. If there is such a path, w is said to be reachable from v.

The notion of reachability is extended in the following ways for a node v and subsets of the nodes S and T:

- S is reachable from v if there exists a $w \varepsilon S$ such that w is reachable from v.
- v is reachable from S if there exists a $w \varepsilon S$ such that v is reachable from w.
- S is reachable from T if there exists a $v \varepsilon T$ and a $w \varepsilon S$ such that w is reachable from v.

A graph is said to be connected if every node is reachable from every other node – that is, if any two nodes are mutually reachable. Likewise if every node in a digraph is reachable from every other node, the digraph is said to be strongly connected.

Given a graph (or digraph) G, the "mutually reachable" relation is obviously an equivalence relation on the vertices of G. For an undirected graph, the equivalence classes under this relation are called the connected components of G. They are the maximal connected subgraphs of G. In the case of a digraph G, the equivalence classes are called the strongly connected components of G and they are the maximal strongly connected subgraphs of G. Also it is important to note that there is an undirected graph underlying any digraph – simply ignore the direction of the arcs. A set of nodes in a digraph is said to be a weakly connected component if it is a connected component of the underlying undirected graph. The phrase "strongly connected component" is often abbreviated as SCC and "weakly connected component" is referred to as WCC.

The Bow-Tie Decomposition

Definition of the Bow-Tie Decomposition

Since its introduction by Broder et al. [16], the idea of using a bow-tie decomposition as a vehicle for understanding the structure of the World Wide web and other directed graphs has been widely used. The original drawing Fig. 6.1 is a familiar feature in many publications (see [5, 7, 22, 25, 31, 35]). In [22], the bow-tie decomposition, which gives a macroscopic view of the web, served as a jumping-off point for an investigation of finer structural details within its components. In an investigation of self-similarity in the web, Dill et al. [20] used thematically unified clusters with a bow-tie structure as building blocks to model the web. The evolution of the bow-tie structure over time was studied by Hirate et al. [31]. Within the application domain, Arasu et al. [5] carried out computational experiments with the PageRank algorithm and some of its variants using the bow-tie decomposition as the model for the large-scale structure of the web. The uneven bow-tie structure of the Java Developer Forum was used in [58] to help test a number of ranking algorithms to identify expertise networks. The bow-tie structure has also shown to be present in core metabolism networks [51]. Thus the bow-tie decomposition has demonstrated its usefulness both in theoretical studies and eminently practical applications.

While the bow-tie structure is frequently cited in the literature, it is generally described in words or by an illustration and has never been precisely defined. It has also never been noted that this structure is really relative to a given strongly connected component. Here we provide the needed formal definition of a bow-tie decomposition relative to a component and an algorithm for computing it.

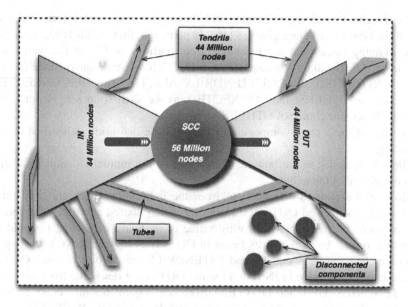

Fig. 6.1 The original bow-tie drawing (depicted in [7])

Let $G = (V, A)$ be a digraph and let S be a strongly connected component of G. The bow-tie decomposition of G with respect to S consists of the following sets of nodes:

$SCC = S$

$IN = \{v \varepsilon V - S \mid S \text{ is reachable from } v\}$

$OUT = \{v \varepsilon V - S \mid v \text{ is reachable from } S\}$

$TUBES = \{v \varepsilon V - S - IN\ OUT \mid$
$\quad v \text{ is reachable from } IN \text{ and}$
$\quad OUT \text{ is reachable from } v\}$

$INTENDRILS = \{v \varepsilon V - S \mid$
$\quad v \text{ is reachable from } IN \text{ and}$
$\quad OUT \text{ is not reachable from } v\}$

$OUTTENDRILS = \{v \varepsilon V - S \mid$
$\quad v \text{ is not reachable from } IN \text{ and}$
$\quad OUT \text{ is reachable from } v\}$

$OTHERS = V - S - IN\ OUT\ TUBES -$
$\quad INTENDRILS - OUTTENDRILS$

This precise definition is in keeping with the original (somewhat informal) definition of the bow-tie structure given in [16]. In particular, there tendrils are described as "containing nodes that are reachable from portions of IN, or that can reach portions of OUT without passage through SCC." No distinction is made in [16] between INTENDRILS and OUTTENDRILS. Also, [16] uses DISCONNECTED where we use OTHERS. DISCONNECTED, as we shall soon see, is not really correct – hence our choice of OTHERS.

The use of the term decomposition in the bow-tie definition is justified by the following:

The sets of nodes in the bow-tie decomposition are mutually disjoint and thus form a partition of the nodes.

Most of the cases are immediate from the definition. There are only three nontrivial cases. IN and OUT are disjoint, for if they shared a node v in common, then S would be reachable from v by virtue of its being in IN and v would be reachable from S by virtue of its being in OUT. Thus v would have to belong to S, which clearly it does not. IN and INTENDRILS are disjoint because OUT is reachable from any node in IN (via S) while OUT is not reachable from any node in INTENDRILS. OUT and OUTTENDRILS are disjoint because every node in OUT is reachable from any node in IN (via S) while no node in OUTTENDRILS is reachable from IN.

A fact which is useful and easy to establish, but which seems to have never appeared in the literature, is the following:

Each block in the bow-tie decomposition of G with respect to S is the union of strongly connected components of G.

Certainly this is true for SCC since by definition it is a strongly connected component of G. IN, OUT, TUBES, INTENDRILS, and OUTTENDRILS are all defined in terms of reachability criteria and any two nodes in the same strongly connected component can reach and can be reached by exactly the same nodes. Thus the assertion holds for these blocks. Finally, OTHERS consists precisely of those nodes which cannot be reached from SCC, IN, or OUT and cannot reach any of those blocks, so the assertion holds for OTHERS as well.

The smallest possible digraph in which each of the bow-tie blocks is nonempty has order 7. It is pictured in Fig. 6.2. A slightly larger example Fig. 6.3 serves to illustrate some of the problems with earlier informal definitions and software. The existing literature does not make the distinction between intendrils and outtendrils that we are making here. More importantly, when the commonly used social network program Pajek [11, 12, 45] is used to analyze this network, it correctly identifies SCC, IN, OUT, and the TUBES but it includes nodes 8 and 10 in its collection of tendrils. Only node 9 is placed in the OTHERS category. This is clearly not correct either according to our definition or the original definition in [16].

In the literature about the World Wide Web, reference is typically made to the bow-tie structure of the web or part of the web. What this means is the bow-tie decomposition relative to the strongly connected component of maximum size. Of course, in general there is no such uniquely defined component of maximum size. There may be many strongly connected components, all of the same maximum size.

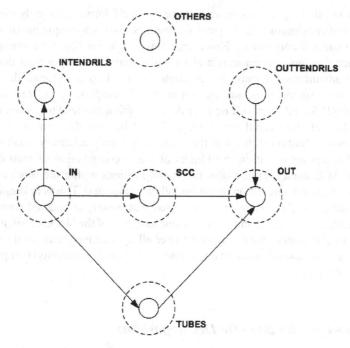

Fig. 6.2 The smallest graph with all bow-tie blocks nonempty

Fig. 6.3 A more detailed
bow-tie

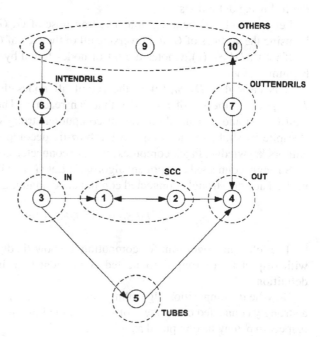

Indeed, in the first figure above, each node by itself forms a strongly connected component of maximum size. In practice, there is always a unique maximum size strongly connected component. However, allowing for the bow-tie decomposition to be relative to any chosen maximal strongly connected component does have significant advantages. It may, for example, be used to investigate the portion of the network surrounding any chosen maximal component, say one in IN or OUTTENDRILS, and the resulting finer decomposition can lead to a more detailed understanding of the overall structure. It should be said that our investigations using this new definition shows that there are usually only relatively small strongly connected components within the blocks of the decomposition of web domains (other than SCC itself), so that bow-tie decompositions within the blocks are less likely to be of great interest than might initially be suspected. This is in keeping with the conclusions of [22], where it is suggested that weakly connected components may serve better as tools for analyzing the fine structure of the blocks. Still, it is quite possible that this pattern may not persist over all application areas, so the concept of a bow-tie decomposition relative to a maximal strongly connected component is well worth keeping.

Algorithms for the Bow-Tie Decomposition

It is easy to find the strongly connected components of a digraph G with the aid of the following definitions.

Let $G = (V, A)$ be a digraph. The transpose of G, G^T, is the digraph formed by using the vertices of G and reversing all of the arcs of G.

If $v \varepsilon V$, $DFS_G(v)$ denotes the set of nodes found by a depth-first search in G beginning at v.

It is clear that $DFS_G(v)$ is the set of all nodes that v can reach and that $DFS_{G^T}(v)$ is the set of all nodes that can reach v. The following algorithm is well known and is a standard way of computing strongly connected components. (Despite its slight shortcomings in the bow-tie decomposition, to the best of the authors knowledge, Pajek computes strongly connected components correctly.)

Strongly connected component algorithm: Let $G = (V, A)$ be a digraph and let $v \varepsilon V$. Then the strongly connected component containing v is

$$DFS_G(v) \cap DFS_{G^T}(v)$$

The following algorithm for computing the bow-tie decomposition of a digraph with respect to a strongly connected component is a direct consequence of the definition.

Bow-tie decomposition algorithm: Let $G = (V, A)$ be a digraph and let S be a strongly connected component of G. Then the bow-tie decomposition of G with respect to S may be computed as follows:

Table 6.1 Western Kentucky
University bow-tie
decomposition

Region	Size
SCC	5,867
IN	104
OUT	19,250
TUBES	2
INTENDRILS	446
OUTTENDRILS	75
OTHER	1,046

1. Set $SCC = S$.
2. Choose $v \varepsilon S$. Then $OUT = DFS_G(v) - S$.
3. Choose $v \varepsilon S$. Then $IN = DFS_{G^T}(v) - S$.
4. For each $v \varepsilon V - S - IN - OUT$, compute the following two Boolean values:

$$IRV = (IN \cap DFS_{G^T}(v) \neq \phi)$$

$$VRO = (OUT \cap DFS_G(v) \neq \phi)$$

Then, since IRV answers the question of whether IN can reach v and VRO answers the question of whether v can reach OUT:

1. IRV and $VRO \Rightarrow v \varepsilon TUBES$
2. IRV and not $VRO \Rightarrow v \varepsilon INTENDRILS$
3. Not IRV and $VRO \Rightarrow v \varepsilon OUTTENDRILS$
4. Not IRV and not $VRO \Rightarrow v \varepsilon OTHER$

A program based on the above algorithm is relatively efficient, with a runtime of $O\left(|V|^2 + |V||A|\right)$, where $|V|$ is the number of vertices of the graph and $|A|$ is the number of arcs. An unoptimized Java implementation was able to compute the bow-tie structure for the Western Kentucky University domain (26,790 nodes, 103,131 arcs) in about 40 s on a 1.60 GHz machine. The results of that decomposition are given in Table 6.1.

These numbers are of some interest because of the contrast with the bow-tie structure of the entire web, where it is estimated that IN, OUT, and TENDRILS are all roughly the same size while SCC is somewhat larger than any of these. They also show that the distinction between INTENDRILS and OUTTENDRILS is a nontrivial one and that they play significantly different roles within the overall network. Both of these aspects deserve further consideration in future attempts to understand the structure of meaningful portions of the web graph.

Figure 6.4 shows the actual structure of the WKU domain bow-tie decomposition. The size of the nodes in that graph gives an indication of the size of the respective blocks. Here it is to be noted that there are links between blocks which are not required by the definition itself – the direct link from IN to OUT, the link from TUBES to INTENDRILS, and so forth. While not required by the definition, neither are they forbidden. Some links are forbidden – there could be no link from OUT to IN, for example.

Fig. 6.4 Structure of the
WKU domain bow-tie
decomposition

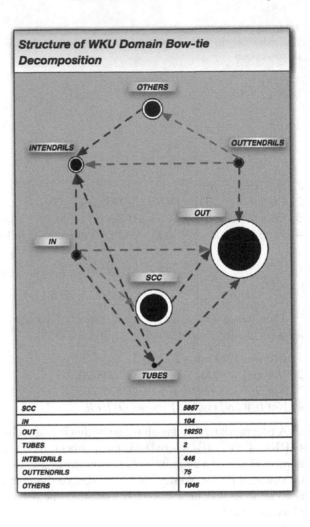

SCC	5867
IN	104
OUT	19250
TUBES	2
INTENDRILS	446
OUTTENDRILS	75
OTHERS	1046

The Daisy Approach

In a very interesting paper [22], Donato et al. use the macroscopic bow-tie
description of the web graph to initiate a more detailed investigation of the pieces
of that decomposition. To illustrate some of the ideas presented there and the utility
of looking at networks in terms of their decompositions, we use the neural network
of C. Elegans [54,55]. For brevity, we will refer to this network as CEN (C. Elegans
Neural). This is a relatively small but nontrivial network with 297 vertices and 2,359
arcs. A sketch of the network in Fig. 6.5 using the Fructerman-Reingold 2D layout
algorithm certainly does not give much insight into its structure. A much better
idea of the nature of the network is obtained through a simplified picture of its
bow-tie structure, shown in Fig. 6.6. In this figure, the SCC component of the bow-
tie has been collasped to a single large node at the center top. The other existing

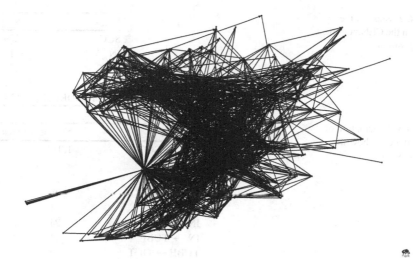

Fig. 6.5 The C. Elegans neural network

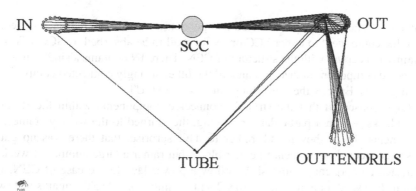

Fig. 6.6 Simplified bow-tie decomposition of the C. Elegans neural network

components are as labeled. Also, edges leading from IN to OUT have been omitted to avoid clutter. This single picture certainly gives one a much better idea of the macroscopic structure of the network, which is further clarified by an enumeration of the sizes of the blocks in the decomposition and the placement of the arcs between and within the blocks. These enumerations are given in Tables 6.2 and 6.3.

Donato et al. went much further than this in their analysis. Their data used very large crawls of the web (from 7.4 million to 203.5 million nodes), and they were interested first in whether the IN and OUT blocks contained any sizeable strongly connected components. They found that they did not and they concluded that there were no reasonable candidates for an SCC inside IN or OUT, which might yield interesting bow-tie structures within those blocks. (This may help explain why in many situations, IN and OUT remain quite large – if, for example, OUT

Table 6.2 Sizes of the blocks in the CEN bow-tie decomposition

Block	Size
SCC	239
IN	16
OUT	27
TUBES	1
OUTTENDRILS	14

Table 6.3 Distribution of arcs in the CEN bow-tie decomposition

Arc type	Number of arcs
SCC → SCC	1,918
IN → IN	3
OUT → OUT	29
SCC → OUT	296
IN → SCC	71
IN → OUT	24
IN → TUBE	1
TUBE → OUT	3
OUTTENDRILS → OUT	14

contained a giant strongly connected component, it would take but one new edge from that component to either SCC or IN for it all to be absorbed by SCC.) This is certainly in keeping with the structure of CEN. There IN contains a single strongly connected component of size two and all the other strongly connected components are singletons. Exactly the same thing happens with OUT.

Having observed that the strongly connected components within the IN and OUT blocks were not particularly revealing, they turned to the weakly connected components. There they found, rather to their surprise, that there was no giant weakly connected component in either block, but rather a large number of weakly connected components whose sizes follow a power law. In the case of CEN, IN contains two weak components of size 2 and 12 singletons. OUT contains just two weak components, including one singleton.

They also classified the vertices in IN and OUT into levels according to their distance from the SCC. Here they found that, even for their large networks, almost all the vertices are to be found in the first few (about 5) small levels. They conclude that IN and OUT are shallow by this measure. For CEN, the situation is about as simple as it get – every node in both IN and OUT is at level 1, so they are all directly connected to the SCC.

Turning their attention to the structure of the SCC itself, they define a vertex in the SCC to be an entry point if it is pointed to by at least one vertex in IN, an exit point if it points to at least one vertex in OUT, and a bridge if it is both an entry point and an exit point. (Note that this usage of the term bridge is not the same as that generally used in graph theory.) For their data they observe a power-law in-degree distribution for entry points, which means that most entry points are pointed to by only a few vertices in IN, but a few will be pointed to by a great many vertices in IN. They found similar results for OUT. In the case of CEN, there are 53 entry

Table 6.4 In-degree
distribution of entry points
in CEN

In-degree	1	2	3	4	5
Number of entry points	43	5	3	1	1

Table 6.5 Out-degree distribution of exit points in CEN

Out-degree	1	2	3	5	6	7	9	10	11	13	14	15	18	108
Number of exit points	2	1	2	6	4	2	2	1	2	1	1	1	1	1

Fig. 6.7 The Daisy structure
of the web [22]

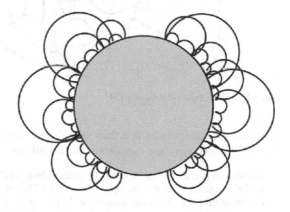

points, 27 exit points, and no bridges. Of the 53 entry points, 42 are pointed to by only one vertex in IN. The in and out degree distributions of entry points and exit points are here quite different and are given in Tables 6.4 and 6.5.

The evidence that IN and OUT consist of a large number of relatively small and relatively shallow pieces (the weakly connected components) led Donato et al. to describe their view of the web as a Daisy. Their original depiction is in Fig. 6.7. While their work concentrated on the web graph, it is clear that the notions they introduced can be applied to any complex network and can certainly help understand their structure and perhaps prove useful as a means of classifying networks.

A Fractal Attack

The scale-free nature of the power-law distributions that seem to constantly arise in the study of complex networks are reminiscent of fractals, where being scale free is a defining characteristic. It is possible that the fact that fractals are self-similar has motivated some researchers to ask whether complex networks might also have self-similar properties. Several scholars have in fact investigated this possibility, including Dill et al. [20] who studied "Thematically Unified Clusters" (TUCs). These are not simply random collections of web pages. A TUC is a group of web pages that share some kind of common trait – it could be that they are linked by content, by location within sites or intranets, by geographic location, or any number of other features. They considered a range of parameters, including degree distributions, connected component sizes, and bipartite cores. They discovered, with

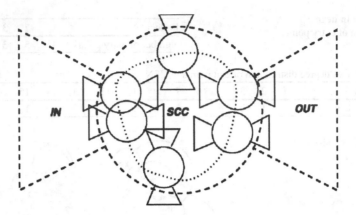

Fig. 6.8 Fractal bow-tie structure [34]

considerable consistency, that their data demonstrated a wide range of self-similar, fractal-like behavior, and supported, among others, the following conclusion:

> The web comprises several thematically unified clusters (TUCs). The common theme within a TUC is one of many diverse possibilities. Each TUC has a bowtie structure that consists of a large strongly-connected component (SCC). The SCCs corresponding to the TUCs are integrated, via the navigational backbone, into a global SCC for the entire web. The extent to which each TUC exhibits the bowtie structure and the extent to which its SCC is integrated into the web as a whole indicate how well-established the corresponding community is.

Figure 6.8 clearly shows the resulting vision of the structure of the web. Although this work focused specifically on the web and some of its subgraphs, the corresponding ideas could be investigated in many other large complex graphs. There is evidence that this fractal structure may be the result of a number of independent stochastic processes operating simultaneously [34]. It should be noted that there has been some disagreement about whether fractal properties do in fact exist. See [50] for a discussion.

Others Worth Mentioning

Björneborn [13, 14] has introduced a novel presentation of the bow-tie decomposition which he calls a corona model because of it resemblance to a solar corona. While it essentially is just a way of redrawing the standard bow-tie, it is very cleverly done and has several advantages over the usual representation. His dissertation [13] contains the most detailed examination of the bow-tie structure of a particular real-world network (UK university subsites) as you are likely to find anywhere.

A conceptual model that might seem superficially similar to the bow-tie was introduced in [49]. It is called the jellyfish model and it was developed for the Internet AS topology. It is a layered model, and their depiction of it, shown in Fig. 6.5 is certainly evocative. The model is based on using a clique of the vertices with the highest degrees as the core (the smallest circle at the top of Fig. 6.9). The

Fig. 6.9 The internet topology as a jellyfish [49]

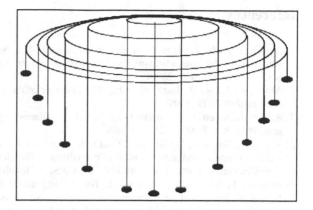

core is layer 0. The vertices adjacent to the core form layer 1, and so on. The layers are the expanding concentric circles surrounding the core. The small solid circles are the degree-1 vertices attached to each layer.

Unlike all the models considered earlier, the jellyfish model applies only to undirected networks. Note that the bow-tie model is essentially useless for undirected networks since all the blocks except for OTHERS collapse into one block in the undirected case. Thus, despite the fact that it applicable to different situations than our other models, when it does apply, the jellyfish model can be a very useful tool.

It is amusing to note that [49] refers to a number of other models which were considered and found wanting: the broom model, the furball model, and the doughnut model.

Conclusions

We have introduced a number of the most important macroscopic ways of viewing large complex networks, including a precise and unambiguous definition of the bow-tie decomposition for a directed graph (and an effective algorithm for producing this decomposition) which should be useful in standardizing discussions of bow-tie structures in the future, the Daisy variant of the bow-tie decomposition, and fractal structures. We also presented the notion of a bow-tie decomposition relative to a particular strongly connected component, which allows for detailed decompositions beyond the gross bow-tie structure. Examples of the types of information that can be obtained from such views were given.

From our discussion and especially from the references, it should be clear that these approaches to understanding the overall structure of complex directed networks have had both wide popularity and wide applicability. Despite the fact that these notions have been in use for some years now, they have by no means outlived their usefulness. In fact, these approaches and others which will doubtless be found later will continue to guide network research for the foreseeable future.

References

1. Adamic, L., Adar, E.: How to search a social network. Soc. Netw. **27**(3), 187–203 (2005)
2. Ahuja, G.: Collaboration networks, structural holes, and innovation: a longitudinal study. Adm. Sci. Q. **45**(3), 425–455 (2000)
3. Albert, R.: Jeong, H., Barabási, A.L.: The diameter of the world wide web. Arxiv preprint cond-mat/9907038 (1999)
4. Albert, R., Albert, I., Nakarado, G.L.: Structural vulnerability of the North American power grid. Phys. Rev. E. **69**(2), 25103 (2004)
5. Arasu, A., Novak, J., Tomkins, A., Tomlin, J.: PageRank computation and the structure of the web: experiments and algorithms. In: Proceedings of the Eleventh International World Wide Web Conference, Poster Track, pp. 107–117. Citeseer, Honolulu (2002)
6. Arquilla, J., Ronfeldt, D., Zanini, M., Naval Postgraduate School Monterey CA Graduate School of Operational, and Information Sciences: Networks, Netwar, and Information-Age Terrorism. Defense Technical Information Center, Fort Belvoir (1999)
7. Baldi, P., Frasconi, P., Smyth, P.: Modeling the Internet and the Web: Probabilistic Methods and Algorithms. Wiley, Chichester/Hoboken (2003)
8. Barabasi, A.L., Albert, R.: Emergence of scaling in random networks. Science **286**(5439), 509 (1999)
9. Barabasi, A.L., Jeong, H., Néda, Z., Ravasz, E., Schubert, A., Vicsek, T.: Evolution of the social network of scientific collaborations. Phys. A Stat. Mech. Appl. **311**(3–4), 590–614 (2002)
10. Barla, P., Constantatos, C.: Airline network structure under demand uncertainty. Transp. Res. E Logist. Transp. Rev. **36**(3), 173–180 (2000)
11. Batagelj, V., Mrvar, A.: Pajek-program for large network analysis. Connections **21**(2), 47–57 (1998)
12. Batagelj, V., Mrvar, A.: Pajek analysis and visualization of large networks. In: Mutzel, P., Jünger, M., Leipert, S. (eds.) Graph Drawing, pp. 8–11. Springer, Berlin (2002)
13. Bjorneborn, L., Danmarks biblioteksskole: Small-World Link Structures Across an Academic Web Space: a Library and Information Science Approach. Department of Information Studies, Royal School of Library and Information Science, Copenhagen (2004)
14. Bjorneborn, L.: 'Mini small worlds' of shortest link paths crossing domain boundaries in an academic Web space. Scientometrics **68**(3), 395–414 (2006)
15. Boyd, D.M., Ellison, N.B.: Social network sites: definition, history, and scholarship. J Comput. Mediat. Commun. **13**(1), 210–230 (2008)
16. Broder, A., Kumar, R., Maghoul, F., Raghavan, P., Rajagopalan, S., Stata, R., Tomkins, A., Wiener, J.: Graph structure in the web. Comput. Netw. **33**(1–6), 309–320 (2000)
17. Caldarelli, G., Marchetti, R., Pietronero, L.: The fractal properties of internet. EPL (Europhys. Lett.) **52**, 386 (2000)
18. Chassin, D.P., Posse, C.: Evaluating North American electric grid reliability using the Barabasi-albert network model. Phys. A Stat. Mech. Appl. **355**(2–4), 667–677 (2005)
19. Cowan, R., Jonard, N.: Network structure and the diffusion of knowledge. J. Econ. Dyn. Control **28**(8), 1557–1575 (2004)
20. Dill, S., Kumar, R., McCurley, K.S., Rajagopalan, S., Sivakumar, D., Tomkins, A.: Self-similarity in the web. ACM Trans. Internet Technol. (TOIT) **2**(3), 205–223 (2002)
21. Dombroski, M., Carley, K.M.: NETEST: estimating a terrorist networks structure. In: CASOS Conference Proceedings, Pittsburgh, p. 2 (2002)
22. Donato, D., Leonardi, S., Millozzi, S., Tsaparas, P.: Mining the inner structure of the web graph. J. Phys. A Math. Theor. **41**, 224017 (2008)
23. Dunne, J.A.: The network structure of food webs. Ecol. Netw. Link. Struct. Dyn. Food Webs. pp. 27–86 (2006)
24. Dunne, J.A., Williams, R.J., Martinez, N.D.: Network structure and robustness of marine food webs. Mar. Ecol. Prog. Ser. **273**, 291–302 (2004)

25. Easley, D., Kleinberg, J.:   Networks, Crowds, and Markets: Reasoning About a Highly Connected World. Cambridge University Press, New York (2010)
26. Erdos, P., Renyi, A.: On random graphs I. Publ. Math. Debr. 6(290–297), 156 (1959)
27. Erdos, P., Rényi, A.: On the Evolution of Random Graphs. Publication of the Mathematical Institute of the Hungarian Academy of Sciences, Citeseer (1960)
28. Gastner, M.T., Newman, M.E.J.: The spatial structure of networks. Eur. Phys. J. B-Condens. Matter Complex Syst. 49(2), 247–252 (2006)
29. Girvan, M., Newman, M.E.J.: Community structure in social and biological networks. Proc. Natl. Acad. Sci. USA 99(12), 7821 (2002)
30. Gross, T., DLima, C.J.D., Blasius, B.: Epidemic dynamics on an adaptive network. Phys. Rev. Lett. 96(20), 208701 (2006)
31. Hirate, Y., Kato, S., Yamana, H.: Web structure in 2005. In: W. Aiello et al. (eds.): WAW 2006, LNCS 4936, pp. 36–46. Springer, Berlin/Heidelberg (2008)
32. Kinney, R., Crucitti, P., Albert, R., Latora, V.: Modeling cascading failures in the North American power grid. Eur. Phys. J. B-Condens. Matter Complex Syst. 46(1), 101–107 (2005)
33. Krebs, V.E.: Mapping networks of terrorist cells. Connections 24(3), 43–52 (2002)
34. Kumar, R., Raghavan, P., Rajagopalan, S., Sivakumar, D., Tomkins, A., Upfal, E.: Stochastic models for the web graph. In: Foundations of Computer Science, 2000. Proceedings. 41st Annual Symposium on, pp. 57–65. IEEE, Los Alamitos (2002)
35. Kumar, R., Raghavan, P., Rajagopalan, S., Tomkins, A.: The web and social networks. IEEE Comput. 35(11), 32–36 (2002)
36. May, R.M.: Network structure and the biology of populations. Trends Ecol. Evol. 21(7), 394–399 (2006)
37. May, R.M., Lloyd, A.L.: Infection dynamics on scale-free networks. Phys. Rev. E 64(6), 66112 (2001)
38. Meyers, L.A., Pourbohloul, B., Newman, M.E.J., Skowronski, D.M., Brunham, R.C.: Network theory and SARS: predicting outbreak diversity. J. Theor. Biol. 232(1), 71–81 (2005)
39. Newman, M.E.J.: Scientific collaboration networks. II. Shortest paths, weighted networks, and centrality. Phys. Rev. E 64(1), 16132 (2001)
40. Newman, M.E.J.: The structure of scientific collaboration networks. Proc. Natl. Acad. Sci. USA 98(2), 404 (2001)
41. Newman, M.E.J.: Spread of epidemic disease on networks. Phys. Rev. E 66(1), 16128 (2002)
42. Newman, M.E.J.: The structure and function of complex networks. Arxiv preprint cond-mat/0303516 (2003)
43. Newman, M.E.J., Girvan, M.: Finding and evaluating community structure in networks. Phys. Rev. E 69(2), 26113 (2004)
44. Newman, M.E.J., Forrest, S., Balthrop, J.: Email networks and the spread of computer viruses. Phys. Rev. E. 66(3), 35101 (2002)
45. Nooy, W., Mrvar, A., Batagelj, V.: Exploratory social network analysis with Pajek. Cambridge University Press, New York (2005)
46. Porter, M.A., Onnela, J.P., Mucha, P.J.: Communities in networks. Not. Am. Math. Soc. 56(9), 1082–1097 (2009)
47. Ressler, S.: Social network analysis as an approach to combat terrorism: past, present, and future research. Homel. Secur. Aff. 2(2), 1–10 (2006)
48. Rothenberg, R.: From whole cloth: making up the terrorist network. New York Times. Connections 24(3), 36–42 (2002)
49. Siganos, G., Tauro, S.L., Faloutsos, M.: Jellyfish: a conceptual model for the as internet topology. J. Commun. Netw. 8(3), 339 (2006)
50. Song, C., Havlin, S., Makse, H.A.: Self-similarity of complex networks. Nature 433(7024), 392–395 (2005)
51. Tanaka, R., Csete, M., Doyle, J.: Highly optimised global organisation of metabolic networks. IEE Proc. Syst. Biol. 152(4), 179–184 (2005)
52. Tu, Y.: How robust is the internet. Nature 406(6794), 353–354 (2000)

53. Vazquez, A., Pastor-Satorras, R., Vespignani, A.: Large-scale topological and dynamical properties of the internet. Phys. Rev. E **65**(6), 66130 (2002)
54. Watts, D.J., Strogatz, S.H.: Collective dynamics of small-world networks. Nature **393**(6684), 440–442 (1998)
55. White, J.G., Southgate, E., Thomson, J.N., Brenner, S.: The structure of the nervous system of the nematode Caenorhabditis elegans. Philos. Trans. R. Soc. Lond. B Biol. Sci. **314**(1165), 1 (1986)
56. Yerra, B.M., Levinson, D.M.: The emergence of hierarchy in transportation networks. Ann Reg. Sci. **39**(3), 541–553 (2005)
57. Zegura, E.W., Calvert, K.L., Donahoo, M.J.: A quantitative comparison of graph-based models for internet topology. IEEE/ACM Trans. Netw. (TON) **5**(6), 770–783 (1997)
58. Zhang, J., Ackerman, M.S., Adamic, L.: Expertise networks in online communities: structure and algorithms. In: Proceedings of the 16th international conference on World Wide Web, p. 230. ACM Press, New York (2007)
59. Zhao, L., Lai, Y.C., Park, K., Ye, N.: Onset of traffic congestion in complex networks. Phys. Rev. E **71**(2), 26125 (2005)

Chapter 7
Enhancing Online Communities with Cycle-Sharing for Social Networks

Nuno Apolónia, Paulo Ferreira, and Luís Veiga

Abstract The Internet has made it possible to exchange information more rapidly on a global scale. A natural succeeding step was the creation of Social Networks where anyone in the world can share their experiences, content, and current information, using only their Internet-enabled personal computer or mobile devices. Under this scope, there are many Social Networks such as Facebook, Orkut, and Youtube each one exporting its own APIs to interact with its users and groups databases. Studies done on Social Networks show that they follow some properties like the Small-World property. Meaning that traversing friendship relations, vast numbers of other users could be reached from each single user (e.g., Friends of Friends), even though users usually only interact (on a daily basis) with a restrict group of friends. Considering that these networks could be regarded as enabling peer-to-peer information sharing (albeit mediated by a centrally controlled infrastructure), employing them for cycle-sharing should be a great improvement for global distributed computing, by allowing public-resource sharing among trusted users and within online virtual communities. Resources from these types of networks can be used to further advance studies in other areas which may be too computational intensive for using a single computer or a cluster, e.g., to process data mined from the various Social Networks. We describe the design, development, and resulting evaluation of a web-enabled platform, called CSSN: Cycle-Sharing in Social Networks. The platform leverages a Social Network (Facebook) to perform discovery of computational resources, thus giving the possibility for any user to submit his own jobs for remote processing. Walls, messages, and comments in Facebook are used as the underlying transport for CSSN protocol messages, achieving full portability with existing Social Networks. Globally, CSSN gives the

N. Apolónia (✉) • P. Ferreira • L. Veiga
INESC ID Lisboa/Technical University of Lisbon, Rua Alves Redol 9,
1000-029 Lisboa, Portugal
e-mail: nuno.apolonia@ist.utl.pt; paulo.ferreira@inesc-id.pt; luis.veiga@inesc-id.pt

A. Abraham and A.-E. Hassanien (eds.), *Computational Social Networks: Tools,*
Perspectives and Applications, DOI 10.1007/978-1-4471-4048-1_7,
© Springer-Verlag London 2012

chance for common users to unleash the untapped computing power hidden in Social Networks, and exploit it using the cycle-sharing paradigm to speedup their own (or common) applications' execution.

Introduction

The computing power has been significantly increased in the past few years; however, there are still many computational problems that need an enormous and increasing amount of computing resources, e.g., applications for scientific research, financial risk analysis, or multimedia video or image rendering and encoding. These resources are composed by computing elements such as CPU, memory, or data storage, and all of them can be found in the millions of desktop computers all around the world. In other words, the needed resources can be gathered from every household or from offices and even from our daily devices, such as notebooks or mobile phones.

The idea to use idle cycles for distributed computing was proposed in 1978 by the WORM computing project at Xerox PARC [31]. It was only after that the scientific community started to see the benefits that such systems can give. Furthermore, the possibility of having supercomputers available was very tempting and made the scientific community realize that they could harvest the idle processing time to suite their own needs. These networks are called Grids [14], a combination of computational resources from multiple administration domains. They employ coordinated resource-sharing and problem-solving environments, which made possible to make distributed processing of large computational (and scientific) problems.

With the Internet, the available resources for such projects were extended. Projects like SETI@Home [3], Folding@Home (folding.stanford.edu), Distributed.net (www.distributed.net) gathered the gigantic potential of using desktop computers from any household (also known as global distributed computing), allowing them to process their data much quicker than in traditional supercomputers. This is usually done by Internet users willing to participate in such projects, that *install* an application, which runs in the background when the computer has idle cycles to spare.

A lesson to be taken from such projects is that to attract and keep users, such projects should explain and justify their goals, research subject, and impacts. Users may not be interested in systems that would steal their idle cycles without their consent (Plura Processing response to the Digsby Controversy in Wordpress.com).

Motivation

The Internet has also enabled information and content sharing by using peer-to-peer (P2P) networks [36]. These networks are usually formed by interconnected home desktop computers. They can be categorized in terms of their formation as being structured or unstructured. Unstructured P2P systems are characterized by having an underlying topology unrelated with the placement of the contents, as opposed to Structured P2P systems where it is attempted to place the contents in locations related with the content identification. Furthermore, optimizations were done to leverage the performance for locating contents and their scalability (in terms of traffic load). The resulting systems are generally called Hybrid P2P systems that highlight two types of users. The users that provide more bandwidth are called super-peers and those with low bandwidths are called peers; the last ones are connected to the super-peers [36].

These networks raise challenges, such as efficient resource discovery. That is, when a peer needs a resource, it asks other peers for it. Some approaches try to minimize the message traffic that can be generated, either by contacting fewer peers (when information is spread to others) or by creating central nodes that have all or partial information for locating the exact resource.

Moreover, the Internet has made it possible to exchange information more rapidly in a global scale. One of the natural steps was the creation of Social Networks, where any one in the world can share their experiences and information using only their Internet enabled personal computer or mobile device (facebook.com/mobile). Under this scope, there are many Social Networks such as Facebook (facebook.com), Orkut, (orkut.com) and Youtube (youtube.com) each one exporting their own *APIs* to interact with their users and groups databases, e.g., Facebook API[1] and OpenSocial.[2] Also, these networks have great potential for financial benefits, such as advertising.

Furthermore, studies show that the Social Networks have some properties like the Small-World property, meaning that there is a small group of users with high connectivity to others and a much larger group with low connectivity. Besides that, even the highly connected users only interact (on a daily basis) with a restrict group of users [39]. Considering that these networks could be regarded as enabling Peer-to-Peer information sharing (albeit mediated by a centrally controlled infrastructure), employing them for cycle-sharing should be a great improvement for global distributed computing, by allowing public-resource sharing among trusted users and within communities.

There are already projects that use Social Network concepts to improve performance on other topics, such as PeerSpective [23] which enhances search results with social information from friends.

Background

In our work, we developed and evaluated a web-enabled platform, called Cycle-Sharing in Social Networks (CSSN), that interacts with a Social Network (Facebook) to be able to locate and search for idle resources among its users. We leverage an existing middleware, Ginger [33, 38], for task (called *Gridlets*) creation and aggregation.

---

[1]Facebook Developers: developers.facebook.com accessed on 05/01/2010.
[2]OpenSocial website: code.google.com/apis/opensocial accessed on 05/01/2010.

CSSN uses a Social Network already established in order to give beneficial results to communities willing to adopt the paradigm of cycle-sharing. Moreover, the users in such networks are mostly linked with each other by friendship and common interests, meaning that users may be more opened to share their resources with their own friends.

The client application developed interacts with Facebook mostly by means of the *Graph* interface which Facebook provides. This interface gives us access to users' information, such as their friends, groups, and Walls. These Walls are the main interactions between the people that use Facebook, meaning that they record messages onto the Wall to be read by the users linked to them.

We designed a communication protocol to allow interaction among the CSSN clients and execute Jobs (sets of tasks) successfully. This means that we use Facebook Walls (users/groups/Application Walls) to send and retrieve messages sent by other CSSN clients. CSSN starts the discovery process by sending a Job search message to the users' Wall in order for the users' friends to read and accept (or deny) the request to use their idle resources. As we also want to gather users' computers as much as possible, we send messages to groups that have users who may be willing to help (or have the Jobs' requirements). Furthermore, we extend the reach of gathering resources to contain friends of friends (FoFs), by contacting FoFs CSSN clients.

In the development of CSSN, our concerns were with the resource discovery and also the manner which a user could submit his own Jobs to be processed on others' computers. Furthermore, to reach as many users and communities as possible, we used Java for portability purposes.

The evaluation of CSSN is comprised of several scenarios, where each one evaluates a portion of our works' goals, in order to know the effects each carries.

In the last scenarios, we augment the network size used, to become more realistic in terms of users' roles (friends, FoFs, group members). In addition, we create *Gridlets* representing tasks to be performed by a known program (Pov-Ray)[3] to render an image. These scenarios were made in order to conclude that CSSN can gain speedups against local execution; however, it is demonstrated that CSSN can be hindered by variables such as Facebook latency, and searching for resources may not return positive results, or even that the number of *Gridlets* may surpass the number of donating users.

Current Shortcomings

The public-resource sharing and cycle-sharing systems that are widely used today are not concerned with the common users' needs. They are mostly used for intensive computational projects (and proprietary) such as Folding@Home, PluraProcessing.

---

[3]Pov-Ray web site: povray.org accessed on 13/10/2010.

Other systems allow common applications to be executed; however, they do not support users' networks already established, meaning that they cannot use Social Networks to be able to gather resources to be used by other interested users (such as friends or communities), while often do not provide a flexible sharing system between users.

Some systems, however, are beginning to use technologies previously unavailable to other projects, in order to cover more Internet users. Such systems can use the users' Browsers to do cycle-stealing instead of addressing the needs of the common users. Moreover, they use remote code embedded on website and games (i.e., Adobe Flash-based games) to gain access to potential idle resources. Furthermore, their resource discovery and scheduling are rudimentary, meaning that they do not rely on established networks of users to do public-resource sharing; instead, users may have to create their own networks. Also, their scheduling process is defined by predesignated users and targets occasional users (which may not be aware of the system).

Contribution

Our main contribution is the CSSN platform with its architecture, messaging protocol, system monitor, and client application. It performs resource and service discovery on top of a Social Network already established. Furthermore, CSSN needs to be able to gather idle cycles from users' computers and communities that would be willing, and capable of executing a Job, in order to achieve cycle-sharing on a Social Network. It can also allow common users to use the cycle-sharing paradigm to speedup their own (or common) applications' execution without the need to create a new network. Meaning that, CSSN can use an already established network as in case of Social Networks (Facebook, MySpace, among others) to interact between users to share their idle cycles.

Related Work

This section offers a review on relevant works and technologies more related to our focus, addressing: (i) Social Networks, (ii) peer-to-peer networks, Grids and Distributed Computing, and (iii) deployment mechanisms and code execution via the web.

Social Networks

Social Networks are popular infrastructures for communication, interaction and information sharing on the Internet. Anyone with a desktop computer and a Browser can access such websites, like Facebook, MySpace, Orkut, Hi5, YouTube, LinkedIn, and many more (List of Social Networks on Wikipedia.org). They are used to interact with other people for personal or business purposes, sending messages, posting them on the website, receiving *links* to other websites or even sharing files between people.

Like in real-life social interactions [30], people tend to interact with many others along their lives, some of those are called friends with whom the interaction may be daily. In the Social Networks, the basic (real life) behaviors or interaction patterns still apply. By grouping people in the same areas or topics, it is easier to exploit those interactions, because people understand better what the distributed tasks will accomplish and are willing to participate. Social Networks have already began to sprout new ideas to exploit them for uses other than human interactions, such as using it for enhancing Internet search [23] and leveraging infrastructures to enable ad hoc VPNs [13].

Small-World networks can be described by the following properties: the local neighborhood is preserved; and the diameter of the network, quantified by the average shortest distance between two vertices, increases logarithmically with the number of vertices. It is then possible to connect any two vertices in the network through just a few links [1]. Growing of such networks can be hindered by two factors: *Aging of the vertices*, where vertices no longer connect to newer vertices; *Cost of adding links to the vertices or the limited capacity of a vertex*, adding links to the networks may not be possible if there are constraints of space/time.

Many Social Networks also have ways of connecting users without being linked as friends; such connections are called groups or communities, where knowledge is exchanged within a specific topic of interest. The creation of such groups and their subsequently taking shape and evolution over time is inherent in the structure of society; this means that people have the tendency of coming together to share knowledge on a particular theme [6]. We give special focus on **Facebook** and **OpenSocial**, explained by their size and possibility of access to user databases, by means of the APIs they export. Facebook claims to have 500,000,000 (as of July 21 of 2010) users and MySpace (one website that uses the OpenSocial API) claiming to have more than 130,000,000 registered users. The potential of these networks for global distributed computing is best compared to other networks.

The Facebook API and the OpenSocial API enables web applications to interact with the server using a *REST*-like interface[4] or in case of Facebook also a *Graph* interface.[5] This means that the calls from outside applications are made over the Internet by sending HTTP GET and POST requests.

An example of a Facebook application is **Progress Thru Processors**.[6] It executes a BOINC system to do distributed computing, when the computer has idle cycles to spare. Through the applications' interface on Facebook, it is able to track contributions from users and share updates with friends to intentionally promote

---

[4]Representational State Transfer: tinyurl.com/6x9ya accessed on 05/01/2010.

[5]OpenGraph Protocol: opengraphprotocol.org accessed on 23/08/2010.

[6]Progress Thru Processors: facebook.com/progressthruprocessors accessed on 05/01/2010.

distributed projects to other users. **PeerSpective**[7] is a Social Network-based web search. It tries to merge the Social Networking with search engines, to improve their ranking system, by understanding how people perform searches. They employ the search results, made by friends, into the ranking system. Overall, they claim that the system can be leveraged to improve the quality of search results for a given group of people. The system works by indexing search content and querying friends for their searches including the extra results, which may be relevant to the question, on the search web page. A lesson to be taken is that *"Social Networks can organize the world of information according to the tastes and preferences of smaller groups of individuals"* [23]. **Social Cloud** [8] is described as being a model that integrates Social Networking, cloud computing [5] and *volunteer computing*. In this model, users can acquire the resources (in this project, the only resource considered is disk space) by exchanging virtual credits, making a virtual economy over the social cloud computing. Users can gather resources from their friends (either by virtual compensation, payment, or with a reciprocal credit model [24]), which allows this model to approach the objectives of public-resource sharing. Furthermore, they state that there are a number of advantages gained by leveraging Social Networking platforms, such as gaining access to a huge user community, exploiting existent user management functionality, and relying on pre established trust formed through user relationships. However, the trusting relationship of friends may not be always the case[8] in Social Networks such as Facebook.

Peer-to-Peer Networks, Grids, and Distributed Computing

Peer-to-peer (P2P) networks and Grids are the most common types of sharing systems. They evolved from different communities to serve different purposes [36]. The Grid systems interconnect clusters of supercomputers and storage systems. Normally, they are centralized and hierarchically administrated, each with its own set of rules regarding resource availability. Resources can be dynamic and thus may vary in amount and availability during time, and have to be known beforehand among the network. Grid systems were created by the scientific community to run computation intensive applications that would take too much time in normal desktops (without being distributed) or on a single cluster, e.g., large-scale simulations or data analysis.

P2P networks are typically made from household desktop computers or common mobile devices, being extremely dynamic in terms of resource types and whose membership can vary in time with more intensity than with Grids. P2P networks are normally used for sharing files, although there are a number of projects using those kinds of networks for other purposes, such as sharing information and

---

[7]PeerSpective: peerspective.mpi-sws.org accessed on 05/01/2010.

[8]How Facebook could make cloud computing better: tinyurl.com/237ddem accessed on 15/10/2010.

streaming (e.g., Massive Multi-player Online games using P2P [16] to alleviate server load, distributing tasks as SETI@Home [3], data streaming for watching TV[9]). The nodes (or peers) are composed by anonymous or unknown users unlike in Grids, which raises its own problems with security or even with forged results [36].

Both Grid and P2P systems have been converging by relaxing rules from Grid systems and opening P2P applications for more computation, and not simply storage. These two distributing systems have different resources, which may indicate a different level of computing power of the nodes comprising each one. However, it is easier to leverage more desktop computers than to have large supercomputers at our disposal. This can make P2P systems aggregate more computing power than the Grid systems.

In **Unstructured P2P systems**, the placement of contents (Files) is completely unrelated to the overlay topology and they must be located (or searched). These systems, such as Gnutella[10] and (FastTrack) KaZaA [18], are generally more appropriate for accommodating highly transient node populations. To search for resources, it is common to use methods such as *Flooding* [26], *Dynamic Querying*,[11] *Random walks* [37], *direct searches* [20] (if statistical information is available), or *forwarding indices* [10]. Moreover, they have obvious implications regarding availability, scalability, and persistence [4]. **Structured P2P systems** are an attempt to improve the scalability issues regarding locating content, that the unstructured systems suffered from, by controlling where contents should be placed at all times. For supporting searches, these systems use namely a distributed routing table (also presented as DHT – Distributed Hash Table) [21], for queries to be efficiently routed to the peer that has the content or the information where the content is located. Every peer that joins the network has partial information where to find the contents (CHORD [35], CAN [27], Pastry [29]) meaning that peers need more information to join the network. These systems are more scalable in terms of traffic load, but still need more auto-organizational capabilities.

There are also **hybrid approaches** created to make up for the lacks that each approach has and still retains its benefits. A common optimization to unstructured systems is to have two types of peers (or nodes): the *super-peers* (peers with higher bandwidth) which would form an unstructured overlay network and the leaves (*peers* with low bandwidth) connected to the super-peers. Thus, flooding of messages is only passed through the super-peers and does not cause problems with peers which cannot handle too many search requests [36]. **Kademlia** [22] uses a group of peers (that are near each other) known as buckets to locate files, avoiding some flooding problems. Also peers may have the ability to change their positioning, enabling them to become part of the overlay network used to coordinate the P2P structure. Furthermore, some hybrid systems use a central server to bootstrap the peers (i.e., eDonkey network [25]).

---

[9]PPStream: ppstream.com accessed on 05/01/2010.

[10]Gnutella Protocol: tinyurl.com/yaz95ep accessed on 07/01/2010.

[11]Dynamic Querying Protocol: tinyurl.com/6jh958q accessed on 05/01/2010.

SETI@Home [3] aims at using globally distributed resources to analyze radio wave signals that come from outer space, hoping to find radio signals originated from other planets on our galaxy.

For this project, having more computing power means it is possible to cover a greater range of frequencies, instead of using supercomputers which owners did not have in abundance [3], they found a way that lets them use computers around the world to calculate those wave signals.

The wave signals are divided in small units of fixed size to be able to distribute among the BOINC clients (that would be located in any user computer operating as a *screen saver* when there are idle cycles). Then, each client computes the results in its spare time and sends it to the central server asking for more work to do. In this process, clients only need to be able to communicate with the server when they finish computations (or for asking more data). The client (application) is platform independent, in order to reach as many Internet users as possible. A ranking system allowed users to compete against other users, to motivate them to use this system. Thus, the most important lesson of SETI@Home project was that to attract and keep users, such projects should explain and justify their goals, research subject, and its impact. **BOINC** (Berkeley Open Infrastructure for Network Computing) [2] is a platform for distributed computing through volunteer computers; it emerged from the SETI@Home project and became useful to other projects.[12] Although each project has its' own topic and therefore their own computational differences, the BOINC system used for each project (client application) has to be unique.

Folding@Home [17] is an example of a BOINC system that studies protein folding, determining whether proteins assemble (or fold) themselves for a certain task or function; misfolding, which occurs when proteins do not fold correctly; and related diseases such as Alzheimer's, ALS, Huntington's, Parkinson's disease, and many types of cancers. The system uses distributed computing to simulate timescales, thousands to millions of times longer than previously achieved, which allows them to simulate actual protein folding and direct their approach to examine folding-related diseases.

Another example of a BOINC system is the **climateprediction.net** [34], that employs climate models to predict the Earth's climate up to the year 2100 and to test the accuracy of such models. This allows them to improve the understanding of how sensitive climate models are to small changes, e.g., in carbon dioxide and sulphur cycles. The project has many similarities with other BOINC systems, but the computational tasks are different. **Distributed Computing Projects** embody another approach to leverage spare cycles across the Internet. The first relevant projects to distributed computing were distributed.net and GIMPS. **Distributed.net** uses computers from all around the world to do brute-force decryption of RSA keys, and attempt to solve other large-scale problems. The initial project was to break the RC5-56bits algorithm, which took 250 days to locate the key (0x532B744CC20999). Other consequential projects like RC5-64bits, Optimal Golomb Rulers (OGR-24,

---

[12]BOINC projects: boinc.berkeley.edu/projects.php accessed on 13/10/2010

OGR-25, OGR-26), which is a mathematical term given to a set of whole numbers where no two pairs of numbers have the same difference, have also been concluded with varying times of 100–3,000 days, and currently they are trying to break the RC5-72bits algorithm and find the OGR-27.

The **GIMPS**[13] project uses the same concept of distributed computing to search for *Mersenne* prime numbers; these numbers are of the form $2^P - 1$ where P is a prime. The last known Mersenne prime (47th) that was found is $2^{43,112,609} - 1$, which has about 12.8 million digits. Both projects use their own Client and Server applications, following the same idea as the BOINC projects.

There are many other projects for distributed computing (List of Distributed Computing projects on Wikipedia.org). However, all of them have only one topic of research (for each project), meaning that each system does not have the flexibility of changing its own research topic. With BOINC Extensions for Community Cycle-Sharing (**nuBOINC** [32]), users without programming expertise may address the frequent difficulties in setting up the required infrastructures for BOINC systems and subsequently gather enough computer cycles for their own project. The nuBOINC extension is a customization of the BOINC system that allows users to create and submit tasks for distributed computing using available commodity applications. They try to bring global distributed computing to home users, using a public-resource sharing approach.

The main concept of **Ginger** (Grid Infrastructure for Non-grid Environments) [28, 33, 38] is that any home user may take advantage of idle cycles from other computers, much like SETI@Home. However, by donating idle cycles to other users to speedup their applications, they would also take advantage of idle cycles from other computers, to speedup the execution for their own applications. To leverage the process of sharing, Ginger introduces a novel application and programming model that is based on the *Gridlet* concept. *Gridlets* are work units containing chunks of data and the operations to be performed on that data. Moreover, every *Gridlet* has an estimated cost (CPU and bandwidth), so that they can try to be fair for every user that executes these *Gridlets*. This project also tries to span the boundaries of the typical grid usage, enabling the Internet users to take advantage of the Grid features, previously unavailable to the common user. The project also employs a P2P model to provide a large-scale deployment in a self-organized way. **Social-P2P** [19] is a social-like P2P algorithm for resource discovery. It mimics the way humans interact in Social Networks. Knowledge is passed on among people in these networks as a means of sharing information; moreover, people recall information in memory to find the right persons to interact with, when searching for a given resource. However, in most circumstances, people recall something because they had similar knowledge, or in the same context of the requesting resource, instead of actually knowing about it. A person may be recalled solely because of the information topics of the requested resource. Social-P2P makes use of this information in order to direct searches appropriately,

---

[13]The Great Internet Mersenne Prime Search: mersenne.org accessed on 05/01/2010.

by having community-based networks, and mimicking human interactions in Social Networks. This algorithm serves as a demonstration that human interaction strategies are successful for resource discovery in P2P networks. Nevertheless, in their simulations, a dynamic environment with only probabilistic request structure and file sharing was considered.

Deployment Mechanisms and Code Execution via the Web

To navigate through websites, for common users, the most common way is to use a *web browser* (i.e., Internet Explorer, Chrome, among others). Browsers are user applications (named clients) that follow generally a client-server architecture and they play an important role to access Internet content and achieve communication between people [7].

Furthermore, browsers and running applications contact servers by using a standard protocol named HTTP (Hypertext Transfer Protocol).[14] This protocol is used for retrieving interlinked resources, called hypertext documents. This protocol follows a request-response sequence of messages, where the basic request methods (or verbs) are *GET, POST, PUT,* and DELETE to, respectively, request a representation of the specified resource, submit data to be processed to the identified resource (this may result in the creation of a new resource or its update), submit a document to be stored in the server, and delete a document stored within the server, respectively.

Other languages can also be used either on the client or on the server, to generate HTML dynamic content [15], e.g., Asynchronous JavaScript and XML (AJAX)[15] being client side, Hypertext Preprocessor (PHP)[16] being server side.

AJAX [9] is an integration of consolidated technologies, such as JavaScript and XML, used to obtain new functionality and more control over the Browsers' contents. It is generally used to develop web applications that serve to interact with web servers without the users' knowledge or perception. It is able to provide the user with a continuous method of interaction (within the browser environment), meaning that the Javascript module fetches web contents and displays it to the user without having to switch to another web page (also called nonflickering effect).

Representational State Transfer (*REST*) [12] is a style of software architecture for distributed Hypermedia (including graphics, audio, video, plain text and hyper links) systems. The main concept is that existing resources can be referenced with a global identifier (e.g., URI in HTTP), and also the exchange of a representation of a resource can be applied without any constraint of state. However, the client may need to understand the format which the information (representation) is returned.

---

[14]HTTP 1.0 specification: www.ietf.org/rfc/rfc1945.txt accessed on 05/01/2010.

[15]AJAX article: adaptivepath.com/ideas/e000385 accessed on 05/01/2010.

[16]PHP website: php.net accessed on 05/01/2010.

Typically, the format used can be one of the following: HTML that consists of a document format with structural markers, XML generally used to represent arbitrary data structures, for example in web services, and JSON (JavaScript Object Notation) as a lightweight data-interchange format, made in order to ease the computational parsing of data. The last one is generally used on the web, because it is simpler for Browsers to parse and generate it, consuming less CPU time than other formats.

The Open Graph protocol was originally created at Facebook, and it is an extension to the HTTP protocol in order to enable web pages to become rich objects in a social environment. Any website can use this technology to organize information in a structured way, similar to Facebook pages. Also, it is built on standards (RDFa)[17] to create a more semantically aware web.

The idea of integrating distributed computing with web browsers has already surfaced on the Internet. An example to this is the Collaborative Map-Reduce[18]; this application code uses Javascript to interact with the web server, requesting jobs to be fulfilled by the users' Browser and posting the results back on the server. This method does not account for the lack of resources that the users' computers might have, or even a cycle-sharing environment. Furthermore, their concern was only to apply the Map-Reduce algorithm [11] on the data collected from the server. The Collaborative Map-Reduce would then use this algorithm combined with the processing power from users' computers from all over the world, to perform the algorithm steps while the user is browsing a website.

Another example of distributed computing using web browsers is Plura Processing,[19] which is a proprietary executable code made to enable idle cycle-stealing. Its main idea is that everyone that browses the Internet has idle cycles that could be used for other purposes, and thus they "steal" idle cycles from users' computers to perform determined tasks. It is claimed that users can sacrifice their CPU time, even without their knowledge, to benefit computationally intensive projects (much like SETI@Home). However, this approach may not be best to suite the users, because they need to understand the tasks' relevance (Plura Processing response to the Digsby Controversy in Wordpress.com). Moreover, they use simple web pages and games (Adobe Flash based) to embed their processing code to execute the needed tasks.

Analysis

Social Networks are popular infrastructures for communication, interaction and information sharing on the Internet. A user only needs his/her Internet enabled device (e.g., desktop computers, notebooks, mobile phones) to access web sites, such as Facebook, MySpace, Orkut, LinkedIn, and many others, to be able to send or receive personal or business information.

---

[17]RDFa standard: www.w3.org/TR/rdfa-in-html access on 23/08/2010.

[18]Collaborative Map-Reduce in the browser: tinyurl.com/ad248t accessed on 05/01/2010.

[19]Plura Processing: pluraprocessing.com accessed on 05/01/2010.

P2P networks, on the other hand, are mostly used for file sharing between users (either with desktop computers or mobile devices). However, these networks can also be used in other situations, such as cycle-sharing.

Some global distributed computing projects make use of distributed computing technologies to solve their computer resource shortage (CPU time) by using the millions of Internet enabled users' computers all over the world. On all these projects, we can say that they do not have the flexibility to change their own research topic (the goal of their data processing), and also only used to further advance their own research.

While there are other systems that give the ability of cycle-sharing to common users, each of them employ their own platforms to enable common applications to be executed on peers, not Social Networks. Moreover, some systems allow interaction only on P2P networks, meaning that their networks have to be created by the users.

Architecture

This work uses a Social Network (Facebook) to discover resources for the execution of Jobs (which are composed of *Gridlets* [38]) submitted by the users, and to discover the computer's full capabilities (e.g., processor information) and users' profiles, such as the groups which they belong to and their friends.

Users should be able to *install* CSSN, which is a web-enabled platform (Fig. 7.1), into their computers. Then, the user has the ability to *log in* into their Facebook account, by means of the *Facebook Connect*, which is a web page given by Facebook to enable the *log in* process for outside applications (known as Facebook applications).

Afterward, the client application is able to interact with the Social Network server, meaning that it intercepts/sends messages from/to other users or groups,

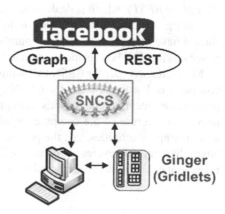

Fig. 7.1 Cycle-sharing in Social Networks global overview

while also discovering users' computer profiles by contacting the *Graph* server. The client application also gives the user the ability to initiate a Job, by using CSSN user interface.

To actually locate resources through the Social Network, CSSN has the ability of searching local resources, by means of the *SIGAR* library, that gives information, such as processor's status, memory available, among others. Such information is sent to other users upon request, or it can also be sent to the users' Wall, in order for everyone (people who have the ability to see the Wall) to get access to it. Note that this information may contain the programs that can be executed by a computer in the network to process *Gridlets*.

Cycle-Sharing in Social Networks must also have access to friends and groups through the Social Network API. It advertises users' availability to others, sending messages, and scheduling tasks (i.e., search for information, *Gridlet* acceptance) on them (Friends, Friends of Friend, Groups) in order to execute the tasks when users can spare their idle cycles (usually when they are in a *idle* or *away* state).

The main approach for CSSN is to have a client application split into two parts: one that interacts with the Social Network and another to interact with the users and the Ginger Middleware (in order to create and regroup *Gridlets*, which is out of the scope of this work [38]).

Design Requirements

The client application interacts with the Social Network (Facebook) through web Protocols named *Graph* and *REST* (which are an added layer to the HTTP protocol). As Facebook is still developing the *Graph* protocol and discontinuing the usage of *REST*, current operations within the client application make use of the first protocol, although some operations can only be executed by *REST*. This requires that the client application has to understand both protocols and interact at the same level (*Graph* or *REST*), which is dealt with the *RestFB* library.[20]

Another requirement for CSSN is to know the computer's information that it should have at its disposal, such as number of processors, available memory, or the programs that can be executed to process *Gridlets*.

Moreover, in order for CSSN to not interfere with the users, normal usage of their computer or Facebook page, the CSSN client schedules *Gridlets* according to user preferences, meaning that friends have priorities for executing their *Gridlets*. Also, to prevent overuse of the computer, while the user is in an *Online* state, CSSN is able to stop its activities, i.e., the processing of requests and *Gridlets* only happens when there are idle cycles to spare. The CSSN client also removes any unnecessary posts that could prevent the normal usage of the Facebook page.

---

[20]RestFb website: restfb.com accessed on 24/08/2010.

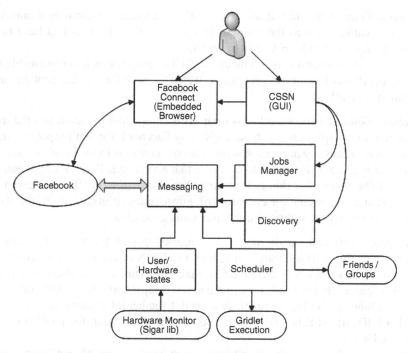

Fig. 7.2 Cycle-Sharing in Social Networks module view

CSSN Architecture

The CSSN architecture, depicted in Fig. 7.1, relies on an interaction with the Social Network through the Social Networks' API (*Graph* or *REST* protocols) for the purpose of searching and successfully executing Jobs; with the Ginger Middleware for *Gridlet* creation and aggregation; and also the user's operating system to acquire the information and hardware states that are needed.

Jobs are considered to be tasks initiated by the users, and containing more than one *Gridlet* to be processed in someone else's computer; all Jobs state what they require in order to execute those *Gridlets*, so that the client application can search for specific users or groups.

A *Gridlet* contains the information necessary to process it, meaning that it has the data file(s) to be transferred to another user and the arguments to be given to the executable program. The process of creating and aggregating the *Gridlets* is managed by the Ginger Middleware and is outside the scope of this work [38].

The architecture for CSSN is comprised of a set of components depicted in Fig. 7.2 and is described as follows.

CSSN (GUI): This module performs the main interaction with the user via a graphic interface. It is responsible to establish the connection to Facebook, by starting the

Facebook Connect module. It also loads all the necessary information onto the client application, such as the configuration of priorities, the Jobs that have been submitted, accepted and *Gridlets* in progress.

The user can submit a new Job using the GUI interface, which is responsible for starting the chain of events for processing that Job (search for users, acceptance and execution of *Gridlets*).

Facebook Connect (Embedded browser): This component authenticates the user to Facebook (it displays the web page given by Facebook for that purpose). Then, it extracts the necessary *access token* for consequent access to the Facebook server. This token is given by Facebook to everyone that accepts this Facebook application, and has to be renewed within a determined timeframe (the timeframe is given by Facebook and not specific for every token). Furthermore, it makes use of the JDIC library[21] to display the website for the user's authentication.

Messaging: This is the main module for interacting with the Social Network. It makes use of the *RestFb* library that creates the JSON or XML objects, which are required to access Facebook *Graph/REST* functions. This module also contains the options necessary to read and write to the users/groups/Application Wall (or feeds) Posts or Comments and removing them as well; to gather information such as users' Facebook ID, friend lists, and groups lists, and also to search for public Objects (Groups, Users).

Furthermore, some Facebook restrictions may apply to the interactions between the module and the Social Network, such as limiting the size of the messages, inability to erase Posts or Comments (made by other users).

The module also contains the schemas applied to the messages sent and retrieved, to specify what actions should be taken.

Jobs Manager: This is the module that runs a cycle of the following tasks (named "checking" cycle).

Verifying submitted Jobs that the user has in progress, and it assembles *Gridlets* to send to other users.

Check for new Jobs from the users' Wall, groups' Wall or Registration Post that can be processed by the users' machine, making sure that the required properties of the *Gridlets* are compatible, and thus accepting a Job.

Verify accepted Jobs, meaning that after accepting a Job a *Gridlet* message should have been sent to the user, although it is not guaranteed that the requesting user still has *Gridlets* to be processed.

Check for Job completion, when the client application has submitted a Job or a *Gridlet*, it should be able to detect if it has been completed. When a *Gridlet* is not completed successfully, the module can resend it to someone that has accepted the Job.

---

[21] JDIC: http://jdic.dev.java.net accessed on 15/10/2010.

Check for messages that the client application needs to redirect to its friends; this method is necessary because Facebook restricts conversations to only the users that are considered friends.

Check for messages that have been redirected to the user, in order for CSSN to answer on the Registration Post (in the Applications' Wall), that was made prior by the requesting user. This adds the functionality of reaching other people rather than only the users' friends, also the content of these messages should be requests to fulfill a Job or to send their computer information to the requesting user.

Also, after CSSN has acquired a *Gridlet* message, it hands it to the scheduler module (described later) for ulterior execution. Moreover, this module has the task to remove all the Posts that are no longer necessary. This module can be stopped if the computer is in an *Online* state, in order to not interfere with the normal computer's usage.

Discovery: This module searches for friends and groups, in order to reach as many people as possible, to complete a Job. It sends messages to friends so that they can redirect those to their own friends (Friends of Friends method), while also sending messages to groups of interest for that specific Job.

This module is responsible to *register* the user in the Applications' Wall, meaning that every user has a Post on this Wall, in order for other users (that are unable to directly contact them), to interact as if they were friends.

User/HW States: This module determines the state of the local resources and takes into consideration the processors' idle times, the Internet connectivity (that is essential to all processes) and the users Facebook state, in order to yield execution to a later time, when the processor has idle cycles to spare. In addition, it sends the state of the CSSN client (*Online*, *Offline*, *Idle*) to the Social Network in order to inform other users of its state. The state *Online* should be active when the user has decided that the client application should run. The *Idle* takes place when the computer has idle cycles to spare, but it does not take into account the fact that the computer is being used and also if the user does wish that the client application needs to be *Offline*, the latter state prevails. The *Offline* state means that the client application does not process any messages or *Gridlets*, stopping all processes related to this fact, because either there is no Internet connection (which is needed on the overall process) or that the user explicitly does not want CSSN to be running.

This module uses a submodule, named Hardware Monitor depicted in Fig. 7.2, that is comprised of the *SIGAR* library, which reports the system information needed to determine the availability of the resources.

Scheduler: This module is an addition to the *Gridlet* processing, making use of the priority lists, while also stopping its process when the computer does not have idle cycles.

The priority list consists of friends and other people added by the user, in order for the client application to use the idle cycles on *Gridlets* belonging to the people with the highest priorities meaning that some *Gridlets* wait for a conclusion of others even if they arrived first.

This module starts a submodule that is responsible for processing the *Gridlet*; it performs data transfer, executes the program that processes the data, and upon completion informs the originator of the *Gridlet* state by sending a message to Facebook telling where it should retrieve the completed *Gridlet* or if the *Gridlet* was not completed successfully (may occur when there is an error on the executing program or client application).

CSSN Communications

CSSN interacts with the user and the Social Network, and therefore a protocol or flow of communication has to be established. The following demonstrates how the creation and execution of the *Gridlets* is being carried out.

The task for creating a Job, which can be comprised of several *Gridlets*, is initiated by the user by submitting the Job on the CSSN GUI. The information for a Job consists of the following items: the program that executes the *Gridlets*; the commands or arguments that are given to that program; the data file(s) that the client application needs to transfer; the number of *Gridlets* that comprises the Job (although this should be determined by the Ginger Middleware); and the requirements to execute the *Gridlets*.

A search for resources is specified by the *Gridlets* requirements, e.g., a Job that consists of generating an image on POV-Ray, which needs 4 processors and 2,048 Mb of memory. The client application uses this information in order to gather users that have such resources (including the processing application) available.

After the user submits a Job, CSSN starts to perform the actions to complete it, such as sending a message onto the users' Facebook Wall and waiting for other users to respond to it; starting the discovery process that is able to find friends and groups that would be interested and/or have the capability of executing the specified Job (as illustrated in Fig. 7.3).

There is an impossibility of directly contacting people and groups that are not in the friends' domain, such as Friends of Friends (FoFs). To handle this, CSSN client routes messages to the users' friends, in order for them to forward those messages to their own friends, making them viable to contact FoFs. The scale for this type of messaging could be larger, i.e., the message could reach people that are our Nth degree friend, but it may end up *Spamming* users, and such actions are considered as a violation of the Facebook Use terms.[22] As such, CSSN only goes as further as FoFs (2nd degree). The client application only contacts the users' groups that are able to help for the specific Job. It searches for computer information in order to determine the ones capable of processing the Job.

The discovery mechanism of CSSN tries to gather as much computer information as possible, and sends messages to the corresponding users and groups. Meanwhile the Job part stays alert for incoming messages on the users' Wall that may carry requests or stating availability.

---

[22]Facebook Use Terms: facebook.com/terms.php accessed on 26/08/2010.

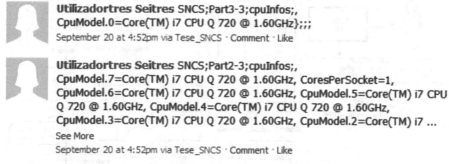

Utilizadortres Seitres SNCS;Part3-3;cpuInfos;,
CpuModel.0=Core(TM) i7 CPU Q 720 @ 1.60GHz};;;
September 20 at 4:52pm via Tese_SNCS · Comment · Like

Utilizadortres Seitres SNCS;Part2-3;cpuInfos;,
CpuModel.7=Core(TM) i7 CPU Q 720 @ 1.60GHz, CoresPerSocket=1,
CpuModel.6=Core(TM) i7 CPU Q 720 @ 1.60GHz, CpuModel.5=Core(TM) i7 CPU
Q 720 @ 1.60GHz, CpuModel.4=Core(TM) i7 CPU Q 720 @ 1.60GHz,
CpuModel.3=Core(TM) i7 CPU Q 720 @ 1.60GHz, CpuModel.2=Core(TM) i7 ...
See More
September 20 at 4:52pm via Tese_SNCS · Comment · Like

Utilizadortres Seitres SNCS;Part1-3;cpuInfos;{CpuVendor.7=Intel,
TotalCores=8, CpuVendor.6=Intel, SNCS=100001446852547,
CpuMhz.7=1596, CpuVendor.5=Intel, CpuMhz.6=1596, CpuVendor.4=Intel,
CpuMhz.5=1596, CpuVendor.3=Intel, CpuMhz.4=1596, CpuVendor.2=Intel,
CpuVendor.1=Intel, CpuMhz.3=1596, CpuVendor.0=Intel, CpuMhz.2=1596,
CpuMhz.1=1596, CpuM...
See More
September 20 at 4:52pm via Tese_SNCS · Comment · Like

Fig. 7.3 Example of the computer information message on Facebook

The people that receive messages (FoFs) and are not capable of directly contacting the originator use the Registration Post on the Applications' Wall to respond to the redirected messages. This serves as a means of interaction with everyone that has the Facebook application (client application), which enables the process of searching for people outside the scope of friendship.

Their client applications then tries to match their own information to the expected Jobs and accept them accordingly, by sending an *Accept* or *Deny* message back to the originator. If the Job has been accepted, the client application try to fetch a *Gridlet* in order to execute it locally.

The transfer of *Gridlet's* data occurs after a client application has retrieved the *Gridlet* message, and determined that it has idle cycles to execute it. The transfer can employ a direct connection between the CSSN clients (acting as peers). This may also be carried out by having a repository server or by sending the data file along with the message (if permitted by the Social Networks' Use terms).

If the CSSN client determines that the execution of a *Gridlet* has failed, due to the processing program returning an error code, it sends a message to the originator informing that the *Gridlet* could not be completed. In case the error was within the client application, such as a client application crash, CSSN can still reacquire the *Gridlet* from the users' Wall, to repeat it, if the message was not deleted.

Afterward, the originator of the Job receives all the *Gridlets* that have been processed, using the same means of transfer, and pass them to the Ginger Middleware for aggregation.

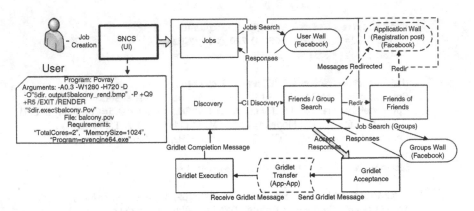

Fig. 7.4 CSSN Prototypical example

Prototypical Example

We describe a more detailed example of a Job submission and the steps CSSN takes to process it, as depicted in Fig. 7.4.

A user submits a Job, using the CSSN GUI, with the following properties.

The client application needs to execute the program named pvengine64.exe, with the arguments "-A0.3 -W1280 -H720 -D -O'$dir.output$balcony_rend.bmp' -P +Q9 +R5 /EXIT /RENDER '$dir.exec$balcony.pov'", meaning that the Pov-Ray program will render an image with $1,280 \times 720$ dimensions, using Anti-aliasing, with high quality and it requires the file balcony.pov to start the process, which should be downloaded from 127.0.0.1:52392/balcony.pov. The user also specifies what the program needs, such as "TotalCores=2", "MemorySize=1024", "Program=pvengine64.exe" and the number of *Gridlets* that comprises this Job.

CSSN then starts the search for resources using the specified requirements; the requirements should be as accurate as possible to search for specific groups and users. To locate the resources, a client starts by sending a Job search message to the users' Wall. Meanwhile, it also requests the computers information (CI discovery) from the people that are in the user's groups, in order to know which of the groups would be willing to accept the Job. Also, it tries to send a message to the user's friends in order for them to redirect to their own friends (FoFs method), waiting for a reply on the Applications' Wall. The last message contains the information necessary to redirect it, i.e., the Post ID for which it should be sent, and the type of message that the user should send (in this case their computer information).

Afterward, CSSN reads the responses to the Job search, which can be accept or deny messages, meaning that even if someone would have the requirements to process the *Gridlets*, a user may not have idle cycles to spare, and thus denying the request. For the users that accept the Job, CSSN sends a *Gridlet* message; until all the *Gridlets* have been sent, this message is then received by the processing client application.

The client application does not verify the correct completion of the *Gridlets*, although this process should be included in order to give greater reliability assurance. However, the reassignment of a *Gridlet* occurs in case the processing client application encounters an error while executing it, sending an error message back to the originator.

In this example, the client application uses a direct transfer method to send the "balcony.pov" file, although other methods can be used such as sending the file to a web server and retrieving the results with the same method. Moreover, the *Gridlet* message contains the necessary information in order for this client application to locate and retrieve the necessary data to be processed.

The CSSN client receiving a request, before it downloads the data file, needs to consider the execution of the *Gridlet*, according to the computers' state and from whom it has originated, creating a queue of *Gridlets* when necessary.

From this example, the client application receiving the request would then call the program pvengine64.exe, that the user specified its location on the "Programs List", i.e., D:\Pov-ray\bin\pvengine64.exe, with the right arguments, waiting until the process finishes. After that, it sends a message to the originators' client application informing that it has completed and where it should retrieve the resulting file, this process also uses the same method as for the transfer of "balcony.pov" file, although it is also considered that other methods can be used.

To finish the interactions between the two users, the originators' client application sends a message to the users' Wall that has completed the *Gridlet*, thanking them for the time they have spent on it, when this is not possible (FoFs case), the message is sent to the originator users' Wall, in order to have a record of people that helped in a Job.

The originator of the Job requires that every *Gridlet* finishes, before it can pass them to the Ginger Middleware. Thus, it waits for all completion messages before it can erase the resulting messages from Facebook. Moreover, while the originator client application is performing this overall process, it also listens for Job search messages that can appear on friends and groups, in order to give its own idle cycles to other users.

Implementation

The implementation of CSSN aims for a simple use by the end-users. Also, the different types of operating systems lead us to favor portability; therefore, we used Java as the main language. We chose to use Facebook over other alternatives, such as OpenSocial-based networks, because Facebook has a higher number of registered users than any other Social Networks. Another consideration was the fact that Facebook exports its own API and many libraries (such as *RestFB*) have been created to facilitate the usage of the API.

This section gives an insight on how the technologies were used, such as *Graph* and *REST* protocols. It also explains the schemas used for the messages sent/received to/from the Social Network chosen. The section ends with a view of some of the constraints that CSSN suffered from using Facebook as the Social Network for users' interactions.

Technology Employed

For the purpose of interacting with the *Graph* and *REST* servers, the client application makes use of the *RestFb* library, that gives a simple and flexible way of connecting to them and conceal the use of XML or JSON objects.[23] However, the functions (using REST) or connections (using Graph) have to be known, in order to use this library, e.g., to read the Posts on a users' Wall using the Graph protocol, we need a users' ID or Name in order for the library to access Facebook and retrieve that users' Wall.

The IDs generated for each object are dependent on the previous objects, meaning that the UID for a Comment on a Post on a Users' Wall would become "UserID_PostID_CommentID" which uniquely identifies the Comment belonging to the Post of that particular users' Wall.

Moreover, Facebook gives the possibility for external client applications to authenticate a user by means of their own Facebook Connect system, which is a web page dedicated for the *Log in* process. Also, for the client applications to gain access to Facebook pages, it has to be authorized by the users and given an *access token*, generated by the use of the *OAuth 2.0* protocol.[24]

For the purpose of displaying the Facebook Connect web page, we make use of the *JDIC* library. This enables us to display a website[25] to the users for the authentication process.

As CSSN also needs to gather the information about the local resources of the users' computer, we make use of the *SIGAR* library.[26] This allows us to easily access a list of local resources each time it is called, such as CPUs, cores, memory. Also, it gives us the ability to know the current states of those resources, i.e., it can give us the available memory at the requesting time, or even the current idle time for each of the available cores or CPUs. This library is also useful for the fact that it can work in multiple environments, such as Windows, Linux, among others, making possible the portability of CSSN to other systems.

---

[23] JSON: json.org accessed on 15/10/2010.
[24] Facebook Authentication methods: tinyurl.com/24edrkg accessed on 27/08/2010.
[25] Tese_CSSN Application Facebook Page: tinyurl.com/6duzlmc accessed on 15/10/2010.
[26] SIGAR library: hyperic.com/products/sigar accessed on 15/10/2010.

Utilizador Sei SNCS;Job;100001089184602;TotalCores=8;Me morySize=4072;Program=pvengine64.exe;

5 seconds ago via Tese_SNCS · Comment · Like

Fig. 7.5 Example of Job Search message on Users' Wall

Message Schemas

CSSN uses Facebook to send and retrieve messages via the Facebook API. It reads Posts (messages that are contained in the users' Wall, groups' Wall) and Comments (messages contained within the Posts), and writes other messages on users' Wall (which is a space that contains messages) either as Posts or Comments.

Posts can only be used between users that are considered friends or in known groups, and therefore the people and groups that the user cannot directly contact do so via the Applications' Wall by commenting on users' Posts (Registration Post). This Post is either created by the users or it can be created automatically by the client application when it needs to reach FoFs. This method is used to bypass the inability of contacting other people rather than just direct friends.

In CSSN, we make use of the *RestFB* library, which gives us the flexibility of contacting Facebook without knowing JSON objects are being sent. Also, the library gives us a generic Java object that it uses to map the JSON objects to it. However, some Facebook objects cannot be mapped to a generic Java object, which requires us to create Java objects compatible with the JSON objects, in order to acquire the information sent from Facebook.

For the communication between the client applications using Facebook, we use our own Schemas. Much because Facebook does not allow some types of message schemas, such as XML based.

These Schemas make use of an ordinary separator of *Strings*, as depicted in Fig. 7.5. Regarding messages that can be longer than the limit imposed by Facebook, such as the Computer information messages (Fig. 7.3), they are split into various messages and an indicator of more messages alike is inserted in the schema ("PartX-Y"), which is read by the client application, informing it is not the only part that has to be fetched, and it needs to fetch Y messages.

These Schemas are very simple and human readable, in order for Facebook to allow them on the website, and not consider them as "Spam" or other type of blocked messages. They are also human readable to assure the users what information is being sent to other users.

The Schemas represented in Figs. 7.5 and 7.6 give us the idea of how it appears to the users in their Walls and in the registration Post in the Applications' Wall (FoFs method), respectively. Moreover, these messages are comprised of the Jobs' requirements and the JobID in case of the Applications' Wall (which contains the UserID). Also, in Fig. 7.6, we can see that the user has responded to the Job Search with an accept message.

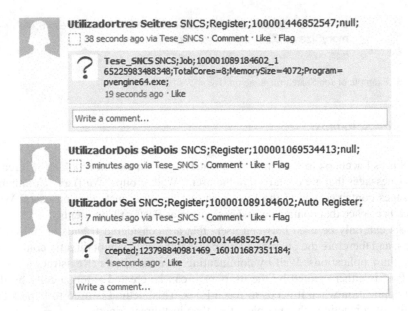

Fig. 7.6 Example of Job Search and Acceptance messages in Applications' Wall

CSSN Constraints

The decision of using Facebook as the Social Network for interactions between people has brought some constraints due to the limitations that Facebook enforces, either with the Use Terms or their API.

In order to interact between users, the client application normally uses the Posts method, which cannot be guaranteed between users that are not friends. As such, we use the method of redirecting messages, by sending it to a friends' Wall, so that the users' client application can direct it to the proper Wall, meaning its friends (the FoFs method). To reduce traffic "spam," we avoid loops in message exchanges among users who are friends.

In the case of sending messages, Facebook has limited the size of the messages that can be sent by outside applications (in the order of 420 characters), and the method used to circumvent it was to split messages in smaller ones, making the client application verify from all the Posts their message type and from whom they belong to.

Evaluation

In this section, we present the evaluation of CSSN regarding its performance, stability and viability for using a Social Network to achieve public-resource sharing. Our focus is demonstrating the practicality of resource and service discovery, by

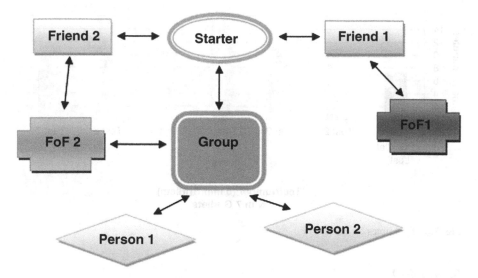

Fig. 7.7 CSSN Scenario 1 view

recruiting as many users as possible to execute *Gridlets*. We also evaluate integration with the normal usage of the Social Network, which in the user's point of view would be the amount of information perceived in the Social Network, which should be kept minimal. Finally, as CSSN is designed to provide idle cycles to be used to process the upcoming *Gridlets* with real world applications, the client application was tested with ray-tracing jobs in a "more realistic" environment as described in this section. In order to perform all the tests, we constructed several scenarios, where the environment for each would change. In these scenarios, we changed the number of users involved and also their roles, i.e., in Scenario 1, as depicted in Fig. 7.7, we considered two friends, two FoF and a group with three users, where one of them was a FoF. The number of *Gridlets* as 7 and the processing time is only 5 min for each *Gridlet*.

In Scenario 2, as depicted in Fig. 7.10, a "more realistic" scenario is considered, where there are Friends, FoF and other people connected by a Group, while also increasing the number of Jobs to 2, and the total number of *Gridlets* to 15, with the same processing time for each *Gridlet* as before.

For the last scenario, we considered to execute *Gridlets* in a real program (Pov-Ray) which renders an image, to understand exactly the consequences of the added overheads of CSSN to the overall process.

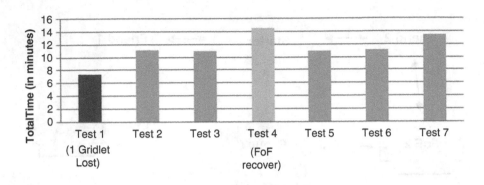

Fig. 7.8 Total times for Scenario 1

Scenario 1

Scenario 1 brings us a view of a Social Network, where the user Starter is connected to two Friends, who are connected to one FoF each and a group with three other people, where one of them is a FoF. The number of *Gridlets* is 7 and their processing time is of only 5 min.

For this scenario, we assume that the client applications have "registered" in the Applications' Wall, that each of the group members has already accepted group membership and that the client application is already running in the users' computers. Moreover, we assume that the time to process a realistic *Gridlet* can be more than 5 min and therefore the time spent is sufficient to determine the viability of using the Social Network to achieve our works' goals, and also the processing time of a *Gridlet* data does not change the inherited overheads of CSSN. In this scenario, the requirements to process a *Gridlet* are "TotalCores=2; MemorySize=4078; Program=Gridlet.exe", and each CSSN client who processes the *Gridlet* is able to accept its conditions (however, they still need to assess if they have idle cycles to spare). In the results for this scenario, as depicted in Fig. 7.8, we can see that the times to complete a Job were in the order of 11 min. Although, in Test 1, the user FoF2 did not receive the last *Gridlet* as it was supposed to, and in Test 4, the user FoF2 crashed and recovered the last *Gridlet* in time to repeat its execution and complete it. These situations show that the total times will be hindered by the fact that people are not always in a *Away* state and also by giving more than one *Gridlet* to the same user, the Job will have longer completion times. However, we cannot always expect to find as many users as the number of *Gridlets* needed to complete a Job.

We can also see that the overhead of CSSN is minimal considering the processing time of the *Gridlets*, which makes it possible to have speedups on data processing. However, we cannot estimate the exact added time of the Social Network usage, since these times can vary with the Social Networks' traffic load at the time of use.

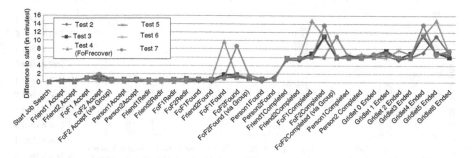

Fig. 7.9 Communication times for Scenario 1

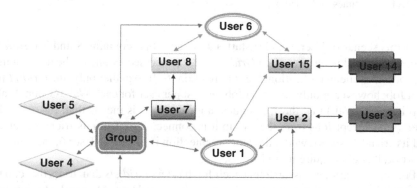

Fig. 7.10 CSSN Scenario 2 view

Figure 7.9 explains in detail how much time each task takes in relation with the starting point. It can take less than 1 min for users' client applications to find and accept new Jobs. The higher spikes are caused by the fact that the client application only found the *Gridlet* some minutes later due to its *Offline* state and between the found tasks and completed tasks (for each user) we can see the processing time of the *Gridlet* (5 min).

Scenario 2

Scenario 2 is an attempt to test CSSN in a more realistic environment, having a more complex network of users. As depicted in Fig. 7.10, we have two users who start a Job (User 1 and 6), where User 1 has three Friends (User 2, 7 and 15), User 6 has two Friends (User 8 and 15). User 2 and 15 have each a FoF not connected to anyone else. Also, we created a group with six people (User 1, 2, 4, 5, 6 and 7). The layout of this network is made in an attempt to maximize the diversity of the users' roles, making it possible for a Job request to reach any kind of users.

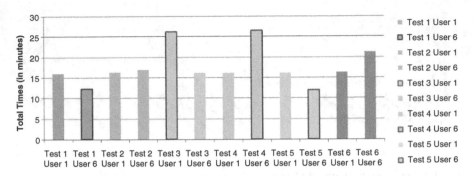

Fig. 7.11 Total times for Scenario 2

In this scenario, User 1 and 6 start a Job each, that contains 8 and 7 *Gridlets*, respectively, making a total of 15 *Gridlets* to be processed by any of the users in this network. The client application does not restrain itself to gather only one *Gridlet* for each Job; however, it only accepts a Job request per user for each Wall (Group, Wall, Applications' Wall) that the Job request appears in. This means that, for example, User 7 can accept Jobs from the Group it is connected to, from its friend (User 1), and its friend (User 8), where the latter connection is of FoF to User 6; thus, in this network, it could acquire four *Gridlets*.

For this scenario, we assume that each Job has less *Gridlets* than users that can be connected to a user submitting requests (e.g., User 1 and User 6), in order to simulate a larger network where the user could have potentially hundreds of connections, that could either accept or deny the request. Each client application must already be "registered" in the Applications' Wall, the group members already established and the client application be running prior to the Jobs submissions. Furthermore, the two Jobs are started roughly around the same time in order for the client applications to retrieve the *Gridlets* in any given order.

The results for Scenario 2, as depicted in Fig. 7.11, bring us closer to understand how CSSN performs in a realistic environment. In this scenario, we can see that the total times can vary depending on factors such as number of *Gridlets*, users' states (*Offline* versus *Online*), number of users/groups involved, Social Network latency, and use of concurrent *Gridlets* (or *Gridlet* queue).

The times on this scenario are around 16 min to complete both Jobs; however, we can see that in Test 1 and 5, the Job initiated by User 6 was completed 5 min earlier than in the other tests; this is due to the fact that the *Gridlets* were evenly distributed among the available users.

In Test 4, as depicted in Fig. 7.12, we can see the added time due to the Social Network latency, where two of the *Gridlets* were retrieved only after all other *Gridlets* were already processed, thus hindering CSSN performance.

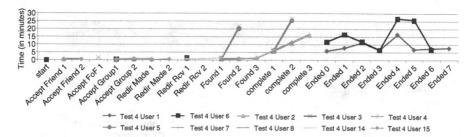

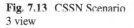

Fig. 7.12 Communication times for Scenario 2 Test 4

Fig. 7.13 CSSN Scenario
3 view

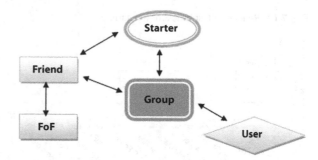

Scenario 3

Scenario 3 was designed in order to evaluate the performance with a real program that renders images. In this scenario, as depicted in Fig. 7.13, we have one friend, one FoF and two users in a group (not counting with the user Starter), where one of them is the friend. The goal of this scenario is to know if CSSN can function with a real processing program, such as Pov-Ray, which is used in the tests. For each test, the number of *Gridlets* to be completed is 4 and their execution times in the processing computers are undefined, as they depend on the computers' hardware states and capabilities. However, the first data file (for Test 1) is smaller than the second one (used in Test 2) and Test 3 uses the same file as the second test, but with different rendering options. Furthermore, we use a direct transfer method to retrieve the data files in both ways (Starter to User and vice versa) for each test. Also, we assume that the client applications are running prior to the start of the Job.

Test 1 is initiated with the property arguments as being:

"-A0.3 -W1280 -H720 -D -O'$dir.output$abyss_rend.bmp' -P +Q9 /EXIT /RENDER '$dir.exec$ abyss.pov' "

and the program property as "pvengine64.exe", which in every CSSN is defined (by the user) in the "Programs list".

For Test 2, the arguments property is altered to become

"-A0.3 -W1280 -H720 -D -O'$dir.output$balcony_rend.bmp' -P +Q9 +R5 /EXIT /RENDER '$dir.exec$balcony.pov' " and with the same program parameter as the latter test.

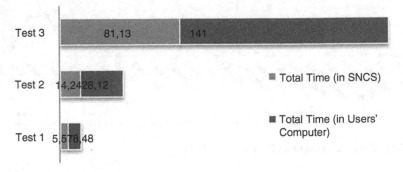

Fig. 7.14 Rendering test times for Scenario 3

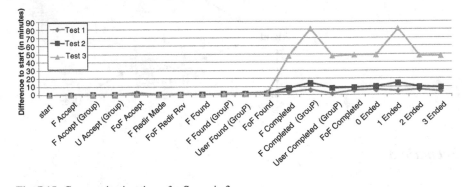

Fig. 7.15 Communication times for Scenario 3

In Test 3, we modify the arguments property to be:

"-A0.0 -W3921 -H2767 -R200 -D -O'$dir.output$balcony_render.bmp' -P +Q9 /EXIT /RENDER '$dir.exec$balcony.pov' ", which modifies the images properties, such as anti-aliases, resolution and how many rays POV-Ray will supersample with when it is anti-aliasing, in order to have a longer running *Gridlet*, and also the program property still remains the same.

The results for Scenario 3 confirmed that CSSN can gain speedups against local execution, as depicted in Fig. 7.14, where we have the total times of Test 1 around 6 min, Test 2 around 14 min and Test 3 with 81 min.

Furthermore, in all the tests, the friend user processes 2 *Gridlets*, meaning that it queues one to be processed when it has idle cycles to spare. We can also see in Fig. 7.15 that although each task can take some time to execute, the average performance can be acceptable for *Gridlets* that have higher processing times.

Moreover, the first test suffers from communication latency, i.e., the task FoF Accept (accepting the Job from the Applications' Wall) takes more time to execute than in the second test.

Test 3 demonstrates that with longer running *Gridlets*, the variables that hinder the overall performance can be amortized by the difference that it would take to process all the data in the user's computer.

Discussion

When comparing with local execution, CSSN decreased the total processing time, compared to what it would have consumed in the users' computers, meaning that CSSN achieves overall speedups on Jobs.

We can also state that the overhead that CSSN imposes on the overall process is minimal compared to the time it takes to process a *Gridlet*, which in realistic terms it can be more than 1 h. However, times can be hindered from the fact that searching for resources may not return positive results, or that the total resources available are less than the number of *Gridlets* to be processed, or even that latency of Facebook servers may vary with their global traffic load.

We can also conclude that the number of messages varies with the number of users (friends, FoFs and groups) that comes in contact with the Job, while varying with the number of *Gridlets* comprising the Job.

We can state that the number of messages sent to Facebook are proportionally increased by the number of users in the network, meaning that a Job may receive as many accepts and denies messages as users in the network. Although, the user may not be aware of this in the long run, because those messages are erased when they are no longer needed, making a clean environment in Facebook, meaning that we can accomplish our goal of making CSSN viable to use Facebook without hindering the usage of the Social Network.

We can also conclude that the method used to contact FoFs hinders the total times, although in our tests the delays were not significant as compared to the overall process.

Moreover, we can confirm that the users can donate their resources (CPU time) for other users' consumption and for users' groups that would have interest in acquiring more processing power. Also, takes advantage of other users' resources with the same interests (or in the same groups) to further speedup their own programs.

In conclusion, even with the latency variables and excess messages introduced by the interaction between users, using a Social Network, CSSN can definitely use the dispersed and idle resources available on these networks to speedup application execution, that would take more time in the users' computer.

Conclusion

In this project, we presented a new method of resource and service discovery through the use of a Social Network. It is also considered that by making use of a Social Network already established, we can involve more people to donate their computers' idle cycles. Also, we analyzed Peer-to-Peer networks and Grids to understand the related problems like efficient resource discovery, while also analyzing Social Networks and user interactions to understand how we can achieve our works' goals.

The idea of distributed computing has enabled other projects to create environments to execute common applications used by desktop computer users. Anyone can join or create their own network to share and receive idle cycles for their own usage. However, this may not be practical for common users, because they might not have the resources or capabilities to gather enough users (or computers) for their problems. This idea suites small networks within communities, or enterprises in order to gather idle cycles for common applications' execution.

Social Networks were a step forward for user interactions in the Internet, since websites, such as Facebook and MySpace are used for personal or business interactions at any given time, i.e., friends interactions or advertising.

Studies done to these networks demonstrate that they follow some properties of Small-World networks. On these networks, a user can reach another with just a few links; moreover, there is a small group of users with many links (to others) and a larger group with fewer links. We can also see this in a P2P perspective, where users with many links are super-peers connected by users with fewer links (peers). This leads us to believe that we could utilize these networks for other purposes, other than messaging and interaction, much like using P2P networks for global distributed computing.

Our work describes Cycle-Sharing in Social Networks (CSSN), a web-enabled platform, which is designed to use Facebook, to search for potential idle resources available on this type of network, also enabling public-resource sharing within a Social Network.

The main approach for CSSN is to have a client application split into two parts. One that interacts with the Social Network using *REST* or *Graph* protocols and another to interact with the users' computers for local resource discovery, and the Ginger Middleware for creation and aggregation of *Gridlets*.

CSSN main concern is to actually achieve resource and application discovery, while being able to perform resource sharing; thus, our works' primary concerns were to utilize users' computers in a way that would help common users to share their resources (when not needed) and to use others' resources to gain computational cycles for their own applications. After a successful submission of a Job, the CSSN requesting client starts a search for resources that could meet the requirements of that particular Job. Moreover, it sends a Job Search message to the users' friends, to groups which could have the capabilities to process the Job, and also to the users' friends of friends (FoFs).

We evaluated CSSN with scenarios to determine how it would manage in such environments. Several scenarios were created in order to test CSSN regarding its performance, stability and viability for using a Social Network to achieve cycle-sharing and resource and application discovery. These ranged from a simple one to derive speedup and latency measurements to more sophisticated ones with more diverse user's roles, and employing real applications such as **Pov-Ray**.

With the obtained results, we can conclude that while the total times for processing a Job gained speedups against local execution in the users' computers, this can be hindered by some variables: latencyof Facebook servers, the fact that searching for resources among Social Networks users may not return positive results, and that the total number of available resources is less than the number of *Gridlets* that comprises a Job.

However, with functional and quantitative evaluation, we can conclude that the results are encouraging despite the overheads introduced by the variable Facebook latency, and the intermediate messaging among FoFs. In fact, with CSSN, Jobs are completed faster than in the user's computer, also releasing it for other tasks. The performance gains would increase with longer running *Gridlets* (more realistically about 1 h) by amortizing overheads attributable to Facebook and communication.

We can conclude that our works' goals have been successfully met. It is possible to utilize a Social Network to perform resource and service discovery, and also global distributed computing. Furthermore, by introducing the concept of global resource sharing to Social Network users, we believe that any common user can utilize CSSN to make use of idle resources scattered across the world to further advance process parallelization and continue decrease in processing waiting times. We also hope that this project may contribute to the study and advancements made to novel cycle-sharing models.

Future Work: In the future, we plan to augment the testing scenarios to address the issues of having a realistic environment, completing it with results of real peoples' usage and longer running *Gridlets*. We intend to extend the use of processing programs to include more common applications, such as video encoding, among others.

Moreover, we believe that Jobs completion and the search for resources would benefit with requirements' semantics, increasing the chance to direct *Gridlets* to peoples' computers that would satisfy the requirements.

Also, the use of topic ontologies would greatly help in determining the number of users that may be able to help in a Job, while also focusing on those users that have more interest in such topics. Thus, CSSN could search for specific groups using the Jobs' topics as a point of reference, in order to obtain the groups that would be more favorable to that particular Job.

Furthermore, we could extend the parameters of cycle-sharing to perform a form of advance scheduling: CSSN would request resources before starting a Job in order to avoid the lack of resources, and decrease the overheads attributable to resource discovery in the Job search requests.

Moreover, to continue further development of CSSN and study on our works' goals, we plan to support other Social Networks, to perform cycle-sharing between the users. Also, we plan to substitute the need of having a stand-alone application, by embedding the CSSN client with the Browser, in order to gather resources and process *Gridlets* while the users are navigating through the Social Network or the Internet.

References

1. Amaral, L.A.N., Scala, A., Barthelemy, M., Stanley, H.E.: Classes of small-world networks. Proc. Natl. Acad. Sci. USA **97**(21), 11149–11152 (2000)
2. Anderson, D.P.: BOINC: a system for public-resource computing and storage. In: Proceedings of the 5th IEEE/ACM International Workshop on Grid Computing, pp. 4–10. IEEE Computer Society (2004)
3. Anderson, D.P., Cobb, J., Korpela, E., Lebofsky, M., Werthimer, D.: SETI@ home: an experiment in public-resource computing. Commun. ACM **45**(11), 56–61 (2002)
4. Androutsellis-Theotokis, S., Spinellis, D.: A survey of peer-to-peer content distribution technologies. ACM Comput. Surv. **36**(4), 335–371 (2004)
5. Armbrust, M., Fox, A., Griffith, R., Joseph, A.D., Katz, R.H., Konwinski, A., Lee, G., Patterson, D.A., Rabkin, A., Stoica, I. et al.: A view of cloud computing. Commun. ACM **53**(4), 50–58 (2010)
6. Backstrom, L.: Group formation in large social networks: membership, growth, and evolution. In: In KDD '06: Proceedings of the 12th ACM SIGKDD International Conference on Knowledge Discovery and Data Mining, pp. 44–54. ACM (2006)
7. Boldrin, F., Taddia, C. and Mazzini G.: Distributed computing through web browser. In: 2007 IEEE 66th Vehicular Technology Conference, VTC-2007 Fall, pp. 2020–2024 (2007)
8. Chard, K., Caton, S., Rana, O., Bubendorfer, K.: Social cloud: cloud computing in social networks. In: 2010 IEEE 3rd International Conference on Cloud Computing, pp. 99–106. IEEE (2010)
9. Crane, D., Pascarello, E., James, D.: Ajax in Action. Manning Publications Co., Greenwich (2005)
10. Crespo, A., Garcia-Molina, H.: Routing indices for peer-to-peer systems. In: International Conference on Distributed Computing Systems, vol. 22, pp. 23–34. IEEE Computer Society (1999, 2002)
11. Dean, J. and Ghemawat, S.: MapReduce: simplified data processing on large clusters. Commun. ACM **51**(1), 107–113 (2008)
12. Fielding, R.T., Taylor, R.N.: Principled design of the modern web architecture. ACM Trans. Internet Tech. **2**(2), 115–150 (2002)
13. Figueiredo, R.J., Boykin, P., Juste, P. and Wolinsky, D.: Integrating overlay and social networks for seamless p2p networking. In: 2008 IEEE 17th Workshop on Enabling Technologies: Infrastructure for Collaborative Enterprises (WETICE'08), pp. 93–98. IEEE (2008)
14. Foster, I., Kesselman, C., Nick, J.M., Tuecke, S.: Grid services for distributed system integration. IEEE Computer **35**(6), 37–46 (2002)
15. Goodman, D.: Dynamic HTML: The Definitive Reference. O'Reilly and Associates, Inc., Sebastopol (1998)
16. Knutsson, B., Lu, H., Xu, W., Hopkins, B.: Peer-to-peer support for massively multiplayer games. In: IEEE INFOCOM, vol. 1, pp. 96–107. IEEE (2004)
17. Larson, S.M., Snow, D., Shirts, M., Pande Vijay, S.: Folding@home and genome@home: using distributed computing to tackle previously intractable problems in computational biology. Arxiv preprint arXiv:0901.0866 (2009)
18. Liang, J., Kumar, R., Ross, K.W.: Understanding kazaa. Manuscript, Polytechnic University (2004)
19. Liu, L., Antonopoulos, N., Mackin, S.: Social peer-to-peer for resource discovery. In: Parallel, Distributed and Network-Based Processing, 2007. PDP'07. 15th EUROMICRO International Conference on, pp. 459–466. IEEE (2007)
20. Lv, Q., Cao, P., Cohen, E., Li, K., Shenker, S.: Search and replication in unstructured peer-to-peer networks. In: Proceedings of the 16th International Conference on Supercomputing, pp. 84–95. ACM, New York (2002)
21. Manku, G.S.: Routing networks for distributed hash tables. In: Proceedings of the 22nd Annual Symposium on Principles of Distributed Computing, pp. 133–142. ACM, New York (2003)

22. Maymounkov, P., Mazieres, D.: Kademlia: a peer-to-peer information system based on the xor metric. In: Proceedings of IPTPS02, Cambridge, vol. 1, pp. 53–65 (2002)
23. Mislove, A., Gummadi, K.P., Druschel, P.: Exploiting social networks for internet search. Proceedings of the 5th Workshop on Hot Topics in Networks (HotNets-V), Irvine, CA, pp. 79–84 (2006)
24. Mowbray, M., Brasileiro, F., Andrade, N., Santana, J.: A reciprocation-based economy for multiple services in peer-to-peer grids. In: Peer-to-Peer Computing, 2006. P2P 2006. 6th IEEE International Conference on, pp. 193–202. IEEE (2006)
25. O'Connor, A., Brady, C., Byrne, P., Olivré, A.: Characterising the eDonkey peer-to-peer file sharing network. In: Techical Reports, Computer Science Department, Trinity College Dublin (2004)
26. Papadakis, C., Fragopoulou, P., Markatos, E., Athanasopoulos, E., Dikaiakos, M., Labrinidis, A.: A feedback-based approach to reduce duplicate messages in unstructured peer-to-peer networks. Integrated Workshop on GRID Research, pp. 103–118 (2005)
27. Ratnasamy, S., Francis, P., Handley, M., Karp, R., Schenker, S.: A scalable content-addressable network. In: Proceedings of the 2001 Conference on Applications, Technologies, Architectures, and Protocols for Computer Communications, pp. 161–172. ACM (2001)
28. Rodrigues, P.D., Ribeiro, C., Veiga, L.: Incentive mechanisms in peer-to-peer networks. In: 15th IEEE Workshop on Dependable Parallel, Distributed and Network-Centric Systems (DPDNS), 24th IEEE International Parallel and Distributed Processing Symposium (IPDPS 2010). IEEE (2010)
29. Rowstron, A., Druschel, P.: Pastry: scalable, decentralized object location, and routing for large-scale peer-to-peer systems. In: Middleware 2001, pp. 329–350. Springer (2001)
30. Scott, J.: Social network analysis. Sociology 22(1), 109 (1988)
31. Shostak, S.: Sharing the Universe- Perspectives on Extraterrestrial Life. Berkeley Hills Books, Berkeley (1998)
32. Silva, J., Veiga, L., Ferreira, P.: Nuboinc: Boinc extensions for community cycle sharing. In Proceedings of the 2008 Second IEEE International Conference on Self-Adaptive and Self-Organizing SystemsWorkshops (SASOW'08), Washington, DC, USA, IEEE Computer Society, pp. 248–253 (2008)
33. Silva, J.N., Ferreira, P., Veiga, L.: Service and resource discovery in cycle-sharing environments with a utility algebra. In: Parallel and Distributed Processing (IPDPS), 2010 IEEE International Symposium on, pp. 1–11. IEEE (2010)
34. Stainforth, D., Kettleborough, J., Martin, A., Simpson, A., Gillis, R., Akkas, A., Gault, R., Collins, M., Gavaghan, D., Allen, M.: Climateprediction. net: Design principles for public-resource modeling research. In Proceedings of the 14th IASTED International Conference on Parallel and Distributed Computing Systems, ACTA Press, Calgary, pp. 32–38 (2002)
35. Stoica, I., Morris, R., Karger, D., Kaashoek, M.F., Balakrishnan, H.: Chord: a scalable peer-to-peer lookup service for internet applications. In: Proceedings of the 2001 Conference on Applications, Technologies, Architectures, and Protocols for Computer Communications, pp. 149–160. ACM (2001)
36. Trunfio, P., Talia, D., Papadakis, H., Fragopoulou, P., Mordacchini, M., Pennanen, M., Popov, K., Vlassov, V., Haridi, S.: Peer-to-peer resource discovery in Grids: models and systems. Future Gener. Comput. Syst. 23(7), 864–878 (2007)
37. Tsoumakos, D., Roussopoulos, N.: A comparison of peer-to-peer search methods. In: Proceedings of the 6th International Workshop on the Web and Databases, pp. 61–66, Citeseer (2003)
38. Veiga, L., Rodrigues, R., Ferreira, P.: GiGi: an Ocean of gridlets on a "Grid-for-the-Masses". In: Proceedings of the 7th IEEE International Symposium on Cluster Computing and the Grid, pp. 783–788. IEEE Computer Society (2007)
39. Wilson, C., Boe, B., Sala, A., Puttaswamy, K.P.N., Zhao, B.Y.: User interactions in social networks and their implications. In: Proceedings of the 4th ACM European Conference on Computer Systems, pp. 205–218. ACM (2009)

Chapter 8
Centrality Robustness and Link Prediction in Complex Social Networks

Søren Atmakuri Davidsen and Daniel Ortiz-Arroyo

Abstract This chapter addresses two important issues in social network analysis that involve uncertainty. Firstly, we present an analysis on the robustness of centrality measures that extends the work presented in Borgatti et al. using three types of complex network structures and one real social network. Secondly, we present a method to predict edges in dynamic social networks. Our experimental results indicate that the robustness of the centrality measures applied to more realistic social networks follows a predictable pattern and that the use of temporal statistics could improve the accuracy achieved on edge prediction.

Introduction

Complex networks are networks which are neither random nor regular. This type of networks are found in many diverse areas such as social networks, transportation airlines, biological networks, etc. This chapter focuses on analyzing some of the properties of complex social networks.

Social Network Analysis (SNA) studies social networks with regard to its structure, functionality, and efficiency in diffusing information. SNA provides the link between sociology and graph theory. In SNA, social networks are represented as graphs, depicting the relations and ties among social actors. The connection between social networks and computational studies is laid out in [20]. SNA has recently attracted attention given the popularity of social network sites on the Internet, the recent worldwide epidemic outbursts, financial fraud scandals, and the coordinated actions performed by international criminal organizations. The study of these social networks helps us to understand the dynamics, structuring, and functioning of social relations.

S.A. Davidsen (✉) • D. Ortiz-Arroyo
Computational Intelligence and Security Laboratory, Department of Electronic Systems,
Aalborg University, Esbjerg, Denmark
e-mail: soren@cislab.org, do@cislab.org

A. Abraham and A.-E. Hassanien (eds.), *Computational Social Networks: Tools,*
Perspectives and Applications, DOI 10.1007/978-1-4471-4048-1_8,
© Springer-Verlag London 2012

Finding central nodes is an important task in SNA that helps analysts to understand how information is diffused in the network, how command control is structured, and what is the effect on the network's structure when such nodes are removed. However, determining the full structure of a network may not be feasible in some cases. For instance, criminal organizations try to hide the structure and hierarchy of their networks from outsiders. Additionally, errors may be introduced when the network is constructed. Errors produce uncertainty with regard to the true structure of the network. Two types of uncertainty may be found during network construction: (1) *node uncertainty*, i.e., uncertainty of a node existence and (2) *edge uncertainty*, i.e., uncertainty about the relation between two nodes.

In [5] Borgatti et al. examined the effect that random errors introduced during network construction have on the performance of some centrality measures. Borgatti essentially found that centrality measures are robust in the presence of errors. However, the networks considered in [5] were random Erdős-Rényi networks. In this chapter, we have extended that work to study complex social networks that are not random.

Networks commonly studied in SNA are static, i.e., the models assume that their structure will not change. Contrarily to static networks, dynamic social networks change with time. In dynamic networks, nodes and edges are periodically added or deleted. An example of a dynamic social network is the network of personal relations that is created during the lifetime of a person. The analysis of dynamic social networks is a relatively new area of research in SNA.

Dynamic networks can be modeled using *temporal graphs*. In this chapter, we use Tang et al.'s *temporal network model* [22] and extend it to predict when a new edge is likely to be added to a network. Our experiments show that there is correlation between: (a) the age of a node and the creation of new edges and (b) last edge creation time and the creation of new edges. We have applied this knowledge to the problem of predicting edges in a temporal graph. Our results indicate that when temporal information is available, it can be used to improve prediction accuracy.

Section "Network Models" introduces the network concepts used in this chapter and section "Related Work" describes most relevant related work. In section "Robustness of Centrality Measures in Complex Social Networks," we examine the robustness aspect and present experimental results. Section "Edge Prediction in Temporal Social Networks" examines temporal networks and presents experimental results on the accuracy of our edge prediction method. Finally, in section "Conclusions and Future Work" we conclude our work and discuss future directions.

Network Models

The most common model of a network is an undirected weighted graph $G(V, E, w)$, where $V = \{v_1, v_2, \ldots, v_n\}$ is the set of vertices, $E = \{e_1, e_2, \ldots, e_m\}$ a set of edges, each edge being a tuple of the two connecting nodes $e_i = (s, t)$, and $w(v, u) \rightarrow [0, 1]$ a function that maps each edge into a weight. The unweighted network is a special case where $\forall (v, u) \in E : w(v, y) = 1$.

While networks in some domains can be described as directed graphs, in this chapter, we will consider only undirected graphs (i.e., for social network analysis, we consider actors to be reciprocally associated). Formally this means $(v, u) \in E \Leftrightarrow (u, v) \in E$.

For simplicity, in the rest of this chapter, we will use indistinctly the terms network and undirected graph, additionally to edge and link to mean the same concepts.

The *order* of a graph is the number of vertices in the graph, $|V|$. The *size* is the maximal number of possible edges in the graph $|E|$. The number of edges is $\frac{|V|(|V|-1)}{2}$. The *density* is the proportion of current edges in a graph to all possible edges that the graph may contain, $\frac{2|E|}{|V|(|V|-1)}$. A graph is *complete* if its density is 1. Low-density graphs are called *sparse*. Nodes are called *adjacent* if there is an edge connecting them.

A graph has a *path* from s (the source node) to t (the target node) if there is a sequence of edges connecting the nodes, $(s, u_0), (u_0, u_1), \ldots (u_{n-1}, t)$ through a finite set of interconnected nodes. The minimum-length path between two nodes s and t is called the *shortest* or *geodesic* path, which we denote $p(s,t)$ and its length $s(s,t)$. A graph is *connected* if all nodes are joined by a path, $\forall v, j \in V : s(v, u) < \infty$. If a graph is not connected, each maximal set of nodes for which a path exists between all of them is denoted a *component*. A *walk* is a path that allows the same edge to be traversed more than once. If a node v has d adjacent nodes, we denote d the *degree* of v, $D(v) = d$. A *triad* is a triangle of three nodes connected to each other by direct edges. The neighbors of a node we call the *neighborhood*, $N(v) = \{u|(v, u) \in E\}$.

An adjacency matrix $A^{n \times n}$ is a useful representation of a network in which each element represents an edge (see Eq. 8.1). The adjacency matrix for an undirected graph is symmetric around the diagonal.

$$A_{vu} = \begin{cases} w(v, u), & \text{if } (v, u) \in E, \\ 0, & \text{otherwise.} \end{cases} \tag{8.1}$$

A *temporal graph* is a graph for which there is an ordered sequence of edges $(e_1, e_2, e_3, \ldots, e_t)$, the index of each edge is the edge's time-stamp, hence the tth edge we denote e_t. $t(v)$ is a function that gives time-stamp when a node v joined the network, and $t(e)$ is the time-stamp when edge e joined the network. We use T to denote the set of time-stamps.

In this chapter, we use Tang et al.'s *temporal network model* [22]. The model describes the temporal network as a sequence of states in which each state contains time-stamps of the events that happen in the network.

The set of observed network states is denoted T, where $T = \{t_0, \ldots, t_{max}\}$. Each state (represented by its time-stamp t) produces a temporary graph to which nodes and edges have been added or deleted. See Fig. 8.1 for a visual example.

A function $t(e)$ yields the time-stamp of the state at which an edge was added to the network. The final network $G(V, E)$ is the union of edges from each state $E_0 \cup \ldots \cup E_t$.

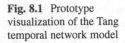

Fig. 8.1 Prototype
visualization of the Tang
temporal network model

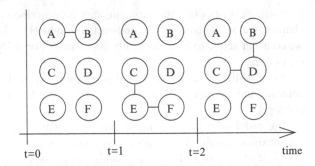

In Tang's model, all nodes are known a priori, i.e., the model does not consider new nodes entering the network. To model new nodes entering a network, we propose to augment Tang's model with a function $t(n)$ similar to $t(e)$, which will allows us to keep track of the time when a node enters the network. We will also use a subscript t for each of the available functions/sets to indicate that network is at state that has a time-stamp t, for example, $s_t(v, u)$ denotes the length of the geodesic between v and u at time t.

Related Work

The study of complex networks is today a well-established field. Early work that defined the *small-world* network effect [17] and the more recent discovery of *scale-free* structures in [1] laid out the groundwork for the study of complex networks. Several recent surveys on complex networks are available, see for instance [4, 10, 18].

Only little work on robustness has been done. Borgatti et al. in [5] generate random graphs to study the performance of centrality measures in the presence of errors. Borgatti classifies errors into two groups: (1) sampling errors and (2) misinformation errors. Sampling errors occur when the observed network is only a partial sample of the true network, i.e., the network misses either nodes or edges. Misinformation errors occur when a network has additional information compared to the real network, i.e., the network may have additional nodes or edges.

The experiments cited in [5] show that as expected errors degrade the performance of the centrality measures employed. However, degradation occurs in a predictable way. Hence, if the proportion of errors in a random network could be estimated, it will be possible to predict the accuracy of the results produced by the centrality measures.

In relation to link prediction, the discovered properties of complex networks lead to proposals of generative models that explain the dynamics of network evolution. For instance, in [23] a generative model for small-world networks was proposed using random rewirings of a lattice. Moreover, in [2] the *preferential attachment* model was suggested to explain how a scale-free structure could emerge.

Many other properties of complex networks have since then been examined. Some of them are *assortative mixing* [18] where types of nodes are taken into account when selecting edges, the *giant component* [4, 18] behavior in a network, *community structures* [18], and more recently a *densifying model* described in [15].

Some approaches include in their generative models the use of dynamic information such as node age or lifetime. Node age was used to predict the clustering coefficient of nodes in [12]. In [7] node lifetime is analyzed to propose a model with decaying degrees. Other research such as those in [8, 9] include using the visualization of changes to calculate network centralities.

The problem of edge prediction has received recently some attention. The problem is described with some detail in [16, 24]. In these works, [16] evaluates current state-of-art methods and [24] creates a classification of the different approaches. The general classes of link prediction considered in [24] are: (a) Class-1, node-wise similarity, where similarities between nodes are determined based on their features, (b) Class-2, topological patterns where similarities between nodes are determined from the structure of the network (locally or globally), and (c) Class-3, probabilistic models, where compressed networks of interactions are learned and used for prediction.

Class-1 has roots in clustering/classification tasks, where we wish to discover hidden relations between a set of otherwise unrelated nodes. Link prediction for this class depends on the availability of a feature vector for each node $f(v) = (f_1, f_2, \ldots, f_n)$, and a similarity measure to determine the vectors' similarity $\text{sim}(f(v), f(u))$. Classical measures such as cosine similarity and the Euclidean distance could be employed. These methods predict a missing edge in the network, when two nodes with high similarity are found. In network analysis, however, this approach is not always applicable, but only in models that include latent spaces, or where physical distance does not matter.

Class-2 employs topological patterns in the network. Some approaches in this class are based on a local heuristic such as "your close neighbors influence you". This is the case described in [16] where a node-proximity measure is developed to find new neighbors and in [6] where a combination of clustering coefficient and hierarchical clustering is used.

Class-3 is a classification task, where examples of network interactions are learned and used for prediction. This approach is described in [11] where a learning algorithm is applied to select neighbors.

While Class-1 depends on node features being available and Class-3 depends on having available examples of node interactions, Class-2 depends only on the network itself. This is a desirable feature, but has some limitations.

Robustness of Centrality Measures in Complex Social Networks

This section describes a method for evaluating the robustness of the centrality measures described in Table 8.1 when applied to non random social networks.

Table 8.1 Commonly used centrality measures and their definition

Measure	Definition	Notes
Degree centrality	$C_D(v) = \frac{D(v)}{n-1}$	
Betweenness centrality	$C_B(v) = \sum_{u \in V} \sum_{z \in V} g_{uz}(v)$	$g_{uz}(v) = 1$ if $v \in p(u,z)$
Closeness centrality	$C_C(v) = \sum_{u \in V} s(v,u)$	
Eigenvector centrality	$x_i = \frac{1}{\lambda} \sum_{j=1}^{n} A_{ij} x_j$	rewritten as $\lambda x = Ax$
Entropy centrality	$C_E(v) = -\sum_{u \in V'} \gamma(u) \times \log_2 \gamma(u)$	$\gamma(v) = \frac{\text{paths}(v_i)}{M}$. V' is V without the node v.

In addition to replicate the results produced by Borgatti in [5] using ER random networks, we want to analyze the robustness of centrality measures on more realistic social networks. One way to do this is by synthesizing network structures that are general models of social networks. Our synthetic networks were selected from three categories described in the literature. Firstly, we generated *scale-free* networks that are used to model collaboration networks using Barabasi's [3] *preferential attachment* model. Secondly, we used the Krebs' community structures described in [14] to generate *Cliques* that model friendship networks and *Core/periphery* networks that can be used to model cohesive social groups.

Section "Synthesizing Complex Networks" describes the methods used to generate the three types of complex networks and section "Experimental Tests" discusses the results obtained in our experiments.

Synthesizing Complex Networks

Clique networks are networks in which several cliques of tightly connected nodes are interconnected loosely. Clique networks are synthesized using a parametric algorithm which groups the nodes of the network into c cliques and then makes random edge creation dependent on whether two nodes are in the same clique or not as shown in Eq. 8.3.

$$re(p) = \begin{cases} 1, & \text{if rand} < p, \\ 0, & \text{otherwise,} \end{cases} \tag{8.2}$$

$$A_{ij} = \begin{cases} re(p_c), & \text{if } C(v_i) = C(v_j), \\ re(p_b), & \text{otherwise,} \end{cases} \tag{8.3}$$

$C(v)$ is a function that returns the clique of the node v. $re(p)$ is a function that returns 1 (indicating an edge in the adjacency matrix) given a uniform random probability distribution p. A is the adjacency matrix representing the network. It is expected that centrality measures in clique networks will behave similarly as when applied to ER networks. The intuitive reason for this is that the centrality measures will pick up nodes that are on the edges of many cliques as the most central. Additionally a clique can be seen as a single node in the network.

Fig. 8.2 A sample function for $P(x) = 0.6$ if $x <$ 40, 0.03 otherwise

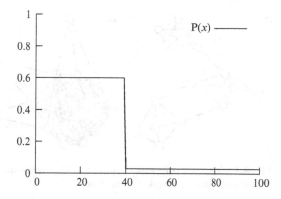

Core/periphery networks are networks in which there is a core of closely connected nodes and a periphery of loosely connected nodes. Core/periphery networks were synthesized as a generalization of ER random networks using a given probability density function P instead of a single probability value p. This is shown in Eq. 8.4 where A is an adjacency matrix. A sample function for P can be seen in Fig. 8.2.[1]

$$A_{ij} = \begin{cases} 1, & \text{if rand} < \min(P(i), P(j)), \\ 0, & \text{otherwise}, \end{cases} \qquad (8.4)$$

When errors are introduced into core/periphery networks, it is expected that the removal of nodes and edges will have less effect on the centrality measures, i.e., the dense core will provide alternative paths for the periphery nodes. However, when errors are added to the core, they could have some impact on the centrality measures.

A simple method to synthesize scale-free networks is given in [21]. The method consists in attaching new nodes at random to previously existing nodes, using the degree of these previously existing nodes as their probability of attachment. This method is described by Eq. 8.5.

$$P_{v_i} = \frac{D(v_i)}{D_{\max}} \qquad (8.5)$$

P_{v_i} is the edge creation probability function on node v_i, D is the degree of a node v_i, and $D_{\max}$ is the highest node degree found in the graph.

Intuitively it is expected that centrality measures will perform better in scale-free networks, given that in its construction few nodes will be very well connected. These few nodes will likely be picked as central nodes by the centrality measures. Hence, the probability of introducing errors in these few nodes is small given the "long tail" of other insignificant nodes. Figure 8.3 shows examples of synthesized networks.

---

[1]It should be noted that this function is dependent on the size of network that has to be generated.

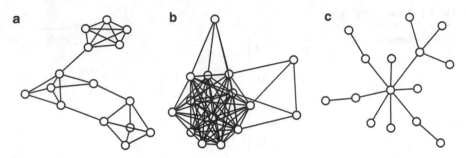

Fig. 8.3 Examples of small, $n = 15$, synthesized networks. (**a**) Clique network. (**b**) Core/periphery network. (**c**) Scale-free

Experimental Tests

Creating synthetic networks is very convenient for experimental purposes. However, it is also important to use real social networks and see how they perform in the presence of errors when compared to synthetic networks. The terrorist network collected by Krebs [13] was chosen as an example of a real network in our experiments. The network has 62 nodes and 155 edges with a density of 0.08 and is shown as Fig. 4 in [13]. The errors introduced to the network are randomly chosen at each iteration.

We performed three types of experiments to determine: (1) the robustness of centrality measures on random complex networks, (2) the robustness of centrality measures using a real network, and (3) the robustness of entropy as a centrality measure

In [5] five different measures are used to determine the accuracy of the measurements obtained in the network containing errors when compared to an error-free (true) network. These measures are:

1. Top 1 – considers only the top node, i.e., the most central node in the true network is also the most central in the network with errors introduced.
2. Top 3 – considers the top 3 nodes, i.e., the most central node in the true network is among the three most central in the network with errors introduced.
3. Top 10% – considers the top 0.1 of nodes, i.e., the most central node in the true network is in the top 10% of the most central nodes in the network with errors introduced.
4. Overlap – considers Jaccard's similarity measure between top 10% nodes, i.e., the overlap between the top 10% nodes in the true network and the top 10% nodes in the network with errors introduced.
5. R^2 – considers Pearson correlation, i.e., the correlation between the centralities of the true network and the centralities of the network with errors introduced.

In this chapter, we will use the same measurements of accuracy.

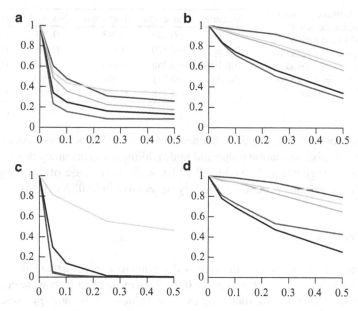

Fig. 8.4 Scatter plots of the average betweenness accuracy as a function of error. Betweenness measures for core/periphery network of size 50, and a density of 0.40. Legend: ■ top 1, ■ top 3, ■ top 10%, ■ overlap, ■ R^2. (**a**) Edge addition. (**b**) Edge removal. (**c**) Node addition. (**d**) Node removal

Experiments with Synthetic Complex Networks

Synthetic complex graphs were created and tests were conducted with each of the complex topologies previously mentioned. Due to lack of space, we only report the results of our experiments using graphs of size $n = 50$, but we have performed other tests with graph sizes of 10, 25, 50, and 100 nodes, obtaining similar results.

Additionally, in all of our experiments, we used only the betweenness centrality measure. This measure was chosen because it is a global measure and because it was also used in [5]. However, we have conducted experiments using betweenness, closeness, and eigenvector centrality obtaining similar accuracies. It is important to remark that contrarily to other measures, degree centrality is easily affected by local changes in the graphs; hence, it is a less predictive measure.

Finally, networks were compared using the same values in density and size. However, in the case of the real network and a random scale-free network, the size and density of the networks used were not the same.

Core/Periphery Networks

To generate core/periphery networks, the P function shown in Fig. 8.2 was used. Figure 8.4 and Table 8.2 show that the accuracy obtained for this kind of network

Table 8.2 Arithmetic mean of the difference between measures of an ER network and a core/periphery network, calculated for betweenness centrality, on graphs with 50 nodes, and 0.40 density

Measure	Edge add	Edge rem	Node add	Node rem
Top 1	−0.309	0.093	−0.398	0.069
Top 3	−0.370	0.048	−0.576	0.040
Top 10%	−0.358	0.046	−0.633	0.037
Overlap	−0.241	0.109	−0.302	0.054
R^2	−0.278	0.085	−0.123	0.085

has a distinctive difference to that obtained with random ER networks. As expected, in the case of misinformation (edge and node addition), the accuracy drops quickly (having an average within $[-0.633, -0.123]$), while in the case of sampling (edge and node removal), the accuracy is slightly better (within $[0.037, 0.109]$).

Clique Networks

To generate clique networks, the required parameters were set to the following values: $s = 0.28$, $p_c = 0.60$, and $p_b = 0.03$. This means that tests were conducted on networks with three to four cliques. The values for p_c and p_b were found experimentally to produce easily visible clique networks. The density of graphs generated with these settings was found to be 0.20 for comparison with ER networks of equal density.

As expected Fig. 8.5 and Table 8.3 show that accuracy is similar to that obtained with random ER networks. These figures show that adding extra nodes or edges has a negative impact on the accuracy, while in the case of sampling accuracy improves. However, this variation is small compared to the case of core/periphery networks. The reason for this could be that an odd size of cliques was used, which could bias one clique to be more central than others.

Scale-Free Networks

To generate scale-free networks no special parameters are needed. The density of the networks is shown in Eq. 8.6.

$$\text{density}(n) = \frac{2(n-1)}{n(n-1)} \tag{8.6}$$

Previous figures show that scale-free networks are very robust to errors. According to Barabási and Bonabeau [3], we should expect that scale-free networks be more robust than random networks, and the experimental results in Fig. 8.6 and Table 8.4 support this assumption. This indicates that centrality measures applied to real networks that have scale-free structure will perform well in the presence of errors.

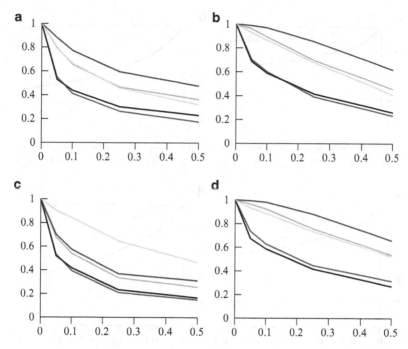

Fig. 8.5 Scatter plots of the average betweenness accuracy as a function of error. Betweenness measures for clique network of size 50, a density of 0.20. Legend: ■ top 1, ▨ top 3, ■ top 10%, ■ overlap, ▨ R^2. (**a**) Edge addition. (**b**) Edge removal. (**c**) Node addition. (**d**) Node removal

	Measure	Edge add	Edge rem	Node add	Node rem
Table 8.3 Arithmetic mean of the difference between measures of an ER network and a clique network, calculated for betweenness centrality, on graphs with 50 nodes, and 0.20 density	Top 1	−0.092	0.043	−0.145	−0.021
	Top 3	−0.116	0.032	−0.235	0.006
	Top 10%	−0.104	0.033	−0.268	0.002
	Overlap	−0.082	0.026	−0.122	0.003
	R^2	−0.132	0.024	−0.071	−0.001

Krebs Terrorist Network

As an example of a real-world network, we have used the Krebs Terrorist Network. As with the synthesized networks, we have introduced random errors in this network, and compared with random errors in an ER network of same size and density.

As expected Fig. 8.7 shows that the accuracy obtained in this network is better compared to that obtained with the ER random network in Fig. 8.8. Since it is difficult to generate a scale-free network with equal size and density as the Krebs network, the comparison with a scale-free network was made using the results presented in Fig. 8.6. Table 8.5 shows that the accuracies are very similar, within [−0.103, 0.078].

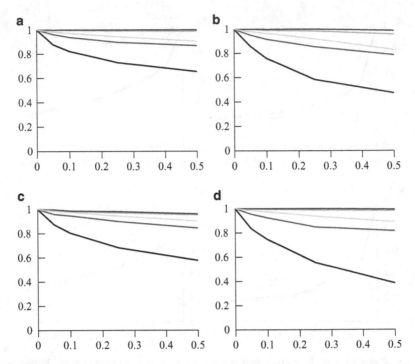

Fig. 8.6 Scatter plots of the average betweenness accuracy as a function of error. Betweenness measures for scale-free network of size 50, with a density of 0.04. Legend: ■ Top 1, ▪ Top 3, ■ Top 10%, ■ Overlap, ▪ R^2. (**a**) Edge addition. (**b**) Edge removal. (**c**) Node addition. (**d**) Node removal

Table 8.4 Arithmetic mean of the difference between measures of an ER network and a scale-free network, calculated for betweenness centrality on graphs with 50 nodes, and 0.04 density

Measure	Edge add	Edge rem	Node add	Node rem
Top 1	0.355	0.279	0.309	0.189
Top 3	0.251	0.224	0.227	0.099
Top 10%	0.222	0.202	0.212	0.091
Overlap	0.295	0.235	0.267	0.148
R^2	0.217	0.243	0.196	0.161

Entropy as Centrality Measure

Our experiments using the entropy measure described in [19] were conducted using the following parameters: (1) network sizes $\in \{10, 25, 50\}$, (2) network densities $\in \{0.05, 0.10, 0.25, 0.50\}$, and (3) error ratios $\in \{0.00, 0.05, 0.10, 0.25, 0.50\}$.

For each combination, 1,000 ER networks were generated and statistics of the entropy measure were collected. Figure 8.9 shows the results from these tests. The experiment shows that the accuracy of entropy under errors declines faster than the other centrality measures, however it still does so in a predictive way.

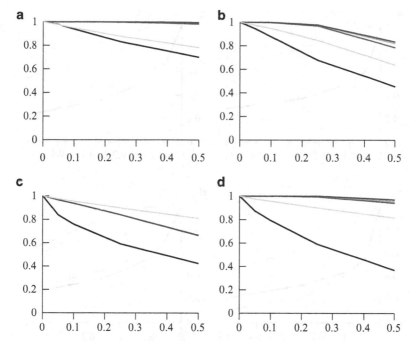

Fig. 8.7 Scatter plots of the average betweenness accuracy as a function of error. Betweenness measures for Krebs Terrorist network of size 62, with a density of 0.08. Legend: ■ top 1, ■ top 3, ■ top 10%, ■ overlap, ■ R^2. (**a**) Edge addition. (**b**) Edge removal. (**c**) Node addition. (**d**) Node removal

Figure 8.9 shows the performance of the entropy measure when applied to an ER graph with a density of 0.05. Figure 8.10 shows that dense graphs produce less variation in the entropy. At densities larger than 0.05, the variation in centrality entropy becomes so small that results of the measure are inconclusive in deciding the most central node. Variation is calculated as the number of different values of $C_E(v)$ (see Fig. 8.1) found in the test networks.

Edge Prediction in Temporal Social Networks

The edge prediction problem can be formally describe as: Given a network $G(V, E)$, where E represents the observed edges, how likely is that an unobserved edge $(v, u) \notin E$ may appear between an arbitrary pair of nodes (v, u).

Section "Temporal Datasets" describes the datasets used in our edge prediction experiments. Sections "Static Network Properties" and "Exploring the Dynamics of the Datasets" describe the static and dynamic parameters that we have used to improve prediction accuracy. Finally, section "Temporal Modeling and Experimental Results" describes the results of our experiments.

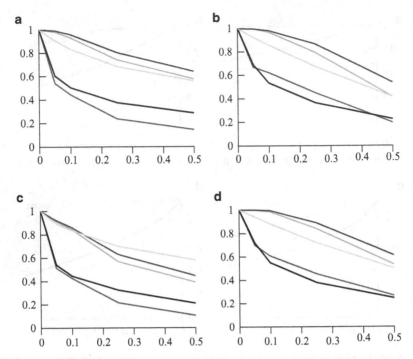

Fig. 8.8 Scatter plots of the average betweenness accuracy as a function of error. Betweenness measures for ER network of size 62, with a density of 0.08. Legend: ■ top 1, ▨ top 3, ■ top 10%, ■ overlap, ▨ R^2. (**a**) Edge addition. (**b**) Edge removal. (**c**) Node addition. (**d**) Node removal

Table 8.5 Arithmetic mean of the difference between measures of a scale-free network with 50 nodes, and a density of 0.04, and the Krebs network, calculated for betweenness centrality	Measure	Edge add	Edge rem	Node add	Node rem
	Top 1	0.064	0.049	−0.048	0.078
	Top 3	0.004	−0.027	−0.099	−0.003
	Top 10%	0.000	−0.035	−0.103	−0.005
	Overlap	0.073	0.055	−0.065	0.020
	R^2	−0.043	−0.058	−0.034	−0.029

Temporal Datasets

We have selected four datasets for our experiments using the following criteria: (1) temporal information must be available, i.e., $t(e)$ must be known, (2) the dataset must contain a statistically significant amount of nodes and edges, and (3) the dataset should be computationally possible to handle.[2]

Given that the number of datasets publicly available that fit these criteria were quite limited, we decided to create our own datasets. The dataset that we called

---

[2]Practical memory limit for holding adjacency matrices in our computing system is less than 25,000 nodes.

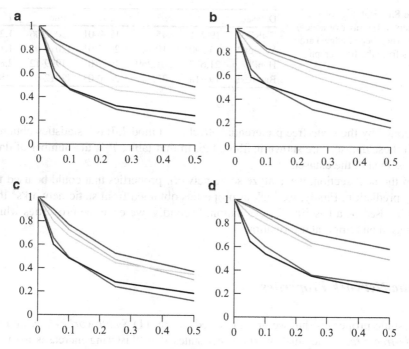

Fig. 8.9 Scatter plots of the average entropy accuracy as a function of error. Entropy measures for ER network of size 50, with a density of 0.02. Legend: ■ top 1, ■ top 3, ■ top 10%, ■ overlap, ■ R^2. (**a**) Edge addition. (**b**) Edge removal. (**c**) Node addition. (**d**) Node removal

Fig. 8.10 Scatter plots of the entropy variation (y-axis) as a function of density (x-axis) in ER networks of size 50. Legend: ■ true, ■ node add, ■ node remove, ■ edge add, ■ edge remove

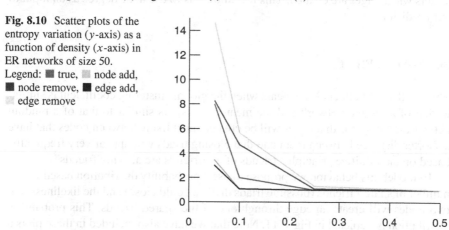

Version2 was obtained from an online IT-news community. The *ENRON* dataset was constructed from the corpus of emails that were made publicly available on the ENRON scandal case. The *HepPh* dataset is a citation graph of papers from the High Energy Physics domain. Finally, we created a synthetic dataset called *Barabasi*

Table 8.6 Statistics of
datasets, n (number of nodes)
and m (number of edges) are
values from the final graph

Dataset	n	m	Start	End	T
ENRON	19,211	45,967	1999-01	2002-06	1,264
Version2	3,390	110,147	2007-01	2010-02	1,145
HepPh	21,627	201,259	1992-03	1999-12	2,847
Barabasi	19,218	30,446	2010-03	2012-05	801

generated by the scale-free preferential attachment model. Basic statistics obtained
from these datasets are shown in Table 8.6. In that table, T is the number of days
represented in the dataset.

In the next section, we analyze some network properties that could be used for
edge prediction. Firstly, we look at properties obtained from static networks[3] that
will be used as a baseline for evaluation. Secondly, we examine properties which
are based on temporal information.

Static Network Properties

The static properties that we are interested in are: (1) *Small-world effect* and (2)
Scale-free effect. The small-world effect states that clustering increases as mean
path length decreases. This fact allows us to make edge predictions based on triads
and hops in the network. The scale-free effect states that nodes prefer high-degree
targets when edges are created. This fact allows us to use node degree as an input to
our predictor.

Small-World Effect

The small-world effect [23] appears when the global clustering coefficient is similar
to that of a regular network and the mean geodesic is similar to that of a random
network. This means that edges will be created most likely between nodes that have
a shorter distance between them and that closing triads will appear very frequently,
based on the intuitive principle "friends of my friends are also my friends".

To model this behavior, we propose to use a probability distribution based on the
number of shared friends (possible triads that we could close) and the likeliness that
two nodes will create an edge through one of the shared friends. This probability
distribution is depicted in Fig. 8.11. Note that we have also included in these plots a
fitness function graph.

The probability distribution used to generate Fig. 8.11 is shown in Eq. 8.8 where
$E_\Delta(x)$ is the set of edges that at time $t - 1$ have x neighbors in common, $n_t(u, v)$ is

---

[3]This approach was used in [16].

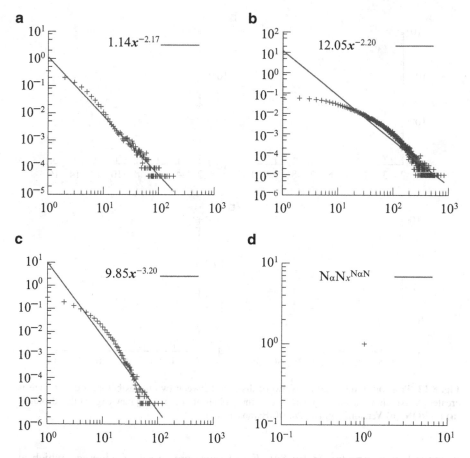

Fig. 8.11 Probability distribution: Closed triads in proportion to number of shared neighbors, x-axis shows the number of shared neighbors, y-axis shows the probability that end nodes create an edge. Note: The scale-free dataset was created with only one edge per new node, hence no triads are closed. (**a**) ENRON. (**b**) Version2. (**c**) HepPh. (**d**) Scale-free

the number of common neighbors for two nodes v and u and $P_\Delta(x)$ is the probability that two nodes with x neighbors in common will create a new edge.

$$n_t(u,v) = |N_t(u) \cap N_t(v)|, \qquad (8.7)$$

$$E_\Delta(x) = \{e_t = (u,v)|n_{t-1}(u,v) = x\}, \quad P_\Delta(x) = \frac{|E_\Delta(x)|}{\sum_i |E_\Delta(i)|} \qquad (8.8)$$

A second probability we are interested in represents the frequency with which a node makes contact with nodes outside the "friend of friends" network. Figure 8.12 shows the probability distribution of the frequency with which relations to far-away nodes in the network are created. We have plotted the probability of linking vs.

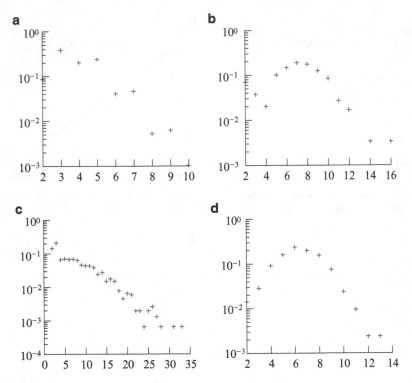

Fig. 8.12 Probability distribution: Network distance between two nodes before a direct edge is created. x-axis shows distance, y-axis shows the probability of creating new edge at this distance. (**a**) ENRON. (**b**) Version2. (**c**) HepPh. (**d**) Barabasi

distance between nodes. In Eq. 8.9, $E_h(x)$ represents a set of edges e_t, which at time $t-1$ have distance x (represented by $s_{t-1}(v, u) = x$). $P_h(x)$ is the probability of creating an edge between two nodes at distance x and $|E|$ is the total number of edges in the graph.

$$E_h(x) = \{e_t = (v, u) \quad | \quad s_{t-1}(v, u) = x\}, \quad P_h(x) = \frac{|E_h(x)|}{|E|} \quad (8.9)$$

It can be noticed from previous figures that the ENRON and HepPh datasets both follow an exponential decaying function, and the Version2 and Barabasi follow something that appears to be a bell-curve function. The Version2 dataset shows the most surprising behavior. In the preferential attachment Barabasi dataset, we would expect a bell-curve distribution, since selecting target nodes happens randomly uniformly. However, in the Version2 dataset, it appears that selecting a target also happens randomly uniformly in the network.

Scale-Free Effect

The scale-free effect means that the degree distribution follows a power-law function $f(x) = ax^{-}k$, which is true for our datasets with $k = [-0.99, 2.01]$. However, what we are interested in is the probability that will indicate how likely a node v is to be attached to another node with a given degree. This probability is calculated in Eq. 8.12. $P_d(x)$ is the probability that a target node with a degree x will create a new edge. $E_d(x, t)$ is the set of edges created where the target node has degree x at time t; $V_d(x, t)$ is the set of nodes available with a degree of x at time t; and $M_d(x)$ is the number of edges created where the target node has degree x in proportion to how many nodes are available in the network with a degree x. Finally, M_D is the sum of all $M_d(x)$ for all x.

$$E_d(x, t) = \{e_t = (u, v) | D_{t-1}(v) = x\}, \tag{8.10}$$

$$V_d(x, t) = \{v_t | D_t(v) = x\}, \tag{8.11}$$

$$M_d(x) = \frac{\sum_t |E_d(x, t)|}{\sum_t |V_d(x, t)|}, \quad P_d(x) = \frac{M_d(x)}{M_D} \tag{8.12}$$

We observe from Fig. 8.13 that all datasets show heavy bias toward creating edges in high-degree nodes. For the ENRON and Version2 datasets, our intuition is that few people tend to communicate very frequently, while the HepPh dataset has few seminal papers. The Barabasi dataset shows the expected behavior given by its definition.

Exploring the Dynamics of the Datasets

In [18] and other related works, the dynamics of static networks are thoroughly examined. Properties such as scale-free preferential attachment, small-world clustering, and density are learned and generative models are proposed to create synthetic networks with similar properties. However, little work has been reported in the literature regarding the dynamics of temporal networks. In this section, an analysis was performed in relation to the temporal aspect of the networks. More specifically, we have explored these aspects:

1. *At what rate are new edges created?* In our temporal network model, a node joins the network, and creates new edges over time. Does this happen in uniformly over time?
2. *Is there a lifetime of nodes?* As a node joins the network and creates edges, it is also deleted at some point. The creation of new edges is uniformly distributed over time.

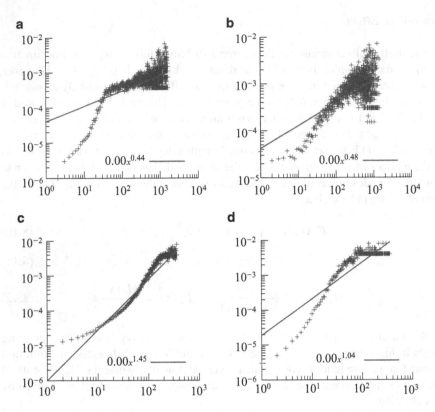

Fig. 8.13 Probability distribution: Degree attachment. x-axis is the degree d and the y-axis the probability of edge creation for the degree. (**a**) ENRON. (**b**) Version2. (**c**) HepPh. (**d**) Scale-free

3. *Do older nodes create more edges?* The preferential attachment model indicates that old nodes are the ones with the highest degree, and therefore are likely to create most edges over time.

Last Edge Creation Time

Last edge creation time is the time that has elapsed from the time a node has created an edge, until the node is connected to a new edge. The intuition used here is that this property will follow the preferential attachment model where nodes with many edges will tend to create new edges more often, and nodes with less edges will wait longer before creating new edges. Figure 8.14 shows the probability distribution described by Eq. 8.14. In Eq. 8.14, g is the time gap since the last edge was created, counted as the number of edges at each t, which had a gap g at $t - 1$.

In Eq. 8.14, g is the time gap since the last edge was created, $E_g(x)$ is the set of edges that had a time gap x at $t - 1$, and E_G the set of edges with all different time gaps at $t - 1$.

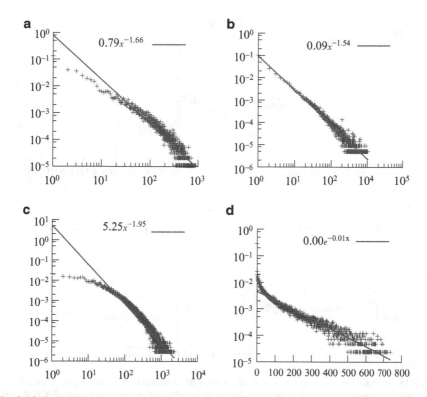

Fig. 8.14 Probability distribution: Gap between edges, x-axis is the gap in t, increasing from left to right, y-axis is the number of edges with the gap, as described by $P_g(x)$. (**a**) ENRON. (**b**) Version2. (**c**) HepPh. (**d**) Scale-free (note, single-log scale)

$$g_t(v) = t - \max\{t(e)|e = (v, u)\}, \qquad (8.13)$$

$$E_g(x) = \{e_t = (u, v)|g_{t-1}(u) = x\}, \quad P_g(x) = \frac{|E_g(x)|}{|E_G|} \qquad (8.14)$$

We can see that all datasets, except the synthetic Barabasi dataset, conform to a power-law distribution, where nodes that create edges often will likely continue doing it and the longer time elapses without new edges are being attached to a node, the less likely this will happen. This is similar to the way degree distribution behaves. Therefore, it is not expected that using this effect will give much better predictions when degree distribution has been already used.

Node Age Edge Creation

The preferential attachment model relies on node degree calcualtions when deciding when to create new edges. Here we examine if there is also a temporal aspect in this

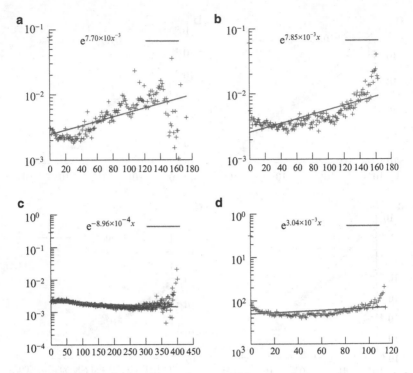

Fig. 8.15 Probability distribution: Mean edges created in proportion to node age, x-axis is the node age a (counting weeks), y-axis is the mean number of edges $P_a(x)$. (**a**) ENRON. (**b**) Version2. (**c**) HepPh. (**d**) Barabasi

type of attachment. The intuitive idea is that old nodes have more "experience" within the network and therefore they are more likely to build new "relations."

We propose calculating the mean number of edges created in proportion to a node's age, as shown in Eq. 8.15. The numerator is the number of edges created with age a.[4] This is then normalized with the number of nodes that have reached all ages E_A. Figure 8.15 shows the plots obtained with each of the datasets. Note that a is counted in weeks for this plot, due to the fact that only few very old nodes are available.

$$E_a(x) = \{e = (u,v)|t(e) - t(u) = x\}, \quad P_a(x) = \frac{|E_a(x)|}{|E_A|} \qquad (8.15)$$

Figure 8.15 shows that we can fit the data of all datasets with an exponential function with different features. ENRON and Version2 datasets have a slightly increasing curve. The Version2 dataset is consistently increasing. This means that

---

[4]$t(e)$ is the time-stamp when edge e was created, and $t(u)$ the time-stamp when u joined the network.

older nodes are more likely to create new edges. Contrarily, the ENRON dataset is generally increasing, except in the oldest nodes. This means that the older a node gets, the more likely it will create new edges, except, if the node is among the oldest. The HepPh dataset, on the other hand, shows a slightly decreasing behavior, but with strong bias to oldest nodes. The intuition for this behavior is that in citation networks, a few old seminal papers will be referenced very often, while in general other papers will be forgotten over time (and thus receive less new edges).

The Barabasi dataset shows an almost straight line, which is what we would expect since the model depends only on the degree.

In summary, all the previous graphs show that we can create either linear, power-law, or exponential functions for the following probability distributions:

- $P_\Delta(x)$ probability of creating an edge given x possible triads between two nodes, where x for two nodes is calculated as shown in Eq. 8.7
- $P_h(x)$ probability of creating an edge given the distance x between two nodes, where x for two nodes is $s_t(u, v)$
- $P_d(x)$ probability of creating an edge on a given target node's degree, where x for a target node is $D_t(v)$
- $P_g(x)$ probability of creating an edge given the target node's last edge creation x, where x is the gap $g_t(v)$ as defined in Eq. 8.13
- $P_a(x)$ probability of creating an edge on a given target node's age x, where x is the age of the target $a_t(u) = t - t(v)$

Temporal Modeling and Experimental Results

In this section, we propose a simple linear regresion model for edge prediction that uses the statistical features obtained from the analysis we have made on the static network and the temporal network discussed in sections "Static Network Properties" and "Exploring the Dynamics of the Datasets", respectively.

The model employs the scoring function shown in Eq. 8.16, where $\mathbb{R}$ is a score that indicates our degree of belief in an unobserved edge (u, v); a higher number indicates higher belief.

$$\text{score}(G_t, v, u) \to \mathbb{R}. \tag{8.16}$$

Each unobserved edge is described with a triplet (v, u, w), where w is the score and u and v are nodes. The set of predicted edges E_p is then constructed by selecting edges with highest scores.

Temporal Link Predictor

This section introduces our novel *temporal link predictor* (tep). The main idea of our predictor is to extract a ranking function from each of the probability distributions used and then aggregate the ranking functions to produce a final score.

Table 8.7 Probability distributions and their fit ranking functions

Probability distribution	Ranking function	Actual used ranking function, $\mu(x)$	
		ENRON	Version2
Triads attachment, $P_\Delta(x)$	μ_Δ	$x^{-2.17}$	$x^{-2.20}$
Distance attachment, $P_h(x)$	μ_h	$e^{-0.65x}$	1
Degree attachment, $P_d(x)$	μ_d	$x^{0.44}$	$x^{0.48}$
Edge creation gap $P_g(x)$	μ_g	$x^{-1.66}$	$x^{-1.54}$
Node age activity $P_a(x)$	μ_a	$e^{0.01x}$	$e^{0.01x}$

Note: distance attachment ranking function for Version2 is fixed to 1 because of bell-curve shape

Table 8.8 Scoring functions

Name	Score-function	Comments
tep_{am}	$\oplus_{am}(\mu_d, \mu_\Delta, \mu_a, \mu_h, \mu_g)$	
tep_{rd}	$\oplus_{am}(\mu_d + \frac{1}{\text{rand}(n)}, \mu_\Delta, \mu_h, \mu_g)$	Use randomness and degree in target node selection.
tep_a	$\oplus_{am}(\mu_a, \mu_\Delta, \mu_h, \mu_g)$	Use only age instead of degree.
tep_{ad}	$\oplus_{am}(\mu_a + \mu_d, \mu_\Delta, \mu_h, \mu_g)$	Use age or degree.
tep_{ngr}	$\oplus_{am}(\mu_a, \mu_d, \mu_\Delta, \mu_h, \frac{1}{\text{rand}(t)})$	Use randomness instead of last edge creation.
tep_{tg}	$\oplus_{am}(\mu_a, \mu_d, \mu_\Delta + \mu_g, \mu_h)$	Bias towards triads or last edge creation.
Adamic/Adar$_2$	$\sum_{z \in N(v) \cap N(u)} \frac{1}{\log D_t(z)} \mu_a \mu_g$	Added temporal for target node.
Adamic/Adar$_3$	$\sum_{z \in N(v) \cap N(u)} \frac{1}{\log(D_t(z)\mu_a(a_t(z))\mu_g(g_t(z)))}$	Added temporal for intermediate node z.

Firstly, for each of the probability distributions that we have used, we extract a linear ranking function, denoted μ.[5] Table 8.7 shows the relation between the probability distributions and the ranking functions for each of the datasets we used for prediction.

Secondly, we aggregated the ranking functions into a set of scoring functions. Table 8.8 lists our proposed functions. $\oplus_{am}$ is an aggregation function based on the arithmetic mean and rand(x) is a random number generator with a uniform probability distribution. The set contains variations, where special attention was placed to separate features or randomize a feature. Additionally our method makes the following two modifications to the Adamic/Adar metric: (1) we apply temporal information to the intermediate nodes, (2) we apply temporal information to the target node only.

The main motivation of this simple model is to determine if temporal information helps to increase overall predictor's performance.

---

[5]This function was found using standard linear least squares method, and the pearson correlation as fitness function between power fit and exponential fit.

Other Predictors

In our experiments, additionally to the temporal link predictor, we use two other models for comparison purposes: (1) a random predictor used as baseline and (2) the Adamic/Adar measure, which received the best scores in [16].

The Adamic/Adar measure is shown in Eq. 8.17. This equation takes into account the common neighbors of two nodes (v, u) and the degree of the common neighbors, weighted by an importance degree function $\frac{1}{\log D(z)}$. We note that $D(z) \geq 2$ and that nodes with few neighbors are favored. $N(v)$ is the set of neighbors for v and $D(z)$ the degree of node z as previously defined.

$$\text{score}_{\text{AA}}(v, u) = \sum_{z \in N(v) \cap N(u)} \frac{1}{\log D(z)} \tag{8.17}$$

In [16] the Adamic/Adar measure performed the best on the chosen datasets, when only graph-structural properties were considered.

Experimental Results

We evaluated the proposed temporal link predictor on our two datasets. However, since our simple linear regression model was not always able to fit the actual network data, it is expected that for some datasets, its accuraccy will be low.

We consider predicting edges a function $f(G_{t-1}, l) \rightarrow \{(u, v) : \text{to appear in } G_t\}$, where l is the number of new edges to be predicted for G_t and G_{t-1} is the graph before time t. The experiments were performed as follows: for each t in T, a network G_{t-1} was constructed, then the set of new edges E_t that will be added to G_t was determined. Then, a the size of the set E_t is used as the number of new edges that will be predicted. E_a will represent the set of new edges actually created between G_{t-1} and G_t.

Table 8.9 shows the output of our evaluation on edge prediction using the ENRON and Version2 datasets.

Using the *tep* predictor, each feature was disabled one by one, in order to evaluate its final influence on the final results. These results are shown in Table 8.9 as tepnofeat where feat is the name of disabled feature. A lower number here means that a feature has more influence, and a higher number less influence, compared to tep_{am}, which includes all features.

It can be noticed that in general the performance obtained was poor. However, this is consistent with the results obtained by [16], given that edge prediction is a hard problem. The results obtained by our predictor when compared with those obtained by the Adamic/Adar method are not consistent. For the ENRON dataset, the performance of our method is better and for the Version2 dataset performance is worse.

Table 8.9 Link prediction results on ENRON and Version2 datasets. *random* is the random predictor, *tep* is the edge predictor presented here. Index is relative to tep_{am}. The highlighted elements are: (1) best overall for the dataset; (2) best *tep* for the dataset

Predictor	ENRON			Version2		
	$E_p \cap E_a$	%	Index	$E_p \cap E_a$	%	Index
Random	15	0.04	0.01	968	1.41	0.14
Adamic/Adar	720	2.13	0.59	**9,230**	**13.46**	**1.31**
tep_{am}	1,212	3.59	1.00	7,067	10.30	1.00
tep_{rd}	766	2.27	0.63	6,941	10.12	0.98
tep_a	369	1.09	0.30	4,027	5.87	0.57
tep_{ad}	459	1.36	0.38	4,669	6.81	0.66
tep_{ngr}	344	1.02	0.28	3,162	4.61	0.45
tep_{tg}	458	1.36	0.38	4,669	6.81	0.66
Adamic/Adar$_2$	747	2.21	0.62	4,979	7.26	0.70
Adamic/Adar$_3$	**1,381**	**4.09**	**1.14**	5,707	8.32	0.81
$tep_{nonodeage}$	973	2.88	0.80	6,812	9.93	0.96
$tep_{notriads}$	951	2.82	0.78	5,474	7.98	0.77
$tep_{nodistance}$	**1,243**	**3.68**	**1.03**	7,069	10.31	1.00
$tep_{nolastedge}$	1,070	3.17	0.88	7,030	10.25	0.99
$tep_{nodegree}$	1,206	3.58	1.00	**8,778**	**12.80**	**1.24**

As a summary our results indicate the following:

- All measures used outperform the random predictor. However, the random predictor performs better on the Version2 dataset.
- There is not big difference in which aggregation operator was used.
- Prediction precision on the Version2 dataset is higher when random features are introduced. Random, tep_{rd}, and tep_{ngr} perform better on the Version2 dataset than the ENRON dataset when random features are used.
- Using the distance feature μ_h does not show good results. It has little or worse effect in both cases.
- The Version2 dataset is less sensitive to not including some features in our predictor, while the ENRON dataset requires as many features as possible.
- The improvement over the Adamic/Adar method is small. However, the Adamic/Adar method has the highest performance on both datasets.
- For the tests performed with features disabled, we determined that the most important features are (in ranked order): (1) ENRON – triads, node age, last edge creation, degree, and distance; (2) Version2 – triads, node age, last edge creation, distance, and degree.

It can be noticed that in all cases, using temporal information will increase the precision. However, a deeper analysis needs to be done to determine which method should be used on a given network.

Conclusions and Future Work

In this chapter, we have analyzed the robustness of centrality measures when errors are introduced in the construction of a complex social network. Our results extend the work performed in [5] by considering non random networks. In the replication of Borgatti's et al. experiments, we observed some discrepancies with our results. This may be due to the slightly different methodologies employed. However, we obtained the same linear predictability in the centrality measures that is described in [5].

Our experiments employed generative models of complex social networks and one real social network. One limitation of generative models is that while the methods for producing complex networks allow constructing networks of any size, they do not allow constructing networks with arbitrary density.

In the second contribution of this chapter, several datasets have been analyzed to obtain temporal and static features that were used in our model to predict edges in a dynamic network. Our predictive model was based on simple linear regression. The model was evaluated with two different datasets of real social networks. Our experiments show that incorporating temporal information can improve precision in prediction. This fact indicates that learning other temporal features may improve the prediction furthermore.

Our prediction model only considers predicting new edges, not if some current edges will be deleted. Changing our model to incorporate this type of prediction may improve its performance.

In our experiments, the time T was defined as 1-day intervals, and the effect of changing this parameter was not investigated. We splitted time into time stamps as was done in [16]; half of the time-stamps were used for learning and the other half for prediction. However, given the nature of the datasets at hand it could happen that the initial construction phase of the network (that is used for learning) had different dynamics than the establized phase (where the predictions are made). This issue needs further investigations.

The evaluation of our edge predictor was done under the assumption that the past behavior that was not included in the dataset will not have any effect in predictor's performance. In [15] it was shown that missing part of the past do not affect in predicting the evolution of a network's diameter.

We noticed that the random predictor performs much better in the Version2 dataset used. It is interesting to note that the Adamic/Adar predictor performs also better on this same dataset. Contrarily, our method performs better on the ENRON dataset. This could be an indication that the Version2 dataset is more random in its structure than the ENRON dataset.

The simple model used in our predictor considers few correlations between features. However, in some type of networks, features are dependent, for instance node lifetime and the degree of the node. Other supervised machine learning methods such as naive bayes could also be incorporated in our preditor to improve its accuracy. Finally, we plan to apply our predictor on more datasets to obtain a more complete characterization of its performance.

References

1. Albert, R., Barabási, A.L.: Emergence of scaling in random networks. Science **286**, 509–512 (1999)
2. Albert, R., Barabási, A.L., Jeong, H.: Mean-field theory for scale-free random networks. Physica A **272**, 173–187 (1999). doi:10.1016/S0378-4371(99)00291-5
3. Barabási, A.L., Bonabeau, E.: Scale-free networks. Sci. Am. **288**(5), 50–59 (2003)
4. Boccaletti, S., Latora, V., Moreno, Y., Chavez, M., Hwang, D.U.: Complex networks: structure and dynamics. Phys. Rep. **424**, 175–308 (2006). doi:10.1016/j.physrep.2005.10.009
5. Borgatti, S.P., Carley, K.M., Krackhardt, D.: On the robustness of centrality measures under conditions of imperfect data. Soc. Netw. **28**(2), 124–136 (2005). doi:10.1016/j.socnet.2005.05.001
6. Clauset, A., Moore, C., Newman, M.E.J.: Hierarchical structure and the prediction of missing links in networks. Nature **453**, 98–101 (2008). doi:10.1038/nature06830
7. Geng, X., Wang, Y.: Degree correlations in citation networks model with aging. Europhys. Lett. **88**, 38002 (2009). doi:10.1209/0295-5075/88/38002
8. Gloor, P.A., Niepel, S., Li, Y.: Identifying potential suspects by temporal link analysis. Technical Reports, MIT CCS (2006)
9. Gloor, P.A., Zhao, Y.: Tecflow – a temporal communication flow visualizer for social network analysis. In: ACM CSCW Workshop on Social Networks, ACM CSCW Conference (2005)
10. Goldenberg, A., Zheng, A.X., Fienberg, S.E., Airoldi, E.M.: A survey of statistical network models. Found. Trends Mach. Learn. **2**(2), 1–117 (2009)
11. Kashima, H., Abe, N.: A parameterized probabilistic model of network evolution for supervised link prediction. In: Proceedings of the 6th International Conference on Data Mining, pp. 340–349. IEEE Computer Society (2006). doi:10.1109/ICDM.2006.8
12. Klemm, K., Eguiluz, V.M.: Highly clustered scale-free networks. Phys. Rev. E **65**(3), 036123 (2002). doi:10.1103/PhysRevE.65.03612
13. Krebs, V.E.: Uncloaking terrorist networks. First Monday **7**(4) (2002)
14. Krebs V., Holley J. : Building Smart Communities through Network Weaving Know the Net. Communities **26**(3), 367–368 (1985). doi:10.1080/00420988920080361
15. Leskovec, J., Kleinberg, J., Faloutsos, C.: Graphs over time: densification laws, shrinking diameters and possible explanations. In: Proceedings of the 11th ACM SIGKDD international conference on knowledge discovery in data mining, pp. 177–187 (2005). doi:10.1145/1081870.1081893
16. Liben-Nowell, D., Kleinberg, J.: The link-prediction problem for social networks. J. Am. Soc. Inf. Sci. Technol. **58**(7), 1019–1031 (2007). doi:10.1002/asi.v58:7
17. Milgram, S.: The small world problem. Psychol. Today **2**, 60–67 (1967)
18. Newman, M.E.J.: The structure and function of complex networks. SIAM Rev. **45**(2), 167–256 (2003)
19. Ortiz-Arroyo, D., Hussain, D.M.A.: An information theory approach to identify sets of key players. In: Intelligence and Security Informatics, vol. 5376/2008, pp. 15–26. Springer (2008). doi:10.1007/978-3-540-89900-6_5
20. Scott, J.: Social Network Analysis: A Handbook, 2nd edn. SAGE, London (2000)
21. Strogatz, S.H.: Exploring complex networks. Nature **410**, 268–276 (2001). doi:10.1038/35065725
22. Tang, J., Musolesi, M., Mascolo, C., Latora, V.: Temporal distance metrics for social network analysis. In: WOSN '09: Proceedings of the 2nd ACM Workshop on Online Social Networks, pp. 31–36. ACM, New York (2009). doi:10.1145/1592665.1592674
23. Watts, D.J., Strogatz, S.: Collective dynamics of small-world networks. Nature **393**, 440–442 (1998). doi:10.1038/30918
24. Xiang, E.W.: A survey on link prediction models for social network data. Technical Reports, The Hong Kong University of Science and Technology (2008)

Part II
Applications

## Part III

Chapter 9
Social Networking Tools for Knowledge-Based Action Groups

William P. Hall, Susu Nousala, Russell Best, and Siddharth Nair

Abstract Urban bureaucrats are often overburdened with limited time and little genuine knowledge relating to decisions they must make within their briefs that impact community members. Consequently, bureaucrats often work at what Herbert Simon called the bounds of their rationality. Community groups concerned with particular issues may emerge that have issue-related local knowledge; and probably also the time and effort to share and assemble such knowledge into practical and informative group proposals. This chapter considers knowledge-based roles and dynamics of community groups, looks at revolutionary socio-technical capabilities able to support and extend group aims effectiveness, and presents a template based on social computing technologies to demonstrate how the technology can be deployed. Properly used, the tools can connect bureaucrats with the power to decide and act

W.P. Hall (✉)
Engineering Learning Unit, Melbourne School of Engineering,
University of Melbourne 2010, VIC, Australia

Kororoit Institute, St Albans, VIC, Australia
e-mail: whall@unimelb.edu.au; william-hall@bigpond.com

S. Nousala
Aalto University, NODUS-Sustainable Design Research Group, Helsinki, Finland

GAMUT, University of Melbourne and Kororoit Institute, St Albans, VIC, Australia
e-mail: susu.nousala@aalto.fi; s.nousala@gmail.com

R. Best
ISEAL, Victoria University, Melbourne, VIC, Australia

Riddells Creek Landcare, Riddells Creek, VIC, Australia
e-mail: russell.best@vu.edu.au

S. Nair
Spatial Information Architecture Lab, RMIT University, Melbourne, VIC, Australia
e-mail: sidhrth@gmail.com

A. Abraham and A.-E. Hassanien (eds.), *Computational Social Networks: Tools,*
Perspectives and Applications, DOI 10.1007/978-1-4471-4048-1_9,
© Springer-Verlag London 2012

with the local knowledge and motivation to make rational decisions about allocation of resources, etc., to deal with various kinds of situations. The template developed for this project demonstrates the capabilities of the cloud computing tools.

Introduction

Urban areas are administratively complex, and bureaucrats are often overburdened when they are working at or beyond what Herbert Simon called the bounds of their rationality [1]. Decisions impacting community group members may be based on little genuine knowledge of issues. Groups concerned with particular issues may emerge in the community. Given their focus and interests, group members will collect issue-related knowledge that can be assembled into proposals. However, it is often difficult for people to form such networks and discover what their various interested members know to construct collective knowledge. Also, such community knowledge is often ignored by governing bodies and their bureaucracies. This chapter reviews this situation from deep theoretical, technological, and practical points of view and shows how simple to use and freely available social networking tools in the cloud can be applied to effectively support knowledge-based community action.

Based on practical [2–18] and theoretical understanding [19–29] of knowledge management in groups and organizations, we consider here some of the knowledge-based roles and dynamics of community groups. We discuss some new cognitive technologies to support the aims of individuals, community groups, and governing bodies in urban and regional hierarchies to extend their effectiveness and abilities to communicate across boundaries. Revolutionary Web 2.0 technologies based in the cloud provide action and other social groups with simple yet sophisticated tools to assemble and support social networks; to collect and assemble personal knowledge; and to transform personal knowledge into community knowledge. Properly implemented in a collaborative environment, Web tools can also be used by bureaucrats and administrators to source local knowledge to support rational decisions about allocation of resources, etc., and to deal with various kinds of emerging situations. The template developed for this project[1] demonstrates cloud computing capabilities of the new tools.

This chapter relates to the sociological concept of "community action." Following Bryant [30], community action means any emergent or externally promoted attempt to involve local people in self-help schemes or to participate in policy making and service provision. A community action group is a network of people formed in a local context to promote, guide, or carry out social, political, or practical objectives. From theoretical and practical points of view, we explore roles

---

[1] See "Template for Knowledge-Based Community Organizations" – https://sites.google.com/site/organizingcommunityaction/

of knowledge and information in (a) forming such groups and (b) achieving goals within the governance frameworks of urban and regional environments. Action groups are at the far end of the spectrum of knowledge-based communities including "communities of interest" (CoI) and "communities of practice" (CoP) [13, 31, 32]. Compared to the well-known CoPs, which often are informal subdivisions within the structural hierarchy of one or more existing organizations, action groups are normally independent, self-governed, and are often formally constituted groups of people with their own self-determined goals. Historically, action groups have emerged in local areas from the face-to-face social interactions and collective work of people sharing common concerns and interests – often as promoted by community "organizers" [33–36].

The new Web-based "social" technologies provide people with powerful cognitive tools to help form and sustain such groups, and to construct, manage, and share knowledge relating to commonly held concerns. The result of combining people and cognitive tools with networking capabilities is the formation of sociotechnical networks with much more power than the people alone would have. The technologies to be discussed here have been tested primarily in community action groups, but provide all kinds of knowledge-based groups with powerful tools for assembling, sharing, and applying knowledge and enabling virtual participation in group activities.

In this chapter, we begin with a theoretical framework for community action, then discuss some of the revolutionary cognitive technologies that provide tools for implementing the theory, and conclude by presenting some preliminary observations from ongoing case studies where the technology has been recently implemented. Given that some of the specific Web technologies we are concerned with here have only become fully functional since 2007–2010, there has been no opportunity to study their use over long time scales.

Theoretical Framework

Communities and Action Groups

Human social systems are based on fractally complex networks of physical, social, and economic interactions. The networks define complex adaptive systems at different hierarchical levels of organization from local groups, formal organizations, and governing bodies. Many of these bodies have properties allowing them to be considered autopoietic (i.e., living [37], see section "Life, Cognition, and Living Knowledge") at a level of hierarchical organization above individual people and below economic or statutory organizations [19–29, 37–45].

All activities maintaining the organized fabric of urban and regional districts are to some degree knowledge-based and would not function without the material implementation of that knowledge. Governing bodies make decisions at many different levels of organization, whether by committees, individual bureaucrats, or designated workers. All decisions boil down to individual people choosing among alternatives based on available knowledge. Under the label "bounded rationality," Herbert Simon explained that the rationality of decisions is limited by the amount of information that can be held in the mind, processed, and understood [1, 9, 24, 25, 46, 47]. If these limits are breached by lack of pertinent information that can be found in the available time or an overload of irrelevant information, decisions become increasingly irrational. However, suboptimal decisions are still almost always better than no decision, so Simon recommends that decision makers should find tools that can help them make the "best" decision one can in the time available, to help "satisfice."

> [T]he elaborate organizations that human beings have constructed ... to carry out the work of production and government can only be understood as machinery for coping with the limits of man's abilities to comprehend and compute in the face of complexity and uncertainty ([1]: p. 354).

> [W]e ... understand today many of the mechanisms of human rational choice. We ... know how the information processing system called Man, faced with complexity beyond his ken, uses his information processing capacities to seek out alternatives, to calculate consequences, to resolve uncertainties, and thereby - sometimes, not always - to find ways of action that are sufficient unto the day, that satisfice. ([1]: p. 368)

Organizations can make more effective decisions by devolving decisions to people who are closer to the problems and presumably have more knowledge and time to consider the particular problem area [9]. Another is to more effectively filter decision-related input to genuinely critical information and tested wisdom [24, 25]. Greiner [48] observed that to grow large, businesses had to survive several revolutionary transformations in management structure to continue growing. We think that successful revolutions represented changes that kept operational decisions within the limits of rational decision making. In other words, decisions need to be made by people who are close to and well informed about the issues being decided [9, 24, 25].

Individual people can work together in the interface between their physical environment and systems of urban and regional governance to ensure local and personal knowledge is available to guide and constrain activities of administrative juggernauts. Within large social systems, action groups can emerge from networks of people with interests in particular problem areas [13, 17, 28]. However, there is a large gap between the emergence of an action group and assembling its members' personal knowledge into coherent objective knowledge to support rational decisions by a bureaucrat or functionary. We next look at some theoretical considerations involved in understanding the nature of this gap and bridging it.

Constructed and Tested Knowledge

What "knowledge" and "information" mean in the organizational knowledge management discipline is contentious [49–51]. Here we adopt Karl Popper's [52] definition that knowledge is "solutions to problems," where the knowledge may be contained in thoughts, in speech, written on paper, or embodied in the structure of an artifact. For living entities, everything involved with maintaining life in a constantly variable environment is a "problem" [53, 54]. In this framework, we consider that "information" refers to variations in the world that may in living things stimulate cognition and add to living entities' knowledge, i.e., Bateson's [55] "differences which make differences." For us, information signifies the content or "meaning" of a message based on its effect on the cognition of the recipient (see Hayles discussion [56: p 55–56]).

Popper [52, 59, 60], as interpreted by Hall [19–23], also usefully divided the world into three ontological domains:

- "world 1" – the world of uninterpreted physical systems and dynamics
- "world 2" – the world of cognitive processes (i.e., cybernetics) together with structural, dispositional, and subjective knowledge (i.e., living knowledge)
- "world 3" – the world of "objective" knowledge (i.e., knowledge that is codified into relatively inert and persistent objects existing in world 1 via printing, computer memories, or DNA)

Donald Campbell [57, 58] coined the term evolutionary epistemology for the understanding he and Popper had that knowledge was something that was cognitively constructed by living entities from their experiences with the world through fallible processes of trial and error learning [61]. Campbell called the process "blind variation and selective retention," and Popper "conjecture and refutation" [62] or "tentative solutions and error elimination" [52]. In evolutionary epistemology, knowledge is constructed via continually iterated cyclical process of cognition resulting in increasingly accurate, although always fallible, understandings of reality. Popper's most detailed exposition what he calls his "general theory of evolution" [52: pp. 241–244]. A more concrete description of the fundamentally cyclic nature of knowledge building in the real world is summarized in John Boyd's OODA Loop process (Fig. 9.1) [19–25, 63–65] that is applicable to both personal and organizational levels of analysis.

This cyclical process of knowledge building involves self-reflection, self-criticism, and self-maintenance that some consider to be viciously circular [e.g., 66–68]. Vollmer argues on philosophical and scientific grounds that such critiques are unfounded as the supposed "circular" processes are "non-vicious, consistent, fertile, self-correcting feedback loops … termed 'virtuous circles'" [69: p. 200]. More simply, knowledge building involves neurological or administrative processing in the physical world [70]. There can be no paradox as the cognitive activities are causally connected to form a "virtuous spiral" process through time [24–26] (Fig. 9.2; see [71] for animations of the concept). Due to time delays in dynamical systems, the world as observed is never the world that is acted upon.

Problem-solving entities (people, organizations) seek to understand the world in ways that will enable them to reach particular "intended future" states, but they exist in an unpredictably changing world, where at any time the situation may diverge to any of many possible "divergent" futures [24, 65, 70–72]. Without continual vigilance, rational orientation and decision, reflected in appropriate action (i.e., via

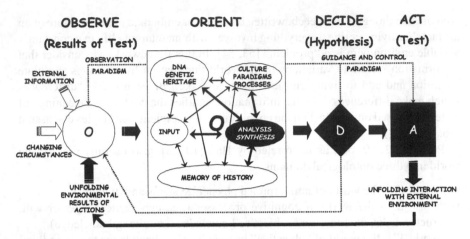

Fig. 9.1 Boyd's problem solving Observe, Orient, Decide, Act (OODA) loop (After [19, 63])

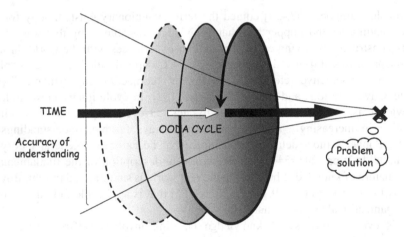

Fig. 9.2 Spiral construction of knowledge through time converging on a solution to a problem (See [13, 24–26, 71])

OODA cycles) to converge on intended futures, stochastic divergence is inevitable. It is here that Simon's [1] bounds to rationality are of particular concern. For them to be effective, decisions must be made in the entity's cognitive system close enough to the interface with the problem that processing is informed with enough relevant observational data without being overwhelmed with irrelevant information [24, 25, 70–72].

Life, Cognition, and Living Knowledge

We have argued elsewhere that cells, people, organizations, and other entities in the complex systems hierarchy of the biological world are all autopoietic or living [19–28]. Autopoiesis (= "self" + "production") is a condition of a complex dynamical system at any level of structural organization that gives it the autonomous ability within its environment to self-produce and maintain its dynamic state of organization. As defined by Maturana and Varela [37–39], systems are autopoietic when they meet six criteria considered necessary and sufficient to recognize when a complex system could be considered to be autopoietic, and thus living [39: p. 192–193]:

- *Bounded* ("the unity [i.e., an entity] has identifiable boundaries"). Varela et al. [39] were concerned that the entity could be discriminated by an external observer. To us this criterion should read, "the entity has *self*-identifiable boundaries."
- *Complex* ("there are constitutive elements of the unity, that is, components"). Biological systems are more than complicated.
- *Mechanistic* ("the component properties are capable of satisfying certain relations that determine in the unity the interactions and transformations of these components"). In other words, the complex entity is a dynamical system, such that components show causal interactions as detailed by Urrestarazu [73, 74].
- *Self-referential or self-differentiated* ("the components that constitute the boundaries of the unity constitute these boundaries through preferential neighborhood relations and interactions between themselves, as determined by their properties in the space of their interactions"). That is, the boundaries of the system are structurally determined.
- *Self-producing* ("the boundaries of the unity are produced by the interactions of the components of the unity, either by transformations of previously produced components, or by transformations and/or coupling of non-component elements that enter the unity through its boundaries").
- *Autonomous* ("all the other components of the unity are also produced by interactions of its components as in [the statement above], and . . . those which are not produced by the interactions of other components participate as necessary permanent constitutive components in the production of other components")

Maturana and Varela [37] consider that cognition begins with the self-defining, self-regulating, and self-producing spiral processes that determine and dynamically maintain the autopoietic condition. In other words, autopoiesis cannot exist or continue without cognitive processes able to build, maintain, and act on knowledge to solve the problems of life. See Popper [52] and "All life is problem solving" [54] for a similar understanding developed completely independently from Maturana and Varela's (or conversely).

Unifying the paradigms of evolutionary epistemology and autopoiesis [22], we recognize three categories of knowledge:

- *Structural* knowledge is embodied in the organized physical structure of a causal network responsible for maintaining autopoiesis in a dynamical system in an instant of time. At one instant the structure is such that it ensures that the causal network maintains autopoiesis in the next instant. In other words, most adjacent possible [75–77] states of the system in the next instant will be states that also propagate the autopoietic organization of the system. Thus, autopoiesis continues as long as the system remains in the basin of a "'strange' or 'chaotic' attractor" [78: p. 178–179]. Loss of autopoiesis is equivalent to disintegration of the system. Natural selection builds increasingly reliable knowledge by eliminating entities unable to maintain themselves in the basin of attraction where autopoiesis is maintained.
- *Dispositional* and *subjective*: Using Popper's terms [52] (and as informed by the theory of autopoiesis [37]) this is knowledge held in the nervous system. Dispositional knowledge relates to dispositions or instincts to act in certain ways, i.e., as built into the inherited or habituated structure of the nervous system; subjective knowledge is the living or conscious knowledge of the individual "subject," readily available to be criticized or improved by learning. All of this is more or less comparable to Polanyi's [79, 80] "tacit" knowledge.
- *Objective* or "*explicit*": encoded forms of knowledge (e.g., in the form of letters on paper, sequences of bits in a computer memory, or sequences of nucleotides in a DNA molecule). Objective knowledge is inert and persistent. As such it can be preserved through time and exchanged across time and the space between living individuals.

Structural, dispositional, and subjective knowledge, together with the cybernetic (cognitive) processes for building, maintaining, and acting on this knowledge, are encompassed within world 2. Popper [52]. places articulated (but not codified) speech in world 3 together with all kinds of persistently codified knowledge. We (following Hall [22] and Ong [81]) place speech in world 2 because sound vanishes from the physical world in an instant and its content persists only through its impact on cognitive processes of living people (world 2).

Living systems emerge and can exist at several different levels of organization in a complex systems hierarchy [20–23, 28, 40–44, 82, 83]. The hierarchy containing living systems ranges from fundamental particles through cells, multicellular organisms, and various kinds and levels of social systems involving organisms to planets, solar systems, galaxies, and the universe [41, 83]. What we see is determined by level of the hierarchy on which we focus (Fig. 9.3). If we focus on, e.g., human organizations, we see organizational systems comprised of components ("subsystems" such as people that may be recognized as systems in their own right if studied at a lower level in the hierarchy). The focal system also exists within an environment (e.g., a national economy) that may also be seen as a system in its own right when examined at a higher level. Koestler [84, 85] (following Simon [42–44]) wrote that a focal system ("holon") formed a triad of the system itself

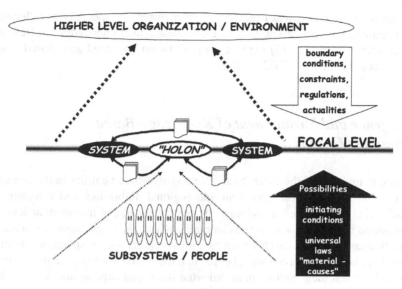

Fig. 9.3 Action groups in the hierarchical structure (After [23, 41])

and its component subsystems, within the higher level organization that formed its environment. Focal levels containing living entities are self-identified. Causal networks of subsystems and components constrain what the holon is capable to do (upward causation), while downward causation from the higher level system constrains what the holon is possible to do.

Simon [42–44] noted that individual systems and levels of complexity can be discriminated by intrinsic interaction frequencies. Systems at a focal level are discriminated by lower frequencies of interactions across their boundaries than between components within them. Simon [43: p. 33] called this "loose coupling." (Maturana [86: p. 54] similarly noted that boundaries of autopoietic system are "surfaces of thermodynamic cleavage.") Hierarchical levels in a holonic triad are discriminated by interaction speeds. Interactions of components in subsystems are generally so fast that (seen from the focal level) they appear to be in internal equilibrium and interact as particles in law-like ways to form the focal system. Similarly, interactions of components forming the supersystem will generally be so slow that the supersystem forms a relatively constant environment for the focal system [43: pp. 10–11; 44]. Simon calls hierarchically complex systems conforming to this situation "nearly decomposable."

For humans, networks of "social" interactions interconnect people via the exchange of knowledge or "content" in worlds 2 and 3 (see section "Constructed and Tested Knowledge") to form higher order social systems (organizations). In peoples' brains, faster networks of interaction interconnect their nerve cells to carry out cognitive processes. In organizations, (1) structural knowledge for autopoiesis is held in dynamically changing logical and physical networks of interactions among members, layout of plant and equipment, etc., (2) dispositional and subjective knowledge in the minds and behaviors of its members – especially as reflected in organizational routines and jargons ("organizational tacit knowledge" in Nelson & Winter's term [87]), and (3) explicit documentation produced and shared among organizational members [20–22, 45].

Emergence and Sustainment of Knowledge-Based Community Groups

We seek to understand the emergence of knowledge-based entities in the hierarchy between individual people and local and regional authorities and governments. Salthe [82] argues that self-sustaining systems can emerge at intermediate levels of organization in the complex systems hierarchy where there are major inefficiencies in the dissipation of potential between existing levels. This corresponds to situations where there is a gap between what people in a local area need and want in terms of affordances from their environment and what the social supersystem is providing. This is often due to gaps in resources and knowledge.

Where individual people form groups to construct, share, and apply knowledge relating to problem situations, Nousala and Hall [28] suggest that they coalesce around a "human attractor" who has a public reputation for interest in that type of problem. People recognize that they share this interest with the attractor and begin to exchange knowledge with her/him, and having been brought together by the attractor, they also begin to network among themselves in various knowledge transfer processes, as illustrated in Fig. 9.4 that shows early stages in the emergence of an autopoietic organization.

"Faces" in Fig. 9.4 are subsystems/people in the emerging group or organization. ("*a*") is a human attractor. ("*b*") is the emerging boundary separating "insiders" who identify themselves as participants for community purposes from "outsiders" in the neighborhood. Faces crossing the boundary ("*c*") are people being recruited and inducted into the community. Bright smiley faces represent people/actors receiving organizational/social rewards for their involvement with the collective need. Open arrows at the top indicate the value/importance of the assembled knowledge as this is ordered and directed to address higher level organizational needs, while arrows at the bottom indicate the importance and roles of historical circumstances in constraining what is possible ("adjacent possible"). Directed lines connecting faces show knowledge transfer between individual actors. Line weights show strengths of the connections. Note that the connections are beginning to form cyclical knowledge processing routines able to be mapped and improved [2, 88].

Figure 9.5 combines the concepts introduced in the previous four figures to illustrate the virtuous knowledge building spiral of an emergent organization responding to environmental imperatives and its internal goals. Each OODA cycle responds to fresh observations where the organizational understanding is analyzed

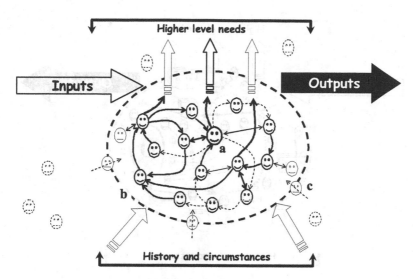

Fig. 9.4 Early stages in the emergence of a knowledge-based community (After [28])

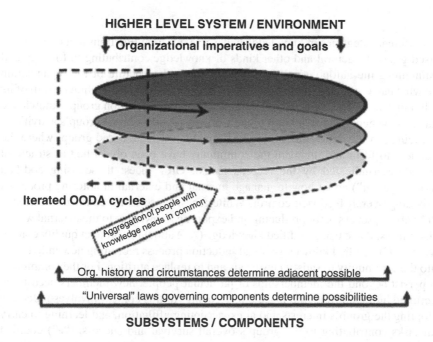

Fig. 9.5 Building organizational knowledge (After [13])

and criticized via orientation processes and tested via selective decisions and actions in the world. On balance, the organization's understanding of the world should be improved with each turn of the spiral.

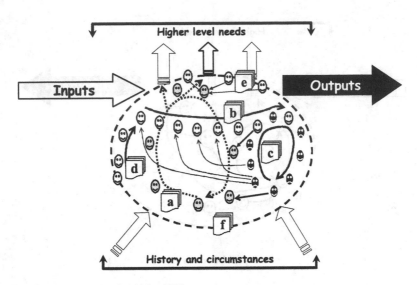

Fig. 9.6 A mature community (After [28])

Different categories of knowledge may serve different functions in a knowledge-based group. Structural and other kinds of knowledge contributing to forming and maintaining the autopoietically functioning network structure of the organization are what makes the functioning group something more than the arithmetic sum of its individual members. Especially in the case of community action groups, knowledge may also be generated for export to the world as products of the group's activities.

Figure 9.6 illustrates this in a fully formed knowledge-based group, where the practices to form and maintain the community have been objectified as structural procedures (indicated by the records icons). Grey faces: those using codified knowledge ("*a*") about how to manage internal and external monitoring processes providing overall feedback control. White faces: those using codified knowledge ("*b*") about processes for producing and exporting knowledge to the external world. Black faces: those using codified knowledge ("*c*") about the product quality control cycle. ("*d*") codified knowledge about induction process recruiting new individuals into the community to satisfy new needs and to replace attrition. For the community to persist beyond the memberships of particular people, new members need to be recruited into the group to replace those leaving. In this context involves inductees adopting the group's interests and aims, accepting affiliation, and learning to carry out tasks contributing to the group's overall survival and success. ("*e*") codified knowledge about environmental monitoring processes. ("*f*") codified and structural knowledge about how to establish and sustain the community itself.

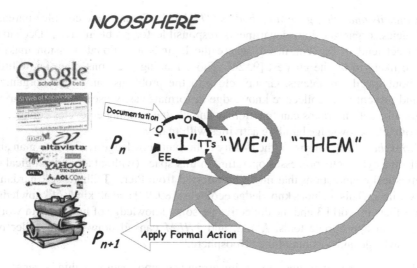

Fig. 9.7 Putting community knowledge into its hierarchical context (From [8])

Application of Actionable Community Knowledge in a Governance Framework

We now consider how emergent knowledge-based community groups fit into and function in the hierarchical complexity of the knowledge ecology [89] of their environments. Urban/regional councils, other administrative bodies and their delegates are responsible to provide services necessary for civil life and for maintaining peoples' health and amenities. When relating to problem areas, functionaries need to know who, what, where, when, why, and how.

Figure 9.7 applies the theoretical framework presented in the previous sections and [6, 8] to knowledge acquisition, building, and acting in the urban environment. We recognize at least three nested epicycles of knowledge-based autopoietic systems that we have also seen in other hierarchical knowledge-based systems, i.e., large engineering organizations [9, 13, 16, 17], industry clusters [5, 7], and academic and scientific research communities [27, 91].

The levels in these hierarchical structures are defined as follows:

- *Individual people* (*"I"*). Individuals concerned by particular problems may assembler explicit knowledge in the form of documents, photographs, maps, records of measurements, etc.; as well as developing his/her personal knowledge. Following Popper [52] this knowledge building may involve cycles of Observing, Orienting, constructing Tentative Theories, and acting to Eliminate Errors.
- *Community action groups* (*"WE"*). Where several people face similar problems, they may share concerns and knowledge leading to emergence of a community group [28]. This may involve sharing personal knowledge and documents to build a group repository. Group success and sustainability will depend on the success of the personal interactions in assembling useful knowledge and action plans.

- *Councils and other governing bodies ("THEM")*. Councils are complex bureaucracies, organized into departments responsible for problem areas. Decisions to act tend to be centralized, where the bounds to rational decision making are likely to be the greatest [9, 24]. Those making decisions often know little about specific problems. Groups close to the problems can collect, organize, and present their collective knowledge in formats easily used by functionaries. Ideally, action groups can function as knowledge building epicycles connecting councils' knowledge building activities with reality.
- *Noosphere* [90]. This is (a) the totality of human knowledge available to man and (b) the cybernetic processes operating in this space (without any teleological or mystical connotations that might be inferred from Pierte Teilhard de Chardan's writings). This includes knowledge ecologies [89, 92] and all kinds of knowledge artifacts in world 3 and the collective personal knowledge of humanity in world 2. With appropriate tools, *I, WE*, and *THEM* can all draw on the collective knowledge and wisdom of the "Noosphere."

The emergence of groups networking around common causes within larger social or ecological systems is probably as old as the origins of human language [81], depending mainly on tacit and verbal knowledge exchange [9, 13–17]. However, as will be discussed in the next section, the development in the last ~30 years of cognitive technologies able to exchange massive amounts of explicit knowledge in a variety of formats has revolutionized the environment for and potential capabilities of knowledge-based groups.

Technologies for Socially Constructing and Sharing Knowledge

In less than a lifetime, the integration of new cognitive tools and knowledge production technologies has extended human cognition far beyond the bounds of human brains. Humans have become "post human," where people and their machines now act as symbiotic super-organisms [56, 93–96]. Similarly, human networks have become "socio-technical," i.e., comprised of people, plus tools, machines, and technologically mediated processes [97]. Over the last 30 years, tools such as personal computers and the Internet are radically revolutionizing people's interactions to organize. Today's organizations potentially command vastly more knowledge to support their actions than was the case three decades earlier.

The Importance of "Free" Applications for the Support of Emergent Action

Genuine community action begins with individual people at the grass-roots level, who desire (and need) to combine their knowledge with the knowledge of other individuals in the community who have similar concerns and interests to act. The essential consideration in this emergent situation is that whatever is initially done to establish an organized action must be done within the personal household budgets of interested and motivated individuals. Institutions, governments, and industrial organizations can spend millions of dollars on integrated knowledge management applications for licensing, implementation, training, and support [3, 4, 11]. Individuals need access to user-friendly applications they can readily implement for no cost other than time and labor. In the remainder of this chapter, we consider only applications that are available "free to the web" for no license costs to individuals and community groups.

A Caveat

There are important caveats regarding the use of "free applications." Genuinely useful tools are created only through the investment of major intellectual effort either by altruistic groups or commercial organizations hoping to use them as vehicles for paid advertising or for marketing paid services. Where products provided by altruistic groups are concerned, there is no guarantee that the group will survive to provide continuing maintenance of the application. Where tools developed by commercial organizations are concerned, the free service may be withdrawn or changed at any time on the whim of the provider.

Although our demonstration below is based on Google's applications as they existed in the latter half of 2010, it should be noted that in February 2011, with no warning, Google (1) made major modifications to the user interface of their flagship document management ("Docs") application. These substantially impaired the functionality of its user interface (even for paid users) – Google Help Forum: "The New Refreshed Documents List is DREADFUL" – http://www.google.com/support/forum/p/Google+Docs/thread?tid=327b78beafe120ba&hl=en; and (2) changed the licensing of their application suite ("Apps") that now requires paid licensing for use by more than ten members ("Update on changes to Google Apps" – email to existing users dated 29 April 2011). The advertised cost for commercial licensing of Google Apps is $50 per user/per year (http://www.google.com/apps/intl/en/group/index.html) or $30 per user/per year for "non-profits" having US IRS 501(c)(3) status with more than 3,000 users. A free Google Apps for Education license is available for those qualifying organizations with fewer than 3,000 users (http://www.google.com/nonprofits/eligibility.html) or non-US, although we could find nothing on Google's web pages explaining how such smaller organizations could obtain licenses. These changes may offer insurmountable obstacles to those attempting to implement Google's tools for at the level of community groups. At the time of writing this, it is still unclear how these changes impact the "sharing" capabilities of sites maintained by a single person – as is the case for the implementations documented below.

Social, Semantic and Cloud Computing Externalize Aspects of Community Cognition

Since 2000 the Web's revolutionary capabilities for extending cognition have continued to evolve at a still increasing pace. Personal computing technologies have vastly extended and revolutionized the cognitive capacities of individual humans [56, 95, 96]. This is turning emergent human social organizations on the borderline of autopoiesis, that to now have been predominantly organized via tacit knowledge exchanges, into much more powerful and robustly sustainable "sociotechnical" organizations. Three new trends of technological understanding and development are coming together to externalize and support cognitive processes at the community level:

- *Semantic Web*, where specialized markup languages allow the significance of components of text to be marked up in ways that computers can understand semantically for further processing [3, 98], with the first "Recommendation" for XML released in 1998 [99]. However, the full potential of the semantic web hoped for by Berners-Lee et al. [98] has still not been realized because of difficulties reconciling logical and dialectical differences between the implementations of XML on different sites [90, 100].
- *Web 2.0*. Web 2.0 or "social computing" does not refer to specific technology developments but rather to the development of aspects of the web that favor virtual collaboration and sharing of electronically delivered content. The term Web 2.0 was invented by O'Reilly in 2001 to cover the whole range of social computing activities [101, 102] Following Miller [103], Web 2.0 thinking seeks to:
  - Free data (e.g., "freedom of information," minimize constraints on data access)
  - Enable virtual applications (e.g., aggregate data and functions from different sources)
  - Facilitate two-way participation (e.g., peer to peer)
  - Focus on user needs not provider wants
  - Build modular applications (facilitate hierarchically complex systems)
  - Share (code, content, ideas)
  - Facilitate communication and community building
  - Facilitate remix and mashup
  - Become smarter (e.g., Amazon's recommendation engines, Google's Page Ranking)
  - Open up the "long tail" (make it cost effective to service small requirements of large number of individuals)
  - Build trust (in individuals, assertions, data and its reuse)

  For community knowledge management, probably the best known and most successful application exemplifying Web 2.0 qualities is Wikipedia [104]. A wiki is a collaborative website where users can easily add to, modify, and comment on content using only a Web browser. Wikis facilitate collaborative collection, generation, review, and distribution of content. They typically allow users to add new content, link to other content within and outside the wiki environment, edit content, organize and structure content, view content and access a history of changes to contributions. Contributions may be authored within the environment or brought in from outside [105].

- *Cloud computing.* The concept first appeared in 2007 [106–108] to cover the idea that data storage and processing will be offloaded onto external repositories and data processing centers [109, 110] users can access the data and control the processing with little more than a web browser and Internet connection. A wide range of applications (apps) are available that can be more-or-less readily integrated to meet most knowledge management needs for knowledge-based groups. The best known cloud-based tool is probably MediaWiki (http://www.mediawiki.org/), which provides the basis for Wikipedia. From the point of implementation by individual users at the community level, its user interface is non-intuitive and does not provide for the easy embedding of tables, calendars, and non-HTML content such as videos and forms that are useful to community groups. On the other hand, although free and useful cloud-based tools are offered by many providers, the major tools we personally experimented with and integrated in 2010 for community use are Google's cloud "Apps" (see caveat in section "A Caveat", above) with social capabilities [10]. These include:

  Google Account (a "single sign-on" server that identifies a user for access to other Google Apps – see Wikipedia: "Google Account")
  - *Gmail* (a cloud-based email server launched as a beta in 2004 and fully released in 2007 – Wikipedia: "Gmail").
  - *Docs* (authoring and repository). Text documents, spreadsheets, and presentations can all be authored and edited in the HTML-based browser environment. Any document type may be stored and managed in the repository (but only Google formatted documents may be edited in the browser rather than using a dedicated application – e.g., MS Word for .doc formats). Docs supports document sharing and collaborative authoring with version tracking. Documents may be shared or not (controlled either at file or folder level and sharing may be limited to specified account holders or may be open to the public). Docs was released to Google Apps users in February 2007. Currently, each Google Account user is automatically granted more than a gigabyte of free repository storage in the cloud. Additional storage can be purchased in increments of 20 GB for (currently) $5.00 per year, electronically payable via Google Account. (Wikipedia: "Google Docs"). Note 1: free tools such as Zotero (http://www.zotero.org/) and Dropbox (http://www.dropbox.com) are substantially better stand-alone tools for managing shared document repositories than Docs, but offer less free storage and connectivity with other tools. As for Google, additional Zotero or Dropbox storage can be purchased – at substantially greater costs than Google charges. Note 2: changes made to the user interface in February 2011 make Docs less user-friendly than it was in 2010.

- *Sites* is a flexible wiki-like collaborative authoring tool for assembling and managing complete web sites based on collections of HTML Web pages. Sites, launched in 2008, has similar access controls to Docs, and (e.g., compared to MediaWiki) will embed and provide access to files held within (and controlled by) Docs. It is ideal for hosting community-based wikis. Usage notes for Google Sites are provided by [111, 112]. (Wikipedia: "Google Sites").
- *Groups*, acquired in 2001, offers a discussion forum format allowing threaded conversations comparable to several other group hosting applications, except that it relies on the members' single-sign-ons maintained in Google Accounts. Groups may be based on controlled subscriptions or open to the public, and may be used to manage sharing for Docs and Sites (Wikipedia: "Google Groups").
- *Translator Toolkit* is Google's multilingual collaborative translation tool hidden behind its normal machine translation function. It facilitates interactive human collaboration and lexicon development around machine generated texts (Wikipedia "Google translator toolkit").
- *Other Google social computing tools integrating with Sites.* There are a variety of other social computing tools in addition to those mentioned above that can be integrated into a Google Sites environment to assist the assembly and management of group knowledge and to produce knowledge-based products to influence decisions of larger organizations [10, 111]. These include Google Maps, Picasa Web Albums, Google Calendar, and YouTube.

Constructing a Template for Community Groups

For community problem solutions to be successful, they need to meet community content management requirements and be supportable. For several years Hall has supported collaboration environments for an informal research group, TOMOK, interested in the theory, ontology, and management of organizational knowledge. After testing several free wiki tools and collaboration environments, the group's first collaboration environment was established on a product called BSCW and marketed by OrbiTeam (http://www.bscw.de/english/product.html). This provided full content management requirements for source references and versioning, tracking and discussion requirements for several coauthored papers, to meet all TOMOK's requirements Although BSCW was available free on trial or for longer periods to unfunded academic groups, TOMOK found the server maintenance and frequent re-licensing requirements beyond our capacity to support.

From January to mid May 2010 Hall constructed a collaboration environment for the TOMOK group using Google Apps, and based on this experience, began experimenting with implementing these tools in community action scenarios.

Fig. 9.8   Test 1: Wiki site constructed for a particular group project

Initial Usability Testing in a Community Action Scenario

Our assumption that the technology would be useable by people with few computer skills has been tested in four new implementations (note: these test that the technology meets theoretical requirements discussed above, and are not studies of the knowledge lifecycles in the groups concerned):

- *Test 1* (Fig. 9.8): Hall established a collaboration site for authors contributing to a special session of Knowledge Cities World Summit, "Putting Community Knowledge in Place," beginning with Google's Wiki template (https://sites.google.com/site/projectwikitemplate_en/). Implementation began 17 May and was complete and shared with other contributors by 26 May.

- *Test 2* (Fig. 9.9): Selected components of Putting Community Knowledge in Place were used as the starting template for a demonstration linked to the present paper that has been shared with the world [111]. Work began 27 June 2010, with the page structure complete by 29 June. Page contents were modified July 5, 8, and 22 as inclusions and linked documents were refined.

- *Test 3*: Starting with a blank Google Site, a new site was created by the Riddells Creek Landcare Group (RCL) with content transferred from the existing RCL Web page hosted on conventional server-based web technologies. The new RCL site includes public pages as well as private pages accessible only to Committee members (http://www.riddellscreeklandcare.org.au/). Beginning with the blank site opened around June 1, members of the RCL Committee transferred most historical documents, project records, financial accounts, and membership list details before the 24 July 2010 AGM. All RCL people who have tested it have found the Google technology intuitively easy to work with – much easier than the prior server-based technology that requires specialist skills to administer.

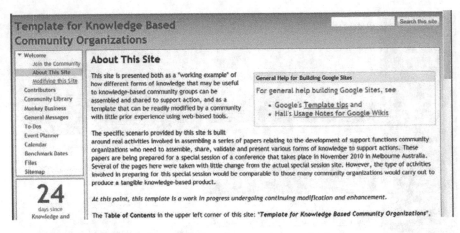

Fig. 9.9 Test 2: Template for knowledge-based community organizations

- *Test 4*: Google Sites was trialed in a committee meeting of an umbrella group of 11 landcare groups to see how easily a group of naïve people with modest computing skills could come to grips with it. The Secretary (representing one group) and representatives of two other groups attended the meeting. Sitting around a kitchen table and networking wirelessly via their notebook computers, participants soon understood the Google Sites' logic. Starting with a blank site, the basic structure for the umbrella group's Web page was built within an hour. This explains the group's aims, describes joint projects and stream observations, establishes a private committee area, and provides links to each of the 11 component groups. For the live site see http://www.jcen.org.au/.

The conclusion from these tests is that anyone able to use an Internet browser on a personal computer should be able to work within a Google Site to make their personal knowledge explicit. As a final comment, we note that Google provides only limited documentation to explain use of sophisticated functions and multiple "add-ins" (i.e., "gadgets"). To partially fill this gap we developed the Template for Knowledge Based Community Organizations [111] that also includes some detailed usage notes [112].

Knowledge Management Capabilities to Support Community Action

For community actions in the real world to successfully achieve their intended effects, they need to be based on tested knowledge of the reality being confronted. As noted above, a wiki provides a framework for the social construction, testing, and criticism of knowledge following a Popperian knowledge development cycle as illustrated in Figs. 9.1 and 9.5. An appropriately implemented wiki should meet most knowledge-related requirements for a community action group. In our personal experience, Google Sites (together with other Google Apps) meets several knowledge management requirements beyond content management for community action groups, all as illustrated in [111]:

- *Observation*: Hall [112] describes how individual users can insert a wide range of materials ranging from original observations to links and embedded documents, or even a "file cabinet" into a web page, ranging from textual notes and observations, individual photographs, photo albums, maps, and even videos (as illustrated by "Monkey Business" in [111]).
- *Orientation and development of tentative theories/solutions*: Web pages offer provisions for people to comment, discuss, and attach additional document files. Message functions can be used for either general discussions at the site level or discussions related to specific project pages, etc., shown on the bottom right of the "Welcome page" (general) and at the bottom of the "Free Technology for the Support of Community Action Groups" page (specific).
- *Decision*: Decisions can be developed via topic page-related discussions or polls based on spreadsheet forms.
- *Action*: Google Sites provides excellent facilities for multilayered presentations. Inviting councillors to join the site may be a deliverable in its own right, as this would give them full access to a submission and layers of supporting information.
- *Monitoring results of actions*: The full capabilities of the observing functions can be used.
- *Recruitment functions*: The site may be shared with "everyone" so it is indexed and discoverable by anyone interested in the group's activities.
- *Membership administrative functions*: New member records can be generated automatically using a Google Spreadsheet form in a web page (as illustrated on the Join the Community page).
- *Financial management*: Financial records, contracts, funding proposals, membership dues, and all other matters of financial interest can be kept in a linked Site accessible only to group officers and committee members.
- *Communication, coordination, and tracking*: There is no mail out function other than change notifications specifically associated with a Google Site. Group members can nominate to be notified of changes to the site as a whole or to designated pages within the site. However, a parallel Google Group (see http://groups.google.com/) can be established and linked to the site to manage a fully functional discussion list.
- *Facilitate internal trust and outside security*: As can be seen from the Join the Community page and various Contributors pages, e.g., Susu Nousala, the Template provides ample possibilities to create a trustworthy persona within the site community. Secure materials can easily be established in linked Sites where the access is password protected and fully controlled. Google's cloud computing "Apps for Government" have been certified for government use under the US Federal Information Security Management Act [113].

- *Provide epistemic structure*: Pages within a Google Site can be readily established in a logical hierarchy reflecting the group's aims and purposes. Documents and cross-links within pages provide additional cognitive associations. If desired linked document libraries can also be established within Google Docs, organized within a hierarchical folder structure (e.g., click the Community Library link). As amply demonstrated in the Template, hyperlinks can be used throughout the site structure to link associated knowledge objects.

Higher Levels of Organization

Although our own studies have focused on the potential uses of cloud computing social technologies at the level of communities emerging at levels of organization between that of individual people and the larger governing organizations such as urban and regional councils and states, such technologies are also being adopted at these higher levels in the USA, at city, county, state, and federal levels. Documented examples implementations are Department of Defense, Social Security Administration, State of Wisconsin, Prince Georges County MD, and the City of Los Angeles among several others [114]. The next step in our explorations of the social dynamics of this technology will be to see if we can build connections between the "WE" and "THEM" epicycles (Fig. 9.7) social knowledge building.

Conclusions and Looking to the Future

Even before the Web was established, it was recognized that interpersonal networking supported by computer systems could help form and sustain community groups [115–117]. As elaborated above, in 2010 no cost and easy to use social technologies appeared that offer extraordinary capabilities for socially constructing, managing, and delivering content for knowledge-based community groups. The tools can easily be used by a single human attractor to create a socio-technical environment advertizing a problem situation and inviting like-minded people to join together to form a community of interest/practice/action. The community and its membership can be easily formalized in the environment that then offers its members an array of powerful tools helping group members to capture observations and existing knowledge to build, criticize, and propose solutions to the identified problems.

Once established, the site and its contents persist as an underlying and evolving structure (a) linking the changing network of community members and (b) containing knowledge relating to the community's imperatives as individual members come and go. Individual humans are dynamic actors in the organizational system, but the evolving knowledge persists to guide and inform members' individual actions relating to the system's goals and to sustain its organization. The sociotechnical knowledge management system can thus contribute greatly to the formation and continuity of the community as an autopoietic organization.

The small organizational networks that tested the technology described here are all components of emerging umbrella groups concerned with monitoring, maintaining, and improving the ecological health of the urban fringe of the Melbourne metropolitan area. These super-organizations are emerging from the overlapping interests of (1) several individual landcare groups (e.g., including Riddells Creek Landcare – *loc. cit.*) combined into umbrella groups covering drainage basins crossing the northern and western suburbs of Melbourne (e.g., Jacksons Creek Econetwork – *loc. cit.*), (2) native plant and animal societies (e.g., the Keilor Plains Group of the Australian Plants Society – http://www. apskeilorplains.org.au/), and (3) an emerging grant-supported group called NatureShare (http://natureshare.org.au/) that is seeking to observe, photograph, and map all Victorian flora and fauna. These last two sites were developed on other (i.e., non-Google) platforms. The NatureShare site was subsequently supported by a Help page developed in Google Sites - https://sites.google.com/site/naturesharehelp/.

It is possible that the social technology described here may powerfully help coordinate all of these group and umbrella interests into a powerful autopoietic supersystem. Over the next years we will be following the development of selected community action groups, the impacts of new technologies on their knowledge lifecycles and successes/failures in achieving their aims, and changes in their knowledge ecologies (e.g., along the lines of [118, 119]).

Finally, we seek to understand how the knowledge building and sharing capabilities of the action groups can be integrated with local and regional governments that are themselves implementing similar social technologies in their own organizations (Fig. 9.7).

Acknowledgments This chapter extends the ideas of our paper for the Third Knowledge Cities World Summit [8]. Hall thanks the Australian Centre for Science, Innovation and Society and the Engineering Learning Unit, both of the University of Melbourne, for facilities and library access. Many of the ideas presented here are based on joint work with Richard Vines and Gavan McCarthy in the eScholarship Research Centre, University of Melbourne, and an earlier collaboration with Vines and Luke Naismith. Face to face and virtual discussions over the years with members of the TOMOK group (Steve Else, Tony Smith, Hugo Urrestarazu, Peter Dalmaris, Joe Firestone, Amir Morris, etc.) and the Melbourne Knowledge Management Leaders Forum helped in development of the ideas.

References

Note: All URLs are valid as at 29/05/2012

1. Simon, H.A.: Rational decision-making in business organizations. Am. Econ. Rev. **69**, 493–513 (1979). [Nobel Memorial Lecture, Economic Sciences, Dec. 8, 1978] http://tinyurl.com/26bhflq
2. Dalmaris, P., Tsui, E., Hall, W.P., Smith, B.: A Framework for the improvement of knowledge-intensive business processes. Bus. Proc. Manag. J. **13**(2), 279–305 (2007). http://tinyurl.com/82hjze8

3. Hall, W.P.: Writing and managing maintenance procedures for a class of warships: A case for structured authoring and content management. Tech. Commun. **48**, 235–247 (2001). http://tinyurl.com/jlhe2

4. Hall, W.P.: Managing maintenance knowledge in the context of large engineering projects – theory and case study. J. Inf. Knowl. Manage. **2**(2), (2003). [Corrected version reprinted in **2**(3):1–17] http://tinyurl.com/3yqh8j

5. Hall, W.P.: Forming new ICT industry clusters in Victoria. Australian Centre for Science, Innovation and Society. Occasional Paper 1 (2006). http://tinyurl.com/89z2pcc

6. Hall, W.P., Kilpatrick, B.: Managing community knowledge to build a better world. Australasian Conference on Information Systems (ACIS), Sydney, Australia, 30th November–2 December, 2011. http://tinyurl.com/6qteaq7

7. Hall, W.P., Nousala, S.: Facilitating emergence of an ICT industry cluster. In: ICE 2007, 13th International Conference on Concurrent Enterprising, Sophia-Antipolis, France, 4–6 June 2007. http://tinyurl.com/2x9czt

8. Hall, W.P., Nousala, S., Best, R.: Free technology for the support of community action groups: theory, technology and practice. In: Knowledge Cities World Summit, Melbourne, Australia, 16–19 Nov 2010. http://tinyurl.com/26f9rnn

9. Hall, W.P., Nousala, S., Kilpatrick, B.: One company – two outcomes: knowledge integration vs corporate disintegration in the absence of knowledge management. VINE: J. Inf. Knowl. Manag. Syst. **39**, 242–258 (2009). http://tinyurl.com/yzgjew4

10. Hall, W.P., Nousala, S., Vines, R.: Using Google's apps for the collaborative construction, refinement and formalization of knowledge. In: ICOMP'10 – 2010 International Conference on Internet Computing, Las Vegas, NV, 12–15 July 2010. http://tinyurl.com/26pklny

11. Hall, W.P., Richards, G., Sarelius, C., Kilpatrick, B.: Organisational management of project and technical knowledge over fleet lifecycles. Aust. J. Mech. Eng. **5**, 81–95 (2008). http://tinyurl.com/5d2lz7

12. Mo, J.P.T., Zhou, M., Anticev, J., Nemes, L., Jones, M., Hall, W.P.: A study on the logistics and performance of a real 'virtual enterprise'. Int. J. Bus. Perform. Manag. **8**(2/3), 152–169 (2006). http://tinyurl.com/yyjx9q

13. Nousala, S.: Tacit knowledge networks and their implementation in complex organisations. Ph.D. thesis, Aerospace, Mechanical and Manufacturing Engineering, RMIT University (2006). http://tinyurl.com/79ejs9x

14. Nousala, S., Jamsai-Whyte, S.: The value of sustainable knowledge transfer methods for SMEs, utilizing socio-technical networks and complex systems. In: 4th International Conference on Knowledge Generation, Communication and Management: KGCM 2010. Orlando, FL, 29 June–2 July 2010. http://tinyurl.com/75r2aw3

15. Nousala, S., Jamsai Whyte, S., Hall, W.P.: Tacit knowledge network development: the comparative analysis of knowledge threads in complex systems. In: Knowledge Cities World Summit, Melbourne, Australia, 16–19 Nov 2010. http://tinyurl.com/82j52hy

16. Nousala, S., Miles, A., Kilpatrick, B., Hall, W.P.: Building knowledge sharing communities using team expertise access maps (TEAM). In: KMAP05 Knowledge Management in Asia Pacific, Wellington, New Zealand, 28–29 Nov 2005. http://tinyurl.com/q4n8y

17. Nousala, S., Miles, A., Kilpatrick, B., Hall, W.P.: Building knowledge sharing communities using team expertise access maps (TEAM). Int. J. Bus. Syst. Res. **3**, 279–296 (2009). http://tinyurl.com/24lf6lt

18. Sykes, M., Hall, W.P.: Generating fleet support knowledge from data and information. In: Australian Conference for Knowledge Management and Intelligent Decision Support ACKMIDS 2003, Melbourne, Australia, 11 and 12 Dec 2003. http://tinyurl.com/ltn2x

19. Hall, W.P.: Organisational autopoiesis and knowledge management. In: ISD'03 12th International Conference on Information Systems Development, Melbourne, Australia, 25–27 Aug 2003. http://tinyurl.com/yehcqz

20. Hall, W.P.: Biological nature of knowledge in the learning organization. Learn. Organ. **12**, 169–188 (2005). http://tinyurl.com/lqz3q

21. Hall, W.P.: Emergence and growth of knowledge and diversity in hierarchically complex living systems. In: Workshop "Selection, Self-Organization and Diversity" CSIRO Centre for Complex Systems Science and ARC Complex Open Systems Network, Katoomba, NSW, Australia 17–18 May 2006. [Revision 4, 3 Nov 2006] http://tinyurl.com/29kpl8d
22. Hall, W.P. Physical basis for the emergence of autopoiesis, cognition and knowledge. Kororoit Institute Working Papers No. 2: 1–63 (2011). http://tinyurl.com/7fcbhfr
23. Hall, W.P., Dalmaris, P., Nousala, S.: A biological theory of knowledge and applications to real world organizations. In: KMAP05 Knowledge Management in Asia Pacific, Wellington, New Zealand, 28–29 Nov 2005. http://tinyurl.com/qflam
24. Hall, W.P., Dalmaris, P., Else, S., Martin, C.P., Philp, W.R.: Time value of knowledge: time-based frameworks for valuing knowledge. In: 10th Australian Conference of Knowledge Management and Intelligent Decision Support, Melbourne, 10–11 Dec 2007.http://tinyurl.com/25z68k
25. Hall, W.P., Else, S., Martin, C., Philp, W. 2011. Time based frameworks for valuing knowledge: maintaining strategic knowledge. Kororoit Institute Working Papers No. 1: 1–28 – http://tinyurl.com/7ca866n
26. Hall, W.P., Nousala, S.: Autopoiesis and knowledge in self-sustaining organizational systems. In: 4th International Multi-Conference on Society, Cybernet and Informatics: IMSCI 2010, June 29th–July 2nd 2010, Orlando, FL, USA. http://tinyurl.com/yztsq4t
27. Hall, W.P., Nousala, S.: What is the value of peer review – some sociotechnical considerations. In: 2nd International Symposium on Peer Reviewing, Orlando, FL, 29 June–2 July 2010. http://tinyurl.com/323v4k3
28. Nousala, S., Hall, W.P.: Emerging autopoietic communities – scalability of knowledge transfer in complex systems. Proc. IFIP Int. Conf Network and Parallel Comp, Shanghai, China, October 18–19, 2008, Washington, DC: IEEE Computer Society, pp. 418–425 (2008). http://tinyurl.com/25khr3o
29. Vines, R., Hall, W.P.: Exploring the foundations of organizational knowledge. Kororoit Institute Working Papers No. 3: 1–39 (2011). http://tinyurl.com/8y6tczq
30. Bryant, R.: Community action. Brit. J. Soc. Work 2, 205–215 (1972)
31. Brown, J.S., Duguid, P.: Organizational learning and communities-of-practice: towards a unified view of working, learning, and innovation. Organ. Sci. 2, 40–57 (1991)
32. Wenger, E.C., Snyder, W.: Communities of practice: the organizational frontier. Harv. Bus. Rev. 78(1), 139–145 (2000). http://tinyurl.com/23jxt72
33. Ball-Rokeach, S.J., Kim, Y.-C., Matei, S.: Storytelling neighborhood: paths to belonging in diverse urban environments. Commun. Res. 28(4), 292–428 (2001). http://tinyurl.com/8ybl427
34. Perkins, D.D., Brown, B.B., Taylor, R.B.: The ecology of empowerment: predicting participation in community organizations. J. Soc. Issue 52(1), 85–110 (1996). http://tinyurl.com/7nago42
35. Pilisuk, M., McAllister, J., Rothman, J.: Coming together for action: the challenge of contemporary grassroots community organizing. J. Soc. Issue 52(1), 15–37 (1996)
36. Walker, S.: Digital design in social action settings: a review through a sociotechnical lens. In: Prato CIRN 2008 Community Informatics Conference (2008). http://tinyurl.com/85zel4g
37. Maturana, H.R., Varela, F.J.: Autopoiesis and Cognition: The Realization of the Living. Reidel, Dordrecht (1980)
38. Maturana, H.R.: Autopoiesis, structural coupling and cognition: a history of these and other notions in the biology of cognition. Cybernet Hum. Know. 9(3–4), 5–34 (2002). http://tinyurl.com/7uqelc8
39. Varela, F., Maturana, H., Uribe, R.: Autopoiesis: the organization of living systems, its characterisation and a model. Biosystems 5, 187–196 (1974)
40. Salthe, S.: Evolving Hierarchical Systems: Their Structure and Representation. Columbia University Press, New York (1985)
41. Salthe, S.: Development and Evolution: Complexity and Change in Biology. MIT Press, Cambridge (1993)

42. Simon, H.A.: The architecture of complexity. Proc. Am. Philos. Soc. **106**, 467–482 (1962). http://tinyurl.com/36r58a7
43. Simon, H.A.: The organization of complex systems. In: Pattee, H.H. (ed.) Hierarchy Theory: The Challenge of Complex Systems, pp. 1–27. George Braziller, New York (1973). http://tinyurl.com/6taasle
44. Simon, H.A.: Near decomposability and the speed of evolution. Indust. Corp. Change **11**(3), 587–599 (2002)
45. Vines, R., Hall, W.P., Naismith, L.: Exploring the foundations of organisational knowledge: an emergent synthesis grounded in thinking related to evolutionary biology. In: actKM Conference, Australian National University, Canberra, 23–24 Oct 2007. http://tinyurl.com/3xpmbc
46. Simon, H.A.: A behavioral model of rational choice. Q. J. Econ. **69**, 99–118 (1955). http://tinyurl.com/27z7jpg
47. Else, S.E.: Organization theory and the transformation of large, complex organizations: Donald H. Rumsfeld and the U.S. Department of Defence, 2001–04. PhD Thesis, Graduate School of International Studies University of Denver, CO (2004). http://tinyurl.com/6xt89m
48. Greiner, L.E.: Evolution and revolution as organizations grow. Harv. Bus. Rev. **76**(3), 55–67 (1998). http://tinyurl.com/6thq7je
49. Stenmark, D.: Information vs. knowledge: the role of intranets in knowledge management. In: Proceedings of the HICSS-35, Big Island, HI, 7–10 Jan 2002. http://tinyurl.com/5qwurc
50. Wilson, T.D.: The nonsense of 'knowledge management'. Info. Res. **8**(1), 1–26 (2002). http://tinyurl.com/2lupn
51. Miller, F.J.: I = 0 (Information has no intrinsic meaning). Info. Res. **8**(1), (2002) http://tinyurl.com/24p7ysf
52. Popper, K.R.: Objective knowledge: An evolutionary approach. Oxford University Press, London (1972)
53. Popper, K.R.: Knowledge and the Mind Body Problem: In Defence of Interaction. Routledge, London (1994)
54. Popper, K.R.: All Life is Problem Solving. Routledge, London (1999)
55. Bateson, G.: Steps to an Ecology of Mind. Chandler, San Francisco (1972)
56. Hayles, N.K.: How We Became Posthuman: Virtual Bodies in Cybernetics, Literature and Informatics. University of Chicago Press, Chicago (1999)
57. Popper, K.R.: Three Worlds: The Tanner Lecture on Human Values. Humanities Center, University of Utah (1978). http://tinyurl.com/yjf7n3x
58. Popper, K.R.: Knowledge and the Body-Mind Problem: In Defence of Interaction. Routlege, London (1994)
59. Campbell, D.T.: Blind variation and selective retention in creative thought as in other knowledge processes. Psychol. Rev. **67**, 380–400 (1960) [Reprinted (1987) in: Radnitzky G, Bartley WW III (eds) Evolutionary epistemology, rationality, and the sociology of knowledge, Open Court, LaSalle, IL pp 91–11]
60. Campbell, D.T.: Evolutionary epistemology. In: Schilpp, P.A. (ed.) The Philosophy of Karl Popper, pp. 413–463. Open Court, LaSalle (1974) [Reprinted in (1987) in: Radnitzky G, Bartley WW III (eds) Evolutionary epistemology, rationality, and the sociology of knowledge, Open Court, LaSalle, IL pp 47–89]
61. Bartly III, W.W.: Philosophy of biology versus philosophy of physics. In: Radnitzky, G., Bartley III, W.W. (eds.) Evolutionary Epistemology, Rationality, and the Sociology of Knowledge, pp. 7–45. Open Court, LaSalle (1987)
62. Popper, K.R.: Conjectures and Refutations: The Growth of Scientific Knowledge. Routledge and Kegan Paul, London (1963)
63. Boyd, J.R.: Unpublished briefings available via Defence and the National Interest (2008). [see titles under "A Discourse on Winning and Losing"] http://tinyurl.com/6x5z45
64. Osinga, F.P.B.: Science, Strategy and War: The Strategic Theory of John Boyd. Eburon Academic Publishers, Delft (2005). [also Routledge, Taylor and Francis Group (2007)] – http://tinyurl.com/26eqduv

65. Philp, W.R., Martin, C.P.: A philosophical approach to time in military knowledge management. J. Knowl. Manag. **13**(1), 171–183 (2009). http://tinyurl.com/2bj7dxm
66. Post, J.F.: Paradox in critical rationalism and related theories. Philos. Forum **3**(1), 27–61 (1971) [Reprinted in Radnitzky G, Bartley WW III (eds) Evolutionary epistemology, rationality, and the sociology of knowledge, Open Court, LaSalle, IL pp 223–251 (1987)]
67. Luhmann, N.: Social Systems. Trans. J. Bednarz, D. Baecker. Stanford University Press, Stanford (1995)
68. Luhmann, N.: The paradox of observing systems. In: Rasch, W. (ed.) Theories of Distinction: Redescribing the Descriptions of Modernity, pp. 79–93. Stanford University Press, Stanford (2002)
69. Vollmer, G.: On supposed circularities in an empirically oriented epistemology. In: Radnitzky, G., Bartley III, W.W. (eds.) Evolutionary Epistemology, Rationality, and the Sociology of Knowledge, pp. 163–200. Open Court, LaSalle (1987)
70. Dalmaris, P., Hall, W.P., Philp, W.R.: The time-value of knowledge: a temporal qualification of knowledge, its issues, and role in the improvement of knowledge intense business processes. In: Proceedings of the 3rd Asia-Pacific International Conference on Knowledge Management (KMAP06), Hong Kong, 11–13 Dec 2006. http://tinyurl.com/5rjrny
71. Hall, W.P., Dalmaris, P., Else, S., Martin, C., Philp, W.: Time value of knowledge: time-based frameworks for valuing knowledge. OASIS seminar presentation, Department of Information System, University of Melbourne, 27 July 2007. http://tinyurl.com/3y6n4y
72. Martin, C.P., Philp, W., Hall, W.P.: Temporal convergence for knowledge management. Australas. J. Inf. Syst. **15**(2), 133–148 (2009). http://tinyurl.com/2azpqrv
73. Urrestarazu, H.: On boundaries of autopoietic systems. J. Autopoietic Theory. 19 May 2004 http://tinyurl.com/4p2rtz
74. Urrestarazu, H.: Autopoietic systems: a generalized explanatory approach – Parts 1&2. Constructivist Foundations 6(3): 307–324 (2011). http://tinyurl.com/7jzg8q; 7(1): 48–67 (2011) – http://tinyurl.com/7pr2ay8
75. Kauffman, S.A.: Investigations. Oxford University Press, Oxford (2000)
76. Kauffman, S.A.: Molecular autonomous agents. Philos. Trans. R. Soc. Lond. A **361**, 1089–1099 (2003)
77. Kauffman, S.A., Logan, R.K., Este, R., Goebel, R., Hobill, D., Shmulevich, I.: Propagating organization: an enquiry. Biol. Philos. **23**, 27–45 (2008). http://tinyurl.com/7nn7eue
78. Kauffman, S.A.: The Origins of Order: Self-organization and Selection in Evolution. Oxford University Press, New York (1983)
79. Polanyi, M.: Personal Knowledge: Towards a Post-critical Philosophy. University of Chicago Press, Chicago (1958)
80. Polanyi, M.: The Tacit Dimension. Routledge & Kegan Paul, London (1966)
81. Ong, W.J.: Orality and Literacy: The Technologizing of the Word. Routledge, London (1982)
82. Salthe, S.: The spontaneous origin of new levels in a scalar hierarchy. Entropy **6**, 327–343 (2004). http://tinyurl.com/3sb989
83. Chaisson, E.J.: Cosmic Evolution: The Rise of Complexity in Nature. Harvard University Press, Cambridge (2001)
84. Koestler, A.: The Ghost in the Machine. Arkana, London (1967)
85. Koestler, A.: Janus: A Summing Up. Random House, New York (1978)
86. Maturana, H.R.: Autopoiesis: reproduction, heredity and evolution. In: Zeleny, M. (ed.) Autopoiesis, Dissipative Structures, and Spontaneous Social Orders. AAAS selected symposium No. 55, pp. 45–79. Westview Press, Boulder (1980)
87. Nelson, R.R., Winter, S.G.: An Evolutionary Theory of Economic Change. Harvard University Press, Cambridge (1982)
88. Dalmaris, P.: A framework for the improvement of knowledge-intense business processes. Ph.D. thesis, University of Technology, Sydney (2006). http://tinyurl.com/89qz27a
89. Pallaris, C., Costigan, S.S.: Knowledge ecologies in international affairs: A new paradigm for dialog and collaboration. SSRN, 21 May 2010. http://tinyurl.com/24ykonk

90. Vines, R., Hall, W.P., McCarthy, G.: Textual representations and knowledge support-systems in research intensive networks. In: Cope, B., Kalantzis, M., Magee, L. (eds.) Towards a Semantic Web: Connecting Knowledge in Academic Research, pp. 145–195. Chandos Press, Oxford (2011). http://tinyurl.com/27qd4of

91. Krippendorff, K.: A dictionary of cybernetics. Principia Cybernetica Web (1986). http://tinyurl.com/23b88ek

92. Turner, D.P.: Thinking at the global scale. Glob. Ecol. Biogeogr. **14**, 505–508 (2005)

93. Licklider, J.C.R.: Man-computer symbiosis. IRE Trans. Hum. Factor. Electron. **1**, 4–11 (1960). http://tinyurl.com/2ah4ysx

94. Pepperell, R.: The Post-human Condition. Intellect Books, Exeter (1995)

95. Hall, W.P.: Tools extending human and organizational cognition: revolutionary tools and cognitive revolutions. Int. J. Knowl. Cult. Change Manag. **6**(6), 1–10 (2006). http://tinyurl.com/qza7q

96. Yakhlef, A.: Towards a post-human distributed cognition environment. Knowl. Manag. Res. Pract. **6**, 287–297 (2008). http://tinyurl.com/28tf4yn

97. Harvey, E.: Technology and the structure of organizations. Am. Soc. Rev. **33**, 247–259 (1968). http://tinyurl.com/2dnwyzp

98. Berners-Lee, T., Hendler, J., Lassila, O.: The semantic Web. Sci. Am. **284**, 35–43 (2001). http://tinyurl.com/2foq7eq

99. W3C: Extensible markup language (XML). W3C Ubiquitous Web domain (2010). http://tinyurl.com/736rl

100. Vines, R., Firestone, J.: Interoperability and the exchange of humanly usable digital content. In: Cope, B., Kalantzis, M., Magee, L. (eds.) Towards a Semantic Web: Connecting Knowledge in Academic Research, pp. 429–489. Chandos Press, Oxford (2011). http://tinyurl.com/acmzpl

101. O'Reilly, T.: What is Web 2.0: design patterns and business models for the next generation of software. Commun. Strat. **65**, 17 (2007). http://tinyurl.com/28bbt7e

102. Gruber, T.: Collective knowledge systems: where the Social Web meets the Semantic Web. J. Web Semantic. **6**, 4–13 (2008). http://tinyurl.com/2ekzrje

103. Miller, P.: Web 2.0: building the new library. Ariadne **45** (2005). http://tinyurl.com/hxssz

104. Wikipedia: Wikipedia: about (2010). http://tinyurl.com/2cof8t8

105. O'Leary, D.E.: Wikis: 'from each according to his knowledge'. Computer **41**(2), 34–41 (2008). http://tinyurl.com/25vq2ks

106. Markoff, J.: Software via the Internet: Microsoft in cloud computing. New York Times, 2 Sept 2007. http://tinyurl.com/27kc67s

107. Lohr, S.: Google and IBM join in cloud computing research. New York Times, 8 Oct 2007. http://tinyurl.com/26jh6ww

108. Lohr, S., Helft, M.: Google gets ready to rumble with Microsoft. New York Times, 16 Dec 2007. http://tinyurl.com/27zuf5

109. Baker, S.: Google and the wisdom of clouds. Bloomberg Businessweek, 13 Dec 2007. http://tinyurl.com/3yhjo7n

110. Raman, T.V.: Cloud computing and equal access for all. In: Proceedings of the International Cross-Disciplinary Conference on Web Access, Bejing, China, 21–22 Apr 2008. http://tinyurl.com/7cqwtvd

111. Hall, W.P., Best, R.: Template for knowledge based organizations (2010). http://tinyurl.com/27rtqj4

112. Hall, W.P. Usage notes for Google wikis (2010). http://tinyurl.com/2b7vjxl

113. Krishnan, K.: Introducing Google apps for government. The Official Google Blog, 27 July 2010. http://tinyurl.com/2elmmyx

114. Kundra, V.: State of public sector cloud computing. Chief Information Officers Council, Office of Management & Budget, Washington, DC (2010). http://tinyurl.com/3x8pqfr

115. Licklider, J.C.R., Taylor, R.W.: The computer as a communication device. Part. Sci. Technol. **76**, 21–31 (1968). http://tinyurl.com/2g87txw

116. Rheingold, H.: The Virtual Community: Homesteading on the Electronic Frontier. Addison-Wesley, Reading (1993). http://tinyurl.com/39les9u
117. Schuler, D.: Community networks: building a new participatory medium. Commun. ACM **37**, 39–51 (1994)
118. Lanzara, G., Morner, M.: The knowledge ecology of open-source software projects. In: 19th Colloq Exploration Euro Group Organiz Studies (EGOS), Copenhagen, Denmark, pp. 19–61, July 03–July 05 2003. http://tinyurl.com/26komso
119. Sowe, S., Stamelos, I., Angelis, L.: Understanding knowledge sharing activities in free/open source software projects: An empirical study. J. Syst. Softw. **81**, 431–446 (2008). http://tinyurl.com/23tgmvn

Chapter 10
Dynamic Web Prediction Using Asynchronous Mouse Activity

Anirban Kundu

Abstract A variety of recent trend predictions for the social Web see an evolution in the making. Social business thrives as more businesses would enter the social Web. Information technology (IT) departments would open up to social Web and adapt the new processes needed for opening up. Social media marketing would use social media differently. In this scenario, dynamic Web prediction comes into the picture for handling the real-time scenario in a smoother way. A typical Web prediction method follows Markov model. A Web page consists of several hyperlinks. Prediction requires complicated methodologies for selection of a particular hyperlink from the pool of hyperlinks of current Web page. Existing approaches forecast only on personal computer in a fruitful manner. In case of public computers, the same machine is used by different users at different time instance. Thus, high-quality prediction is not possible in this situation. In this chapter, a novel strategy on Web prediction is suggested using the real-time characteristics of users. Overall, four events have been demonstrated and further compared for finding the most efficient technique of Web prediction having least processing time. The proposed technique requires no Web-log. Mouse movement and its real-time direction are utilized for the prediction of the next probable Web page. Mouse position is tracked as an alternative of using traditional Markov model. Entirely dynamic Web prediction scheme is introduced in the proposed approach due to the fact that Web-log has not been utilized. Minimization of total number of hyperlinks to be selected is the main aim of the proposed approach for accomplishing superior precision in dynamic prediction mode. The proposed approach shows the step-wise build-up of a concrete Web prediction agenda applicable in both personal and public environment. An earlier version of this work has been published in [1]. This version

A. Kundu (✉)
Netaji Subhash Engineering College, West Bengal University of Technology, Kolkata,
West Bengal 700152, India

Innovation Research Lab (IRL), Capex Technologies, Howrah, West Bengal 711103, India
e-mail: anik76in@gmail.com

A. Abraham and A.-E. Hassanien (eds.), *Computational Social Networks: Tools,*
Perspectives and Applications, DOI 10.1007/978-1-4471-4048-1_10,
© Springer-Verlag London 2012

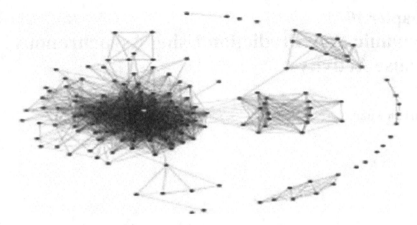

Fig. 10.1 Abstraction of a typical social network

mainly concentrates on social networking. The proposed research also attempts to improve Web prediction technique focusing on the specialized methodologies with the objective of increasing its precision. This approach reduces the users' perceived latency with no additional cost over the basic mechanism.

Introduction

A social infrastructure containing of individuals or organizations called "nodes" which are interconnected is presented. Social relationships are viewed in terms of network theory consisting of nodes and ties. Nodes are the individuals within the network and ties denote the relation among them. The nodes to which individuals are tied are their social contacts (refer Fig. 10.1).

The shape of the social network helps an individual to determine its usefulness. Smaller, tighter networks can be less useful to their members than networks with lots of loose connections to individuals outside the main network. More open networks, with many weak ties and social connections, are more likely to introduce new ideas and opportunities to their members than closed networks with many redundant ties [2–5]. Social networking is the grouping of distinct users into definite clusters. Social networking is feasible in person, especially in the place of work, universities, and high schools. It is most popular in case of online activities of geographically distributed users. World Wide Web (WWW) is filled with millions of individuals looking to meet other people, to gather and share information and experiences, develop friendships, find employment, business-to-business marketing, and so on. Web sites are typically used for online social networking. These Web sites are known as "Social Sites." Social networking Web sites act as an online community of Internet users. Online community users share common interests in several fields.

The user gets the permission from the Web-master for accessing a particular social networking Web site. This socialization includes reading the profile pages of other users of the society and possibly even contacting them.

Social networking is all about communication. People with common interests are able to share information with each other via a huge variety of social networking Web sites which are created specifically to make sharing, communicating, and creating information as simple and efficient as possible. "Facebook," "LinkedIn," and "Twitter" are examples of social networking. Web-based tools are being used for communication and collaboration for achieving social networking which consists of a lot of user-generated contents and their related feedbacks with real-time interactivity. It shows the overall group activity of a cluster having common interests. There are various types of sharing of interests in social networking utilizing proper online system. Social networking involves clustering specific individuals or organizations for ease of connectivity. Some social networking Web sites focus on particular interests; whereas at the same time, there are others that do not. The Web sites having no particular focus are referred to as traditional social networking Web sites in which memberships are usually open for everybody without any authentication. This means that anyone can become a member, no matter what their hobbies, beliefs, or views are. Once a user gets inside the online community, he can begin to create his own network of friends and eliminate members that do not share common interests or goals. In its simplest form, a social network is a map of specified ties, such as friendship, between the online nodes being considered. The nodes to which a user is connected are actually the social contacts of him. The network also measures the value of a user for getting involved in the social network.

People have exploited the idea of social network for over a century to connect complex sets of relationships between members of social systems at all scales, from interpersonal to international. In 1954, J. A. Barnes started using the term systematically to denote patterns of ties, encompassing concepts traditionally used by the public and those used by social scientists: bounded groups (e.g., tribes, families) and social categories (e.g., gender, ethnicity). Several scholars have already expanded the use of systematic social network analysis [6]. Social network analysis has now moved from being a suggestive metaphor to an analytic approach to a paradigm, with its own theoretical statements, methods, social network analysis software, and researchers. Analysts reason from whole to part; from structure to relation to individual; from behavior to attitude. They typically either study whole networks, all of the ties containing specified relations in a defined population, or personal networks, the ties that specified people have, such as their personal communities [7].

The distinction between whole networks and personal networks has depended largely on how analysts were able to gather data. That is, for groups such as companies, schools, or membership societies, the analyst was expected to have complete information about who was in the network, all participants being both potential egos and alters. Personal/egocentric studies were typically conducted when identities of egos were known, but not their "alters." These studies rely on the egos to provide information about the identities of alters and there is no expectation that the various egos or sets of alters will be tied to each other. A snowball network refers to the idea that the "alters" identified in an egocentric survey then become egos themselves and are able in turn to nominate additional alters. While there are severe logistic limits to conducting snowball network studies, a method for examining hybrid networks has recently been developed in which egos in complete networks can nominate alters otherwise not listed who are then available for all subsequent egos to see [8]. The hybrid network may be valuable for examining whole/complete networks that are expected to include important players beyond those who are formally identified. For example, employees of a company often work with non-company consultants who may be part of a network that cannot fully be defined prior to data collection.

Prediction [9, 10] of upcoming needs remains an open challenge for researchers. Numerous procedures had been configured in recent past for Web-oriented prediction using sequential routing patterns from server log files, combined with Web site topology. Web prediction is a mechanism to derive the Web page (link) the user is going to open (click) next from the present Web page. The rapid expansion of the WWW [11] has created an opportunity to propagate and gather information online [12–14].

This chapter is organized as follows: section "Existent Approaches of Web Prediction" briefly exposes some existing strategies of Web prediction. Section "Proposed Work" shows the proposed work along with four procedures which support different levels of Web-based prediction. Experimental results have been depicted in section "Experimental Results". Conclusion of the proposed Web prediction is shown in section "Conclusion". The final section lists the acknowledgments.

Existent Approaches of Web Prediction

In the present world, there are a lot of existing methods used for prediction such as Markov model, number of Web pages viewed and by creating an algorithm from the user's record [15–17]. Popularity-based prediction model for Web pre-fetching is discussed in [18]. It is really a tough job to understand and further model the user-based online behavior. When a user observes a Web page on the computer screen, the prediction mechanism predicts the next Web page and downloads the content in computer memory. When the user clicks the link, the respective content comes on the screen without waiting for it to download. In the real world, the correctness of Web prediction is not 100% as it is very difficult to predict the only link among several links which are present on a particular Web page. One of the useful methods used for Web prediction is Markov model. Markov model is a statistical model in which the system being modeled is assumed to be a Markov process with unobserved state. Markov model can be considered as the simplest dynamic Bayesian network. The page rank of a Web page as used by "Google" is defined by a Markov chain. It is the probability to be at Web page i in the stationary distribution on the following Markov chain on all (known) Web pages. If N is the number of known Web pages, and a Web page i has ki links, then it has transition probability $[(\alpha/ki) + (1 - \alpha)/N]$ for all pages that are linked to and $[(1 - \alpha)/N]$ for all pages that are not linked to. The parameter α is taken to be about 0.85. Many researchers use different techniques which usually employ Markov model of order-k for predicting the next Web page in real time. Navigational behavior of the user is being recorded in the Web-log as an input for Markov model. Several clustering [19–21] techniques have been established for prediction purpose for Web data mining [22]. N-gram is another important factor for the researchers for predicting results using comparative analysis [23]. Typically, Web prediction plays an important role by predicting and fetching the probable Web page of next request in advance, resulting in reducing the user latency. The users surf the WWW either by entering URL or search for some topics or through links of the same topics. Existing clustering techniques are also used for the accumulation of the similar Web pages. Similar Web pages of same type reside in the same cluster. The cluster containing Web pages has the similarity with respect to the topic of the session. The Clustering algorithms considered in the market are K-Means and K-Medoid. Overall, the typical and existing prediction algorithms follow the Web-log as well as the comparative analyses.

The WWW has created an opportunity to disseminate and gather information online from a vast database of information. This motivates the researchers to study Web usage behavior of the Web users by reducing the access latency using efficient Web prediction technique. Researchers use different techniques which usually employs Markov model of order-k for next Web page prediction in real time [15, 24]. Navigational behavior of the user is being recorded in Web-log as an input for Markov model. The main limitation of Markov model is as follows: lower order Markov models are coupled with low accuracy, whereas, higher order Markov models are associated with high state-space complexity, and also the sequences are not available in the Web-log. This problem motivates us for innovation some other features to be considered for better prediction accuracy. Web surfers either enter URL or search topic or go by navigation through link.

There are broadly three categories of prediction approaches of Web page pre-fetching:

(a) Client-based approach: This pre-fetching model is based on navigation behavior of a specific server which is stored in cache at client's side. This model is aimed for a particular user or group of users (where Web pages are accessed through proxy server).

(b) Server-based approach: This model is based on navigation behavior of a specific server for the Web pages hosted on that server. In this case, different clients use the same server and same Web site. Priority may be given to some clients, which should be considered while predicting Web pages for the particular server.

(c) Client-Server-based approach: As the name suggests, this model is the combination of the above two models.

The differences between static prediction and dynamic prediction are as follows:

Static prediction uses actual rather than forecasted values. It can only be used when the actual data are available in the prescribed system. These are also known as "1-step ahead" or "rolling" forecasts. Dynamic prediction calculates forecasts for periods after the first period in the sample by using the previously forecasted values of the lagged left-hand variable. These are also called "n-step ahead" forecasts. Both of these methods forecast the value of the disturbance caused by the specific user, if the equation has an autoregressive or moving-average error specification. Overall, Static prediction modeling is used to represent the structural constituents of a software system but dynamic prediction modeling is used to represent the behavior of a structural constituents in real-time basis.

In this chapter, the proposed approach is client-based methodology. It aims at the navigational behavior of clients combining the respective interest. The idea of using mouse direction for predictive crawling is an innovative process. As many users use a machine (public computer), it is nearly impossible to find out a particular prediction algorithm for that machine. It is possible to increase the efficiency in prediction for the respective users using mouse direction, since the previous Web-log might not satisfy the behavior of the current user. A real-time Web page prediction model giving significant importance to the user's interest using the navigational behavior of the user has been proposed. In this chapter, a new concept of Web prediction has been depicted without exploiting the existing Web-log of a machine or server.

Proposed Work

The proposed approach targets for generating Web prediction in a dynamic manner. The algorithms behind these approaches are mentioned in [1]. Predictions are made based on users' behavior of using mouse at real time. This approach shows the mouse activity for prediction of next Web pages contrasting typical approaches of Web prediction. It recommends a set of URLs as a trust-based recommendation system. Here, trust means the confidence level of the user about the selection among the prescribed URL list generated by the proposed schemes. Maximum research efforts related to Web prediction focus on the improvement of theoretical indexes of the prediction algorithm such as precision and recall. A client-based software module is utilized for prediction in real time. This module acts like a prediction engine which is responsible for making overall prediction. The communication between a specific user and Web browser at client-side is held responsible for taking the run-time decision about the user's future activities as a forecast. The prediction engine behaves like a controller unit which actually selects one or more Web links from the currently operated Web page. No other existing approaches use this concept. A Web page maintains a lot of Web links. It is hard to forecast the exact

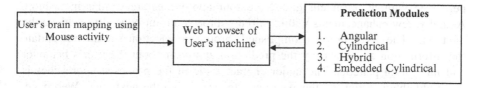

Fig. 10.2 Basic interaction between user and proposed modules

link among the list of URLs of the particular Web page for the apprehensive user. Prediction occurs only when the mouse is active. The aim is to choose the user's next destination over the Internet using a smart plan. So, the system should select the appropriate URLs and put them in a queue. The proposed prediction program predicts Web links by using the movement of the mouse. The mouse movement and its relative direction are the key points in this approach. This method does not depend on Web history. It only depends on the mouse movement and the corresponding angle made by the respective user such that if the user accesses a machine for the first time, the accuracy would not be lesser. In this system, the idea is to scrutinize the Web links of a particular part of the Web page being demonstrated as per the mouse behaviors. A mouse is moved by the user as required. Thus, the major issue in case of this type of Web-based prediction is tracking the mouse location. This procedure is active in nature for predicting Web link for next layer of visualization of Web pages in respect of the user. Web-log is not used for storing previously traversed data of the user. All other existing procedures use Web-log in a typical fashion. Thus, the approach is innovative in respect of dynamism. If the user selects a particular Web link while the browser is downloading another Web page as background prediction process, the background process is interrupted immediately to satisfy the user's real request at that moment. The prediction queue is erased as an emergency action.

The Web links are considered and downloaded as back-end job after the initial progress of the mouse right away. The highlighted area on the particular Web page would be generated as the mouse starts moving. This highlighted area remains same until the mouse traversed the defined edge of highlighted segment in all the proposed procedures. As a result, fixed bandwidth is devoted in case of limited mouse fluctuations. When a user first opens a Web page, all the Web links of that particular Web page are inactive until the mouse moves. The scanning mechanism starts working for predicting Web links as soon as the mouse is moved from its initial position. At first, a part of Web page is searched for fetching the Web links using mouse movement based on the direction. Prediction queue consists of Web links of the highlighted part of the Web page based on the mouse movement in a particular direction.

Four different procedures have been used for reducing the latency per user's click on the specific URLs of a Web page in case of dynamic prediction. Basic interaction between user and proposed modules has been shown in Fig. 10.2. Here, the latency reduction is the ratio of the latency perceived using pre-fetching to the latency perceived without pre-fetching. All the four approaches are similar in fashion. Actually, few enhancements within initial approach are introduced to achieve the next one. The predictions accomplished through a selection should not update the information assembled by the prediction approach about the user's behavior and navigation patterns. The major characteristic of the proposed approaches is the highlighted section on the Web page for predicting the next stage Web page. By enhancing approaches, the stress has been put to modify the shaded area for achieving better prediction.

Web page is considered as a typical graph containing vertical and horizontal lines having equal spacing in the proposed approach. Each small box or unit generated by the horizontal and vertical lines of the graph is considered as block. The number of blocks of a graph directly varies with the number of URLs on the Web page. Now, if "X" number of blocks are occupied by the specific URL on any Web page, then it is to be considered that the URL length is of "X" unit. Similarly, in each type of proposed approaches, it can be measured using the number of blocks of the highlighted area on the Web page that which approach consumes lesser number of URLs for prediction purpose. It is being calculated in the following approaches for measuring the size of the highlighted region on the Web page depending on the mouse activity of the user at any time instance. If the size of the highlighted area is small, it can be presumed that the number of URLs within that shaded area would be less. Thus, the prediction would be higher.

In the subsequent sub-sections, the impact of the proposed techniques in the prediction related performance has been shown. The precision is increased as the prediction techniques become more sophisticated. Typically, a parser module is utilized for extraction of URLs from the selected region on the Web page. After that, URLs are placed in the queue for further prediction.

Overall activity of proposed approaches has been depicted in Fig. 10.3.

Angular Approach

Angular approach is treated as the initiation of the proposed techniques for achieving prediction in a satisfactory level in any situation. Typically, predictions are made based on previous experience and pre-fetching techniques. Everything is static. In this chapter, dynamic predictions have been introduced. Since dynamic prediction is considered in this case, the prediction module decides what Web links are going to be highlighted. An angular area of a Web page is focused for scanning Web links. Figure 10.4 shows a Web page in a particular instance. The arrow indicates the direction of mouse. An angular area is created immediately on the Web page by prediction method. All the Web links within the highlighted angular part of the Web page are being activated and are further put into the prediction queue. The angle should be predefined for a particular size of monitor of computer system along with the resolution of the system. If the system is changed or modified or even the resolution is changed, then the prescribed angle should be modified based

Fig. 10.3 Prediction activity
based on proposed modules

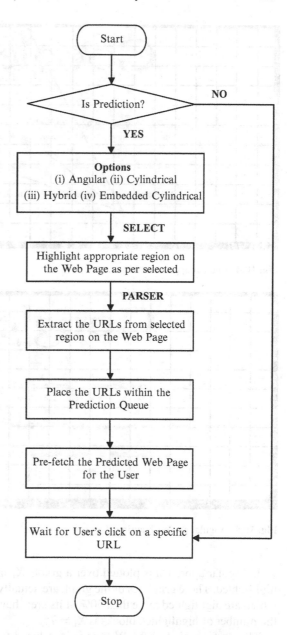

on the system analysis. Highlighted part is shown as the active area in Fig. 10.4. The user would not be able to see the lines and the activated area, since these are all hidden in nature. All Web links are activated within this shaded area. So, the program only predicts Web pages among those activated links for the particular position and direction of mouse.

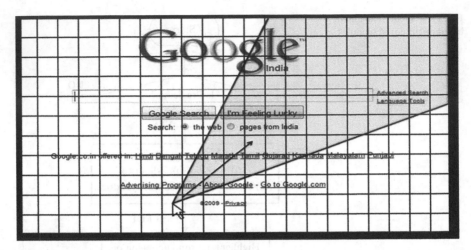

Fig. 10.4 Angular approach at time T

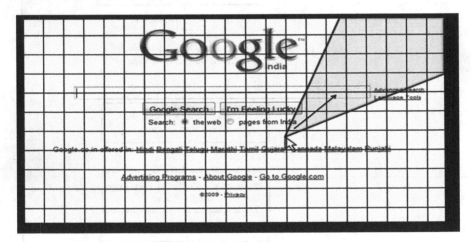

Fig. 10.5 Angular approach at time $T + 1$

If angular approach is plotted over a graph, X_1 number of blocks is going to be highlighted. These grid lines or the graph are actually hidden to the user. The blocks, which are highlighted more than 50% of its area, have been considered. In Fig. 10.4, the number of highlighted blocks is $X_1 = 76$.

The useful region of the Web page is reduced for selection of Web links as the user moves the mouse towards the flanks of the Web page. The Web links residing outside the active area become inactive and would be removed from the prediction queue. Figure 10.5 is the next position of Fig. 10.4. Here, the mouse direction is not changed by the user as shown by arrow. The activated area is reduced as the mouse moves towards the edges of the Web page. The number of Web links to be predicted is reduced as a consequence.

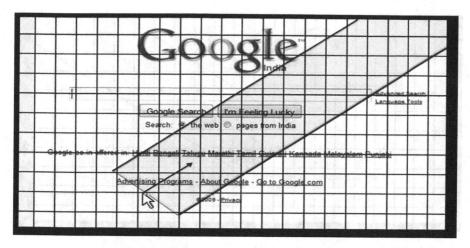

Fig. 10.6 Cylindrical approach at time T

If the user does not click on any of those predicted links and suddenly changes the mouse direction, the projected angular area would also be modified following the current mouse direction. The prediction program immediately creates the angular area in the direction of the mouse and the same process would occur again. Every time the user changes the mouse direction, the area for scanning would also be changed, if and only if the mouse is crossed any of the edges of the highlighted section.

It is pragmatic based on experimental data on mouse progress that the users move mouse in a particular direction as concentrated on a specific task. The user observes the objective point on the Web page and immediately establishes a neural connection between the brain of the user and the particular hand controlling the mouse. Thus, mouse is moved to the particular direction to reach the destination on the Web page based on synchronization. It is also observed that the mouse is not moved in other arbitrary directions at the time of doing specific job by the user. The users try to click on a specific URL on the Web page to see the next Web page on the Web browser. Thus, 'θ' (50) degree is considered for the angular measurement on average as per the real-time observations on 10,000 instances. The user typically moves the mouse in a particular direction with a tolerance of '$\theta/2$' (25) degree in both left and right side.

At the next time instance "$T + 1$" in Fig. 10.5, the number of highlighted blocks is $X_1 = 32$. Therefore, at time "$T + 1$," the prediction would be higher than at "T." Further, cylindrical approach has been introduced in the next sub-section.

Cylindrical Approach

In procedure 2, the highlighted angular area is replaced by an area of two parallel lines. Figure 10.6 is a snapshot of a particular time instance. The arrow indicates the direction of the mouse and the shaded portion is the activated area of the Web page.

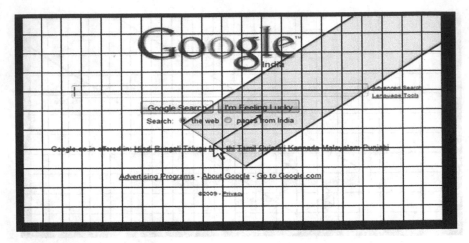

Fig. 10.7 Cylindrical approach at time $T + 1$

In this case, the functional parts are similar in working except the shape of the highlighted area on the Web page. The URLs are selected and then stored in the queue as earlier. As the mouse moves towards the edges of the Web page, the area is reduced and the links coming out of the area would be inactive. Figure 10.7 is another snapshot taken after Fig. 10.6 with less number of links.

If cylindrical approach is plotted over a graph, X_2 number of blocks is going to be highlighted. These grid lines or the graph are actually hidden to the user. The blocks, which are highlighted more than 50% of its area, have been considered. In Fig. 10.6, the number of highlighted blocks is $X_2 = 59$.

The higher prediction ratio is achieved by this cylindrical approach. Number of effective URLs would be lesser as compared to angular approach of section "Angular Approach" as the mouse is moved towards the edge of the Web page. The actual reason of achieving better prediction percentage depends on the geometrical nature that has been exploited in this technique. Angle is the most important aspect in case of angular approach of section "Angular Approach". The number of URLs is pretty less within the highlighted section in the nearby region of the current position of the mouse pointer. Whenever the user moves the mouse to any direction on the specific Web page, lots of URLs fall within the scope of the highlighted angular section while the angular lines approach towards the ending of the Web page. Thus, more number of URLs has to be measured at the time of prediction computation. In case of cylindrical approach, the number of URLs is not more than the expected, since fixed parallel lines have been used for highlighting the effective area. This type of offset method is more supportive for determining the predicted Web page as the next Web page. 'X' (2) inch is considered as the offset value depending on real-time mouse movement of 15,000 instances.

At the next time instance "$T + 1$" in Fig. 10.7, the number of highlighted blocks is $X_2 = 44$. Therefore, at time "$T + 1$," the prediction would be higher than at "T." Further, hybrid approach has been introduced in the next sub-section.

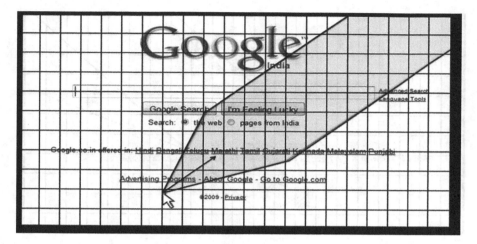

Fig. 10.8 Hybrid approach at time T

Hybrid Approach

This model is a mixed concept of the previous two procedures and also more efficient for predicting Web pages with better accuracy. Figure 10.8 shows the basic idea of hybrid approach. Initially, angular area is considered for URL scanning and then the area to be scanned would be parallel. Apparently, the hybrid approach seems to be the merging of angular approach and cylindrical approach. Both the approaches have same negative points. All the disadvantages have been overcome in this approach. The effective region for URL scanning is reduced in this approach compared to earlier mentioned approaches. Number of URLs to be selected would be less as highlighted region is minimized. So, number of Web pages to be considered for prediction is also lesser resulting in higher prediction accuracy.

To find out why this case is better than the previous two approaches those two previous cases have been projected in a single frame which is shown in Fig. 10.9. The solid lines are covering the activated area which is the main concept of this case. The dotted lines are indicating the portions that are being neglected. If the angular area is being used, some extra and unnecessary portions of the Web page have to be scanned. It includes some extra links in the prediction queue (like 'Advance Search', 'Language Tools'). In case of cylindrical approach, two parallel lines have been used. These lines include many extra links those are nearby the mouse pointer but not needed for prediction queue (like 'Hindi', 'Bengali', 'About Google'). At the time of mouse movement in a particular direction, the user could not be able to move the mouse in the perpendicular direction in respect of mouse pointer origin. Thus, it is wastage of memory to store those links. So by this approach, the number of links would be reduced and it would be easier to predict next stage Web links with less number of URLs. In Fig. 10.9, the 'X' marked areas are being neglected and the '$\sqrt{}$' marked areas are being highlighted for future prediction as a whole.

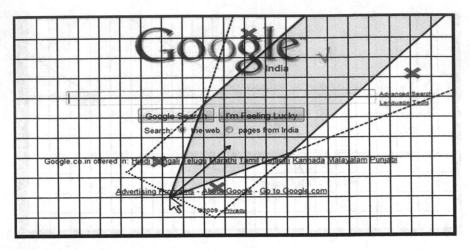

Fig. 10.9 Hybrid approach at time $T + 1$

If hybrid approach is plotted over a graph, X_3 number of blocks is going to be highlighted. These grid lines or the graph are actually hidden to the user. The blocks, which are highlighted more than 50% of its area, have been considered. In Fig. 10.8, the number of highlighted blocks is $X_3 = 56$.

At the next time instance "$T + 1$" in Fig. 10.9, the number of highlighted blocks is $X_3 = 50$. Therefore, at time "$T + 1$," the prediction would be higher than at "T." At the same time, the figure also shows the irrelevant sections which are to be rejected using cross (X) sign. Further, embedded cylindrical approach has been introduced in the next sub-section.

Embedded Cylindrical Approach

It is being observed through practical experiment that all the users maintain a certain path while using the mouse. The fluctuation of the mouse varies from user to user while moving to a particular direction. In this case the area between parallel lines of section "Cylindrical Approach" is divided further using another inner cylindrical section. So, four parallel lines are considered as a result and the angular section is also used at the origin or starting point of the mouse (cursor) as discussed in earlier sub-sections. In Fig. 10.10, the arrow shows current mouse direction along with the activated (shaded) area taken in a particular time instance.

After initial mouse movement, effectively three areas are created, such as one inner area and two outer areas as shown in Fig. 10.10. Here the inner parallel lines scan a smaller area. If the fluctuation of mouse is less for any user, then by this idea it would be easier to predict links for the prediction program. In this case, there would be three prediction queues, such as (1) Primary, (2) Left Secondary, and (3) Right

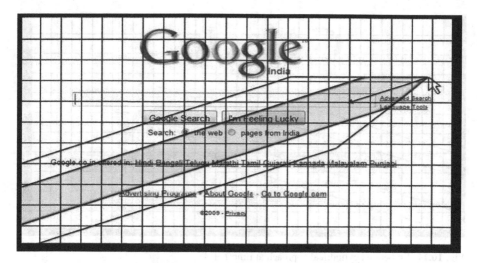

Fig. 10.10 Embedded cylindrical approach at time T

Secondary. The total area covered by the outer lines would be scanned while initial movement of the mouse is detected. But only inner area would be activated and links inside it would be added within the primary prediction queue (like, 'Advanced Search', 'Language', 'Hindi', 'Bengali', and 'Telugu'). The links of the left outer area (with respect to the mouse direction) would be added in the left secondary prediction queue (like, 'Marathi', 'Tamil', 'Gujarati', and 'Advertising Programs') and links of the right outer area (with respect to the mouse direction) would be added similarly in the right secondary queue. There are no links on that area of the Web page as shown in Fig. 10.10.

If embedded cylindrical approach is plotted over a graph, X_4 number of blocks is going to be highlighted. These grid lines or the graph are actually hidden to the user. The blocks, which are highlighted more than 50% of its area, have been considered. X_4 can be of three (3) types, such as $X_{4(0)}$, $X_{4(1)}$ & $X_{4(2)}$. Here, $X_{4(0)}$ represents only the inner cylindrical section. $X_{4(1)}$ represents the left section of the outer cylinder. $X_{4(2)}$ represents the right section of the outer cylinder. In Fig. 10.10, the number of highlighted blocks is $X_{4(0)} = 34$.

Figure 10.11 shows the variety of mouse movement by the user. Mouse might be moved with some variation depending on the behavior of the user. So, prediction accuracy would be less, if the effective (shaded) area is generated every time the user moves the mouse in different directions. That is why in this procedure, a tolerance is given to the movement of the mouse to increase the accuracy. If the user takes the mouse beyond that predefined range (tolerance), then only the effective area would be changed. The area for scanning the URLs is created after the first mouse movement. Once the inner area is activated, the mouse can move in any forward direction as shown by the arrows in Fig. 10.11. The activated area would not be changed until the mouse crosses the borders of the inner cylindrical area.

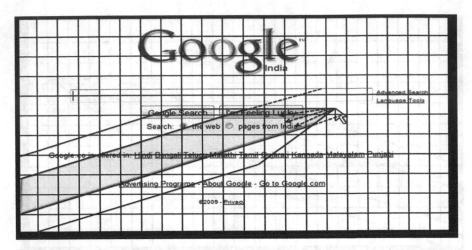

Fig. 10.11 Embedded cylindrical approach at time $T + 1$

If the mouse is moved within the inner cylindrical part of the effective area, primary prediction queue is only considered for updating and prediction of the next stage Web page. Left Secondary or Right Secondary prediction queue would be considered for prediction, while the mouse moves beyond its inner cylindrical part and reaches the outer cylindrical section. In all the cases whether the primary queue or any secondary queue is considered, the initial effective area would only be changed in respect of the forward movement of the mouse. But, the inner and outer parallel lines of the effective area would not be modified at all. Those lines remain same. The angular part of the mouse's origin (cursor) is moved forward with the mouse. So, effectively there are some changes in the prediction queues. Thus, the current effective area looks different as compared to its original shape. Actually, 'θ' (50) degree angle is always fixed with fixed parallel lines. So, the respective angular lines intersect the fixed parallel lines based on the present position of the mouse. As a result, the effective area looks like Fig. 10.11.

Figure 10.12 shows the previous mouse position using a circle. The dotted lines are the borders of the inner area. Previously the mouse was inside the inner area, so there was no change in the activated area. It is shown in the figure that the mouse is crossed the left border (with respect to mouse direction) of the inner area. As a result, the left border of the inner area is immediately removed and a new area is activated bordered by the right border of the inner area and the left border of the outer area. If the mouse crosses the right border of the inner area, the newly activated area would be bordered by the left border of the inner area and the right border of the outer area. In this case, after the newly created active area, the links of the left secondary queue is added to the primary queue and the right secondary queue would be deleted.

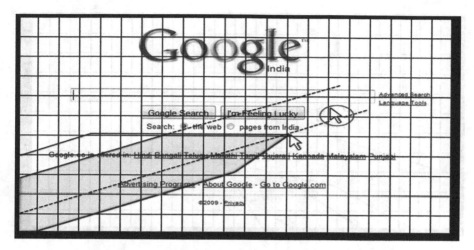

Fig. 10.12 Embedded cylindrical approach at time $T + 2$

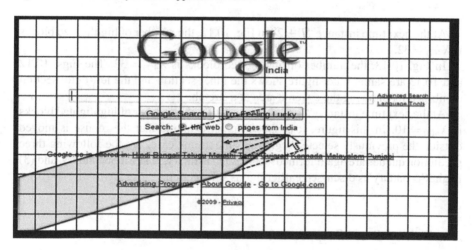

Fig. 10.13 Embedded cylindrical approach at time $T + 2$

Figure 10.13 shows another perspective of Fig. 10.12. In the new active area also the mouse can move in any forward direction and there would not be any change in this area until the mouse is crossed the border of that area.

If the user does not click any link in this effective area and the mouse crosses the border again, then the total mechanism would be repeated from that point as shown in Fig. 10.14. The previous mouse position is shown by the circle and dotted lines are the borders of the previous active area. The arrow is the direction of the mouse just after it crosses the border.

At the next time instance "$T + 1$" in Fig. 10.11, the number of highlighted blocks is $X_{4(0)} = 25$. Therefore, at time "$T + 1$," the prediction would be higher than at "T."

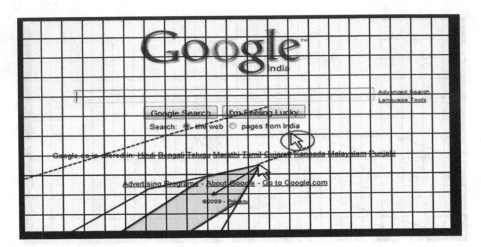

Fig. 10.14 Embedded cylindrical approach at time $T + 3$

At the next time instance "$T + 2$" in Fig. 10.12, the number of highlighted blocks is $X_{4(1)} = 32$.

In Fig. 10.13, the number of highlighted blocks is $X_{4(1)} = 32$. The Figs. 10.12 and 10.13 are same. Later figure shows the inner section and the left-outer section combined for showing the covered area at a stretch.

At the next time instance "$T + 3$" in Fig. 10.14, the number of highlighted blocks is $X_{4(0)} = 10$. In this figure, it is shown as an example that the mouse is moved outside the previously selected region as an extreme case. So, the following three prediction queues are again formed, such as (1) Primary, (2) Left Secondary, and (3) Right Secondary as discussed earlier in this sub-section.

Analysis of Overall Approach

As per discussion, it is clear that X_2 is less than X_1 as the highlighted section would be more in case of angular approach. Similarly, X_3 is less than X_2. It means that hybrid approach shows less highlighted section as compared to cylindrical approach.

Therefore, X_3 is less than X_1.

Similarly, in case of embedded cylindrical approach, the highlighted area would be further reduced. So, $X_{4(0)}$ is less than X_3; $X_{4(1)}$ is less than X_3; $X_{4(2)}$ is less than X_3.

Therefore, $X_{4(0)}$ is less than X_2 and X_1.
Therefore, $X_{4(1)}$ is less than X_2 and X_1.
Therefore, $X_{4(2)}$ is less than X_2 and X_1.

Hence, $X_{4(0)}$, $X_{4(1)}$, $X_{4(2)}$ consist of less number of blocks on any graph with respect to X_3 or X_2 or X_1.

Therefore, in this case, total number of highlighted URLs is minimal. Thus, the prediction ratio achieved should be highest in this case.

Experimental Results

We present the important factors that affect the performance of Web prediction algorithms. The first factor is the order of dependencies within the range of highlighted section of the Web page. Based on the different approaches, distinct types of highlighted section have been generated on the specific Web pages which are to be used for predicting next level Web documents of user's interest.

The experimental results have been collected from the following machine configuration:

Color quality $= 32$ bit;
Screen resolution $= 1{,}024 \times 768$;
Refresh rate $= 60$ Hz;

Effectiveness of the pruning criterion has been examined within the proposed methodologies or events for reducing the number of Web links or URLs for achieving better prediction ratio in run-time. It is being observed that proposed approaches are better than typical approaches. 'Embedded Cylindrical Approach' exhibits best result in the prescribed limited experimentation. Real as well as synthetic data sets are tested. The highlighted sections of the Web page are being treated as the most important factors for determining the probable Web page at the next time instance. The URLs which fall outside the shaded portion of the Web page are treated as insignificant entities. The experiment has been carried out on downloaded Web pages of distinct domains. Prediction accuracy of proposed approaches on Web pages has been shown in Table 10.1. Prediction accuracy directly varies to the number of URLs of the particular Web page. Embedded cylindrical approach shows the best result with respect to other approaches. Web-log of the proxy server has been considered to compare the existing and proposed approaches. For prediction accuracy calculation test data set has been referred. Table 10.2 shows test Web-log data of transition probability and corresponding prediction accuracies. It is evidenced from Table 10.3 that Web-log is insufficient for prediction of next Web-page. Better result has been achieved in proposed approach than typical approaches for predicting next Web-page by introducing dynamic prediction using mouse movement with its directions. The experimental results have been manually evaluated. Here, Prediction accuracy means the ratio between number of correct predictions and number of total predictions. Among the large data sets, a few have been shown on the following tables for representing the superiority of proposed approaches over the existing ones. 1st order Markov model, 2nd order Markov model and Prediction by Partial Match (PPM) model do not support the

Table 10.1 Test data on Web page prediction accuracy based on proposed approaches

Web page	No. of URLs	Angular approach		Cylindrical approach		Hybrid approach		Embedded cylindrical approach	
		Selected URLs	P.A. (%)	Selected URLs	P.A. (%)	Selected URLs	P.A. (%)	Selected URLs	P.A. (%)
orkut.com	7	3	57	2	71	2	71	1	85
wikipedia.org	10	6	40	6	40	4	60	2	80
java.com	25	8	68	7	72	5	80	3	88
nptel.iitm.ac.in	32	10	68	10	68	9	71	5	84
oracle.com	48	25	47	15	68	12	75	7	85

Table 10.2 Test Web-log (static) data for transition probability and prediction accuracy

Current Web-page	Next Web-page	Transition probability	Static prediction accuracy	Dynamic prediction accuracy
2	3	0.50	0.60	0.82
2	5	0.50	0.40	0.81
4	10	0.66	0.33	0.82
4	5	0.33	0.66	0.80
5	7	0.50	0.75	0.83
5	6	0.50	0.25	0.80

Table 10.3 Average prediction accuracy in different prediction mode

Prediction mode	1st order Markov model	2nd order Markov model	Prediction by partial match (PPM) model	Proposed approach
Static	66%	66%	71%	$\geq$80%
Dynamic	Not supported	Not supported	Not supported	$\geq$80%

dynamic prediction mode as they are not designed based on the real-time scenario. These methods only support the static scenario. That means Web-log or some equivalent data-log is required to handle the situation. On the contrary, proposed methods show real-time results on prediction by analyzing the mouse movement of the concerned users. The characteristic behavior of the user plays an important role in prediction.

The number of URLs considerably impacts the performance of these types of prediction algorithms. This is in accordance with associated work on association rule mining. Therefore, the efficiency is improved by the proposed prediction methods which actually prune the irrelevant Web links based on the user's customization. Moreover, highlight techniques are being modified efficiently considering the current Web page structure in every step of the rule discovery algorithm. Evaluation of the examined prediction algorithms is being concluded by presenting some experiments that were executed using real Web server traces. In the following, due to space limitations, the results obtained from one trace are being presented.

Figures 10.15 and 10.16 show the static and dynamic prediction samples respectively. In both the figures, the 'Y' axis represents the percentage of prediction and the 'X' axis represents a few models which are mentioned in Table 10.3. In these two figures, on the 'X' axis, '1' represents "1st Order Markov Model"; '2' represents "2nd Order Markov Model"; '3' represents "Prediction by Partial Match (PPM) Model"; and, '4' represents "Proposed Approach."

Conclusion

In this chapter, better dynamic prediction on Web pages has been achieved. This paper describes a social network mining approach using real-time dynamic prediction. The problem of predictive Web pre-fetching is considered, that is,

Fig. 10.15 Static prediction accuracy samples

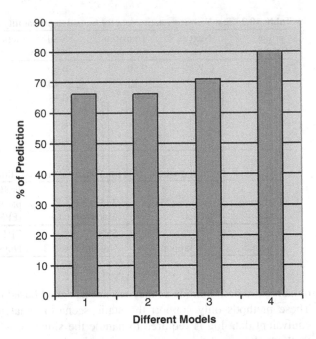

Fig. 10.16 Dynamic prediction accuracy samples

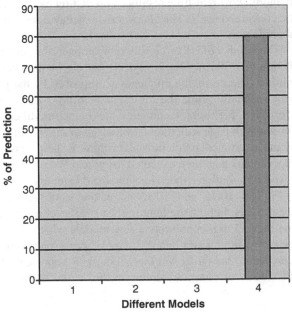

of deriving users' future requests for Web documents. In total, four events have been depicted in this work for accomplish better competence. Mouse association is exploited for predicting future Web pages. Efficient prediction schemas have been shown based on the extraction of URLs highlighted by mouse movement. Dynamic prediction suits the Web's hyper-textual nature and reduces significantly the perceived latency. Angular, cylindrical, hybrid, and embedded cylindrical approaches have been expressed for visualizing the Web prediction using self-motivated nature of user. With the increasing numbers of Web services and service users on WWW, predicting Quality of Service (QoS) for users would greatly aid service selection and discovery in respect of users' psychology. Proposed method is effective for both personal access and public access to a computer. Value of 'θ' and 'X' are being considered based on the experimental observations for the specific machine configuration mentioned in section "Experimental Results". All the proposed approaches exhibit better results than typical prediction methods. Main target is highlighting an optimal segment on the selected Web page for predicting next Web page for the specific user. Step-wise increment in prediction accuracy has been depicted using the proposed approaches. User profiles have been used to get higher accuracy. This data offers information for extending the proposal and apply this method in some areas like marketing and/or Web usability in the field of social networking.

Acknowledgements The author would like to acknowledge the many helpful suggestions of the participants of *The International ACM Conference on Management of Emergent Digital EcoSystems (MEDES 2010)*, Bangkok, Thailand, on earlier paper based on which this chapter is designed.

References

1. Kundu, A., Guha, S., Mitra, A., Mukherjee, T.: A new approach in dynamic prediction for user based web page crawling. In: The International ACM Conference on Management of Emergent Digital EcoSystems (MEDES 2010), Bangkok, Thailand, pp. 166–173, 26–29 Oct 2010
2. http://en.wikipedia.org/wiki/Social_network
3. Barnes, J.A.: Class and committees in a Norwegian Island Parish. Hum. Relat. **7**, 39–58 (1954)
4. Berkowitz, S.D.: An Introduction to Structural Analysis: The Network Approach to Social Research. Butterworth, Toronto (1982). ISBN 0–409–81362–1
5. Brandes, U., Erlebach, T. (eds.): Network Analysis: Methodological Foundations. Springer, Berlin/Heidelberg (2005)
6. Freeman, L.: The Development of Social Network Analysis. Empirical Press, Vancouver (2006)
7. Wellman, B., Berkowitz, S.D.: Social Structures: A Network Approach. Cambridge University Press, Cambridge (1988)
8. Hansen, W.B., Reese, E.L.: Network Genie User Manual. Tanglewood Research, Greensboro (2009)
9. Mukhopadhyay, D., Mishra, P., Saha, D.: An agent based method for web page prediction. In: 1st KES Symposium on Agent and Multi-Agent Systems – Technologies and Applications, AMSTA 2007 Proceedings, Wroclow, Poland, Lecture Notes in Computer Science, May 31–June 1 2007, pp. 219–228. Springer, Berlin (2007)
10. Mukhopadhyay, D., Dutta, R., Kundu, A., Kim, Y.: A model for web page prediction using cellular automata. In: The 6th International Workshop MSPT 2006 Proceedings, 20 Nov 2006, pp. 95–100. Youngil Publication, Republic of Korea (2006). ISBN 89–8801–90–0, ISSN 1975–5635

11. Page, L., Brin, S.: The anatomy of a large-scale hypertextual web search engine. In: 7th International World Wide Web Conference, Brisbane, Australia, pp. 107–11, 14–18 Apr 2008
12. Huberman, B.A., et al.: Strong regularities in world wide web surfing. Science **3**, 95–97 (1998)
13. Davison, B.D.: Learning web request patterns. In: Web Dynamics – Adapting to Change in Content, Size. Topology and Use, pp. 435–459. Springer, Berlin/New York (2004)
14. Duchamp, D.: Prefetching hyperlinks. In: USENIX Symposium on Internet Technologies and Systems, Boulder, CO, pp.127–138, Oct 1999
15. Pitkow, J.E., Pirolli, P.: Mining longest repeating subsequences to predict world wide web surfing. In: USENIX Symposium on Internet Technologies and Systems, Boulder, CO, pp. 139–150, Oct 1999
16. Kroeger, T.M., Long, D.D.E., Mogul, J.C.: Exploring the bounds of web latency reduction from caching and prefetching. In: USENIX Symposium on Internet Technologies and Systems, Monterey, CA, Dec 1997
17. Palpanas, T.: Web Prefetching Using Partial Match Prediction. Technical Report CSRG-376, Graduate department of Computer Science, University of Toronto, 1966
18. Xin Chen, X., Zhang, X.: A popularity-based prediction model for web prefetching. IEEE Comput. Soc. **36**(3), 63–70 (2003)
19. Rasmussen, E.: Clustering algorithms. In: Information Retrieval, pp. 419–442. Prentice Hall, Eaglewood Cliffs (1992)
20. Hearst, M.A., Pedersen, J.O.: Reexamining the cluster hypothesis: scatter/gather on retrieval results. In: Proceedings of the 19th Annual International ACM SIGIR Conference, Zurich, June 1996
21. Wang, Y., Kitsuregawa, M.: On combining link and contents information for web page clustering. In: 13th International Conference on Database and Expert Systems Applications DEXA2002, Aix-en-Provence, France, pp. 902–913, Sept 2002
22. Gupta, G.K.: Introduction to Data Mining with Case Studies. Prentice Hall of India, New Delhi (2006)
23. Su, Z., Yang, Q., Lu, Y., Zhang, H.: Whatnext: a prediction system for web requests using N-gram sequence models. In: First International Conferences on Web Information Systems and Engineering Conferences, Hong Kong, pp. 200–207, June 2000
24. Kroeger, T.M., Long, D.D.E., Jeffrey, C.M.: Exploring the bounds of web latency reduction from caching and pre-fetching. In: USENIX Symposium on Internet Technologies and Systems, Monterey, CA, Dec 1997.

Chapter 11
PPMN: A CityWide Reliable Public Wireless Mesh Network

Ali Asghar Khodaparast and Azade Kavianfar

Abstract In the near future, wireless modems will be used in every house to connect to the Internet through service providers in both urban and rural areas. Since user bandwidth for connection to the Internet is limited, a large fraction of each modem's bandwidth is not used. In this chapter, we show how to make a reliable public cooperative network of these wireless users to exchange intra-city data traffic without using service providers. For this reason, we introduce and analyze a network architecture called PPMN. The architecture includes a routing algorithm, a forwarding incentive mechanism, a security system, and a resiliency scheme. Design challenges are discussed in each case. Two resiliency schemes, (1) multipath routing and (2) OHOF, are reviewed which should be used together to provide an acceptable level of reliability in PPMN.

Introduction

Every residential area will soon be full of IEEE802.16 users covered by BSs (base stations) belonging to different service providers and DSL/cable users as well (Fig. 11.1). Each BS/ISP covers a limited area and gives service to a number of users. Users are mostly fixed and do not encounter energy shortage. For every user, the bandwidth for connecting to BS/ISP is an expensive resource whereas users have a significant amount of bandwidth to their neighbors in a way that all wired/wireless users in a residential area can sustain a huge volume of intra-city data

A.A. Khodaparast (✉)
Amirkabir University of Technology, Tehran, Iran
e-mail: aa_khodaparast@yahoo.com

A. Kavianfar
Guilan University, Rasht, Iran
e-mail: azadeh_kaviyanfar@yahoo.com

A. Abraham and A.-E. Hassanien (eds.), *Computational Social Networks: Tools, Perspectives and Applications*, DOI 10.1007/978-1-4471-4048-1_11,
© Springer-Verlag London 2012

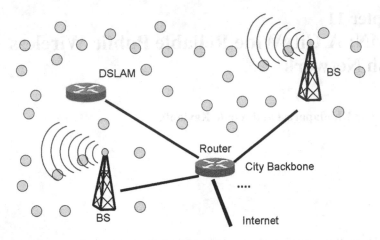

Fig. 11.1 A typical view of users and service providers in a residential area

traffic. To utilize this free bandwidth, a number of users under the same authority may compose a private wireless mesh network but such a network is not scalable.

For example, let us consider a city containing four million users in the near future when the penetration of broadband access reaches 100%. If we assume that each four users use a shared connection, then as many as one million 1-Mbps connections are typically required in the city. That means the ISPs have to provide 1-Tbps bandwidth to the city whereas a large portion of the bandwidth is used for applications such as IP-Telephony and local media broadcasts that generate intra-city traffic.

In this chapter, we introduce an architecture to make a cooperative wireless mesh network called PPMN [1] (public peer-to-peer mesh network) composed of all users in the residential area. Users can be under any authority and have wired or wireless connection to the Internet, but they need IEEE802.16 wireless modems to connect to PPMN. They have to forward internal data traffic themselves. As a result, it is not required to transfer internal traffic through ISPs except for critical information. Despite traditional customer-provider networks, adding a user to PPMN increases available bandwidth and number of links in the network. We discuss the design of PPMN in section "PPMN Design." Section "Routing Protocol" introduces the routing algorithm. Section "Forwarding Incentive Mechanism" discusses how an incentive can be used in PPMN. Section "Security" discusses security issues in PPMN. Section "Resiliency" introduces a number of resiliency mechanisms. Section "Conclusions" finally concludes the chapter.

PPMN Design

In a public network, users are dynamic and unreliable. A user may frequently join the network and then leave it. Users are typically selfish and try to use bandwidth but not to give bandwidth. A user may even attack the network or attack another

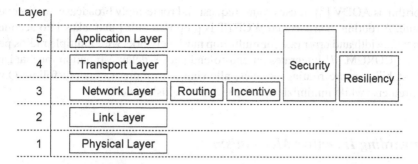

Fig. 11.2 Node's protocol layers in PPMN

user. To cope with these problems, PPMN must have a reliable resistant design. In this section, we introduce the components required in PPMN and review what is done so far in the literature on each component.

A number of public mesh networks are recently deployed in some cities (such as PWMN [2]). Users are free to join these networks and use its free internal bandwidth and contents. However, such a network uses the same protocols as a private network with trusted users. For example, PWMN uses the OSPF routing protocol [3] which is not suitable for public networks. Thus, such a public network does not consider reliability, fairness, security, and resiliency.

Figure 11.2 illustrates the protocols which are used by a node in PPMN. All the protocols work the same as the TCP/IP network model [4] except for the following components in order to achieve an acceptable level of reliability and stability in PPMN:

- Routing protocol
- Forwarding incentive mechanism
- Security scheme
- Resiliency scheme

Routing Protocol

The routing algorithm must not impose too much load on nodes by sending control messages. Some nodes have access to the internet through ISPs and some do not. It must be possible that they all connect to the PPMN. Routing is extensively studied in wireless ad hoc networks. Most the existing algorithms are distributed in a way that they broadcast routing messages throughout the network to discover a route. In contract, we require a centralized algorithm in PPMN that helps security and stability. Section "Routing Protocol" introduces such a routing algorithm.

Here we review a number of routing protocols which are generally designed for wireless ad hoc networks. The most famous and the simplest distributed routing algorithm is AODV [5]. It uses route-request and route-reply broadcasts to discover a route. A routing metric called WCETT is proposed in [6] that takes into account both bandwidth and error rate for multi-hop mesh networks with multiple radios per node. QUORUM [7] integrates an end-to-end packet delay estimation mechanism with stability-aware routing policies, allowing it to more accurately follow QoS requirements while minimizing misbehavior of selfish nodes.

Forwarding Incentive Mechanism

There must be an incentive mechanism in PPMN that encourages nodes to forward packets originated from other nodes. Although incentive mechanisms are already studied in peer-to-peer networks and wireless ad hoc networks, not all of them suit PPMN. Section "Forwarding Incentive Mechanism" discusses how an incentive can be used in PPMN.

Schemes that stimulate cooperation and mitigate the detrimental effect of uncooperative nodes in mobile ad hoc network can be classified as (1) incentive schemes and (2) reputation schemes. Incentive schemes [8–10] use some form of currency to enforce nodes' cooperation. Nodes get the currency upon serving the network and use it to gain service from the network. If a node does not have enough budgets, it will not get any service from the network. Reputation schemes [11, 12] use the nodes' reputation to forward packets through the most reliable nodes. Nodes maintain the reputation of other nodes based on direct observation or the exchange of reputation messages with other nodes.

Security Scheme

Since PPMN consists of nodes under different authorities, it needs a registration scheme to keep track of nodes. Then, security issues can be handled. Section "Security" discusses security issues in PPMN. Authors in [13] categorize security solutions in public networks into three categories: identity, trust-reputation, and incentives. The research that is done in the identity category focuses on researching solutions that achieve anonymity and access control. In the trust-reputation category, the research focuses on trying to achieve availability and authenticity using trust systems. The research that is categorized in the incentives category deals with trying to achieve fair trading and availability of peers by researching various ways to incite peers to contribute to the system.

Resiliency Scheme

Since nodes are neither trusted nor reliable in PPMN, there must be a resiliency scheme to guarantee a level of reliability for a data transfer session. We review a number of resiliency mechanisms in section "Resiliency" which can be used in PPMN. They operate in layer 2 and layer 3 according to the model illustrated in Fig. 11.2.

In general, the existing resiliency mechanisms in data transmission can be classified in the following categories:

1. Packet retransmission
2. Data redundancy
3. Path redundancy
4. Resiliency against attacks

Now, we review the existing mechanisms belonging to these categories.

Packet Retransmission. In general, the receiver notifies the sender which packets were received correctly or informs the sender which packets were not received even though they were sent and thus need to be retransmitted. An example of this category is the sliding window mechanism [4].

Data Redundancy. FEC [14] is a system of error control whereby the sender adds redundant data to its messages, also known as an error correction code. This allows the receiver to detect and correct errors without the need to ask the sender for retransmission. HARQ [15] uses the same idea for incremental redundancy. Network coding [16] also exploits data redundancy to achieve resilience.

Path Redundancy. There is extensive research aiming at finding two link-disjoint paths for data transfer, one as the active path and the other as the backup path which is used when the active path fails [17]. Authors in [18] propose a generic resilient multipath routing scheme for mobile ad hoc networks with the aim of ensuring network throughput in both adversarial and node failure scenarios. OR is another form of path redundancy discussed in section"One-Hop Opportunistic Forwarding."

Resiliency Against Attacks. Authors in [19] investigate resilience to security attacks in ad hoc networks. SEMAP [20] is a secure enhancement mechanism based on Attacking Point which converts the possibility of security threat to a concrete metric. It can exclude the nodes that will be the objects of adversaries from the network before actual routing process.

Routing Protocol

In this section, we introduce an algorithm to find a path between a source node and a destination node in PPMN considering the following issues. These issues direct us to choose a centralized hierarchical approach. The central nature enables control over routing messages, whereas hierarchy distributes the load on routing controllers:

- Routing between two nodes must not impose load on other nodes. A malicious node may use this idea and broadcast routing messages over the network while there is no efficient mechanism in the literature to control how much a particular node broadcasts over the network where the routing scheme is distributed (such as AODV [5]). For example, a malicious node first consumes all its broadcast quota inside a network area and then moves to another area where no neighbor has knowledge about its quota to generate new broadcasts.

- No node should be able to inject false routing information into the network. If the routing scheme is distributed, then the information carried by a routing message cannot be verified or authenticated in most cases. For example, if a malicious node mentions that it has a route to a far node, its neighbors are not able to verify this claim but a central controller who has knowledge about all the nodes is able to do that.
- The discovered route must satisfy the cooperative conditions of intermediate nodes.
- Selfishness restricts routing message propagation (e.g., RouteRequest in AODV) in the network.
- Routing should be scalable and thus needs hierarchy.
- Routing scheme should be load-efficient and as fast as possible. Exchanging routing information with a local routing controller through ISP provides this goal.
- Since most 802.16 users are mostly fixed and use it as a broadband connection, churn rate in PPMN is not as high as other peer-to-peer systems (such as public file sharing [21]).

In the following subsections, we present a routing algorithm which is specifically design to operate in PPMN.

Routing Model

Each ISP contains an LRC (local routing controller) and there is one GRC (global routing controller) in the city (Fig. 11.3). There is a hierarchy. An LRC composes a domain and controls and performs local routing operations in its domain whereas the GRC performs inter-domain routings. An LRC knows the topology in its domain whereas the GRC only knows the top-level interconnections between the domains. A directed link from node a to node b in a topology graph means that node b is willing to forward node a's packets. LRCs and the GRC are connected to the city backbone and only update topology changes. A user needs the following items to be able to use PPMN:

- An IEEE802.16 wireless modem.
- A connection to the city backbone. This connection can be wired or wireless provided by an ISP or by another PPMN node.

Each LRC belonging to an ISP is responsible for routing in a domain containing the following nodes:

- Subscriber nodes of the ISP
- Nodes which are not subscribed to any ISPs but try to discover a route by sending RouteRequest to a subscriber node of the ISP

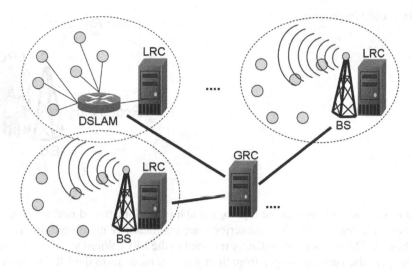

Fig. 11.3 An illustration of routing domains in PPMN. Two domains are logically distinct but may have physical overlap

Increasing number of domains generates a bigger top-level topology graph and thus increases the load on the GRC. Therefore, we should not assign a separate domain to small ISPs in a large city. Instead, we aggregate small neighbor ISPs in a single domain with one LRC. Furthermore, we assume that physical overlap of domains are not too much in a way that the number of intra-domain links is at least ten times more than the number of inter-domain links in the PPMN.

A session is defined as the duration of data transfer between a source node and a destination node in PPMN. A full-duplex route is established for a session such that both the source and the destination can send packets to each other. The source embeds the route into packets such that intermediate nodes are able to forward the packet without doing routing.

Bandwidth is reserved along the route. The amounts of bandwidth reserved along the forward path and the backward path depend on traffic symmetry of the application. For example, IP-Telephony is symmetric but FTP is asymmetric. Even if the application is highly asymmetric, ACK packets (used in section "Session Resiliency" and TCP) are at least transferred along the non-loaded path.

Local Routing

When a node starts up, when it is going to change its forwarding policy to neighbors, or when it detects a change in neighbors, it sends a TopologyReport message to the LRC of the domain. A TopologyReport message contains the descriptions of links which the node provides along with the node's willingness to forward packets on

Fig. 11.4 Local routing steps

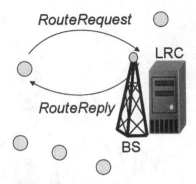

those links. The LRC makes the topology graph of its domain and updates it upon changes. In a domain, wireless subscribers are continuously monitored by the BS and their On/Off status is immediately reported to the LRC. Wired subscribers have to send periodic Hello messages from their wireless modems to the LRC to update their On/Off status but wireless subscribers do not. Every node has to periodically broadcast Hello message to discover neighbors.

When a subscriber node needs to discover a route, it sends a RouteRequest message to the corresponding LRC. A node without subscription has to find a subscriber node as a gateway to the LRC. It has to pay for the routing packets which the subscriber node forwards for it. The LRC makes the topology graph of both subscriber and non-subscriber nodes in the domain. When an LRC receives a RouteRequest message where both the source and the destination are located in its domain, it locally computes a route and sends the route back to the source. In short, local routing steps are as follows (Fig. 11.4):

1. The source sends a RouteRequest message to the LRC.
2. The LRC locally computes a route.
3. The LRC sends the route back to the source.

Global Routing

The city's GRC makes the top-level topology graph of the city containing only the interconnections between the domains and updates it upon changes. Each LRC reports changes in its connections to other domains to the GRC. When an LRC receives a RouteRequest message in which the destination is located outside its domain, it sends the RouteRequest to the GRC. Global routing steps are as follows (Fig. 11.5):

1. The source sends a RouteRequest message to its LRC.
2. The LRC sends a RouteRequest message to the GRC.
3. The GRC computes a top-level route.

Fig. 11.5 Global routing steps

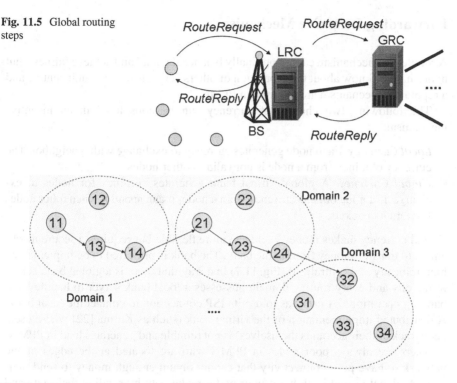

Fig. 11.6 An illustration of routes in PPMN

4. The GRC sends the route back to the LRC.
5. The LRC separately asks the LRCs of the intermediate domains to complete the route by inserting intermediate nodes in the route.
6. The LRC sends the route back to the source.

For example, Fig. 11.6 shows the following routes:

- A local (intra-domain) route: $< 11 \rightarrow 13 \rightarrow 14 >$
- A top-level inter-domain route: $< 11 \rightarrow Domain(1) \rightarrow Domain(2) \rightarrow Domain(3) \rightarrow 32 >$
- A detailed inter-domain route: $< 11 \rightarrow 13 \rightarrow 14 \rightarrow 21 \rightarrow 23 \rightarrow 24 \rightarrow 32 >$

Using this mechanism, most the routing tasks are distributed among LRCs, and the GRC does a minimal amount of calculations and receives a minimal amount of topology updates during network operation. This makes the routing scheme scalable. A top-level topology update is required when there is a change in interconnections between the domains. Since we expect multiple connections between two neighbor domains, no top-level topology update is required when a single top-level connection changes. Thus, we do not expect a high rate of top-level topology updates.

Forwarding Incentive Mechanism

A reputation mechanism cannot optimally balance the load and achieve fairness, but nodes have to know about the reputation of others. Therefore, both an incentive and a reputation mechanism are required in PPMN.

The following two choices of currency can be considered in an incentive mechanism:

- *Local Currency.* Each node generates currency to exchange with a neighbor. The currency obtained from a node is not valid to other nodes.
- *Global Currency.* A global virtual bank generates currency for nodes to exchange. If a node obtains currency from a node, it can spend it when other nodes forward its packets.

Global currency makes money exchange more flexible but requires a secure mechanism to transfer money from/to the bank. The bank is preferred to be implemented hierarchically and centralized (Fig. 11.7) in a way that there is a global bank server in the city and every routing domain possesses a local bank server to handle local banking operations. A user has to use its ISP connection to contact the local bank. A distributed implementation of the virtual bank (such as Karma [22] where users keep track of their accounts themselves) is not reliable and generates load in PPMN.

There are always poor nodes in PPMN who are located at the edges of the network or have poor connectivity that cannot obtain enough money to send their data. A global virtual bank helps poor nodes make debt by sending their data and then pay back by forwarding packets for others or by exchanging real money. This mechanism increases throughput and requires a tough registration scheme where each node has a permanent unique ID to keep track of node accounts in the virtual

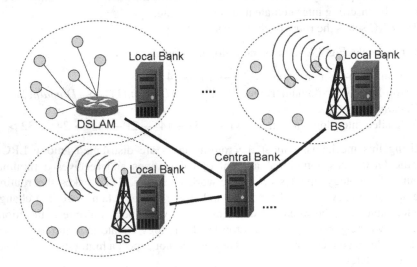

Fig. 11.7 An illustration of bank distribution in PPMN

bank. The perfect case for PPMN would be the case in which every node has an account in the bank. Each node is charged for sending packets and is rewarded by forwarding packets for others. Account balances are annually computed such that some nodes have to pay real money to the bank and some nodes receive real money from the bank. Nodes located in the center of PPMN are probably on the shortest paths of most the flows. Thus, a node in the central areas is able to earn money.

The source is a node that starts the session. Depending on the application, traffic direction can be from the source to the destination, from the destination to the source, or both. In all the three cases, the source node has to pay to the intermediate nodes for all the exchanged packets. The destination node can be a public server that may claim money from the source. Thus, PPMN naturally supports network services. For example, a user is able to provide a public storage and automatically earn money.

There are two cases for intermediate nodes' payoffs:

- *Fixed Payoff.* All the intermediate nodes receive the same payoff per unit data.
- *Variable Payoffs.* Nodes are free to claim different unit payoffs.

In the case of variable payoffs, a poor node is able to decrease its payoff to ensure its route will be accepted by the source and a node located in the center is able to increase its payoff since it is probably in the shortest paths of many traffic flows, and thus, it is probably in the least-price paths of many traffic flows if it slightly increases its unit payoff. Such a system must guarantee that the exact price agreed before transmission is paid after successful transmission. Knowledge about topology and payoffs of other nodes helps a node to justify its payoff since that node looses the route by specifying a too high payoff and is underpaid by specifying a too low payoff.

In the case of variable payoffs, the LRC has to updates payoffs before every data transfer. This operation generates load and startup delay. Any load on nodes because of control information can be a source of unfairness and network abuse. In general, we conclude that a global currency incentive scheme with a fixed payoff suits PPMN.

An established route has a price which is relative to its length. A route has minimal QoS requirements that may not be satisfied along the shortest path because of congestion. Thus, the GRC and LRCs must handle route requests in a way that different sources get fair path lengths. This is the same goal which traffic engineering algorithms try to achieve [23]. In case of multipath routing, the controllers should compute two paths of similar prices for each RouteRequest.

Global currency enables mobility. A mobile node can stay at a place for awhile as a fixed node until it earns enough budgets, and then, it is able to move and spend its budget at another place. However, the routing controllers should not insert a mobile node (when moving) in routes since the links which a mobile node creates are transient.

When a controller assigns a route to a traffic flow, it has to reserve bandwidth on that route for the flow and direct upcoming flows toward the paths with available bandwidth. A source that has established a route to a destination may send nothing on that route and pay nothing while the route is consuming resources. To prevent this kind of misbehaviors, the source should pay a constant price for each unit time interval in which it holds the route, in addition to the payment which it makes for packet forwarding.

Security

There must be a scheme in PPMN to ensure security and safety of established routes and prevent/resist misbehaviors/attacks. Because of the virtual banking, every node has to register with the GRC using its MAC address as a unique ID along with the name and the address of the owner just like telephone registration. In other words, each node owner has to go to the GRC office to register its MAC address. Then, that node is able to join the PPMN.

Key Management

A key management scheme [24] suitable for non-trusted environments should be used to enable encryption in PPMN. The scheme must guarantee that keys are confidentially established and updated. The following kinds of keys are essential in PPMN:

1. *Session Key.* A new key should be established between the source and the destination for each data transfer session. Every packet generated between the source and the destination of the session is encrypted using session key.
2. *Initial Session Key* (described below).
3. *Pairwise Key.* A node has to separately establish a pairwise key with each neighbor so that routing information exchanged between two neighbors is not exposed to other neighbors.
4. *Routing Key.* Each node has to establish a routing key with the corresponding LRC to ensure secure routing operations. This key has to be updated periodically.
5. *Bank Key.* Each node has to establish a bank key with the bank server to ensure secure money exchange. This key has to be updated periodically.

There are a number of key-exchange mechanisms (e.g., Diffie-Hellman [25] and SPEKE [26]) that provide key establishment between two nodes without transferring the real key across the network. Such a mechanism transfers a number of messages between the two nodes to establish a common key. To protect the key-establishment messages from malicious intermediate nodes, these messages are encrypted. The two nodes initially have no common key. They request a trusted key server for an initial key to encrypt key-establishment messages. Once the session key is established, they release the initial key and use the session key afterward. Although extracting the session key from key-establishment messages is too hard, it is preferred that no node should be able to have both the encrypted key-establishment messages and the initial key. Otherwise, that node can extract the plain key-establishment messages. Since key-establishment messages are transferred along a PPMN path, the key server which is the only node who knows the initial key is not able to receive them. This mechanism ensures that the session key is not exposed to anyone other than the source and the destination.

Misbehaviors and Attacks

A single node or a group of cooperative nodes can harm the system in one of the following ways:

- *Sybil Attack.* This is an easy attack in most peer-to-peer systems in which a node joins the system with different identities [24, 27]. Since nodes are identified by their MAC addresses, this is not possible in PPMN.
- *Frequent Departures.* This action imposes heavy load on the system since it requires frequent topology updates and path recoveries. To avoid this misbehavior, there should be a minimum time interval in which a node can join PPMN. Neighbors do not send TopologyReport messages until a node reach a stable state and an LRC does not accept frequent TopologyReport or Hello messages from a single node.
- *False Misbehavior Report.* A report to a controller that indicates a node is misbehaving and lowers the reputation of that node. To prevent false reports, the system should only accept reports that contain evidence. Such evidence-based reports are proposed in [8, 9].
- *False Money-Exchange Report.* A number of mechanisms [8, 10] have been proposed to guarantee proper money exchange after a data transmission session.
- *False Failure Report.* We discuss how to reject this kind of false reports in section "Reporting Mechanism."
- *Misforwarding.* A malicious node can do selective forwarding [24], disordering packets, or degrading the service quality of a flow. Detecting such kind of attacks is so hard since congestion can cause the same consequences as well and misbehavior reports are mostly not trusted.
- *False Routing.* This happens when a node injects false routing information into the system. If a node lies about a neighbor to an LRC, then that neighbor may tell the truth and then the false information will be rejected. When both the neighbor nodes lie and establish a fake link, they are not able to make extra payoff and the fake link will be detected since it does not satisfy the QoS requirements of passing flows. This kind of attacks is categorized in [24] and is prevented in PPMN since routing messages are fully controlled.

Resiliency

In this section, we introduce a number of resiliency mechanisms which are specifically designed for PPMN. An efficient resiliency scheme for PPMN is to use all these mechanisms together.

Session Resiliency

Since not all kinds of failure/misbehavior can be prevented, an established session should be resilient to them. In this section, we introduce a multipath session resiliency scheme [1] in PPMN to cope with (1) node departure/failure, (2) misforwarding, (3) misreporting, and (4) congestion (QoS degradation).

Two paths of similar length and price between a given source node and a destination node are discovered on demand (Fig. 11.8). Then, the source and the destination initially transmit data along these paths in a round-robin manner. Then, they adapt data transmission rate along the two paths according to path price and bandwidth. When the source discovers a path performs poorly in comparison with the other one, it releases the path and requests the LRC for another path. This mechanism is based on the fact that misforwarding and congestion in a network have the common symptoms of disruption of data communication which manifests itself in the form of reduced throughput. Both the source and the destination continuously monitor the throughput of each path. The destination reports the throughput of a path to the source along the other path. In this way, no intermediate node is able to alter the reports or to generate fake throughput reports.

To acknowledge arrived packets, the receiver (the source or the destination) sends ACK packets (as specified in TCP) along the two paths in a round-robin manner to the sender. We assume that packet content is encrypted so that intermediate nodes are not able to understand the content or determine which packets are being acknowledged.

If packet(i) is lost, then packet(j) where $j > i$ which is received successfully will become useless. This is the base of the selective forwarding attack in which a malicious intermediate node drops a few number of selected packets in a session to effectively disturb the whole session. In this case, the two paths have approximately

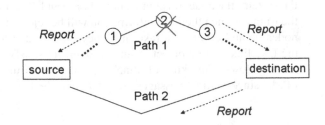

Fig. 11.8 Reports when node(2) fails or leaves

the same throughput since the losses affect data transmission along both the paths. A solution to this is that the receiver gains knowledge about the sequence of packets that arrive from each one of the paths and immediately requests the sender for retransmission if an out of order packet arrives since it indicates that a packet is lost. Once a path is established, the source and the destination secretly agree on a series of sequence numbers with which packets are sent on that path. This series is updated when the sender decides to change data transmission rate on that path. Another solution is to create content redundancy between the two paths. If a packet is lost along a path, it can be recovered from the contents received along the other path.

This mechanism can be incorporated in the routing algorithm. The two paths should be maximally disjoint. There should be a time interval in which no more than one route request is accepted from one node.

This level of reliability works perfect for applications such as web, file transfer, and telnet. However, there are real time applications such as telephony that require not much bandwidth but more reliability. This can be achieved using a low bandwidth reliable path through ISPs and one high bandwidth path inside PPMN. This strategy is also useful when at most one path is found in PPMN between the source and the destination. To increase reliability and decrease cost, control messages such as acknowledgments and reports are transferred along the low-speed ISP path and data messages are transferred along the high-speed PPMN path. In general, one of the following sets of paths can be selected for a session:

- Two paths in PPMN
- A low-speed path through ISPs and a high-speed path through PPMN
- One path through ISPs

Reporting Mechanism

Reporting to a controller is required in one of the following cases. A report of any kind may be falsely generated:

1. Failure.
2. Misbehavior and reputation.
3. Money exchange. A number of mechanisms are proposed in the literature [8, 10] to guarantee proper money exchange and avoid fraud.

When node(i) along one of the established paths between a source and a destination fails or departs, the following three reports are generated (Fig. 11.8):

1. Node(i − 1) sends a failure report to the source along the same path.
2. Node(i + 1) sends a failure report to the destination along the same path.
3. Then, the destination sends a failure report to the source along the other path.

This mechanism makes the source confident that both the reports which it receives are not fakes. Then, the source informs the LRC of the node failure and asks for another path. The LRC directly checks node(i)'s status and discover whether the source, the destination, or an intermediate node is telling the truth. This mechanism provides resiliency to failure/departure and works well even in the cases depicted in Fig. 11.10 when a session encounters multiple failures/departures at the same time.

Since misbehaviors cannot be proved, this kind of report is not trusted. Reputation systems solve this problem by using a voting mechanism in which a number of nodes are asked about a particular node. In PPMN, only two neighbors along a path are able to monitor an intermediate node and then voting cannot guarantee that a node is misbehaving to get a bad reputation. Therefore, a bad/negative reputation does not work. For this reason, most reputation systems only consider positive reputation where the reputation of a node will never become less than zero [27]. Thus, we suggest that the reputation system in PPMN is designed in a way that an LRC sets node's reputation according to the way that the node handles the sessions to which it is assigned. In response, the more reputation a node has, the cheaper and the shorter paths it gets for data transfer.

One-Hop Opportunistic Forwarding

Opportunistic routing (OR) and network coding (NC) are two state-of-the-art techniques to improve the fault-tolerance of wireless mesh networks. In contrast to traditional routing which forwards packets along a fixed path from a source to a destination, OR [28] opportunistically exploits multiple paths between the source and the destination. OR broadcasts the packet first and then decides the next hop among all neighbors that hear the packet successfully, thus providing more chances for a packet to make some progress toward the destination. In NC [16], a forwarding node encodes a number of packets into a single coded packet and then broadcasts the packet to all its neighbors. This reduces the number of transmissions needed for forwarding packets and hence increases the effective capacity of the network. If each plain packet appears in multiple coded packets, a level of redundancy is created in the network. This redundancy makes the network resistant against packet loss.

A malicious node can easily make coded packets non-decodable to receivers [29]. To prevent this, there must be a mechanism that may increase overhead. Thus, this is an open problem whether NC is useful in a public network. In contrast, we use the idea of OR and introduce a resiliency mechanism called one-hop opportunistic forwarding (OHOF) that does not contain routing. It can be incorporated in a unicast routing algorithm to improve resiliency and load balance. Original OR cannot be used in PPMN because of the fact that it does not control packet forwarding and a packet may get far from its original path. Thus, it is possible that copies of a single packet overload the network.

We assume that the data transfer path is embedded in packets. When a node is going to forward a packet to the next hop, it broadcasts the packet (Fig. 11.9). In addition to the next hop, every node with the following conditions receives the packet:

Fig. 11.9 The OHOF
mechanism with one next hop
and two neighbors

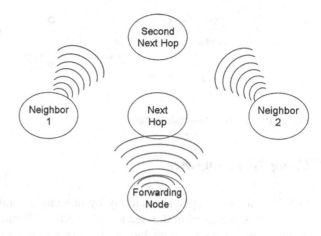

1. It is a neighbor of all the three nodes: forwarding node, next hop, and second next hop.
2. It has available bandwidth.

Such a neighbor (whether it is the next hop or not) waits a random time interval until it hears another node sending the packet to the second next hop. Otherwise, it takes the wireless channel and forwards the packet to the second next hop. When a neighbor receives a packet that is not a neighbor of the packet's second next hop, it simply drops the packet. This avoids packets from getting away from their original path and prevents redundant transmissions.

If two neighbors of the forwarding node are too far or if directional antennas are used, then they are not able to monitor each other and they may both forward the packet. To cope with this problem, each neighbor has to check with the second next hop before forwarding whether the second next hop is receiving the packet now or has previously received the packet. When the second next hop successfully receives the packet, it broadcasts a confirmation message to all its neighbors to stop trying to forward the packet.

When an intermediate node is congested, it makes delay in forwarding packets, and thus, its non-congested neighbors do the forwarding. Since 802.16 modems have high transmission range, it is expected that a single node has several neighbors and then OHOF will significantly improve tolerance to failure and congestion. Since a path gets wider using OHOF, the two disjoint paths are preferred to be zone-disjoint than being link-disjoint.

Since packets may be forwarded by different nodes during a session, OHOF requires a per-packet money-exchange scheme to ensure intermediate nodes receive appropriate payoffs. A neighbor node that has forwarded a single packet and is not in the path should be able to receive its payoff. When a packet is forwarded at a hop in the path, a number of nodes receive it. The money-exchange scheme must guarantee that the node who delivers the packet to the next hop earns the money.

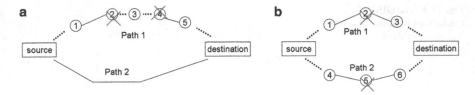

Fig. 11.10 Two node failures/departures

Using Them Together

PPMN achieves acceptable reliability by utilizing a combination of the resiliency mechanisms presented in this section and section "Resiliency Scheme." Each one of the mechanisms recovers lost packets in specific situations. For example in Fig. 11.10, a 2-path session encounters two synchronous failures/departures. Then, we have:

1. If the two failures/departures occur on the same path (Path 1 in Fig. 11.10a), then OHOF may not be able to forward the packets on that path. In this case, the lost packets are retransmitted on the other path as a result of multipath routing.
2. If the two failures/departures occur on different paths (both Path 1 and Path 2 in Fig. 11.10b), then multipath routing does not work. In this case, OHOF can successfully forward packets on the paths by using the neighbors of the failed nodes.
3. If more than two failures/departures occur on both the paths in a way that no packet can be transferred, then the source asks another path from its LRC to continue the data transfer.

Conclusions

In this chapter, we introduced an architecture to construct a public peer-to-peer mesh network called PPMN of independent 802.16 users. The architecture is composed of a routing protocol, a forwarding incentive mechanism, a security scheme, and a resiliency scheme:

- The routing algorithm is scalable and able to control routing control messages. It is different from the other routing algorithms in the way that it is compatible to the security goals of public peer-to-peer systems.
- Since the GRC only discovers routes on a graph containing the routing domains as vertices, and the number of domains is expected to be less than 50 in a city, the load on the GRC is not considerable.
- A forwarding incentive mechanism with global currency and fixed payoff should be used to increase flexibility and support mobility.

- A key management scheme suitable for non-trusted environments should be used to enable encryption in PPMN.
- We discussed a simple key-establishment mechanism to ensure no third person is able to find the session key between a source and a destination.
- Five kinds of keys are essential in PPMN.
- We described possible kinds of misbehaviors and attacks in PPMN.
- Reports from nodes to ISPs, controllers, or the virtual bank should provide evidence to be accepted. We introduced such a reporting mechanism in case of node failure/departure.
- Two resiliency schemes, (1) multipath routing and (2) OHOF, are introduced which should be used together to provide an acceptable level of reliability in PPMN.

As future work, researchers may work on the following topics:

- An improved key management scheme which is compatible to the non-trusted environment of PPMN
- A secure money-exchange scheme that allows per-packet money-exchange reports and does not impose high load on the network
- Improving the routing scheme to support more anonymity of nodes.

Acknowledgements A.A. Khodaparast would like to thank *Icce Chen* for her encouragement and efforts in preparing this chapter.

References

1. Kavianfar, A., Habibi, J.: PPMN: a resilient public peer-to-peer mesh network of IEEE802.16 Users. In: International Conference on Computer Design and Applications, IEEE Computer Society (2009)
2. Patras Wireless Metropolitan Network. http://www.pwmn.net
3. Moy, J.: OSPF Version 2. The Internet Society, RFC 2328 (1998)
4. Tanenbaum, A.: Computer Networks, 4th edn. Prentice Hall PTR, Upper Saddle River (2003)
5. Perkins, C., Royer, E.: Ad hoc on-demand distance vector routing. In: The 2nd IEEE Workshop on Mobile Computing Systems and Applications, New Orleans (1999)
6. Draves, R., Padhye, J., Zill, B.: Routing in multi-radio, multi-hop wireless mesh networks. In: MobiCom'04, New York (2004)
7. Kone, V., Das, S., Zhao, B., Zheng, H.: QUORUM – QUality Of service RoUting in wireless Mesh networks. MONET **12**(5), 358–369 (2007)
8. Chen, T., Zhong, S.: INPAC: an enforceable incentive scheme for wireless networks using network coding. In: The 29th IEEE International Conference on Computer Communications (INFOCOM), San Diego (2010)
9. Choi, H., Enck, W., Shin, J., McDaniel, P., La Porta, T.: ASR: anonymous and secure reporting of traffic forwarding activity in mobile Ad Hoc networks. Wirel. Netw., ACM/Kluwer **15**(4), 525–539 (2009)
10. Zhang, Y., Lou, W., Liu, W., Fang, Y.: A secure incentive protocol for mobile ad hoc networks. ACM Wirel. Netw. **13**(5), 663–678 (2007)

11. Michiardi, P., Molva, R.: Core: a COllaborative REputation mechanism to enforce node cooperation in Mobile Ad Hoc Networks. In: IFIP-Communication and Multimedia Security Conference. IEEE (2002)
12. Bansal, S., Baker, M.: Observation-based Cooperation Enforcement in Ad Hoc Networks. Technical Report, Stanford University (2003)
13. Risson, J., Moors, T.: Survey of research towards Robust peer-to-peer networks: search methods. Technical Report UNSW-EE-P2P-1-1, University of New South Wales (2004)
14. Wicker, S.: Error control systems for digital communication and storage. Prentice-Hall, Englewood Cliffs (1995). ISBN:0-13-200809-2
15. Soljanin, E.: Hybrid ARQ in wireless networks. In: DIMACS Workshop on Network Information Theory, Piscataway (2003)
16. Fragouli, C., Katabi, D., Markopoulou, A., Medard, M., Rahul, H.: Wireless network coding: opportunities and challenges. In: Military Communications Conference (IEEE MILCOM'07). IEEE (2007)
17. Bhandari, R.: Survivable Networks: Algorithms for Diverse Routing. Kluwer, Boston (1999)
18. Kesavan, M., Swarup, D., Andiappan, K.: A generic resilient multipath routing mechanism for failure prone Ad Hoc networks. In: The International Conference on High Performance Computing (HiPC), Goa (2005)
19. Aad, I., Hubaux, J., Knightly, E.: Denial of service resilience in Ad Hoc networks. In: ACM MobiCom'04, Philadelphia (2004)
20. Lu, Z., Huang, C., Wang, F., Rong, C.: SEMAP: improving multipath security based on attacking point in Ad Hoc networks. In: The 5th International Conference on Autonomic and Trusted Computing (ATC-08), Oslo (2008)
21. Baldoni, R., Mian, A., Scipioni, S., Piergiovanni, S.: Churn resilience of peer-to-peer group membership: a performance analysis. In: IWDC'05, Kharagpur, 226–237 (2005)
22. Vishnumurthy, V., Chandrakumar, S., Sirer, E.: Karma: a secure economic framework for peer-to-peer resource sharing. In: Economics of Peer-to-Peer Systems, Berkeley (2003)
23. Girish, M., Zhou, B., Hu, J.: Formulation of the traffic engineering problems in MPLS based IP networks. In: the Fifth IEEE Symposium on Computers and Communications (ISCC 2000), Antibes (2000)
24. Karlof, C., Wagner, D.: Secure routing in wireless sensor networks: attacks and countermeasures. In: 1st IEEE International Workshop Sensor Network Protocols and Applications, IEEE (2003)
25. Diffie, W., Oorschot, P., Wiener, M.: Authentication and authenticated key exchanges. Des. Codes Cryptogr. 2(2), 107–125 (1992)
26. MacKenzie, P.: On the security of the SPEKE password-authenticated key exchange protocol. Technical Report 2001/057, Lucent Technologies (2001)
27. Vroonhoven, J.: Peer to peer security. In: 4th Twente Student Conference on IT, Enschede (2006)
28. Biswas, S., Morris, R.: ExOR: opportunistic multi-hop routing for wireless networks. In: ACM SIGCOMM'05, Philadelphia (2005)
29. Jaggi, S., Langberg, M., Katti, S., Ho, T., Katabi, D., Medard, M., Effros, M.: Resilient network coding in the presence of byzantine adversaries. IEEE Trans. Inf. Theory 54(6), 2596–2603 (2008)

Chapter 12
Applications of Social Networks in Peer-to-Peer Networks

Jiaqing Huang, Qingyuan Liu, Zhibin Lei, and Dah Ming Chiu

Abstract When peer-to-peer (P2P) networks meet *social networks* (for instance, Facebook), the former develops new characteristics. A notable change is that peers would use real names in social networks, and hence the P2P networks become naturally clustered according to the human relationship imported from the social networks. Conceivably, social network theories can be applied to improve the performance of P2P networks. This chapter introduces the social network theories, including *small world* (six degrees of separation), *weak ties*, *structural holes*, and others, and their applications in P2P networks. Specifically, the chapter describes applications of social networks in P2P networks using *network coding* as well as social networks in P2P *content-centric networking* (CCN) or *named data networking* (NDN), which is a brand-new framework for future communications.

J. Huang (✉) • Q. Liu
Department of Electronics and Information Engineering, Huazhong University of Science and Technology (HUST), Hubei Provincial Key Lab of Smart Internet Technology, Wuhan, 430074, P.R.China
e-mail: jqhuang@mail.hust.edu.cn

Z. Lei
Hong Kong Applied Science and Technology Research Institute Company Limited (ASTRI), 2 Science Park East Avenue, Shatin, NT, Hong Kong
e-mail: lei@astri.org

D.M. Chiu
Department of Information Engineering, Chinese University of Hong Kong (CUHK), Shatin, NT, Hong Kong
e-mail: dmchiu@ie.cuhk.edu.hk

A. Abraham and A.-E. Hassanien (eds.), *Computational Social Networks: Tools, Perspectives and Applications*, DOI 10.1007/978-1-4471-4048-1_12,
© Springer-Verlag London 2012

Introduction

With the upsurge of Web 2.0 presently, such as Facebook (http://www.facebook.com/), MySpace (http://www.myspace.com/), Kaixin (http://www.kaixin001.com/), Renren (http://www.renren.com/), *social network* becomes a hot research topic. The movie *The Social Network* in 2010, which retells the origins of Facebook how to produce huge Internet society with about 500 million persons, also fuels the interests of research on social network theories and their applications in real networks.

The typical characteristic of Web 2.0 is *user generated content* (UGC). That is, users not only read the contents from Internet, but also generate the contents to Internet. For instance, users can publish their own articles in *Twitter* and *blog*. Thus, there comes a new era, so-called Web 2.0. In comparison, previous Internet can be called Web 1.0, such as *portal* websites Yahoo.com, Sina.com, Sohu.com. In Web 1.0, users can only read instead of generating contents from the portal websites. Web 2.0 is closely related to *social networks* in that users would use real names, in order to make friends and friends' friends.

One essential difference between social networks and Web 1.0 is person-centric (see Fig. 12.1). In real human society, people cluster together with regard to similar/same interests, goals and so on. In social networks, users would use real names. Thus, it is similar for users to make friends through social networks and through real human society. Consequently, social networks also have clustered characteristic of real human society. This clustered social property is of great significance to plan the physical networks (see the section "Advantages of Social Networks").

Social networks and peer-to-peer (P2P) networks are naturally matched. Because Client/Server framework cannot support large amount of traffic, especially for exchanging video files among large amount of people, P2P technologies become necessary to meet the requirement to improve the throughput. However, one drawback of P2P is no *trust* so that there are many *free-riders* in P2P networks. This hardly happens in social networks. Due to usage of real names in social networks,

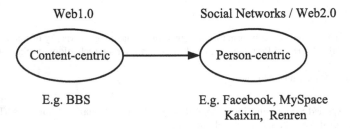

Fig. 12.1 From content-centric to person-centric

users must keep their *credits* just like they do in the real human society. It can reduce the problem of selfishness to a great extent. This chapter focuses on the applications of social networks in P2P networks.

Next, advantages and disadvantages of social networks are summarized as follows.

Advantages of Social Networks

- *Increase Searching Efficiency*
  Social networks are clustered, for instance, in terms of similar interests. Consequently, it is of higher efficiency to search in the correlative cluster than to search blindly in the overall networks.
- *Stimulate Incentives to Collaborate*
  Users in social networks must keep their credits because they should use real names in order to make friends as well as friends' friends. Furthermore, they are willing to help others in order to obtain help from others when needed. This stimulates the incentives to collaborate rather than cheat each other under the circumstances of anonymous login. Take P2P file sharing as example; it results in the least free-riders.

  In addition, users in social networks will help each other in terms of different events. That is, User A helps User B in terms of Event 1; User B will help User A in terms of Event 2. A case in point is cross-channel caching in P2P VoD system: Peer A who watches Channel 1 can help cache the content of Channel 2, because Peer B who watches Channel 2 has ever help cache the content of Channel 1. The main reason here is that users will collaborate with each other because they want to keep the balance of *trust* among them in social networks.
- *Improve Network Planning*
  It is difficult for Internet Service Provider (ISP) to design a network to meet all demands of different scenarios, since it is difficult to propose a traffic model that is suitable for all scenarios. However, the clustered property of social networks can bring about the possibility. Take a social group of university students as example, a peak traffic among this group can be predicted when a new movie about a love story is released. Speaking on an average, young students are fond of love stories. When one student think it is a good movie, he will surely recommend it to his classmates; his classmates will recommend it to their classmates. Thus, the traffic in this group will be predicted to increase sharply. Then, ISP can adopt corresponding policies to adjust in advance. Therefore, the traffic models based on social networks can be used to improve the network planning.
- *Improve Accuracy of Recommendations*
  Different social groups have different interests. However, it has similar interests inside one group. This provides opportunities for accurate business recommendations. If one user of a social group buys a commodity, a merchant can anticipate that other members of this group must be the potential buyers with high

probability. Then, the merchant can send recommendations to these potential buyers. Actually, social networks are great helpful for data mining or opinion mining.

Disadvantages of Social Networks

* *Privacy/Security*
  One vulnerable aspect of social networks is privacy. All personal information in social networks are real. Thus, social networks pose higher risk of security. Hence, it is necessary to have well-designed secure mechanisms for social networks. Furthermore, social networks need fine-grained access control mechanisms to personal information with respect to a large number of varieties of users. In general, there is a trade-off between keeping privacy and searching efficiency.

The rest of the chapter is organized as follows. In section "Social Network Theories", the primary theories of social networks are illustrated. In section "Social Networks in P2P Networks", the applications of social networks in P2P networks are described. Finally, section "Conclusions" draws the conclusion.

Social Network Theories

This section describes the primary theories of social networks, including small world, weak ties, structural holes, and tipping point.

Small World

Several milestones of *small world* are introduced as follows.

* *Six Degrees of Separation*
  In 1967, Stanley Milgram, a social psychologist in Harvard University, proposed a concept called *six degrees of separation* [1] that declares that the average length to reach any stranger is about six. The experiment method is as follows: (1) Ask subjects to deliver mail to a stranger by means of delivering to subjects' acquaintances; (2) Count the average hops between every subject and the stranger. The result is about *six*.

  In 2001, Watts [2–4] adopted e-mail to explore the phenomenon of *six degrees of separation*. The results is about *five* to *seven*. The detailed process was published in *Science* [2].

The essential point of small world is not the exact number of six, five, or seven, because it is nothing compared with 6,000,000,000 human being in the earth, just like an ant with an elephant. To some extent, any phenomenon can be called small world if the number of the phenomenon is tiny enough compared with a very large group.

- *Rule of 150 (Dunbar's Rule)*
  The anthropologist Robin Dunbar stated that the optimal number of small companies and organizations is approximately 150, namely *Rule of 150* [5]. It is a theoretical cognitive limit to the number of people with whom one can maintain stable social relationships. Keeping things under 150 seems to be the best and most efficient way to manage a group of people [5].

  Rule of 150 can be applied to understand six degrees of separation. Suppose a person, named Tom, recognizes 149 friends. Each of these 149 friends also has 149 friends, respectively. By six hops, Tom can recognize $149^6 = 10,942,526,586,601$ friends, which are far more than all the human being in the earth currently. It seems easy to understand the feasibility of six degrees of separation.

Metrics of Small World

- *Average Shortest Path Length*
  The shortest path length is the length between any two nodes in the networks [6]. Average shortest path length of the whole networks is the average of all individual shortest path lengths. The lower average shortest path length, the faster searching speed.
- *Cluster Coefficient*
  The cluster coefficient C of the whole network is the average of all individual clustering C_i, i.e., $C = \frac{1}{k_i} \sum C_i$. C_i is defined as

$$C_i = \frac{E_i}{k_i(k_i - 1)/2},\qquad (12.1)$$

  where k_i is the number of total nodes of the whole network; E_i is the number of actually existed edges among these k_i nodes; $k_i(k_i - 1)/2$ is the total number of edges among these k_i nodes. The high cluster coefficient means the high connectedness.
- *Distribution of Degree*
  Node degree k means how many edges are connected to a node, including incoming and outgoing edges. The degree distribution of the whole network is of great crucial metric, marked as *distribution function* $P(k)$. There are two kinds of degree distributions:

  - *Poisson Distribution* (see Fig. 12.2a)
    Denote $\langle k \rangle$ as the average node degree of the whole network. The Poisson distribution denotes that the majority of nodes have approximately the same

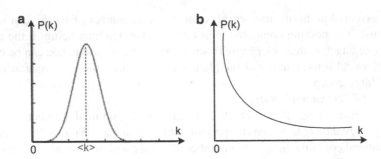

Fig. 12.2 Node degree distribution. (**a**) Poisson distribution. (**b**) Power-law distribution

degree. The number of majority of nodes' degree reaches the peak when $k = \langle k \rangle$. The cases in point are random networks and small world networks (Watts-Strogatz (WS) model) [6].

– *Power-law Distribution* (see Fig. 12.2b)

The degree distribution $P(k)$ has power-law of k, i.e.,

$$P(k) \sim k^{-\gamma} , \qquad (12.2)$$

The main characteristic is that lots of nodes have low node degree and few nodes have high node degree, for instance, scale-free networks [7].

Principles of Small World

This section describes a small world network in terms of Watts-Strogatz (WS) model [8]. We also compare it with a regular network and a random network (see Fig. 12.3), where p is the probability of rewiring [8].

- *Regular Network* (Fig. 12.3a)
  Take a ring lattice as example here. It has high cluster coefficient but high average shortest path length, according to Fig. 12.4.
- *Random Network* (Fig. 12.3b)
  It connects each pair of nodes randomly. It has low average shortest path length but low cluster coefficient, according to Fig. 12.4.
- *Small World Network* (Fig. 12.3c)
  It adopts rewiring with probability p ($0 < p < 1$). An example of rewiring is given in Fig. 12.3d: original AA' is rewired to AA"; original BB' is rewired to BB"; original CC' is rewired to CC". After rewiring, the properties of resultant network, i.e., a small world network, can have low average shortest path length and high cluster coefficient (see Fig. 12.4). That is, it has both advantages of short path and high connectedness. Furthermore, this improved performance is obtained only by means of a few rewiring. It indicates that we may improve

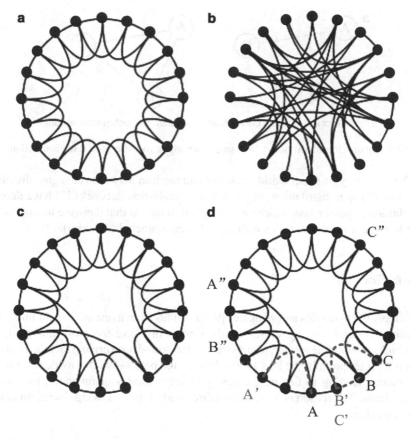

Fig. 12.3 Small world network. (**a**) Regular network ($p = 0$). (**b**) Random network ($p = 1$). (**c**) Small world network ($0 < p < 1$). (**d**) Rewiring

Fig. 12.4 Small world network by rewiring

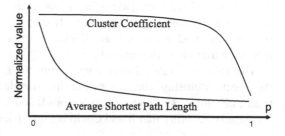

performance of current network without rebuilding from the scratch. On the contrary, we may only do small modifications, for instance, changing some connections of current network (i.e., rewiring). That is a alluring hint.

In addition, when the rewiring probability p is zero, a small world network reduces to a regular network. When p is 1, the small world network corresponds to a random network.

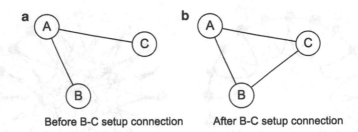

Before B-C setup connection   After B-C setup connection

Fig. 12.5 Triadic closure. (**a**) Before B–C setup connection. (**b**) After B–C setup connection

The similarity of small world networks and random networks is degree distribution, i.e., Poisson distribution. In comparison, scale-free networks [7] have degree distribution of power-law, which has a long tail. It means that there are lots of nodes with low degree and few nodes with high degree (namely hub nodes).

Weak Ties

The theory of strong ties and weak ties [9,10] comes from a research on finding jobs. Commonly understanding, close friends presumably have the most motivation to help find a new job. However, Mark Granovetter found a surprising fact through his dissertation research in the late 1960s. That is, the persons who provide for crucial information leading to finding the new jobs are distant acquaintances, instead of close friends. The reason is what will be discussed in the following – strength of the weak ties [10].

Triadic Closure

As shown in Fig. 12.5a, node A has a connection with node B, at the same time, node A has a connection with node C. If we watch the network over a longer time span, we will find that node B and C will set up a connection (see Fig. 12.5b). Thus, it forms a triangle in the network.

The term of *triadic closure* comes from the fact that the B–C connection has the effect of "closing" the third side of this triangle [9]. The physical significance of triadic closure is as follows. If two persons B and C have a same friend A, there is an increased possibility that B and C will become friends themselves as time goes on.

Structural Holes

According to Fig. 12.5a, there is a *hole* between node B and node C. Then node A is the intermediate node for B and C. Thus, node A is very significant for communication between B and C. Hence, node A has some superiority because of a *structural hole* [11].

Fig. 12.6 Structure hole

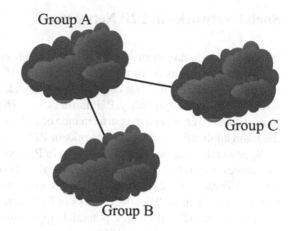

We may also extend three-nodes to a network with groups (see Fig. 12.6). There are three groups in this network. Group A has a connection with Group B and with Group C. However, there is a structure hole among Group B and Group C.

Power of the Weak Ties

We come to discuss two notions, intra-group and inter-group. According to Fig. 12.6, there are many connections in each intra-group. Users in the intra-group contact frequently due to similar/same interests. Thus, the relationship in the intra-group is called as *strong ties*. In comparison, the relationship in the inter-group is called as *weak ties*. For example, the connection between Groups A and B is a weak tie. The physical significance of strong ties and weak ties is as follows. In general, intra-group and inter-group can be considered as *homogeneous* group and *heterogeneous* group. Therefore, strong ties in the intra-group (i.e., homogeneous group) can be used to improve throughput. Weak ties in the inter-group (i.e. heterogeneous group) can be used to improve the variety of searching, which results in increasing the hit rate of searching.

Tipping Point

The theory of tipping point [5] describes how a previously rare phenomenon becomes rapidly and dramatically popular. In general, there are three factors for epidemic: (1) the law of the few; (2) stickiness and (3) power of the context. We only discuss the first factor here. The law of the few shows that few people, however, has significant impact on epidemic. These few people corresponds to hub nodes that have high node degree. Thus, they can propagate the messages very conveniently and quickly. To some extent, it proposes almost same ideas as power-law degree distribution.

Social Networks in P2P Networks

There are two classifications of P2P applications: (1) non-real-time P2P file downloading, such as BitTorrent and (2) real-time P2P streaming, including P2P live streaming and P2P Video-on-demand (VoD). In addition, we also need to solve the issues of P2P security/privacy, P2P fairness, etc. The emergence of social networks has profoundly enhanced the performance of P2P networks. This section introduces the main applications of social networks in P2P networks.

Specifically, section "Social Networks in P2P Networks using Network Coding" introduces the relationship between social networks and P2P networks using *network coding* [12–23], which is a breakthrough in *network information theory*. Furthermore, section "Social Networks in P2P Content-Centric Networking/Named Data Networking" introduces potential applications of social networks in P2P *content-centric networking* (CCN) or *named data networking* (NDN) (http://www. named-data.net/index.html) [24], which is a brand-new framework for future communications.

Social Networks in P2P File Downloading

Improve P2P Searching Efficiency

Due to the clustered characteristic of social networks, it is not necessary search blindly through the whole P2P networks. This social property enhances the effectiveness of P2P searching.

Community-Based Mechanism to Improve P2P Searching Efficiency

A community-based trust mechanism [25] includes two kinds of reputation according to the peers. One is inter-community reputation, which is calculated by super nodes in each community. It is relatively a kind of global currency. The other is intra-community reputation, which means the transaction between the peers who have similar interests or semantics locally. As shown in Fig. 12.7, peers with similar interests will be gathered to one social community. In addition, there is one super node in each community and these super nodes form the upper-tier of the P2P system. The rest nodes are ordinary nodes and they are unstructured.

Unlike normal P2P network system, users in the semantic-based community P2P social network seem to communicate with others more effectively. For instance, the users in Community4 all like classic music. When they want to obtain similar information, they can broadcast the request to the users in the Community4, instead of broadcasting to the users in the global network. Because of all the users in the same community have similar interests, they can support data more reliably. In

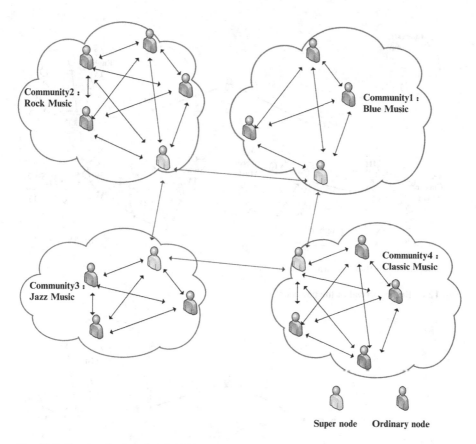

Fig. 12.7 Community-based social P2P network architecture

addition, super nodes in different communities can calculate the credibility through the whole network. This probably makes the credibility more accurate.

The join process to a social community of a new user can be described as follows. The algorithm based on social networks in [26] is implemented in terms of similar interests. The benefit of the algorithm is that all the nodes contribute to the network. As shown in Fig. 12.8, if the new user wants to join the network, it will first connect with the super node who knows the interests of the whole network. Then the super node tells the user which community it may participate in. For instance, the new user is interested in classic music, so the super node returns a message with join information. After that, the new user continues to connect with the representative of the Community C2 that knows the interests of each sub-community. Later the new user obtains the information about the sub-community that has the same interest. The hub is the representative of each sub-community which has abundant resources. If there are two communities with the same interests, the new user will send control messages to both hubs. Which community it will attend depends on the number of

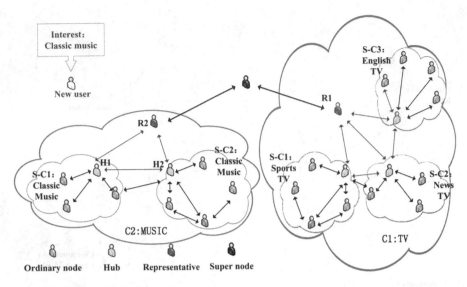

Fig. 12.8 Before arrival of the new user

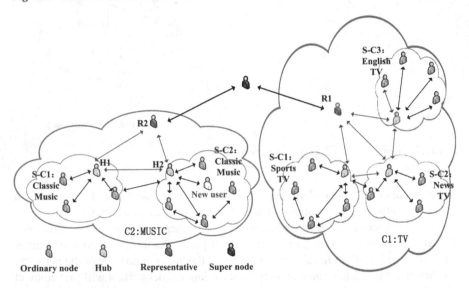

Fig. 12.9 After arrival of the new user

hops. We assume that the new user connects H2 with *2-hop* cost and connects H1 with *3-hop* cost , thus it will join the S-C2(Classic Music), as shown in Fig. 12.9.

In the searching algorithm, the hub node will not send queries to its neighbor hubs because the representative node will send a copy to them. Thus, the hub will not relay the queries any more. This probably reduces the cost among the hubs. In addition, the nodes in the same community are more likely to find the cooperated peers that they have similar interests.

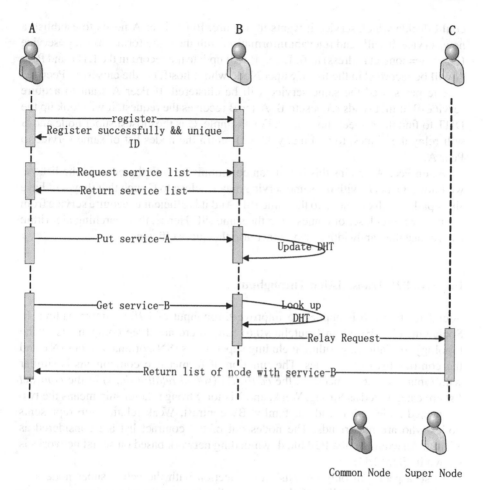

Fig. 12.10 DHT-based mechanism to improve searching efficiency in SCOPE

DHT-Based Mechanism to Improve P2P Searching Efficiency

SCOPE [27] adopts distributed hash table (DHT) to manage data of users and contents. It defines rules to maintain a spontaneous social network system by updating its information. DHT is used to store distributed data and look up the information of services. And its code only runs on super nodes. The DHT information is stored by (key,value) pair format, where DHT key is service name and DHT value is user's information. Figure 12.10 shows the procedures of peers' activity.

First, a peer joins the system, denoted as peer A. Suppose both B and C are super nodes. Peer A sends register information to B, then B returns Peer A with the unique ID after Peer A registers successfully. Second, Peer A requests the list of service name that includes all the services in the system. After obtaining this list, Peer A could decide which service it wants to acquire. But if Peer A needs to establish a new service, it will send relevant information with the same format as (key=service ID, value=contact address) to B. Later, B will update the record in the DHT and Peer A will be recorded in the list of Super Node whose hostID is the closest to Peer A.

The peers used the same service will be clustered. If Peer A want to acquire service-B, it first sends request to B. After B receives the request, it will look up the DHT to find the correct super node. For example, C is the closest super node and B will relay the request to C. Finally, C will return the nodes list of same service to Peer A.

When Peer A obtains this list, it can communicate with the peers in the list. As we know, the peers with the same service may be close to C such that they will have short path length or belong to the same ISP. And it is efficient to acquire service from the peer who is closer or comes from the same ISP. Hence, this searching algorithm can reduce the bandwidth cost and increase the query efficiency.

Improve P2P Transmission Throughput

Social relationship is applied to improve throughput of P2Pfile downloading. In SocialGnutella (based on Gnutella v0.6) [28], there are three components of the topology formation algorithm, including super nodes (SN), ordinary nodes (N), and the contract list of the nodes. The function of former two components is similar with Gnutella v0.6. Especially, the *contracts* (*social relationships*) in the *contract list* are categorized as Strong, Weak, and Visitor. Strong relationship means the two connected nodes are friends or family. By contrast, Weak relationship represents nodes who are not friends. The nodes out of the contract list are considered as Visitor. An example of a P2P file downloading network based on social networks is shown in Fig. 12.11.

First, a peer will only establish a connection with the active super node as a friend in the contract list. If the contract list has no friend, the peer will join another super node as a visitor. Second, after establishing successfully, searching file mechanism of SocialGnutella is identical to the Gnutella v0.6. There are some differences in terms of transmitting file, in particular, *Relay Download*. The super node can control its bandwidth by limiting the share size. Thus, the sharing will not significantly affect the super node. For instance, the super node will download from the responder with Strong relationship and upload files as much as its available bandwidth. Otherwise, the nodes with Weak relationship are limited to a certain value for transmitting files.

If both nodes are behind the NAT, they need the help of super node as a intermediary (see Fig. 12.12). First, the requester N1 will send a relay message to SN1 that is in its contract list. Then SN1 will decide whether to download the file or not by the rest of available bandwidth. If the N2 is a friend of SN1, the relationship between them is strong, thus SN1 will download the file from N2 as soon as possible if the available bandwidth is enough. Otherwise, if N2 is a common neighbor of SN1, SN1 will not support bandwidth more than 5 kbps (a value can be configured).

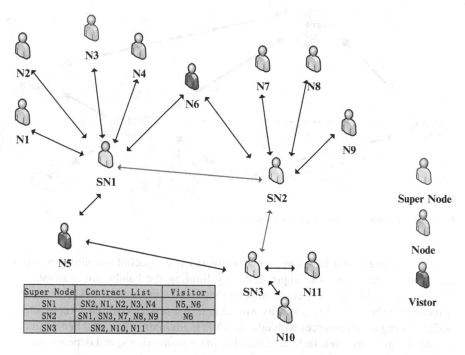

Super Node	Contract List	Visitor
SN1	SN2, N1, N2, N3, N4	N5, N6
SN2	SN1, SN3, N7, N8, N9	N6
SN3	SN2, N10, N11	

Fig. 12.11 SocialGnutella: a social network based P2P file downloading system

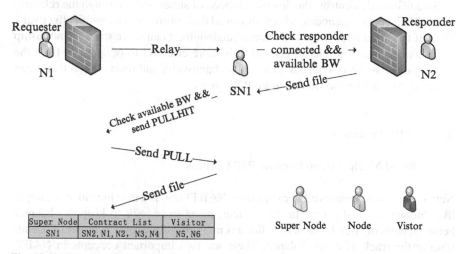

Super Node	Contract List	Visitor
SN1	SN2, N1, N2, N3, N4	N5, N6

Fig. 12.12 Example of relay download

After receiving file successfully, SN1 will pull the file to the requester. In the same way, SN1 also needs to check the bandwidth by the relationship with N1. When N1 receives a PULLHIT message from SN1, it will reply a PULL message. Finally, the relay progress is finished.

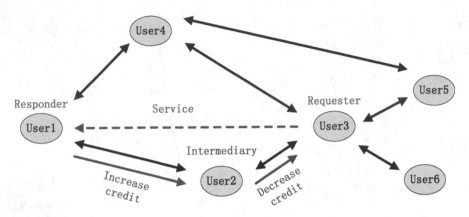

Fig. 12.13 Example of credit transfer in social network

The new algorithm based on social networks (i.e., SocialGnutella) can avoid performance degradation of super nodes by limiting the bandwidth available for relay service. Otherwise, it could happen that a large number of NATed contacts consume up the entire link capacity available to the super node. This keeps super nodes sharing their resources with others, while maintaining their own benefit at the declared minimum level. In SocialGnutella, the transmission speed depends on the relationship between nodes and their super nodes.

SocialGnutella controls the download speed of super nodes through the relationship with the common nodes, which improved their utility of bandwidth effectively. Thus, if the super node has the abundant bandwidth, it can serve strong relationship nodes as much as possible. In general, it is more effective to obtain data from the super nodes that always have both abundant bandwidth and resources so that it can enhance the performance of the entire P2P system.

Improve P2P Fairness

Credit-Based Mechanism to Improve P2P Fairness

Networked asynchronous bilateral trading (NABT) [29] is a new incentive paradigm like "networked tit-for-tat". In this system, peers use *credit* to keep the balance between pairs of friends. In NABT, there is no global currency. Each pair of friends reserve the track of credit balance. There are two important concepts in NABT. One is asynchronous trading that means the responder will not provide the service if requester acquires data exceed the credit. The other is intermediaries, which increase the market efficiency by relaying trading.

As shown in Fig. 12.13, there is not direct connection between User1 and User3. If User3 wants to download data from User1, they will need the help of User2 as an intermediary. After determining relay routing, User1 will first upload the file to

User2. Then User2 will relay it to User3. In this procedure, the credit between User2 and User1 will increase while the credit between User2 and User3 will decrease. In other words, with the credit increased, User2 is willing to support data to User1 next time. On the contrary, after several trading between User2 and User3, the credit between them has decreased below the minimum, User2 will not support to relay data to User3. As a result, we may recognize that the credit between the intermediary and the requester will enhance after each relay trading. This will encourage cooperation between two friends or between friends of friends. With the credit mechanism, peers are likely willing to support data to their friends and in turn, they could obtain more resources under the help of friends of friends. Additionally, if User4 wants to download data from User1, they can connect each other directly.

NABT [29] also adopts a simple additive increase multiplication decrease (AIMD) adjustment algorithm to avoid uncooperative users (e.g., free-riders). For example, if User1 transmits data to User4 successfully, the credit between them will increase by one factor. Otherwise, if User1 is a free-rider, it will not support any data for other users so its link credit will decrease by another factor. At last, those free-riders will not be connected with other users next time. Therefore, peers are willing to support more services to their friends or relay trading.

Owning to intermediaries, they increase the number of credits that can be passed between direct neighbors. It also increases the number of potential trading partners. Moreover, reputation can help solve cheating behaviors, because the credit of a cheating peer will decrease whenever it does not fulfill the transaction. In addition, these uncooperative behaviors will also lead to a dispute among the peers on the credit transfer path.

NABT [29] has proved that social networks can help in P2P file downloading systems. Through social networks, users can acquire useful data more quickly and effectively with the help of intermediaries. At the same time, the reputation mechanism can reduce the behaviors of free-riding and cheating. In consequence, it can enhance the performance of P2P systems.

Community-Based Trust to Improve P2P Fairness

As described in the previous section (see Fig. 12.7), there exist a community based trust in [25]. Take Community4 as example, as shown in Fig. 12.14, if user E wants to request data from others in the community, it will first send searching request to all the neighbors, such as A, B, C, and D. If the neighbors have data, they will send response messages. User E will rank the local reputation of each responder, and then choose a user whose reputation is high, which is D in the table in this example. Intra-community user reputation is calculated by direct reputation, recommendation reputation, indirect reputation, believe ratio about evaluation credit of other users. If a user want to increase its local reputation, it will improve transaction with other users. By contrast, the local reputation of the free-riders, such as malicious users

Fig. 12.14 Peers in the same
community

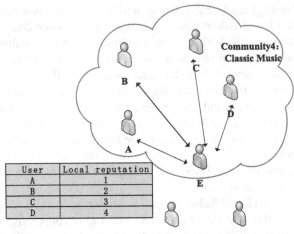

User	Local reputation
A	1
B	2
C	3
D	4

Super node   Ordinary node

and white-washing users, will decrease quickly by unsatisfied transactions. Finally, they cannot obtain data from other users.

Inter-community reputation is calculated by local reputation and recommendation reputation, similarity of two communities, global reputation. Global reputation is not direct, it may evaluate by the third community. The similarity is important, just like local community. If the similarity of two communities is higher, it means that their interests are more similar. Thus, their resources are reliable. Although four communities (in Fig. 12.7) are interested in different kinds of music, their similarity is high and they more likely have high inter-community reputation.

As shown in Fig. 12.15, if the user O3 in the Community3 needs the reputation of O4 in community4, it will send request to the super node S3. Then, S3 will send the request to the super node S4 of the community4. Subsequently, S4 will send back the O4's reputation to S3. Finally, O3 acquires the reputation of O4.

This community-based trust mechanism can reduce the malicious behaviors effectively in P2P social network by inter-community reputation and intra-community reputation. If a user does not transact with others successfully, its reputation will decrease rapidly. As a result, other users in the community will not communicate with it any more. It will lead to a smaller impact on the whole system. At last, the malicious user will be abandoned by the system.

Social Networks in P2P Streaming

Lin et al. [30] apply social networks and game theory to improve fairness of P2P streaming. A cheat-proof and attack-resistant incentive mechanism is proposed to make the performance of P2P social network effective. Case I (see Fig. 12.16): in a searching round, if Peer A sends a request to Peer B, and Peer B refuses the request.

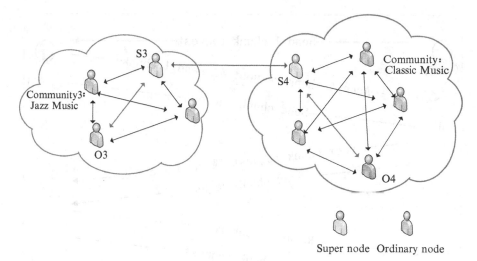

Fig. 12.15 Peers in different communities

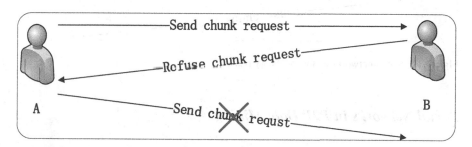

Fig. 12.16 Social networks and game theory (Case I)

In the next searching round, Peer A will not request Peer B any more. Case II (see Fig. 12.17): if Peer B accepts the request and then sends a chunk, Peer A will send a chunk as well. Otherwise, if Peer B refuses to send a chunk, Peer A will not send a chunk either. This mechanism may reduce the number of free-riders in P2P live streaming who only wants to acquire chunks but not provide.

There is a parameter that limits the number of chunks transmitted between two peers. For instance, if Peer A sends ten chunks to Peer B but only five of them are useful. Peer B sends nine chunks to Peer A but six of them are useful. As a result, Peer A will not be allowed to send chunks to Peer B because the data from Peer A is considered distrusted. This probably reduces the behavior of malicious users who send pollution messages. The ultimate aim is to decrease the number of peers with bad behaviors to zero. Those methods can efficiently improve the trust among peers and reduce the malicious users and free-riders.

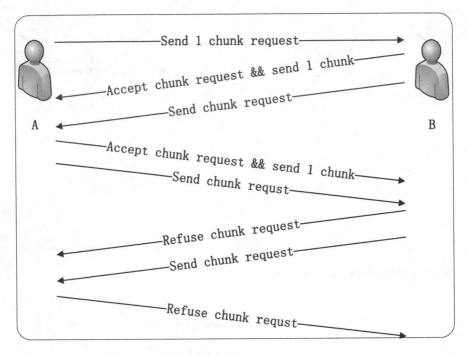

Fig. 12.17 Social networks and game theory (Case II)

Social Networks in P2P Data Mining

Social networks and semantic overlay networks are combined to apply in P2P data mining. Two-layer architecture was proposed in [31]. One is social network (SN) layer. The users in this layer connected randomly or maybe they are friends. The other is semantic overlay network (SON) layer (see Fig. 12.18). The users in this layer are clustered with respect to their interests. As shown in Fig. 12.18, users colored yellow are in one SON and the rest blue users are in another SON. Suppose the white user have common interests with both two SONs.

Here, it is noted that each node has two identities in this system. The function of SN layer is to share information conveniently among nodes. And it is based on the properties of small world. The function of SON layer is to improve query efficiency. If a node wants to join the SN, it only randomly connects two nodes and then makes several connections with some nearest neighbors. For instance, after node C joins the system, it will connect with nodes A and B. In addition, there is a semantic vector (SV) whose function is to record the interest information and a list of nodes that have the same interests. Euclidean distance is used to distinguish the similarity between two SVs. When a new node wants to join the SV that is too large, the SV will separate into two sub-SVs according to their content.

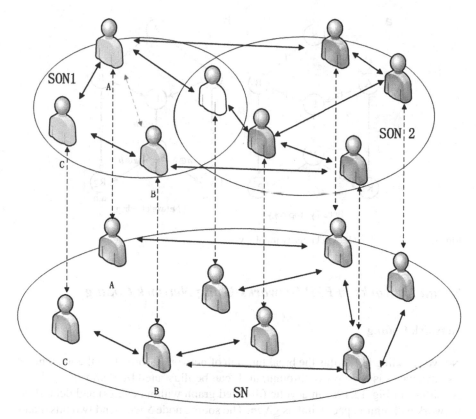

Fig. 12.18 Semantic overlay network (SON) layer and social network (SN) layer

In order to reduce the overhead of control messages, each node usually forwards share information at most six times. After a node receives share information, it only broadcasts to the neighbors in the contact list in the SN layer. If the node has received the same share data, it will not relay to others. This approach probably facilitates the spread of new share file knowledge because most nodes in SN have short paths. SON layer uses rumor spreading to forward knowledge. Users are classified to three states and they can forward share data on the basic of their interests at a certain probability. This approach probably reduces the data traffic that some users are not interested in.

When nodes want to search data, it will first check whether the query is in its SON. If so, it will broadcast the query to its neighbors and find the node that has the most similarity. If not, it will first search for the similar SON and send the query to that SON. To obtain better performance, each searching will be recorded in the vector for next query.

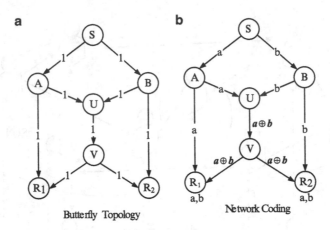

Fig. 12.19 Network coding in butterfly topology

Social Networks in P2P Networks Using Network Coding

Network Coding

Network coding [12–16] is the breakthrough of network information theory. One of its advantages is to improve throughput. It can be illustrated by *Butterfly* topology. As shown in Fig. 12.19a, an acyclic (directed graph without cycles) and delay-free network with unit-capacity link is given. The source node S will send two bits a and b to Sink R_1 and Sink R_2. Let us consider what the average maximum throughput is in Butterfly topology [17].

Because the link UV is a bottleneck, it can only transmit one bit each time if only routing is allowed. Thus, sink R_1 can get 2 bits a and b while sink R_2 can get only 1 bit b. Or, sink R_2 can get 2 bits a and b while sink R_1 can get only 1 bit a. Hence, the average maximum throughput of the sinks R_1 an R_2 is 1.5 bits/sink.

If *network coding* is adopted, the average throughput of sink R_1 an sink R_2 can reach 2 bits/sink. As shown in Fig. 12.19b, the intermediate node U does encoding ($a \oplus b$), and node V multicasts this encoded message to sink R_1 and sink R_2. Thus, sink R_1 can decode to get a and b after receiving a and $a \oplus b$. Likewise, sink R_2 can decode to get two bits a and b after receiving b and $a \oplus b$.

In essence, network coding can allow *information* to be compressed, whereas *commodity* can not be compressed in classical information theory. Therefore, *network coding theory* is also called *network information flow theory*.

Random Network Coding (RNC)

Above network coding belongs to the centralized code construction algorithm. In order to apply to decentralized networks, such as P2P networks, it is necessary

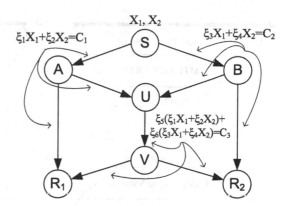

Fig. 12.20 Principle of random network coding

to construct distributed network coding algorithm. That is random network coding (RNC) [18]. The main idea of RNC is as follows. The source will send combination (i.e., by means of linear network coding) to its outgoing links, while the non-source nodes will combine messages from its incoming links and forward combinations to its outgoing links.

As shown in Fig. 12.20, an acyclic graph with unit capacity is given. Suppose that the source node S will send two messages X_1 and X_2 to two sinks (R_1 and R_2) by means of RNC. Coefficients $\xi_1 \sim \xi_6$ will be chosen randomly in finite field F. The procedure is as follows: S sends combination $C_1 = \xi_1 X_1 + \xi_2 X_2$ to node A and sends combination $C_2 = \xi_3 X_1 + \xi_4 X_2$ to node B; node A sends combination C_1 to node U and Sink R_1; node B sends combination C_2 to node U and sink R_2; node U combines two combinations from its incoming links AU and BU, then U creates a new combination $C_3 = \xi_5 C_1 + \xi_6 C_2$ and sends it to sinks R_1 and R_2.

As for sink R_1, it receives two combinations as well as their corresponding coefficients so that sink R_1 can decode X_1 and X_2 using *Gauss-Jordan elimination*, i.e., to solve the following two equations. Note, the higher independency of the coefficients, the higher successful decoding probability.

$$\begin{cases} C_1 = \xi_1 X_1 + \xi_2 X_2 \\ C_3 = (\xi_5 \xi_1 + \xi_6 \xi_3) X_1 + (\xi_5 \xi_2 + \xi_6 \xi_4) X_2 \end{cases}, \qquad (12.3)$$

As for sink R_2, it can decode X_1 and X_2 in the similar way.

Social Networks in P2P Networks Using RNC

The typical instance of P2P file downloading using RNC is Avalanche [19]. The typical instance of P2P live streaming using RNC is R^2 [20]. The typical instance of P2P VoD using RNC is UUSee [21]. In addition to considering computation cost of coding and decoding, another crucial issue is successful decoding probability at the receiving nodes. Wu et al. [22] present that topology of P2P live streaming shows some properties of small world. Chen et al. [23] use experimental results to

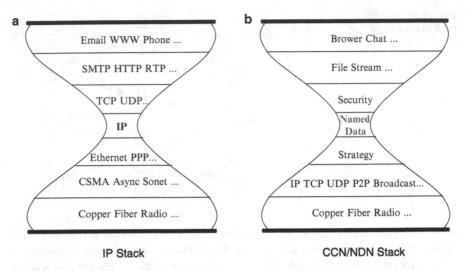

Fig. 12.21 Comparison between IP stack and CCN/NDN stack

show that it will have high successful decoding probability in small world networks than in random networks. This result may be explained by the small world theory. The small world network has high cluster coefficients (i.e., high connectedness) so that it is of high probability to have more edge-disjoint paths. Consequently, the independency is of high probability for receiving nodes to decode successfully. Thus, social networks can help P2P networks using random network coding.

Social Networks in P2P Content-Centric Networking/Named Data Networking

Content-centric networking (CCN) or *Named data networking* (NDN) (http:// www.named-data.net/index.html) [24] is a brand-new framework for the future communications. The main idea of CCN/NDN is to replace *where* with *what*. In other words, CCN/NDN focuses on *content* instead of *location* (in terms of IP). Subsequently, it is of better abstraction for CCN/NDN to use *named data* rather than *named hosts* (in terms of IP). The comparison between IP stack and CCN/NDN stack is shown in Fig. 12.21. The thin '*waist*' of CCN/NDN stack is *named data* instead of IP. That is why CCN is also called named data networking (NDN). Another excellent property of CCN/NDN is that it is sufficiently compatible with IP. Consequently, CCN/NDN can be deployed incrementally based on existing infrastructure [24].

There are two types of packets in CCN/NDN [24]: interest packets and data Packets (see Fig. 12.22). A data consumer sends request for content by broadcasting

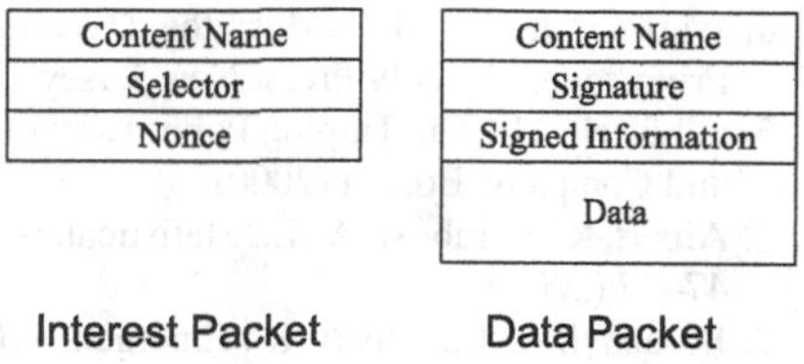

Fig. 12.22 Two types of
CCN/NDN packets

Content Name
Selector
Nonce

Interest Packet

Content Name
Signature
Signed Information
Data

Data Packet

interest packets over all available connectivity. Any data producer/owner hearing the interest will response with data packets. The advantage of above mechanism in terms of content is high probability of sharing. Because interest and data identify the content being exchanged by name, multiple nodes interested in the same content can share transmission. For instance, many data consumers read the same newspaper or watch the same YouTube video [24]. In addition, CCN/NDN that uses named data also helps to find the content more quickly/actually than IP when using DHT.

Social networks and CCN/NDN are naturally matched. On one hand, CCN/NDN uses contents (i.e., named data) and interests. On the other hand, social networks have many clusters in terms of same/similar interests. If one member in a cluster is interested in certain content, other members in the same cluster will also be interested in same content. If CCN/NDN is adopted in this social network, the CCN/NDN data packets can serve for almost all the members in this cluster. This results in great saving in terms of bandwidth.

Conclusions

This chapter introduces the primary social network theories and their applications in P2P networks. It can be seen that there exists a trade-off between searching efficiency and protecting privacy in social networks. Specifically, social networks can be combined with CCN/NDN technology, which is a brand-new framework for future communications.

Acknowledgements This research was supported by National Natural Science Foundation of China (No.60872005). The authors would like to thank anonymous reviewers for their precious comments. The authors would also like to acknowledge Editor Ajith Abraham for this book publishing.

References

1. Milgram, S.: The small world problem. Psychol. Today **1**(1), 60–67 (1967)
2. Dodds, P.S., Muhamad, R., Watts, D.J.: An experimental Study of search in global social networks. Science **301**(5634), 827–829 (2003)
3. Watts, D.J.: Six Degrees. W.W. Norton & Company, New York (2004)

4. Watts, D.J.: Small Worlds: the Dynamics of Networks Between Order and Randomness. Princeton University Press, New Jersey (2004)
5. Gladwell, M.: The Tipping Point: How Little Things Can Make a Big Difference. Little, Brown and Company, Boston (2000)
6. Albert, R., Barabási, A.-L.: Statistical mechanics of complex networks. Rev. Mod. Phys. **74**(1), 47–97 (2002)
7. Barabási, A.-L., Albert, R.: Emergence of scaling in random networks. Science **286**, 509–512 (1999)
8. Watts, D.J., Strogatz, S.H.: Collective dynamics of "small-world" networks. Nature **393**, 440–442 (1998)
9. Easley, D., Kleinberg, J.: Networks, Crowds, and Markets: Reasoning About a Highly Connected World. Cambridge University Press, New York (2010)
10. Granovetter, M.S.: The strength of weak ties. Am. J. Sociol. **78**, 1360–1380 (1973)
11. Burt, R.S.: Structural Holes: The Social Structure of Competition. Harvard University Press, Cambridge (1995)
12. Ahlswede, R., Cai, N., Li, S.-Y.R., Yeung, R.W.: Network information flow. IEEE Trans. Inf. Thy. **45**(4), 1204–1216 (2000)
13. Yeung, R.W., Li, S.-Y.R., Cai, N., Zhang, Z.: Network coding theory. Found. Trends Commun. Inf. Technol. **2**(4), 241–381 (2005)
14. Yeung, R.W.: Information Theory and Network Coding. Springer, New York (2008)
15. Fragouli, C., Soljanin, E.: Network coding fundamentals. Found. Trends Netw. **2**(1), 1–133 (2007)
16. Ho, T., Lun, D.S.: Network Coding: An Introduction. Cambridge University Press, Cambridge/New York (2008)
17. Huang, J., Gobana, T.: Network information flow and its wireless applications. In: Misra, S., Misra, S.C., Woungang, I. (eds.) Selected Topics in Communication Networks and Distributed Systems, pp. 463–483 . World Scientific Publishing Co. Pte. Ltd., Singapore/Hackensack (2010)
18. Ho, T., Médard, M., Koetter, R., Karger, D.R., Effros, M., Shi, J., Leong, B.: A random linear network coding approach to multicast. IEEE Trans. Inf. Theory **52**(10), 4413–4430 (2006)
19. Gkantsidis, C., Rodriguez, P.R.: Network coding for large scale content distribution. In: IEEE INFOCOM'05, Miami (2005)
20. Wang, M. Li, B.: R^2: Random push with random network coding in live Peer-to-Peer streaming. IEEE J. Sel. Areas Commun. **25**(9), 1655–1666 (2007)
21. Liu, Z., Wu, C., Li, B., Zhao, S.: UUSee: large-scale operational on-demand streaming with random network coding. In: IEEE INFOCOM'10, San Diego (2010)
22. Wu, C., Li, B., Zhao, S.: Magellan: charting large-scale Peer-to-Peer live streaming topologies. In: 27th International Conference on Distributed Computing Systems, Toronto (2007)
23. Chen, W., Liu, Y., Wang, H.: Impact on streaming media performance based on network coding by topology structure. Comput. Eng. (In Chinese) **35**(14), 130–131, 134 (2009)
24. Jacobson, V., Smetters, D.K., Thornton, J.D., Plass, M.F., Briggs, N.H., Braynard, R.L.: Networking named content. In: ACM CoNEXT'09, Rome (2009)
25. Yu, J., Wang, J., Liu, X., Yu, M., Zhao, Z., Zhang, Y.: Community-based trust mechanism in P2P social networks. In: IEEE International Conference on Wireless Communications, Networking and Information Security, Beijing, pp. 669–673 (2010)
26. Modarresi, A., Mamat, A., Ibrahim, H., Mustapha, N.: How community-based peer-to-peer social networks can affect query routing? In: International Conference on Networked Computing and Advanced Information Management, Gyeongju, pp. 432–437 (2008)
27. Mani, M., Nguyen, A.-M., Crespi, N.: SCOPE: a prototype for spontaneous P2P social networking. In: IEEE International Conference on Pervasive Computing and Communications Workshops, Mannheim, Germany, pp. 220–225 (2010)
28. Altmann, J., Bedane, Z.B.: A P2P file sharing network topology formation algorithm based on social network information. In: IEEE INFOCOM Workshops, Rio de Janeiro, pp. 1–6 (2009)

29. Liu, Z., Hu, H., Liu, Y., Ross, K.W., Wang, Y., Mobius, M.: P2P trading in social networks: the value of staying connected. In: IEEE INFOCOM, San Diego, pp. 1–9 (2010)
30. Lin, W.S., Zhao, H.V., Liu, K.J.R.: Incentive cooperation strategies for peer-to-peer live multimedia streaming social networks. IEEE Trans. Multimed. **11**(3), 396–412 (2009)
31. Saberi, S., Trunfio, P., Talia, D., Fesharaki, M.N., Badie, K.: Using social network and semantic overlay network approaches to share knowledge in distributed data mining scenarios. In: International Conference on High Performance Computing and Simulation (ICHPCS), Caen, pp. 536–544 (2010)

Chapter 13
Intelligent Social Network of Devices

Arpan Pal, Chirabrata Bhaumik, Priyanka Sinha, and Avik Ghose

Abstract People participate in social networks today whereas devices do not. Devices can generate a lot of data that can augment information in a social network. This chapter deals with how devices can contribute to a social network used by people. It describes the need for devices to detect user activity and allow other users to interact using that information, thereby creating an immersion of the real and virtual worlds. It discusses the enabling technology and associated problems in making a social network of devices work. Further, it outlines benefits to people participating in an intelligent social network of devices.

Introduction

Devices may form a network and exchange information amongst them to sense and actuate each other. Such devices can be car infotainment and telematics platforms, smart phones, set top boxes (STB) of different variety (cable, satellite, IPTV and over-the-top) and consumer electronic products (CEP) like refrigerator, microwave, television (TV), air conditioner, etc. For example, an intelligent refrigerator can sense the load and perhaps even differentiate amongst some food items. This information can be sent for analysis via a home gateway. Analytics will have a history of the refrigerator load for that user and correlate it with a chat session or online calendar to be aware of an upcoming party. Once it receives this information, it will adjust its cooling system to ensure drinks are chilled the party.

Current social networks allow people to upload their daily life updates for friends and families to view and comment (like Facebook™, Orkut™, Twitter™, Myspace™, Friendster™, etc.). They also allow people to engage in virtual

A. Pal • C. Bhaumik • P. Sinha (✉) • A. Ghose
Tata Consultancy Services, Plot C, Block EP, Salt Lake Electronics Complex, Kolkata 700091, West Bengal, India
e-mail: arpan.pal@tcs.com; c.bhaumik@tcs.com; priyanka27.s@tcs.com; avik.ghose@tcs.com

A. Abraham and A.-E. Hassanien (eds.), *Computational Social Networks: Tools, Perspectives and Applications*, DOI 10.1007/978-1-4471-4048-1_13, © Springer-Verlag London 2012

activities like games, chats, watching of videos in a virtual social community. However, most of these updates are generated by people who input this data through a physical computing device and very little of their daily status updates are enhanced by intelligent devices around them. At some point people will find that they spend a disproportionate amount of time trying to involve themselves with their virtual lives that it starts hampering their real lives. By relieving some of this stress via intelligent devices, it will create for a richer virtual experience as well as save people's time. This chapter will discuss how devices can discover and update people's context like presence as they move to different locations, real life activities (such as TV watching) and moods. It will also depict how people react to such updates and thereby interact with each other. For example, while watching TV, the TV can tweet the program you are watching onto Twitter. This informs your followers and friends of the same. When these friends are watching the same channel as you, they become "closer" friends in the virtual world and your "trust" in them automatically upgrades.

The rest of this chapter is organized as follows. Section "Technology" outlines the various technologies involved with an intelligent social network of devices. Section "Use Cases" describes use cases benefiting people that may be possible using such devices. Finally, in section "Conclusion" we conclude with our experiences with such a system.

Technology

This section discusses the various technologies related to enabling intelligent social networks of devices to function. It mentions problems specific to devices. We assume that all concerned devices have some form of connection to a local network or Internet. In the case of devices in a home, a device with home gateway functionality that interacts with all the devices can be assumed as well.

To become part of web applications, devices will need a way to communicate with internet services. This can be done using Representational State Transfer (REST) and CEA 2014 standard [1] HTML. This section details these technologies first. Next, OAuth is slowly becoming the standard in authenticating and authorizing online activity in social networks. We describe the OAuth mechanism and outline its problems and possible workarounds in relation to devices. Thereafter, we explore the problem of identifying who is the physical (virtual) owner of the device whose information it handles. Lastly we propose architecture for this system of intelligent devices participating in social networks.

REST

REST is a software architectural style for distributed hypermedia systems like the World Wide Web. The term originated in a 2000 doctoral dissertation Architectural Style and the Design of Network-based Software Architectures about the web written by Roy Fielding [2], one of the principal authors of the HTTP protocol specification, and has quickly passed into widespread use in the networking community. It is a light weight architecture and generic for information exchange in comparison to standards like Simple Object Access Protocol (SOAP) [3]. This makes REST a good choice for interchanging information for devices, especially since some of them may be resource constrained.

REST is intended to evoke an image of how a well-designed Web application behaves: a network of web pages (a virtual state-machine), where the user progresses through an application by selecting links (state transitions), resulting in the next page (representing the next state of the application) being transferred to the user and rendered for their use [4]. In simpler terms, a web app consists of a set of web pages. These web pages represent states of the application. Clicking on links in the web pages causes a transition from one web page, that is, state to another.

REST strictly refers to a collection of architectural principles called the Principled Design of the Modern Web Architecture. This term is also used to describe any simple interface that uses XML, YAML, JSON or plain text over HTTP without an additional messaging layer such as SOAP. These two meanings can conflict as well as overlap. It is possible to design any large software system in accordance with Fielding's REST architectural style without using the HTTP protocol and without interacting with the World Wide Web. It is also possible to design simple XML + HTTP interfaces that do not conform to REST principles, and instead follow a RPC model. The two different uses of the term REST cause some confusion in technical discussions.

The key design principles that REST's scalability and growth can be attributed to are:

1. Application state and functionality is divided into resources.
2. Every resource is uniquely addressable using a universal syntax for use in hypermedia links.
3. All resources share a uniform interface for the transfer of state between client and resource, consisting of

   (a) A constrained set of well-defined operations.
   (b) A constrained set of content types, optionally supporting code-on-demand.

4. A protocol that is

   (a) Client/Server
   (b) Stateless
   (c) Cacheable
   (d) Layered

REST founders claim that REST [2]:

- Provides improved response times and server loading characteristics due to support for caching.
- Improves server scalability by reducing the need to maintain communication state. This means that different servers can handle initial and subsequent requests.

- Requires less client-side software to be written than other approaches, because a single browser can access any application and any resource.
- Depends on less vendor software than mechanisms that layer additional messaging frameworks on top of HTTP.
- Provides equivalent functionality when compared to alternative approaches to communication.
- Does not require a separate resource discovery mechanism, due to the use of hyperlinks in content.
- Provides better long-term compatibility and evolvability characteristics than RPC. This is due to:

  - The capability of document types such as HTML to evolve without breaking backwards-or-forwards-compatibility, and
  - The ability of resources to add support for new content types as they are defined without dropping or reducing support for older content types.

REST detractors note the lack of tool support and the scarcity of truly RESTful applications deployed on the web of today. HTTP defines the GET, POST and PUT requests. Some claim that REST is applicable to GET, but unproven for other state transfer operations such as PUT. POST is often considered the only necessary client-to-server state transfer operation, and is treated as a mechanism to tunnel arbitrary method invocations across HTTP.

It is evident that the REST server is a simple web server supporting very minimal web methods as show in Fig. 13.1. Its feasibility is supported by [5] that describe REST in a low power sensor network setting. Furthermore, mongoose [6] is an example of a small footprint REST web server for resource constrained embedded devices. This paves the way for the REST client and server to be implemented in devices that would need to exchange information. For an IP-enabled refrigerator, as a REST client, it can update its sense data to analytics REST server. To actuate the refrigerator to chill drinks for a party, the analytics REST client can converse with the refrigerator's REST server.

CE-HTML

CE-HTML is a standard for web interfaces for consumer electronics (CE) devices as specified by the CEA 2014 standard [1]. It is fast gaining as the interface of choice on television (TV), set top boxes (STB) and other CE devices. It requires a web browser to be built-in the device. This browser should be able to render XHMTL/CSS. It should be able to interpret Ecmascript 262 which is a variant of Javascript. It should support XMLHttpRequest to send http requests and handle its responses from within the script. This allows rich interactive user interfaces (UI) and apps to be built. Web pages that conform to CE-HTML standard have a MIME type of "application/ce-html + xml." CE-HTML uses profiles that express the capabilities of the device. For example, on TV and STB, it exposes an embedded object tag. This object tag can control the video output. It allows for resizing and

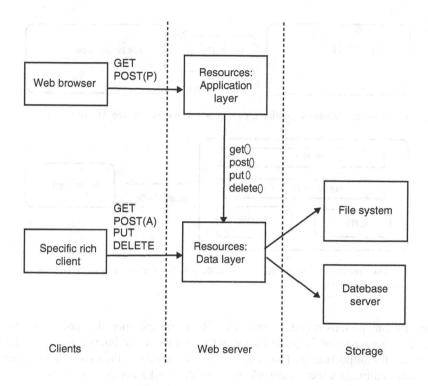

Fig. 13.1 The protocol flow of REST

positioning of the TV video output on any part of the screen as embedded within a web page. OreganMedia [7] is one such browser for STB. For an IP-enabled refrigerator, the display UI on the front of the refrigerator could be in CE-HTML.

On STB, CE-HTML, allows blending video content with web content. However, it does not allow applications access to the video frames. This limits the type of applications to those that cannot derive context from the TV video. They can draw user context from the electronic program guide (EPG), the Internet but not from the TV video. Therefore, presently, CE-HTML cannot be used for synchronous (where device context is used) applications when content from the device is not accessible, such as video frames in TV.

OAuth for CE devices

Introduction

OAuth is an authentication and authorization standard for web-services. There are currently three versions available: 1.0, 1.0a and 2.0. Twitter™ & Google™ currently use version 1.0a, while Facebook™ has adapted version 2.0. Most of

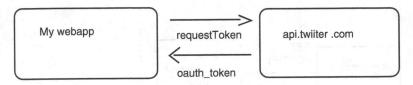

Fig. 13.2 A twitter webapp requesting for a request token using its web 2.0 API

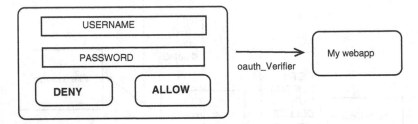

Fig. 13.3 Once the authorization URL is visited, the final verifier information is sent and a session oauth_token is requested

the implementations require a callback URL to be specified that points to a web server where control is passed after authorization. User intervention is usually required for authorization. This scheme has not considered the existence of devices communicating in a social network. We consider workarounds to the same.

Protocol Overview

- The first HTTP request for OAuth is a request for a temporary token as shown in Fig. 13.2
- The next step is authorization of that temporary oauth_token with the web 2.0 service as shown in Fig. 13.3. In order to authorize, the user is asked for its username and password to choose to allow or deny access to its data.
- With the authorized oauth_token and oauth_verifier, the access token is now demanded from the web-service.

All these requests use a HMAC-SHA-1 signed authorization header. The authorization header uses the access token and secret to sign. A detailed explanation of OAuth 1.0a for Twitter[TM] can be found at the web page describing authentication for Twitter[TM] [8].

Implementation Challenges and Workarounds

Problem Statement

Devices that communicate with social networks need to be able to use OAuth. In order to implement OAuth in Javascript, the HTTP headers need to be set correctly and the base string needs to be constructed right. Compound to this the lack of support for cross domain XMLHttpRequests in the Opera browser. The Opera browser is one of the popular choices in embedded systems such as STBs. Cross domain XMLHttpRequests would be required if the web application is a set of web pages local to the device.

Implementing OAuth in C language can be considered as most embedded web browsers running on IPTC set top boxes expose native C APIs. Liboauth [9] is an open source C library specifically designed to handle oauth. Liboauth uses the library libcurl [10]. Presently, we have found that with the latest libcurl builds, handling of OAuth http requests is not handled correctly.

Solution

There is an alternative manner for devices to access web 2.0 APIs of popular web services. It is by introducing a proxy webapp on a server that interacts with the social network API and serves the data from it to clients on the devices. There are numerous open source libraries that implement various versions of OAuth. Therefore, the easiest way to obtain user specific data from popular web services is to host a webapp. This webapp would then expose web pages to which requests can be directed from the devices. As described above, in order to authorize a request token, a user needs to enter their username and password and click on "Allow." On a STB, this may be a one time setup. On first boot, the username and password may be set and the access token cached. As long as the box is powered up thereafter, no further login needs to happen. The username and password are cached in persistent storage by the Opera browser wand and on future reboots, the user just needs to click on "Allow," thereby reducing the number of key presses that make for comfortable data entry.

Sample Implementations

There are various libraries available that implement OAuth in different languages. For example, Facebook[TM] has an open source Javascript API. For Twitter[TM], open source Java[TM] libraries such as Scribe [11] and Twitter4J [12] are available.

Facebook[TM] Javascript SDK

For Facebook[TM], to initially login:

- FB.init is called first with the API key to initialize the library.
- FB.login is called to then authorize. This throws a popup from the server to login and allow access to the app. When the callback is involved with a success, the API can be used to query for meaningful results.

Once logged in, Facebook™ API can be used via FB.api. This includes both graph API and old REST API calls. For example, to view the updated wall status messages as a ticker on the bottom of the TV, we can obtain the home news feed, using FB.api(me/home, handlerFunction). The web server address URL also needs to be updated on the Facebook™ developer applications Connect URL setting for the whole setup to work.

Twitter™ Using Java

In case of Twitter™, we use the Scribe library [13] and Java Server Pages (JSP). On the web server we maintain the users' consumer key, consumer secret, access token and other information in a file. When the STB user first accesses the webapp to login to use Twitter, the webpage is redirected to authorization of the oauth_token by Twitter. Once logged in, the webapp is able to correctly sign any request headers on behalf of the user. Applications of this are for example, the STB may tweet the current program being watched by sending a request to http://api.twitter.com/1/statuses/update.json. At the same time, the users' public timeline may be available as a ticker at the bottom of the screen by sending a request to http://api.twitter.com/1/statuses/home_timeline.json. This timeline gives both the users own statuses as well as those the user is following.

Authentication and Registration

All devices in the system under consideration are IP-enabled having some form of connection to a local network or Internet. In order for devices to become part of a social network they need to be tagged to a consumer. This gives rise to the problem of identifying which group(s) of users a device belongs to. Who is the physical (virtual) owner of the device whose information it handles? This problem includes identifying the physical community to which a device belongs as well as storing and managing of user profiles. For example, a wifi refrigerator may have to choose between the different neighboring wireless networks and will need user input in associating with the right one. It may also need a one time registration of who uses the microwave to enable personal settings.

This requires a one time authentication and registration on a device. We assume that all these devices have some form of UI, either via the web or command line interface (CLI) or onboard display, etc. XML or JSON allows structured data to be represented, transformed and used by all applications. We expect XML or JSON to be the form in which data is interchanged between connected devices. All semantic information is expected to be captured and communicated in XML or JSON.

Internet of Things

In computing, the Internet of things, also known as the Internet of objects, refers to the networked interconnection of everyday objects. It has been described as a self configuring wireless network of sensors whose purpose would be to interconnect all things. The concept is attributed to the former Auto-ID center, founded in 1999, based at the time at the Massachusetts Institute of Technology (MIT). As of now, Internet of objects encompasses all the embedded devices and networks that are natively IP-enabled and Internet-connected, along with the Internet services monitoring and controlling of those devices. It is made up of IP-enabled embedded devices connected to the Internet that includes sensors, machines, active positioning tags, radio-frequency identification (RFID), etc. [14]. The devices that we consider participating in social networks invariably are all IP-enabled and hence form an Internet of things. For example, an IP-enabled refrigerator is a thing as is a IP-enabled microwave oven. Both these items when connected to the Internet, become capable of interacting not with just each other, but also analytical servers, and can decide without human intervention to operate them or change their operational settings.

Although the idea is simple, its application is difficult. If all objects in the world were equipped with minuscule identifying devices, we can become more dependent on them to ease our daily lives. Such a system could greatly reduce the chances of a company running out of stock or wasting products, as all involved parties would know exactly which products are requires and consumed. Mislaid items and physical theft would be affected by the fact that the location of an item would be known at all times.

If all objects of daily life were equipped with radio tags, they could be identified and inventoried by computers. Finding their physical location would be as easy as a database query. The next generation of Internet applications using Internet Protocol Version 6 (IPv6) would be able to communicate with devices attached to virtually all human-made objects because of the extremely large address space of IPv6. This system would therefore be able to identify any physical object.

The Internet of things will likely be a non-deterministic and open network. It will consist of auto-organized or intelligent entities such as web services and service oriented architecture (SOA) components, virtual objects such as avatars. These will be interoperable and able to act independently. They would be able to access context, circumstances and their environments. They would use that to pursue their own objectives or cooperate towards a shared goal.

The system will likely be an example of event-driven architecture. The meaning of an event will not necessarily be based on a deterministic or syntactic model but would instead be based on the context of the event itself: this will also be a semantic web. Consequently, it will not necessarily need common standards that would not be able to address every context or use; some actors such as services, components, avatars will accordingly be self-referenced and, if ever needed, adaptive to existing common standards. Predicting everything would be no more than defining a "global finality" for everything that is just not possible with any of the current top-down approaches and standardizations. In semi-open or closed loops, that is, value chains, whenever a global finality can be settled, it will therefore be considered and studied as a complex system due to the huge number of different links and interactions between autonomous actors, and its capacity to integrate new actors. At the overall stage, that is, full open loop, it will likely be seen as a chaotic environment since systems have always finality.

In an Internet of things, the precise geographic location of an object and also the precise geographic dimensions of an object will be critical. Currently, the Internet has been primarily used to manage information processed by people. Therefore, facts about a thing, such as its location in time and space, has been less critical to track because the person processing the information can decide whether or not that information was important to the action being taken, and if so, add the missing information or decide to not take the action. Note that some things in the Internet of things will be sensors, and sensor location is usually important. If in the Internet of things, things are able to take actions on their own initiative, this human-centric mediation role is eliminated, and the time-space context that we as humans take for granted must be given a central role in this information ecosystem. Just as standards play a key role in the Internet and the Web, geo-spatial standards will play a key role in the Internet of things.

System Architecture for Social Network of Devices

For all the devices in a home or in any vicinity to be connected via IP (as per norms of Internet of Things), and exchange information through a simple REST based implementation, there is the need for a central hub which will act as a server for all such REST services which are called the devices to POST their experience, that is, the devices can share their current status or participate in decision making via the REST server.

The concept is that each device will gather data from users' interaction with it. For example, a refrigerator will record that a user is putting in extra food, that is, greater than the users "usual" food storage. Similarly, the washing machine will record that the load is more than usual. This information will be computed upon to detect events that will be posted to a residential gateway as an experience. The gateway shall collect a series of such experiences to create a story using semantic analysis and then expose it to the social network of the user. It may take the help of an analytical server in an offshore cloud environment as well.

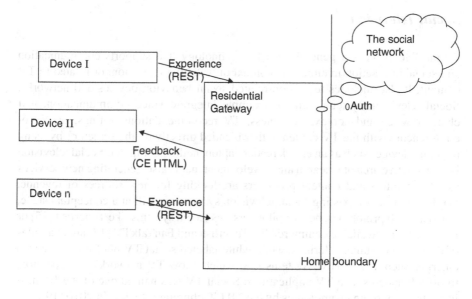

Fig. 13.4 System architecture for Social Network of Devices

Use Cases

One of the goals of a social network of devices is to reduce the workload on people and increase meaningful interactivity between them. This leads to immersion in applications, that is, being able to bridge the real world with the virtual world with two way communication between the two. For example, gaming has become more social and immersive with real physical devices being used to track virtual movements in games (Fig. 13.4).

TV applications are becoming more context-aware by utilizing context sensitive information. Software can extract context from TV via online character recognition (OCR) of text in the video, by detecting the channel logo in analog TV and also by pulling in information from the EPG. This context provides the starting point with which related interesting information is gathered from other web services. It is then used to suggest actions, do background tasks such as downloading related videos, or even overlaying that information over the TV.

As devices become intelligent by being social, they can take decisions as well and thus reduce our work. They shall have all the capability to make everyday mundane decisions. By profiling different users of a device, they can make meaningful predictions in user behavior that would give a more pleasant, less intrusive experience.

This section enlists potential use cases and advantages people will most likely get if they make use of such ubiquitous devices participating in social networks.

Social Television

Social Television is a general term for technology that supports communication and social interaction in either the context of watching television, or related to TV content. It also includes television-related social behavior, devices and networks. Social television systems can for example integrate voice communication, text chat, presence and context awareness, TV recommendations, ratings, or video-conferencing with the TV content either blended directly on the screen or by using ancillary devices such as an ebook reader, laptop, netbook or tablet. Social television is a very active area of research and development that is also generating new services as TV operators and content producers are looking for new sources of revenue. While a number of existing social television systems are still at a conceptual stage, or exist as lab prototypes, beta or pilot versions recent systems like Tunerfish [15] or Boxee [16] are available commercially. Tunerfish and FanTalkTV [17] are examples of direct-to-consumer offerings, while white-labeled social TV platforms have also emerged such as LiveHive Systems [18] which allow TV networks and operators to offer branded social TV applications. Social TV was named one of the 10 most important emerging technologies by the MIT Technology Review in 2010 [19].

The concept of socializing around TV content is old. But Social TV is increasing interactivity around shared programming both live and time-shifted. In an attempt to recapture the social aspects of television lost since the advent of multiple-screen households, which discourage gatherings to watch television together, social television aims to connect viewers with their friends and families even when they are not watching the same screen. As a concept, social television is not linked to a specific architecture such as cable, IPTV, peer-to-peer delivery, or internet television. Nor is it necessarily limited to a traditional television screen, but could also be presented on a computer or handheld device such as a cell phone, tablet or netbook.

Social TV started in the early 2000s with limited success as the creation of the shared connections was cumbersome with a remote control and the UI design made the interaction disruptive to the TV experience. Social networking has made Social TV suddenly feasible, since it already encourages constant connection between members of the network and the creation of like minded groups. The shared content and activities often relate to TV content.

The market of Social TV is growing fast and multiple startups have recently appeared in the field. According to a Parks Associates Industry Report [20], over one-fourth of users ages 18–24 are interested in having more social features integrated into their TV-experience. The most desired social experience was in multiplayer games, though a close second was to chat with others who were watching the same program. Generation Y, those currently 18–28 years old, have been found to actually access the internet more often than they watch television. The same research shows that 42% of the members of this generation access an Internet video at least monthly. And the industry is taking note: popular video sites are now more and more allowing viewers to interact.

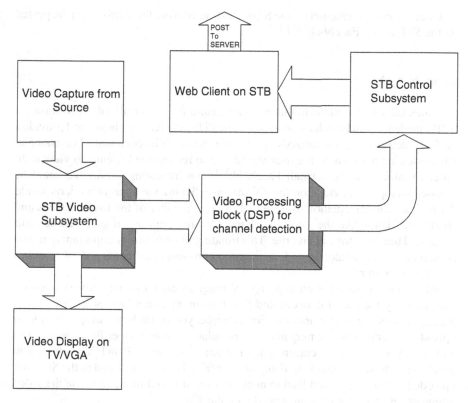

Fig. 13.5 Posting of current channel by STB

The main research areas include the creation of a simple user experience across multiple platforms that encompass aspects of development platforms, devices and networks. Also necessary are easy ways to filter casual acquaintances their social network from "real" friends or affinity circle members, with whom an individual would actually want to share thoughts or comments in a more private environment. Also because of the multiplicity of platforms recent work has also addressed the networking fundamentals behind Social TV.

Posting of Current Channel by STB

The following provides an insight into how device interactivity can enrich social networking. The use case provides an infrastructure for STB to update a server with viewership data for a particular user. This leads to a social database of people watching the same channel which helps realize an implementation of social TV networking on broadcast TV. Brief architecture of the device is shown below in the Fig. 13.5.

Once the current channel on the STB is extracted from the video, it can be posted on the STB users' Facebook™ id.

Connected TV

A connected TV is a platform that enabled creation of personalized applications. It is IP-enabled. It can be enhanced to pair with all the devices in a home and provide a unified gateway to a personalized experience at home for its occupants. For example, while viewing a TV show the user would like to recommend friends to view it. In order to inform others, a small Facebook™ icon indicating like/unlike could be blended on top of the video on the TV screen. Clicking the appropriate icon would disseminate the information to friends. If a large number of the user's friends and friends of friends like the same or related TV programming, it soon reaches cult status and becomes the hot favorite. This trending information is important to media companies, and can take immediate action on product placements and ad revenues based on such trends.

Pushing information of an ongoing TV program onto a social network allows a user to query the social network and find how many and which of its friends are watching the same to talk about it. For example, you could be viewing a broadcast episode of StarTrek which may not be as popular as the live Super Bowl, in general, and most people may be currently talking about the Super Bowl. Therefore, you would be interested in knowing if any of your friends were interested in the StarTrek episode instead. This could lead to another form of social interaction via the video phone or cell phone or chat integrated with the TV.

Games consoles that attach to TV are also devices that provide video input to the TV. These consoles such as the Nintendo Wii [21], the Xbox Kinect [22] allow multiplayer options and their games are immersive. Connected TV also allows for immersive apps on TV. At present it is possible to OCR any text that appears on the TV frame via set top boxes [23]. The EPG information is also available in such boxes as is a graphics plane blended with the video screen. This allows overlaying of the TV screen with an EPG that has been enhanced with information from the web, EPG and the OCRed text. As an example, if a movie is being played with no EPG information and there is a text on the video identifying the movie, then this text can be OCRed to obtain movie information. This text can be used to query a Web 2.0 service such as IMDB that returns comprehensive information about the movie. This TV contextual information can be used by users to obtain further information. Users can read trivia related to the cast, download subtitles in the languages not provided by the content provider but available on the web.

This context from the TV can be directly linked to applications in surrounding devices that may or may not be paired with the TV. The currently viewed program information can be posted on the viewer's social network. Then, the viewer's social network can be queried for friends currently viewing the same. This information can be blended on the TV screen as shown in Figs. 13.6 and 13.7 (these screenshots are applications on the low cost platform [23]). This allows the viewer to call them or chat with them on their mobile phone or tablet.

Fig. 13.6 Twitter^{TM} notification of followers are watching the same channel

Fig. 13.7 Facebook^{TM} strip to share with friends or indicate likeness of current program

Distant Learning

In distant learning, when a coursework is being played on the TV, a test can be sent to the nearest computing device simultaneously, allowing for continuous assessment. This computing device would need to be paired to the TV beforehand for the test to be sent automatically. Just as game scores are shared on Facebook™, these scores can also be published at the discretion of the student.

Social Living

The concept of social living is that your social behavior may be used as criteria using which you get to know your friends a little better through their interests and quickly find new friends with similar tastes as you. A Facebook™ friend who happens to keep watching the same TV programs as you do is potentially a better, closer friend to hang out with perhaps than the others.

The Facebook™ LivingSocial [24] app allows you to catalog books, movies, albums, video games, restaurants, ski slopes, TV shows, and iPhone apps. These are part of one's daily life.

The fact is that users use their mobile phones when finding/entering a restaurant/cafeteria. Users use their DVD/Blu-Ray players to watch movies and other devices like Personal Media Player (PMP) to listen to music and probably their set top box to follow TV shows. Hence, the use of these to determine a users' social behavior and affinity towards certain types of people would require that these data reach the social network from the respective devices.

The car is a system enclosed with lots of devices. In recent times, with advancement in communication technology and social networking, a connected social network of cars allows for a lot of social activities especially for passengers. The in vehicle entertainment device could have access to the rest of the cars devices. For example, it could be connected to the Global Positioning System (GPS), the accelerometer, the onboard controller of the car. Each of these devices can be IP-enabled and form a connected network. This would allow all the devices to interact with each other and allow transfer of data amongst them. It would allow the in vehicle entertainment device to be aware of the speed, rotations, fuel, efficiency, route, location and all other sensors in the car. This car's devices can then communicate to cars in collocated/remote areas. Long term evolution (LTE) Connected Car concept [25] is making it possible to have cars connected to the Internet.

Communicating collocated cars can share information about traffic and other road conditions such as potholes. The traffic and pothole information can be analyzed by the onboard GPS or guidance system real-time for effortless driving. This traffic information can be aggregated and analyzed by servers for route optimizations and jam warnings. Peoples driving histories can also be made available for auto u insurance companies and automobile manufacturers for accurate driving records and conditions. This is possible when the car's device is connected to the Internet and is exposing simple REST APIs that can be queried for data.

An application that could be enabled by connected cars is being able to dynamically schedule people in transit. If there is a party of strangers from different places meeting up (such as an online community, meeting offline), despite having agreed to meet up at a specific time and place, some may not make it in time. They and their modes of transportation can then form a social network to keep track of where they are, how long they are going to be in transit, who will take more time in reaching, thus allowing the group to modify plans on the fly. This application is similar to tracking goods, materials or documents being transported in supply chain management (SCM). In SCM, there are cases where deadlines can be missed and on the fly rescheduling and rerouting of materials may need to be done. Connected vehicles can help discover and recover from such cases faster.

In connected cars that are collocated, information such as amount of remaining oil and charge (for electric cars) can be recorded. If a car has a predefined destination, then it can estimate its own oil or charge usage. This allows it to barter off its potentially unused oil or charge to nearby cars which may not be able to reach a gas or charging station in time enroute to its destination.

Unified Messaging: Presence Through Devices

Unified messaging integrates messaging and communications from varied electronic devices in a single interface and make it available to various devices. The aim is to make communication seamless, no matter what the method. The missing piece not mentioned that allows these technologies to be delivered together is "presence." If friends and colleagues are "aware" of each other's state (e.g., available, busy, in a meeting, or offline), they can then choose the most appropriate communication method to use and therefore ensure effective communication.

With intelligent devices, presence detection and notification would be possible. Devices with communications capabilities can detect if another is within close physical proximity. A person usually carries a device on person which is connected always. This device is usually the mobile phone. The TV and the phone can be paired via bluetooth or wifi. Now, while watching TV, the phone need not ring and disturb the viewer. The TV can take over the informational functions of the phone. Any notification or calling function can now make use of the potentially larger screen area of the TV. For example, if there are new emails to be read, they can come up as a notification on this TV overlayed on top of the currently running video. If the user wants, she can choose to see this message on the cell phone. If the TV has a video conferencing facility like Skype^{TM}, calls can be converted to a TV based video conference instead of a voice call on the phone. The UI design of such a system would take into account that all the associated notifications and actions are geared towards making the entire experience the least intrusive to one's current mood, situation and ecosystem of devices. When the user moves out of the room and into another, that rooms devices will pair up. If there is a TV in this room, it could also automatically tune to the channel the user was just watching.

When the person walks to his or her car, then the cars infotainment device can take over the phones data functionalities as well. Since the presence is now detected here, calls may be routed to the cars phone depending on the urgency of the call as well as road conditions. If the driver is trying to negotiate sharp turns or potholes, an intelligent busy message is composed on the fly and the caller is informed of the same. If the driver is cruising on the highway without much traffic, the call goes through. This is possible since the cars onboard phone which is the present device, is able to communicate to the cars other electronic machinery thereby giving it enough data to be able to take an intelligent decision of the current surroundings. When at work, the office computer would be able to detect its presence and thereby route all calls to that person here. It would also be able to handle all kinds of notifications on the desktop itself and direct calls to the desk phone. Such an architecture and system would be possible as all devices are IP-enabled, and can send discovery signals periodically to discover and pair up with devices that come into close proximity of each other to exchange data.

Second Life

Second life is an online multiplayer social game. It involves mirroring real life activities in a virtual setting. There are virtual properties being created, bought and sold. There are avatars that describe the characters appearance. Social activities of all kinds abound. This platform is entirely virtual. Only its participants, humans, are real. By introducing intelligent devices into this game, it would bridge the real and the virtual. There need not be any restriction in building 3D models of real homes and offices in Second Life. Presence of a person can be tracked in the real world and updated in Second Life. A person usually carries around a mobile phone. From this, the persons' location can be gathered. A one to one mapping may be kept of the persons real location and second life location, so that people attempting to look up this person can just send out a virtual query in second life and be returned with real physical coordinates. It would also integrate with the persons messaging system for unified messaging.

Instant Rating

Internet enabled devices can potentially allow its users to tag each of its events as a "like" or "unlike." These user choices can be propagated to the social networks such as Facebook[TM]. Every instant in the real world can then be possibly tagged as "like" and "unlike" in Facebook[TM]. Consider a situation where a user is at a party where web enabled cameras are clicking and uploading pictures of the party occasionally to social networking websites. This would be possible with web 2.0 REST APIs and OAuth. Before uploading though, instead of uploading random pictures, people present at the party can be notified of their pictures. This would allow them to "like" or "unlike" a particular picture of theirs, giving valuable feedback to the camera to decide whether to upload the picture or not. This notification can be sent via bluetooth to mobile phones as the people and the pictures are in close proximity to each other. A similar situation arises with scenic places. Pictures can be geotagged while uploading from their cameras and therefore, new tourist places can be discovered. This can be enabled with geocoding of pictures as available via Zonetag [26] or Placelab [27].

Restaurants

At places to eat that are currently experiencing a rush, it gets difficult to find a place to sit. We hardly find ourselves able to accept sitting along with strangers at the same table. With intelligent devices and social networks, we can identify as we walk into a busy restaurant, who among the ones dining may be our closest friends. Once we know a table that has some empty seating and that the others at the table are close to us, we can sit together not as strangers but as friend of friends. This application may be especially helpful in school cafeterias and bars where we would be open to meet new people. There are currently mobile location based dating services such as MeetMoi [28] and SKOUT [29] that intelligently match, alert and allow meeting new people instantaneously.

Conclusion

In conclusion this chapter has covered the various aspects of creating and using an intelligent social network of devices. It depicts that there is a need for such ubiquity to exist as it enhances existing systems. It then lists out relevant technologies and their shortcomings. Finally, advantages and specific use cases are described to support the benefits due to such a system.

References

1. CEA-2014-B: Web-based Protocol and Framework for Remote User Interface on UPnPTM Networks and the Internet (Web4CE). Consumer Electronics Association, Arlington (2010)
2. Fielding, R. (2000) Architectural styles and the design of network-based soft-ware architectures. Ph.d. dissertation, University of California, Irvine

3. SOAP Version 1.2 Part 0: Primer. http://www.w3c.org/TR/2007/REC-soap12-part020070427/ (2007)
4. What is REST. http://rest.blueoxen.net/cgi-bin/wiki.pl?WhatIsREST
5. Yazar, D., Dunkels, A.: Efficient application integration in IP-based sensor networks. In: Proceedings of ACM BuildSys 2009, First ACM Workshop on Embedded Sensing Systems for Energy-Efficiency in Buildings, Berkeley, CA (2009)
6. Mongoose. http://code.google.com/p/mongoose/
7. Oregan Media Browser. http://oregan.net/oreganmediabrowser.php
8. Twitter Authentication. http://dev.twitter.com/pages/auth
9. OAuth Library Functions. http://liboauth.sourceforge.net/
10. Libcurl – the multiprotocol file transfer library. http://curl.haxx.se/libcurl/
11. Extensible OAuth library for Java. http://github.com/fernandezpablo85/scribe
12. Twitter4J – A Java library for the Twitter API. http://twitter4j.org
13. Twitter Scribe library. https://github.com/fernandezpablo85/scribe/wiki/getting-started
14. Shelby, Z., Bormann, C.: 6LoWPAN: The Wireless Embedded Internet. John Wiley & Sons Ltd, Chichester (2009)
15. Tunerfish. http://www.tunerfish.com/
16. Boxee. http://www.boxee.tv/
17. Fan Talk TV. http://www.fantalk.tv/
18. Live Hive Systems. http://www.livehivesystems.com/
19. Bulkeley, W.M.: TR10: social TV. Relying on relationships to rebuild TV audiences. In: Technology Review: 10 Emerging Technologies. MIT, Cambridge (2010)
20. Dennisov, A.: Social Media & User-Generated Content. Parks Associates, Dallas (2009)
21. Wii at Nintendo. http://www.nintendo.com/wii
22. Kinect for Xbox 360. http://www.xbox.com/en-US/kinect
23. Pal, A., Prashant, M., Ghose, A., Bhaumik, C.: Home infotainment platform – a ubiquitous access device for masses. In: Communications in Computer and Information Science. Springer, Berlin/Heidelberg (2010)
24. Living Social. http://apps.facebook.com/livingsocial
25. LTE Connected Car. http://www.ngconnect.org/ecosystem/connected-car.htm
26. Zonetag. http://zonetag.research.yahoo.com
27. LaMarca, A., Chawathe, Y., Consolvo, S., Hightower, J., Smith, I., Scott, J., Sohn, T., Howard, J., Hughes, J., Potter, F., Tabert, J., Powledge, P., Borriello, G., Schilit, B.: Place lab: device positioning using radio beacons in the wild. Lect. Notes Comput. Sci. **3682**, 116–133 (2005)
28. Meet Moi. http://www.meetmoi.com/
29. Skout. http://www.skout.com/

Chapter 14
Social Network-Based Media Sharing in the Ubiquitous Environment: Technologies and Applications

Xun Luo

Abstract Ubiquitous computing paradigm fundamentally changed the relationship between humans and computers. In the ubiquitous environment, computing functionalities are naturally integrated with the surrounding objects rather than being isolated units by themselves. Instead of requiring humans to learn how to use computers, intelligence in the environment is smart enough to automatically sense and serve users' needs. Since the origination of ubiquitous computing concept in the late 1980s, a great amount of research and development efforts have taken place in this field, and the paradigm has undergone substantial evolvement. As new technologies and application models keep emerging and growing mature, many of the old goals envisioned by ubiquitous computing researchers have turned into realities, and novel ones become focused on, making the paradigm an actively moving target to be pursued. In recent years, media sharing established itself as a hot topic in the ubiquitous computing community, thanks to the power of several critical driving forces. An especially important one among these forces is social networking. In this chapter, we first present the background of ubiquitous environment, social networks, and media sharing. In this part we illustrate why and how social network-based media sharing is destined to be indispensable in the ubiquitous environment. Several representative applications are subsequently examined in depth as case studies. The last part of the chapter gives an overlook of future directions envisioned from an expert's eye.

Background

We start by introducing the background of three concepts: ubiquitous environment, social networks, and media sharing. For each concept, both theoretical definitions and one or more real-life scenarios are given.

X. Luo (✉)
Office of the Chief Scientist, Qualcomm Inc., San Diego, USA
e-mail: xun.luo@ieee.org

A. Abraham and A.-E. Hassanien (eds.), *Computational Social Networks: Tools, Perspectives and Applications*, DOI 10.1007/978-1-4471-4048-1_14, © Springer-Verlag London 2012

Ubiquitous Environment

The term "ubiquitous computing," or shortened as "ubicomp," was coined by Mark Weiser around 1988, who was then the Chief Technologist at Xerox Palo Alto Research Center (PARC) [1]. As Mark Weiser and the pioneers envisioned, ubicomp is a post-desktop model of human-computer interaction in which information processing has been thoroughly integrated into everyday objects and activities. In the course of ordinary activities, someone "using" ubiquitous computing engages many computational devices and systems simultaneously, and may not necessarily even be aware that they are doing so. This model is usually considered an advancement from the desktop paradigm. More formally ubiquitous computing is defined as "machines that fit the human environment instead of forcing humans to enter theirs."

The ubiquitous computing paradigm is also described as pervasive computing, ambient intelligence, where each term emphasizes slightly different aspects. When primarily concerning the objects involved, it is also physical computing, the Internet of Things, haptic computing, and things that think. Rather than propose a single definition for ubiquitous computing and for these related terms, a taxonomy of properties for ubiquitous computing has been proposed, from which different kinds or flavors of ubiquitous systems and applications can be described.

Mark Weiser proposed three basic forms for ubiquitous system devices: tabs, pads, and boards.

- Tabs: wearable centimeter-sized devices.
- Pads: handheld decimeter-sized devices.
- Boards: meter-sized interactive display devices.

These three forms proposed by Weiser are characterized by being macro sized, having a planar form, and incorporating visual output displays. More recently, Stefan Posland, a researcher at the University of London, relaxed each of these three characteristics and expanded this range into a much more diverse and potentially more useful range of ubiquitous computing devices. Hence, three additional forms for ubiquitous systems have been proposed [2]:

- Dust: Miniaturized devices can be without visual output displays, e.g., Micro-Electro-Mechanical Systems (MEMS), ranging from nanometers through micrometers to millimeters.
- Skin: Fabrics based upon light emitting and conductive polymers, organic computer devices, can be formed into more flexible non-planar display surfaces and products such as clothes and curtains. MEMS device can also be painted onto various surfaces, so that a variety of physical world structures can act as networked surfaces of MEMS.
- Clay: Ensembles of MEMS can be formed into arbitrary three-dimensional shapes as artifacts resembling many different kinds of physical object.

Posland's proposals extended the ones originally proposed by Weiser. Although the dust, skin, and clay devices still seem to be futuristic based on today's

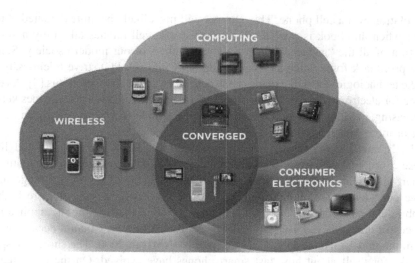

Fig. 14.1 Convergence of the three "C"s: computing, communications, and consumer electronics

technologies, we can confidently assert that they will become realities in the near future. A strong supporting evidence is that after 20 years of scientific research and engineering development, the contemporary devices have implemented almost all the functionalities that Weiser described, at comparable or even higher levels.

There have been two remarkable evolutions observed for electronic devices (also called the more fancy name "gadgets" by some people) during the last decade. First of all, with the plummeting of processor cost, increasing of processor speed and miniaturization of processor size, three categories of electronic devices started to show convergence. These three categories are Computing, Communications, and Consumer Electronics, or simply put as the three "C"s. Figure 14.1 illustrates this trend. As shown in the figure, computing devices used to include PCs, workstations, and other forms of computers; communications devices used to mainly cover wireless and wired phones; and consumer electronics devices used to incorporate a wide range of special-purpose product lines such as digital cameras, media players, GPS, and so on. With the developments in processor design and fabricating technologies, computing devices start to gain flexible connectivity and rich multimedia processing capabilities, making themselves able to fulfill communications and media-processing tasks. For similar reasons, communications and consumer electronics devices become more and more powerful in general-purpose processing, and begin to be able to accomplish computing-intensive tasks. The boundaries among the three "C"s have been truly blurred. Nowadays, it is often difficult to put a certain electronic device with one "C" label. For example, a GPS device which has Bluetooth radio and an mp3 player embedded clearly qualifies the classification criteria for computing, communications, and consumer electronics devices.

The second evolution of electronic devices is that their deployed quantities have grown explosively. In 2007, an IDC survey reported that half of the world population own a cell phone. This number will most likely be quite outdated at the time when this book is published. And of course, cell phones take only a small portion of all the "gadgets" owned by the members of our modern society. Some non-profit task forces such as One Laptop Per Child (OLPC) strive relentlessly to make technologies available to everyone despite of their economic status [3]. As the price for electronic devices keeps dropping and the craving for these devices keeps increasing, it will not be too far from seeing each and every of us accompanied by one or more "gadgets."

Let's now re-visit Weiser's definitions of Tabs, Pads, and Boards, and link these conceptual definitions with real-life devices that have corresponding features. Smart phones implement the Tabs concept well: they are of centimeter-range size, have considerable computing and multimedia processing power, and are highly mobile and pocketable. In 2009, Qualcomm released the first mobile application processor that achieved 1-GHz clock speed. This is only less than a decade away from the first 1-GHz desktop CPU released by AMD in 2000. The short timespan speaks for itself about how fast smart phones have evolved. On the other hand, global smart phone shipments have maintained a steady upward trend. In 2007, annual shipments of smart phones outnumbered laptops for the first time – 116 million for smart phones and 108 million for laptops. After that crossover, the gap between smart phone and laptop shipments has continued to grow larger. A revolutionary product in the history of smart phones, as commonly regarded, is the Apple iPhone. Powered by the novel features such as multi-touch gesture interaction and third-party application support, over 70 million iPhones have been sold from its announcement in October 2010.

Apple safeguarded its leadership role in technology innovation and launched iPad, a tablet computer in April 2010. Almost all the aspects of "Pads" concept are embodied in this product. The iPad is of decimeter-range size, has a processor of 1-GHz clock speed, and is designed for perfect handheld use. Although tablet PCs have existed in market for quite a long time, iPad was the first tablet computer that gained true success with regard to number of users. The success of iPad stimulated a wave of tablet computer product development. During the 2011 annual Consumer Electronics Show held in Las Vegas, over a 100 tablet computer models were exhibited by various manufacturers.

Devices that resemble closest to "Boards" concept are probably the smart TVs and high-resolution display walls. A decade ago, an overwhelming majority of TVs were analog and CRT tubes were the display components for them. Contemporary TVs equip themselves with wireless or ethernet connectivity, as well as state-of-art media processors. TV vendors are trying best to add intelligence to their products with the hope to make TVs the center of home computing experience. With these demands going on, two Internet giants have released their products to cater the need for smart TVs. As shown in Fig. 14.2, the Yahoo! TV gadgets are pure software applications that can be executed on TVs with media processor, while the Google TV can be either a software solution just like Yahoo! TV gadgets or a software/hardware combined solution that runs on OEM-made set-top boxes.

Fig. 14.2 Yahoo! TV gadgets and Google TV

Fig. 14.3 A large tiled display wall with 18 display units (Picture courtesy of Tom DeFanti, UCSD/Calit2)

In the academic arena, researchers have been actively exploring the opportunities for high-resolution display walls [4]. These display walls are usually constructed using a group of cluster-driven single display units, with advanced rendering and displaying management middleware. The back-end computer cluster provides abundant computing power to the walls, making them unquestionably high-end with regard to both displaying and computing aspects. Figure 14.3 shows such a display wall built by the researchers at the California Institute for Telecommunications and Information Technology (Calit2), a research institution at the University of California, San Diego (UCSD). The display wall has been serving as the platform for many research disciplines such as visualization, interaction, video analytics, and scientific collaboration.

It is deemed by many scientists that high-resolution tiled displays are the precursors of smart walls and windows of the future.

After the in-depth discussion of ubiquitous devices, the concept of ubiquitous environment becomes clear: it is the environment within which ubiquitous devices exist, interact with each other seamlessly, and serve the users' needs in a natural fashion. Figure 14.4 shows several representative user interfaces for contemporary TVs, a.k.a the "Boards" in Weiser's nomenclature. These user interfaces are

Fig. 14.4 Representative 10-foot user interfaces

designed to be used at normal viewing distance of TVs, and thus gained the name "10-foot User Interfaces." Some more advanced ubiquitous devices, such as the Microsoft Kinect [5], are device-free and respond to user's full body motion for human-computer interaction. It is also worth pointing out another important concept which is related to the ubiquitous environment: cloud computing. The fundamental concept of cloud computing is that the computing is "in the cloud" i.e. the processing (and the related data) is not in a specified, known, or static place(s). This is in opposition to where the processing takes place in one or more specific servers that are known. With cloud computing, the ubiquitous environment surrounding a user is not only just the environment within physical proximity but also the resources and ubiquitous devices available through "cloud access."

As illustrative examples for the ubiquitous environment concept, we present two real-life scenarios: at home and on-the-go. In the at home scenario, the TV in the living room, the smart phone accompanying the user, and a network connected picture frame in the bedroom are the ubiquitous devices in the user's vicinity. The three devices automatically link with each other through a home wireless access point, and formed the ubiquitous environment at home to serve the user's needs. In the on-the-go scenario, the mobile phone carried by the user automatically joins a peer-to-peer network formed by other mobile phones in the proximity; these phones then intelligently share video and music files with each other, catering to the owners' needs. As we can see from these scenarios, ubiquitous environments can be based on a relatively fixed infrastructure, or ad hoc formations of a set of ubiquitous devices and the services provided by them. More details about these two scenarios will be discussed later in this chapter.

Fig. 14.5 An example of social network structure (Picture courtesy of Wikipedia)

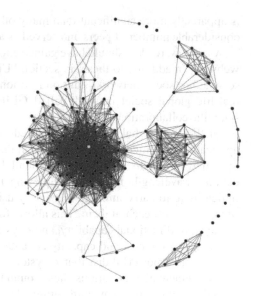

Social Networks

In 2010, Columbia Pictures released the movie *The Social Network* which achieved a remarkable box office success. This movie based itself on the social-networking website Facebook, about the Internet tycoon's founding and related lawsuits. Whether or not the movie plot reflects the true stories of Facebook is a matter of controversy. However, as the large number of audience manifested, few would argue that social networking has become a common part of our daily life. The Facebook website alone has over 600 million active registered users as of January 2011 [6]. Other representative social networking websites include MySpace, LinkedIn, just to name a few. The most common forms of social structure on these websites are friendship and professional networks.

Although people often refer to "social networking websites" as "social networks," concept of the latter is actually much broader than that of the former. In general, a social network is a social structure made up of individuals (or organizations) called "nodes," which are tied (connected) by one or more specific types of interdependency, such as friendship, kinship, common interest, financial exchange, dislike, sexual relationships, or relationships of beliefs, knowledge, or prestige.

Figure 14.5 illustrates an example of social network structure, from which some interesting characteristics can be observed. Comparing to traditional points of view, social networks provide drastically different perspectives to look at the relationship among social entities. In a social network, a specific individual node can be analyzed by how it is impacted by its connected peers, or vice versa. The yellow node in Fig. 14.5 (shown as a lighter node in black-and-white prints) is apparently more significant than many other nodes, because it is connected to a considerable number of peers and served as a hub in the social network.

As of now, readers should have gained enough familiarity with social networking websites. In addition to these, in section "Ubiquitous Environment," we have also seen ad hoc social networks built on location proximities. In the following, another real-life global social network called GLIF [7] is described which is based on scientific collaborations.

GLIF (The Global Lambda Integrated Facility) is a worldwide laboratory for application and middleware development that utilizes a network of interconnected optical wavelengths (also known as lambda grids). In fibre optic telecommunications, wavelength-division multiplexing is a technology that enables a single optical fibre to carry multiple signals by using different wavelengths (or colours) of laser light for each of them. This allows for a significant increase in transmission capacity, bi-directional capability, and physical separation of channels. GLIF takes advantage of the cost and capacity advantages offered by optical multiplexing, in order to build powerful distributed systems that utilize processing power, storage, and instrumentation at various sites around the globe. The aim is to encourage the shared use of resources by eliminating a lack of network capacity as the traditional performance bottleneck.

The GLIF participants are organizations that share the vision of optical interconnection of different facilities, and who voluntarily contribute network resources (equipment and/or lambdas) and/or actively participate in activities in furtherance of these goals. Seamless end-to-end connections require a high degree of interoperability between different transmission, interface, and service implementations, and also require harmonization of contracting and fault management processes. The GLIF Technical and Control Plane Working Groups are technical forums for addressing these operational issues.

Clearly, the GLIF can be abstracted into a social network representation (V, E) which consists of a set V of network nodes and a set E of edges connecting nodes in V. As shown in Fig. 14.6, each GLIF participant on the map is a node in V. Because the institutions in the U.S. outnumber other geographical areas in the world, node density in the GLIF social network is higher in the USA than any other countries and regions. Furthermore, the US institutions have formed some "inner social networks" of their own. National LambdaRail (NLR) [8] is one of such "inner social networks." NLR is owned by the US research and education community and is the ultra high-performance, 12,000-mile innovation platform for a wide range of academic disciplines and public-private partnerships. Figure 14.7 displays a map of NLR.

It starts to get interesting when discussion about how the set of edges E in the GLIF social network should be defined starts. As mentioned earlier, edges in the social network denote interdependencies among the network nodes. Different types of interdependency thus lead to different defined edge sets. One way to look at interdependencies is to make observations at different layers. If the study is undertaken at the infrastructure layer, then each lambda in the infrastructure can be treated as an edge between two nodes. For example, each of the optical

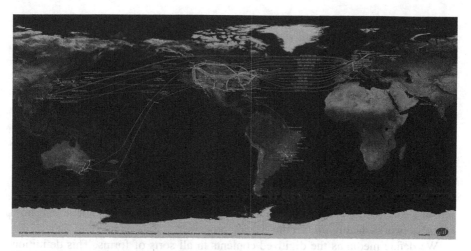

Fig. 14.6 The world map of GLIF infrastructure (Picture courtesy of GLIF)

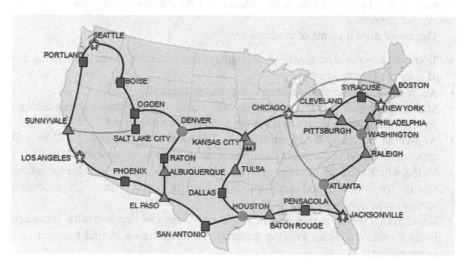

Fig. 14.7 National LambdaRail (NLR), an inner social network of the GLIF (Picture courtesy of NLR)

network links between two GLIF local node clusters: Chicago and Atlanta is an edge accordingly. However, if the service and application layer is examined, then the interdependencies become scientific services provided and consumed. As a result of this view angle, the edges are defined differently as well. Not surprisingly, the service and application layer structure of the GLIF social network features large distinctions from the structure seen at infrastructure layer.

To summarize, social networks can be formed among individuals or organizations. They can be based on ad hoc encounters as well as well-established fixed connections. With same set of nodes in a social network, different views at the nodes' interdependencies will yield to different representations of the social network structure.

Media Sharing

Concepts of ubiquitous environment and social networks provide the necessary knowledge to look at the subject topic of this chapter, which is social network-based media sharing in the ubiquitous environment. In this section, we first describe categories of media based on two classification criteria. After that we explain the reasons why media sharing is important in the ubiquitous environment, and how social networks deeply impact the sharing process.

We define media as the digitized contents in all sorts of forms. This definition thus excludes the legacy "media" term which only covers traditional forms of printed or hand-produced material. Media can be categorized by the *forms* and *sources* of contents.

The major digital forms of contents are:

- Text, which is the representation of language in a textual medium through the use of a set of signs or symbols.
- Audio, which is the audible sound and/or sound signal.
- Still image, which may be two-dimensional, such as a photograph, screen display, and as well as three-dimensional, such as a statue or hologram.
- Animation, which is the rapid display of a sequence of images of 2-D or 3-D artwork or model positions in order to create an illusion of movement.
- Video, which is the technology of electronically capturing, recording, processing, storing, transmitting, and reconstructing a sequence of still images representing scenes in motion.
- Interactivity, which designates the forms that users can become fully immersed in their experiences by viewing material, commenting on it, and then actively contributing to it.

And the major sources of contents are:

- Mass media, which are maintained and distributed by corporations.
- User-generated contents (UGCs), which are produced and maintained by individuals.

Mass media usually follow one-way distribution channels, from the administration corporations to the recipients. Under normal cases, production of mass media needs professional skills, dedicated equipments, and considerable operation cost. In contrast, UGCs are conversational, which means that they flow in two-way distribution channels. Being conversational is a key characteristic of so-called Web 2.0 which encourages the publishing of one's own content and commenting on other people's. UGCs can be produced without sophisticated skills and/or equipments,

Table 14.1 Specialties of PCs, TVs, and phones

Type	Display size	Mobility	A/V quality	Power sensitivity
PC	OK	OK	OK	None (PC), small (Laptop)
TV	Good	Poor	Good	None
Phone	Poor	Good	Poor	High

Table 14.2 Usage convergence matrix for PCs, TVs, and phones

	PC	TV	Phone
PC	–	Internet-based TV or embedded tuner card	Skype
TV	Internet browsing	–	Skype
Phone	Smart phones	Mobile TV	–

and publishing to the public incurs minimum or no cost to the user. Because of the easiness of producing and administrating UGCs, the amount of them exploded in the pass decade. The powerful media capturing and authoring capabilities on personal devices further fostered this trend. The most representative UGC website YouTube which hosts mostly video contents, reported in 2010 that every minute 24-h length of video contents were uploaded to its servers. The corresponding bandwidth consumed is by no means small – in 2007, YouTube generated the same amount of traffic as the whole Internet did in 2000.

With the diversity of forms and plethora of sources, media sharing becomes essential to, as well as beneficial for, ubiquitous environments. It is essential to the ubiquitous environments for several reasons. The first one is that with device feature convergence, media production and consuming capabilities are getting common for ubiquitous devices. It is possible for any device in the environment to be a media source, a media sink, or a combination of both. Sharing media across devices is thus a basic functionality of the environment. The other reason is that despite of feature convergence, the devices still have different specialties. Complete replacement of one device with another is not happening for now and will not be likely in the future. For example, PCs, TVs, and phones are the most common devices seen in a home environment, known as the "three screens." The specialties of these three kinds of devices are shown in Table 14.1. In the mean time, the usage convergence matrix for them are shown in Table 14.2. It can be apparently observed that although the usages of them do have some overlap, for anyone among the three to be omnipotent in serving all of user's needs is yet not practical.

Yet another reason is that in the ubiquitous environment, users are the center of the computing process rather than the devices. When a user has produced media or wanted to consume media, it is most natural for the device that can best cater for the user's needs to serve him/her, instead of imposing the obligation of choosing devices to the user. Ideally, when the user moves in the environment, his/her personal media should follow and be available when needed without any delay. For this purpose, the devices in a ubiquitous environment need to be capable of sharing media in a smart fashion among themselves.

The benefits of media sharing are twofold for the ubiquitous environments. As media act directly on the perceptual inputs of humans, they are among the most attractive user experiences. Media sharing thus helps to accelerate the transition of computing paradigm from desktop-based to ubiquitous environment-based. Also, efficient media sharing puts high requirements on intelligent context awareness and natural human-computer interaction. The effort to fulfill these requirements will push ubiquitous computing research continuously moving forward.

Why media sharing in the ubiquitous environments is preferably social network-based? Because social networks help to answer several important questions for this procedure:

- Whom to share the media with?
- What should be shared?
- When is the optimal time for media sharing?
- Where is the best venue for media sharing?

It is straightforward that the social networks that a user belongs to give direct answer for the first question, and provide critical hints to the other three.

Applications

At Home

Many smart devices exist in a typical home or home office environment. For example, in the living room, there are TVs, BlueRay players, stereo speakers, and game consoles. In the study room, there are PCs, laptops, and printers. Digital photo frames and music players are normally found in the bedroom. With friends visiting, the home or home office environment have both static and dynamic social network flavors.

To manage the challenge of media sharing across devices which are using multiple technologies and manufactured by various venders, the Digital Living Network Alliance (DLNA) proposed a set of frameworks, which share the same name with the alliance. Figure 14.8 illustrates the DLNA solutions.

On-the-Go

There are billions of mobile devices carried and used by the people across the globe. This has enabled the development of mobile P2P applications for mobile phones. These new mobile P2P systems seem promising in a new domain of applications based on physical location and context, together with the possibility of using a wide variety of wireless radio access technologies. As Fig. 14.9 illustrates, peer-to-peer

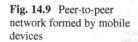

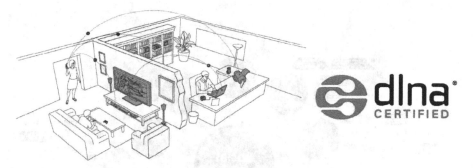

Fig. 14.8 The DLNA solution (Picture courtesy of DLNA)

Fig. 14.9 Peer-to-peer
network formed by mobile
devices

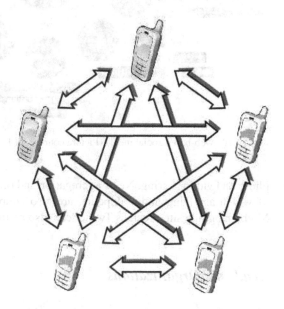

content distribution is a very interesting paradigm in cellular environments because
the bandwidth available to the content server according to the with demand. This
feature ensures a wide range of applications for peer-to-peer systems in mobile
environments.

Web Communities

Figure 14.10 shows some popular social media websites. It includes common examples of the popular social networking sites like Friendster, Facebook, MySpace.
Social media also includes YouTube, Photobucket, Flickr, and other sites aimed at

Fig. 14.10 Web-based social media (Picture courtesy of FredCavazza.net)

photo and video sharing. News aggregation and online reference sources, examples of which are Digg and Wikipedia, are also counted in the social media bucket. Micro-blogging sites such as Twitter can also be included as social media.

Academic Organizations

The NSF-funded OptIPuter project [9] enables user-controlled 10-Gbps dedicated light paths to provide direct access to global data repositories, scientific instruments, and computational resources from OptIPortals, PC clusters which provide scalable visualization in user's campus laboratories (Fig. 14.11). This 5-year project was initiated in 2003 and since then, numerous scientific applications of several disciplines have been designed and deployed on this global "OptIPlatform."

Future Directions

After reviewing the background and applications for social network-based media sharing in the ubiquitous environment, we try to look beyond the status quo of

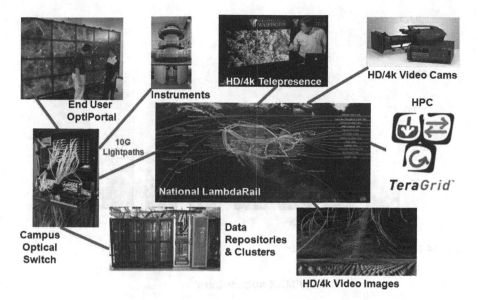

Fig. 14.11 The NSF Optiputer project (Picture courtesy of Larry Smarr, UCSD/Calit2)

this topic and predict some future directions. These forward-looking statements are by no means guaranteed to be comprehensive and accurate, but they reflected the authors' opinions as a field expert with best attempt.

Wireless Broadband

The penetrations of mobile computing devices, services provided over the air and wireless broadband will continue to exhibit strong momentums. In 2007, cell phone ownership had exceeded 50% globally. As Figs. 14.12 and 14.13 illustrate, worldwide 3G subscribers are projected to be about 2.4 billion by 2013, and LTE and WiMax subscribers are estimated to be 24 and 54 millions, respectively, by 2012. In year 2017, mobile devices will most likely be the dominating gadgets people use for their daily life computing tasks. Wireless broadband will connect everyone and every device, making social networks invisibly integrated with the infrastructure, and media sharing unnoticeable but silently prevalent.

Readers should also be aware that the American National Broadband Plan has several important goals to be achieved in the next decade:

- Goal 1: At least 100 million U.S. homes should have affordable access to actual download speeds of at least 100 Mbps and actual upload speeds of at least 50 Mbps.

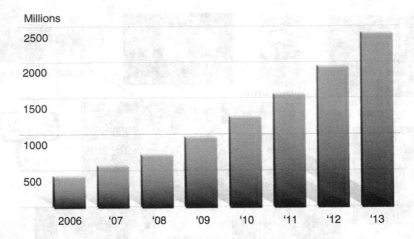

Fig. 14.12 3G subscribers worldwide

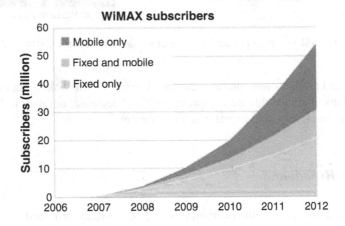

Fig. 14.13 WiMax subscribers worldwide

- Goal 4: Every American community should have affordable access to at least 1 Gbps broadband service to anchor institutions such as schools, hospitals, and government buildings.

New Models of Sharing

Innovations in the models of social network-based media sharing have just begun, and are yet a long way from reaching their mayday. The rapid growth of new companies providing novel sharing experience underscores this trend. Probably, sharing will evolve on two axis: the perspectives of social networking will drastically increase and the types of ubiquitous devices to participate sharing will witness a comprehensive extension. The Dust, Skin, and Clay devices will have their roles played on this important stage.

Standardization

Just like the needs for computer network interoperability led to specification standardization, the same needs for social networks will also push related standards to be developed. Currently, the processes to implement social networks and the media sharing applications on top of them are still free arts. In the future, not far from now with ubiquitous devices deployed everywhere and things-to-things research becoming sufficiently mature, compliance with published standards will be compulsory for almost all device and service venders.

Vertical Integration

The layer boundaries between physical networks and social networks will be at least largely blurred, if not vanish at all. It will be not easy to tell whether the utilization of social networks is at the infrastructure level, the service level, or the application level. The social networks concept will be integrated vertically into every aspect of computing and communication.

Conclusion

We conclude this chapter with an old but candid saying:

The world is but a little place, after all.

References

1. Weiser, M., Gold, R., Brown, J.S.: The origins of ubiquitous computing research at PARC in the late 1980s. IBM Syst. J. **38**(4), 693 (1999)
2. Poslad, S.: Ubiquitous Computing Smart Devices, Smart Environments and Smart Interaction. Wiley, Chichester (2009). ISBN: 978-0-470-03560-3
3. One Laptop per Child. http://one.laptop.org. Accessed 29 May 2012
4. Jeong, B., Renambot, L., Jagodic, R., Singh, R., Aguilera, J., Johnson, A., Leigh, J.: High-performance dynamic graphics streaming for scalable adaptive graphics environment. Proceedings of SC '06, Tampa (2006)
5. Microsoft Kinect for Xbox 360. http://www.xbox.com/en-US/kinect/. Accessed 29 May 2012

6. MSNBC: Goldman to Clients: Facebook Has 600 Million Users. MSNBC (2011)
7. Brown, M. (guest ed.): Blueprint for the future of high-performance networking. Commun. ACM (CACM) **46**(11), 30–77 (2003)
8. HPCWire news article, National LambdaRail Supercharges Infrastructure, April, 2009. http://www.hpcwire.com/hpcwire/2009-04-28/national_lambdarail_supercharges_infrastructure.html. Accessed 29 May 2012
9. Smarr, L.L., Chien, A.A., DeFanti, T., Leigh, J., Papadopoulos, P.M.: The OptIPuter. Commun. ACM **46**(11), 58–67 (2003)

Chapter 15
Customer Interaction Management Goes Social: Getting Business Processes Plugged in Social Networks

Michaela Geierhos and Mohamed Ebrahim

Abstract Within this chapter, we will describe a novel technical service dealing with the integration of social networking channels into existing business processes. Since many businesses are moving to online communities as a means of communicating directly with their customers, social media has to be explored as an additional communication channel between individuals and companies. While the English-speaking consumers on Facebook are more likely to respond to communication rather than to initiate communication with an organisation, some German companies already have regularly updated Facebook pages for customer service and support, e.g. Telekom. Therefore, the idea of classifying and evaluating public comments addressed to German companies is based on an existing demand. In order to maintain an active Facebook wall, the consumer posts have to be categorised and then automatically assigned to the corresponding business processes (e.g. the technical service, shipping, marketing, accounting, etc.). This service works like an issue tracking system sending e-mails to the corresponding person in charge of customer service and support. That way, business process management systems which are already used to e-mail communication can benefit from social media. This allows the company to follow general trends in customer opinions on the Internet; moreover it facilates the recording of two-sided communication for customer relationship management and the company's response will be delivered through consumer's preferred medium: Facebook.

M. Geierhos (✉)
CIS, Centre for Information and Language Processing, Ludwig-Maximilians-Universität München, Oettingenstr. 67, D-80538 München, Germany
e-mail: michaela.geierhos@cis.uni-muenchen.de

M. Ebrahim
IPSC, European Commission, Joint Research Centre – Ispra site, Institute for the Protection and Security of the Citizen, T.P. 267, I-21027, Ispra, VA, Italy
e-mail: mohamed.ebrahim@jrc.ec.europa.eu

A. Abraham and A.-E. Hassanien (eds.), *Computational Social Networks: Tools, Perspectives and Applications*, DOI 10.1007/978-1-4471-4048-1_15,
© Springer-Verlag London 2012

Introduction

In January 2011, there were more than 14 million active Facebook users in Germany.[1] Each of them writes approximately 25 comments per month and is a member of 13 groups.[2] More than 1,145 million people worldwide[3] use social networking sites such as Facebook,[4] Twitter,[5] MySpace,[6] and Foursquare[7] because something incredible happened: Anyone can communicate almost anywhere, any time with anyone using image, text and sound. For this reason, it is assumed that social networks will evolve into a common communication channel – not only between individuals but also between customers and companies.

Using the traditional communication channels such as telephone and e-mail, there are already established approaches and systems to incoming requests: so-called contact centres. They are used by companies to manage all client contact through a variety of mediums such as telephone, fax, letter, e-mail and online live chat. Contact centre agents are therefore responsible for assigning all customer requests to internal business processes. However, social networking has not yet been integrated into customer interaction management tools. In order to complement their current marketing and business development activity with social media and other online marketing activities, companies expand their focus on social networks such as Facebook, Twitter and Xing.[8] Until now, the dialogue with customers is still one-sided and not designed as a two-way process addressing the customer on the same communication channel.

Considering that Facebook alone has more than 500 million users in December 2010, it becomes apparent that Facebook currently is the most preferred medium by consumers and companies alike. Since many businesses are moving to online communities as a means of communicating directly with their customers, social media has to be explored as an additional communication channel between individuals and companies. While the English-speaking consumers on Facebook are more likely to respond to communication rather than to initiate communication with an organisation [4], the German-speaking community in turn directly contacts the companies. Therefore, some German enterprises already have regularly updated Facebook pages

---

[1]http://facebookmarketing.de/zahlen_fakten/facebook-nutzerzahlen-2011

[2]http://facebookmarketing.de/zahlen_fakten/facebook-infografik-und-statistiken

[3]http://www.radicalgeography.co.uk/brandnewworldcardsort.doc

[4]http://www.facebook.com

[5]http://twitter.com

[6]http://www.myspace.com

[7]http://foursquare.com

[8]http://www.xing.com

for customer service and support, e.g. Telekom (German Telecom),[9] Vodafone,[10] O$_2$[11] or Nokia.[12]

Facebook is now Germany's most popular social networking site. Many German companies – especially in the telecommunication sector – maintain active Facebook profile pages. Since the German and, for example, the Australian Facebook communities are complete opposites behaviourally because 89% of the Australian consumers only respond to communication and only 11% initiate communication with a company [4], we cannot concentrate on the English-speaking Facebook users. Due to our observations of customers' behaviour on Facebook in the USA and the UK, we must admit that the Australian pilot study [4] is quite representative for the English-speaking Facebook communities. We therefore focus on German Facebook users searching the dialogue with companies' customer support services.

In this chapter, we will describe a new approach to customer interaction management by integrating social networking channels into existing business processes. Until now, contact centre agents still read these messages and forward them to the persons in charge of customers in the company. They also answer simple questions by themselves. This process is very time-consuming and error-prone because of the employee's high workload. It can therefore happen that customer requests "stray" for a long time in the company before reaching the person responsible for it, which can sometimes lead to loss of clients [33]. But with the introduction of Web 2.0 and social networking clients are more likely to communicate with the companies via Facebook and Twitter instead of filling data in contact forms or sending e-mail requests.

The major difference of our method with respect to previous best practice is that customer posts have to be categorised and then automatically assigned to the corresponding business processes (e.g. the technical service, shipping, marketing, accounting, etc.). Furthermore, we do not use traditional algorithms like the Naive Bayes [27, 29] or Support Vector Machine classifier [3, 30]. We strike a new path and use so-called local grammars [11, 12], a kind of recursive transition networks [31], for classification purposes (cf. section on "Applying Local Grammars for Feature Extraction"). We minimise the error rate in the assignment of messages by substituting the manual classification step for an automatically done extraction and categorisation of consumer requests. This service works like an issue tracking system sending e-mails to the corresponding person in charge of customer service and support. This allows the company to follow general trends in customer opinions on Facebook; moreover it facilites the recording of two-sided communication for customer relationship management and the company does real-time customer interaction management (CIM) via Facebook.

Here we present an application monitoring social network sites, especially company profiles, in order to automatically assign the correct customer request to the corresponding person responsible in company. The structure of this chapter and its examples are chosen to remind readers that social network mining is always a reverse engineering task: First, there is the study of existing social networks, then a task-specific use case is defined and finally, competing software applications are examined carefully. Unfortunately, there is no existing software providing the same features our future system will do. So we have to start with a mock-up before discovering the techniques and resources behind the application.

Starting to Mock-up a Monitoring Demo for CIM

Customer interaction management (CIM) is handled by an application which is responsible for managing the interaction between an organisation and its clients. In general, a CIM application is used by the agents in a contact centre while communicating with the customers. Such systems handle communication across multiple different channels, such as e-mail, telephone, Instant Messaging, letter, etc.

What we do now is to integrate social networking into CIM applications by adding another communication channel. Since CIM applications and contact centre agents have already been used to e-mail communication, our approach foresees to emulate an issue-tracking system sending e-mails with Facebook posts to the corresponding person in charge of customer service and support. Figure 15.1 shows *how* our system shall *be*. This mock-up of a social network monitoring tool for customer interaction management was created for unit testing.

Before specifying the architecture of our monitoring application, we will have a closer look on the non-functional requirements of our system. We therefore define a list of constraints being valid for this mock-up described in this section.

Constraints

Using the following trigger questions, we want to explain how our system has to behave considering human and other factors:

Human Factors

Q   *What type of user will be using the system?*
A   Contact centre agents and person in charge of customer service and support will use this application.

Q   *Is it particularly important that the system be easy to learn?*
A   An intuitive user interface is absolutely necessary. As shown in Fig. 15.1 the contact centre agents get pre-classified consumer requests (cf. issue, e.g.

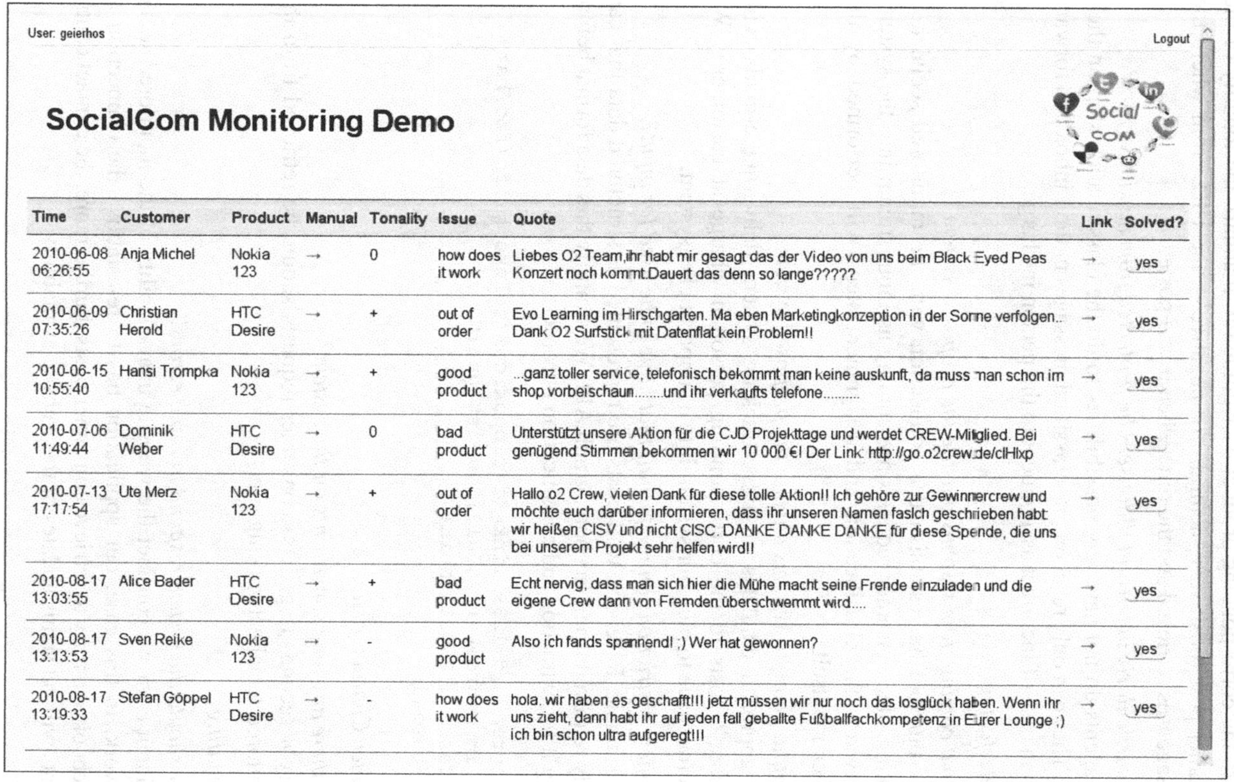

SocialCom Monitoring Demo

Time	Customer	Product	Manual	Tonality	Issue	Quote	Link	Solved?
2010-06-08 06:26:55	Anja Michel	Nokia 123	↑	0	how does it work	Liebes O2 Team,ihr habt mir gesagt das der Video von uns beim Black Eyed Peas Konzert noch kommt.Dauert das denn so lange?????	↑	yes
2010-06-09 07:35:26	Christian Herold	HTC Desire	↑	+	out of order	Evo Learning im Hirschgarten. Ma eben Marketingkonzeption in der Sonne verfolgen. Dank O2 Surfstick mit Datenflat kein Problem!!	↑	yes
2010-06-15 10:55:40	Hansi Trompka	Nokia 123	↑	+	good product	...ganz toller service, telefonisch bekommt man keine auskunft, da muss man schon im shop vorbeischaun.......und ihr verkaufts telefone.........	↑	yes
2010-07-06 11:49:44	Dominik Weber	HTC Desire	↑	0	bad product	Unterstützt unsere Aktion für die CJD Projekttage und werdet CREW-Mitglied. Bei genügend Stimmen bekommen wir 10 000 €! Der Link: http://go.o2crew.de/cIHixp	↑	yes
2010-07-13 17:17:54	Ute Merz	Nokia 123	↑	+	out of order	Hallo o2 Crew, vielen Dank für diese tolle Aktion!! Ich gehöre zur Gewinnercrew und möchte euch darüber informieren, dass ihr unseren Namen falsch geschrieben habt: wir heißen CISV und nicht CISC. DANKE DANKE DANKE für diese Spende, die uns bei unserem Projekt sehr helfen wird!!	↑	yes
2010-08-17 13:03:55	Alice Bader	HTC Desire	↑	+	bad product	Echt nervig, dass man sich hier die Mühe macht seine Freunde einzuladen und die eigene Crew dann von Fremden überschwemmt wird.....	↑	yes
2010-08-17 13:13:53	Sven Reike	Nokia 123	↑	-	good product	Also ich fands spannend! :) Wer hat gewonnen?	↑	yes
2010-08-17 13:19:33	Stefan Göppel	HTC Desire	↑	-	how does it work	hola, wir haben es geschafft!! jetzt müssen wir nur noch das losglück haben. Wenn ihr uns zieht, dann habt Ihr auf jeden fall geballte Fußballfachkompetenz in Eurer Lounge :) ich bin schon ultra aufgeregt!!!	↑	yes

User: geiethos   Logout

Fig. 15.1 SocialCom monitoring demo for customer interaction management; this user interface was developed within the collaborative research project SocialCom funded by the German Federal Ministry of Economics and Technology

"out of order" or *"bad product"*) from a monitored social networking site (Facebook). Our tool provides additional information such as the customer's name, the product name mentioned in the request (e.g. *"HTC Desire"*), a short link to the corresponding product user guide (cf. manual), the tonality of the customer post (positive/+, neutral/0 or negative/-), the URL from where the message was retrieved and the time when it was posted.

Q *Is it particularly important that users be protected from making errors?*
A The agents do not have any possibilities to do the classification step on their own. They can only react on pre-classified messages in their inbox and forward them in case of incorrect assignment to the person in charge.

System Interfacing

Q *Is input coming from systems outside the proposed system?*
A Since our tool has established a connection with the monitored social networking site, consumer requests are coming as input stream into the system. Afterwards the classification and assignment steps will performed by the application itself.

Q *Is output going to systems outside the proposed system?*
A Our approach emulates an issue-tracking system delivering e-mails with Facebook posts to the corresponding person in charge at customer's. We therefore have to plug our system into a support ticket system.

Q *Are there restrictions on the format that have to be used for input?*
A For example, Facebook wall posts are represented as structured data that can easily retrieved from Facebook graph API. We simplify this data format before using it for extraction and classification purposes:

```
<thread id=1289 link="facebook.com/telekomhilft/foo/bar">
Tim Schroeter|200012|Das ist gut!
Jessica|200013|Nein!
</thread>
```

Performance Characteristics

Q *Are there any time constraints on the system?*
A Every *n* seconds (e.g. 10 s) consumer requests should be retrieved from the monitored social networking site.

Error Handling

Q *How should the system respond to input errors?*
A As input error we consider the website unavailability of the monitored social network. In this case, our application has to re-establish the connection to Facebook and retry to retrieve consumer posts. Furthermore, the contact centre agents will get status updates of the website availability.

System Modifications

Q *What parts of the system are likely candidates for later modification?*

A If the Facebook graph API changes, we will have to update the component collecting the customer requests. Moreover, the products can change in the telecommunication sector.

Q *What sorts of modifications are expected?*

A We expect modifications in configuration. Furthermore, upgrades will be necessary with respect to fluctuating (sector-dependant) vocabulary used for classification.

These system design issues are essential for the architecture of the application. We only discussed the most important questions because we started with a mock-up of a social network monitoring tool for customer interaction management by skipping non-functional requirements such as recoverability, security, backup, capacity, documentation and all the rest of it.

System Architecture

In Fig. 15.2, we illustrate the work flow of our system. Since customers first share their problems with a social networking community before directly addressing the company, the social networking site will be the interface between customer and company. For instance, Facebook users post on the wall of a telecommunication company messages concerning tariffs, technical malfunction or bugs of its products, positive and negative feedback (cf. step 1 in Fig. 15.2).

The collector should download every *n* seconds (e.g. 10 s) data from the monitored social networking site (cf. step 2 in Fig. 15.2). Above all, it should be possible to choose the social networking site, especially the business pages, to be monitored. This can be configured by updating the collector's settings. In order to retrieve data from Facebook, we use its graph API as described in section "Constraints". In step 3, customer messages will be stored in a database. After simplifying their structure (cf. *System Interfacing* in section "Constraints"), the requests have to be categorised by the classification module (cf. step 4 in Fig. 15.2). During the classification process, we assign both semantic and application/business tags (cf. section "Classification: Assignment to Business Tags") as features to the user posts before restoring them in a database (cf. step 5 in Fig. 15.2). According to the tags the messages are assigned to the corresponding business process in step 6. This *n* : 1 relationship is modelled in the contact centre interface before passing these messages as e-mail requests to the customer interaction management tool used in contact centres (cf. step 7 in Fig. 15.2). Finally, the pre-classified e-mails are automatically forwarded to the persons in charge of customer service and support.

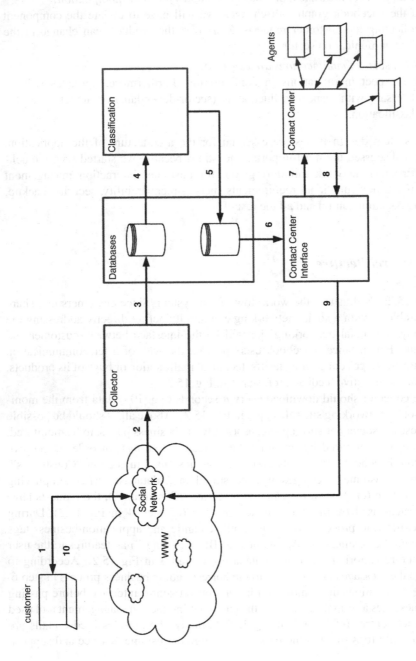

Fig. 15.2 System architecture: how the system is supposed to be

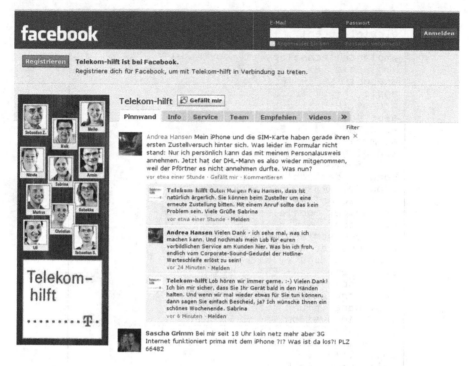

Fig. 15.3 Facebook wall for customer service and support provided by the German Telecom

Those agents reply to the client requests and their responses will be delivered via e-mail to the contact centre before being transformed to social network messages in step 8 and send back to the Facebook wall in step 9. Afterwards, the Facebook user can read his answer (cf. step 10 in Fig. 15.2).

In this section, we only provided a short overview of our system architecture which is described in more detail in later sections.

Linguistic Variation and Change in Social Networks

Before thinking about the classification approach we have to study the linguistic phenomena typically appearing in social communication. But there is one basic concept we have to discuss first: the notion of *social network sublanguage*.

Definition 15.1 (Social network sublanguage). Sublanguages are specialised language subsets which are distinguished by a special vocabulary and grammar from the general language [15,16]. With respect to social networks, a sublanguage is characterised by a certain number of phrases or a grammar and special vocabulary [10], e.g. *"Nokia ServicePoint"*.

```
alcatel,.N+HERSTELLER
alcatel-lucent,.N+HERSTELLER
altek,.N+HERSTELLER
ambiance technology,at mobile.N+HERSTELLER
amoisonic,.N+HERSTELLER
anycool,.N+HERSTELLER
apple,.N+HERSTELLER
archos,.N+HERSTELLER
asus computer,asus.N+HERSTELLER
asus,.N+HERSTELLER
at mobile,.N+HERSTELLER
audioline,.N+HERSTELLER
bang & olufsen,.N+HERSTELLER
beaucom deutschland,beaucom.N+HERSTELLER
beaucom,.N+HERSTELLER
bell technology,.N+HERSTELLER
bellpepper mobile,bellpepper.N+HERSTELLER
bellpepper,.N+HERSTELLER
benq deutschland,benq mobile.N+HERSTELLER
benq mobile,.N+HERSTELLER
benq,benq mobile,.N+HERSTELLER
benq-siemens,.N+HERSTELLER
blau mobilfunk,.N+HERSTELLER
bodyphone gmbh & co. kg,bodyphone.N+HERSTELLER
bodyphone,.N+HERSTELLER
bonac innovation,.N+HERSTELLER
bosch,.N+HERSTELLER
dancall,.N+HERSTELLER
dbtel,.N+HERSTELLER
dell,.N+HERSTELLER
deutsche telekom,t-com.N+HERSTELLER
```

Fig. 15.4 Sample instances of the attribute class *"manufacturer"* providing part-of-speech (N) and semantic (HERSTELLER) information; HERSTELLER is German for *"manufacturer"*

Sublanguage Analysis

Social network sublanguage occurs on the Facebook walls as well as on Twitter and other social networking sites. Regarding the Facebook pages, we try to discover relationships between clients and products, customers and technical problems, products and features that will be used for classification purposes.

```
# like(Person, Product)
# dislike(Person, Product)
# problem(Person, Product)
# wanttobuy(Person, Product)
```

But the variety of organisation-specific standard phrases (*frozen expressions*) and vocabulary that frequently emerge on Facebook walls are clustered into *attribute classes* during the training step of our system. For instance, the classes *manufacturer* (cf. Fig. 15.4), *brand name, mobile phone model* (cf. Fig. 15.5) and *mobile accessories* totally contain about 4,000 specialised words and phrases.

```
samsung drift,.N+HANDY_MODELL+SAMSUNG
i7110,samsung i7110.N+HANDY_MODELL+SAMSUNG
samsung i7110,.N+HANDY_MODELL+SAMSUNG
i7410,samsung i7410.N+HANDY_MODELL+SAMSUNG
samsung i7410,.N+HANDY_MODELL+SAMSUNG
i8910 hd,samsung i8910 hd.N+HANDY_MODELL+SAMSUNG
samsung i8910 hd,.N+HANDY_MODELL+SAMSUNG
impact,samsung impact.N+HANDY_MODELL+SAMSUNG
samsung impact,.N+HANDY_MODELL+SAMSUNG
impact b,samsung impact b.N+HANDY_MODELL+SAMSUNG
samsung impact b,.N+HANDY_MODELL+SAMSUNG
impact sf,samsung impact sf.N+HANDY_MODELL+SAMSUNG
samsung impact sf,.N+HANDY_MODELL+SAMSUNG
innov8 i8510,samsung innov8 i8510.N+HANDY_MODELL+SAMSUNG
samsung innov8 i8510,.N+HANDY_MODELL+SAMSUNG
jet 2gb,samsung jet 2gb.N+HANDY_MODELL+SAMSUNG
samsung jet 2gb,.N+HANDY_MODELL+SAMSUNG
jet 8gb,samsung jet 8gb.N+HANDY_MODELL+SAMSUNG
samsung jet 8gb,.N+HANDY_MODELL+SAMSUNG
```

Fig. 15.5 Sample instances of the attribute class *"mobile phone model"* providing part-of-speech (N) and semantic (HANDY_MODELL+SAMSUNG) information; HANDY_MODELL is German for *"mobile phone model"*. These examples show only Samsung mobile phones

There are more linguistic phenomena apart from domain-specific vocabulary we have to deal with when analysing social network communication such as orthographic variation, misspelling, creative grammar application, neologism (e.g. *SW flashung* instead of *SW flashing*), various product names (e.g. *Nokia Extrapower DC-11+N8, Nokia Extrapower DC-11, Nokia Extrapower N8*) and even capitalisation is ignored.

All attribute classes (cf. sample classes in Figs. 15.4 and 15.5) form closed semantic classes characterised by lexica of limited size. We created several specialised dictionaries for simple terms as well as for multi-word terms which can deal with a substantial part of the above-mentioned sublanguage and which conform to the DELA lexicon format [6, 14] and which are modelled as finite automata [21].

The convention of dictionary development according to the DELA format enables the use of local grammars [11, 12] within the LGPL (GNU Lesser General Public License) software Unitex [25]. This platform provides all linguistic tools necessary for the processing of big corpora and enables the efficient handling of electronic lexica. Additionally, the development of local grammars, represented by graph structures (cf. Figs. 15.6 and 15.7), is supported by a graphical development tool.

Sublanguage and Local Grammars

All relations outlined in the previous section form closed semantic classes characterised by lexica of limited size and a limited number of syntactic patterns. Hence,

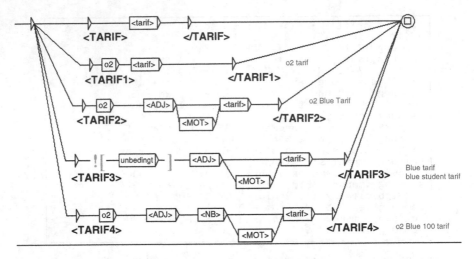

alten Tarif in den ⟨TARIF3⟩Blue Tarif⟨/TARIF3⟩ gewechselt.{S}
Der ⟨TARIF3⟩Blue Tarif⟨/TARIF3⟩ läuft 24 Monate.{S}
interessiere mich für den ⟨TARIF2⟩o2 Blue Tarif⟨/TARIF2⟩.{S}
ich habe Interesse an dem ⟨TARIF2⟩o2 blue flex Tarif⟨/TARIF2⟩.{S}
werde den ⟨TARIF2⟩O2 Blue Tarif⟨/TARIF2⟩ abschließen.{S}
welchen ⟨TARIF1⟩O2 Tarif⟨/TARIF1⟩ für Samsung Galaxy?{S}

Fig. 15.6 Local grammar for the recognition of mobile phone tariffs provided by the company O_2; this state transducer shows a regular expression used for the recognition of German mobile phone tariffs where ⟨NB⟩ stands for a numeric group, ⟨MOT⟩ for an alphabetic group and ⟨ADJ⟩ for an adjective listed in the lexicon for German; a sample output is shown below; moreover TARIF is German for *"tariff"*

we consider them and the following ones describing tonality as a sublanguage in the meaning of Harris [15].

```
# positive(Person, Phone, Content)
# positive(Person, Tariff, Content)
# neutral(Person, Phone, Content)
# neutral(Person, Tariff, Content)
# negative(Person, Phone, Content)
# negative(Person, Tariff, Content)
```

Hunston and Sinclair [17] showed that it is possible to consider local grammars as small sublanguages and therefore, for a given domain (here, telecommunication in social networks), it is possible to build large-scale local grammars covering at best the entire sublanguage.

Formally, local grammars are recursive transition networks [31]. The construction and manipulation of those are facilitated by the free software tool Unitex [25]. They are not intended to describe the entire grammar of a language, but they can be

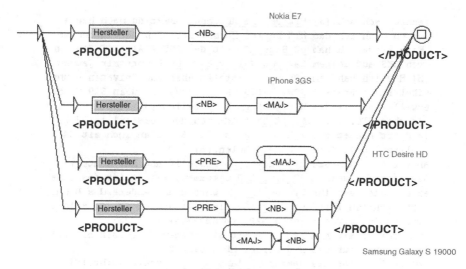

Fig. 15.7 Local grammar for the recognition of mobile phone models; ⟨NB⟩ recognises any sequence of digits; ⟨PRE⟩ recognises any sequence of letters that begins with an upper case letter; ⟨MAJ⟩ recognises any sequence of letters in upper case; "Hersteller" identifies manufacturers

successfully used to describe the syntax and vocabulary of linguistic phenomena related to a specialised domain [5]. In this context, they perfectly fit into the extraction process and enable us to restrict our analysis to the relevant facts.

From a technical point of view, local grammars are used in a cascading style. Each level of the cascade relies on the results of the previous level. The first levels enable us to identify and annotate simple entities (e.g. person names, products, tariffs) (Fig. 15.8).

The next levels in local grammar application broaden these entities so as to cover all the predicative relations above-mentioned (*like, dislike, problem, wanttobuy*).

Internal and External Indicators for Named Entity Recognition

Internal evidence is derived from within the sequence of words that comprise the name. (...) By contrast, external evidence is the classificatory criteria provided by the context in which a name appears. [22]

Others experimented with several lexicon sizes and discovered that a large comprehensive lexicon cannot improve considerably the precision or recall of a NER system [23]. Hence, we also pursue this strategy and compile the internal and external indicators into the corresponding attribute classes (Table 15.1). Moreover, the list of indicators is open-ended and managed within different files – a sublist per attribute class (e.g. *"manufacturer"* (cf. Fig. 15.4), *"brand name"*, *"mobile phone model"* (cf. Fig. 15.5) and *"mobile accessories"*. Some examples for external indicators are shown below:

```
iemlich schwach.{S} HTC Desire HD wann kommst du nach hause ;
rosten wenn ich das HTC Desire HD mit der o2 blue flat nehme
Eine Frage ich hab O2 Blue 100 mit der SMS FLAT iNET Flat ur
von MMS auf meinem Samsung Galaxy S I9000.Könnte mir jemand
{S} Hey ich hab ien iPhone 4 bestellt aber aus Privaten grünc
tikel Farbe Preis 1 SONY ERICSSON VIVAZ RUBIN rubin 319,00 EU
erweile überall das HTC Desire HD bestellen.{S}
ola über HTC... :-( Nokia N8 finde ich doch besser! ;-)[] [/]
ia Markt bietet das iPhone 4 jetzt für 579 € an auch mit 24 M
wollte ich mir ein iPhone 4 holen.{S}
ab vor 4 Wochen das HTC Desire HD bestellt und hab heute von
Simkarte für meinen O2 Blue 100 bekommen, leider ist das eine
er 6 Wochen auf ihr HTC Desire HD warten und andere das Handy
denten in den Tarif o2 Blue 100 Flex für Studenten wechseln!{
rung online mit dem iphone4??? warum???{S}
one schickt mir ein iPhone 4 mit sichtbaren Materialfehler.{S
igator auch für das HTC Desire HD geben?{S}
ndroid 2.2) für das Samsung Galaxy S I9000 von o2 gibt?{S}
Kundenbetreuer den o2 Dienst ACR kennt.{S}
:-({S} An alle die Samsung Galaxy S I 9000 haben bitte das r
```

Fig. 15.8 Mobile phone models recognised by the local grammar shown in Fig. 15.7

Table 15.1 Examples of external indicators for attribute classes

Attribute class	Vocabulary
Manufacturer	X *Handy* (X mobile phone; e.g. Nokia)
	X *Vertragshandy* (X contract phone; e.g. Motorola)
	X-*Vertrag läuft aus* (X contract coming to an end; e.g. Apple)
Mobile phone model	*Vertragshandy* X *defekt* (Contract phone X out of order)
	verschicke MMS mit meinem X (send MMS via X; e.g. Apple iPhone)
	kaufe mir ein X (buy an X; e.g. Samsung Galaxy)

A Necessary Machine Learning Stage

The relevance of the contextual analysis and, therefore, of the quality of the automatic extraction of telecommunication patterns out of customer requests, is all the more satisfactory as we have at our disposal large knowledge bases of lexical entries. Thus, the more instances that are present in the object classes, the more relevant the extractions are and the more rudimentary the contextual analyses necessary for disambiguation are.

However, the manual development of resources remains a very expensive process which does not fulfil all the constraints implied by the implementation of an industrial application. Therefore, the automatic acquisition of linguistic resources is a necessary stage. The notion of sublanguage [15, 16] opens up prospects that allow us to imagine a partial, if not complete, automation of the formalisation process.

Indeed, the closing property, as well as the semantic homogeneity of documents coming from a specific sublanguage, lead us to believe in the efficiency of machine learning methods. Riloff and Jones [28] and Grishman [10] explored this hypothesis and obtained promising results.

> The input to our algorithm is a set of unannotated training texts and a handful of 'seed' words for the semantic category of interest. [28]

At no time did Riloff and Jones [28] refer to the notion of sublanguage. Nevertheless, both the method (distributionalism) and the context (specialised discourse) remind us of the works by Harris [15, 16]. The work presented in their study relies on specialised corpora: Th description of corpora includes two sets: one is from Internet pages presenting companies and the other from newspaper articles about terrorist attacts. Both text collections were provided for the shared tasks during the last Message Understanding Conferences. The procedure comprises three steps: The first step relies on a small lexicon of domain-specific terms; all the noun phrases containing them are extracted. At the same time, this process applies a series of heuristics in order to abstract linguistic patterns generalising extracted phrases. Second, these patterns are applied to the training corpus and the most productive ones will be kept as extraction patterns. Finally, the extracted data is used to enrich the semantic lexicon and identify new phrases.

Within the framework of this study, we have considered a bootstrapping method, which is inspired from the procedures we have just mentioned, and that aim at the acquisition of both lexical entries and predicative relations.

Bootstrapping for Synonymic Predicate Extraction

For the recognition of synonymic relations related to initial verbs (e.g. *"mögen"/like*) we designed a method based on the iterative bootstrapping technique described by Gross [13]. The entire process of synonymic candidates extraction is quite complex and requires the enrichment of internal contexts by the detection of specific external contexts, and vice versa.

Classification via Local Grammars

Since we analyse Facebook wall posts in the telecommunication sector, we started to create a corpus of consumer requests by collecting messages around the topic *mobile phone*.

1 : Ich hab auch n ganzen Tag gewartet am Mittwoch :(Ein Tipp wann es heute losgeht für die Kinotickets in Stuttgart wäre supi! :D

2 : ich hab da mal noch ne frage zu morgen: wann is denn bei Linkin Park morgen einlass?!? 20 uhr - oder schon früher?!?

3 : ich hab den code für das a-ha konzert erst eben gelesen, tolle überraschung aber auf der seite steht es ist zu spät ....? :(

4 : Ich hab den ganzen Tag im Netz gesucht und außer eurem online angebot noch keinen Store in Gelsenkirchen und umgebung(Gladbeck , Bottrop , Herten) wo Ich mir Das HTC HD 7 Kaufen kann! Ab wann stehts denn in den Läden???

5 : ich hab den tarif "O2 Blue 100 Flex Online" und heute meine Immatrikulationsbestätigung abgeschickt. Die Frei-sms in alle Netzte, 120 Freiminuten, Flat ins o2 Netzt und Internetflat hab ich jedoch seitdem ich die Karte aktiviert habe oder??

6 : ich habe eine normale sim card, hätte aber gerne eine micro sim-card. kostet das etwas? wenn ja wieviel?

7 : Ich habe am 11.11.2010 telefonisch meinen Vertrag verlängert und ein iPhone im O2 Blue-Tarif bestellt. Leider habe ich seither nix mehr von Euch gehört. Tarifumstellung ist noch nicht erfolgt, sowie Vertragsverlängerung auch noch nicht. Auf der Hotline habe ich nach 30 Min. Wartezeit aufgelegt..... Das iPhone sollte spätestens Dienstag geliefert werden. Ich hoffe die Bestellung kam wirklich durch!

Fig. 15.9 Corpus sample consisting of customers requests obtained from O_2's Facebook wall

Training Data

In the absence of a reference corpus or any benchmark, we build a corpus containing about 73,000 words. These texts were gathered via the Facebook graph API, reduced to the customer messages and later manually labelled (Fig. 15.9).

Applying Local Grammars for Feature Extraction

We used linguistically motivated local grammars to describe telecommunication contexts of customer requests and to detect the product and tariff identifiers within these contexts. Local grammars [11, 12] enable the description of a local context and restrict the emergence of certain lexical or syntactical features to a window of predefined size. Thus, they avoid or reduce ambiguities that occur for a simple keyword search.

Feature Extraction

In order to apply these graphs (e.g. Figs. 15.6 and 15.7 amongst others), the clients' Facebook wall posts have to be passed through the following processing pipeline of the Unitex system:

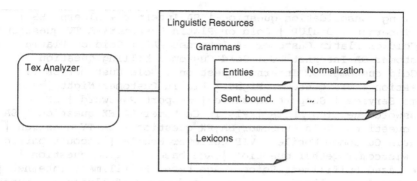

Fig. 15.10 Overview of Unitex' architecture

1. *Conversion*: Converts the text into Unicode (UTF-16-LE)
2. *Normalisation*: Normalises the special characters, white spaces and line breaks
3. *Sentence*: End of sentence detection
4. *Tokenisation*: Tokenises the text according to the alphabet of the investigated language
5. *Dictionary*: Performs a lexical analysis by comparing tokens to lexical entries and assigns to each word its possible grammatical categories
6. *Concordance*: Construct concordance or merge transducer output with original text

Unitex takes as input plain text in UTF-16-LE and gives as output a concordance or a merged text. Technically speaking, there is also detailed information available on the matches and their offsets. This information is usually used by the Unitex module concord but can be used in one's own program as well (Fig. 15.10).

The lexical analysis is directly followed by the step of information extraction via local grammars. Each piece of structured information is covered by different extraction units.[13] We created a system of local grammars which works iteratively and sometimes cascaded [9]. The cascaded grammars are executed with different priorities. For example, we developed local grammars to extract job descriptions with eight levels of priority. The graphs of level $n + 1$ are only applied if the grammars of level n with higher priority generate no recall.

The main task of feature extraction is to normalize the extracted sequences and to eliminate duplicates as well as incompletely recognised units. Because sequences are recognised simultaneously by alternative paths of the graphs that work as annotation transducers a decision on the match strategy had to be made. As results on test data have shown that the longest match strategy delivered the best performance, we decided to use it.

---

[13] Among them are, for example, person, product, tariff, mobile phone model, and manufacturer.

---

billing consolidation question | SA Internet + Altern. BB |
SA Internet + DialUP | Gold or Platin Customer SA TV question
| Gold or Platin Customer SA Internet MAC | Gold or Platin
Customer SA Internet PC | Gold Customer billing question
| Gold customer SF Internet question | Gold Customer SF TV
question | VIP Customer Night | Platin Customer Night |
Home Service | Support Password | Support Password | SF
Password question ALLIP | Platin Customer SA FX question | SA
FX question | Gold Customer SA FX question | SA TV question |
Platin Customer Mobile | VIP Customer Mobile | account barred
| Swisscom Together question | Age based Billing question |
Age based Fulfillment Voice | Age based Fulfillment Internet |
Age based Fulfillment TV | Age based any Fulfillment | Support
Password | SA question | SA Equipment | SA Internet MAC |
SA question | any SF question | Gold Customer SF question
| SF question | SF question + TV customer | Gold customer
SF FX question | SF FX question | SF Internet question | SF
TV question | high churn risk | SF question | FTTH billing
question | Senior customer Wline | billing question | Case
Assurance | Case ONP | Case Saver Desk | Case Move | Case DSL
- not new customer | Case DSL Activation | Case TV - not
new customer | Case TV activation | Case Mutation FX | Case
Carrier Preselection | Case Abuse | SF question | No Input on
IVR | Support Password

Fig. 15.11 Sample set of semantic tags used by contact centre agents at *Swisscom*

Feature Selection

By selecting the appropriate set of features (*semantic tags*), we can reach an accurate classification.

Definition 15.2 (Semantic tag). Keywords used for tagging the content of a message. There is usually more than one semantic tag belonging to a customer request specifying his concern.

Furthermore, semantic tags are totally independent from business processes. The assignment of this $n : 1$ relationship will be done during the classification step. Therefore, there is no need to update semantic tags (Fig. 15.11). We distinguish between semantic and application tags. Whereas semantic tags are rather generic, application tags represent special business processes. Thus, we also call them business tags.

Classification: Assignment to Business Tags

The retrieved feature value sets are then fed into a classification algorithm that provides a *first decision* on the basis of weighted features as for whether a customer message demands an answer (in case of requests) or not (in case of recommendations). In the next step, our classification is not binary any more.

By adapting the algorithm of Lee [20, p. 31] originally used for business website classification, we can set a threshold per weighted feature to decide if a customer request has to be categorised as, for example, "technical service", "billing", "shipping" or "marketing" problem. The number of business tags or classes respectively depend on the variety of business processes the company has to deal with.

The assignment of messages to business tags is a $n : 1$ relationship because only one agent should be responsible and reply to this request. Of course, persons in charge of customer service and support will answer many requests per day. That is why no double assignment is allowed: No message will be integrated in more than one business process because clients should get only one reliable answer instead of two contradictory statements.

Discussion on Linguistic Approaches and Modularity

The linguistic approach, also called knowledge-based extraction, is based on the development of grammars, and requires the combination of an introspective approach and a methodology based on a corpus, more precisely a specialised corpus. This type of work, however, requires much time and effort as the process is iterative. Each rule must be tested and debugged many times. In addition, the performance of the system is highly dependent on the linguist responsible for its development.

While it is clear by now that we cannot replace the linguist with a machine without compromising the quality of the language description, the machine can help at different levels in the work of formalisation to automate or simply facilitate the process. Thus, Yangarber and Grishman [32] describe the operation of a graphical user-interface – PET – for semi-automatic knowledge acquisition. Based on examples of events and a description of informational structures expected, PET creates the appropriate pattern to achieve the extraction. It also suggests some generalisations to increase the coverage. This idea of semi-automatic acquisition was also considered in [7, 26] and [24].

In the context of a monolithic analysis, this process could not be used. The linguistic knowledge that needs to be integrated into the extraction patterns is too vast and the resulting inferences and generalisations are too complex to be precise. PROTEUS [32], the extractor for which PET was developed, shows a modular architecture, separating general (invariant) and specialised (domain-dependent) knowledge. In this way, the formalisation of the extraction patterns (specialised knowledge) is easier because it does not have to cope with general lexical and syntactic considerations. In this way, PET works with a much smaller number of items which are more easily manipulated.

If we do not consider other approaches to semi-automatically acquire extraction patterns, the central principle of our studies will be modularity, which is often called the linguistic aspect in other related work [2, 18, 19].

For a long time, a clear priority was given to statistical methods, certainly due to their apparent automatism. Depending on the circumstances of the acquisition, this automatism may nevertheless be very tedious. Appelt and Israel [1] describe two such situations that can arise during the development of an extractor for named entities. If the case sensitivity – for this system the original specification – is reversed, a statistical method will only have to reapply its learning algorithm to its training corpus with the capitalisation removed. On the other hand, the knowledge-based approach will be forced to rewrite its rules. The first situation, hence, favours a statistical approach, but if the scope of the system needs to be extended, a linguistic approach will only have to extend the coverage of its grammar; as opposed to statistical methods which will have to build a new training corpus.

In recent years, computational linguistics has begun to consider a potential integration of statistical and linguistic solutions to profit from the benefits of both. In the area of information extraction, this idea results in the combination of the descriptive power of linguistic solutions and the convenience of statistical acquisition. Note that other recent developments [8] already embody this concept.

First Prototype

Working in conjunction with our partner organisation who has years of experience in prototyping, we established the first prototype shown in Fig. 15.12. It provides the same functionalities as our mock-up in Fig. 15.1.

Conclusions and Directions for Future Research

In this chapter, we described a new technical service dealing with the integration of social networking channels into customer interaction management tools. The idea of classifying and evaluating public comments addressed to German companies is based on an existing demand. In order to maintain an active Facebook wall, the consumer posts have to be categorised and then automatically assigned to the corresponding business processes represented by the person in charge of customer service and support. This service works like an issue tracking system sending e-mails to the corresponding agents. That way, customer interaction management systems which are already used to e-mail communication can benefit of social networking. This allows the company to record two-sided communication for customer relationship management and the agent's response will be delivered through consumer's favourite social medium.

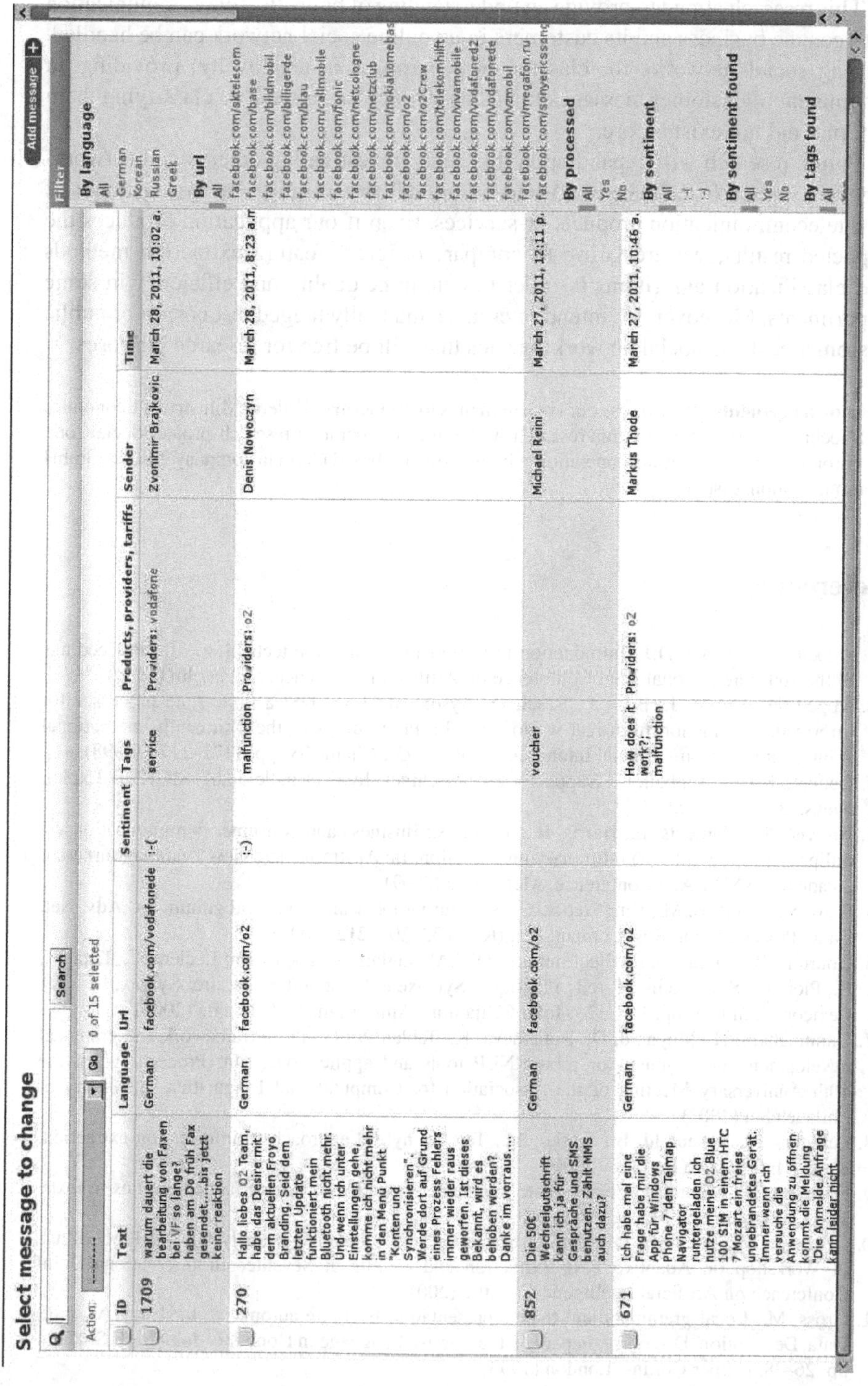

Select message to change

Action: —————— [Go]   0 of 15 selected   [Search]   Add message [+]   Filter

ID	Text	Language	Url	Sentiment	Tags	Products, providers, tariffs	Sender	Time
1709	warum dauert die bearbeitung von Faxen bei VF so lange? haben am Do früh Fax gesendet....bis jetzt keine reaktion	German	facebook.com/vodafonede	:-(	service	Providers: vodafone	Zvonimir Brajkovic	March 28, 2011, 10:02 a.
270	Hallo liebes O2 Team, habe das Desire mit dem aktuellen Froyo Branding. Seid dem letzten Update funktioniert mein Bluetooth nicht mehr. Und wenn ich unter Einstellungen gehe, komme ich nicht mehr in den Menü Punkt "Konten und Synchronisieren". Werde dort auf Grund eines Prozess Fehlers immer wieder raus geworfen. Ist dieses Bekannt, wird es behoben werden? Danke im verraus....	German	facebook.com/o2	:-)	malfunction	Providers: o2	Denis Nowoczyn	March 28, 2011, 8:23 a.m
852	Die 50€ Wechselgutschrift kann ich ja für Gespräche und SMS benutzen. Zählt MMS auch dazu?	German	facebook.com/o2		voucher		Michael Reini	March 27, 2011, 12:11 p.
671	Ich habe mal eine Frage habe mir die App für Windows Phone 7 den Telmap Navigator runtergeladen ich nutze meine O2 Blue 100 SIM in einem HTC 7 Mozart ein freies ungebrandetes Gerät. Immer wenn ich versuche die Anwendung zu öffnen kommt die Meldung "Die Anmelde Anfrage kann leider nicht	German	facebook.com/o2		How does it work?; malfunction	Providers: o2	Markus Thode	March 27, 2011, 10:46 a.

By language
All
German
Korean
Russian
Greek

By url
All
facebook.com/aktelcom
facebook.com/base
facebook.com/bildmobil
facebook.com/billigerde
facebook.com/blau
facebook.com/callmobile
facebook.com/fonic
facebook.com/netzcologne
facebook.com/netzclub
facebook.com/nokiahomebas
facebook.com/o2
facebook.com/o2Crew
facebook.com/telekomhilft
facebook.com/vvamobile
facebook.com/vodafoned2
facebook.com/vodafonede
facebook.com/vzmobil
facebook.com/megafon.ru
facebook.com/sonyericsssnc

By processed
All
Yes
No

By sentiment
All

By sentiment found
All
Yes
No

By tags found
All

Fig. 15.12   First prototype of a social network monitoring tool for customer interaction management

This research aimed to provide an understanding of how effective communication between the business and its customers in an online social network can be handled. Mining social networks for classification purposes is no novelty; providing an assignment of customer messages to business processes instead of classifying them in topics did not exist before.

Future research will expand upon this study, investigating other social networking sites (apart from Facebook) and additional organisations across a range of non-telecommunication products or services. Even if our application produces the expected results, we are going to compare different feature extraction methods and classification algorithms in order to determine quality and efficiency in some experiments. Moreover, we intend to create a manually tagged test corpus of public customer posts on social networking sites that will be free for research purposes.

Acknowledgements We express our sincere thanks to the German Federal Ministry of Economics and Technology for financing this research within the collaborative research project SocialCom. Our prototype was created in cooperation with the Munich-based German company Telenet GmbH Kommunikationssysteme.

References

1. Appelt, D.E., Israel, D.J.: Introduction to information extraction technology. In: Proceedings of the 16th International Joint Conference on Artificial Intelligence, Stockholm (1999)
2. Appelt, D., Hobbs, J., Bear, J., Israel, D., Tyson, M.: FASTUS: a finite-state processor for information extraction from real-world text. In: Proceedings of the Thirteenth International Joint Conference on Artificial Intelligence (IJCAI-93), Chambéry, pp. 1172–1178 (1993)
3. Bennett, K.P., Campbell, C.: Support vector machines: hype or hallelujah? SIGKDD Explor. Newsl. **2**, 1–13 (2000)
4. Browne, R., Clements, E., Harris, R., Baxter, S.: Business and consumer communication via online social networks: a preliminary investigation. In: Australian and New Zealand Marketing Academy (ANZMAC) Conference, Melbourne (2009)
5. Bsiri, S., Geierhos, M., Ringlstetter, C.: Structuring job search via local grammars. Adv. Nat. Lang. Process. Appl. Res. Comput. Sci. (RCS) **33**, 201–212 (2008)
6. Courtois, B.: Dictionnaires électroniques DELAF anglais et français. In: Leclère, C., Laporte, E., Piot, M., Silberztein, M. (eds.) Lexique, Syntaxe et Lexique-Grammaire; Syntax, Lexis & Lexicon-Grammar, pp. 113–123. John Benjamins, Amsterdam/Philadelphia (2004)
7. Cunningham, H., Maynard, D., Bontcheva, K., Tablan, V.: GATE: a framework and graphical development environment for robust NLP tools and applications. In: Proceedings of the 40th Anniversary Meeting of the Association for Computational Linguistics, University of Philadelphia (2002)
8. Feldman, R., Rosenfeld, B., Fresko, M.: Teg – a hybrid approach to information extraction. Knowl. Inf. Syst. **9**(1), 1–18 (2006)
9. Friburger, N., Maurel, D.: Finite-state transducer cascades to extract named entities in texts. Theor. Comput. Sci. **313**, 93–104 (2004)
10. Grishman, R.: Adaptive information extraction and sublanguage analysis. In: Proceedings of Workshop on Adaptive Text Extraction and Mining at Seventeenth International Joint Conference on Artificial Intelligence, Seattle (2001)
11. Gross, M.: Local grammars and their representation by finite automata. In: Hoey, M. (ed.) Data, Description, Discourse, Papers on the English Language in Honour of John McH Sinclair, pp. 26–38. Harper-Collins, London (1993)

12. Gross, M.: The construction of local grammars. In: Roche, E., Schabes, Y. (eds.) Finite-State Language Processing, pp. 329–354. MIT Press, Cambridge (1997)
13. Gross, M.: A bootstrap method for constructing local grammars. In: Contemporary Mathematics: Proceedings of the Symposium, University of Belgrad, Belgrad, pp. 229–250 (1999)
14. Guenthner, F.: Electronic Lexica and Corpora Research at CIS. Int. J. Corpus Linguist. 1(2), 287–301 (1996)
15. Harris, Z.S.: Mathematical structures of language. Intersci. Tracts Pure Appl. Math. 21, 152–156 (1968)
16. Harris, Z.S.: Language and information. Bampton Lect. Am. 28, 33–56 (1988)
17. Hunston, S., Sinclair, J.: A local grammar of evaluation. In: Hunston, S., Thompson, G. (eds.) Evaluation in Text: Authorial Stance and the Construction of Discourse, pp. 74–101. Oxford University Press, Oxford (2000)
18. Jacobs, P.S., Rau, L.F.: The GE NLToolset: a software foundation for intelligent text processing. In: Proceedings of the 13th International Conference on Computational Linguistics, Helsinki, pp. 373–375 (1990)
19. Jacobs, P.S., Krupka, G., Rau, L., Mauldin, M., Mitamura, T., Kitani, T., Sider, I., Childs, L.: GE-CMU: Description of the SHOGUN system used for MUC-5. In: Proceedings of the Fifth Message Understanding Conference, Baltimore, pp. 109–120 (2001)
20. Lee, Y.S.: Website-Klassifikation und Informationsextraktion aus Informationsseiten einer Firmenwebsite. Ph.D. thesis, Ludwig-Maximilians-Universität München (2008)
21. Maurel, D., Guenthner, F.: Automata and Dictionaries. Texts in Computing Science, vol. 6. King's College Publications, London (2006)
22. McDonald, D.: Internal and external evidence in the identification and semantic categorization of proper names. In: Boguraev, B., Pustejovsky, J. (eds.) Corpus Processing for Lexical Acquisition, pp. 21–39. MIT Press, Cambridge (1996)
23. Mikheev, A., Moens, M., Grover, C.: Named entity recognition without gazetteers. In: Proceedings of the Ninth Conference of the European Chapter of the Association for Computational Linguistics, Bergen, pp. 1–8 (1999)
24. Patwardhan, S., Riloff, E.: Learning domain-specific information extraction patterns from the web. In: IEBeyondDoc '06: Proceedings of the Workshop on Information Extraction Beyond the Document, pp. 66–73. Association for Computational Linguistics, Morristown (2006)
25. Paumier, S.: Unitex user manual 2.1 (2010). http://igm.univ-mlv.fr/~unitex/UnitexManual2.1.pdf
26. Poibeau, T.: Extraction d'information: du texte brut au web sémantique. Hermès, Paris (2003)
27. Rennie, J.D.M., Teevan, J., Karger, D.R.: Tackling the poor assumptions of Naive Bayes text classifiers. In: Proceedings of the Twentieth International Conference on Machine Learning, Washington, pp. 616–623 (2003)
28. Riloff, E., Jones, R.: Learning dictionaries for information extraction by multi-level bootstrapping. In: Proceedings of the 16th National Conference on Artificial Intelligence (AAAI-1999), Orlando, pp. 474–479 (1999)
29. Rish, I.: An empirical study of the Naive Bayes classifier. In: IJCAI-01 Workshop on "Empirical Methods in AI". Seattle, Washington, USA (2001)
30. Steinwart, I., Christmann, A.: Support Vector Machines. Information Science and Statistics. Springer, New York (2008)
31. Woods, W.A.: Transition network grammars for natural language analysis. Commun. ACM. 13(10), 591–606 (1970)
32. Yangarber, R., Grishman, R.: NYU: description of the proteus/PET system as used for MUC-7 ST. In: Proceedings of the Seventh Message Understanding Conference. Fairfax, VA, USA (1998)
33. Yoon, D., Choi, S.M., Sohn, D.: Building customer relationships in an electronic age: the role of interactivity of e-commerce web sites. Psychol. Mark. 25, 602–618 (2008)

Chapter 16
Real Emotions for Simulated Social Networks

Pietro Cipresso, Luigi Sellitti, Nadia El Assawy, Federica Galli, Anna Balgera, Jean Marie Dembele, Marco Villamira, and Giuseppe Riva

Abstract In this study we analyzed how to consider real emotions in complex networks. The main idea is to understand subjects' behaviors in specific situations, such as social network sites navigation, to use these information in modeling complex phenomena. We suggest the use of agent-based models, since this is a flexible and powerful tool in complex systems modeling; moreover such models are able to include behavioral cues for heterogeneous agents: this is an important property above all considering the study of networked agents representing subjects and relationships.

To have a precise idea about the subjects' behavior during social network site navigation, we used wearable biosensors in an experiment with 28 subjects to assess cardiorespiratory aspects (using a belt respiration sensor and a electrocardiogram), and facial cues (using two facial electromyography sensors). Subjects showed an

P. Cipresso (✉)
Applied Technology for Neuro-Psychology Lab, IRCCS Istituto Auxologico Italiano,
Via Pellizza da Volpedo 41, 20149 Milan, Italy
e-mail: p.cipresso@auxologico.it

L. Sellitti • N. El Assawy • F. Galli
Division of Neurology and Neurorehabilitation, San Giuseppe Hospital, IRCCS Istituto
Auxologico Italiano, Piancavallo (VB), Italy
e-mail: l.sellitti@auxologico.it; nadiaea@tiscali.it; f.galli@auxologico.it

A. Balgera • M. Villamira
IULM University, Via Carlo Bo, 8, 20143 Milan, Italy
e-mail: anna.balgera@iulm.it; marco.villamira@iulm.it

J.M. Dembele
Université Cheikh Anta Diop, Dakar, Republic of Senegal
e-mail: dembele@ird.sn

G. Riva
Psychology Department, Catholic University of Milan, Italy, Largo Gemelli, 1, 20123 Milan, Italy
e-mail: giuseppe.riva@unicatt.it

A. Abraham and A.-E. Hassanien (eds.), *Computational Social Networks: Tools,*   391
Perspectives and Applications, DOI 10.1007/978-1-4471-4048-1_16,
© Springer-Verlag London 2012

optimal experience during navigation and this information gave us the chance to discuss an example of information diffusion using both a mathematical model and an agent-based model.

Introduction

Emotions exist in human beings and cover a main, relevant portion on the processes of attention/perception, motivation, decision making (aware and unaware), and behavior (aware and unaware).

Emotions are also observed in some animals, but there is heated debate concerning the level of evolution at which we can speak about emotions (insects, mammiferous, etc.); as a general rule, it seems that the "weight" of emotions in determining behavior is raised with the evolution of the species [7, 15, 22, 24].

From evolutionary and utilitaristic standpoints, it can be said that, if a feature (to have emotions and feelings, which are, by definition, different from rationality and logic) remains and really develops during species evolution, this means that this feature is useful for the survival and success of that species, otherwise: the feature would have disappeared (or, at least, been reduced) or the species would be extinct [20, 32, 42].

Social networking sites such as Facebook are becoming relevant in many aspects of communication, interaction, human behavior, and even personality [14, 17, 18, 29, 30, 33, 43, 44]. In order to understand subjects' emotions during navigation in social networking sites, we did an experiment on 28 healthy subjects using biosensors to evaluate affective states during such navigation. This approach give us a deeper idea of subjects' states in a more objective way than just ask them. We tried to verify the hypothesis that Facebook navigation make users engaged and, in particular, we compared this states with Relax and Stress states, as suggested in literature [26].

The idea is to extract information about the subjects' behavior, based on objective parameter. Once obtained such "behavioral parameters" related to Facebook use, it is possible to create mathematical model to foreseen simple social behavior and diffusion. A first step is to study diffusion processes through social networking sites using the affective states information to create a set of "simple behavioral rules" in an interactional complex system model.

Emotions in Real Social Networks

In this chapter we will analyze the use of social networks in a group of subjects. In particular Psychophysiological reaction during free navigation in the Facebook website are recorded and post-analyzed. Results from this analysis will be useful to understand subjects' behaviors during Facebook navigation.

Fig. 16.1 The affective
space, based on Lang [19]

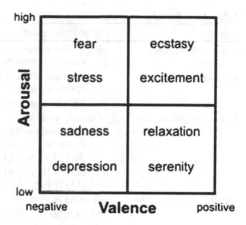

Psychophysiology and Affective States

One of the most used methods in order to identify affective states in subjects during
an experimental session, is consider two dimensions of "activation": *physiological
arousal* and *emotional valence*. In Fig. 16.1 an intuitive identification of affective
states based on these two dimensions.

These activation can be accurate measured through biosensors, obtaining signals
that can give many information after a signal processing procedure that requires
many mathematical and computational techniques. Briefly, *physiological arousal*
can be measured using Electroencephalogram (EEG), Galvanic Skin Response
(GSR), Electrocardiogram (ECG), Pulip Dilation (PD) and Respiration signal
(RSP); from the other side *emotional valence* can be measured through EEG,
self-reports, facial expression identification, eye-blinks, eye-blink startle, and facial
EMG corrugator and/or zygomatic (Table 16.1).

Cardio-respiratory activity is monitored to evaluate both voluntary and autonomic effect of respiration on heart rate in both physical and virtual environment
interactions, analyzing both R-R interval (from electrocardiogram) and respiration
(from chest strip sensor) and their interaction. Furthermore standard HRV spectral
methods indexes and akin can be used to evaluate the autonomic nervous system
response [1, 28] (Fig. 16.2).

Spectral analysis can be performed by means of spectral methods with custom
software. The rhythms will be classified as very low frequency (VLF, <0.04 Hz),
low-frequency (LF, from 0.04 to 0.15 Hz) and high frequency (HF, from 0.15 to
0.5 Hz) oscillations [1, 38] (Fig. 16.3).

Moreover the quantification of respiratory sinus arrhythmia (RSA) provides
information about the mechanisms involved in respiratory coupling [25].

Table 16.1 Signal processing

Signal	Signal processing
Electrocardiogram (ECG) Respiration	HRV = heart rate variability; HF = high frequency; LF = low frequency; PNN50 = percentage of successive normal interbeat intervals differing by at least 50s (correlated with HF HRV); SDNN = standard deviation of normal-to-normal beats; RSA = respiratory sinus arrhythmia.
Electroencephalogram (EEG)	Cross-spectral analysis and asymmetry analysis. Matrixes can be computed for bands delta (2–3.5 Hz), theta (4–7.5 Hz), alpha1 (8–10 Hz), alpha2 (10–12), combined alpha 1 and alpha 2 (8–12 Hz), beta1 (12–16 Hz), beta2 (16–20 Hz), beta3 (20–24 Hz), beta4 (24–28 Hz), beta5 (28–32 Hz), low beta (13–21 Hz), high beta (22–32 Hz) and global beta (13–32 Hz).
Electro dermal activity	Number of response; Mean value of GSR; Amplitude of response; Rising time of response; Energy of response.
Electromyography	Double-threshold detection; Wavelet Transform; Wigner-Ville distribution; Choi-Williams method.
Eye-tracker	Pupil dilation Gazes Eye-blinks

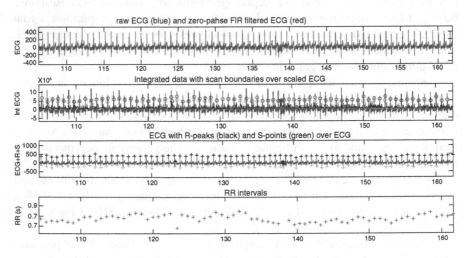

Fig. 16.2 Fast Fourier transform filtering and general peaks detection

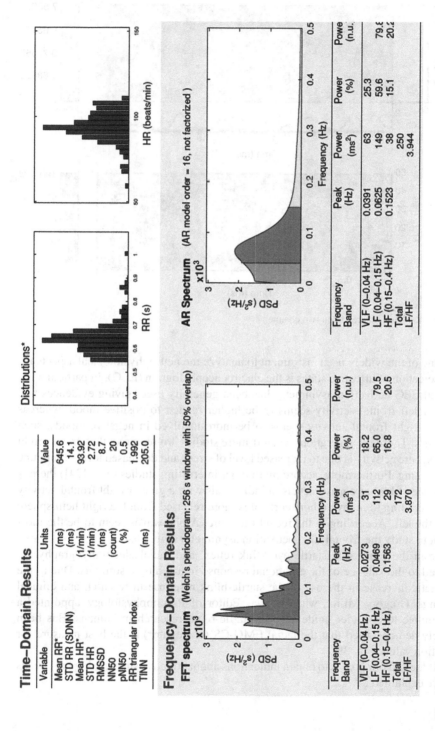

Fig. 16.3 Heart rate variability (*HRV*) analysis

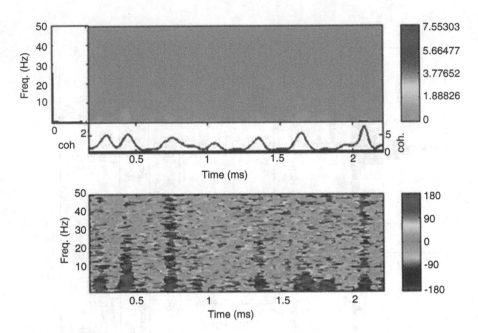

Fig. 16.4 Phase coherence on two channel

One of the widely used instrument to analyze the neurophysiological aspects for the detection of affective states is the electroencephalogram (EEG). In particular the frontal EEG activation asymmetry has been generally used, giving evidences that greater left frontal activity seems to be higher related to positive mood, whereas greater right frontal activity seems to be more involved in negative moods, such us stress. There are indications, even if more studies are required, that greater right hemisphere activity is due to increased level of stress and decreased level of immune functioning. Furthermore, according to other interesting studies (e.g., [24]) there is evidence of higher cortisol levels in individuals with a greater right frontal activity and according to many authors cortisol is more released from the right hemisphere than the left. According to the recent literature, Alpha waves seem to be the most adapt to study the frontal EEG activation asymmetry (Fig. 16.4).

From the other side startle eye-blink reflex, and facial electromyography are related to the valence of the emotional response induced by a stimulus. Due to the dramatic increase in the use of the startle-blink response in research and clinical settings, Gregory Miller, when he was Editor of Psychophysiology, appointed a committee to consider guidelines for startle-blink research in humans. Has been widely demonstrated that the facial EMG-CS (corrugator) is the best measure for emotion valence [4, 39].

At the end our goal is to obtain indications about affective states, using the signals above explained .

To compute spectral analysis, let consider $f(t)$ on $(-\infty, +\infty)$, with a nucleus:

$$k(p, x) = k(\lambda, t) = e^{-i\lambda t} \qquad (16.1)$$

where $1/i = -i$ is imaginary unity and λ is angular frequency. doing the transformation above, we will get

$$F(x) = \int_{-\infty}^{\infty} f(x)e^{-i\lambda t} dt \qquad (16.2)$$

if the integral exists for each value of λ, $F(x)$ is said Fourier transform.

Of course for each direct transform exists an inverse one $F(t) \rightarrow f(t)$. This is obtained through the following integral

$$f(t) = \frac{1}{2\pi} \int_{-\infty}^{\infty} F(\lambda) e^{i\lambda t} d\lambda \qquad (16.3)$$

said inverse Fourier Transform.

Emotions in Facebook

In order to evaluate affective states of subjects during Facebook navigation, we prepared a psychophysiological setting to perform an experimental session. Our hypothesis is that Facebook have an activating effect on subjects, in term of physiological arousal, but we also suppose that subjects have a positive emotional valence. According to Lang model (see Fig. 16.1) this would configure the subjects in a state of ecstasy/excitement. In recent researches [13, 35] has been widely demonstrated that this situation represents an optimal experience for the subjects and this would be one of the reasons for which users continue to use Facebook.

Materials and Methods

Subjects

Twenty-eight healthy subjects (16 females and 12 males) constituted the participants, with ages between 19 and 55, with an average of 29. They were all volunteers from Ospedale San Giuseppe of Piancavallo (VB), recruited among the hospital staff (nurse, guardian, doctors, . . .). Exclusion criteria were related to the states of their cardiac, eye, mental and psychological health. They were requested not drink caffeine or alcohol and not to smoke prior to the experimental test to avoid any effects of these substances on the central autonomic nervous system.

Procedures

Subjects who met the experimental criteria were contacted via email and/or telephone to schedule a meeting at the Neurophysiology Laboratory, located in the Hospital at the Department of Neurology. They were welcomed by a technical specialized in neurophysiologist and a physician, who assisted them for the duration of all laboratory sessions. The experimenter was instructed to maintain a neutral voice tone and a neutral behavior while the subjects were being exposed to experimental stimuli. When they arrived at the Neurophysiology Laboratory, the participants were asked to sit down in front of a computer, and they were told about the general goals of the research investigation, the procedures to be used, and the concerns for study involvement. All subjects were required to sign a release form. While explaining the broad function of electrodes, the subjects were prepared in order to collect the psychophysiological indexes.

Procedure

The subjects were asked to relax for 5 min in front of a monitor showing panorama slide shows with a soft music in order to help them in the relaxing exercise. According to literature a relaxing session at the beginning of the experimental session can substitute the standard baseline [26]. After this session the subjects were asked to log in to Facebook and freely navigate for 5 min with the PC in front of them. Once finished the 5 min [26] of Facebook navigation the Subjects were asked to execute a Stroop task [34, 37, 45], this cognitive task give us a reference systems for the cognitive stress evaluation.

At the end of the experimental session, the experimenter helped subjects in removing all electrodes and patches, while explaining the scientific rationale for the use of the stimuli and the aims of the experiment. No further meeting were scheduled.

Every recording was marked through a synchronization algorithm [8] realized (by using Matlab 7.2 – The Mathworks, Inc.; Natick, MA) for the alignment of the stimulus with all the psychophysiological signals. To improve the precision of such algorithm the Subjects was asked to eye-blink rapidly five times before each stimulus; using electrodes near the eyes (EOG, namely Electrooculogram) connected to all other biosensors, this operation guarantee a precision of 1/100 of second and this allow a better analysis and success of experiment.

Once extracted, all biosignals were worked in Matlab and branched in three category: Relax (R), Facebook (F), and Stress (S). These three categories are the best we can use, according to Lang model, in order to identifying the affective state most related to Facebook use. In fact Relax and Stress sessions represents a sort of extreme measures of physiological arousal (the minimum with relax and the maximum with the stress). In such way, adding the information of emotional valence, we can try to identify better the users' state during Facebook navigation.

Computationally, each category contain all psychophysiological signals of that session and can be processed for heart rate variability (HRV) analysis and other signal processing procedure in order to extract a series of index for the statistical analysis [38].

Measurement of the Physiological Signals

The responses of the central and peripheral nervous system were measured by means of ECG (electrocardiogram), two facial EMG (electromyography): corrugator and zygomatic, EOG (electrooculogram), and RSP (chest respiration). Signals were acquired by means of a Polisomno device certified for medical use. Then, the signals were processed with custom software developed using Matlab, and SPSS v. 17.0 to compute the statistical analyses. The sampling frequency for measuring the physiological signals was set at 256 Hz (every 3.90625 ms).

Data Analysis

Since this study implicated many measures involved in psychophysiological mechanisms, we performed a principal component analysis (PCA) to decrease the number of dependent variables. We used a Varimax rotation method with Kaiser Normalization (SPSS v. 17).

Analyzing Rotated Component Matrix (rotation converged in five iterations), we had a reduced number of factors. Actually analyses performed with an higher number of variables reveled a redundancy in results, above all for cardiovascular indexes. The reason of such result is that many cardiorespiratory patterns reflect similar conditions in subjects and thus calculating different kind of indexes we are actually considering the same phenomenon and its representation.

Results

We compared the following indexes for the three conditions: HR (heart rate), Max NN, Min NN, Range, Mean NN, Median NN, Average HR, SDNN, SD of delta NN, Ratio, RMSSD, NN50, Spectral intervals, Mean spectrum, NN, Total power, VLF, LF, HF, LF/HF. RM vs FM vs SM. This index showed a statistical significance in the within-subjects design. The results of a repeated measure ANOVA gave a statistical significance for most of the indexes. Moreover, a discriminant analysis showed that 81.8% of groups classify correctly (according to Lambda Wilks, $p < .001$). We are interested in discriminant analysis because this is our starting point in order to build a classifier based on fuzzy rules or neural networks, as showed in Fig. 16.5. In fact if it is possible to discriminate among affective states, then it is possible to identify the dynamic of variation during experiment and could be possible to build a simulated system including both artificial agents and real human being interacting cotemporary to better study computationally social networks.

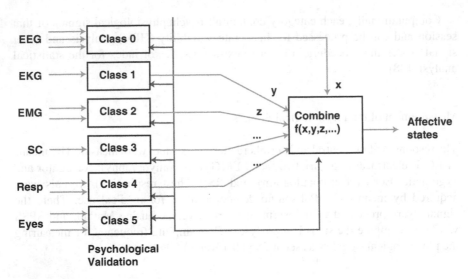

Fig. 16.5 From psychophysiological signals to affective state definition. The combination is generally calculated with fuzzy system, neural networks, and support vector machines [31]

Following some graphics to show the general trend. In Fig. 16.6 we can see that heart rate is moderate in relax session and accelerated in stress session. Thus, as expected in exiting, engaging or stressful situations the heart rate increase, and this justify the middle position of Facebook session.

In Figs. 16.7 and 16.8 we are considering two cardiovascular indexes: NN50 is a time related index, and LF/HF is a spectral index (related to sympathovagal balance). Both this indexes are related to stress level: with higher stress we expect lower NN50 and higher LF/HF.

Discussion

A greater physiological arousal in the subjects during Facebook navigation, is evident (see for example HR index in Fig. 16.6). According to Lang model (see Fig. 16.1), this higher physiological arousal during the navigation could reflect a fear/stress or an ecstasy/excitement, depending on emotional valence. We can see emotional valence from Facial EMG corrugator. Unfortunately this index have no statistical significance ($p > .05$).

Nonetheless is quite evident, from cardiovascular indexes, that Facebook condition does not generate stress or fear in subjects: Figs. 16.7 and 16.8 show a clear differentiation from stress of the Facebook condition, showing the highest NN50 (Lower values of NN50 would be a sign of higher mental stress) and a sympathovagal balance level quite similar to the Relax condition (Higher LF/HF is a sign of higher stress).

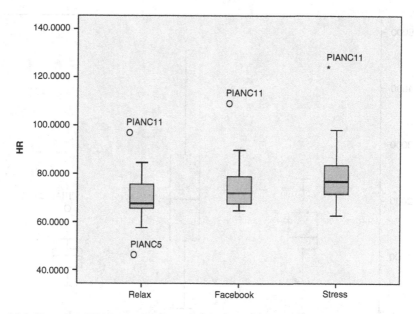

Fig. 16.6 Heart rate (*HR*) in a well-known index of physiological arousal, as defined before. We can see that an higher level of arousal is associated to facebook and stress session, than the relax one. Higher level of arousal in facebook is probably associated to an engagement state

Simulated Social Networks

Emotions affect the human beings' behaviors. In this sense emotions can be "included" as a variable of models of human behavior. It is easy to understand, for example, that the behavior of a stressed subject in a social network, such as Facebook, will be different from the behavior of an engaged subjects, that is enjoying doing this.

Social Networks and Complex Systems

Around us there are many systems, that are constituted by many elements, that are difficult to map and, surely, almost impossible to model. It is, however, necessary to try to specify which is the difference between complicated systems and complex systems. A complicated system, is composed by elements independent from each other. So, if we remove an element from this system, we make this system simpler but, basically, we do not change the system's general behaviors. In a complex system interdependencies between elements is essential to form "the whole" and this will not exists anymore removing an element from it.

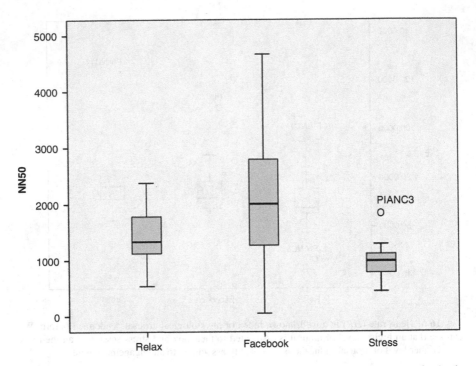

Fig. 16.7 Lower values of NN50 would be a sign of higher mental stress. As we can facebook session is the less stressful, supporting the hypothesis that users are engaged and not stressed

So, complexity is an essential property of the system, "complication" is not. A complex systems does not exists anymore removing an element, whereas a complicated system continues to exists, even if a little bit changed. Complex words are irreducible.

To understand the behavior of the complex systems we have to analyze both the behavior of single elements and the connection among them, in the process of forming the system [16].

Complex networks are the backbone of complex systems; network anatomy is important to characterize because structure affects function, and vice versa.

Social networks, such as Facebook, can be represented mathematically in order to understand their evolution, dynamical processes, diffusion over the network structures, and many other issues. Thus, it is possible to create a mathematical model (a matrix) containing the relationship that we want to study (e.g. friendship in Facebook), and consequently analyze this matrix to understand, through well-known indexes, important characteristics of the studied network, such as centrality analyzed with "Betweenness", "Closeness", and "Degree" measures.

We could be interested in study how behavior of single nodes in a network can affect all the structure and/or some processes through the network, such as diffusion. In this case could be useful to create an agent-based model with simulated networks [10].

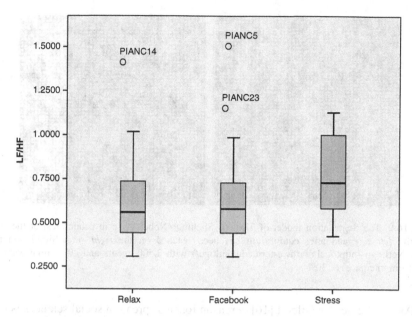

Fig. 16.8 Higher level of sympathovagal balance (*LF/HF*) would be a sign of higher mental stress. Our data, also with this index, seems to be coherent with our hypotheses

Agent-Based Models

Modeling using agent-based objects[1] proceeds by bottom-up in the understanding of complex systems.

Practically we create a computer program containing program parts representing artificial agents, shaping this agents in an environment and being them endowed of some rules, we let them interact each other over time in the so-called agent-based simulation, building in this way an artificial laboratory to experiment social and economic phenomena or whatever else we are interesting in to observe [10, 36].

This new approach, unlike most mathematical and statistical models, allow us – for example – to build heterogeneous agents, to work in situations "far from equilibrium", and to consider in the model the consequences of interactions among agents [12].

Agent based models are becoming very used in economic and social sciences; e.g., in a review of a recent book on CAS by John H Miller and Scott E. Page, Kenneth J. Arrow, winner of the Nobel Prize in economics, says "the use of computational, especially agent-based, models has already shown its value in illuminating the study of economic and other social processes." [27].

---

[1] According to John H. Miller and Scott E. Page, this could be a better name to identify agent-based models, furthermore is useful to distinguish bottom-up modeling (e.g., artificial adaptive agents) and bottom-up simulation (e.g., artificial life).

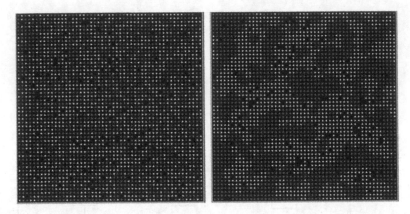

Fig. 16.9 The Segregation model of Thomas Shelling (Nobel Prize in economics) at the start on the *left side* and after equilibrium has been reached on the *right side*. Simulation ran with NetLogo (http://ccl.northwestern.edu/netlogo/) with 2.500 agents and "%-similar-wanted" (uniform tolerance) of 30%

As highlighted by Gilbert [16], a reason for this spread in social sciences is that an agent based simulation allow us to build models where individual entities and their interactions are directly represented.

This bottom-up approach is useful to understand the emergence of a complex systems creating the interacting elements at low-level and looking for this emergence running simulations over time, manipulating agent behavior to understand which combination of environment, rules and agents let complex system emerge (Fig. 16.9).

In an agent-based social simulation we represent a sort of "social reality" and, we are not interested in insert all features of "real system" in our model, but we are interested in the few features, elements and interactions that allow us to observe the emergent phenomenon that we are trying to understand. We practically build our models from the bottom-up.

According to this construction we can think to agent-based simulations such as experiments on complex systems, but some considerations are necessary. For example, many complex systems are experimented with agent-based or other methodologies since these are such that it is not possible to do differently; think to disaster, even if it is possible to plan evacuation situation simulating with human beings the event, is not ethic to generate the real conditions, causing many people dying. Thus an agent-based simulation is well suited in such phenomena representation, since give us a practically instruments to manage the scenarios.

Agent-based simulations give us the possibility to change initial conditions, input, behaviors, interactions, structures, environment and other "parameter" to have a large series of scenarios and not and unique solution. This last is both a great limit and one of the greatest resource of agent-based models.

According to Miller and Page, "no single theoretical tool is suitable for all needs, and we are certainly not claiming that agent-based object modeling is an exceptions.

Table 16.2 Modeling Potential

Traditional tools	Agent-based tools
Precise	Flexible
Little process	Process oriented
Timeless	Timely
Optimizing	Adaptive
Static	Dynamic
1, 2, ... or ∞	1, 2, ..., N agents
Vacuous	Spacey/networked
Homogeneous	Heterogeneous

Adapted by John H Miller and Scott E. Page

We do, however, suggest that the constellation of features offered by such models represents a very appropriate set from which to gain new insights into complex adaptive social systems." (Table 16.2)

Since agent-based is often modeled through code to run a simulation, we need to consider "coding" problems and errors in our model.

It is enough important to keep in mind also Axelrod when he says "Achieving internal validity is harder than it might seem. The problem is knowing whether an unexpected result is a reflection of a mistake in the programming, or a surprising consequence of the model itself. [...] As is often the case, confirming that the model was correctly programmed was substantially more work than programming the model in the first place."

The errors are unavoidable, but thanks to the flexibility of agent-based modeling the applications are wide and growing in social sciences and many other fields. In fact agent-based modeling compose of many different kind of scientist, such as social scientist, engineers, philosophers, economists, psychologists, mathematicians, biologists, physicists, computer scientist, sociologist, and so on. This is not surprisingly in complex systems perspective [23]. Surly science is disciplinary but we have to remember that the reality is a unique one (Fig. 16.10).

An agent-based model consist of many agents interacting in an environment. The agents can represents individual people, firms, nations, and other aggregate. These agents exchange information, rules, behaviors, and so on. Agent-based model differs from other computational model above all for this possibility to model an interaction between agents [21].

A Short Review of Modeling Tools

Thanks to nowadays computational capabilities and a wider interest in complex adaptive systems in more and more fields, in the last few years have been developed many tools allowing many individual to create models for many applications. It is possible to use many toolkits, framing, environment, programming language,

Fig. 16.10 A well-known example of emerging organization. On the *left side* a simulation in StarLogoTNG, representing the behavior of termites assembling wood chips into piles, following a very limited set of simple rules. On the *right side* a real termitaria (mounds)

and libraries, depending on needs and the features coming into situations. We cannot of course review every tool used in complex systems and for that tool here examined will be given only few information reporting the official website for more explorations.

Complex systems modeling require a computer, thus a first step concern the operative system in which we go to operate. Both client and servers are well-suited for agent-based modeling; of course if we need to have high computationally necessity and we are going to plan to use many computer in cluster, a server-based system could be a good choice.

Standard complex systems modeling require a single computer. There is a large choice of operative systems. Let us see briefly some. Most tools run under Windows and Linux. Many tools have versions for Macintosh with both PowerPC processors and Intel Processors. Other operative systems very used in complex systems modeling are Unix, OS/2, OS/370, OS/400, HPUX, SunOS, DOS, AIX, BSD, and many others.

A different discussion deserve applications running on a Java Virtual Machine (JVM), that allow a program – within some limit – to be platform independent, as its slogan highlight: "write once, run everywhere".

Most of operative systems have one version of JVM. In complex systems modeling a programming language, among other solutions, could be a good one. Generally to program give more flexibility of simpler toolkit, but requires experience and the capacity to transforms ideas in block diagrams, pseudo-code and eventually executable code. On the other hand the many toolkit easy-to-use nowadays available provide good chances to model ideas also to non-computer scientist interested in emergences and complexity issues instead of algorithmic optimization and other informatics issues. The problem in simple toolkits is that many times these are not so flexible as we desire for some model.

These considerations have been in the mind of many researcher in complexity field and in effect in the last few years have been developed easy-to-use tools with high capabilities and flexibility to model complexity. However there are not best choices in this moment; it depends on methodologies, preferences, knowledge, costs (in terms of money, time, efforts, capabilities, and so on), model requirements, and many other factors. Moreover, are coming into existence more and more specific tools born to analyze particular phenomena and situations, modeling them. An example by Pietro Terna could be jES (Java Enterprise Simulator project[2]) descript in official website to be "both to simulate the activities and the consistent emerging results – of an actual enterprise and to build virtual or hypothetical enterprises." jES has been written in Java and based on the Swarm libraries'.

Swarm (www.swarm.org) is a software package for agent-based (and individual-based) models to study complex systems. Swarm can be used with many operative systems, among them Linux, Mac and Windows (using Cgiwin to have Linux API emulation layer providing substantial Linux API functionality) and can be programmed using Java or OjectiveC. Using Swarm it is possible to create many simulation and use the computer as a laboratory to model complex systems. Swarm is quite old, but he has a great and large community. Moreover Swarm has inspired many models (e.g., HeatBugs) and tools to model.

One fast and flexible "Swarm son" is Mason (Multi-Agent Simulator Of Neighborhoods... or Networks... or something..., as in the official website). Mason is well suited for general purpose complex systems model, can be programmed with Java and can implement machine learning, other AI (Artificial Intelligence), and social networks. From a graphical point of view, Mason, can manage 2D and 3D visualization and generate many type of output (images, video, charts, and so on). Mason is really good special with swarm simulations also with millions of artificial agents.

Many other tools are comparable with Mason. No one (for the moment) is absolutely the best, as already said, it depends on model we have to build.

Another tools, programmable with Java, is RePast (Recursive Porous Agent Simulation Toolkit), a really good tools above all for its integration with other (also network and mathematical) tools. RePast is particular indicated for social sciences.

Sometimes it is useful over that impressive to visualize a simulation in 3D. As previously seen many tools give this possibility. A further example is given by Breve, a 3D environment for multi-agent simulations and artificial life, where agent behavior can be programmed with Python.

---

[2]http://web.econ.unito.it/terna/jes/

Another purpose of 3D simulation has StarLogo TNG (the next generation), where the idea is to teach complex systems and basic computer programming, with simple blocks, to K-12 students, like Open StarLogo (an open source version of StarLogo series developed at MIT) and AgentSheets.

One of the most popular agent-based simulation tool is NetLogo. It is enough flexible and can be programmed with an integrated friendly language. Run on any JVM. It is free for educational and research purpose but it is not open source. May not be the most suitable for large and complex model.

Most of tools we have seen have some feature (e.g., modules and libraries) to analyze networks. However, sometimes, a specific tool could be a better choice, also to benefit of large community of user, in this specific field.

One of older and well-known tool is UCINet.[3] Other tools are, Pajek,[4] NetworkX (in Python), ORA,[5] SocNetV,[6] the statnet[7] suite of packages in R,[8] and many others. For visualization, SocioMetrica, SoNIA (Social Network Image Animator), and iGraph (also with R, Python and Ruby).

In complex systems modeling, often, there is a large use of Matlab and Mathematica, two very useful software that gave many possibility to model networks, agent-based simulation, PDE (partially differentially equations), and so on. In general they allow to work in many mathematical and statistical fields and so in literature, and in this chapter too, there is a large use of them, even if they are not free.

Finally, a special mention deserves Python (devoted to mythic "Monty Python's Flying Circus" TV series), a programming language freely usable and distributable, even for commercial use.

Developed by Guido van Rossum, more than 10 years ago, Python popularity has grown over the time and is becoming, always more, a good alternative to well-known C++ and Java.

A useful package that will be largely used in this chapter is NetworkX, "a Python package for the creation, manipulation, and study of the structure, dynamics, and functions of complex networks" as we can read in the official website (under the slogan "high productivity software for complex networks").

From Psychophysiology to Networked Emotion

In the previous section we showed how to use agent-based models to represent social phenomena, also considering the structure of social relationship through complex networks. The experiment we did and reported in section "Emotions in Real Social

---

[3] http://www.analytictech.com/ucinet/ucinet.htm

[4] http://vlado.fmf.uni-lj.si/pub/networks/pajek/

[5] http://www.casos.cs.cmu.edu/projects/ora/

[6] http://socnetv.sourceforge.net/

[7] http://cran.r-project.org/web/packages/statnet/

[8] http://en.wikipedia.org/wiki/R_programming_language

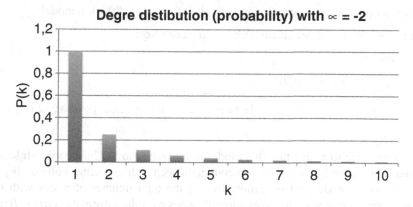

Fig. 16.11 The power law tail of scale free network

Networks" of this chapter, give many useful information that can be used to build models of behavior in Facebook. Knowing the affective state of a subject during Facebook navigation we can try to predict some behaviors and reactions to actions as they come. For example we could to study how an information received by a subject during his Facebook navigation diffuse through the Facebook network of friend and friend of friend, and so on. It is possible to predict the spread of such information through Facebook using mathematical model or also agent based model, as we will see following.

Mathematical Model

Let consider to be in a Barabasi-Albert network (i.e. a scale-free network) built iteratively in this way: from a small number of node (one), we add, at every time step, a new node with one edge that links it to an already present node *i*. The attachment is done preferentially with a probability

$$\Pi(k_i) = \frac{k_i}{\sum_j k_j} \tag{16.4}$$

with k_i the degree of the node *i*. This construction gives a distribution of the degrees independent from the number of links a new node can have with the present nodes (Fig. 16.11).

$$P(k) \approx k^{-\alpha}, 2 \leq \alpha \leq 3 \tag{16.5}$$

Let us now consider the following simple information diffusion model:

```
For each node without the information

  Begin

     Look at neighbors;
     If a node has the information
     Then receive the information with the probability λ;

  End
```

It is possible to notice that this model is equivalent to the Susceptible-Infected model in a network. In a homogeneous network (with the same number $\langle k \rangle$ of vertices for all nodes) let us denote by $I(t)$ the total number of nodes with the information, in that way the proportion of nodes with the information $i(t)$ is $I(t)/N$ where N is the total number of nodes. The evolution equation of $i(t)$ is then given by (16.3), with λ the diffusion probability of the information and $(1 - i(t))$ the proportion of nodes susceptible to receive the information.

$$\frac{di(t)}{dt} = \lambda i(t) \langle k \rangle (1 - i(t)) \tag{16.6}$$

However in a heterogeneous network, like ours, the average degree $\langle k \rangle$ is not relevant,[9] so it is more convenient to compute $i_k(t)$ the density of nodes having the information and a degree k:

$$i_k(t) = I_k(t)/N_k \tag{16.7}$$

with N_k the number of nodes with degree k and $I_k(t)$ the number of nodes with degree k and with the information. In this case, the equation of density is as follow [5]:

$$\frac{di_k(t)}{dt} = \lambda \theta_k(t) k (1 - i_k(t)) \tag{16.8}$$

$\theta_k(t)$ (rather than $i(t)$) is the density of nodes with the information and also with neighbor of degree k, and $(1 - i_k(t))$ (rather than $(1 - i(t))$), the rate of nodes susceptible to receive the information and having a degree k. Barthélémy and Colleagues [2, 3] give a solution of the Eq. 16.8:

$$i_k(t) = i_0 \left[1 + \frac{k \langle k \rangle}{\langle k^2 \rangle - \langle k \rangle} (e^{t/\tau} - 1) \right] \tag{16.9}$$

where $\tau = \frac{\langle k^2 \rangle}{\lambda(\langle k^2 \rangle - \langle k \rangle)}$ and i_0 is the initial condition.

---

[9] $\langle k \rangle (1 - i(t))$ is no more an exact expression of the receivable information.

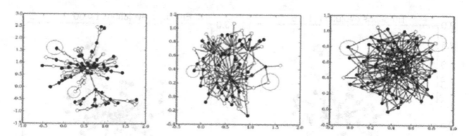

Fig. 16.12 Barabàsi-Albert network with out-degree 1, 2, and 3

Agent-Based Model

The mathematical model represent some limitations due to difficult in considering behavior of single nodes. In an agent-based model it is easier to include a sort of behavior (based on simple rules) in agents. Moreover, it is also possible to have agents with neural networks (able to learn from experience) and to build genetic algorithms to let network structure evolve [6, 11, 40–42].

Let suppose that information diffusion processes are different for stressed subjects and engaged subjects. From a specific study, such as the one described in section "Emotions in Real Social Networks", it is possible to establish such behavior and to transpose this in the model.

Thus, in the agent-based model, we define interaction among agents. Each agent has a "self state" variable that provides information that each agent has or does not have. Moreover, the agent has a list of neighbors representing the list of agents to which he is linked through network. We define another variable giving the "emotional state" of the agent [9].medskip

```
class agentClass:
  def __init__(self,id, state_agent, neighbors, emotion,
emotion_degree:
    self.id = id
self.state = state_agent# knows or not
self.neighbors = neighbors# list of neighbors
self.emotion_degree = emotion_degree# engaged or stressed
```

Each agent must decide whether to diffuse the information to their neighbors. This decision depends on the variable *emotion_degree*. If *emotion_degree* is positive, then the agent will diffuse information to their neighbors; otherwise, he or she will not (Fig. 16.12).

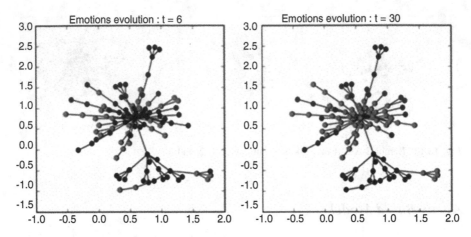

Fig. 16.13 An example of evolution of emotion

Thus, under the following "mechanical" algorithm, we define diffusion and reciprocal diffusion of agents as follows (Fig. 16.13):

```
# both are engaged
if agent.emotion_degree < 0 and neighbor.emotion_degree
< 0:
neighbor.emotion_degree = (neighbor.emotion_degree +
agent.emotion_degree) / 2

# the next one is under stress
if agent.emotion_degree < 0 and neighbor.emotion_degree
>= 0:
neighbor.emotion_degree = neighbor.emotion_degree +
agent.emotion_degree

# both are under stress
if agent.emotion_degree >= 0 and
neighbor.emotion_degree >= 0:
neighbor.emotion_degree = (neighbor.emotion_degree +
agent.emotion_degree) / 2

# the next one is engaged
if agent.emotion_degree >= 0 and
neighbor.emotion_degree < 0:
neighbor.emotion_degree = neighbor.emotion_degree +
agent.emotion_degree
```

In the implementation of our model, we used two visualizations of the same network. One visualization was for diffusion of information, and the other was for the diffusion of emotions. The model depends on time and interaction among artificial agents, following simple predefined rules (Fig. 16.14).

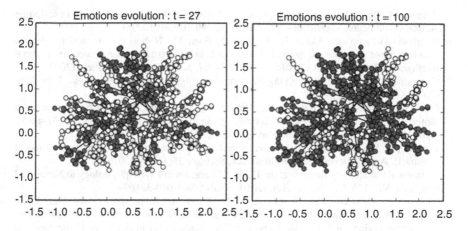

Fig. 16.14 Evolution of emotion: another structure with more agents

Conclusion

According to Christakis and Fowler our friends and their friends and their friends affect our happiness! (Three Degrees of Influence Rule). Happy and unhappy people cluster among themselves. Unhappy people are on periphery of the network.

Furthermore, Christakis reports that a person is 15% more likely to be happy if directly connected to a happy person (1°), at 2° 10% more likely to be happy, at 3° 6% more likely to be happy, and each unhappy friend deceases the likelihood of happiness 7%.

Using these and other information about social networks and running experiments like the one in section "Emotions in Real Social Networks", it is possible to have more input on subjects' behavior during social networks site navigation. This could help in building models of specific situation. Moreover it is possible to think to monitor with biosensors subjects during specific behaviors in order to have a more precise model. Finally a great chance could come from study real interaction using both psychophysiology and network analysis simultaneously.

References

1. Barbieri, R., Triedman, J.K., Saul, J.P.: Heart rate control and mechanical cardiopulmonary coupling to assess central volume: a systems analysis. Am. J. Physiol.-Regul. Integr. Comp. Physiol. **283**, R1210–R1220 (2002)
2. Barthélémy, M.: Spatial networks. Phys. Rep. **499**, 1–101 (2011)
3. Barthélémy, M., Barrat, A., Pastor-Satorras, R., Vespignani, A.: Velocity and hierarchical spread of epidemic outbreaks in scale-free networks. Phys. Rev. Lett. **92**, 178701 (2004)
4. Blumenthal, T.D., Cuthbert, A.B.N., Filion, B.D.L., Hackley, S., Lipp, D.O.V., Van Boxtel, F.A.: Committee report: guidelines for human startle eyeblink electromyographic studies. Psychophysiology **42**, 1–15 (2005)

5. Boguna, M., Pastor-Satorras, R., Vespignani, A.: Absence of epidemic threshold in scale-free networks with degree correlations. Phys. Rev. Lett. **90**, 028701 (2003)
6. Burghouts G.J., op den Akker, R., Heylen, D., Poel, M., Nijholt A.: An action selection architecture for an emotional agent. In Russell and Haller (eds.) Recent Advances in Artificial Intelligence, Proceedings of FLAIRS 16, pp 293–297. Menlo Park: AAAI Press (2003)
7. Ciarrochi, J., Mayer, J.D.: Applying Emotional Intelligence. Psychology Press, New York (2007)
8. Cipresso, P., Mauri, M., Balgera, A., Romanò, E., Villamira, M.: Synchronization of a biofeedback system with an eye tracker through an audiovisual stimulus marker [Abstract]. Appl. Psychophysiol. Biofeedback, Springer **35**(4), 331 (2010)
9. Cipresso, P., Villamira, M.: Physiological correlates for an agent-based computational model [Abstract]. Appl. Psychophysiol. Biofeedback, Springer **35**(4), 331 (2010)
10. Cipresso, P.: Modeling Emotions at the Edge of Chaos. From Psychophysiology to Networked Emotions. VDM Verlag, Saarbrucken (2010). ISBN 978-3-639-30169-4
11. Cipresso, P., Dembele, J.M., Villamira, M.A.: An emotional perspective for agent-based computational economics. In: Vallverdù, J., Casacuberta, D. (eds.) Handbook of Research on Synthetic Emotions and Sociable Robotics: New Applications in Affective Computing and Artificial Intelligence. IGI Global, Hershey (2009). ISBN 978-1-60566-354-8
12. Cipresso, P., Villamira, M.A.: Human behaviour and organisational framework: a multi-agent approach to shape information management systems. In: Proceeding of European Conference on Information Management and Evaluation, Montpellier, France. Academic Conferences, Reading (2007). ISBN: Print 978-1-905305-54-4, CD 978-1-905305-55-1
13. De Manzano, O., Theorell, T., Harmat, L., Ullén, F.: The psychophysiology of flow during piano playing. Emotion **10**(3), 301–311 (2010)
14. DiMicco, J., Millen, D.R.: Identity management: multiple presentations of self in facebook In: Proceedings of the 2007 International ACM Conference on Supporting Group Work, FL, pp. 383–386 (2007)
15. Elman, J.L.: Finding structure in time. Cogn. Sci. **14**, 179–211 (1990)
16. Gilbert, N.: Agent-Based Models. Quantitative Applications in the Social Sciences. SAGE Publications, London (2008)
17. Lampe, C., Ellison, N., Steinfield, C.: A face(book) in the crowd: social searching vs. social browsing. In: Proceedings of the 2006 20th Anniversary Conference on Computer Supported Cooperative Work, pp. 167–170. ACM Press, New York (2006)
18. Lampe, C., Ellison, N., Steinfield, C.: The benefits of facebook "friends": social capital and college students' use of online social network sites. J. Comput.-Mediat. Commun. **12**(4), 1143–1168 (2007)
19. Lang, P.J.: The emotion probe. Studies of motivation and attention. Am. Psychol. **50**(5), 372–385 (1995)
20. Lazarus, R.S.: Psychological Stress and Coping Process. McGraw-Hill, New York (1966)
21. LeBaron, B.: Agent based computational finance: suggested readings and early research. J. Econ. Dyn. Control. **24**, 679–702 (2006)
22. LeDoux, J.: Fear and the brain: where have we been, and where are we going? Biol. Psychiatry **44**, 12 (1998)
23. Leijonhufvud, A.: Agent-based macro. In: Tesfatsion, L., Judd, K.L. (eds.) Handbook of Computational Economics, vol. 2, pp. 1625–1637. North-Holland, Amsterdam (2006)
24. Lewis, M., Haviland-Jones, J.M., Feldman Barrett, L. (eds.): Handbook of Emotions, 3rd edn. Psychology Press, New York (2008)
25. Magagnin, V., Mauri, M., Cipresso, P., Mainardi, L., Brown, E.N., Cerutti, S., Villamira, M., Barbieri, R.: Heart rate variability and respiratory sinus arrhythmia assessment of affective states by bivariate autoregressive spectral analysis. Comput. Cardiol. **37**, 145–148 (2010)
26. Mauri, M., Magagnin, V., Cipresso, P., Mainardi, L., Brown, E.N., Cerutti, S., Villamira, M.A., Barbieri, R.: Psychophysiological signals associated with affective states. Conf. Proc. IEEE Eng. Med. Biol. Soc. **2010**, 3563–3566 (2010)

27. Miller, J.H., Page, S.E.: Complex Adaptive Systems. Princeton University Press, Princeton (2007)
28. Nolan, R.P.: Heart rate variability biofeedback as a behavioral neurocardiac intervention to enhance vagal heart rate control. Am. Heart J. **149**(6), 1137 (2005)
29. Orr, E.S., Sisic, M., Ross, C., Simmering, M.G., Arseneault, J.M., Orr, R.R.: The influence of shyness on the use of facebook in an undergraduate sample. Cyberpsychol. Behav. **12**(3), 337–340 (2009). doi:10.1089/cpb.2008.0214
30. Park, N., Kee, K.F., Valenzuela, S.: Being immersed in social networking environment: facebook groups, uses and gratifications, and social outcomes. Cyberpsychol. Behav. **12**(6), 729–733 (2009). doi:10.1089/cpb.2009.0003
31. Picard, R.: Affective Computing. MIT Press, Cambridge (1997)
32. Power, M., Dalgleish, T.: Cognition and Emotion. From Order to Disorder. Psychology Press, New York (2008)
33. Riva, G.: Social Networks. Il Mulino, Bologna (2010)
34. Roberts, K.L., Hall, D.A.: Examining a supramodal network for conflict processing: a systematic review and novel functional magnetic resonance imaging data for related visual and auditory stroop tasks. J. Cogn. Neurosci. **20**(6), 1063–1078 (2008)
35. Sas, C., Dix, A., Hart, J., Su, R.: Emotional experience on facebook site. In: Proceedings of the 27th International Conference Extended Abstracts on Human Factors in Computing Systems, pp. 4345–4350. ACM Press, New York (2009)
36. Simon, H.: Models of Bounded Rationality, vol. 3. MIT Press, Cambridge (1997)
37. Stroop, J.R.: Studies of interference in serial verbal reactions. J. Exp. Psychol. **18**, 643–662 (1935)
38. Task force of the European Society of Cardiology and the North American Society of Pacing and Electrophysiology: Standard of measurement, physiological interpretation and clinical use. Circulation **93**, 1043–1065 (1996)
39. Tassinary, L.G., Cacioppo, J.T., Wanman, E.J.: The skeletomotor system: surface electromyography. In: Cacioppo, J.T., Tassinary, L.G., Berntson, G.G. (eds.) Handbook of Psychophysiology, 3rd edn, pp. 267–299. Cambridge University Press. Pages, New York (2007)
40. Terna, P., Boero, R., Morini, M., Sonnessa, M.: Modelli per la complessità. La simulazione ad agenti in economia. Il Mulino, Bologna (2006)
41. Tesfatsion, L.: Agent based computational economics: a constructive approach to economic theory. In: Tesfatsion, L., Judd, K.L. (eds.) Handbook of Computational Economics, vol. 2, pp. 831–880. North-Holland, Amsterdam (2006)
42. Villamira, M., Cipresso, P.: Bio-inspired ICT for evolutionary emotional intelligence. In: Serra, R., Villani, M., Poli, I. (eds.) Artificial Life and Evolutionary Computation, pp. 143–154. World Scientific Pub Co Inc, Singapore/Hackensack (2010)
43. Wise, K., Alhabash, S., Park, H.: Cyberpsychology, behavior, and social networking **13**(5), 555–562 (2010). doi:10.1089/cyber.2009.0365
44. Mauri, M., Cipresso, P., Balgera, A., Villamira, M., Riva, G.: Cyberpsychology, behavior, and social networking **14**(12), 723–731 (2011). doi:10.1089/cyber.cyber.2010.0377
45. Cipresso, P., Serino, S., Villani, D., Repetto, C., Sellitti, L., Albani, G., Mauro, A., Gaggioli, A., Riva, G.: Is your phone so smart to affect your states? An exploratory study based on psychophysiological measures. Neurocomputing **84**, 23–30 (2012). doi:dx.doi.org/10.1016/j.neucom.2011.12.027

Chapter 17
Social Networks for Learning: Breaking Through the Walled Garden of the VLE

Karen Jones, Rhian Pole, Stephen Hole, and James Williams

Abstract e-Learning is ubiquitous. The virtual learning environment (VLE) is the mainstay of UK universities e-learning provision. However, its' deployment is often standardised and pedestrian; typically resources are made more available to the learner without necessarily adding value to the learning. Many contemporary theorists in e-learning advocate learning environments developed using social network technologies and Web 2.0 tools, to encourage learners to customise and personalise their learning environment. A key tenet of any social network is communication. Learners, as 'digital natives', routinely use social networks to communicate with friends and family. To harness and exploit the communication and collaborative qualities of a social network, a university SLE prototype was developed and is evaluated in this chapter. Learners become active participants in the learning process. They access public internet content to practice independent information-search and -discernment skills, which they can share with others, breaking through the 'walled garden' of the VLE.

Introduction

According to Holmes and Gardner [1], 'e-learning offers new opportunities for both educators and learners to enrich their teaching and learning experiences, through virtual environments that support not just the delivery but also the exploration and application of information and the promotion of new knowledge'. However, in O'Hear's [2] view, 'the early promise of e-learning...has not been fully realised...for many [it] has been no more than a hand-out published online,

---

K. Jones (✉) • R. Pole
Swansea Business School, Swansea Metropolitan University, Wales, UK
e-mail: karen.jones@smu.ac.uk

S. Hole • J. Williams
School of Applied Computing, Swansea Metropolitan University, Wales, UK

A. Abraham and A.-E. Hassanien (eds.), *Computational Social Networks: Tools, Perspectives and Applications*, DOI 10.1007/978-1-4471-4048-1_17,
© Springer-Verlag London 2012

coupled with a simple multiple-choice quiz. Hardly inspiring...'. Yet, by using social networks and web services, 'e-learning has the potential to become far more personal, social and flexible' [2]. O'Hear advocates e-learning 2.0, which 'takes a "small pieces, loosely joined" approach that combines the use of discrete but complementary tools and web services – such as blogs, wikis, and other social software – to support the creation of ad-hoc learning communities'. Indeed, social software can initiate new ways of learning as it incorporates a range of tools which allow learners to interact and share data with other learners, primarily via the web [3]. Walton et al. [4] contend that social learning technologies used in an educational context can 'create a new, dynamic and engaging learning environment for tomorrow's students'.

This contemporary approach to learning using social software, represents a fundamental shift in the way people learn and so must be put into the context of the variety of approaches to learning and teaching that are available. Traditional approaches to learning and teaching are teacher-driven where 'teacher knows best' [5, 6] and learners passively 'receive' information. However, in the last decade or so there has been an increasing trend towards social constructivist approaches that empower learners to build on past experience through individual and group activities [7]. Abadzi [8] contends that the role of a social constructivist teacher is to take a back seat in the *teaching* but instead to provide the *social* environment and supportive resources that will afford students the freedom to actively control, direct and make sense of their own learning. An associated approach is the discovery learning method, in which students are encouraged to discover new information for themselves or in groups [9]. Whilst such collaborative and enquiry based activities may well take place face-to-face, a technology-based network can provide a structured and supportive learning environment [7, 10–12].

Virtual learning environments (VLE), described by the British Educational Communications and Technology Agency (BECTA) as 'standardised, computer-based environments that support the delivery of web-based learning and facilitate online interaction between students and teachers' [13], are being used routinely in schools and higher education organisations to support this process [7, 10–12]. However, while VLEs typically provide the functionality to upload course content for learners and monitor usage they generally have limited, if any social network functionality [14]. Hart advocates a social learning environment (SLE), which she describes as 'a social network application in which individual learners and groups of learners can meet to collaborate in the creation of materials and resources, share resources, knowledge and experiences, and learn from one another' [14]. Hart adds that through social interaction with tutors and other learners, SLE-based activities can improve learners' personal and professional productivity in both formal and informal ways. 'In other words, a SLE does not manage, control and track users but rather provides an open environment for them to work and learn collaboratively' [14]. A SLE then, is a social network that comprises a number of social elements, including networking, social bookmarking, communicating and collaborating with others, blogging, podcasting and RSS feeds.

From an educational perspective, there may be limited value to learning environments by themselves [15]; Pole and Jones [16] contend that resources can be more *available* to students without necessarily adding *value* to the learning. Motivational features, such as chat facilities and discussion boards, need to be embedded in the learning environment to stimulate learners to engage with it [17]. However, Woodill [18] cautions that just because people are using 'social media', it does not mean that 'social learning' is taking place. Consequently, care must be taken in the design of the SLE to include elements that engage learners and motivate them to participate in discovery learning.

This chapter reviews the literature to explore the notion and rationale for e-learning and the inherent benefits and challenges associated with VLEs and SLEs. The chapter then describes the development of a social network application for discovery learning in the context of a higher education (HE) ICT module. The eTUTOR (Education Through Ubiquitous Technologies and Online Resources) project, was funded by the Joint Information Systems Committee (JISC) through the Next Generation Technologies and Practices strand of the Users and Innovation Programme.

e-Learning and Learning Environments

What Is e-Learning?

Traditionally, learners have needed to meet at the same time and place to exchange knowledge, thereby allowing learning to take place. However, with the sophistication and ubiquity of technology, which is not location specific, it is now possible for individuals to learn anything, anywhere at any time, a development termed e-learning [19]. e-Learning is defined by Bullen and Janes [20] as 'learning which takes place when internet technologies are used to facilitate, deliver, and enable learning processes over a distance'. However, there is no agreement in the literature as to a single definition of e-learning. Mann [21] for example, contends that 'in the EU "e-learning" is defined as a form of distance learning, with learning materials accessed from the web or from a CD via a computer. Typically, tutors and learners communicate with each other using e-mail or discussion forums'. Yet, this suggests that only distance learning is considered e-learning and that the internet is essential for communication. Stockley's [22] definition is much broader as he suggests that e-learning is 'the delivery of a learning, training or education program by electronic means' and is not restricted to the internet, but involves 'the use of a computer or some other electronic device to provide training, educational or learning material'; this can include CD-ROM, DVD, intranet and mobile phone technology [22].

JISC [23] places the emphasis more specifically on the 'learning' and not the 'technology' by defining e-learning as 'learning facilitated and supported through the use of information and communications technology'. It can cover a spectrum of activities from the use of technology to support learning as part of a 'blended' approach (a combination of traditional and e-learning approaches), to learning that is delivered entirely online. Whatever the technology, however, 'learning is the vital element'. According to Holmes and Gardner [1], 'e-learning offers new opportunities for both educators and learners to enrich their teaching and learning experiences, through virtual environments that support not just the delivery but also the exploration and application of information and the promotion of new knowledge'.

However, for the purposes of this chapter, the deliberately open-ended and flexible definition by Horton [19] will be adopted, where e-learning is considered 'the use of information and computer technologies to create learning experiences'.

Rationale for e-Learning

Siemens [24] suggests that the two primary values of e-learning are to make learning more accessible and more effective. He describes these roles as:

1. To *extend* learning (effectiveness). This role involves the addition of discussion forums/email/virtual presentations, software simulations, etc. to existing learning. Holmes and Gardner [1] describe this mix of conventional face-to-face learning (often classroom-based) with e-learning, (which may be at a distance) as *blended* learning.
2. To *replace* traditional learning (accessibility). 'Pure' e-learning in this role is a replacement to traditional learning. The learner may have access to classroom courses, but is able to self-select the schedule to make e-learning more convenient.

Many UK universities have developed a blended approach to e-learning, using technology to extend the existing provision. The combination of e-learning resources and traditional teaching materials and strategies is intended to maximise the advantages of both methods and overcome the associated disadvantages of each approach individually [16].

e-Learning is widely acknowledged to have many advantages for students, teachers and educational organisations and has consequently resulted in many universities rushing to join the e-learning market to enjoy the associated benefits. For example, as Salmon [25] suggests, e-learning can facilitate 'flexibility' and 'adaptability to audience'. Similarly, Aswathappa [26] purports that whilst e-learning is consistent for all learners, it allows individual students to set the pace to meet their own learning needs and styles, but with built-in guidance. According to Zhang et al. [27], computing technologies 'are providing a diverse means to support learning in a more personalised, flexible, portable, and on-demand manner'. The mainstay of UK universities' technological e-learning provision is the virtual learning environment (VLE).

The Virtual Learning Environment Goes Social

The Joint Information Systems Committee (JISC) [28] suggests that the term VLE refers 'to the 'online' interactions of various kinds which take place between learners and tutors'. Fry et al. [12] add that the VLE is a 'menu-based or point and click interface for constructing an online course area without the need for specialist web development skills'. The primary functions of a VLE are to deliver controlled access to structured course materials, to track students, provide learning support, a medium for communication and links to other administrative systems [11]. An alternative classification by El-Ghareeb [29] categorises the main functions of a VLE into Course, Exam, Assessment and Collaboration sectors, with each sector offering extensive component functionality; for example, Course Authoring and Student Tracking functionality would be included in the Course sector and the Communication sector would contain forums and chat rooms. Most VLEs act as a repository for course materials but also have the capability to provide student results, conduct e-Assessment and host forum-based discussions. Indeed, the Higher Education Academy (HEA) [30] suggests that it is the inclusion of communication tools that differentiates a VLE from other forms of e-learning. However, it is difficult to gauge how widely communication tools such as online forums, wikis, blogs, podcasts, etc., are being used in VLEs since there is little published evidence of their use [3].

According to Zhang et al. [27], a VLE supports traditional learning approaches in that it can reinforce basic principles studied in lectures by providing for instance, practical exercises, online testing, links to other websites and additional resources (such as industry publications and software) should students wish to explore the themes. There are numerous other advantages associated with VLEs, which include that student access is widened, that it promotes active and independent learning, there is the potential to support large student cohorts and learning materials can take a variety of forms and media thereby providing a range of materials to fit different learning styles [15, 30]. Such a student-centred approach allows students to learn at their own pace and at a time to suit themselves, thereby enhancing their experience of the programme studied. Lecturers benefit because content is easily updated and there are fewer disruptions caused by students requesting copies of notes due to absence; this enables lecturers to spend more time conducting research and enhancing learning materials/strategies [16].

According to Farmer and Tilton [31], in 2001, 19% of universities and colleges did not use a VLE but by 2005 only 5% were without the VLE. During the same time period, a decline was noted in the use of proprietary VLEs from 93% to 57% [31]. VLEs are typically categorised as open source, commercial (proprietary) and/or free. Open source VLEs provide the source code to developers to enable the manipulation and enhancement of the environment; they are often, but not always, free and examples include Moodle and Sakai. Alternatively, commercial VLEs are purchased under licence, typically closed-source but with the provision of technical support; Blackboard and Janison are examples. Free VLEs typically do not provide the source code or charge for usage but can be downloaded and used without limit; an example is the KnowlEdge eLearning Suite [29]. Between 2001 and 2005, there was a rise in the use of open source VLEs from zero to 11% and locally/self-developed VLEs increased from 7% to 30% [31]. Fry et al. [12] suggests this trend is the result of commercial systems being overly prescriptive while Toole [32] suggests that the need for VLEs is lessened because new web based online learning environments/applications can be created using software and services readily available on the internet [33].

Despite all the benefits associated with VLEs, there are also challenges. VLEs can become a dumping ground for traditionally designed materials, there may be copyright issues, off campus access can be problematic, planned online support is required, educators and learners must be trained and there is often reduced face to face contact [15, 30]. In a survey conducted by Pole and Jones [16], lecturers believed that the use of a VLE encourages 'handholding' of students and the inhibition of independent thought. e-Learning suits best those students who are self-motivated, yet these are seen to be in the minority. Furthermore, the VLE does not generally facilitate immediate, two-way communication and can result in a lack of personal contact and feedback; students can feel isolated as they cannot always interact with their peers.

Moreover, Pole and Jones [16] contend that VLE resources can be more *available* to learners without necessarily adding *value* to the learning. Indeed, van der Klink and Jachems [34] caution that 'a lack of clarity of the institutional role of e-learning is increasingly likely to result in its use solely to supplement face-to-face teaching without adding any value to the learning process'. Whilst lecturers may perceive a positive gain from the highly structured and accessible online environment, Holmes and Gardner [1] argue that this might restrict innovation and spontaneity of delivery of content. Indeed, when questioned about the challenges involved in the use of e-learning, some lecturers stated that they needed more time and resources to develop the materials [16]. This concurs with Bullen and Janes' [20] contention that due to time constraints few education providers are able to identify innovative or even appropriate roles for e-learning.

A social learning environment (SLE) could mitigate some of the problems above. Hart [14] defines a SLE as 'a place where individuals and groups of individuals can come together and co-create content, share knowledge and experiences, and learn from one another to improve their personal and professional productivity; and is also a place that can be used both to extend formal content-based e-learning to provide social interaction with the learners and tutors, as well as to underpin informal learning ... In other words a SLE does not manage, control and track users but rather provides an open environment for them to work and learn collaboratively'. A SLE comprises a number of social elements, including social networking, social bookmarking, communicating and collaborating with others, blogging, podcasting and RSS feeds. Anderson, cited by Minocha [3] describes Educational Social Software as a set of networked tools that support and encourage individuals to learn together while retaining individual control over their time, space, presence, activity, identity and relationship.

Why Use Social Networks and Web 2.0 in Education?

If educators are to be learner-centric, they should use the communication methods that are popular with learners, and that are in accord with learners' activities outside their studies. Today's learners, described by Prensky [35] as 'digital natives', use technology in a variety of different ways to meet their needs. For example, they may share images/photographs captured using mobile phones sent via MMS or uploaded to social networks, watch YouTube video clips, share ideas by chatting to each other using text messaging (SMS) or instant messaging services such as MSN Messenger, Blackberry Messenger and social networks features such as Facebook Chat [3]. The adage 'if you can't beat them, join them' springs to mind. However, Prensky [35] describes many teaching staff as 'digital immigrants', that is, they are not as *au fait* with the use of such technologies as the learners, or are resistant to learn [36] yet everyone needs to be computer literate and able to work collaboratively in the workplace [37].

A fundamental principle of a Web 2.0 social network is its read/write facility, enabling participant interaction and collaboration [3]. Social network technology can support group interaction and thus counter the isolation of self-paced e-learning by fostering a learning community providing mutual support [38]. According to Wenger [39], learning occurs in *communities of practice*, where the practice of learning is the participation in the community. Members who have a shared interest or competence, interact and learn together and develop a shared repertoire of resources (experiences, tools and ways of addressing recurring problems). In the Web 2.0 era, a learning activity is a *conversation* between the learner and other members of the community that consists not only of words but of images, video, multimedia and more. In so doing, a rich variety of dynamic and interconnected resources is formed, created not only by experts, but by all members of the community, including learners [40]. Furthermore, as the interactive nature of social networks facilitates collaborative work, group tasks such as projects and reports may be of a higher quality than if individuals had worked alone (synergistic effects) [37]. In addition to higher quality learning outcomes, participants in the process benefit from both peer recognition and peer review, both excellent preparation for more modern collaborative teamwork [37]. Moreover, the social software allows individual contributions to be tracked for assessment purposes, if desired [3].

Leslie and Landon, cited by Minocha [3] argue that because people can communicate widely with other community members, they can move beyond the more limited circle of their immediate contacts. Thus social networks help to create both an environment and an infrastructure for 'informal and borderless learning' [3]. Minocha [3] describes the rationale for social networking as a virtuous circle, in which the learner generates something of personal use, which benefits the larger network as a whole, which in turn creates additional value for the original user.

According to Mejias [41], the use of social networks develops in learners the practical research skills needed to make best use of online information networks and engages students in 'learning to learn'. He adds that social networks facilitate distributed research, in which 'the power of many' exposes the individual learner to far more research, resources and ideas than they could possibly generate on their own. However, while the movement away from VLEs to internet based social networks exposes students to greater opportunities for research and collaboration, it leads BECTA [37] to comment 'the Web 2.0 tension to be managed is one between welcoming the diversity of Web 2.0 publication, while recognising the need to help students navigate it with confidence and a critical attitude'.

Pedagogy and the 'Fit' with Social Networks for Learning

Mainstream educational learning theories include behaviourism, cognitivism and constructivism. The behaviourist approach focuses on learners' observable behaviour and the stimuli and responses involved in changing behaviour. Whereas behaviourism does not attempt to understand internal thought processes (black box thinking), cognitivist theorists attempt to understand the mental process of learning, so that the process can be improved. Both these schools of thought place the learner as a passive recipient of knowledge from external sources, that is, that responsibility rests with the teacher to deliver knowledge while the learner passively internalises it [42]. Conversely, constructivism depicts the learner as an active participant in the search for knowledge and that the learner directs his or her own problem-solving process [3].

Social networks and Web 2.0 are closely aligned with modern thinking about educational practice, and in particular the social constructivist and socially-oriented approaches [3]. Such paradigms promote that effective learning requires opportunities for learners to be independent in their study and research, have a wider range of expressive capability and more collaborative ways of working, all of which are facilitated by Web 2.0 tools in social networks [43]. Developing the skills of problem solving, research and collaborative working also equips learners well for the world of work.

The underlying pedagogy is considered by other educational theorists however, who comment that Web 1.0 is aligned with constructivism allowing the individual to search actively for information and knowledge. Siemens [42] proposes that Web 2.0 methods and tools permit the educational process to transcend constructivist theories by moving on from isolated, individual activity to interactivity amongst a community of collaborating learners termed 'collaborative constructivism' or 'connectivism' [3].

Table 17.1 provides a summary of the Web 2.0 principles aligned with pedagogical aspirations for social learning as specified by Walton et al. [44].

In order to create a social network learning framework several components are required [44]:

– *Technology*: rather than a 'one-size fits all' centralised, institutional system, there must be a move towards more loosely-coupled, personalised learning

Table 17.1 Social learning: Web 2.0 principles aligned with pedagogical aspirations [44]

Web 2.0 characteristics	Key pedagogical characteristics
User-generated content	Personalised, adaptive
Power of the crowd	Authentic, 'real', situated
Data on an epic scale	Active, experiential,
Architecture of participation	Collaborative, sum is greater than the parts
Network effects	Communicative, peer supported
Openness	Reflective, cumulative

environments, using third party applications and widgets as well as bespoke developed tools, to create personal learning spaces, including, for example, the learner's profile.

- *Content*: users need to be encouraged to actively participate with others in the search for, customisation and generation of content. For this they require unrestricted access to content in a variety of formats and the tools to aid its discovery. This is a barrier in some institutions due to network restrictions [36], the 'potential conflict between the opportunities provided by exposing learners to public internet content and the comparative safety of the "walled garden" VLE of the institution' [3], and the fear that learners will source or produce inappropriate material [37].

- *Pedagogy*: learning in personalised social networks tends to be unstructured and informal, based around peer to peer dialogue and independent study. Learners generally value *some* structure and support which can be achieved through the use of appropriate tools and narrative structures. Indeed, Crook et al. [37] point out that even with increased 'learner centeredness', there will still be significant demands on teachers to provide structure and facilitate the learning. Walton et al. [44] evaluate the paradox of discovery learning 'how can I inquire about something which I don't know anything about?' Often the initial, tentative exploration about an unfamiliar subject will be deeper and faster when familiar social networks are engaged. It is essential that learners have access to suitable content and are supported in identifying good content and finding consistent and timely ways of accessing it.

- *Community*: social networks and Web 2.0 applications succeed through the strength of the communities they foster. These social networks need not be limited to one educational module, programme or university – they could be global [44].

Web 2.0 services will doubtless increase in complexity and scale during the coming years as users continue to creatively adapt new tools to produce knowledge, leverage collective intelligence, and build social capital [38]. Educational institutions use of social networks and Web 2.0 tools appears to have been mainly positive and they are continuing to develop their provision [3]. There may be a 'peak of inflated expectations' as discussed by Armstrong and Franklin [36] but given the current governmental and environment pressures on higher education there is an urgent requirement to establish new forms of learning that meet the need of the new generations of learners whose experience has been fundamentally influenced by the internet and Web 2.0 social technologies [44].

The eTUTOR Project

The previous sections of this chapter have evaluated the benefits and challenges inherent in e-learning, and particularly those associated with VLEs and SLEs, as described in the literature. This section describes the application of those concepts in the development of a social learning environment for a university computing module. The project was termed the eTUTOR (Education Through Ubiquitous Technologies and Online Resources) project, funded by JISC through the Next Generation Technologies and Practices strand of the Users and Innovation Programme.

Background to the eTUTOR Project

In anticipation of next generation technologies and practices in the development of e-learning, the eTUTOR project was developed to evaluate the use of current technology in the context of educational learning. It addressed the contention that in the future, the creation of an online learning environment and the sourcing of online learning content and resources, will be predominantly facilitated through the use of freely available web services and web-based materials [45]. The project used free social network software and web services coupled with search engine functionality to create an online learning environment in which a learner-centric discovery learning pedagogy would apply. The intention was to facilitate access to open educational resources available globally rather than individuals creating their version of that content locally. It was acknowledged that the quality of resources gathered might not be consistent because the ability to aggregate Web 2.0 services would not be as far advanced as required for quality educational delivery. However, an assessment of current capability would be valuable in anticipation of predicted future trends [46–48].

There has been a great deal of previous work on learning environments developed using social software, including a number of JISC funded initiatives [49]. The eTUTOR project benefited from the outcomes of these projects and used the information provided when planning the learning environments used. There have also been a number of projects looking at the functionality of Web 2.0 services and their potential to contribute to online learning environments [40]. The functionality of commercial VLEs includes synchronous and asynchronous communications, learning content and resource hosting and management, database and information management and a number of services. All of these services can be provided individually through Web 2.0 applications and the project had the objective of exploring the ability to aggregate them into a fully functional SLE [45].

The Project Aim and Rationale

According to JISC [49], the broad aim of the eTUTOR project was to apply the principles of the e-Framework to 'explore the possibility of creating an effective online learning environment from currently available Web 2.0 services and social network software, and to use this environment to deliver quality assured learning modules using existing online content and resources'. The rationale for the eTUTOR project grew from the work of the Wales e-Training Network (WeTN) online delivery programme and ran in parallel with the JISC *WALES* project which evaluated social network software in the support of online learners; as a consequence, a number of innovative directions for the future of education were revealed [45], some of which were investigated in this project.

The context for the project was the growing open educational resource movement. MIT's Open Courseware initiative, for example, provides their learning materials free online. Similarly, the global Open Courseware Consortium, whose main contributor in the UK is the Open University through its OpenLearn Unit, is committed to sharing high quality content freely with all and its objectives align well with the rationale for the eTUTOR project. Open Educational Resources generate economies of scale in collaborative e-learning content development and are operationally scalable as networks become larger, which is likely given that it is claimed that web-based learning will eventually become a globally networked service [47].

A further consideration is that resources with the potential for use in an educational context are being generated and made available on the web every day. It is also evident that such resources are being increasingly identified, catalogued and presented automatically by search portals. The providers of these services are already beginning to recognise the value of structuring their presentations for educational use [45, 50], potentially minimising individual lecturer course material preparation time. Moreover, a significant proportion of the learning resources sourced from the web would be from non-educational sources, that is, information and guidance materials created by all manner of organisations for their own purposes but useful to students to place their learning in a contemporary, real-life context.

'The existence of open online courseware on a global scale means that learning resources are there to be discovered by learners' [45]. The use of the internet by individuals seeking knowledge and skills, for whatever reason, can result in informal learning and therefore, the effectiveness of learning online is increasing dramatically. Thus, the discovery learning approach of the eTUTOR project aligns formal learning much more closely with informal learning by adopting the same approach that learners use when they routinely search the internet.

Although there is much debate regarding the best learning approaches, the effectiveness of discovery and inquiry-based learning is widely promoted, for instance, through the work of Piaget [51], Bruner [52] and Papert [53]. Yet, Mayer [54], although criticising discovery learning, advocates guided instruction and in doing so, strengthens the argument that discovery learning aids cognitive development. Learners new to discovery learning need more guidance and that is the approach taken in the eTUTOR project. Toole [45] contends that 'there is a growing consensus in the e-learning community that discovery learning will be a central feature of future globalised education'.

Design and Implementation of the SLE

This section describes the design alternatives and selections made in the creation of two modules of the eTUTOR SLE prototype: *Personal Computer and Internet Technology* and *Computer Games Development*. The design decisions are detailed below, using the *Personal Computer and Internet Technology* module screenshots to illustrate points made.

In accord with the aim of the project, the design of the eTUTOR SLE conforms to the e-Framework for Education and Research, an initiative that promotes technical interoperability and reusability through service-oriented approaches [1, 26]. The project adopted a service oriented architecture approach that is based on 'innovation in assembly', and where development tools are reused in a variety of ways and scenarios, as advocated by Weller [55] and broadens the notion of VLE 2.0; this concept can be considered as a precursor to SLE 2.0.

According to Chatti [56], two types of mashup (a combination of data or functionality from more than one external source to create a new service) can be considered when constructing a SLE. The first, uses developers' programming skills to embed Application User Interfaces (APIs) such as iGoogle, NetVibes and Yahoo widgets and services, including Del.icio.us, Flicker and GoogleMaps. However, as the SLE is likely to be used by developers with little or no programming skills, this project used the second type of mash-up, using easy-to-use widgets and feeds to aggregate information from different sources, which requires no programming knowledge.

The Host Environment

There are many social network applications online that include the communication and resource presentation features that can support online learning and complement or rival, traditional VLEs. A number of options were compared for use in the eTUTOR project, including KickApps, pbWiki and Crowdvine; the evaluation criteria included level of functionality (e.g. social communication tools including

Add as friend feature, Web 2.0 collaborative tools, coursework submission options such as wall, blog, forum), the ability to embed widgets, having an educational version that did not carry advertising and free from cost. Initial experimentation compared Wetpaint and Ning; for this module, Ning, a free social network solution, was selected as it was deemed to be easiest to build, manage and use, providing more easy-to-use social and collaboration tools for users. Ning appeals to people who want to create their own unique social networks around specific interests, which could be an educational network for example. It enables users to customise their own visual design and choice of features with little or no knowledge of web design. Educators around the world, technical and non-technical, are using Ning to develop educational resources. Furthermore, learners are likely to be familiar with and comfortable using the popular leading social network sites such as Facebook and MySpace, and so there is likely to be some transferability of usability skills to the Ning environment [57].

Ning has a modern look and feel, with full use of Web 2.0 features allowing customisation of the community site. The social networks running on Ning's service are developed with Open Source PHP, giving advanced users the flexibility to deploy their programming skills, though no programming is required. Like Facebook, there is a large variety of interactive widgets available for Ning, which are very easy to install/embed by both learner/user and tutor/administrator. Consequently, the environment is ideal for educators to rapidly create an interactive social learning environment. However, unlike Facebook, learners using Ning, have their own customisable page and are able to change the colour of many elements, such as the text, headers, background or tables to suit their own look and feel.

Figure 17.1 illustrates the home page of the *Personal Computer and Internet Technology module* of the eTUTOR social learning environment developed in Ning. The page is divided into discrete sections, which accommodate all the aspects of the SLE including: Introduction text, Events, Chat, Notes, Members, Discovery Map, Videos, Latest Activity, Forum, Blog, etc.

The development of the SLE using Ning was relatively speedy and the management of the environment was very easy. For educators with little prior knowledge Ning is highly suitable as a development platform for the creation of a social learning environment.

Mind Mapping Software

This project required the creation of a customised gateway to web-based learning resources and consequently a suitable navigation structure was required that was clear, self-explanatory and easy-to-use. Early experimentation led to the decision to *visually* portray the structure and specifically to adopt mind-map representations of the module curriculum [45].

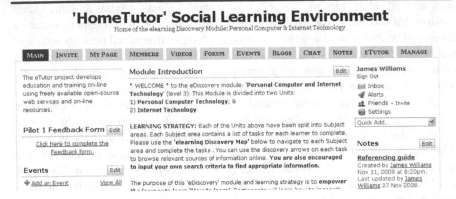

Fig. 17.1 Learning environment home page [58]

There are many mind mapping tools available online, though Mindomo and MindMeister were chosen for evaluation for this project. The criteria used for comparison and the results are illustrated in Table 17.2.

Based on the evaluation in Table 17.2, MindMeister was chosen because of its' ease of use, the ability to create multi-layered maps and because it facilitates real-time collaboration by enabling multiple people to simultaneously work on the same mind map and see each other's changes in real-time. The immediacy of MindMeister's facility to share information is a social feature that allows learners to feel supported by each other while the collaboration aspects hone their group working skills.

An online mind-map entitled 'Discovery Map' was created using MindMeister. The design focused on the 'learning outcomes' of the modules, that is, the knowledge and practical skills that a learner would be able to demonstrate on completion of the module. A structured sequence of learning activities in numerical order guided the learners towards achieving the outcomes of the module. For example, the *Personal Computer Technology andInternet Technology* module required partitioning to display the course content so the module was first subdivided into two units, namely *Personal Computer Technology* and *Internet Technology* (Fig. 17.2).

The mind-map depicts a set of linked nodes, with every node representing one module topic for research and tasks for completion. Each individual node provides URL-enabled arrow icons containing pre-defined search strings linked to a search engine results page that when selected, presents appropriate learning resources related to the learning activity for the topic. Thus the search engines results are customised for the particular resources being researched and the learners have opportunities to further refine the search to 'discover' more specific content [57], as shown in Fig. 17.3. The learner can then use the search results to complete the learning activities (tasks). This Discovery Map provides a coherent pathway through the units, their topics and learning activities, in a user-friendly format.

Table 17.2 Mind mapping software evaluation [57]

Criteria	Evaluation
1. Ease of use:	Although Mindomo offers a wonderful array of tools, significantly greater than MindMeister, this was its downfall. MindMeister is significantly easier to use and offers all the essential features deemed necessary to achieve the project's requirements
2. Hyperlinks:	It is very easy to assign a hyperlink to a node. The user can either click on the 'hyperlink' icon in the main horizontal menu or alternatively utilise the hyperlink accordion menu on the left. However, using Mindomo it is not possible to create a link inside a node, instead a small square link box is created at the side of the node. This feature is very useful but not user-friendly as there is nothing to indicate that it is a hyperlink
3. Upload/attach learning resources:	Online mind mapping software can be used not only to structure a course, list favourite website links or organise tasks/projects, but also as a document repository to organise lecture/tutorial files for example. This feature is available in the premium version of both MindMeister ($4 a month) and Mindomo ($6 a month). It is very easy to add attachments to a node using MindMeister
4. Multi-layered Maps:	MindMeister also allows you to link to multiple mind-maps, allowing the creation of multi-layered maps. This feature is very useful as a tutor can present the user learner with increasing amounts of information regarding the learner's interest
5. Synchronous collaboration:	MindMeister allows multiple people to collaborate on the same map in real time, Mindomo does not. MindMeister gives the author of a map the ability to share with multiple people who can then work on the map at the same time

The Discovery Map aims to encourage and empower learners to seek out information for themselves. However, as learners go through the discovery learning tasks, they do require support from the online tutor, mainly in two forms: via forums and messages posted in the learning environment and weekly chat sessions. Each learner had a personal blog where they were to post a brief report on the outcomes of each task as they completed them. They were also required to post a weekly reflective blog entry and to contribute to a collaborative forum, sharing insights, problems and solutions with the tutor and their peers. This social engagement helped ensure that learners did not feel isolated.

Search Engine Selection for Customised Searches

Given that the MindMeister nodes provide URL-enabled arrow icons containing pre-defined search strings, a key decision in the development process was the

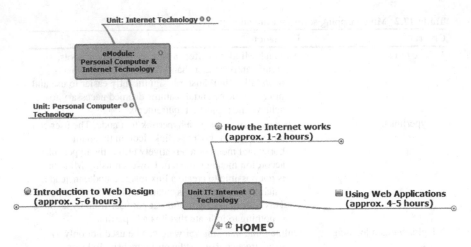

Fig. 17.2 Module and unit maps [58]

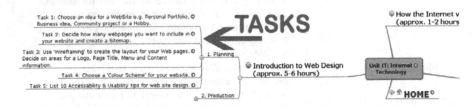

Fig. 17.3 e-Learning discovery map learning activities [58]

selection of a suitable search engine. A number of search engines were evaluated to assess their appropriateness for use in this project, including Google the search engine market leader (see Fig. 17.4), and other search engines that have different approaches, such as Ask and Yahoo. Google Customised Search Engine (CSE) was selected because its search for resources can be configured to be very specific and it can be further refined by users to prioritise good quality resources.

Learners need guidance in web searching techniques and tools to help them to discover the online resources. Typically, students do not have the knowledge or formal learning to allow them to create their own sophisticated search strings. Two possible search method solutions were evaluated: Customised Google Search Engine (CSEs) and Customised Google Search String. An experiment compared the effectiveness of each approach, and based on the appropriateness of the websites listed in the search results for each learning activity, the Customised Google Search Strings results seemed to present links that were more relevant to the learning activity. The Discovery Map was then created to organise and list the learning activities. The tutor/developer tested and inserted appropriate Google search strings for each of the learning activity nodes on the map as illustrated in Fig. 17.5 [58].

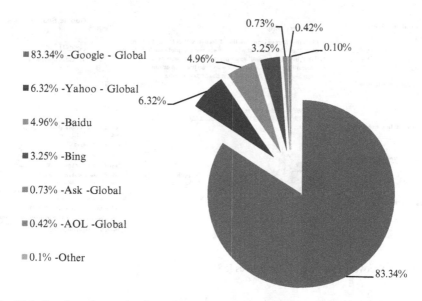

■83.34% -Google - Global

■6.32% -Yahoo - Global

■4.96% -Baidu

■3.25% -Bing

■0.73% -Ask -Global

■0.42% -AOL -Global

■0.1% -Other

Fig. 17.4 Search engine market share (September, 2010) (Data derived from [59])

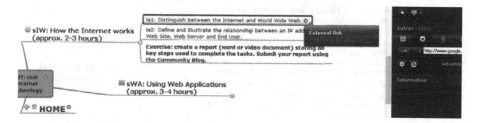

Fig. 17.5 MindMeister.com mind map – Google search strings [58]

Each time the learner clicks on a node, a Google search result page appears, allowing the learner to examine the search result list and use the information to complete the learning activity, thereby developing their knowledge and skills. The learner may also continue to refine the search by editing the individual search strings, thus becoming more skilled in discovery learning techniques.

All three Discovery Map search methods can be included in a single page: Google Search, Custom Google Search and Pre-defined Google Search String (as shown in Fig. 17.6). The inclusion of all three methods enables learners to recognise and use search method alternatives, and to select their preferred method.

As learners select successive nodes, more detail is revealed. Figure 17.7 shows the learning activities associated with a particular node.

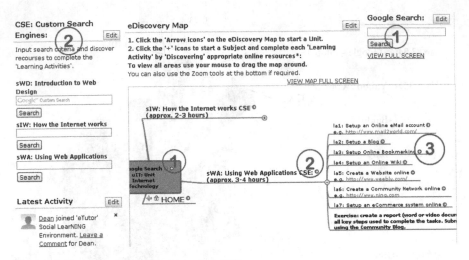

Fig. 17.6 Discovery map search alternatives [58]

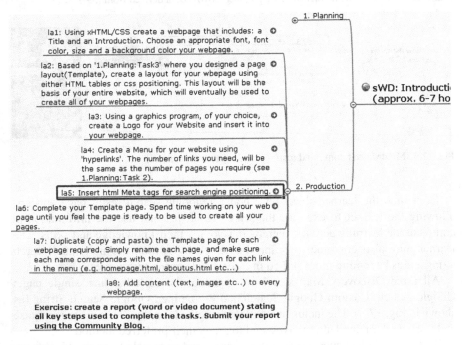

Fig. 17.7 A typical learning activity [58]

Results and Evaluation

This section describes the results of the eTUTOR project, including developer testing and feedback, usability testing with four expert users, a questionnaire survey involving 20 undergraduate learner respondents, and supplemented by users' blog and forum posts. All results and respondent comments are sourced from the pilot report of the eTUTOR Project [58].

The Social Learning Environment

The eTUTOR system is ideal for educators to rapidly and easily create a SLE and provides a suitable platform for any type of collaborative exercise, whether it is for learning, commercial or leisure projects; the creation of a Ning network only takes a few minutes. The functionality and potential of Ning is only limited by the number of widgets that can be obtained or created and given that new widgets are continually being developed, the possibilities are endless [57]. Using the Ning platform, it feels like there is a free development team constantly updating and evolving the system as the web itself continues to expand and evolve to meet the need for greater social tools, richer and more engaging user experiences. The management of the SLE is also very easy. The Ning system provides a central 'Manage' page for the Network creator, as can be seen in Fig. 17.8:

After only using the SLE during tutorial sessions over a 2 week period, 80% of undergraduate respondents found the SLE easy-to-use while 85% of learners thought the use of a social network enhanced their learning. This may be because social networks make learning fun, more interesting and stimulating for the student. Students liked the user friendly dashboard style of Ning, where content was organised on one page, similar to other social network sites such as iGoogle, Facebook and MySpace. Respondents also commented positively on having their own individual page and map to organise their resources, the implied schedule of tasks that could be viewed as a whole and favourite internet sites (favourites). The easy-to-use software encouraged wider adoption of the technology, with some students using it to organise aspects of their personal lives.

The Ning environment allows participants to leave comments on forums, blogs, private messaging and personal wall spaces to support the learning of others. This opportunity for collaborative learning and social commentary was clearly valued by undergraduate respondents. Learners' favourite features include the informal but productive community culture, ease of communication with others and social features such as Buddypoke. Indeed, most learners valued the social aspects of the learning environment and none mentioned feeling 'isolated', an oft-cited drawback associated with e-learning. The Web 2.0 social network allowed for asynchronous communication and collaborative learning within individual student groups and between multiple groups of students. Using these communication tools, feedback

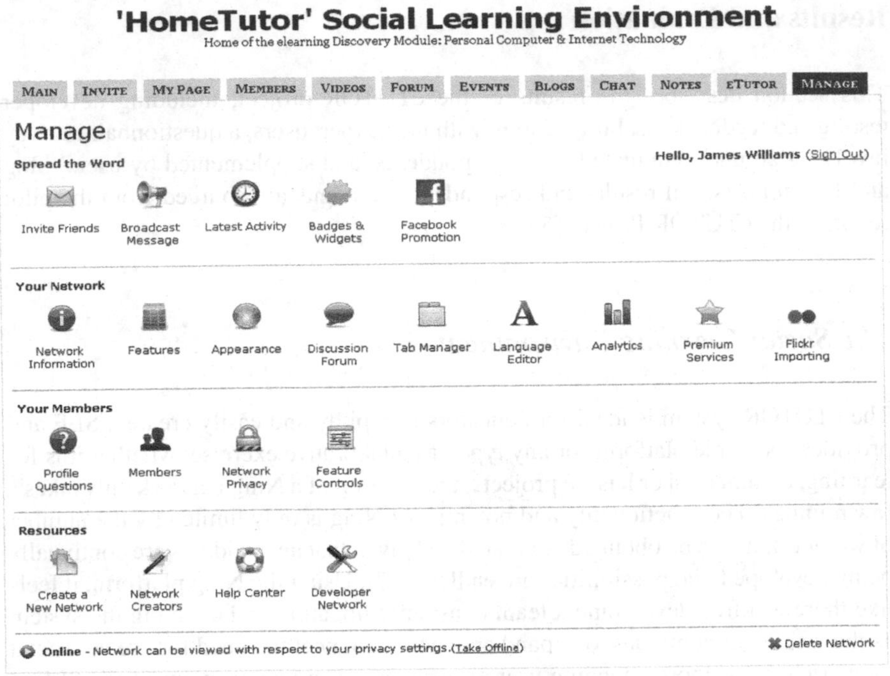

'HomeTutor' Social Learning Environment
Home of the elearning Discovery Module: Personal Computer & Internet Technology

| MAIN | INVITE | MY PAGE | MEMBERS | VIDEOS | FORUM | EVENTS | BLOGS | CHAT | NOTES | eTUTOR | MANAGE |

Manage

Spread the Word   Hello, James Williams (Sign Out)

Invite Friends   Broadcast   Latest Activity   Badges &   Facebook
                  Message   Widgets   Promotion

Your Network

Network   Features   Appearance   Discussion   Tab Manager   Language   Analytics   Premium   Flickr
Information   Forum   Editor   Services   Importing

Your Members

Profile   Members   Network   Feature
Questions   Privacy   Controls

Resources

Create a   Network   Help Center   Developer
New Network   Creators   Network

 Online - Network can be viewed with respect to your privacy settings.(Take Offline)   ✖ Delete Network

Fig. 17.8 Ning social learning environment management system [58]

from learners indicate that they enjoy supporting each other through the learning activities in an open social community environment. Feedback on learning activities can be uploaded in audio or video format. Respondents liked the multimedia aspects, including video links to online tutorials, the ability to link preferred resources to the learners personal home page and using 3D interactive applications.

The ability of the learner to achieve the learning outcomes of a module largely depends on their personal motivation. However, the tutor's ability to create an open and supportive community learning environment, where the learners are assisted to manage themselves and their time effectively, is also crucial. The module incorporated a 'self-reflective blog', which when used as part of the module's assessment, encouraged in learners, skills of self-evaluation. Learners commented that this motivated them to break the work down into regular, self-paced learning packages. The tutor witnessed an increase in independent learning and positive reflection. The emphasis on the search for credible information encouraged students to cite all sources used, thereby demonstrating the breadth of their research and improving their referencing skills.

However, at the time of writing, Ning did not provide a method to store and organise large amounts of learning resources, although there were widgets available, or one could have been created. However, the improved quality of up-to-date learning resources online means the need to create learning repositories continues to diminish. There were few responses regarding the learners' least favourite aspect of the SLE though several learners commented on the amount of email notifications they received when groups of which they are members updated discussion forums, etc. This issue was easily resolved by showing students how to change the email settings but it did reveal a training need that will need to be addressed in future induction sessions. However, most learners are very familiar with the interfaces of social network sites such as Facebook, and required no initial training on how to use the network. one learner did comment that 'I have got used to the structure of Blackboard'. One respondent did not like the 'work' involved with the community, though overall feedback was positive, including comments such as 'it's all good'.

The Discovery Mind Map

The Discovery Map displayed the module learning activities and learning resources for the topics in a single, clear and structured interactive graphical interface. It enabled the learners to proceed through the sequence of tasks for each subject in a user-friendly and structured form to achieve the learning outcomes of the module. Eighty-five percent of learners found the map easy to use. Some found the map's visual nature aesthetically appealing and felt that the ability to view all topics in a single view was one of the most useful features; in particular they liked that they could expand and collapse nodes at will to display content. In addition, learners commented positively on the ease of access to resources, provision of tutorials in both file and weblink format, both of which show the value learners place on receiving information/tutorials from educators. From this perspective, discovery learning is valuable to supplement learning activities and traditional handouts and indicates that a blended rather than pure e-learning approach can be the most effective solution.

It can be argued that the Discovery Map is not any better than a traditional VLEs ability to list resources in a typical file directory fashion. There is no real difference between the map and a traditional structured list of learning activities with accompanying hyperlinks, which of course can easily be created in Blackboard or any electronic document. However, learners preferred the interactive and graphical nature of the map. It is an alternative that gives the learner the ability to organise and present a large amount of learning resources on one page, in one interactive graphical representation, that also allows the learners to contribute and be a part of the resources provided.

Customised Searches

A learning activity was selected and a search string was constructed using the keywords relating to the learning activity: 'create a webpage using xHTML'. The

Table 17.3 Search method effectiveness test [58]

Search Engine	Relevant links (x/10)	Analysis
Test 1: Google Search	2	Using key words from the learning activity 2 out of 10 sites were deemed relevant to the learning activity i.e. a link that provided the practical information on the first click and without purchasing a book. The search provided many links guiding the user to commercial sites that sell learning guides on xHTML and CSS
Test 2: Custom Search Engine (CSE)	8	The same Google search string was used from the previous search but within a specially created custom search engine. Eight out of ten search results were deemed relevant. However several links were from the same tutorial websites. Websites were selected for the CSE based on industry experience and the most relevant were chosen from the top ten Google page results
Test 3: Refined Search String	7	Using the same method as test 1, but with a refined search string (basic xHTML tutorial), 7 out of 10 search results were deemed relevant to the learning activity. There was only one repeat learning resource
Test 4: Refined CSE string	10	Using the previous refined search string within a CSE, 10 out of 10 of the search results were relevant to the activity. Although several results were from the same tutorial sites, this happened much less than the CSE only method. Overall, a greater variety of relevant results and less repetition

single search string was used in four different ways to obtain the search results from Google in order to compare the number and relevance of the entries in each search result list (Table 17.3).

Based on this analysis, using a refined search string with a Custom Search Engine greatly increases the quality of the learning resources presented to the learner, and is the most effective discovery learning method tested. As identified previously, the use of customised search strings enables the learner to rapidly home-in on the most valuable resources. Customised search strings can be added to any level of the Discovery Map, from centre node to individual learning activities or indeed anywhere on the Ning environment. For example, they can be added underneath the map thereby enabling the learner to simultaneously view the learning activities whilst using the search engine. However, use of this method impeded learners' ability to create effective search strings for *themselves*, and given that the ability to search creatively is an essential skill, the creation of a CSE customised for particular learning outcomes or learning activities in which learners create their own search strings, is recommended [57].

Discovery Learning

Discovery learning facilitated and structured by the tutor using Web 2.0 technologies produced high quality online resources that improved the learning process. However, the role of the tutor was crucial in guiding the learner through the learning process, from goal setting, time management and encouragement to achieve their goals. One of the most useful features of the social network according to learners' feedback was the regular contact and clarification of learning activities from the tutor that helped them to stay focused. Learners were encouraged to solve problems through social collaboration with peers and independent self-reflection before contacting the tutor. In addition to building social team-working and problem solving skills, this method ensured the tutor was not over-burdened by learner communication and was able to answer questions on the support forum or via email at his or her convenience. Furthermore, the use of the community network communication tools (e.g. for individual Modules) empowers the module lecturer/tutor with tools such as 'community broadcast messages', 'group messaging', or simply 'send a message to an individual student', enhanced support and monitoring, which will ultimately increase retention.

Eighty-five percent of undergraduate learners responded that use of the discovery learning SLE enhanced their learning. During usability testing, one expert learner commented:

> For both tasks I began by looking at the web pages provided by the tuned Google search engine that the mind map takes the learner to. I then followed any further links, web pages, videos etc. provided by the suggested web pages . . . Even though the timescale given on the mind map was 1-2 hrs I easily spent 3-4 hours on the two tasks combined. This was due to the fact that I would click on hyperlinks within the suggested web pages to dig deeper into the subject, as well as using Google to search for more specific areas related to the tasks. This shows discovery learning has taken place at least with me and this would be of great benefit for "real learners".

It is an accessible source for online tutorials making it easier to work at home, or any convenient place yet still being part of a learning community. Learners commented that when learning with peers, they felt more motivated and less likely to procrastinate. As previously identified, social and collaborative learning technology offers a peer- and tutor-supportive learning environment. 'Peer-to-peer support is a positive aspect of learning; the awareness that peers are struggling with the same difficulties is important' [60]. It is vital for the tutor/moderator to create a social and professional learning culture, and in a supportive manner to help students to maintain their focus on learning activities. The system allowed the tutor to review easily student progress, particularly via the weekly blog and provided a useful monitoring tool to identify which learners required help and/or encouragement. This was also a very constructive teaching and learning strategy for a more traditionally delivered module to ensure students make better use of their own study time. The learners' 'My Page' and 'My Map' could be used to create a personal learning plan and to store a portfolio of accomplishments/work completed. Initially the tutor or 'learning coach' can help the learner to set goals and plan study-time; learners can then take control of the direction of their own learning and later reflect on their achievement using their blog facility.

Conclusion

The advent of social networks and Web 2.0 technologies has marked a watershed in the role and impact of technology in higher education that will result in a fundamental shift in the way we learn. Web 2.0 technology has the potential to transform education and provide a response to the challenges of a changing education landscape, environment and stakeholder expectations. For learners, social networks facilitate a connectivist, discovery learning approach in which they control the direction and pace of their own learning, using technologies that are familiar in everyday life. In addition, social networks foster a learning community that provides a (safety) net of peer collaboration, review and support, in which participants access, generate and share resources widely. As well as learning the social software tools that are increasingly used and in demand by employers, learners also hone their research and group work transferable skills, making them more employable and useful in the workplace.

For educators, many of the attributes associated with the use of Web 2.0 tools in social learning environments provide a neat 'fit' to the constructivist pedagogy advocated by many contemporary educational theorists. The role of the educator becomes that of facilitator rather than teacher, as the expectation of students is that they become much more actively involved in their own learning. They are able to engage learners in an interactive dialogue and provide early feedback and advice on learner progress. However, some of the principles and approaches in the socially-networked, Web 2.0 domain do not sit easily within a higher education context. The changing methods of teaching and the design and assessment of online, collaborative learning activities, for example, can be challenging and there may be an adverse impact on workloads. However, in determining their strategies for future success and sustainability, higher education institutions, and those who work in them, must respond to the challenge by establishing a customer/learner-centric approach and new forms of learning using Web 2.0 technologies.

Rather than using a VLE, the eTUTOR project described in this chapter is a social learning environment developed using learning content and resources primarily sourced from the internet and assembled on a foundation of a free social network (Ning). Such environments can be constructed with relative ease by users with little or no knowledge of web design. This provides the flexibility and freedom for users to incorporate as many or as few services that they deem to be relevant and appropriate for their needs, from a diverse range, without relying on specialist skills. There are two distinct eTUTOR stakeholder groups: the tutor as developer and the learner and tutor as users. The developer can create the social learning environment with ease and the user is motivated to collaborate with other users. As the tutor has a dual role, inefficiencies or weaknesses in the SLE will become apparent during use (user role) and s/he will be able to take corrective action (as the developer).

The project provided the learner with a customised gateway to online learning resources that were harvested and presented for use using search engine applications. The social learning environment and online mapping software offered an engaging, rich, social learning experience for learners facilitated by an online tutor, to promote an open and supportive culture of collaboration. A tutor can provide high-quality learning resources relevant to the learning outcomes from the internet and present them in a structured format, whilst highlighting the importance of collaboration and independent discovery learning and personal creativity. Using the SLE, students develop research techniques and improve their content discernment skills i.e. the ability to select wisely appropriate sources of information. They are encouraged to solve problems through self-reflection and social collaboration before contacting the tutor. This method builds self-confidence/esteem and team-working skills. Through the completion of the learning activities, students develop a positive, pro-active attitude. The project presents an effective Web 2.0 solution for collaborative community- and technology-enhanced discovery learning.

The social learning environment is ideal for the Facebook generation as it is based on the tools that they use to communicate in their social lives and does not constrain them to methods of learning that they perceive to be old-fashioned. The learner-to-learner and learner-to-tutor relationships are enhanced due to the close collaborative style of working together; this also encourages learners to be self-motivated and to collaborate with peers safe in the knowledge that the tutor is also there to support them (e-guide on the side). This solution is suitable for any project that requires electronic collaboration and information management while providing opportunities for personalised, adaptive learning using a variety of learning tools derived from free, open source, ubiquitous social networks.

References

1. Holmes, B., Gardner, J.: E-Learning: Concepts and Practice, p. 14. Sage Publications, London (2006)
2. O'Hear, S.: Seconds out, round two. Education Guardian, 15 Nov (online). Available at http://education.guardian.co.uk/elearning/story/0,10577,1642281,00.html (2005). Accessed 8 Jan 2011
3. Minocha, S.: Joint Information Systems Committee (JISC) report, (2009) A study on the effective use of social software by further and higher education in the UK to support student learning and engagement (online). Available at http://www.jisc.ac.uk/whatwedo/projects/socialsoftware08.aspx (2009). Accessed 8 Jan 2011
4. Walton, A., Weller, M., Conole, G.: Social: learn – widening participation and sustainability of higher education. In: Proceedings of EDEN 2008: Annual Conference of the European Distance and E-Learning Network, Lisbon, Portugal, p. 1, June 2008
5. Thorpe, M., Edwards, R., Hanson, A. (eds.): Culture and Processes of Adult Learning. Routledge, London (1993)

6. Tomei, L.A.: Designing Instruction for the Traditional, Adult, and Distance Learner: A New Engine for Technology-Based Teaching. IGI Global, Hershey (2010)
7. Levy, cited Brine, A. (ed.): Handbook of Library Training Practice and Development, vol. 3. Ashgate Publishing Ltd, Farnham (2009)
8. Abadzi, H.: Efficient Learning for the Poor: Insights from the Frontier of Cognitive. World Bank Publications, Washington (2006)
9. Kern, D.E.: Praxis II: Principles of Learning and Teaching. Wiley Publishing Inc., Hoboken (2006)
10. Baziukaite, D., Vaira, Z., Idzelyte, D.: A tool to support self-education in lifelong learning. In: Iskander, M. (ed.) Innovative Techniques in Instruction Technology, E-learning, E-assessment. Springer, New York (2008)
11. Blanco, A., Torrente, J., Moreno-Ger, P., Fernandez-Manjon, B.: Bridging the gap: adaptive games and student-centered VLEs. In: Spaniol, M., Li, Q., Klamma, R. (eds.) 'Advances in Web Based Learning', ICWL 2009: 8th International Conference Aachen, Germany, August 2009 Proceedings. Springer, Berlin (2009)
12. Fry, H., Ketteridge, S., Marshall, S.: A Handbook for Teaching and Learning in Higher Education: Enhancing Academic Practice, 3rd edn, p. 87. Routledge, Abingdon (2009)
13. British Educational Communications and Technology Agency (BECTA): Virtual and managed learning environments, January (Online). Available at http://foi.becta.org.uk/download.cfm?resID=15963 (2003). Accessed 19 Feb 2010
14. Hart, J.: Building a social learning environment – for free or at low cost, part 1: using free, public social media tools. Inside Learning Technologies Magazine, October (online). Available at http://c4lpt.co.uk/articles/bsle1.html (2009). Accessed 25 Mar 2010
15. O'Leary, R.: Virtual learning environments. LTSN Generic Centre and ALT [Online]. Available at http://www.alt.ac.uk/docs/eln002.pdf (2002). Accessed 19 Feb 2010
16. Pole, R., Jones, K.: An evaluation of the effectiveness of e-learning in higher education: a case study of a computing department. In: Recent Advances in Computing and Management Information Systems, pp. 365–374. ATINER, Greece (2009)
17. Jones, cited in de Cássia Veiga Marriott, R., Torres, P.L.: Handbook of Research on E-Learning Methodologies for Language Acquisition. IGI Global, Hershey (2009)
18. Woodill, G.: Elements for constructing social learning environments. Workplace Learning Today, Brandon Hall Research (online). Available at http://www.brandon-hall.com/workplacelearningtoday/?p=9692 (2010). Accessed 8 Jan 2011
19. Horton, W.: E-Learning by Design, p. 1. Pfeiffer, San Francisco (2006)
20. Bullen, M., Janes, D.P.: Making the Transition to E-learning: Strategies and Issues, p. 176. Information Science Publishing, London (2007)
21. Mann, B.L.: Selected Styles in Web-Based Educational Research, p. 19. Information Science Publishing, London (2006)
22. Stockley, D.: E-learning definition and explanation (online). Available from: http://derekstockley.com.au/elearning-definition.html (2006). Accessed 10 Nov 2010
23. Joint Information Systems Committee (JISC): e-learning (online). Available from: http://www.jisc.ac.uk/whatwedo/themes/elearning.aspx (2010). Accessed 22 Sept 2010
24. Siemens, G.: The role of e-learning (online). Available at http://www.elearnspace.org/blog/archives/000623.html (2003). Accessed 9 Jan 2011
25. Salmon, G.: Reclaiming the territory for the natives, online learning: exploiting technology for training, p. 4 (online). Available at http://www.atimod.com/research/presentations2002.shtml (1999). Accessed 14 Dec 2010
26. Aswathappa, K.: Human Resource and Personnel Management: Text and Cases. Tata McGraw-Hill, New Delhi (2005)
27. Zhang, D., Zhao, J.L., Zhou, L., Nunamaker Jr., J.F.: Can e-learning replace classroom learning? Commun. ACM 47(5), 75–79 (2004)
28. Joint Information Systems Committee (JISC): Briefing paper 1: MLEs and VLEs explained, March 31, (online). Available at http://www.jisc.ac.uk/whatwedo/programmes/buildmlehefe/lifelonglearning/mlebriefingpack/1 (2009). Accessed 15 Jan 2010

29. El-Ghareeb, H.A.: E-learning and management information systems: universities need both. eLearn Magazine, ACM, Sept 29, (online). Available at http://elearnmag.org/subpage.cfm?section=articles&article=961 (2009). Accessed 19 Feb 2010
30. Higher Education Academy (HEA): Using the virtual learning environment, 30 June (online). Available at http://www.ukcle.ac.uk/resources/tlr/vles.html (2010). Accessed 9 Jan 2011
31. Farmer, J., Tilton, J.: The use of virtual learning environment software in UK Universities 2001–2005. Industrial Media and Magic Inc Technical Briefs, 16 June (online). Available at http://www.immagic.com/eLibrary/ARCHIVES/GENERAL/IMM/I060616F.pdf (2006). Accessed 9 Jan 2011
32. Toole, A.M.: Globalised learning: are institutions facing an educational tsunami? In: Proceedings of the ALT-C: Rethinking the Digital Divide, Leeds, 9–11 Sept 2008 (2009)
33. Lockyer, L., Bennett, S., Agostinho, S., Harper, B.: Handbook of Research on Learning Design and Learning Objects: Issues, Applications and Technologies. IGI Global, London (2008)
34. van der Klink, Jachems (2003) in O'Donoghue, J.: Technology Supported Learning and Teaching: A Staff Perspective p. 38. Information Science Publishing, London (2006)
35. Prensky, M.: Digital natives, digital immigrants. On Horiz., MCB University Press, 9(5), (2001) (online). Available at http://www.marcprensky.com/writing/prensky%20-%20digital%20natives,%20digital%20immigrants%20-%20part1.pdf. Accessed 9 Jan 2011
36. Armstrong, J., Franklin, T.: A review of current and developing international practice in the use of social networking (Web 2.0) in higher education, a report commissioned by the committee of enquiry into the changing learner experience (online). Available at http://www.franklin-consulting.co.uk/ (2008). Accessed 9 Jan 2011
37. British Educational Communications and Technology Agency (BECTA) Report, Crook, C., Cummings, J., Fisher, T., Graber, R., Harrison, C., Lewin, C., Logan, K., Luckin, R., Oliver, M., Sharples, M.: Web 2.0 technologies for learning: the current landscape – opportunities, challenges and tensions (online). Available at http://partners.becta.org.uk/uploaddir/downloads/page_documents/research/web2_technologies_learning.pdf (2008). Accessed 8 Jan 2011
38. Kamel Boulos, M.N., Wheeler, S.: The emerging web 2.0 social software: an enabling suite of sociable technologies in health and health care education. Health Inf. Libr. J. 24(1), 2–23 (2007)
39. Wenger, E.: Communities of practice (online). Available at http://www.ewenger.com/theory/ (2006). Accessed 8 Jan 2011
40. Downes, S.: Learning networks in practice. In: British Educational Communications and Technology Agency (BECTA), 2007. Emerging Technologies for Learning, vol. 2 (online). Available at http://partners.becta.org.uk/page_documents/research/emerging_technologies07_chapter2.pdf (2007). Accessed 8 Jan 2011
41. Mejias U.: Teaching social software with social software. Innovate: J. Online Educ. 2(5), (2006) (online). Available at http://innovateonline.info/pdf/vol2_issue5/Teaching_Social_Software_with_Social_Software.pdf. Accessed 9 Jan 2011
42. Siemens, G: Connectivism: a learning theory for the digital age. Elearnspace everything elearning, Dec 12 (online). Available at http://www.elearnspace.org/Articles/connectivism.htm (2004). Accessed 9 Jan 2011
43. Dalsgaard, C.: Social software: e-learning beyond learning management systems. Eur. J. Open Distance E-Learning (2006) (online). Available at http://www.eurodl.org/materials/contrib/2006/Christian_Dalsgaard.htm (2006). Accessed 9 Jan 2011
44. Walton, A., Weller, M., Conole, G.: Social: learn – widening participation and sustainability of higher education. In: Proceedings of. EDEN 2008: Annual Conference of the European Distance and E-Learning Network, Lisbon, Portugal, June 2008
45. Toole, T.: Education through ubiquitous technologies and online resources (eTutor): JISC project final report, pp. 7–8 (online). Available at http://reports.jiscemerge.org.uk//18-eTutor-Education-Through-Ubiquitous-Technologies-and-On-line-Resources.html (2009). Accessed 7 Jan 2011

46. Atkins, D.E., Brown, J.S., Hammond, A.L.: A review of the open educational resources (OER) movement: achievements, challenges, and new opportunities, Feb (online). Available at http://learn.creativecommons.org/wpcontent/uploads/2008/03/areviewoftheopeneducationalresourcesoermovement_bloglink.pdf (2007). Accessed 7 Jan 2011

47. Waters, J.K.: Web 2.0 event draws the bleeding-edge cloud crowd. Application development trends, 29 April (online). Available at http://adtmag.com/articles/2008/04/29/web-20-event-draws-the-bleedingedge-cloud-crowd.aspx (2008). Accessed 7 Jan 2011

48. Joint Information Systems Committee (JISC): Enhancing learner progression through personalised learning environments: final report (online). Available at http://www.jisc.ac.uk/whatwedo/programmes/elearningcapital/xinstit1/elp2.aspx. Accessed 8 Jan 2011

49. Joint Information Systems Committee (JISC): eTutor – education through ubiquitous technologies and on-line resources (online). Available at http://www.jisc.ac.uk/whatwedo/programmes/usersandinnovation/etutor.aspx. Accessed 7 Jan 2011

50. Google for Educators: (online). Available at http://www.google.com/educators/index.html (2011). Accessed 7 Jan 2011

51. Piaget, J.: To Understand Is to Invent. The Viking Press, Inc., New York (1972)

52. Bruner, J.S.: The act of discovery. Harv. Educ. Rev. 31(1), 21–32 (1961)

53. Papert, S.: Computer-based microworlds as incubators for powerful ideas. In: Taylor, R. (ed.) The Computer in the School: Tutor, Tool, Tutee, pp. 203–210. Teacher's College Press, New York (1980)

54. Mayer, R.: Should there be a three-strikes rule against pure discovery learning? The case for guided methods of instruction. Am. Psychol. 59(1), 14–19 (2004)

55. Weller, M.: VLE 2.0 and future directions in learning environments. In: Philip, R., Voerman, A., Dalziel, J. (eds.) Proceedings of the First International LAMS Conference 2006: Designing the Future of Learning, Sydney, 6–8 Dec 2006: LAMS Foundation, pp. 99–106 (online). Available http://lamsfoundation.org/lams2006/pdfs/Weller_Lams06.pdf (2006). Accessed 18 Feb 2010

56. Chatti cited in Syvänen, A., Muukkonen, J., Sihvonen, M.: Are the open issues of social software-based personal learning environment practices being addressed? In: Proceedings of the 13th International MindTrek Conference: Everyday Life in the Ubiquitous Era, pp. 142–148 (2009)

57. Pole, R., Hole, S., Jones, K., Williams, J., Toole, T.: eDiscovery learning: an evaluation of web 2.0 technology to enhance learning. In: Proceedings for the 'e'Teaching and Learning Workshop 2010, Higher Education Academy Subject Network for Information and Computer Sciences (HEA-ICS), University of Greenwich, London (2010)

58. JISC, Williams, J.: eTutor project pilot evaluation report: a free, easy and effective web 2.0 solution for discovery e-learning, 13 March (online). Available at http://etutor.pbworks.com/w/page/6146602/Evaluation%20and%20Reporting (2009). Accessed 9 Jan 2011

59. Netmarketshare: Search engine market share (online). Available at http://marketshare.hitslink.com/search-engine-market-share.aspx?qprid=4# (2010). Accessed 27 Oct 2010

60. Liccardi, I., Ounnas, A., Pau, R., Massey, E., Kinnunen, P., Lewthwaite, S., Midy, M., Sarkar, C.: The role of social networks in students' learning experiences. In: Proceedings of ITiCSE-WGR'07 Working Group Reports on Iticse on Innovation and Technology in Computer Science Education (online). Available at http://portal.acm.org/citation.cfm?id=1345442 (2007). Accessed 10 Jan 2011

Chapter 18
Social Networks and Recommender Systems: A World of Current and Future Synergies

Kanna Al Falahi, Nikolaos Mavridis, and Yacine Atif

Abstract Recently, there has been a significant growth in the science of networks, as well as a big boom in social networking sites (SNS), which has arguably had a great impact on multiple aspects of everyday life. Since the beginnings of the World Wide Web, another fast-growing field has been that of recommender systems (RS), which has furthermore had a proven record of immediate financial importance, given that a well-targeted online recommendation often translates into an actual purchase. Although in their beginnings, both SNSs as well as RSs had largely separate paths as well as communities of researchers dealing with them, recently the almost immediate synergies arising from bringing the two together have started to become apparent in a number of real-world systems. However, this is just the beginning; multiple potentially beneficial mutual synergies remain to be explored. In this chapter, after introducing the two fields, we will provide a survey of their existing interaction, as well as a forward-looking view on their potential future.

Introduction

Network science, arguably having its beginnings in the 1700s with Euler's Seven Bridges of Knigsberg [1], has passed through a number of important stages, including the creation of graph theory [2], the sociogram, and the advent of social network analysis [3], culminating in the recent boom and solidification as a discipline. Just a little after, some of the most important recent results, such as

K.A. Falahi (✉) • N. Mavridis • Y. Atif
UAE University, Al Ain, United Arab Emirates
e-mail: K.alfalahi@uaeu.ac.ae; NikolaosM@uaeu.ac.ae; Yacine.Atif@uacu.ac.ae

A. Abraham and A.-E. Hassanien (eds.), *Computational Social Networks: Tools, Perspectives and Applications*, DOI 10.1007/978-1-4471-4048-1_18,
© Springer-Verlag London 2012

the development of scale-free networks [4], the first social networking sites (SNS), started to appear [5], and within less than a decade, Facebook has more than 6% of the world's population as active users.[1]

In parallel to these developments, since its early ARPAnet days (1969), the Internet, even more so after the creation of the World Wide Web (1991) and the wide-spread use of early graphical browsers (mosaic, 1993), has rapidly been utilized as an important platform for a host of activities that are essential to modern daily life: communication, information-seeking, education, as well as, quite importantly, business and e-commerce. One of the most important aspects implicated in successful e-commerce is the ability to identify products or services (items) in which people (users) might be interested in to estimate their interest ratings, and then to recommend such items to users, in order to have the users potentially purchase the items.

This is the central problem that recommender systems (RS) are targeting and it is quite an important problem, for users, merchants, as well as society at large. When it comes to merchants, the immediate and tangible economic benefits of a successful recommendation in terms of increasing sales and creating revenue are obvious. When it comes to users (potential buyers), nowadays, they are often overwhelmed with a multitude of choices and options in their online business experiences, while at the same time they have limited resources and free time to invest in the selection process. Hence, there is an increasing need for using recommendation support to overcome this problem and provide users with personalized recommendations on different items such as books, movies, music and news. Furthermore, the basic ideas behind recommender systems can be applied not only narrowly to purchasing and business, but can be extended to a wider context, for example within the social realm, in which such systems could recommend acquaintances for personal or professional relations, which could potentially increase collective social capital [6].

In terms of their underlying theory driving their implementation, Recommender Systems (RS), although having their roots in a number of disciplines, such as forecasting theories [7], information retrieval [8], approximation theory [9] and consumer choice modeling [10], started solidifying as an area in the 1990s, and today are at the heart of many multibillion dollar e-businesses, such as Amazon [11], Netflix and MovieLens [12]. At the heart of the problem of creating a successful recommendation is the ability to generalize from known or estimated attributes of items and users, and possibly also from existing ratings, in order to predict yet unknown ratings of items from users, towards the ultimate goal of a successful purchase. Thus, in order to create such a successful recommendation, one needs to possess information (data) as well as processes (algorithms): the required information usually consists of a database of users and items, together with adequate attributal information about them, and possibly similarity spaces for the two domains (users and items), as well as an algorithmic/mathematical means of creating and updating predictions on the basis of this information.

---

[1]http://www.facebook.com/press/info.php?statistics

And this is exactly the first obvious point of beneficial contact between social networking sites (SNS) and recommender systems (RS): there is a wealth of information about users, their attributes and preferences, as well as their relations, within social networking sites (Synergy I). Furthermore, a second easy observation that provides a strong basis for synergies has to do with social networking sites as a popular locus for online life: users spend an important percentage of their online time [13] in SNS. Thus, SNS are an ideal platform, not only for gathering information useful for creating recommendations, but for actually presenting these recommendations to users (Synergy II). Furthermore, in social networking sites, there is a need for recommendation not only of products and services but of individuals or groups, with which the user can potentially became related to, in a personal or professional fashion. And this creates the third domain of strong potential synergies (Synergy III) between RS and SNS, as we shall discuss, together with other potential synergies.

The rest of this chapter is organized as follows: The section "Social Networks" presents background on relevant research on social networks and sites, while sections "Recommendation Techniques" and "Recommender Systems Limitations" discusses recommender systems with their underlying techniques and algorithms as well as the limitations in these systems. In section "Recommender Systems in Social Networks", after talking about shortcomings of recommender systems, we discuss how these have been and can be potentially further addressed through their synergies with social networks, followed by sections on future work and conclusion

Social Networks

In the traditional way, businesses use to reach consumers via advertisements through TV and radios cannot satisfy all users as they are generally broadcasted to all users regardless of their personal preferences. The online space provides more efficient approach by allowing users to view products based on their desires especially with the usage of social networks. The web has become more social and data is generated in real time. Famous social networks, such as Facebook and Twitter, are good examples for such evolving social web. These social network websites provide a rich environment for performing recommendations.

Social Networks Definition

Social networks are built from a group of people who share the same interests, backgrounds, and activities. In social networks, people can communicate with each other in many ways. They can socially share and upload files such as images, videos, and audios to their profiles. Social networks consist of nodes that are the actors in the network. These nodes might be a user, a company etc. The nodes are linked to each other through connections or ties. In social networks, these connections represents the relationships between nodes as friendship, partnership, kinship, etc. The number of nodes is changing and expanding specially on the web as new web pages and profiles created everyday [14].

There are different properties that social networks provide here we will define two main concepts:

1. Profiling where each user has his own profile, which represents the user's preferences and interests
2. Linking between users, which make it easier to analyze relationships among users
3. The ease of data extraction from social network sites

User Profile

Usually individual corporations such as Google and Yahoo! moderate online social networks sites. Most of social networks provide their functionalities for free to the users. Though some social networks need the users to register in order to gain access to the full facilities of the website. Personal information about each user is stored in his/her profile. A profile is a collection of user information that shapes the user identity on the Internet [15]. These profiles contain information about the user as well as his/her interests.

User Connections

The main goal of social networks it to connect people, thus each user in a social network can establish a link with other users in the network. Figure 18.1 shows the different relationships that occur in social networks. An example would be the concept of following in Twitter where a user (creator) can follow other users (targets). A full connection between the creator and the target is established if both are following each other. In the case of Twitter example, the full connection will allow additional functionalities such as the ability of sending private messages between users. Users create these connections in order to follow each others' contributions, especially if they are of the same interest.

Data Extraction

Data extraction from social network sites is easy, as many studies done in the field of data collection and extraction from social network have shown is done through introduction of datasets. One dataset is presented in [16] where the researchers introduced a social network dataset based on Facebook. They studied the users, interest as well as the relationships between them.

Fig. 18.1 Social graph: the
pattern of social relationships
in social networks

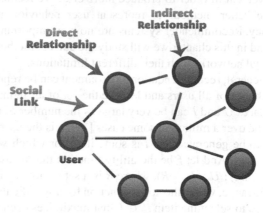

Fig. 18.1 Social graph: the pattern of social relationships in social networks

Understanding the structure of social networks will help evaluating the strength, weaknesses, opportunities and threats associated with them. Many such works have been done in the field of social networks analytics. One of the most popular papers is Milgram's "The Small-World Problem" [17] where the earliest experiment about the six degrees of separation was investigated. Milgram studied the average path length for social networks in the United States and suggested that we live in a small world. Watts also studied the mathematical analyses of the small world structure [18] as he examined the small world systems and discussed the problem of measuring the distances in social world and he studied examples of real small-world networks.

Recommendation Techniques

In mid-1990s recommender systems started to evolve as an independent research area as researchers started to focus on business ratings [19–22]. The problem with recommender systems is related to rating items that have not been seen by the user. When the recommender can estimate the rating for these unrated items, then it can recommend new and varied items to the users [19]. Different algorithms have been introduced over the last decade, both in academia and industry. Online vendors such as Amazon and Netflix used some of these recommender systems for commercial purposes. These systems are used to predict user interest in a new item based on his previous ratings on other items. Customers become more satisfied when the system predicts more.

These companies invest in improving such systems to have accurate items recommendations. For example, Netflix announced an open competition in 2006 with a prize of US $1,000,000 for the best algorithm that predicts user interests in a movie.[2] Recommender systems have attracted much attention since the publication of the first papers in collaborative filtering [20–22], but they still need further improvement in order to produce more effective results [19]. These improvements include better methods to represent user behavior and improve the prediction accuracy. Recommender systems are now an important part of many e-commerce sites and in this chapter we will study the current methods of recommender systems for social networks with their different limitations.

In general, recommendation environment can be represented as follows [19]: Let U be the set of all users and let I be the set of all items that can be recommended. The spaces U and I can be very large as the number of users and items respectively might be over a million in some cases [19]. u is the user for whom recommendation needs to be generated and i is some item for which we would like to predict u's preferences. And let f be the utility function that measures the importance of item i to user u ($f: U \times I \Rightarrow R$), where R is a set of nonnegative ordered values within a specific range, where the utility function for a specific item is represented by ratings. We need to select the item $i' \in I$ that maximizes each user $u \in U$ utility. This can be represented through the following formula.

$$\forall u \in U, i'_u = \mathrm{argmax}_{ei \in I} \, f(u, i) \qquad (18.1)$$

There are different ways to calculate the utility function. It can be defined by the user or calculated by an application [19]. User ratings are triplets (u,i,r) where r is the value assigned by the user u, to a particular item i. Usually this value is a fixed subset of the real numbers or a binary variable. In the user's space U, each user is represented by a profile that includes different attributes such as the user ID, age, gender, income, etc. a simple profile could contain the user ID only. Also each item in the items space I is represented by a set of characteristics. For example when recommending books each book can be represented by its ID, title, author, etc. Fig. 18.2 shows the users and items in the $U \times I$ space.

The problem with recommender systems is that the utility function f is not defined on the whole space $U \times I$ but on a part of it [19]. When the utility function is represented by ratings generated by the users, then the users will rate items that they previously seen while the other set of items is still unexplored and unrated. An example of user-item rating matrix is represented in Table 18.1 for a book recommendation application as on Amazon. Ratings are scaled from 1 to 5. The symbol ϕ indicates that the user did not rate the corresponding book. Therefore, the recommender system must predict the missing ratings for each user-book combination and perform an appropriate recommendation based on that.

The problem of unrated has been approached in two different ways: (1) specifying heuristics that define the utility function and empirically validating its performance and (2) estimating the utility function that optimizes certain performance criterion, such as the mean square error. Recommender systems are classified

---

[2]http://www.netflixprize.com

Fig. 18.2 Users and items in the $U \times I$ space

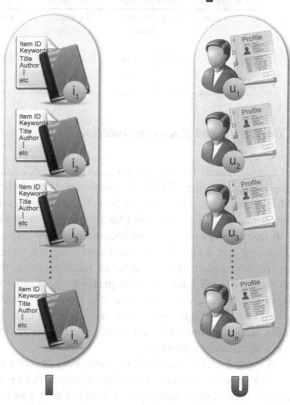

Users x Items Space

Table 18.1 A fragment of a rating matrix for a book recommender system

User	Freedom	The warmth of other suns	Unbroken	Matterhorn
John	1	5	4	ϕ
Alice	3	3	5	2
Mark	ϕ	4	ϕ	4
Bill	4	5	1	3

according to their way of estimating unrated ratings. Next we will present the different classifications and will survey these different techniques used to perform recommendations. Table 18.2 summarizes the recommendation techniques used in content-based recommendation and collaborative recommendation . Recommender systems are classified into the following types [9]:

1. Content-based recommendations
2. Collaborative recommendations
3. Hybrid approaches

Table 18.2 Recommendation techniques

Technique	Background	User input	Process
Content-based	Features on items in I	U's ratings of items in I	Generate a classifier that fits u's ratings behavior and use it on i
Collaborative	Ratings from U on items in I	Ratings from u on items in I	Identify users in U similar to u, and extrapolate from their ratings on i

Content-Based Recommendation

In content-based recommendation, users are recommended items based on their previous preferences [23–25]. In another way, the utility function $f(u, i)$ of an item i for a user u can be estimated based on the ratings assigned by the user u to all the items $i_n \in I$ that are similar to item i. For example, to recommend a book i to user u, the content-based recommender system will get the previously rated books by user u and then the books with highest similarity to the user preferences are recommended. In content-based recommenders the recommendation is based on the item itself rather than the preferences of other users [23, 24, 26]. Moreover, in this approach, users can help the system in providing initial ratings and the system can build a unique characteristic for the user preferences without matching them with someone else's interests [24]. Figure 18.3 represents the content-based recommendation approach.

A typical system would show a summary of items to the user and allow the user to click on an item to get detailed information. For example, Amazon would present a page with books summary and then the user would select one book to read the details and purchase the book if interested. As websites represent the items in a graphical way, but in the server these items are stored in databases. As we said earlier, there could be millions of items in the database, so we need to find a way to show a part of them to the user [27].

Content-based systems are based on previous researches done in the field of information retrieval, so they focus on recommending items that contain textual information as in documents and websites (URLs) [19]. They improved over the traditional information retrieval approaches by using user profiles [19], which contain information about the user tastes and preferences. These profiles can be generated using implicit (learning from users behaviors) or explicit (through questionnaires) approaches. Items are stored usually in databases. Each item is represented by a set of variables, attributes or characteristics. And each record will contain a value for each attribute. The table uses a unique identifier for each item to distinguish items that have common values such as title. The data is called structured if the items are described by the same set of attributes and the value range of these attributes is known [27]. The data is unstructured if there is no attribute names with well-defined values. Instead, they contain a paragraph or a text that describes the

Fig. 18.3 Content-based
recommendations

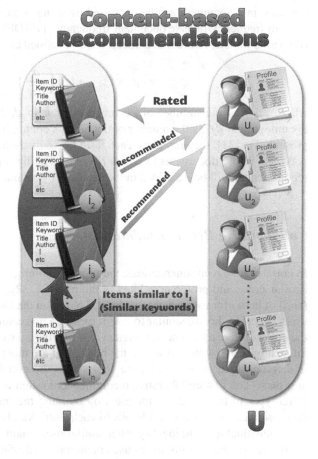

item, such as news articles. Analyzing natural language is very complex as the same word could have many meanings. For example, Grey would represent a color and a name, and power and electricity would refer to the same thing. Some data is represented in a semistructured way as they have some attributes with defined values and free text fields [27].

As we mentioned before, content-based recommender uses text-based items. The content of these items is represented through keywords. One example is LIBRA, which is a content-based book recommender proposed by Mooney and Roy[24] that uses information extraction techniques in order to extract information from Amazon for each title. Also in Fab System, the content is represented by the most 100 major words in order to recommend web pages to users. Similarly, Items are represented through keywords in [28] and the Syskill and Webert system [23] represents documents with the 128 most informative words. The importance of a keyword in a document can be measured by using some weighting measures such as term frequency/inverse document frequency (TF-IDF) measure [8, 30]. The TF-IDF value for a keyword k in a document d is defined as follows:

$$w_{k,d} = tf_{k,d} * \log\left(\frac{n}{df_i}\right) \tag{18.2}$$

where $tf_{k,d}$ is the number of occurrences of k in d, N is the total number of documents and df_i is the number of documents containing k. of the other methods presented in [31], they represent each term t by a distribution of terms (vector) that is typical of the documents in which t occurs. The limitation of the content-based recommender will be described in the discussion section.

Collaborative Recommendations

In collaborative recommendations, the user is recommended items that people with similar tastes and preferences liked in the past [21, 32]. In other words, the utility $f(u,i)$ of item i for user u can be estimated based on the ratings assigned to item i by users $u_n \in U$ who are similar to u. For example, to recommend a book i to user u, the collaborative recommender system will find the set of users who share the same interest in books with user u then the books that are most liked by the similar users is recommended to user u. Figure 18.4 shows the collaborative recommendation approach. The first collaborative recommender system is Grundy [14], which uses stereotypes to build models for users by building the individual user models and then use them to recommend books to each user. Another system is Tapestry that uses individual users to identify other similar users manually [15]. GroupLens [33] is also one of the first groups to use collaborative filtering for Usenet news. Other early collaborative filtering recommender systems are Video Recommender [20] and Ringo [22]. Other recommender systems proposed such as Amazon book recommendation systems, PHOAKS that is used to help people find information on the WWW [34] and the joke recommender system Jester [35].

Collaborative recommendation can be divided into two categories: (1) memory-based and (2) model-based. In memory-based algorithms [21, 22, 32, 36, 37] the unknown rating of an item i for a user u is calculated based on the ratings of other users, who are similar to user u, for the same item i. The similarity between users is calculated as a distance measure. Different user similarity measures could be used as long as the result is normalized with a normalization factor [19]. One of the similarity measures that could be used is the correlation where Pearson correlation coefficient is used to measure similarity [21, 22]. Another similarity measure is cosine-based [25, 32] where the two users are represented as two vector in m-dimensional space and the similarity is measured by computing the cosine angle between them [19]. Model-based algorithms [32, 35, 38–43] use ratings to build a model, which is used then in predictions [19]. Different approaches

Fig. 18.4 Collaborative recommendations

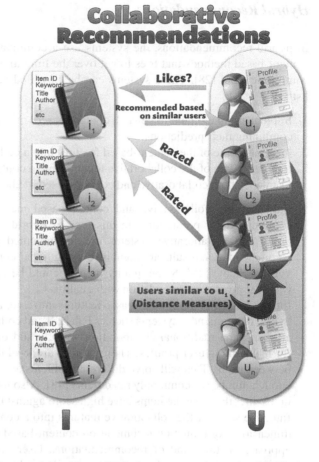

are introduced to learn the model such as [32] that proposed two probabilistic models: cluster model (where similar users are clustered into classes) and Bayesian network, where the rating value of each item is determined through the states of each node. Statistical model is proposed in [43] where they compared different algorithms such as K-means and Gibbs sampling that are used to predict the model parameters. Other collaborative filtering techniques are proposed such as Bayesian model [44], probabilistic relational model [39], linear regression [25] and maximum entropy model [42]. The main difference between memory-based and model-based algorithms is that model-based algorithms estimate the ratings through using statistical and machine learning approaches to learn a model from the underlying data, while the former use some heuristic rules to predict the ratings. It is possible to combine both techniques [45] (memory-based and model-based), which will result in more reliable recommendations than using one technique alone. Collaborative recommendation systems also suffers from limitations as mentioned in [28] and [46]. We will describe these limitations in the discussion section.

Hybrid Recommendations

In hybrid recommendations, the systems use a combination of collaborative and content-based methods that tries to get over the limitations of both the systems by combining them [28]. These systems can be classified according to the following list [19]:

1. Implementing collaborative and content-based methods separately and then combining their predictions
2. Integrate some of the content-based features into a collaborative approach
3. Integrate some of the collaborative features into a content-based approach
4. Combines both collaborative and content-based methods

1. Implementing collaborative and content-based methods separately and then combining their predictions: In this type of hybrid recommendation, content-based and collaborative systems are implemented separately and then the recommendation results are combined using linear combination, ratings [47] or voting scheme [48]. Some quality metrics could be applied to choose the best way that gives recommendation with quality.
2. Integrate some of the content-based features into a collaborative approach: Many hybrid recommender systems such as Fab [28] and collaboration via content [48] are using the traditional collaboration with the aid of content-based approach for maintaining user profiles. These profiles are used then to measure similarity between users. This will solve different problems as when not many users have enough number of commonly rated items [48]. Also users will be recommended items directly when the items have high score against the user profile [28].
3. Integrate some of the collaborative features into a content-based approach: The dimensionality reduction technique on content-based profiles is the most used approach in this kind of recommendations. User profiles are represented as vectors and some normalization techniques is used to reduce the dimensionality as in [49] that uses latent semantic indexing (LSI) to create a collaborative view of a collection of user profiles which results in improving the performance that using only content-based approach.
4. Combines both collaborative and content-based methods: Many researchers use this approach as they propose to combine collaborative and content-based approaches as in [50, 51] where a combined probabilistic method is proposed to combine collaborative and content-based recommendations. Knowledge-based techniques [52] could be used in hybrid recommendation to address some of the limitations such as new user and new item problems [19]. One example of knowledge-based recommender systems is Entre [53] that uses the knowledge cuisines and food to recommend restaurants to the users. Just these types suffer from the need for knowledge acquisition [19].

Different researchers [28, 48, 49] and [54] compared the performance of hybrid recommendations against the collaborative and content-based approaches. They found that hybrid approaches can provide more accurate recommendations than using just collaborative or content-based methods [19].

Recommender Systems Limitations

There are different limitations for using recommender systems. The most two distinct but related well problems are new user and new item problems. A new user with few ratings becomes hard to recognize in recommender systems. Similarly a new item with few ratings cannot be easily recognized by the recommendation system, so there is a need to encourage users to rate items in such systems [53]. In this section, we will discuss these limitations for each recommendation technique and we discuss how to extend these systems.

Content-Based Recommendation

Content and Keywords Limitations

To perform content-based recommendation, the system needs the list of important keywords associated to an item. To find this list, item contents need to be represented in a format that is automatically parsed by computers as in texts or assign the keywords manually to the items [19]. Keyword extraction techniques such as information retrieval are used in recommender systems. But these techniques cannot be applied on data types other than texts such as video, audio or graphics, which lead to a limitation on content-based recommender systems. Another problem occurs when two items are assigned the same set of keywords, which makes them indistinguishable since the content-based systems uses these keywords to predict recommendations. Using the same set of keywords will lead to inaccurate results as the systems will not be able to distinguish between well-written book for example and badly written book [22].

Insufficient Recommendations for New Users

To have accurate a reliable recommendation, the user needs to rate sufficient number of items, as this is the base for content-based recommendations. The system will not be able to predict good recommendations if the user is new in the system and he rated only a few items.

Collaborative Recommendation

Insufficient Recommendations for New Users

As with the content-based recommendation, in order for the system to predict accurate recommendations, it needs first to understand the user's preferences based on the ratings he gave. Researchers used different ways to solve this problem, such as using hybrid recommendation approaches through combining content-based and collaborative techniques as discussed in the sections "Social Networks" and "Recommendation Techniques."

Insufficient Ratings for New Users

Collaborative recommender systems perform recommendation based on user preferences; so for a new item to be seen and recommended by the system a sustainable number of users must rate it. Hybrid recommendation approaches are also used to solve this problem as discussed in the sections "Social Networks" and "Recommendation Techniques".

Recommender Systems in Social Networks

What Can Social Networks Provide to Recommender Systems?

In our daily life, we rely on recommendations from other acquaintances to choose the best products to buy. Nowadays people are depending on the Internet to make their decisions. The Internet alone could not provide the users with sufficient suggestions for their needs as it contains many products and services. So social networks become pivotal for generating recommendations, as integrating recommender systems in social networks will add new intuitions and observation that cannot be achieved through using traditional recommenders. Which produces more accurate and efficient recommendations results? We will summarize these intuitions in the following points: (1) relations between users; (2) improve performance; (3) better recommendation for unrated items; (4) user content-based as recommendation source.

Relations Between Users (Social Influences)

Traditional recommender systems do not take the social relationships between users into consideration [55] even though the studies of measuring the importance of social influence [56, 57] has been performed long time ago. When friends tend to recommend products, other friends will accept these recommendations most of the times, as they trust each other. Businesses that adopted in their recommender systems the relation between humans have achieved a huge success. For example, Hotmail used social influence to reach 12 million subscribers just in 18 months with a marketing budget of US $50,000. Hotmail spread all over the world even in countries they did not make any advertisements such as Sweden and India [58]. This shows that people relations are powerful when making decisions on buying products [55].

Improve Performance

Integrating social networks will improve the performance of recommender systems on different levels as (1) prediction accuracy and (2) similarity between friends [55].

Prediction Accuracy

Understanding the relations between users and their friends as well as the information obtained about them can improve the knowledge about user behaviors and ratings [55]. As a result, predicting user preferences will become easier to infer, which will improve the prediction accuracy.

Similarity Between Friends

Through using social networks, recommender systems will no longer need to use similarity measures in order to measure the similarity between users [55]. When two people are friends, in social networks, we can infer that they share the same interest.

Better Recommendation for Unrated Items

When integrating recommender systems with social networks, the recommender system will be able to recommend items to users even if they have not rated them. This happens based on the preferences of the user's friends [55].

User Content-Based as Recommendation Source

There are two main sources for traditional recommender systems, which are the free text fields and the ratings [59]. Comments are used in e-commerce websites to increase the revenue [60, 61]; they allows users to get the experience of other users with a certain product [62], which makes this method very popular to be integrated in e-commerce websites. But those customer reviews are not accurate as a study showed that the ratings are either of extremely high or extremely low [63]. For that, some studies proposed to use social networks as a data source [59]. They used different text mining techniques, as well as web logs and trustful social networks for allowing the customers to get accurate and satisfaction reviews.

How Can Recommender Systems Use Social Networks to Perform Recommendations?

The different properties of social networks encourage the research in the field recommender systems integration with social networks. These studies are varied and spread over wide areas such as, network value, trust, social tagging, etc.

There are different studies [64, 65] for measuring the network value from analyzing the ability of the customers to influence their friends to buy new products. According to [64], the customers with high influence could leverage the profit of the company.

Trust is also another field related to integrating recommender systems with social networks. It is defined by [66] as the level of subjective probability where each agent helps another agent to accomplish a future behavior. And in social networks the users prefer to get recommendations from their friends. The social relations between users in social networks infer new studies in the field of recommending with trust. People prefer to get recommendations from their friends rather than from a general recommender system [67]; moreover, users prefer to get recommendations from trusted systems [68] and there is a strong relationship between user similarity and trust [69]. In [70] they proposed a distributed trust-based recommendation system on a social network. In their method, the social network needs to have friendship-trust values associated with each field. Then they used a model to compute the trust values between nonadjacent nodes. Each node is assigned a knowledge base to list the vendor preferences (assigned with rating) that the node has for various products and services.

Recommending Users and Groups

In social networking sites, there is a need for recommending users or groups with which the user can potentially became related to, in a personal or professional fashion. There are many researches related to recommending users. Most of these researches build their models based on Facebook and Twitter as they are the most well-known social networks nowadays. One research [71] proposed Twittomender that recommends Twitter users to each other. They used content-based search to check the content of the tweets and collaborative filtering to check the followees and followers of users as well as some hybrid strategies to perform the recommendation. In [72] the authors implemented a system to recommend friends on MySpace. They address issues related to the size of the graph, as it was very huge, keeping the graph up to date and producing friends recommendations using the graph. The system consists of the friend graph manager that manages corresponding portion of the friend graph, the recommendation generator, the recommendation repository manager, and the feedback manager. The challenge with recommending users is how to preserve the privacy of those users specially with the increasing identity theft and web crimes. If the users do not trust the systems, there will be missing attributes that will weaken the generated recommendations.

Future Works

Recommender systems have bright future especially when they combined with social networks. These social networks can provide real time information, relations and connections between different users in the network. Moreover, social networks improved the recommender systems and leveraged them to a new level. So there is a need to study these social networks to understand more the different relations between users. Recommender systems are used now in many businesses to allow businesses to increase traffic, have greater engagement with users, customize the user experience and gain financial benefits [73]. These recommender systems will have potential importance in the future and would be used in (1) engines that identify content on the Internet, (2) the entertainment industry where everything will move to on demand, and (3) advertisement industry [73]. Moreover, adding recommender systems to search engines will generate a new area in which recommender systems would grow. In our future work, we will extend the chapter to cover more issues in recommender systems such as social tagging, scalability, and privacy as these are important issues that need to be addressed and studied extensively.

Conclusion

Much research has been done in the field of recommender systems that helped in improving such systems to produce accurate recommendation results. Social networks and virtual communities with their capabilities of providing user profiles and relations between users added a new way of performing recommendations. In this chapter, we presented social networks and recommender systems. Recommender systems are used in many applications and industrial companies such as Amazon [11] and MovieLens [12]. We discussed the different techniques used for recommendations and categorized them as follows: (1) content-based recommendations, (2) collaborative recommendations and (3) hybrid recommendations. There are limitations in content-based and collaborative recommendations. Hybrid recommendations are used to address the problems of collaborative and content-based approaches such as new user and new item problems. We also discussed the importance of integrating recommender systems in social networks and the different researches done in that field. Real-life recommender systems are very complex and therefore need advanced techniques that can consider many factors during the recommendation process. This leads to the need for developing more advanced recommender systems that can satisfy the customers by providing accurate recommendation based on the different preferences of these users.

References

1. Alexanderson, G.: Euler and königsberg's bridges: a historical view. Bull. Am. Math. Soc. **43**(4), 567–573 (2006)
2. West, D.B.: Introduction to Graph Theory, 2nd edn. Prentice Hall, Upper Saddle River (2000)
3. Wasserman, S., Faust, K.: Social Network Analysis: Methods and Applications. Cambridge University Press, Cambridge/New York (1994)
4. Pastor-Satorras, R., Vespignani, A.: Epidemic spreading in scale-free networks. Phys. Rev. Lett. **86**(14), 3200–3203 (2001)
5. Boyd, D., Ellison, N.: Social network sites: definition, history, and scholarship. J. Comput. Mediat. Commun. **13**(1), 210–230 (2007)
6. Chen, J., Geyer, W., Dugan, C., Muller, M., Guy, I.: Make new friends, but keep the old: recommending people on social networking sites. In: Proceedings of the 27th International Conference on Human Factors in Computing Systems. CHI '09, pp. 201–210. ACM Press, Boston (2009)
7. Armstrong, J.S.: Principles of Forecasting: A Handbook for Researchers and Practitioners. Kluwer Academic Publishers, Boston (2001)
8. Salton, G.: Automatic Text Processing: the Transformation, Analysis and Retrieval of Information by Computer. Addison-Wesley Publishing, Reading (1989)
9. Powell, M.J.D.: Approximation Theory and Methods. Cambridge University Press, Cambridge/New York (1981)
10. Thaler, R.: Toward a positive theory of consumer choice. J. Econ. Behav. Organ. **1**(1), 39–60 (1980)
11. Linden, G., Smith, B., York, J.: Amazon.com recommendations: item-to-item collaborative filtering. IEEE Internet Comput. **7**(1), 76–80 (2003)
12. Miller, B.N., Albert, I., Lam, S.K., Konstan, J.A., Riedl, J.: Movielens unplugged: experiences with an occasionally connected recommender system. In: Proceedings of the 8th International Conference on Intelligent User Interfaces. IUI '03, pp. 263–266. ACM Press, New York (2003)
13. Bellman, S., Lohse, G.H., Johnson, E.J.: Predictors of online buying behavior. Commun. ACM. **42**(12), 32–38 (1999)
14. Rich, E.: User modeling via stereotypes. Cogn. Sci. **3**(4), 329–354 (1979)
15. Goldberg, D., Nichols, D., Oki, B. M., Terry, D.: Using collaborative filtering to weave an information tapestry. Commun. ACM. **35**(12), 61–70 (1992)
16. Lewis, K., Kaufman, J., Gonzalez, M., Wimmer, A., Christakis, N.: Tastes, ties, and time: a new social network dataset using facebook.com. Soc. Netw. **30**(4), 330–342 (2008)
17. Milgram, S.: The small-world problem. Psychol. Today **2**, 60–67 (1967)
18. Watts, D.J.: Small Worlds: the Dynamics of Networks Between Order and Randomness, illustrated edn. Princeton University Press, Princeton (1999)
19. Adomavicius, G., Tuzhilin, A.: Toward the next generation of recommender systems: a survey of the state-of-the-art and possible extensions. IEEE Trans. Knowl. Data Eng. **17**(6), 734–749 (2005)

20. Hill, W., Stead, L., Rosenstein, M., Furnas, G.: Recommending and evaluating choices in a virtual community of use. In: Proceedings of the SIGCHI Conference on Human Factors in Computing Systems, pp. 194–201. ACM Press/Addison-Wesley Publishing Co., New York/Wokingham (1995)
21. Resnick, P., Iacovou, N., Suchak, M., Bergstrom, P., Riedl, J.: Grouplens: an open architecture for collaborative filtering of netnews. In: Proceedings of the 1994 ACM Conference on Computer Supported Cooperative Work. CSCW '94, pp. 175–186. ACM Press, New York (1994)
22. Shardanand, U., Maes, P.: Social information filtering: algorithms for automating 'word of mouth'. In: Proceedings of the SIGCHI Conference on Human Factors in Computing Systems, pp. 210–217. ACM Press, Addison-Wesley Publishing Co., New York/Wokingham (1995)
23. Pazzani, M., Billsus, D.: Learning and revising user profiles: the identification of interesting web sites. Mach. Learn. **27**(3), 313–331 (1997)
24. Mooney, R.J., Roy, L.: Content-based book recommending using learning for text categorization. In: Proceedings of the 5th ACM Conference on Digital Libraries. DL '00, pp. 195–204. ACM Press, New York (2000)
25. Sarwar, B., Karypis, G., Konstan, J., Reidl, J.: Item-based collaborative feeiltering recommendation algorithms. In: Proceedings of the 10th International Conference on World Wide Web. WWW '01, pp. 285–295, ACM Press, New York (2001)
26. Lang, K.: Newsweeder: learning to filter netnews. In: Proceedings of the 12th International Conference on Machine Learning, pp. 331–339. Morgan Kaufmann Publishers Inc., San Francisco (1995)
27. Pazzani, M., Billsus, D.: Content-based recommendation systems. In: Brusilovsky, P., Kobsa, A., Nejdl, W. (eds.) The Adaptive Web Methods and Strategies of Web Personalization, vol. 4321, pp. 325–341. Springer, Berlin/Heidelberg (2007)
28. Balabanovi, M., Shoham, Y.: Fab: content-based, collaborative recommendation. Commun. ACM. **40**(3), 66–72 (1997)
29. Cai, Y., Leung, H.-F., Li, Q., Tang, J., Li, J.: Recommendation based on object typicality. In: Proceedings of the 19th ACM International Conference on Information and Knowledge Management. CIKM '10, pp. 1529–1532, ACM Press, New York (2010)
30. Cantador, I., Bellogín, A., Vallet, D.: Content-based recommendation in social tagging systems. In: Proceedings of the 4th ACM Conference on Recommender Systems. RecSys '10, pp. 237–240, ACM Press, New York (2010)
31. Wartena, C., Slakhorst, W., Wibbels, M.: Selecting keywords for content-based recommendation. In: Proceedings of the 19th ACM International Conference on Information and Knowledge Management. CIKM '10, pp. 1533–1536. ACM Press, New York (2010)
32. Breese, J.S. Heckerman, D., Kadie, C.: Empirical analysis of predictive algorithms for collaborative filtering. In: Cooper, G.F., Moral, S. (eds.) Proceedings of the 14th Conference on Uncertainty in Artificial Intelligence. UAI-98, University of Wisconsin, Madison, pp. 43–52 (1998)
33. Konstan, J.A., Miller, B.N., Maltz, D., Herlocker, J.L., Gordon, L.R., Riedl, J.: Grouplens: applying collaborative filtering to usenet news. Commun. ACM. **40**(3), 77–87 (1997)
34. Terveen, L., Hill, W., Amento, B., McDonald, D., Creter, J.: Phoaks: a system for sharing recommendations. Commun. ACM. **40**(3), 59–62 (1997)
35. Goldberg, K., Roeder, T., Gupta, D., Perkins, C.: Eigentaste: a constant time collaborative filtering algorithm. Inf. Retr. J. **4**(2), 133–151 (2001)
36. Delgado, J., Ishii, N.: Memory-based weighted majority prediction for recommender systems. In: ACM SIGIR'99 Workshop on Recommender Systems: Algorithms and Evaluation. ACM, New York (1999)
37. Nakamura, A., Abe, N.: Collaborative filtering using weighted majority prediction algorithms. In: Proceedings of the 15th International Conference on Machine Learning. ICML '98, pp. 395–403. Morgan Kaufmann Publishers Inc., San Francisco (1998)
38. Billsus, D., Pazzani, M.J.: Learning collaborative information filters. In: Proceedings of the 15th International Conference on Machine Learning. ICML '98, pp. 46–54. Morgan Kaufmann Publishers Inc., San Francisco (1998)

39. Getoor, L., Sahami, M.: Using probabilistic relational models for collaborative filtering. In: Proceedings Workshop on Web Usage Analysis and User Profiling. WEBKDD '99. Springer, Berlin/New York (1999)
40. Hofmann, T.: Collaborative filtering via gaussian probabilistic latent semantic analysis. In: Proceedings of the 26th Annual International ACM SIGIR Conference on Research and Development in Informaion Retrieval. SIGIR '03, pp. 259–266. ACM Press, New York (2003)
41. Marlin, B.: Modeling user rating profiles for collaborative filtering. In: Proceedings of the 17th Annual Conference of Neural Information Processing Systems. NIPS '03. MIT Press, Cambridge (2003)
42. Pavlov, D., Pennock, D.M.: A maximum entropy approach to collaborative filtering in dynamic, sparse, high-dimensional domains. In: Becker, S., Thrun, S., Obermayer, K. (eds.) NIPS, pp. 1441–1448. MIT Press, Cambridge, MA, USA (2002)
43. Ungar, L., Foster, D., Clustering methods for collaborative filtering. In: Proceedings of the Workshop on Recommender Systems at the 15th National Conference on Artificial Intelligence. AAAI'98. AAAI Press, Menlo Park (1998)
44. Chien, Y.H., George, E.I.: A bayesian model for collaborative filtering. In: Proceedings of the 7th International Workshop Artificial Intelligence and Statistics, Fort Lauderdale. Morgan Kaufmann, San Francisco (1999)
45. Pennock, D., Horvitz, E., Lawrence, S., Giles, L.C.: Collaborative filtering by personality diagnosis: a hybrid memory- and model-based approach. In: Proceedings of the 16th Conference on Uncertainty in Artificial Intelligence. UAI 2000, pp. 473–480, Stanford University, Stanford (2000)
46. Lee, W.S.: Collaborative learning for recommender systems. In: Proceedings of the 18th International Conference on Machine Learning. ICML-2001, vol. 2001, pp. 314–321. McGraw-Hill, Williamstown, MA, USA (2001)
47. Claypool, M., Gokhale, A., Miranda, T., Murnikov, P., Netes, D., Sartin, M.: Combining content-based and collaborative filters in an online newspaper. In: Proceedings of ACM SIGIR Workshop on Recommender Systems. SIGIR '99, Berkeley, CA, USA (1999)
48. Pazzani, M.: A framework for collaborative, content-based and demographic filtering. Artif. Intell. Rev. 13(5/6), 393–408 (1999)
49. Soboroff, I., Nicholas, C.: Combining content and collaboration in text filtering. In: Proceedings of the IJCAI-99 Workshop on Machine Learning for Information Filtering, Stockholm, Sweden (1999)
50. Popescul, A., Ungar, L.H., Pennock, D.M., Lawrence, S.: Probabilistic models for unified collaborative and content-based recommendation in sparse-data environments. In: Proceedings of the 17th Conference in Uncertainty in Artificial Intelligence. UAI '01, pp. 437–444. Morgan Kaufmann Publishers Inc., San Francisco (2001)
51. Schein, A.I., Popescul, A., Ungar, L.H., Pennock, D.M.: Methods and metrics for cold-start recommendations. In: Proceedings of the 25th Annual International ACM SIGIR Conference on Research and Development in Information Retrieval. SIGIR '02, pp. 253–260, ACM Press, New York (2002)
52. Burke, R.: Knowledge-based recommender systems. In: Encyclopedia of Library and Information Systems, vol. 69. Marcel Dekker Inc., New York (2000)
53. Burke, R.: Hybrid recommender systems: survey and experiments. User Model. User-Adapt. Interact. 12(4), 331–370 (2002)
54. Melville, P., Mooney, R.J., Nagarajan, R.: Content-boosted collaborative filtering for improved recommendations. In: Proceedings of the 18th National Conference on Artificial Intelligence. AAAI2002, pp. 187–192. AAAI Press, Menlo Park (2002)
55. He, J., Chu, W.W.: A social network-based recommender system (snrs). Ann. Inf. Syst. Spec. Issue Data Min. Soc. Netw. Data. 12, 47–74 (2010)
56. Subramani, M.R., Rajagopalan, B.: Knowledge-sharing and influence in online social networks via viral marketing. Commun. ACM. 46(12), 300–307 (2003)
57. Yang, S., Allenby, G.M.: Modeling interdependent consumer preferences. J. Mark. Res. 40(3), 282–294 (2003)

58. Jurvetson, S.: What exactly is viral marketing? Red Herring **78**, 110–112 (2000)
59. Bank, M., Franke, J.:   Social networks as data source for recommendation systems in: E-commerce and web technologies. Lect. Notes Bus. Inf. Process. **61**, 49–60 (2010)
60. Hu, N., Liu, L., Zhang, J.J.: Do online reviews affect product sales? The role of reviewer characteristics and temporal effects. Inf. Technol. Manag. **9**(3), 201–214 (2008)
61. Ghose, A., Ipeirotis, P.G.: Designing novel review ranking systems: predicting the usefulness and impact of reviews. In: Proceedings of the 9th International Conference on Electronic Commerce. ICEC '07, pp. 303–310. ACM Press, New York (2007)
62. David, S., Pinch, T.J.: Six degrees of reputation: the use and abuse of online review and recommendation systems. First Monday **11**(3) (2005). http://firstmonday.org/htbin/cgiwrap/bin/ojs/index.php/fm/article/view/1590/1505
63. Hu, N., Pavlou, P.A., Zhang, J.: Can online reviews reveal a product's true quality?: empirical findings and analytical modeling of online word-of-mouth communication. In: Proceedings of the 7th ACM Conference on Electronic Commerce. EC '06, pp. 324–330. ACM Press, New York (2006)
64. Domingos, P., Richardson, M.: Mining the network value of customers. In: Proceedings of the 7th ACM SIGKDD International Conference on Knowledge Discovery and Data Mining. KDD '01, pp. 57–66. ACM Press, New York (2001)
65. Richardson, M., Domingos, P.: Mining knowledge-sharing sites for viral marketing. In: Proceedings of the 8th ACM SIGKDD International Conference on Knowledge Discovery and Data Mining. KDD '02, pp. 61–70. ACM Press, New York (2002)
66. Gambetta, D.: Can we trust? In: Trust: Making and Breaking Cooperative Relations, pp. 213–237. Basil Blackwell Publishers, New York (1988)
67. Sinha, R., Swearingen, K.: Comparing recommendations made by online systems and friends. In: Proceedings of the DELOS-NSF Workshop on Personalization and Recommender Systems in Digital Libraries, Dublin (2001)
68. Swearingen, K., Sinha, R.: Beyond algorithms: an hci perspective on recommender systems. In: Proceedings of the ACM SIGIR 2001 Workshop on Recommender Systems, New Orleans. ACM Press, New Orleans, Louisiana, USA (2001)
69. Ziegler, C.N., Lausen, G., Analyzing correlation between trust and user similarity in online communities. In: Proceeding of the 2nd International Conference on Trust Management, vol. 2995, pp. 251–265. Springer, Berlin/Heidelberg (2004)
70. Sarda, K., Gupta, P., Mukherjee, D., Padhy, S., Saran, H.:   A distributed trust-based recommendation system on social networks. In: Proceedings of the 2nd IEEE Workshop on Hot Topics in Web Systems and Technologies (2008)
71. Hannon, J., Bennett, M., Smyth, B.: Recommending twitter users to follow using content and collaborative filtering approaches. In: Proceedings of the 4th ACM Conference on Recommender Systems. RecSys'10, pp. 199–206. ACM Press, New York (2010)
72. Moricz, M., Dosbayev, Y., Berlyant, M.: Pymk: friend recommendation at myspace. In: Proceedings of the 2010 International Conference on Management of Data. SIGMOD '10, pp. 999–1002, ACM Press, New York (2010)
73. Guy, I., Jaimes, A., Agulló, P., Moore, P., Nandy, P., Nastar, C., Schinzel, H.:   Will recommenders kill search?: recommender systems – an industry perspective. In: Proceedings of the 4th ACM Conference on Recommender Systems. RecSys '10, pp. 7–12. ACM Press, New York (2010)

Index

A. Abraham and A.-E. Hassanien (eds.), *Computational Social Networks: Tools,*
Perspectives and Applications, DOI DOI 10.1007/978-1-4471-4048-1,
© Springer-Verlag London 2012